Sensible Politics

Sensible Politics

Visualizing International Relations

WILLIAM A. CALLAHAN

OXFORD
UNIVERSITY PRESS

OXFORD

UNIVERSITY PRESS

Oxford University Press is a department of the University of Oxford. It furthers the University's objective of excellence in research, scholarship, and education by publishing worldwide. Oxford is a registered trade mark of Oxford University Press in the UK and certain other countries.

Published in the United States of America by Oxford University Press
198 Madison Avenue, New York, NY 10016, United States of America.

© Oxford University Press 2020

CIP data is on file at the Library of Congress
ISBN: 978-0-19-007174-5 (pbk)
ISBN: 978-0-19-007173-8 (hbk)

1 3 5 7 9 8 6 4 2

Paperback printed by Sheridan Books, Inc., United States of America
Hardback printed by Bridgeport National Bindery, Inc., United States of America

To my teachers Mike Shapiro and Andy Lawrence,
and to my students in IR318

CONTENTS

List of Figures   ix
Preface   xi
Acknowledgments   xv

Introduction: Visualizing International Relations   1

PART I   VISIBILITY/VISUALITY: A FRAMEWORK FOR ANALYSIS

1. Visibility: The Social Construction of the Visual   19

2. Visuality: The Visual Performance of the International   32

3. Dynamic Dyads: Visibility/Visuality and East/West   46

PART II   VISUAL IMAGES

4. Methods, Ethics, and Filmmaking   61

5. Visualizing Security, Order, and War   90

6. Visual Art, Ethical Witnessing, and Resistance   117

PART III   VISUAL ARTIFACTS AND SENSORY SPACES

7. Maps, Space, and Power   147

8. The Sartorial Engineering of Race, Gender, and Faith   178

9. Walls as Barriers, Gateways, and the Sublime   209

10. Gardens in Diplomacy, War, and Peace   239

11. Visibility, Visuality, and Mass (Self)Surveillance   271

PART IV   CONCLUSION

Conclusion: Sensible Politics   303

Selected Bibliography   317
Index   341

LIST OF FIGURES

1.1   Lorraine O'Grady, "Art Is . . . (Girlfriends Times Two)" (1983/2009)   23
2.1   "Europe in 2035," map 2 (2012)   33
2.2   Jia Zhangke, *Smog Journeys* (2015)   41
4.1   "To fully carry out a patriotic public health movement" (1963)   87
5.1   Bill Anders, *Earthrise* (1968)   93
5.2   George N. Barnard, *City of Atlanta GA No. 2* (1866)   103
5.3   Benjamin West, *The Death of General Wolfe* (1770)   104
5.4   Screenshot of *Health Services in The Islamic State* (2015)   110
5.5   Screenshot of *Administration of Bakeries and Ovens* (2015)   113
6.1   Selfie of Ai Weiwei offering tea and a blanket to a refugee, *Human Flow* (2017)   133
6.2   Drone's-eye view of a refugee camp, *Human Flow* (2017)   134
7.1   Chinese U-shaped line map on PRC passport (2016)   150
7.2   Perpetual All-under-the-Heavens Map of the Unified Great Qing Empire (1811)   158
7.3   Ch'eonhado (ca. 19th century)   161
7.4   Map of Civilization and Barbarians (1136 CE)   164
7.5   Map of China's Lost Sovereign Land and Maritime Territories (1927)   168
8.1   *NiqaBitch Shakes Paris* (2010)   179
8.2   A "white British Muslim convert" (2015)   183
8.3   "Ten Types—One People" pageant winners (1955)   189
8.4   De-veiled woman in *The Battle of Algiers* (1966)   192
8.5   Visual cultural resistance by Princess Hijab   197
8.6   Official mural for the Beauty Engineering Project, Kashgar (2015)   200
9.1   Immigration counter at Haikou International Airport, China (2016)   213
9.2   Inside and Outside the Gate of Mountains and Seas (1760)   216
9.3   Ana Teresa Fernández, *Borrada* (2010)   219

9.4   Chinese ambassador presents Great Wall tapestry to Foreign Ministry of Pakistan (2014)   221

9.5   Cai Guo-Qiang, *Project to Extend the Great Wall of China by 10,000 Meters: Project for Extraterrestrials No. 10* (1993)   235

9.6   Negotiating a border wall (2016)   236

10.1   *Disaster in Jinling*, Nanjing Massacre Memorial (2017)   261

10.2   *Disaster in Jinling*, close up (1999)   261

10.3   Peace Tower (2009)   262

10.4   Peace through strength (2013)   263

10.5   Yasukuni Shrine, Tokyo (2004)   265

10.6   Yasukuni Shrine, Sacred Pond Garden (2016)   267

11.1   "Some tips for internet" at a Chinese hotel (2018)   287

C.1   Patricia Nixon at the US-Mexico border (1971)   309

PREFACE

Sensible Politics argues that students of social theory and international relations (IR) need to appreciate politics as a multisensory performance. This quest to de-center discursive analytical strategies is the result of my practical experience as a student and a teacher; in 2010–2011, I took a course titled Japanese Garden Design in Kyoto and one called Filmmaking for Fieldwork in Manchester, and since 2014 I have taught the course on Visual International Politics at the London School of Economics.

As a student in the garden design and ethnographic filmmaking classes, I lis-tened to lectures and studied texts to survey history and theory, but the most inter-esting part of the courses was their practical instruction. Filmmaking for Fieldwork is organized around making a set of three films, including the final assignment of conceptualizing, shooting, and editing an original documentary short; mine was about pre-teen "girl geeks" who meet on weekends at a museum to do scientific experiments. In the other course, we performed the aesthetics of Japanese gar-dens by trimming an imperial garden in Kyoto, and in the "final exam" each stu-dent designed and constructed a garden in the mountains above the city. People built different styles and types of gardens. To create a water garden of waterfalls and pools, I re-arranged rocks and plants along a stream in the valley, while a classmate integrated rocks, plants, and human artifacts to build a garden on the mountainside. But we both played with the same conventions to create an aesthetic view of "na-ture." In both classes I not only learned new ideas and information, but viscerally felt the giddiness and cringes of multisensory experiences in ways that arrested rational understanding.

I try to reproduce this thinking/feeling dynamic each year in my Visual International Politics class, in which students engage in both the discursive anal-ysis of visual images and the creative production of a short documentary film. It's fascinating to see how students struggle with the challenge of telling stories vis-ually, and heartening to see how happy they are with the resulting film. Learning (and then teaching) these aesthetic conventions and practical techniques—which generally are not discussed in academic literature—pushed me to think about meaning, value, and politics in less textual and more multisensory ways. These experiences thus raised many of the questions addressed in *Sensible Politics*. They led directly to the book's chapters that explore film-making and garden-building as theory-building practices. And they also inform the book's more general questions about theory, method, and ethics: What is the relation between the verbal and the visual, meaning and feeling, the iconic and the everyday, and the West and the non-West?

I am happy to be part of the recent advances in visual IR and visual culture studies that take seriously the role of images in international politics. But this book is also a reaction to frustration with (1) the narrow focus on visual images of war and violence that come from Euro-American sources and (2) dominant strategies that turn visuals into texts for discursive analysis. While filmmaking highlights the importance of visual images, garden-building points to a politics of visual artifacts and multisensory spaces that also appreciates sound, smell, touch, and taste. The Asian studies and ethnographic focus of the gardening and filmmaking courses underlined how concepts, practices, and experiences emerge from beyond Euro-America. To put it another way, while my previous research used theory (e.g., poststructuralism) to explain "China," this book uses "China" (and other non-Western examples) to make theory. *Sensible Politics* revisits previous work in which I conducted discursive analysis of visual images and artifacts—that is, the politics of films, maps, and gardens—but addresses these topics in new ways to explore them as visual and multisensory experiences and performances, where "sensible" also means an attention to everyday pragmatic practices.

In addition to highlighting the multisensory politics of sight, sound, smell, and touch, the garden-building final exam also demonstrated the need to appreciate the spatial and temporal limits of the practice. We were allotted half a day to design and build our gardens. Because I chose to build a large water garden in a deep valley, it got dark before I could finish. My classmate's garden, on the other hand, was not only beautiful but also complete. That classmate better understood the performative possibilities of this late Autumn assignment: the tiny garden on a West-facing hillside took advantage of the golden light of the setting sun. The lesson for me is that you need to get the right balance of time, space, and place; a professional doesn't just create a compelling garden, but makes it the right size in the right place so it can be finished on time.

Visual and multisensory politics is a growing field that addresses an entangled ecology of concepts, practices, and experiences. Rather than build a huge garden to reproduce this expanding world, *Sensible Politics* is a medium-sized project that considers a particular set of concepts, practices, and experiences to make some general points about meaning, value, and ethics. This book aims to decenter our understanding of social theory and international politics by (1) expanding from the verbal to include the visual and the multisensory, (2) expanding from Eurocentric investigations of visual IR to a more comparative approach that looks to Asia and the Middle East, and (3) shifting from critical IR's focus on inside/outside and self/Other distinctions to see politics in terms of creative processes of social-ordering and world-ordering.

ACKNOWLEDGMENTS

I am happy to acknowledge the friends and colleagues who have helped me write *Sensible Politics*. Many people have given generous feedback and support over the years, and I want to especially thank Elena Barabantseva, Roland Bleiker, David Brenner, Cho Young Chul, Andy Lawrence, and Michael J. Shapiro. I also thank the students in my Visual International Politics class for helping me work through the arguments in this book. At Oxford University Press, I thank David McBride and Emily Mackenzie for their enthusiasm and support for this project.

For hosting presentations and for feedback on chapters, I thank Jonathan Luke Austin, Tarak Barkawi, Geremie R. Barmé, Oleg Benesch, Franck Billé, Kelly-Jo Bluen, Clemens Buettner, Kevin Carrico, Pheng Cheah, Timothy Cheek, Carina Chotirawe, Gloria Davies, Andrew Dellatola, Prasenjit Duara, Mark C. Elliott, Magnus Fiskesjö, Simon Glezos, Sophie Harman, Christopher R. Hughes, Lene Hansen, Mark Hoffman, Emma Hutchison, Justyna Jaguscik, Leigh Jenco, Malte Philipp Kaeding, Wybe Kuitert, Milli Lake, Wendy Larson, Martin Lavicka, James Leibold, Andy Hanlun Li, Debbie Lisle, Timothy Luke, Aaron McKeil, Katharine M. Millar, Guanpei Ming, Darren Moon, Naruemon Thabchumpon, Iver Neumann, Kiri Paramore, Pinitbhand Paribatra, Stephanie Perrazzone, Frank Pieke, Claire Roberts, Carlos Rojas, Andrea Riemenschnitter, Florian Schneider, Shawn Smallman, Kaat Smets, Graeme Smith, Vira Somboon, Song Xinning, Verita Sriratana, Sukunya Bumroongsook, Sumalee Bumroongsook, David Tobin, Rex Troumbley, Heidi Wang-Kaeding, Jeffrey Wasserstrom, Cynthia Weber, Peter Wilson, Christian Wirth, Yue Zhuang, and Jinghan Zeng. The editors and reviewers at *Millennium* (2014), *International Political Sociology* (2017), and the *Review of International Studies* (2018) also helpfully shaped this work.

Valuable research assistance was provided by Lana Bilalova, Daniel Fitter, Kim Min-Kyoo, Andy Li, Till Schöfer, and Yi Jael Tan.

Although I didn't know it at the time, two research grants aided this book. The Leverhulme Trust fellowship supported my participation in The Japanese Gardens intensive seminar at the Kyoto University of Art & Design in 2010 and in the Filmmaking for Fieldwork intensive seminar at the University of Manchester in 2011. The Asia Research Institute at the National University of Singapore supported a visiting research professorship (2012–2013), during which I started the research for this book. The International Relations Department of the London School of Economics and Political Science generously supported the "Visual International Politics" workshop in 2016, the book scrub in 2019, and two undergraduate research assistants. The LSE's Knowledge Exchange and Impact fund supported the production of my film *Great Walls: Journeys from Ideology to Experience* (2019), which was an important part of the book's research project.

Chapters 4, 9, and 10 are refined versions of, respectively, the following publications:

"The Visual Turn in IR: Documentary Filmmaking as a Critical Method," *Millennium* 43:3 (2015):891–910.
"The Politics of Walls: Barriers, Flows, and the Sublime," *Review of International Studies* 44:3 (2018):456–481.
"Cultivating Power: Gardens in the Global Politics of Diplomacy, War and Peace," *International Political Sociology* 11:4 (2017):1–20.

I thank the publishers for their permission to use this material.

Finally, I thank Sumalee for all her help and support: Chaiyo!

Introduction

Visualizing International Relations

Sensible Politics argues that visual international politics is important and different. First, the visual is important; in our post-literate age, most people get their information about international affairs from visual media. Images thus shape our view of the world, by making some things visible while at the same time making other things invisible. As illustrated by the widely circulated photograph of the dead toddler Alan Kurdi lying on a beach in Turkey during Europe's migration crisis in 2015, iconic photographs can put issues on the international relations (IR) agenda, even provoking Chancellor Angela Merkel to allow over one million refugees into Germany. This attention to the politics of framing—who and what are included inside the frame of the political, and how people and issues are excluded from the international—shows how visual media impact international politics. Iconic images can be very powerful, even demanding an ethical and political response. This book therefore shows what images can tell us about the elite politics of the state and foreign policy, as well as about the non-elite "intimate geopolitics" seen in everyday self/Other and inside/outside relations. It follows the "aesthetic turn" in IR to argue that the practice of representation is the site of politics. This attention to the social construction of the visible is what I call the "visibility strategy," and it is a powerful and popular approach to visual international politics.

Second, *Sensible Politics*'s contribution is not just that images matter, but that they matter in different ways from what we're used to and have come to expect. To get a critical appreciation of international politics, we need to do more than "add visuals and stir." This book argues that visual images and artifacts provide an opportunity to appreciate international politics in a different register that values both thinking and feeling; it also looks beyond iconic images to the performative experiences of visual artifacts such as veils, walls, and gardens. *Sensible Politics* thus explores how visuals are more than the technical issue of a new way of transmitting information in a "battle of images." Because visuals can viscerally move us in unexpected ways, the book argues that they need to be appreciated not just in terms

Sensible Politics. William A. Callahan, Oxford University Press (2020). © Oxford University Press.
DOI: 10.1093/oso/9780190071738.001.0001

of their ideological-value, but also in terms of their affect-work: not just what they mean, but also how they make us feel, both as individuals and as collectives. The horrible photo of Alan Kurdi did not simply provide information for a greater understanding of the plight of migrants; it viscerally moved and connected people in ways that mobilized "affective communities of sense."

Although it is common to respond to the challenges of the "post-truth" era by deconstructing "fake news," *Sensible Politics* argues that political critique also needs to creatively produce sensory artifacts that can move and connect people to fight such populism. While much visual IR research focuses on inside/outside and self/Other as sites of identity, security, and exclusion, *Sensible Politics* also works to reframe the questions (and answers) to highlight how visual images and multisensory artifacts are better appreciated in terms of ordering processes: social-ordering and world-ordering. Ordering here is less a technical problem and more a political and moral performance, in which people actively visualize the world they want to live in, as well as the societies that they don't want to see and feel. The book thus explores not only how visuals illustrate international events as visual texts, but also how they can actively create international politics as nonverbal and nonnarrative performances and experiences. While the visibility strategy works to reveal the social construction of the visible, here we examine the visual construction of the social—and the multisensory performance of the international. This is what I call the "visuality strategy," and *Sensible Politics* pursues it to highlight the broader issues of how visual images and multisensory artifacts can actively provoke "affective communities of sense" that complicate what can (and cannot) be seen, said, thought, and done.

The importance of nonverbal, nonlinear, and nonnarrative visual politics is a tough argument to make. It's easy to point out the irony of writing a book about nonverbal politics. But the objective of *Sensible Politics* isn't just to convince readers cognitively, but also to start to move and connect them affectively. As the book's chapters illustrate, the purpose is not to switch from one approach to another—from visibility to visuality, from ideology to affect, from images to artifacts—but to appreciate how international politics can come alive in different ways through the productive tension of visibility/visuality, ideology/affect, and images/artifacts. In other words, the goal is to make readers not only think visually, but also feel visually—and to creatively act visually for a multisensory appreciation of politics.

To summarize, *Sensible Politics* makes four key scholarly contributions:

(1) To show how visual international politics is important, it provides a critical examination of how images shape the way we think about IR in our post-literate age, in which, for most people, visual media are the main source of information about the world (i.e., the visibility strategy).

(2) To show how visual international politics is different, it explores how visuals don't just illustrate international events as visual texts but also can actively

create international politics as nonverbal and nonnarrative experiences and performances (i.e., the visuality strategy).

(3) Recognizing that visual IR is dominated by symbolic analyses of "visual images"—photographs, film, online video, television, and visual art—*Sensible Politics* expands the critical gaze to consider how "visual artifacts" and sensory spaces—maps, veils, walls, gardens, and cyberspace—can shape international political phenomena, our perception of them, and popular responses to them.

(4) Since critical analysis is dominated by deconstructions of "Western" visual images, the book explores how an examination of non-Western visual images and artifacts challenges our understanding of international politics.

The third and fourth scholarly contributions have been implicit thus far and thus require further discussion. Both address the empirical issue of what counts as a source for visual international politics: just images, or artifacts, too? And what happens when we employ Asian and Middle Eastern examples to argue general points about IR?

Expanding analysis from two-dimensional visual images to three-dimensional visual artifacts aids the switch from the symbolic analysis of the politics of representation to the affect-work done in multisensory spaces where one can be an observer, a participant, and when things go awry, even a target. It follows from Cynthia Enloe's argument that to gain a critical bottom-up understanding of international politics, we need to switch from research in the halls of power to taking "notes in a brothel, a kitchen, or a latrine."[1] As Chapter 4, "Methods, Ethics, and Filmmaking," shows, it is profitable to appreciate such fieldwork sites as sensory spaces, material modalities, and visual artifacts that can be experienced both individually and collectively. Attention to visual artifacts does not deny that many people experience them as moving and still images, for example, videos of people partying on the Berlin Wall in 1989. And this works the other way around, too. Visual images can take on material form as artifacts and practical experiences; photographs are also material artifacts that people produce, display, archive, and exchange. *Sensible Politics*'s goal is to appreciate visual artifacts as sensory spaces in which international politics is represented, performed, and experienced through more embodied, affective, and everyday encounters on the local, national, and world stages. Here "sensible politics" isn't just sensory, but looks beyond icons and ideology to the pragmatic politics of everyday life.

The fourth contribution of *Sensible Politics* is an empirical expansion of sources from familiar sites in Euro-America to new and different sites in Asia and the Middle East. Eurocentrism increasingly is seen as a problem in IR, and much visual IR addresses this issue through a robust critique of Euro-American images

---

[1] Cynthia Enloe, "The Mundane Matters," *International Political Sociology* 4:5 (2011): 446.

of the non-Western Other. My concern is that Eurocentrism is not simply about content—such as analysis of the global power of Hollywood—but also about theory and method, in which the "West as method" dominates discussions of Asia as well as of Euro-America. How can we address this Eurocentrism of theory and method? One response is to reverse the East/West power dynamic to see China/ Asia not just as the site of alternative perspectives, but also as the source of a ready-made, comprehensive, alternative theory: for example, China's All-under-Heaven (Tianxia) system as an alternative to the Westphalian system. However, rather than replacing "Eurocentric" theory with "Sinocentric" theory, *Sensible Politics* aims to explore visual international politics through an assemblage of concepts that are Chinese, Asian, Islamic, Western, traditional, and contemporary. The goal here is to use Asian and Middle Eastern concepts, practices, and experiences as a critical jux-taposition to decenter (but not necessarily discard) critical IR discourse that char-acteristically generalizes from Euro-American examples.

Since my expertise is in Chinese and Asian politics, the analysis often starts from that point. This oblique entry into social theory and international politics underlines how the critique of "Western universals" cannot produce any new universal theory. It also highlights the value of a comparative approach to visual IR that engages with different places and times, in ways that acknowledge the partiality of the project. To put this another way, it's one thing to open the critical door to new conditions of possibility, as many theorists suggest. It's another to walk through the door to do the detailed empirical research that is necessary to see how alternative social orders and world orders are being visualized in the present: for example, the Islamic State's utopian Caliphate, a revived Chinese world order, Russian Eurasianism, and partic-ipatory surveillance on the World Wide Web.

Positionality and Theory

East/West and West/non-West are presented here not as exclusive binary oppositions, but as fluid dynamics (explained more in Chapter 3, "Dynamic Dyads: Visibility/Visuality and East/West"). This is not just an academic argument, but also a personal one. Growing up in the "utopia" of a middle-class small town in suburban New Jersey, I experienced a heavy dose of what I now understand as white privilege and male privilege. This has greatly benefited my life-chances and continues to frame my professional research opportunities (in ethically problem-atic ways). I try to address this privilege first by acknowledging and problematizing it. I also try to take a critical view of the male gaze and the white/colonial gaze by taking seriously the concepts, practices, and experiences offered by feminist theory and Asian studies. My interest in everyday politics, intimate geopolitics, body pol-itics, reason/emotion, and world-making comes from a long-term engagement with women's studies and feminist theory. My interest in social relations (rather than binary oppositions), reflexivity, social-ordering and world-ordering, and cultural governance/resistance comes as much from my time spent in China, Taiwan, and Thailand as it does from post-positivist theory classes. My experience living for many years in a multi-generational Sino-Thai household continues to guide my understanding of Confucianism, Buddhism, and family as much as my academic studies of Asian thought and society.

This engaged positionality works itself out theoretically in *Sensible Politics*'s attention to identity politics—the politics of "visible minorities," for example—as well as its concern with the problems raised when identity becomes reified into a multicultural menu of essentialized choices. The book thus aims to pursue what Michael J. Shapiro calls a "critical attitude" of self-reflection that goes beyond "merely serving particular social segments or disempowered groups." Instead, it needs to "present a challenge to identity politics in general, . . . even those on which some social movements are predicated." Rather than stake out political positions, *Sensible Politics* seeks to "displace institutionalized forms of recognition with *thinking*. To think (rather than to seek to explain) in this sense is to invent and apply conceptual frames and create juxtapositions that disrupt and/or render historically contingent accepted knowledge practices."[2]

The chapters of *Sensible Politics* employ such new conceptual dynamics and unexpected juxtapositions first to deconstruct how state and corporate power promote ideology by making some things visible and other things invisible; it thus makes visible both the hidden power relations and a different range of actors and issues. It then addresses the more difficult task of appreciating how visuals can work in nonlinear, nonnarrative, and nonverbal ways that excite affect through visceral connections and performative experiences. Importantly, this critical attitude of self-reflection works against the analytical urge to make simple reversals—from West to East and from Right to Left—to complicate our appreciation of the sensible politics of entangled relations.

The role of theory here is not to provide comprehensive or universalizable explanations. Rather than engage in high theory, the concepts in *Sensible Politics* often are taken from what some media theorists call "medium theory" (pun intended). The book figures concepts in terms of dynamic dyads—for example, visible/visual, center/periphery, concealing/revealing, loosening/tightening—that often grow out of the practical conventions that guide picture-taking, film-making, map-making, veil-wearing, wall-building, garden-building, and Web-surfing. Craftspeople here intentionally create meaning; but meaning and value also emerge through the social practices of the exchange and circulation of visual images and multisensory artifacts.

[2] Michael J. Shapiro, *Studies in Trans-Disciplinary Method: After the Aesthetic Turn* (New York: Routledge, 2013), pp. 8, xv.

The goal is not a universal "theory of pictures" but, as W. J. T. Mitchell explains, to "picture theory" itself in a complex and entangled way and thus "to 'perform' theory as a visible, embodied, communal practice, not as a solitary introspection of a disembodied intelligence."[3] While critical theory characteristically works to problematize conventions in order to speak truth to power, this book is skeptical of such emancipatory projects. Rather than criticize conventions, it seeks to recognize them, see how they work, and play with them to see how they can creatively make interesting and different social orders and world orders. This is where the symbolic analysis of visual images is complemented by the practical experience of building theory through, for example, making films and building gardens.

Likewise, *Sensible Politics* does not aim to offer a comprehensive survey of the growing field of visual international politics. Rather, it seeks to act as a provocation that challenges the assumption of what counts as "visual" in international politics, that is, photography and film from Euro-American sources. As the title *Sensible Politics* suggests, the book is also self-critical of the ocular-centrism of visual IR research. Its focus, especially in the first few chapters, certainly is on the visual in international politics as a way to highlight and critique the hegemony of verbal strategies of analysis. This project addresses the visual in much more detail than the other senses, for two reasons: (1) visual culture studies provides a fertile terrain to start the discussion of sensible politics, and (2) visual IR remains an under-studied field.

The goal of *Sensible Politics*, however, is to expand from the verbal to include the visible and the multisensory; the visual here is but one entry into the larger field of sensible politics, where the hear-able, smell-able, touch-able, and taste-able matter alongside the see-able. Film and video, remember, include sounds (both verbal and nonverbal) as well as images. The book's chapters that discuss walls and gardens highlight the multisensory regimes of what Jacques Rancière calls the "distribution of the sensible."[4]

The focus on the visual, therefore, is only a problem (i.e., ocular-centrism) if it marginalizes the appreciation of other senses; for example, if it silences other voices. The analytical framework developed in Part I—the visibility strategy's analysis of the social construction of the visible and the visuality strategy's appreciation of the visual performance of the international—can also be employed to understand and appreciate the international politics of other senses, such as the social construction of the audible and the sonic construction of the international. The purpose of *Sensible Politics* is not to create a new hegemonic approach, but to appreciate politics in terms of a complex multisensory ecology. In this way, the project also moves from criticizing how elites use visual images to manipulate the masses to considering how

[3] W. J. T. Mitchell, *What Do Pictures Want? The Lives and Loves of Images* (Chicago: University of Chicago Press, 2005), p. 355.

[4] Jacques Rancière, *The Politics of Aesthetics: The Distribution of the Sensible*, translated by Gabriel Rockhill (London: Continuum International Publishing Group, 2004).

these multisensory experiences can move and connect people in affective networks and communities of sense. *Sensible Politics* is about multisensory politics, but it also concerns "sensible" in the sense of the pragmatic politics of everyday life.

Structure and Content of the Book

In terms of organization, *Sensible Politics* is neither a linear narrative that develops arguments in a progressive style nor an assemblage of stand-alone essays that dance around certain themes. Theories and methods are introduced in the first four chapters and then are developed in later chapters to show how the visibility/visuality dynamic comes alive through a diverse set of images and artifacts. Theory here is valuable when it works to make the familiar strange and the strange familiar. The chapters move back and forth between familiar sites of hard politics—war, maps, border walls—and strange sites of aesthetics—visual art, women's fashion, gardens. They work to see the aesthetics in politics and the politics in aesthetics. Because few people now read a book from beginning to end, there is some repetition of theoretical arguments across the chapters, but following Mark Twain, I hope that such repetitions actually rhyme in interesting ways: "History doesn't repeat itself, but it often rhymes."

This introduction is a sampling of arguments that are made in more detail (and with copious references) in the first three chapters and throughout *Sensible Politics*. The main body of the book is divided into four parts: Part I, "Visibility/Visuality: A Framework for Analysis"; Part II, "Visual Images"; Part III, "Visual Artifacts and Sensory Spaces"; and Part IV, "Conclusions."

Part I includes three chapters—Chapter 1, "Visibility: The Social Construction of the Visual"; Chapter 2, "Visuality: The Visual Performance of the International"; and Chapter 3, "Dynamic Dyads: Visibility/Visuality and East/West"—which unpack arguments raised in the introduction. While it is popular to use the term "visuality" to discuss how images are more than objective reflections of reality, Part I argues that we need to differentiate between "meaning" and "doing." Chapter 1 develops the visibility strategy, which aims to shift the critical gaze away from empiricism's attention to the "what" issues of accurately reflecting reality to consider the "who, when, where, and how" issues of how images take on meaning through the social construction of the visual. It traces the strategy's suspicion of images, arguing that this is part of a wider critique of the ocular-centrism of European thought. To solve the problem of visual images, Chapter 1 explores how critics use the hermeneutic mode of analysis to reveal hidden ideological meaning and thus speak truth to power.

While Chapter 1 examines what is important about visual IR, Chapter 2 explores what is different about visual IR: that is, how images can actively create sensible politics as visual performances that viscerally move and connect people. It develops the visuality strategy's analysis of how images take on meaning and value through the visual construction of the social and the multisensory performance of the international. It thus expands from Chapter 1's symbolic analysis of visual images to consider how "visual artifacts"—maps, veils, walls, gardens, and cyberspace—can shape IR as material modalities and sensory spaces that are experienced both individually and collectively in affective communities of sense. In this way, it moves from assessing the ideological-value of visuals to appreciating their affect-work. Chapter 2 thus challenges the critique of ocular-centrism by outlining how the visuality strategy can help us appreciate how multisensory spaces can provoke social orders and world orders as affective communities of sense.

Rather than see visibility and visuality as opposing strategies, Chapter 3 argues that both are valuable for an analysis of sensible politics. It figures them as complementary opposites that are joined in the productive tension of a dynamic dyad. It shows how dynamic dyads offer a critical approach to Eurocentrism and East/West figurations and introduces some of the other dynamic dyads—inside/outside, Civilization/barbarism, civility/martiality—that are further developed in later chapters. In this way it looks to Chinese concepts, practices, and experiences to engage in a comparative analysis of visual international politics.

Part I's analysis illustrates that it is not helpful to switch from one approach to another: from visibility to visuality, from ideology to affect, from images to artifacts. It seeks to appreciate how visual international politics comes alive through the productive tension of visibility/visuality, ideology/affect, and images/artifacts. Part I thus presents both a literature review of visual culture studies and visual IR research and an original analytical framework for understanding visual international politics.

Part II engages with existing debates in visual international politics through chapters addressing the aesthetic turn in IR (Chapter 4), visual securitization (Chapter 5), and ethical witnessing (Chapter 6). To make these arguments, it uses a range of visual images—photographs, documentary films, feature films, online videos, and visual art—to discuss visibility/visuality and ideology/affect. Using these examples, Part II argues that we need to shift from the verbal to the visual in our analysis of international politics.

Part II starts with Chapter 4, "Methods, Ethics, and Filmmaking." One of the main analytical approaches to visual international politics is the "aesthetic turn in IR," which argues that we need to more directly address the interpretive aspects of politics and to look at poetry, art, and film as alternative sources of international politics. The chapter analyzes research films in IR to evaluate these hermeneutic approaches, arguing that the visual turn in IR is more than an elaboration of the aesthetic turn. While analyses of visual culture that deconstruct the "social construction of the visual" are characteristically suspicious of the power of images, the chapter argues that making films provides a creative opportunity to explore the "visual construction of the international," especially in terms of affect, bodily sense, and experience.

The chapter develops these theoretical discussions through an autoethnographic account of the methods used to produce a research film. Chapter 4 thus shows what research filmmaking can "do" by providing an innovative method for creating new sites and sensibilities of international politics.

Chapter 5, "Visualizing Security, Order, and War," critically examines another dominant approach to visual international politics: securitization theory, which argues that visual images can shape foreign policy events through their immediacy, circulation, and ambiguity. It uses the North Korea-US national security crisis provoked by the feature film *The Interview* (2014) to question securitization's focus on the state, official elites, and the close relationship between existential threats and security problems. It then introduces the cultural governance/resistance conceptual dynamic to examine how Islamic State videos witnessed the creation (and destruction) not just of a sovereign state, but also of a new social order/world order: the transnational utopia of the Caliphate. Chapter 5 thus shows, on the one hand, the visibility strategy's hermeneutic approach to reading visual securitization, and on the other, the visuality strategy's attention to the broader issues of how social-ordering and world-ordering images can provoke affective communities of sense that complicate what can (and cannot) be seen, said, thought, and done.

Chapter 6, "Visual Art, Ethical Witnessing, and Resistance," engages with another popular approach to visual international politics: visuals as a site of resistance to power, both through producing critical artwork and by ethically witnessing international crises. To trace these issues, it analyzes the work of Ai Weiwei, a world-famous artist-activist whose ethical witnessing creatively resists China's authoritarian party-state. It shows how Ai's art presents ideological resistance to state power, in both the traditional sense of liberal resistance to authoritarian state oppression and the hermeneutical sense, in which it is necessary to decode his work for its "meaning" as the social construction of the visual. The chapter then considers how Ai's documentary film *Human Flow* (2017) provokes transnational resistance through its "visual construction of the social" and of the global. Chapter 6 thus considers how visual art can serve as an ethical witness to resist reigning political regimes, as well as how it can excite affective communities of sense to creatively resist reigning political aesthetics.

Part II thus accomplishes two things. First, it critically engages with existing scholarship on visual IR that looks to the aesthetic turn, securitization, and ethical witnessing. It does this through an analysis of visual images that develops the visibility/visuality and ideology/affect dynamics, while also introducing the cultural governance/resistance dynamic. Second, in this way, *Sensible Politics* expands from verbally-inflected analysis to appreciate how visual images can mean and do things in a different way.

Part III moves beyond existing debates in visual IR to see how visual artifacts can provoke a different kind of sensible politics. The chapters highlight a broad range of visual and multisensory experiences—making maps, wearing a veil, building a wall, enjoying a garden, surfing the Web—to argue that visual artifacts not only mean things but can also "do" things and "make" things in nonnarrative, multisensory, and performative ways. Part III's short introduction explains what is new and different about visual artifacts and sensory spaces. Part III then continues to develop the visibility/visuality, ideology/affect, and cultural governance/resistance dynamics while introducing specific conceptual dynamics for each chapter: center/periphery for maps (Chapter 7), concealing/revealing for women's fashion (Chapter 8), loosening/tightening for walls (Chapter 9), civility/martiality for gardens (Chapter 10), and back to visibility/visuality for surveillance (Chapter 11). Part III, again, deliberately juxtaposes the familiar and the strange, with chapters switching from hard politics to high aesthetics and back again. Importantly, it starts and ends with examples—maps and cyberspace—that complicate the verbal/visual and image/artifact distinctions, in order to develop the analysis of multisensory space.

Part III begins with Chapter 7, "Maps, Space, and Power," highlighting how cartography is a practice in which the visual and the verbal coexist in objects that can be both two-dimensional visual images and three-dimensional visual artifacts and material modalities. Since the 1980s, critical cartography has questioned mimetic understandings of maps as accurate representations of the earth to show how maps are social constructions that reflect broader political and cultural agendas. This chapter builds on this questioning to show how maps themselves can also "do" things as visual artifacts, especially when they are empire-maps and world maps. Maps are an important part of warfare and lawfare (the use of law for strategic purposes), and the chapter proposes the new concept "map-fare" to explore how maps visually construct the social—and the imperial. It introduces and develops the center/periphery dynamic of empire-maps to question the inside-outside logic of national maps. In particular, it considers how the center/periphery logic of Chinese empire-maps is visually shaping the People's Republic of China's (PRC's) current world-ordering projects, in comparison with a briefer consideration of map-fare in Russia and the Islamic State. The chapter argues that map-fare is about more than ideas; the world-ordering of such maps is starting to be enforced on the ground in Ukraine and the South China Sea. The chapter concludes that we need to understand maps as active interventions that can shape international politics, because such map-fare combines word and image, and image and artifact, to visualize and promote particular (imperial) world orders.

Chapter 8, "The Sartorial Engineering of Race, Gender, and Faith," explores visual body politics through the unlikely juxtaposition of young women (1) wearing Islamic veils and (2) participating in beauty pageants. These two practices are exemplary cases of the visibility strategy, especially where veil-wearing's invisibility tactic makes women hypervisible. The chapter uses the conceptual dynamic of concealing/revealing to analyze how various groups—women and men, states and corporations—expend considerable resources negotiating, performing, legislating, policing, and resisting such sartorial practices. Using examples from Europe, the Middle East, and Asia, the chapter first decodes how such practices take on meaning as the individual choices of many women, then considers how the discursive structures of the male gaze and the white/colonial gaze can shape these choices. While much of the debate is located in Europe and the Middle East and is framed by the East/West distinction, the chapter juxtaposes these sites with China to show how structures and agents are mutually constituted through cultural governance and resistance. Finally, the chapter examines how these sartorial performances visually construct the social and the international: you don't just take the veil, the veil also takes you in an experience that is creative as well as disciplinary. Because these are not just visual performances, but also involve touch, the chapter develops the idea of visual artifacts as material modalities. It argues that such material sartorial performances push us to think visually and feel visually in unexpected ways. In other words, does veiling, as a performance of both invisibility and hypervisuality, mark the ethical limits of visual international politics?

Chapter 9, "Walls as Barriers, Gateways, and the Sublime," examines how, as Donald Trump's presidential campaign showed, walls are a hot topic. While "globalization," with its free flow of capital and goods, characterized international politics after the end of the Cold War, the twenty-first century has witnessed a reassertion of cultural, legal, and physical barriers. It is common to criticize such post–Cold War walls, especially the US-Mexico barrier and Israel's West Bank barrier, as ineffective and immoral. This chapter, however, problematizes such arguments by using the unlikely juxtaposition of the Great Wall of China and the conceptual dynamics of gaps and loosening/tightening to explore (1) how walls can be a rational security policy; (2) how they are not simply barriers, but can be complex gateways for flows; and (3) how walls are not simply texts waiting to be decoded but are also sites of nonnarrative and nonlinear affective experience that can even excite the sublime. This critical juxtaposition of walls first explores what they can tell us about the politics of borders, identity, and foreign policy, then considers how, as infrastructures of feeling, walls are examples not simply of ideology, but also of the affective experience of horror and wonder.

Chapter 10, "Gardens in Diplomacy, War, and Peace," notes that while gardens are typically appreciated as peaceful spaces of apolitical serenity, they also can provide new sites and sensibilities that complicate our understanding of international politics. Although gardens are a popular location for diplomatic performances (e.g., the Treaty of Versailles after World War I), the international politics of gardens itself is under-researched. The chapter thus examines gardens as contingent social constructions of social-ordering and world-ordering that both shape and participate in international politics. In particular, it develops the civility/martiality dynamic to explore the sensible politics of how two key national war memorial sites—the Nanjing Massacre Memorial in China and the Yasukuni Shrine in Japan—work as gardens to creatively perform international politics in unexpected ways. Chapter 10's conclusion shows how we can use this analytical framework to better understand (and feel) the sensible politics of other key national memorial spaces, such as the National September 11 Museum and Memorial in New York. As with picture-taking, film-making, map-making, veil-wearing, and wall-building, here garden-building is theory-building: by producing new sites and sensibilities, it creatively shapes our understanding of international politics.

Part III ends with Chapter 11, "Visibility, Visuality, and Mass (Self)Surveillance," which, like Chapter 7, addresses a crossover domain in which the visual and the verbal can coexist in media that can be both two-dimensional visual images and three-dimensional visual artifacts—as well as nondimensional sensory (cyber) spaces. As in Chapter 8, the analysis turns the question of visibility around: not just what we see, but how we are seen, including how we are constituted through various gazes. Chapter 11 explores this through an analysis of the visual international politics of surveillance that looks to historical and social trends. Although it is common to focus analysis and critique on the United States/West, the chapter shows how China is at the cutting edge of surveillance practices both at home and abroad. While most analyses of surveillance look to technology and security, this chapter explores the "culture of surveillance," wherein surveillance is an interactive practice of social-ordering and world-ordering. It examines the visibility/visuality and ideology/affect dynamics through the juxtaposition of European, American, and Chinese surveillance concepts, practices, and experiences. To avoid the problems of an East-West binary opposition, the chapter employs three historical models of social-ordering: the pre-modern society of sovereignty, the modern society of discipline, and the contemporary networked society of control. In this way, it compares how surveillance provokes censorship, self-discipline, and creative social-ordering in China and Europe. The conclusion is that these are political rather than technical or cultural issues, and that it is important to move beyond questions of cybersecurity to appreciate surveillance as a social-ordering and world-ordering project. The visual politics of surveillance thus is not just about how we are captured by the surveillant gaze; it is also about visualizing what kind of world we want to live in, as well as what kind of world we don't want to see and feel.

Part III develops the concept of "visual artifacts" and uses the visibility/visuality framework to analyze them. It highlights how visual artifacts not only mean things but can "do" things in nonnarrative, multisensory, and performative ways. Once again, it stresses how Asian and Middle Eastern visual artifacts provide important concepts, practices, and experiences that can aid us in understanding sensible politics both beyond Eurocentrism and within Euro-America. In this way, Part III argues that to understand social theory and international politics, we need to expand from analysis of visual images to appreciate visual artifacts as material modalities and sensory spaces.

Part IV includes "Conclusion: Sensible Politics." It notes that many of the book's chapters speak to each other (e.g., veils are walls, and gardens require wall-building) and considers how film-making and garden-building experiences can reframe questions of theory, method, and ethics. It recounts how using the visibility and the visuality strategies to examine images and artifacts from Euro-America, the Middle East, and Asia allows us to address questions of ideology and affect in interesting ways. It argues that we need to think beyond critical IR's focus on inside/ outside and self/Other as sites of identity, security, and exclusion, to better appreciate how visual images and multisensory artifacts are involved in much broader projects of social-ordering and world-ordering. While it is common to respond to the challenges of the "post-truth" era by deconstructing "fake news," the conclusion argues that political critique also needs to creatively produce sensory artifacts that can move and connect people to creatively build affective communities of sense to fight such populism. Although the book focuses on visual IR to critique verbally-inflected modes of analysis, it concludes that we also need to expand from our focus on the visual to appreciate multisensory IR, while reconsidering the role of the verbal/multisensory dynamic in international politics. Finally, it argues that it is best not to frame sensible politics merely as a subdiscipline of IR, because sensible politics can serve as an oblique entry into a broader consideration of social theory and international studies.

PART I

VISIBILITY/VISUALITY

A Framework for Analysis

One eye sees, the other feels.

—Paul Klee

The attack on the office of the French satirical magazine *Charlie Hebdo* in 2015 demonstrated how visual images—including cartoons—play an increasingly important role in shaping international political events and our understanding of them. Gunmen associated with al-Qaeda in Yemen stormed the Paris office of this magazine, killing twelve people, including the editor, cartoonists, columnists, and the police who were guarding them. And this was not an isolated case: in 2005 the "Muhammad cartoons" published in a Danish newspaper provoked protests in five Muslim-majority countries, resulting in torched diplomatic missions and nearly 250 deaths, while in 2013 Edward Snowden's revelations about the US National Security Agency's global mass surveillance project provoked an international debate about security, privacy, and global governance.

The influence and impact of the visual on international politics continues to grow. In 2017 Cisco predicted that by 2021, 82 percent of all Internet traffic will be video, up from 73 percent in 2016.[1] As this example shows, the technical change in visual media is not only swift but increasing in speed; any prediction about the growth and spread of visual media quickly becomes

---

[1] "Cisco Visual Networking Index: Forecast and Methodology, 2016–2021" (September 15, 2017) https://goo.gl/SrpKbL (accessed January 8, 2018).

outdated. In addition to the quantitative speed of technological change, visual artifacts have provoked qualitative shifts. On the one hand, smartphone cameras have empowered people to tell their own stories in a new global visual economy that runs parallel to the state and corporate media institutions that dominated the twentieth century. For some, this provides the opportunity for a new, unified world, in which the emerging global society is transnational and visual.[2] The challenges for this global society are technical: overcoming the digital divide between rich and poor, North and South. But they are also political. There is a persistent anxiety over the power of the visual image; while some are concerned about the Islamic State and its successors using visuals to recruit new terrorists, others are concerned about how hidden powers can manipulate voters through "fake news" on the Internet, such as in the Brexit vote and the Trump election.

This speaks to what is different about the visual: it has a way of viscerally grabbing people in ways that are both immediate and intense, with the capacity to provoke "affective communities of sense." Indeed, while warnings are rare for verbal descriptions of atrocities, it is common to see explicit warnings about visual images, for example, **"Warning: Graphic images some viewers might find disturbing.**"[3] In his response to the Muhammad cartoon controversy, United Nations secretary general Kofi Annan spoke to this new visual form of transnational political action: "Incidents like a caricature of the Prophet, or a death threat to the artist who drew it, make far more impact on the popular imagination than pious statements issued by foreign ministers and secretaries-general."[4]

Part I enters into the debate over the power of the image by addressing the theoretical and methodological issues raised in the introduction. (There is some repetition of the introduction's chapter summaries here, so if you just finished reading them, please skip to Chapter 1.) It considers what is important and what is different about the visual's impact on international politics. Although it is popular to use the term "visuality" to discuss how images are more than objective reflections of reality, Part I argues that we need to differentiate between "meaning" and "doing." Chapter 1 explores "visibility"

---

[2] Nicolas Mirzoeff, *How to See the World* (New York: Pelican Books, 2015), p. 6.

[3] Roger Tooth, "Graphic Content: When Photographs of Carnage Are Too Upsetting to Publish," *The Guardian* (July 23, 2014) https://www.theguardian.com/world/2014/jul/23/graphic-content-photographs-too-upsetting-to-publish-gaza-mh17-ukraine (accessed October 17, 2017).

[4] Kofi Annan, quoted in Lene Hansen, "Theorizing the Image for Security Studies: Visual Securitization and the Muhammad Cartoon Crisis," *European Journal of International Relations* 17:1 (2011):68.

to show the hermeneutic search for the meaning of visual images, while Chapter 2 explores "visuality" to appreciate critical aesthetic explorations of how visual artifacts can themselves actively "do" things, often in unexpected ways. Chapter 1 is part of the "visual turn" in international politics that has inspired the serious study of photographs, film, television, online video, maps, visual art, and cartoons/graphic novels. Chapter 2 expands from the symbolic analysis of such "visual images" to develop the concept of "visual artifacts" as material modalities and sensory spaces, for example, maps, veils, walls, gardens, and cyberspace. The first two chapters thus flesh out the visibility/visuality dynamic's relational understanding of the visual and the social; in addition to tracing the "social construction of the visual," they argue that we need to appreciate the "visual construction of the social" and the visual performance of the international. They also examine the interplay of ideology and affect in sensible politics: the visibility strategy works to reveal hidden ideologies, while the visuality strategy appreciates how visuals can move and connect people in "affective communities of sense."

Chapter 3 examines how the visibility/visuality relation is different from the fixed binary distinctions characteristic of Enlightenment modernity. It explores the uneasy relationships between word and image and between ideology and affect to suggest that we need to think in terms of dynamic dyads that are relational, contextual, contingent, and fluid. It argues that dynamic dyads offer a critical approach to Eurocentrism and East/West figurations and introduces other important conceptual dyads—inside/outside, Civilization/barbarism, civility/martiality—that are developed in later chapters. *Sensible Politics* thus engages in comparative analysis that looks to different times and places in order to problematize the present.

The chapters in Part I show how the analysis of visual IR does not require a shift from one approach to another: from visibility to visuality, from ideology to affect, from images to artifacts. Rather, *Sensible Politics* seeks to appreciate how social theory and international politics are provoked and performed through the productive tension of visibility/visuality, ideology/affect, and images/artifacts. It argues that these dynamic dyads provide an analytical framework for the book's exploration of the sensible politics of both iconic images and everyday experiences. Here "sensible" refers both to sensory politics and the pragmatic politics of the everyday.

While visual culture studies is dominated by the disciplines of media studies, cultural studies, and art history, Part I shows the value of figuring visual international politics in a transdisciplinary context that also looks to history, sociology, border studies, Asian studies, and visual anthropology, as well as the conventions and creative practices of picture-taking, film-making, map-making, veil-wearing, wall-building, garden-building, and Web-surfing. Part I thus presents a literature review of visual research done in art history, media and communications, and IR, as well as an original analytical framework for understanding visual international politics.

1

Visibility

The Social Construction of the Visual

The task of *Sensible Politics* is to deconstruct visual images in order to lay bare the ideologies that they illustrate. But it also has the more creative goal of seeing how visual artifacts are more than illustrations of ideology, because they can have their own agency: visuals can actually "do" things, and "make" things. It is popular to use the term "visuality" to discuss how images are more than objective reflections of reality.[1] But for this analysis, I differentiate between "meaning" and "doing"; here "visibility" involves the search for the meaning of the visual, while "visuality" entails an appreciation of how visual artifacts can themselves actively "do" things, often in unexpected ways. The visibility/visuality dynamic builds on W. J. T. Mitchell's dialectical understanding of the relation of the visual and the social: he argues that in addition to tracing the "social construction of the visual," we also need to appreciate the "visual construction of the social."[2] In other words, it is necessary to not simply deconstruct how visual images reflect social, political, and economic power relations; we also need to consider how they can visually provoke new and different social, political, and economic dynamics. While the analytical and political goal of visibility is to "speak truth to power," the aim of visuality is more akin to Umberto

---

[1] Nicholas Mirzoeff, *How to See the World* (New York: Pelican Books, 2015); Hal Foster, ed., *Vision and Visuality* (Seattle: Bay Press, 1988); John Berger, *Ways of Seeing* (London: Penguin Books, 1972); Debbie Lisle, "Learning How to See," in *Routledge Handbook of International Political Sociology*, edited by Xavier Guillaume and Pinar Bilgin, (London: Routledge, 2016), pp. 299–308. For another definition of visuality that stresses its coercive aspects, see Nicholas Mirzoeff, *The Right to Look: A Counterhistory of Visuality* (Durham, NC: Duke University Press, 2011), pp. 13–34.

[2] W. J. T. Mitchell, *What Do Pictures Want? The Lives and Loves of Images* (Chicago: University of Chicago Press, 2005), pp. 343ff.; also see David Campbell, "Geopolitics and Visuality: Sighting the Darfur Conflict," *Political Geography* 26 (2007):379; Rune S. Andersen, Juha A. Vuori, and Can E. Mutlu, "Visuality," in *Critical Security Methods: New Frameworks for Analysis*, edited by Claudia Aradau, Jef Huysmans, Andrew Neal, and Nadine Voelkner (New York: Routledge, 2013), pp. 85–117; Gillian Rose, *Visual Methodologies: An Introduction to Researching with Visual Materials*, 4th ed. (London: Sage, 2016), p. 10.

Sensible Politics. William A. Callahan, Oxford University Press (2020). © Oxford University Press.
DOI: 10.1093/oso/9780190071738.001.0001

Eco's understanding of semiotics as "the discipline studying everything which can be used in order to lie"[3]—especially when we understand lying as an alternative mode of truth-telling. While visibility deconstructs, visuality creates.

To understand this seemingly straightforward visibility/visuality dynamic, it is helpful to consider how it grows out of complex theoretical and methodological debates, particularly discussions about the relation of word and image, ideology and affect, and hermeneutics and critical aesthetics. Rather than suggesting that either visibility or visuality is the definitive strategy for studying visual international politics, Part I considers how they complement each other; instead of understanding them as competing definitions, it is profitable to figure them as a contingent complementary dynamic.[4]

Visibility and visuality are both critical approaches to the mimetic understanding of knowledge as the "mirror of nature," in which visual images are evaluated in terms of how accurately they reflect reality.[5] As Michael J. Shapiro notes for photography, "Of all the modes of representation, it is the one most easily assimilated into the discourses of knowledge and truth, for it is thought to be an unmediated simulacrum, a copy of what we consider the 'real.'"[6] The reality-effect of photography and film is important because once these images are seen as empirically reflecting objective truth, they can be used as "evidence" to judge criminality and deviance in both domestic and international space; the police use visual technologies to profile ethnic and racial minorities, and the national security state uses satellite photography to sort out rogue states—and rogue peoples, such as migrants—from normal ones.[7]

[3] Umberto Eco, *A Theory of Semiotics* (Bloomington: Indiana University Press, 1976), p. 7.

[4] W. J. T. Mitchell, *Iconology: Image, Text, Ideology* (Chicago: University of Chicago Press, 1988), p. 9.

[5] Richard Rorty, *Philosophy and the Mirror of Nature* (Princeton, NJ: Princeton University Press, 1981); Martin Jay, *Downcast Eyes: The Denigration of Vision in Twentieth-Century French Thought* (Berkeley: University of California Press, 1994); Roland Bleiker, *Aesthetics and World Politics* (London: Palgrave Macmillan, 2012).

[6] Michael J. Shapiro, *The Politics of Representation: Writing Practices in Biography, Photography and Policy Analysis* (Madison: University of Wisconsin Press, 1988), p. 124.

[7] Shapiro, *The Politics of Representation*, 135, 141; also see Fraser MacDonald, Rachel Hughes, and Klaus Dodds, eds., *Observant States: Geopolitics and Visual Culture* (New York: I. B. Taurus, 2010); David Shim, *Visual Politics and North Korea: Seeing Is Believing* (London: Routledge, 2013); James Leibold, "Surveillance in Xinjiang: Ethnic Sorting, Coercion, and Inducement," *Journal of Contemporary China* (May 31, 2019):1–15, https://doi.org/10.1080/10670564.2019.1621529 (accessed August 23, 2019); Martina Tazzioli and William Waters, "The Sight of Migration: Governmentality, Visibility, and Europe's Contested Borders," *Global Society* 30:3 (2016):445–464; James Scott, *Seeing Like a State; How Certain Schemes to Improve the Human Condition Have Failed* (New Haven, CT: Yale University Press, 1998).

For the "visibility strategy," the goal is to understand how the meaning of an image is not referential to the "real" world, but is constructed by its social context.[8] The task is to show how the meaning of the image grows out of an overarching "scopic regime," the "who, what, where, and when" of its production, mediation, and consumption.[9] Rather than accept the objective truth of photographs, it is necessary to see them as partial images that not only include people, places, events, and institutions, but also exclude them. Alan Trachtenberg explains how historians and photographers both are confronted with an "opaque mass of facts." To make them intelligible, "[t]he historian employs words, narrative, and analysis. The photographer's solution is in the view-finder: where to place the edge of the picture, what to exclude, from what point of view to show the relations among the included details." The compositional conventions of photography thus are not simply technical, but political: "[T]he viewfinder is a polit-ical instrument, a tool for making a past suitable for the future."[10]

The camera viewfinder's convention of the single-point linear perspective, which is now taken for granted as "natural" in visual culture, is interesting because it has its own history. It was first systematized in fifteenth-century Europe, then "conquered the world of representation under the banner of reason, science, and objectivity (with help of European imperialism)."[11] Cartesian perspectivism's "tyranny of the picture"[12] led Martin Heidegger to declare that we are living in the "age of the world picture," which "does not mean a picture of the world but the world conceived and grasped as a picture."[13] Hence, rather than a singular "world-mirroring," we need to think about how world-picturing functions as "world-making."[14] As we will see in Chapter 7's discussion of maps, there is a close relation between your view of the world and your worldview.[15] The philosophical and technical ability to picture the

[8] Rose, *Visual Methodologies*, 2; Stuart Hall, ed., *Representations: Cultural Representations and Signifying Practices* (London: Sage, 1997).

[9] Jay, *Downcast Eyes*.

[10] Alan Trachtenberg, *Reading American Photographs: Images as History, Matthew Brady to Walker Evans* (New York: Hill and Wang, 1989), p. xiv; also seeRoland Bleiker and Amy Kay, "Representing HIV/AIDS in Africa: Pluralist Photography and Local Empowerment," *International Studies Quarterly* 51 (2007):140.

[11] Mitchell, *Iconology*, 37. Also see Antoine J. Bousquet, *The Eye of War: Military Perception from the Telescope to the Drone* (Minneapolis: University of Minnesota Press, 2018), pp. 21–39; Berger, *Ways of Seeing*, 16ff.; Hal Foster, "Preface," in *Vision and Visuality*, edited by Hal Foster (Seattle: Bay Press, 1988), p. xiv.

[12] Mitchell, *Iconology*, 37; also see Gearóid Ó Tuathail, *Critical Geopolitics* (Minneapolis: University of Minnesota Press, 1996); Jay, *Downcast Eyes*.

[13] Martin Heidegger, *The Question Concerning Technology, and Other Essays* (London: Garland Publishing, 1997), p. 130; also see Mitchell, *What Do Pictures Want?*, xiv.

[14] Mitchell, *What Do Pictures Want?*, xv; Nicholas Onuf, *World of Our Making* (Columbia: University of South Carolina Press, 1989).

[15] See Jordan Branch, *The Cartographic State: Maps, Territory, and the Origins of Sovereignty* (New York: Cambridge University Press, 2014), p. 36.

world as a whole was a "defining element" of European modernity, and mapping the world as a picture enabled European powers to colonize the globe.[16] These new maps not only shaped the material politics of claiming imperial space and sovereignty, but also worked to "colonize the imagination" of both the conquered and the conquerors.[17]

To decolonize the imagination from the scopic regime of Enlightenment modernity, it is helpful to think of visual images in terms of the inside/outside dynamic seen in the practice of framing. Like the camera's viewfinder, the frame is compositional, and it also is ideological.[18] Inside/outside, in many ways, is the master distinction of philosophy, social life, and IR, especially when it works in terms of the self/Other dynamic.[19] To put it another way, the frame determines the limits of visibility/invisibility, and thus the limits of politics: who is included and who is excluded, what is revealed and what is concealed, who/what is veiled and who/what is unveiled.[20] The photograph tells us who we are (and who we aren't); this is the ideology of the image.[21]

Indeed, one way of understanding the US civil rights and women's rights movements is to see how African-Americans and women, who have been historically excluded from politics, empowered themselves by getting into the cultural, social, and political picture frame.[22] Lorraine O'Grady's "Art Is . . ." (1983) project operationalized the technique of framing by mounting a nine-by-fifteen-foot

[16] John Agnew, *Geopolitics: Re-visioning World Politics*, 2nd ed. (London: Routledge, 2003), pp. 15–16.

[17] Walter D. Mignolo, *The Darker Side of the Renaissance: Literacy, Territoriality, and Colonization* (Ann Arbor: University of Michigan Press, 1995), p. 218.

[18] Rose, *Visual Methodologies*, 20; Judith Butler, *Frames of War: When Is Life Grievable?* (London: Verso, 2016); Fraser MacDonald, Rachel Hughes, and Klaus Dodds, "Introduction," in *Observant States: Geopolitics and Visual Culture*, edited by Fraser MacDonald, Rachel Hughes, and Klaus Dodds (New York: I. B. Taurus, 2010), pp. 2, 12.

[19] Gaston Bachelard, *The Poetics of Space* (Boston: Beacon Press, 1964), pp. 211–231; R. B. J. Walker, *Inside/Outside: International Relations as Political Theory* (Cambridge, UK: Cambridge University Press, 1993); William E. Connolly, *Identity\Difference: Democratic Negotiations of Political Paradox*, expanded ed. (Ithaca, NY: Cornell University Press, 2002), pp. 36–63; W. J. T. Mitchell, *Picture Theory: Essays on Verbal and Visual Representation* (Chicago: University of Chicago Press, 1995), p. 42; MacDonald et al., "Introduction," 13; Lilie Chouliaraki, *The Ironic Spectator: Solidarity in the Age of Post-humanitarianism* (Oxford: Polity Press, 2013); Lene Hansen, "Theorizing the Image for Security Studies: Visual Securitization and the Muhammad Cartoon Crisis," *European Journal of International Relations* 17:1 (2011):58.

[20] See R. B. J. Walker, *Out of Line: Essays on the Politics of Boundaries and the Limits of Modern Politics* (New York: Routledge, 2016), p. 26; Butler, *Frames of War*; MacDonald et al., "Introduction," 6; Robert Hariman and John Louis Lucaites, *The Public Image: Photography and Civic Spectatorship* (Chicago: University of Chicago Press, 2016), p. 215.

[21] Hall, *Representations*, 128, 166; Roland Barthes, *Camera Lucida* (New York: Hill and Wang, 1981), p. 28.

[22] Mirzoeff, *How to See the World*, 48; Hansen, "Theorizing the Image for Security Studies," 58.

Figure 1.1 Lorraine O'Grady, "Art Is . . . (Girlfriends Times Two)" (1983/2009). Courtesy Alexander Gray Associates, New York

antique-style gold frame on a float in Harlem's African-American Day Parade.[23] O'Grady's purpose was to include people who typically are excluded from the avant-garde art world by literally framing their neighborhood with the large frame and framing individual people with smaller frames that were carried by fifteen dancing actors. As documented in photographs, this performance art piece was experienced as joyous, playful, and empowering (see figure 1.1).

The struggle for visibility continues in gendered images as well; the British Film Institute noted that there were proportionally fewer women acting on screen in 2017 (30 percent) than in 1913 (31 percent)—although in 2017 many more women were included behind the camera.[24] The politics of visibility/invisibility can also be seen in the controversies about "whitewashing" and cultural appropriation in the cinema, for example, Scarlett Johansson playing a Japanese character in *Ghost*

[23] Lorraine O'Grady, "Art Is . . ." (1983/2009) http://lorraineogrady.com/art/art-is/ (accessed September 23, 2017).

[24] "British Cinema's Gender Imbalance Worse in 2017 Than 1913, Says BFI Study," *The Guardian* (September 20, 2017) https://www.theguardian.com/film/2017/sep/20/british-cinema-gender-imbalance-worse-2017-bfi-filmography (accessed September 22, 2017).

in the Shell (2017)[25] and Matt Damon as pre-modern China's "white savior" in *The Great Wall* (2016).[26]

While O'Grady's "Art Is . . ." (1983) project had dancing African-American actors include Italian-American cops in the celebratory golden frame, more recently framing has shifted to include documenting police brutality against blacks. This "citizen documentation" movement works to erase the invisibility of police shootings, with activist groups providing video-training as well as creating and distributing "smartphone apps that allow onlookers to observe, record and report."[27] Likewise, as Sarah Glidden's award-winning *Rolling Blackouts: Dispatches from Turkey, Syria, and Iraq* shows, citizen journalists are using the long-form graphic reportage genre to get a more diverse range of people into discussions of international politics.[28] In this way, visuals don't just represent the international, but creatively provoke it: in the twenty-first century, to transform local political violence into a global political event, you need a visual (a video, a photograph).[29] The Forensic Architecture project takes this to the next level by using a multimedia strategy to make visible violence, war, and environmental problems, with the goal of providing evidence for "international prosecutors, human rights organizations and political and environmental justice groups." In this way, Forensic Architecture "actually seeks to invert the practice of forensics as currently exercised [by the state], and return the forensic gaze . . . to monitor state agencies (and sometimes corporations)."[30]

[25] Sarah Ahern, "Asian American Media Group Accuses Scarlett Johansson of 'Lying' About 'Ghost in the Shell' Whitewashing Controversy," *Variety* (March 15, 2017) https://variety.com/2017/film/news/scarlett-johansson-ghost-in-the-shell-whitewashing-1202020230/amp/ (accessed September 23, 2017).

[26] Julie Carrie Wong, "Asian Americans Decry 'Whitewashed' Great Wall Film Starring Matt Damon," *The Guardian* (July 29, 2016) https://www.theguardian.com/film/2016/jul/29/the-great-wall-china-film-matt-damon-whitewashed (accessed September 23, 2017).

[27] Matt Pearce, Molly Hennessy-Fiske, and Erica Evans, "As Police Shootings Continue, Bystanders Get More Sophisticated at Filming Altercations," *Los Angeles Times* (July 7, 2016) http://www.latimes.com/nation/la-na-video-shooting-20160707-snap-story.html (accessed July 9, 2016). Also see Jonathan Finn, "Seeing Surveillantly: Surveillance as Social Practice," in *Eyes Everywhere: The Global Growth of Camera Surveillance*, edited by Aaron Doyle, Randy Lippert, and David Lyon (London: Routledge, 2012), pp. 76–77.

[28] Sarah Gliddens, *Rolling Blackouts: Dispatches from Turkey, Syria, and Iraq* (New York: Drawn & Quarterly, 2016). Graphic reportage was pioneered by Joe Sacco and Guy Delisle; see Joe Sacco, *Palestine* (New York: Jonathan Cape, 2003); Guy Delisle, *Pyongyang: A Journey in North Korea* (New York: Jonathan Cape, 2006).

[29] Rune Saugmann Andersen, "Videos," in *Making Things International 1: Circuits and Motion*, edited by Mark B. Salter (Minneapolis: University of Minnesota Press, 2015), p. 260.

[30] Forensic Architecture (no date) https://www.forensic-architecture.org (accessed December 7, 2018); Eyal Weizman, *Forensic Architecture: Violence at the Threshold of Detectability* (Cambridge, MA: Zone Books, 2017), pp. 9–10, 64.

The politics of visibility involves more than efforts to get in the picture frame. Rather than thinking of the inside/outside logic of the frame in terms of absolute exclusion— that is, invisibility—it is also important to consider how the frame works to include some people in hierarchical social orders. Hence visibility is more than the statistics of inclusion that measure it according to gender, race, ethnicity, ability, class, age, sexuality, and so on. We need to focus more on the conditions of visibility and thus the social construction of visual: "the way in which images visualize (or render invisible) social difference."[31] In this way we can determine the hierarchies of visibility and the ideologies that they naturalize. As Susan Sontag argues, "In teaching us a new visual code, photographs alter and enlarge our notions of what is worth looking at and what we have a right to observe. They are a grammar and, even more importantly, an ethics of seeing."[32]

Indeed, in addition to bringing empowerment, being in the picture can be dangerous. The history of warfare is also the history of visibility: "Battlefields were visualized first in the mind's eye of the general; then from the air by balloons, aircraft, satellites and now drones."[33] To frame is to target, in which the military-industrial-media complex "seamlessly merge[s] the production, representation, and execution of war."[34] Here the statecraft of the national security state is closely linked to the stagecraft of the media industry, merging the reel with the real.[35]

The hidden visibility politics of statecraft/stagecraft was graphically shown in the film *Wag the Dog* (1997), in which the White House distracts voters from an emerging sexual scandal by creating a war. Importantly, this war does not exist on the ground, but only in virtual visual media space. The film shows how the statecraft of national security is created through the stagecraft of constructing "the appearance of a war."[36] As the president's fixer explains to the Hollywood producer, we need to think of war "as a pageant, we need a theme, a song, some visuals. We need, ya know—it's a pageant!"

Stagecraft as statecraft can also be seen in military parades, which now are designed for a television audience rather than the dignitaries assembled in the viewing stands. While it is an honor to be invited to watch China's military parades in person, it is also literally a pain in the ass; you have to get there very early, go

---

[31] Rose, *Visual Methodologies*, 11; Hansen, "Theorizing the Image for Security Studies," 63.

[32] Susan Sontag, *On Photography* (New York: Penguin, 1977), p. 3.

[33] Mirzoeff, *How to See the World*, 15. Also see Bousquet, *The Eye of War*.

[34] David Campbell, "Cultural Governance and Pictorial Resistance: Reflections on the Imaging of War," *Review of International Studies* 29 (2003):62; James Der Derian, *Virtuous War: Mapping the Military-Industrial-Media-Entertainment Network* (New York: Routledge, 2009).

[35] See Der Derian, *Virtuous War*; MacDonald et al., "Introduction," 10, 12; Campbell, "Cultural Governance and Pictorial Resistance."

[36] In Barry Levinson, dir., *Wag the Dog* (New Line Cinema, 1997); also see Campbell, "Cultural Governance and Pictorial Resistance," 58.

through invasive security checks, and sit for hours on hard wooden benches.[37] But as a two-minute documentary film produced by the *Guardian* shows, fast-cut editing and emotive music can make a boring parade look cool.[38] Actually, this is not a new practice. Leni Riefenstahl's *Triumph of the Will* (1935) is best understood not as a documentary film recording of the Nazi Party's Nuremberg Rally in 1934; rather, it was the opposite, because the rally was staged for the film: "[T]he ceremonies and precise plans of the parades, marches, processions, the architecture of the halls and stadium were designed for the convenience of the cameras." As Sontag concludes, "In *Triumph of the Will*, the document (the image) is no longer simply the record of reality; 'reality' has been constructed to serve the image."[39]

In the twentieth century, the framing of the battlefield became blurred, thus making surveillance of everyone one of the "foremost activities of the state in a bid to sustain or acquire power through the cogency of the visual."[40] The scopic regime, however, has a much longer history. As feminist analysis of visual art and film has shown, women's visibility is determined by the "male gaze," in which "men act and women appear."[41] The man is the bearer of the look; hence we do not have "images of women, but images as women."[42] In a similar way, the "colonial gaze" works to make non-Europeans visible in specific hierarchal ways.[43] As Edward Said explains, the Occident figures the Orient as part of imperial self/Other relations: the West is strong, masculine, rational, and scientific only when contrasted against the East as weak, feminine, mysterious, and exotic.[44] These imperial conventions still inform a photojournalism that visualizes "Africa" as a site of war, famine, and disease that is either a barbaric Other in the mainstream press or the site of Euro-American humanitarian intervention in the critical press.[45] This is not simply a problem of correcting whitewashing by getting more positive images of Africans into the global media, or even getting more Africans behind the camera. We can see this as the

[37] David Shambaugh, *China Goes Global: The Partial Power* (New York: Oxford University Press, 2013), pp. 1–4.

[38] See Dan Chung, "China's 60th Anniversary National Day—Timelapse and Slow Motion," *The Guardian* (October 1, 2009) https://vimeo.com/6853452 (accessed April 12, 2017).

[39] Susan Sontag, "Fascinating Fascism," *New York Review of Books* (February 6, 1975):1–20.

[40] MacDonald et al., "Introduction," 4. Also see David Lyon, *The Culture of Surveillance: Watching as a Way of Life* (Cambridge, UK: Polity Press, 2018); Leibold, "Surveillance in Xinjiang."

[41] Laura Mulvey, "Visual Pleasure and Narrative Cinema," *Screen* 16:3 (1975):6–18; Berger, *Ways of Seeing.*

[42] Mitchell, *What Do Pictures Want?*, 35.

[43] Frantz Fanon, *Black Skin, White Masks* (New York: Grove Press, 2008); Malek Alloula, *The Colonial Harem* (Minneapolis: University of Minnesota Press, 1986); also see Mirzoeff, *The Right to Look.*

[44] Edward Said, *Orientalism* (New York: Vintage, 2004).

[45] Campbell, "Geopolitics and Visuality"; Bleiker and Kay, "Representing HIV/AIDS in Africa"; Sophie Harman, "Making the Invisible Visible in International Relations: Film, Co-Produced Research and Transnational Feminism," *European Journal of International Relations* (2017):1–23.

site of intersectional entanglement, where the visibility of women, race, and faith erupts in the politics of veiling: Are veiled women victims of patriarchy, or are they empowered by performatively demonstrating their faith? Or something else?

Visibility, once again, is a structural issue of how the visible is socially constructed. These structures determine resistance. While it is common to declare that we need to "tear down the Wall"—both Reagan's demand of Gorbachev in 1987 and the pope's demand of Trump in 2016—sometimes women fight to maintain their veils.[46] The struggle over visibility thus can be violent. In the sixteenth century, Irish leaders resisted English conquest by beheading the first English cartographic surveyor; they didn't want their country "discovered."[47] Discussing the messy intersectional problems of voyeurism raised by critical exhibits of European imperialism in Africa, Mieke Bal argues that rather than more or better photos, we need fewer images: "a thoughtful, sparse use of visual material where every image is provided with an immediately accessible critique that justifies its use with specificity."[48] This suspicion of images is part of a more general critique of the ocular-centrism of Enlightenment and post-Enlightenment thought.[49] Visual images here are problematic because they encourage a "particular sensibility, one habituated to thinking less and feeling more, to quick response over deliberative action."[50] Images thus are dangerous and need to be controlled.

Hermeneutics: The Method for Visibility

One of the great debates in visual culture is about the relation between word and image.[51] Gotthold Ephraim Lessing's classical understanding of painting and poetry explains "the relationship between words and images as potentially a war, but one which he wants to prevent by establishing firm, clear boundaries."[52] Michel Foucault likewise sees the relation between word and image in terms of territorial battle: "a whole series of intersections—or rather attacks launched by one against the other, arrows shot at the enemy target, enterprises of subversion and destruction, lance blows and wounds, a battle."[53] While the idiom tells us that "a picture is worth a

[46] See Jennifer Heath, ed., *The Veil: Women Writers on Its History, Lore, and Politics* (Berkeley: University of California Press, 2008).

[47] Ó Tuathail, *Critical Geopolitics*, 3–5.

[48] Mieke Bal, "The Politics of Citation," *Diacritics* 21:1 (1991): 41.

[49] See Jay, *Downcast Eyes*.

[50] Roxanne L. Euben, "Spectacles of Sovereignty in Digital Time: ISIS Executions, Visual Rhetoric and Sovereign Power," *Perspectives on Politics* 15:4 (2017):1011.

[51] See Mitchell, *Iconology*; Mitchell, *Picture Theory*; Mitchell, *What Do Pictures Want?*

[52] Mitchell, *Picture Theory*, 70.

[53] Michel Foucault, *This Is Not a Pipe* (Berkeley: University of California Press, 1982), p. 26. Also see Mitchell, *Picture Theory*, 70–71.

thousand words," the urge to control visuals, seen in Bal's comment, reflects a general suspicion among critical scholars toward images and other visual artifacts.[54] Michael Ignatieff's oft-cited dismissal of the visual in favor of the verbal is exemplary: "The entire script of the CBS nightly half-hour news would fit on three-quarters of the front page of the *New York Times*."[55]

Here the argument is that the meaning of an image grows out of its textual context, especially through captioning. As Nicholas Mirzoeff explains, "[V]isual culture is the relation between what is visible and the names that we give to what is seen."[56] The idea is that the image cannot speak for itself and thus needs textual intervention to fix meaning and understanding.[57] To put it another way, visual images are best understood as illustrations of verbal arguments. This focus on the textual grounding of visual images is popular in IR scholarship about the global politics of images, especially for the analysis of iconic photographs.[58] Visual images thus can be dangerous; because the emotions of the "unlettered masses" can be manipulated by a well-crafted image, hermeneutics seeks to deconstruct images to reveal their hidden power relations.[59] The solution to the problem of visuals is to cultivate visual literacy, which enables us to speak truth to power.

To critique the power of images, visual culture scholars thus seek to problematize the empiricist methodology that works to accurately reflect reality by "systematically achieving representations of experience by using reliable (that is repeatable) techniques of observation."[60] According to Roland Barthes, images are myths that turn "culture into nature or, at least, the social, the cultural, the ideological,

[54] See Jay, *Downcast Eyes*; Mitchell, *Iconology*; Jessica Evans and Stuart Hall, eds., *Visual Culture: The Reader* (London: Sage, 1999); Rose, *Visual Methodologies*.

[55] Quoted in Bleiker, *Aesthetics and World Politics*, 34.

[56] Mirzoeff, *How to See the World*, 11; Mitchell, *Picture Theory*; Mitchell, *What Do Pictures Want?* For a different view, see Robert Hariman and John Louis Lucaites, *No Caption Needed: Iconic Photographs, Public Culture, and Liberal Democracy* (Chicago: University of Chicago Press, 2011).

[57] Hansen, "Theorizing the Image for Security Studies," 53; Mitchell, *Iconology*; Mitchell, *Picture Theory*; Mitchell, *What Do Pictures Want?*, 140; Campbell, "Geopolitics and Visuality"; Campbell, "Cultural Governance and Pictorial Resistance," 72; Michael C. Williams, "Words, Images, Enemies: Securitization and International Politics," *International Studies Quarterly* 47 (2003):511–531; Rose, *Visual Methodologies*, 16, 236; Roland Bleiker, "Pluralist Methods for Visual Global Politics," *Millennium* 43:3 (2015):875.

[58] See Williams, "Words, Images, Enemies"; Hansen, "Theorizing the Image for Security Studies"; Campbell, "Geopolitics and Visuality," 272; Campbell, "Cultural Governance and Resistance," 72; Michael J. Shapiro, *Studies in Trans-Disciplinary Method: After the Aesthetic Turn* (New York: Routledge, 2013).

[59] Mitchell, *Picture Theory*, 1; also see Mitchell, *What Do Pictures Want?*, 33; Hansen, "Theorizing the Image for Security Studies," 56; Emma Hutchison, *Affective Communities in World Politics: Collective Emotions After Trauma* (Cambridge, UK: Cambridge University Press, 2016), pp. 142ff..

[60] Michael J. Shapiro, *Cinematic Geopolitics* (London: Routledge, 2009), p. 5.

the historical into the 'natural.'"[61] Images thus do not reflect truth, but rather are distractions in a society of spectacle that works according to the rule of simulation and the logic of surveillance.[62] Rather than being active citizens, people here are passive spectators, manipulated by the culture industry into false consciousness.[63] As Walter Benjamin famously wrote, "All efforts to render politics aesthetic culminate in one thing: war."[64]

To decipher such deceptive images, the hermeneutic mode employs a "politicized reading practice."[65] In this sense, we take "photography" literally as "writing with light" to foreground the importance of word over image. Critical analysis thus examines "the political rhetoric of photography" to evaluate

> photographic statements on the basis of their tendency to either reproduce dominant forms of discourse, which help circulate the existing system of power, authority and exchange, or to look at them on the basis of their tendency to provoke critical analysis, to denaturalize what is unproblematically accepted and to offer thereby an avenue for politicizing problematics.[66]

To understand the power of visual images, then, we need to discover the structures of political and economic power that undergird them and unearth the narratives that give them meaning. The politics of visibility thus is the politics of representation, where representations do not simply reflect the world but are social constructions that lend meaning and value to things. Representations are polysemous, containing the possibility of multiple meanings, and thus demand interpretation.[67] Lene Hansen thus argues that the Muhammad cartoon crisis, which the Danish foreign minister called his country's greatest crisis since World War II, was a "crisis of representation."[68] Once again, to understand visual international politics,

---

[61] Roland Barthes, *Image/Music/Text* (New York: Hill and Wang, 1977), p. 165. Also see Roland Barthes, *Mythologies* (New York: The Noonday Press, 1972), p. 142.

[62] See Guy Debord, *The Society of the Spectacle* (Cambridge, MA: MIT Press, 1995); Jean Baudrillard, *Selected Writings*, edited by Mark Poster (Cambridge: Polity, 1988); Michel Foucault, *Discipline and Punish: The Birth of the Prison* (New York: Vintage, 1977); Paul Virilio, *The Vision Machine* (Bloomington: Indiana University Press, 1994).

[63] Jacques Rancière, *The Emancipated Spectator*, translated by Gregory Elliott (London: Verso, 2011), pp. 2–3; Jay, *Downcast Eyes*; Mitchell, *Picture Theory*, 1, 30; Mitchell, *What Do Pictures Want?*, 33, 342; Hutchison, *Affective Communities*, 145.

[64] Walter Benjamin, *Illuminations*, edited by Hannah Arendt (New York: Schocken, 1968), p. 242.

[65] Shapiro, *The Politics of Representation*, 131.

[66] Shapiro, *The Politics of Representation*, 130.

[67] Shapiro, *The Politics of Representation*, 124ff.

[68] Hansen, "Theorizing the Image for Security Studies," 62.

we first need to appreciate the social construction of the visual and then engage in a politicized reading practice to interpret its meaning and reveal its ideology.

Wag the Dog provides a rich example because it shows how such a hermeneutic mode of inquiry works. First, it shows the problem of scandal faced by the incumbent president and the solution proffered by his advisers to hide the scandal not through denial, but by deploying an even bigger news story—here, a war in an obscure location—to distract the voting public. Second, by laying bare the social, political, economic, and cultural construction work necessary to manufacture the (false) images of war, the film is an act of resistance to the combined cultural governance of the White House and Hollywood.[69] The film thus shows how culture is transformed into nature by demonstrating how the "truth claims" of war are actually social constructions that hide ideology. The ideology is not capitalism or communism, but the elite power politics of a society of the spectacle. As Edward S. Herman and Noam Chomsky argue, mass media "manufactures consent" for the status quo.[70] In *Sensible Politics*, "ideology" also refers to the broader sense of how we understand meaning linguistically through structures and codes, which can be deconstructed.

A similar hermeneutic strategy can be seen at work in critical approaches to material objects such as veils. In their analysis of the trend in continental Europe to ban the veil, many critical scholars conclude that we should not concentrate on veiling itself because it distracts us from the real issues of the day: the physical violence and poverty suffered by women, racism in the West, and the political contradictions that define the liberal polity.[71] Likewise, we should not be distracted by the physical infrastructure of walls—the US-Mexico barrier or Israel's West Bank barrier—because their politics is found in unearthing the discursive distinctions that symbolically support such barriers: the social and political power to include/exclude, unite/divide, and reveal/conceal.[72]

Critique here is what Mitchell describes as "iconoclasm": the goal is to deconstruct the image to discover its hidden meaning and thus lay bare its ideology.[73] Although critical of empiricist methods of cause-and-effect, hermeneutics works to draw discursive links between images and power.[74] In visual IR, often

---

[69] See Campbell, "Cultural Governance and Pictorial Resistance."

[70] Edward S. Herman and Noam Chomsky, *Manufacturing Consent: The Political Economy of the Mass Media* (New York: Pantheon Books, 1988).

[71] Heath, *The Veil*; Joan Wallach Scott, *The Politics of the Veil* (Princeton, NJ: Princeton University Press, 2007); Christian Joppke, *Veil: Mirror of Identity* (Cambridge, UK: Polity, 2009).

[72] See Wendy Brown, *Walled States, Waning Sovereignty* (New York: Zone Books, 2014); Eyal Weizman, *Hollow Land: Israel's Architecture of Occupation* (London: Verso, 2007); Thomas Nail, *Theory of the Border* (New York: Oxford University Press, 2016); Yara Sharif, *Architecture of Resistance: Cultivating Moments of Possibility within the Palestinian/Israeli Conflict* (London: Routledge, 2017).

[73] Mitchell, *Iconology*, 3.

[74] Bleiker, "Pluralist Methods," 884.

these are links between images and policy. For example, there is much discussion of the "CNN-Effect," in which images drive policy; that is, whether (or not) the spectacle of war, famine and other atrocities, displayed first on twenty-four-hour cable news programs and now on popular YouTube and social media sites, is able to mobilize the viewing public—and ultimately their political leaders—to respond to injustice.[75] As seen in the preceding discussion, another response to the power of images is to think more about which visuals to employ and how many. Thus to critique the power of mainstream media and Hollywood movies, some commentators appeal to "slower" genres: photographs over film, documentary photos over photojournalism, and visual art over film and photography.[76] Hermeneutics thus engages in "thinking visually" by seeing images in terms of their (con)textuality so as to deconstruct and reveal their underlying ideology.

Conclusion

Chapter 1 develops the visibility strategy as part of a new analytical framework for understanding visual international politics. As part of a critique of empiricism's treatment of images as sources of knowledge that accurately reflect reality, it examines how images take on meaning through the "social construction of the visible." Politics thus is about the empowerment of getting inside the frame of the visible, as well as the problems of becoming a target of dominant gazes. Although this chapter concentrates on visual IR, the structural logic of social construction can also be used to understand the workings of other senses, for example, the social construction of the audible.

The chapter traces the visibility strategy's general suspicion of images, arguing that this is part of a wider critique of the ocular-centrism of European thought. To solve the problem of visual images, Chapter 1 explores how critics use the hermeneutic mode of analysis to reveal hidden ideological meaning and thus speak truth to power. Because images can be used by elites to emotionally manipulate the masses, the visibility strategy argues that they need to be critiqued and controlled.

---

[75] Piers Robinson, *The CNN Effect: The Myth of News Foreign Policy Intervention* (London: Routledge, 2002); Hariman and Lucaites, *The Public Image*; Bleiker and Kay, "Representing HIV/AIDS in Africa."

[76] See Susan Sontag, *Regarding the Pain of Others* (New York: Penguin, 2003), p. 77; Andersen et al., "Visuality," 6; Bleiker, *Aesthetics and World Politics*; Euben, "Spectacles of Sovereignty"; Frank Möller, *Visual Peace: Images, Spectatorship, and the Politics of Violence* (London: Palgrave Macmillan, 2013).

2

Visuality

The Visual Performance of the International

As we saw in Chapter 1, the visibility strategy aims to shift the critical gaze away from content to context—that is, from empiricism's attention to the "what" issues of accurately reflecting reality to consider the "who, when, where, and how" issues of the social construction of the visual. My argument is not that the visibility strategy or its hermeneutic methods are "wrong," but that they are not enough. While "thinking visually" is important, we also need to appreciate the importance of "feeling visually" in international politics. Critical inquiry here changes from asking how the image is constructed to how it makes you feel. Feeling thus is not simply emotions produced by elite manipulation; rather, "feeling visually" appreciates how visuals themselves can be performative, can do things and make things, and thus visually provoke social-ordering and world-ordering practices. The guiding metaphor shifts from the precarious fixity of "framing" to the productive contingency of "moving" and "connecting": connecting people through moving images, moving bodies, moving emotions, and even moving policy.[1] Here we shift from the visibility strategy's analysis of the social construction of the visible to the visuality strategy's appreciation of how images take on meaning and value through the visual construction of the social and the visual performance of the international.

To understand how the visuality strategy works, it is helpful to look at an odd set of maps called "Europe in 2035" that were published in 2012 (see figure 2.1).[2] This exercise in medium-term futurology employs visual artifacts not simply to represent the world or an ideology, but to "do" something: to creatively make a new regional order, and perhaps a new world order. In general, the maps show Western European nation-states fracturing along subnational lines (although Germany and

---

[1] See Brian Massumi, *Parables for the Virtual: Movement, Affect, Sensation* (Durham, NC: Duke University Press, 2002); Judith Butler, *Frames of War: When Is Life Grievable?* (London: Verso, 2016).

[2] See Frank Jacobs, "What Russia Could Look Like in 2035 If Putin Gets His Wish," *Foreign Policy* (June 4, 2014) http://foreignpolicy.com/2014/06/04/what-russia-could-look-like-in-2035-if-putin-gets-his-wish/ (accessed June 6, 2017).

Sensible Politics. William A. Callahan, Oxford University Press (2020). © Oxford University Press.
DOI: 10.1093/oso/9780190071738.001.0001

Figure 2.1 "Europe in 2035," map 2 (2012). Courtesy *Ekspress Gazeta*

Ireland expand), while Russian territory grows to include much (although not all) of the former Soviet Union. Indeed, the futurology project successfully predicted Russia's annexation of Crimea in 2014. Meanwhile, countries that have been "disloyal" to Moscow are dismembered, especially Poland, Ukraine, Latvia, Lithuania, and Estonia. As Frank Jacobs concludes in an online article about the maps in *Foreign Policy*, "This cartographic fantasy panders to Russia's foreign-policy frustrations by predicting future defeats for its 'enemies' and future victories for itself."[3]

Here, the dream of a glorious future is intimately tied to the nightmare of the recent past. Recall Vladimir Putin's declaration that "the collapse of the Soviet Union was the biggest geopolitical catastrophe of the [twentieth] century. For the Russian people, it became a real tragedy. Tens of millions of our citizens and countrymen found themselves outside Russian territory. The epidemic of disintegration also spread to Russia itself."[4] Russian public intellectuals such as Alexander Dugin provide more nuanced arguments for this expansionist ideology of "Eurasianism" and policy prescriptions for "New Russia" that include vast maps that are remarkably similar to Samuel P. Huntington's mapping of Russian Orthodox civilization.[5] Indeed, reportedly a large map of the Soviet Union still hangs on the wall of Russia's visa office in New York.

Of course it is easy to dismiss such maps as unscientific fantasies that are merely propaganda. Indeed, if we use hermeneutic methods to deconstruct the maps, we can see how *Foreign Policy* was duped into broadcasting to an international audience the "fake news" of right-wing propaganda from Russia. Jacobs's English-language article reports on a Russian-language article from Russia's most popular sensationalist tabloid, *Ekspress Gazeta*.[6] But *Ekspress Gazeta* is not the original source for these maps, which first appeared on a popular Ukrainian website, *Obozrevatel'*. While the authorship of the *Ekspress Gazeta* article is anonymous, the author of "Europe in 2035" in *Obozrevatel'* is Igor Lecev, who describes himself as "a deeply intelligent, talented, and, above all, humble journalist . . . [who] is passionate about literature (author of the novel '23'), horror films, and women."[7] Hence, rather than present

[3] Jacobs, "What Russia Could Look Like in 2035."

[4] Quoted in Claire Bigg, "World: Was Soviet Collapse Last Century's Worst Geopolitical Catastrophe?," Radio Free Europe (April 29, 2005) https://www.rferl.org/a/1058688.html (accessed October 7, 2017).

[5] See Alexander Dugin, *Eurasian Mission: An Introduction to Neo-Eurasianism* (London: Arktos Media, 2014); Steven Seegel, *Mapping Europe's Borderlands: Russian Cartography in the Age of Empire* (Chicago: University of Chicago Press, 2012); John Agnew, *Geopolitics: Re-visioning World Politics*, 2nd ed. (London: Routledge, 2003).

[6] "Rossiya pomenyaet Kavkaz na Belorussiyu i Ukrainu" [Russia swaps the Caucasus for Belarus and Ukraine], *Ekspress Gazeta* (July 9, 2012) http://www.eg.ru/daily/politics/32691/ (accessed April 28, 2012). Many thanks to Daniel Fitter for translating these Russian-language sources.

[7] Igor Lecev, "Evropa 2035: iz otkrýtýkh istochnikov TsRU i GRU" [Europe 2035: From CIA and GRU open sources], *Obozrevatel'* (July 3, 2012) https://www.obozrevatel.com/abroad/01548-evropa-2035-iz-otkryityih-istochnikov-tsru-i-gru.htm (accessed April 28, 2017).

a sober analysis of Europe's future that is based on interpreting secret Russian intelligence sources, the "Europe in 2035" maps were created by a Ukrainian horror novelist. Although it appears to be an official plan for Putin's preferred world order, it could very well be a prank.

But the impact of the "Europe in 2035" maps is not limited to empiricist questions about their scientific accuracy, hermeneutic questions about their secret hidden sources, or even questions about authorial intent. The maps took on weight and influence not based on their truth-value or ideological-value, but because they circulated around cyberspace, first in Russian-language networks through the online tabloid newspaper and then around the world again through *Foreign Policy*'s online English-language article. Because of their prominent display on an influential Western media platform, the "Europe in 2035" maps then gained even more traction back in Russia. "Europe in 2035" was popular in Russia because it speaks to (and further mobilizes) already-existing segments of elite and public opinion that long for "New Russia."[8] It was important in the West because it speaks to (and mobilizes) already-existing segments of elite and public opinion that are concerned about such a resurgent Russia. In both cases, it underlines how visual artifacts can mobilize people in ways that differ from state policy decisions that are the result of rational policy analysis or critical textual analysis. These affective communities of sense were excited not necessarily because the maps were given meaning by texts. Although the maps have textual labels, they are in Russian and thus for an international audience do not function as captions to anchor the images' meaning. People thus responded viscerally to what they saw, rather than rationally to what they understood. The maps became important not due to their truth-value or ideological-value, but through "their capacity for circulation and exchange."[9] The "Europe in 2035" episode also shows how almost anyone—including a young Ukrainian horror novelist—now can make a map that does things: here provoking new social configurations of Russian-European-American relations far beyond the imagination or intent of any particular actor. This odd episode shows how visual images can work in nonnarrative and nonlinear ways to construct social relations by provoking emotions—pride, awe, disgust, outrage, fear, and hope—that are themselves political performances. In this way, the "Europe in 2035" maps work to create new visions of social order and world order.

The visuality strategy thus sets aside the iconoclastic view of images that figures the visual as a dangerously powerful mode of manipulation and domination, to consider what images can do and what they can make.[10] Once again, it examines how

---

[8] See Andrei P. Tsygankov and Pavel A. Tsygankov, "National Ideology and IR Theory: Three Incarnations of the 'Russian Idea,'" *European Journal of International Relations* 16:4 (2010):663–686.

[9] Foucault, *Archeology of Knowledge*, quoted in Michael J. Shapiro, *Studies in Trans-Disciplinary Method: After the Aesthetic Turn* (New York: Routledge, 2013), p. 4.

[10] Jacques Rancière, *The Emancipated Spectator*, translated by Gregory Elliott (London: Verso, 2011), p. 96.

the visual constructs the social, especially how the visual can provoke new social-ordering and world-ordering dynamics. The logic of the sensory construction of the social is not limited to the visual but can be used for other senses, such as the sonic performance of the social—and of the international.

Critical Aesthetics: Methods for Visuality

As W. J. T. Mitchell points out, it is easy to confuse a cogent analysis of the social construction of the image with achieving enduring political impact: "We are all familiar with this 'Eureka!' moment, when we reveal to our students and colleagues that vision and visual images, things that (to the novice) are apparently automatic, transparent, and natural, are actually symbolic constructions, like a language to be learned, a system of codes that interposes an ideological veil between us and the real world." While it is certainly necessary to trace the source of, for example, the "Europe in 2035" maps, "[t]here is an unfortunate tendency to slide back into reductive treatments of visual images as all-powerful forces and to engage in a kind of iconoclastic critique which imagines that the destruction or exposure of false images amounts to a political victory."[11] To switch from meaning to doing and from ideology to affect, Mitchell suggests that we shift from the search for the universal "theory of pictures" to "picture theory" itself in a complex and entangled way, and thus "'perform' theory as a visible, embodied, communal practice, not as a solitary introspection of a disembodied intelligence."[12]

To appreciate how the visual can provoke new social relations, we can move toward a "critical aesthetic" mode of inquiry that includes (1) a switch from the search for meaning to an appreciation of what visuals can "do" and (2) a switch from privileging the word over the image to see a more uncertain relation of word and image, (3) which enables a shift from the search for ideology to an appreciation of how the visual works affectively to move people and connect them in affective communities of sense; finally, (4) this critical aesthetic mode refocuses the critical gaze from the reformist politics of empowerment by shifting to see critique in terms of unsettling reigning "distributions of the sensible."[13]

---

[11] W. J. T. Mitchell, *What Do Pictures Want? The Lives and Loves of Images* (Chicago: University of Chicago Press, 2005), pp. 344, 351; also see Fraser MacDonald, Rachel Hughes, and Klaus Dodds, "Introduction," in *Observant States: Geopolitics and Visual Culture*, edited by Fraser MacDonald, Rachel Hughes, and Klaus Dodds (New York: I. B. Taurus, 2010), p. 14.

[12] Mitchell, *What Do Pictures Want?*, 355; also see W. J. T. Mitchell, *Picture Theory: Essays on Verbal and Visual Representation* (Chicago: University of Chicago Press, 1995), p. 6.

[13] See Jacques Rancière, *The Politics of Aesthetics: The Distribution of the Sensible*, translated by Gabriel Rockhill (London: Continuum International Publishing Group, 2004); Meg McLagan and Yates McKee, eds., *Sensible Politics: The Visual Culture of Nongovernmental Activism* (New York: Zone Books, 2012); Rune S. Andersen, Juha A. Vuori, and Can E. Mutlu, "Visuality," in *Critical Security*

When I speak here of "aesthetics" in global politics, I am not discussing a theory of beauty, but am more concerned with modes of social-ordering and world-ordering that raise ethical questions.[14] While the "aesthetic turn" in IR generally concentrates on criticizing empiricism to allow space for hermeneutic interpretation,[15] critical aesthetics is different; it questions both empirical and hermeneutic modes of inquiry. As Michael J. Shapiro argues, "[T]o interrogate statements is not to discover either fidelity of what they are about (the empiricist focus on representation) or their intelligibility when their silent context is disclosed (a hermeneutical focus on disclosure)."[16] Rather, as Jacques Rancière suggests, we need to critically analyze politics in terms of particular "aesthetic regimes" that are "a mode of articulation between ways of doing and making, their corresponding forms of visibility, and possible ways of thinking about their relationships."[17] This aesthetically-inflected politics thus is a specific "distribution of the sensible": "the delimitation of spaces and times, of the visible and the invisible, of speech and noise, that simultaneously determines the place and the stakes of politics as a form of experience."[18] Sensible politics, therefore, is found not just in the partisan struggle for institutional power, but also in the configuration of space and sensibility that provokes specific social orders and world orders. It takes shape in either "policing" the hegemonic distribution of the sensible or challenging it through dissensus, a redistribution of the sensible that "disrupt[s] the relationship between the visible, the sayable, and the thinkable."[19] Aesthetically-inflected politics here emerges in active multidimensional performances that take in all senses of material experience.[20] *Sensible Politics* thus is not only about "what can be sensed" but also concerns "what makes sense" in the pragmatic politics of everyday life.[21]

The critical aesthetic mode thus involves a reconfiguration of the word/image relation. While narrative theory argues that we need to interpret the meaning of texts in relation to other texts—that is, intertextuality—the visuality strategy examines

Method: New Frameworks for Analysis, edited by Claudia Aradau, Jef Huysmans, Andrew Neal, and Nadine Voelkner (New York: Routledge, 2013), pp. 85–117.

[14] David L. Hall and Roger T. Ames, *Anticipating the Han: Thinking Through the Narratives of Chinese and Western Culture* (Albany: State University of New York Press, 1995); Rancière, *The Politics of Aesthetics*; Rancière, *The Emancipated Spectator*; Roland Bleiker, *Aesthetics and World Politics* (London: Palgrave Macmillan, 2012); Shapiro, *Trans-Disciplinary Method*.

[15] See, for example, Bleiker, *Aesthetics and World Politics*, 1–47.

[16] Shapiro, *Trans-Disciplinary Method*, 4.

[17] Rancière, *The Politics of Aesthetics*, 10.

[18] Rancière, *The Politics of Aesthetics*, 13.

[19] Rancière, *The Politics of Aesthetics*, 63.

[20] Rancière, *The Politics of Aesthetics*, 40–41; also see Judith Butler, *Gender Trouble: Feminism and the Subversion of Identity* (New York: Routledge, 2006).

[21] Davide Panagia, *The Political Life of Sensation* (Durham, NC: Duke University Press, 2009), p. 3. Also see McLagan and McKee, *Sensible Politics*.

how images don't simply illustrate texts, but also look to other images in a process of "intervisuality" wherein an "image never stands alone. It belongs to a system of visibility."[22] As Lene Hansen explains, the pictures of emaciated people in concentration camps in the Bosnian war were compelling, in part, because they intervisually evoked iconic photos of people liberated from Nazi death camps in World War II.[23]

In the *Empire of Signs*, Roland Barthes suggests another appreciation of the word/image relation. This idiosyncratic work about his experiences in Japan creatively mixes personal writing with photographs and drawings for a new form of critique in which "[t]he text does not gloss the images, which do not illustrate the text. For me, each has been no more than the onset of a kind of visual uncertainty."[24] This unstable relation of word and image creates fruitful ambiguity. Commenting on a Japanese calligraphic painting, Barthes asks: "Where does the writing begin? Where does the painting begin?"[25] To answer this question, Barthes moves away from hermeneutics to suggest that such a critique "paints more than it digs."[26] Value here emerges in the visceral movement and bodily connections mobilized by this particular redistribution of the see-able and the say-able.

The hermeneutics/critical aesthetics distinction is also an iteration of the long-standing philosophical debate over whether value resides in deep principles or in activities on the surface. Jürgen Habermas praises ancient Greece and other Axial Age civilizations for "br[eaking] open the chasm between deep and surface structure, between essence and appearance, which first conferred the freedom of reflection and the power to distance oneself from the giddy multiplicity of immediacy."[27] Friedrich Nietzsche, on the other hand, argued that it is a mistake to assume that value is hidden in the depths. He felt that the "giddy multiplicity of immediacy" is not a problem, but an opportunity: "Oh, those Greeks! They knew how to *live*: what is required is to stop bravely at the surface, the fold, the skin, to worship appearance, to believe in shapes, tones, words, in the whole Olympus of appearance!"[28] While hermeneutics textualizes images to reveal their deep hidden meaning, critical aesthetics generally looks for value at the surface in embodied, affective, and everyday encounters on the local, national, and world stages.

---

[22] Rancière, *The Emancipated Spectator*, 99.

[23] Lene Hansen, "Theorizing the Image for Security Studies: Visual Securitization and the Muhammad Cartoon Crisis," *European Journal of International Relations* 17:1 (2011):53.

[24] Roland Barthes, *Empire of Signs* (New York: Hill and Wang, 1982), p. xi.

[25] Barthes, *Empire of Signs*, 21.

[26] Roland Barthes, "Inaugural Lecture: College de France," in *A Barthes Reader*, edited by Susan Sontag (London: Vintage, 2000), p. 475.

[27] Jürgen Habermas, *Time of Transitions*, translated and edited by Max Pensky (Cambridge, UK: Polity Press, 2006), p. 160.

[28] Friedrich Nietzsche, *The Gay Science*, edited by Bernard Williams (Cambridge, UK: Cambridge University Press, [1887] 2001), pp. 8–9.

In this way, films can be valuable not necessarily for the meaning of their narrative content, but for their affective dynamics. For example, in discussing a film's critical contribution, Shapiro explains that "[w]hile the narrative of the film reaches no dramatic conclusion, the film's landscape and close-up face and body shots carry the burden of its political thinking."[29] In this decentered world, "time is a function of the cuts and juxtapositions of the editing rather than linear flowing of the movement of the characters."[30] Shapiro thus encourages us to "avoid argument-marking meta-statements" in order to allow "juxtapositions [to] carry much of the burden of the analyses."[31] Chapter 4's discussion of methods, for example, traces how research filmmaking can enable us to appreciate the power of the nonlinear, nonlinguistic, and nonrepresentational aspects of experience: the laughs, sighs, shrugs, cringes, and tears that are provoked in the on-camera interview process, which then can be edited into an engaging set of images that, in turn, can produce laughs, cringes, and tears in the film's audience. Here we move from an empirical/hermeneutic process of making subjects more "visible" to the critical aesthetic mode of exploring the "visuality" of how images themselves can "do" things through nonlinear and non-narrative dynamics.[32] Rancière thus argues that politics emerges not through representation, but through mis-en-scène.[33]

The critical aesthetics mode, therefore, enables us to explore how the visual provokes social-ordering and world-ordering through opening up new affective registers. In this sense, it operationalizes "*aisthitikos*—the ancient Greek word/concept from which aesthetics is derived—[that] refers to the pre-linguistic, embodied, or feeling-based aspect of perception."[34] "Affect" is a broad and contested concept.[35] It generally seeks to shift critical focus from facts to feelings, from stable individual identity to multiple flows of encounter, from texts to nonlinear, nonlinguistic, and nonrepresentational genres, from abstract rational knowledge to embodied forms

---

[29] Shapiro, *Trans-Disciplinary Method*, 23.

[30] Shapiro, *Trans-Disciplinary Method*, 24.

[31] Shapiro, *Trans-Disciplinary Method*, 31.

[32] Gillian Rose, "On the Relation between 'Visual Research Methods' and Contemporary Visual Culture," *The Sociological Review* 62:1 (2014):36–41.

[33] Rancière, *The Emancipated Spectator*, 67.

[34] Shapiro, *Trans-Disciplinary Method*, 15.

[35] See Massumi, *Parables for the Virtual*; Brian Massumi, *Politics of Affect* (Cambridge, UK: Polity, 2015); Emma Hutchison, *Affective Communities in World Politics: Collective Emotions After Trauma* (Cambridge, UK: Cambridge University Press, 2016); Jean-François Lyotard, *Discourse, Figure*, translated by Antony Hudek and Mary Lyndon (Minneapolis: University of Minnesota Press, 2011); Roland Bleiker and Emma Hutchison, eds., "Forum: Emotions and World Politics," special issue, *International Theory* 6:3 (2014):490–594; Gregory J. Seigworth and Melissa Gregg, "An Inventory of Shimmers," in *The Affect Theory Reader*, edited by Melissa Gregg and Gregory J. Seigworth (Durham, NC: Duke University Press, 2010), pp. 1–25; Brian L. Ott, "Affect," in *Oxford Research Encyclopedia of Communication* (Oxford: Oxford University Press, 2017), pp. 1–26.

of experience, and thus from ideology to affect. Brian Massumi famously argues that affect is an "intensive force" that emerges through the visceral resonance of connecting bodies at "the intersection of matter, movement, aesthetics, and sensation."[36] Affect theory generally differentiates between emotion and affect, seeing emotion as the internal subjective content of the individual, while affect emerges as a social experience as bodies connect in an "affective economy."[37] This is a complex argument, and the lesson that I take from it is that affect is a useful concept for appreciating how visual artifacts can act as material modalities and sensory spaces that move and connect people both individually and collectively.

Affect theory is often discussed in terms of visual experiences because, as Massumi notes, they are "central to an understanding of our information- and image-based late capitalist culture."[38] This is because visuals move people in ways that make them "feel a connection with others" in a visceral way: "If seeing is believing, then seeing is also feeling."[39] For example, *Smog Journeys* (2015), a short advocacy film that top Chinese director Jia Zhangke made for Greenpeace, does not use words or a linear narrative to discuss China's environmental problems. It is a "silent movie" that juxtaposes a series of images and (nonverbal) sounds of polluted/clean air, rich/poor people, and urban/rural life-worlds. The political work of the film emerges through these relations, and especially in the juxtaposition of the tragic image of a sick baby's staccato cough against the comic scene of models promoting fashionable face-masks on the catwalk[40] (see figure 2.2). This film is a great example of the audio-visual creation of meaning and feeling, because it shows the social construction of the audible and the sonic construction of the social. This is a different sort of public service announcement (PSA): rather than work through providing evidence and argumentation, the film mobilizes a reaction (and perhaps political action) by provoking a visceral response that connects people. As photojournalist Don McCullin explains, "Photography for me is not looking, it's feeling. If you can't feel what you're looking at, then you're never going to get others to feel anything when they look at your pictures."[41]

For the hermeneutics mode, this would be a problem: hegemonic powers use emotional images to manipulate the general public. But with affect theory, feelings are valued in a different register of experience that moves and connects people.

[36] Massumi, *Parables for the Virtual*, 28; also see Rancière, *The Politics of Aesthetics*, 39; Ott, "Affect," 13.

[37] Massumi, *Parables for the Virtual*, 28; Ott, "Affect," 3; Sarah Ahmed, *The Cultural Politics of Emotion* (Edinburgh: Edinburgh University Press, 2004), pp. 44–49.

[38] Massumi, *Parables for the Virtual*, 27.

[39] Anderson et al., "Visuality," 13.

[40] Jia Zhangke, dir., *Smog Journeys* (Beijing: Greenpeace, January 21, 2015) https://www.youtube.com/watch?v=zfF7ZmKMUX0 (accessed October 17, 2017).

[41] Quoted in David Campbell, "Cultural Governance and Pictorial Resistance: Reflections on the Imaging of War," *Review of International Studies* 29 (2003):68.

Figure 2.2 Jia Zhangke, *Smog Journeys* (2015). Courtesy Greenpeace East Asia

Judith Butler, for example, traces how photographs of torture and suffering can generate affective intensities through an emotional economy of grief.[42] Emma Hutchison goes further to examine the affective register as collective sociality in international politics, in which intense experiences can mobilize "affective communities."[43] As Adam Curtis's innovative documentaries show, international politics is also about dreams, nightmares, and feelings that move people, connecting and repelling them.[44] Mitchell thus argues that pictures themselves can have the agency to desire, while Rancière celebrates how spectators are active and political in "communities of sense."[45] Sensible politics thus is collective, affective, and multisensory in the way that it productively provokes "affective communities of sense" in both elite forums and the pragmatic everyday.

Critical aesthetics also enables us to take seriously the visual and multisensory politics of material things such as maps, veils, walls, and gardens by allowing us to

---

[42] Butler, *Frames of War*.

[43] Hutchison, *Affective Communities*, 4.

[44] Adam Curtis, dir., *The Power of Nightmares* (London: BBC, 2004); Adam Curtis, dir., *Bitter Lake* (London: BBC, 2015).

[45] Mitchell, *What Do Pictures Want?*; Rancière, *The Emancipated Spectator*; Jacques Rancière, "Contemporary Art and the Politics of Aesthetics," in *Communities of Sense: Rethinking Aesthetics and Politics*, edited by Beth Hinderliter, William Kaizen, Vered Maimon, Jaleh Mansoor, and Seth McCormick (Durham, NC: Duke University Press, 2009), p. 31. Also see Michael J. Shapiro, *The Political Sublime* (Durham, NC: Duke University Press, 2018); Lilie Chouliaraki, *The Ironic Spectator: Solidarity in the Age of Post-humanitarianism* (Oxford: Polity Press, 2013); Robert Hariman and John Louis Lucaites, *The Public Image: Photography and Civic Spectatorship* (Chicago: University of Chicago Press, 2016); Frank Möller, *Visual Peace: Images, Spectatorship, and the Politics of Violence* (London: Palgrave Macmillan, 2013).

get beyond the interpretive search for meaning to consider what work these visual artifacts can do, including how they can "picture" theory.[46] A map thus is more than a reflection of the contemporary world. As Cordell D. K. Yee explains, it also can "serve as an instrument of political persuasion, give form to emotional states, or even afford access to transcendent beings."[47] Maps thus aren't just images that represent ideology, because they also can circulate affect as material artifacts in the classroom, that students touch and that touch students. As heavily-designed spaces that forge particular relations between the see-able, hear-able, smell-able, and the touch-able, visual artifacts such as war memorials, monuments, walls, and gardens are also exemplary distributions of the sensible. These infrastructures of feeling have what Jane Bennett calls "*Thing-Power*: the curious ability of inanimate things to animate, to act, to produce effects dramatic and subtle."[48] Rather than see visual culture in terms of "just the study of images or media"—and rather than see visual international politics in terms of the state-centric study of violence, war, and security—visual artifacts show that it is necessary to consider visual IR in terms of the "everyday practices of seeing and showing."[49] Once again, "sensible politics" is more than sensory; it looks beyond icons and ideology to address "what makes sense" in the pragmatic politics of everyday life.

Expanding analysis from two-dimensional visual images to three-dimensional visual artifacts aids the switch from the symbolic analysis of the politics of representation to the affect-work done in multisensory spaces wherein one can be an observer, a participant, and—when things go awry—even a target. Attention to visual artifacts does not deny that many people experience them as moving and still images, for example, videos of people partying on the Berlin Wall in 1989. And it works the other way around, too. Visual images can take on material form as artifacts and practical experiences; an important part of "going to the movies"

[46] MacDonald et al., "Introduction," 15.

[47] Cordell D. K. Yee, "Concluding Remarks: Foundations for a Future History of Chinese Mapping," in *The History of Cartography*, Vol. II, Book II, *Cartography in the Traditional East and Southeast Asian Societies*, edited by J. B. Harley and David Woodward (Chicago: University of Chicago Press, 1994), p. 228.

[48] Elena Barabantseva coined the phrase "infrastructure of feeling." Jane Bennett, *Vibrant Matter: A Political Ecology of Things* (Durham, NC: Duke University Press 2010), p. 6. Also see Hutchison, *Affective Communities*, 128; Caitlin Hamilton, "The Everyday Artefacts of World Politics: Why Graphic Novels, Textiles and Internet Memes Matter in World Politics" (PhD dissertation, University of New South Wales, 2016); Mark B. Salter, "Introduction: Circuits and Motion," in *Making Things International 1: Circuits and Motion*, edited by Mark B. Salter (Minneapolis: University of Minnesota Press, 2015), pp. vii–xxii; Carlos Rojas, *The Great Wall: A Cultural History* (Cambridge, MA: Harvard University Press, 2010); Wybe Kuitert, *Japanese Gardens and Landscapes, 1650–1950* (Philadelphia: University of Pennsylvania Press, 2017).

[49] Mitchell, *What Do Pictures Want?*, 343; Nicholas Mirzoeff, *How to See the World* (New York: Pelican Books, 2015); Shapiro, *Trans-Disciplinary Method*, xiii.

is its collective social experience, and "with still photographs the image is also an object, light-weight, cheap to produce, easy to carry about, accumulate, store. . . . To collect photographs is to collect the world."[50] The goal thus is to appreciate visual artifacts as material modalities and sensory spaces in which international politics is represented, performed, and experienced through more embodied, affective, and everyday encounters on the local, national, and world stages.

In a broader sense, the shift from meaning to doing and from ideology to affect entails a reconfiguration of the political away from the issues of framing seen in the visibility strategy. Certainly, focusing on including a more diverse selection of people in the picture frame has been an effective strategy for positive social change.[51] But what Allan Sekula criticized as the "find-a-bum school of concerned photography" shows how "photographs are not necessarily more politicized and less ideological when they are explicitly called upon on behalf of a political-reform issue."[52] In other words, images of refugees in need of international aid can easily serve to reify the existing social hierarchies of rich/poor, safety/danger, and here/there.[53] A "critical attitude" of self-reflection thus needs to go beyond "merely serving particular social segments or disempowered groups." Instead, it needs to "present a challenge to identity politics in general, . . . even those on which some social movements are predicated." Rather than stake out political positions, the goal here is to "displace institutionalized forms of recognition with *thinking*. To think (rather than to seek to explain) in this sense is to invent and apply conceptual frames and create juxtapositions that disrupt and/or render historically contingent accepted knowledge practices."[54] Instead of working through either empiricist explanation or hermeneutic interpretation, critical aesthetics can provide a "heterogeneous assemblage" that works to arrest common sense—even the common sense of Left-Right politics used to critique Donald Trump's Great Wall of America.[55]

[50] Susan Sontag, *On Photography* (New York: Penguin, 1977), p. 3.

[51] Mitchell, *What Do Pictures Want?*, 350.

[52] Allan Sekula, quoted in Michael J. Shapiro, *The Politics of Representation: Writing Practices in Biography, Photography and Policy Analysis* (Madison: University of Wisconsin Press, 1988), pp. 162, 130.

[53] Roland Bleiker and Amy Kay, "Representing HIV/AIDS in Africa: Pluralist Photography and Local Empowerment," *International Studies Quarterly* 51 (2007):146ff.; David Campbell, "Geopolitics and Visuality: Sighting the Darfur Conflict," *Political Geography* 26 (2007):357–382; R. B. J. Walker, *Inside/Outside: International Relations as Political Theory* (Cambridge, UK: Cambridge University Press, 1993).

[54] Shapiro, *Trans-Disciplinary Method*, 8, xv; also see Seigworth and Gregg, "An Inventory of Shimmers," 11.

[55] Roland Bleiker, "Pluralist Methods for Visual Global Politics," *Millennium* 43:3 (2015):882–883; Gilles Deleuze and Felix Guattari, *A Thousand Plateaus: Capitalism and Schizophrenia* (London: Athlone Press, 1996), pp. 3–25, 377.

If we set aside, for a moment, the familiar measures of partisan politics, how does the critical aesthetic mode of inquiry evaluate things? How does it figure the relation between the sensible and international politics? One way is to shift from the symbolic vocabulary of representation, meaning, and ideology toward a sensible materialist appreciation of intensity, resonance, rhythm, and vibration. To grasp the power of affect, we do not look for "conformity or correspondence, but rather . . . resonation or interference, amplification or dampening."[56] Barthes thus calls on us to conduct an "inventory of shimmers, of nuances, of states, of changes" that is attuned to the giddiness of unexpected and inexplicable experiences.[57] As Mitchell explains, "It isn't simply that the words contradict the image, and vice versa, but that the very identities of words and images, the sayable and the seeable, begin to shimmer and shift in the composition, as if the image could speak and the words were on display."[58] According to Michel Foucault, the weight of discursive formations, including visual artifacts, is a "value that is not defined by their truth, that is not gauged by the presence of a secret content; but which characterizes their place, their capacity for circulation and exchange."[59] Rather than test the truth-value of data or the truth-claims of representations, it seeks to appreciate the "shimmer-value" of heterogeneous visceral encounters that move and connect people in affective communities of sense. This book's discussion of maps in Chapter 7, for example, examines how cartographs can creatively generate alternative world orders in the South China Sea. It looks to the family resemblances seen in a set of maps from early modern and modern East Asia to show how they collectively produced, promoted, and circulated an affective atmosphere that mobilized communities of sense. Rather than search for the "original map" as objective evidence to prove sovereign territorial claims, the chapter argues that these maps "intervisually" resonate with each other to celebrate China's imperial expansion, to lament its lost territories, and to fight to recover them.

The critical aesthetic mode thus highlights how international politics takes shape through sensibility, experience, performativity, and social-ordering and world-ordering in affective communities of sense. These contingent dynamics resonate with each other in complex ways as an assemblage that offers no stable account of causality.[60] Hence, while the international politics of visuality is often overlooked, even in critical IR, because of its indirect impact on global affairs, *Sensible Politics* argues that visuality can do international politics in a broader way by provoking affective communities of sense that complicate what can (and cannot) be seen, said, thought, and done.[61]

---

[56] Massumi, *Parables for the Virtual*, 25.
[57] Quoted in Seigworth and Gregg, "An Inventory of Shimmers," 11.
[58] Mitchell, *Picture Theory*, 68.
[59] Foucault, *Archeology of Knowledge*, quoted in Shapiro, *Trans-Disciplinary Method*, 4.
[60] Bleiker, "Pluralist Methods," 882.
[61] Rancière, *The Politics of Aesthetics*, 13; Rancière, "Contemporary Art and the Politics of Aesthetics," 31; William E. Connolly, *Identity\Difference: Democratic Negotiations of Political Paradox*, expanded ed. (Ithaca, NY: Cornell University Press, 2002); Bleiker, "Pluralist Methods," 874.

Conclusion

While Chapter 1 considers what is important about visual IR, Chapter 2 explores what is different about visual international relations: how visual images don't just illustrate international events as visual texts, but can actively create international politics as visual performances that viscerally move and connect people in unexpected ways. The chapter shifts from the visibility strategy's focus on the social construction of the visible to the visuality strategy's appreciation of how images take on meaning and value through the visual construction of the social. While the visibility strategy looks to the inside/outside dynamics of framing, the visuality strategy examines how the visual can provoke and perform new social-ordering and world-ordering activities. Chapter 2 thus develops the idea of sensible politics as a collective, affective, and multisensory dynamic that excites "affective communities of sense" in both elite forums and everyday life. *Sensible Politics* is about multisensory politics; it also looks beyond icons and ideology to "what makes sense" in the pragmatic politics of the everyday.

Chapter 2 also expands on Chapter 1's symbolic analysis of "visual images"—photos, film, television—to develop the concept of "visual artifact": maps, veils, walls, gardens, and cyberspace. It argues that such three-dimensional visual artifacts can shape IR as material modalities, sensory spaces, and infrastructures of feeling that are experienced both individually and collectively. To evaluate how visual images and artifacts don't just mean things, but can actively do things, the visuality strategy moves beyond assessing their ideological-value to appreciate their affect-work: not just what they mean, but also how they make us feel. Chapter 2 thus challenges the critique of ocular-centrism by outlining how the visuality strategy can help us appreciate affective communities of sense in a different register. The goal is to make readers not only think visually, but also feel visually—and act visually for a multisensory appreciation of politics.

Certainly Chapter 1's discussion of hermeneutics is too narrow; many of the theorists described in this analysis would say that they are exploring aesthetics. Similarly, Chapter 2's discussion of affect theory is too wide; it includes emotions, whereas some affect theorists argue that affect and emotion need to be differentiated. But I find the ideology/affect and hermeneutics/critical aesthetics distinctions useful for differentiating between strategies that turn visuals into meaningful texts in order to reveal their hidden ideology and those that work to appreciate visuals as multisensory affective performances that excite social orders and world orders.

3

Dynamic Dyads

Visibility/Visuality and East/West

What is the relation between visibility and visuality? From the discussion in Chapters 1 and 2, it would be easy to conclude that critical aesthetics is the proper mode for appreciating visual international politics. Indeed, the two chapters' brief summary of hermeneutics and critical aesthetics risks descending into a caricature of pitched battles between words and images. Rather than see visibility and visuality in terms of theoretical battles between opposing positions, perhaps it's better to understand them in terms of a historical development from empiricism, to hermeneutics, and finally to critical aesthetics. Indeed, this movement can be seen in the intellectual trajectories of many of the key theorists discussed in Chapters 1 and 2, who typically started out using hermeneutic methods, then developed more critically aesthetic modes for appreciating the visual.[1]

But *Sensible Politics* figures visual international politics neither in terms of pitched battles nor through historical evolution. What we have is an uneasy relation between visibility and visuality: as W. J. T. Mitchell explains, although he aimed to "move away from meaning and power, [he] kept circling back to semiotics, hermeneutics, and rhetoric."[2] Certainly one reason for this is that the political-economy of the academy values verbally-inflected knowledge production over visually-oriented work.[3] For me, however, it is more than the logistical issue of which genre to employ. As Chapter 4 on methods recounts, I am part of a growing group of scholars who explore international politics not only through writing books, but by making research films. The argument of this chapter (and this book) thus is that we need to explore sensible politics in terms of both visibility and visuality for theoretical and methodological reasons. Only in this way can we benefit from understanding visual

[1] See, for example, the works of W. J. T. Mitchell, Michael J. Shapiro, and Susan Sontag.

[2] W. J. T. Mitchell, *What Do Pictures Want? The Lives and Loves of Images* (Chicago: University of Chicago Press, 2005), p. 46.

[3] See Nicholas Mirzoeff, *An Introduction to Visual Culture*, 2nd ed. (New York: Routledge, 2009), p. xiv.

Sensible Politics. William A. Callahan, Oxford University Press (2020). © Oxford University Press.
DOI: 10.1093/oso/9780190071738.001.0001

international politics in terms of both the "social construction of the visual" and the "visual performance of social orders and world orders."

This visibility/visuality dynamic works itself out in several ways. While hermeneutics privileges the verbal, and affect theory the sensory, some theorists seek to see visual artifacts in terms of an organic combination of word-image, as seen with Roland Barthes's appreciation of calligraphic paintings.[4] Jacques Rancière and Michael J. Shapiro both aim to loosen the hierarchy of word over image by figuring the relation as a contingent dynamic, so as to probe "the relationship between the visible, the sayable, and the thinkable."[5] Mitchell suggests that we think in terms of "image/text," because "all media are mixed media."[6] Since words and images are in an "infinite relation" wherein "neither can be reduced to the other's terms," Michel Foucault argues that we should treat this "incompatibility as starting point, rather than as an obstacle."[7]

In light of this hopeful vagueness, it is helpful to consider concrete examples that play with word and image, and with meaning and doing. For example, the Chinese character for map, *tu* (图, which is also used in Korean and Japanese), speaks to a double-coded understanding of visibility's "social construction of the visual" and visuality's "visual provocation of social relations." As a noun, *tu* means a picture, a diagram, a chart, a table, and a map, while as a verb it means to anticipate, to hope, to scheme, to plan, to plot against, and even to covet.[8] As the "Europe in 2035" maps discussed in Chapter 2 show, cartographs certainly provide information and meaning, but they also can—at the same time—express emotions and desires that covet and scheme in ways that move and connect people in affective communities of sense.

The distinction between hermeneutics and critical aesthetics was discussed in Chapters 1 and 2 in terms of Euro-American critical thought and its various reactions to the theories of objective knowledge and transcendent truth. Classical Chinese thought is interesting because it addresses many of the same issues but

[4] Roland Barthes, *Empire of Signs* (New York: Hill and Wang, 1982), p. 21.

[5] Michael J. Shapiro, *The Politics of Representation: Writing Practices in Biography, Photography and Policy Analysis* (Madison: University of Wisconsin Press, 1988), p. 162; Jacques Rancière, *The Politics of Aesthetics: The Distribution of the Sensible*, translated by Gabriel Rockhill (London: Continuum International Publishing Group, 2004), p. 63.

[6] Mitchell, *What Do Pictures Want?*, 5.

[7] Michel Foucault, *The Order of Things* (New York: Pantheon, 1970), pp. 9–10.

[8] See Cordell D. K. Yee, "Chinese Maps in Political Culture," in *The History of Cartography*, Vol. II, Book II, *Cartography in the Traditional East and Southeast Asian Societies*, edited by J. B. Harley and David Woodward (Chicago: University of Chicago Press, 1994), p. 79; Laura Hostetler, *Qing Colonial Enterprise: Ethnography and Cartography in Early Modern China* (Chicago: University of Chicago Press, 2001), p. 3. Also see Gearóid Ó Tuathail, *Critical Geopolitics* (Minneapolis: University of Minnesota Press, 1996), p. 2; Craig Clunas, *Pictures and Visuality in Early Modern China* (London: Reaktion Books, 1997), pp. 104–108.

from a different starting point: that is, of an immanent world that is based on contingent human relations rather than Enlightenment modernity's external measures of
truth.[9] Knowledge production here "is both descriptive and normative. It suggests
how things ought to be" and thus combines meaning and doing.[10]

Rather than figuring word/image relations in terms of an uneasy armistice or a
fierce battle, "the distinction between word and visual image, so strong in the Western
tradition, is not nearly as sharp in China. . . . [Thus] the usual oppositions between
visual and verbal, cartographic and pictorial, mimetic and symbolic representation may
not apply."[11] While the verbal generally takes precedence in Enlightenment thought,
in Chinese aesthetics the verbal and the visual often work together through a non-
hierarchical co-presence. For example, it is common for a scroll painting to have both
an image and a poem, in which "[t]he picture is not an illustration of the poem, nor is
the poem a commentary on the picture."[12]

Although this lack of clarity can be criticized as "vague," David L. Hall and Roger
T. Ames explain that classical Chinese thought's lack of "univocally defined terms" actually is its strength; as a non-transcendent thought system, it works through analogy
rather than principles and through historical models rather than abstract norms.[13] This
analogical system functions according to an "ongoing process of correlation and negotiation" in which different things and experiences become noteworthy through juxtaposition.[14] "Reasoning" does not refer to measurement against external standards,
but rather "entails an awareness of those constitutive relationships which condition
each thing and which, through patterns of correlation, make its world meaningful and
intelligible."[15]

Once we shift from looking for causality to valuing correlative relations, a greater
appreciation of the relationality of dynamic dyads such as inside/outside is necessary. As we saw in Chapter 1, understanding inside/outside as a complex, overlapping, and contingent relation is popular in critical IR literature. As R. B. J. Walker
argues, inside/outside marks a distinction between domestic politics and international politics that is not only territorial but also social; "inside" denotes safety,

[9] David L. Hall and Roger T. Ames, *Anticipating the Han: Thinking Through the Narratives of Chinese
and Western Culture* (Albany: State University of New York Press, 1995); Craig Clunas, "Reading Wen
Zhengming: Metaphor and Chinese Painting," *Word & Image* 25:1 (2009):96–102.

[10] Hall and Ames, *Anticipating the Han*, 216.

[11] Cordell D. K. Yee, "Chinese Cartography among the Arts: Objectivity, Subjectivity,
Representation," in *The History of Cartography*, Vol. II, Book II, *Cartography in the Traditional East and
Southeast Asian Societies*, edited by J. B. Harley and David Woodward (Chicago: University of Chicago
Press, 1994), p. 128.

[12] Clunas, "Reading Wen Zhengming," 101, 99.

[13] Hall and Ames, *Anticipating the Han*, 212, 217; Clunas, "Reading Wen Zhengming," 98.

[14] Hall and Ames, *Anticipating the Han*, 214.

[15] Hall and Ames, *Anticipating the Han*, 215.

law, and sovereignty, while "outside" marks danger, violence, and anarchy.[16] Politics emerges in the negotiations that occur each time this unstable social distinction is asserted, especially when it defines self/Other and friend/enemy relations.

Inside/outside is even more central to Chinese political discourse as *nei/wai*.[17] According to Thomas A. Metzger, dynamic dyads such as *nei/wai*-inside/outside are key to social life in China, organizing relations between individuals, families, and clans, all the way up to relations between different peoples and different states.[18] Other dynamic dyads include *wen/wu* (civil/military) and *Hua/yi* (Civilization/ barbarism), which likewise directly engage in social-ordering and world-ordering. *Hua/yi* functions in familiar ways to construct the barbaric Other so as to exclude them from the Civilized self.[19] In other words, Civilized China only takes shape when it is distinguished from barbarism through a set of dynamic dyads, with "China being internal, large, and high and barbarians being external, small and low."[20] Civilization/barbarism dynamic is not merely useful for understanding pre-modern China's relations with its neighbors; China's top international lawyers continue to use "barbarian" as a technical term in arguments to discourage neighboring states from making rival territorial claims.[21]

This contemporary example shows how contingent relations with difference can become ossified into fixed binary oppositions of self/Other and friend/enemy. In Euro-America this works itself out through self-criticism that figures the Western

[16] R. B. J. Walker, *Inside/Outside: International Relations as Political Theory* (Cambridge, UK: Cambridge University Press, 1993).

[17] See Lien-sheng Yang, "Historical Notes on the Chinese World Order," in *The Chinese World Order: Traditional China's Foreign Relations*, edited by John King Fairbank (Cambridge, MA: Harvard University Press, 1968), pp. 20–33; Ge Zhaoguang, *Lishi Zhongguo de nei yu wai: Youguan "Zhongguo" yu "zhoubian" gainian de zai chengqing* [Inside and outside in historical China: Re-clarifying the concepts of "Middle Kingdom" and "periphery"] (Hong Kong: Chinese University Press, 2017).

[18] Thomas A. Metzger, *Escape from Predicament: Neo-Confucianism and China's Evolving Political Culture* (New York: Columbia University Press, 1977), p. 84.

[19] See Yang, "Historical Notes"; Magnus Fiskesjö, "On the 'Raw' and the 'Cooked' Barbarians of Imperial China," *Inner Asia* 1:2 (1999):139–168. Although there is now debate about whether we should translate ancient terms such as "Yi" as "foreigner" rather than "barbarian," this argument misses the point that in such a hierarchical world order, outsiders are by definition barbarians. See, for example, Lydia H. Liu, *The Clash of Empires: The Invention of China in Modern World Making* (Cambridge, MA: Harvard University Press, 2004).

[20] Yang, "Historical Notes," 20; also see Fiskesjö, "On the 'Raw' "; William A. Callahan, *Contingent States: Greater China and Transnational Relations* (Minneapolis: University of Minnesota Press, 2004).

[21] Jianming Shen, "China's Sovereignty over the South China Sea Islands: A Historical Perspective," *Chinese Journal of International* 94 (2002):103, 104, 118; Zhiguo Gao and Bing Bing Jia. "The Nine-Dash Line in the South China Sea: History, Status, and Implications," *The American Journal of International Law* 107:1 (2013):100.

self as barbaric in relation to a Civilized East.[22] Unfortunately, such "Occidentalism" not only reverses the Civilization/barbarism distinction but also reinforces its binary opposition logic, thus obstructing more fruitful possibilities. Dynamic dyads thus are not a dialectic opposition in which visual politics is "moved forward by the productive and destructive interaction of opposed forces."[23] The point of figuring sensible politics in terms of dyads is not emancipation or progress, but to loosen up their dynamic relations in ways that question both self/Other and Other/self relations and to critique the social orders, the world orders, and the affective communities of sense that they produce and perform.[24]

Another interesting dynamic dyad is *wen/wu*, which can work in more nuanced ways that resist simple reversal and ossification. *Wen* generally means literary, civilian, and civilization, while *wu* generally means physical, military, and martial.[25] The two concepts certainly can be understood as opposites, but not necessarily in the sense of the mutually exclusive binary opposition of an either/or zero-sum battle between civil and military. *Wen/wu* does not necessarily contrast the roles of different autonomous actors, such as the soldier and the civilian. Likewise, *wen/wu* does not map easily onto gendered distinctions: feminine-civil and masculine-martial.[26] Rather, the ideal person in pre-modern China, Japan, and Korea harmonized a dynamic balance of civility and martiality, as both a poet and a warrior. World-ordering, national governance, family relations, and personal self-cultivation all were guided by this quest to harmonize the complementary opposites of literary and martial performances.[27]

Hence, rather than function according to the fixed binary distinctions characteristic of Enlightenment modernity, such dynamic dyads are relational, contextual, contingent, and fluid, often with a productive tension between the ideal and lived experience.[28] What is most interesting about these dyads is their general *lack* of stable canonical definition; there is no orthodoxy, and the dynamic dyads' contingent flexibility demands that we appreciate each dynamic through continual interpretive practice and affective experience.[29] Rather than analyze according to

---

[22] Tzvetan Todorov, *The Fear of Barbarians: Beyond the Clash of Civilizations* (Chicago: University of Chicago Press, 2010); Erik Ringmar, *Liberal Barbarism: The European Destruction of the Palace of the Emperor of China* (New York: Palgrave Macmillan, 2013).

[23] Mirzoeff, *Introduction to Visual Culture*, 9.

[24] Rancière, *The Politics of Aesthetics*, 48–49.

[25] Kam Louie, *Theorizing Chinese Masculinity: Society and Gender in China* (Cambridge, UK: Cambridge University Press, 2002), p. 10.

[26] Louie, *Theorizing Chinese Masculinity*, 9–11.

[27] Louie, *Theorizing Chinese Masculinity*, 11, 15–17; Oleg Benesch, "National Consciousness and the Evolution of the Civil/Military Binary in East Asia," *Taiwan Journal of East Asian Studies* 8:1 (2011):133–137.

[28] Metzger, *Escape from Predicament*, 84; also see David L. Hall and Roger T. Ames, *Thinking Through Confucius* (Albany: State University of New York Press, 1987).

[29] See Benesch, "National Consciousness," 165.

instrumental rationality and causality, these correlative dyads require concrete and detailed thinking and feeling.[30] Dynamic dyads thus are more about making sense of experience and less about determining stable truth-claims; they help us to "picture theory"[31] by appreciating the workings of the conventions of picture-taking, film-making, map-making, veil-wearing, wall-building, garden-building, and Web-surfing.

This book thus argues that to appreciate the workings of ideology and affect, detailed empirical study is necessary and valuable. One way to problematize the search for universal theory is to examine how sensible politics emerges in specific times and places. David Campbell, for example, conducts a detailed empirical study to show how a different kind of picture-taking was required in the mid-2000s to address atrocities in Sudan. While standard humanitarian war photography pictures the conflict through the frame of suffering women and children in refugee camps, Campbell argues that if the issue is "war crimes," then picture-taking has to adjust to provide specific sorts of photographs that can be used as "evidence" in international tribunals. A "forensic" approach to this particular situation thus required pictures of "Sudanese helicopter gunships strafing villages, Janjaweed militia dividing goods they have looted, as well as their human victims and the ordnance that has killed and injured them."[32] The performativity of picture-taking here is an empirical question.[33] In this way, methods of visual international politics move from the empirics of positivism to the symbolic analysis of hermeneutics to recover the empirical study of material modalities and sensory spaces through the critical aesthetic mode.

East/West as a Conceptual Dyad

Readers may have noticed that this book has yet to discuss or display images of 9/11 or Abu Ghraib. While it is common to see such horrific images on book covers and discussed in the opening pages of visual international politics texts,[34] I have avoided

[30] Hall and Ames, *Anticipating the Han*, 215; Roxanne L. Euben, "Spectacles of Sovereignty in Digital Time: ISIS Executions, Visual Rhetoric and Sovereign Power," *Perspectives on Politics* 15:4 (2017):1007–1033.

[31] Mitchell, *What Do Pictures Want?*, 355; also see W. J. T. Mitchell, *Picture Theory: Essays on Verbal and Visual Representation* (Chicago: University of Chicago Press, 1995), p. 6.

[32] David Campbell, "Geopolitics and Visuality: Sighting the Darfur Conflict," *Political Geography* 26 (2007):378–379; Eyal Weizman, *Forensic Architecture: Violence at the Threshold of Detectability* (Cambridge, MA: Zone Books, 2017).

[33] See Rune S. Andersen, Juha A. Vuori, and Can E. Mutlu, "Visuality," in *Critical Security Methods: New Frameworks for Analysis*, edited by Claudia Aradau, Jef Huysmans, Andrew Neal, and Nadine Voelkner (New York: Routledge, 2013), p. 107.

[34] Emma Hutchison, *Affective Communities in World Politics: Collective Emotions After Trauma* (Cambridge, UK: Cambridge University Press, 2016), p. 1; David Campbell and Michael J. Shapiro, "Guest Editor's Introduction: Securitization, Militarization and Visual Culture in the Worlds of

these images because this starting point characteristically puts discussion on a particular path that conceals as much as it reveals. Namely, it focuses critical attention on
"America/the West," where image politics is dominated by the "military-industrial-
media-entertainment network" that joins Hollywood, corporate America, and the
Pentagon.[35] Eurocentrism increasingly is seen as a problem in IR, and much visual
IR thus addresses this issue through a robust critique of Euro-American images of
the non-Western Other.[36]

My concern is that Eurocentrism is not simply about content—for example,
analysis of the global power of Hollywood—but also about theory and method. As
Kuan-Hsing Chen argues, the "West as method" dominates discussions of Asia as
well as of Euro-America.[37] This problematic emerges when top (Western) theorists
are confronted with their lack of interest in topics outside Euro-America. In her
discussion of the politics of walls, for example, Wendy Brown doesn't feel the need
to look beyond her European and American examples, but suggests that "someone
should."[38] Thomas Nail is more circumspect about his lack of interest in politics beyond Euro-America: while "focusing mainly on the West . . . risks perpetuating a
pernicious Eurocentrism," he argues that it's justified because he is deconstructing
(Western) hegemony and empire.[39] In his *Introduction to Visual Culture*, Mirzoeff
answers potential complaints about his textbook's lack of Asian content in a
different way:

Post-9/11," *Security Dialogue* 38:2 (2007):131–137; Gabi Schlag and Anna Greis, "Visualizing
Violence: Aesthetics and Ethics in International Politics," *Global Discourse* 7:2–3 (2017):193–200;
Roland Bleiker, "Mapping Visual Global Politics," in *Visual Global Politics*, edited by Roland Bleiker
(London: Routledge, 2018), p. 4; Michael J. Shapiro, *Cinematic Geopolitics* (London: Routledge,
2009), p. 1; Mirzoeff, *Introduction to Visual Culture*, book cover; Fraser MacDonald, Rachel Hughes,
and Klaus Dodds, "Introduction," in *Observant States: Geopolitics and Visual Culture*, edited by Fraser
MacDonald, Rachel Hughes, and Klaus Dodds (New York: I. B. Taurus, 2010), p. 5; Frank Möller,
Visual Peace: Images, Spectatorship, and the Politics of Violence (London: Palgrave Macmillan, 2013), p. 6.

[35] James Der Derian, *Virtuous War: Mapping the Military-Industrial-Media-Entertainment
Network* (New York: Routledge, 2009); David Campbell, "Cultural Governance and Pictorial
Resistance: Reflections on the Imaging of War," *Review of International Studies* 29 (2003):57–73.

[36] Thomas Nail, *Theory of the Border* (New York: Oxford University Press, 2016); Fraser MacDonald,
Rachel Hughes, and Klaus Dodds, eds., *Observant States: Geopolitics and Visual Culture* (New York: I.
B. Taurus, 2010); David Shim, *Visual Politics and North Korea: Seeing Is Believing* (London: Routledge,
2013); Jung-Bong Choi, "Mapping Japanese Imperialism onto Postcolonial Criticism," *Social Identities*
9:3 (2003):327; Edward Said, *Culture and Imperialism* (New York: Vintage Books, 1994), pp. xii, xxii–
xxiii; Bleiker, "Mapping Visual Global Politics," 26.

[37] Kuan-Hsing Chen, *Asia as Method: Toward Deimperialization* (Durham, NC: Duke University
Press, 2010), p. 216.

[38] Wendy Brown, *Walled States, Waning Sovereignty* (New York: Zone Books, 2014), p. 78.

[39] Nail, *Theory of the Border*, 223.

I am, for example, very much aware that I do not have a great deal of expertise in Asian visual culture (and none at all in Asian languages) and it is not widely represented in this book. That in no way means that I think it is unimportant: to the contrary, I hope someone writes an account of visual culture from the Chinese, Indian or Japanese point of view.[40]

For such critical theorists, the non-West is a curious place for "area studies" (i.e., requiring exotic language abilities), which can provide a particularist perspective but not interesting concepts—let alone general theory.

How can we address this Eurocentrism of theory and method? One response is to reverse the East/West power dynamic to see China/Asia not just as the site of alternative experiences, but as the source of a ready-made, comprehensive alternative theory: for example, China's All-under-Heaven (Tianxia) system as an alternative to the Westphalian system.[41] Such "Asian alternatives" promise to emancipate the world from the "problem" of America/the West.[42] The problem with such empirical reversals is that Eurocentrism is characteristically replaced with an Asia-centrism that is still, as Chen puts it, "obsessed" with the West.[43] For example, to invoke an Asian alternative, L. H. M. Ling reduces IR in Euro-America to "HEW: Hypermasculine-Eurocentric Whiteness."[44] Or more to the point, while there was a vociferous response in 2016 to one article in *Third World Quarterly* that made "the case for colonialism,"[45] there has been little or no critical response to a

---

[40] Mirzoeff, *Introduction to Visual Culture*, xiv; also see Nicholas Mirzoeff, *The Right to Look: A Counterhistory of Visuality* (Durham, NC: Duke University Press, 2011), p. xvi.

[41] See, for example, Tingyang Zhao, "Rethinking Empire from a Chinese Concept 'All-under-Heaven' (Tian-xia)," *Social Identities* 12:1 (2006):29–41; David C. Kang, *East Asia Before the West: Five Centuries of Trade and Tribute* (New York: Columbia University Press, 2010); Wang Ban, ed., *Chinese Visions of World Order: Tianxia, Culture, and World Politics* (Durham, NC: Duke University Press, 2017).

[42] See, for example, Prasenjit Duara, *The Crisis of Global Modernity: Asian Traditions and a Sustainable Future* (Cambridge, UK: Cambridge University Press, 2015); L. H. M. Ling, *The Dao of World Politics: Towards a Post-Westphalian, Worldist International Relations* (London: Routledge, 2014); Pinar Bilgin and L. H. M. Ling, eds., *Asia in International Relations: Unlearning Imperial Power Relations* (London: Routledge, 2017); Martin Jacques, *When China Rules the World: The End of the Western World and the Birth of a New Global Order*, 2nd ed. (London: Penguin, 2012); Yan Xuetong, *Ancient Chinese Thought, Modern Chinese Power* (Princeton, NJ: Princeton University Press, 2011); Qin Yaqing, *A Relational Theory of World Politics* (Cambridge, UK: Cambridge University Press, 2018).

[43] Chen, *Asia as Method*, 1, 215. Also see Choi, "Mapping Japanese Imperialism"; Arif Dirlik, *The Postcolonial Aura: Third World Criticism in the Age of Global Capitalism* (Boulder, CO: Westview Press, 1998).

[44] Ling, *The Dao of World Politics*, 4.

[45] Bruce Gilley, "The Case for Colonialism," *Third World Quarterly* (September 8, 2017):1–17; Adam Lusher, "Professor's 'Bring Back Colonialism' Call Sparks Fury and Academic Freedom Debate," *The Independent* (October 12, 2017) http://www.independent.co.uk/news/world/americas/colonialism-academic-article-bruce-gilley-threats-violence-published-withdrawn-third-world-quarterly-a7996371.html (accessed December 14, 2017).

tidal wave of texts (both texts from establishment intellectuals in China and critical IR texts from Euro-America) that promote a Chinese model of "benevolent" imperial governance that is suitable for the twenty-first century.[46] This follows from a general trend in critical literature that frames imperialism as a uniquely Western practice, often focusing only on the modern Anglo-French experience.[47] Criticism of "Western imperialism" here focuses more on "the West" than on "imperialism" itself, resulting in the popularity of Chinese imperial models of world order that we see today.

Sensible Politics aims to avoid such East/West and self/Other reversals.[48] Like Nail's confessions of his own Eurocentric limitations, political theory and IR theory are full of apologies for not going beyond the Western canon. As Brown and Mirzoeff suggest, the hope is that "natives" from beyond Euro-America can inform the Western academy about possible theoretical contributions from Chinese, Islamic, Indian, African (and so on) "traditions."[49] But for comparative political theorists such as Leigh Jenco, this is problematic. In *Changing Referents: Learning Across Space and Time in China and the West*, she argues that we need to get beyond a container-style geopolitical organization of knowledge-production in which the choice is between the "modern West" and "traditional China."[50] Jenco describes how in the late nineteenth century critical intellectuals in China dealt with the challenge of the West/modernity by creatively combining various different strands of thought: neo-Confucianism, Daoism, Marxism, liberalism, multiculturalism, and so on. The result of this complex and critical cross-cultural engagement is a new form of global thought that draws on various distinct traditions but is not reducible to any one singular tradition. It thus draws on different times and places to critique the present.

Sensible Politics likewise seeks to learn from Middle Eastern, Chinese, and Asian concepts, practices, and experiences of visual international politics as a way to

---

[46] See the sources in notes 41 and 42.

[47] Mirzoeff, *The Right to Look*, xv–xvi; Choi, "Mapping Japanese Imperialism"; Allen Chun, *Forget Chineseness: On the Geopolitics of Cultural Identification* (Albany: State University of New York Press, 2017), pp. 16–17; Said, *Culture and Imperialism*, xii, xxii–xxiii.

[48] This is part of a problematization of geopolitical binary oppositions, including North/South.

[49] See, for example, Fred Dallmyr and Zhao Tingyang, eds., *Contemporary Chinese Political Thought: Debates and Perspectives* (Lexington: University Press of Kentucky, 2012); Peter Katzenstein, ed., *Civilizations in World Politics: Plural and Pluralist Perspectives* (New York: Routledge, 2010); Diego von Vacano, "The Scope of Comparative Political Theory," *Annual Review of Political Science* 18 (2015):465–80.

[50] Leigh Jenco, *Changing Referents: Learning Across Space and Time in China and the West* (New York: Oxford University Press, 2015). Also see Chen, *Asia as Method*, 253; Clunas, "Reading Wen Zhengming," 100; Roxanne L. Euben, *Enemy in the Mirror: Islamic Fundamentalism and the Limits of Modern Rationalism; A Work of Comparative Political Theory* (Princeton, NJ: Princeton University Press, 1999).

resist the hegemonic Eurocentric framing of analysis. However, the goal is not to replace "Western" concepts with "Chinese" ones, because that risks reproducing the power of hegemonic domination. Rather than replacing "Eurocentrism" with "Sinocentrism," *Sensible Politics* aims to explore visual international politics through an assemblage of concepts that are Chinese, Asian, Western, traditional, and contemporary. Such a critical juxtaposition can decenter (but not necessarily discard) critical IR discourse that characteristically generalizes from Euro-American examples. Since my expertise is in Chinese and Asian politics, the analysis often starts from that point.

In this way, we can take Asian and Middle Eastern concepts, practices, and experiences seriously by analyzing their dynamics. Since the goal is not to replace one meta-theory with another, the task is to denature habitual practices, including those in China, Asia, and the Middle East. If we return to Chapter 1's discussion of Hollywood cinema's "whitewashing" with this denaturing strategy in mind, we can see how Matt Damon's role in *The Great Wall* takes on new significance when understood in terms of China's own Civilization/barbarism (*Hua/yi*) dynamic. In Zhang Yimou's film, Europeans are presented as the Other: dirty, conniving, greedy thieves, whom the Chinese leader calls "barbarians." As Damon's character readily admits: "We really do smell."[51] The European characters are only redeemed when they accept the Chinese way of loyalty and trust; as Damon asks the Chinese general, "*Xinren* [trust], did I say it right?" This drama thus repeats the enduring Chinese narrative of dirty barbarians who are grateful for being "Civilized" by a benevolent China. Hence, while it's reasonable for Asian-Americans to complain that Matt Damon was cast in a Chinese story, we should also recognize how the story itself reproduces China's hierarchical Civilization/barbarian dynamic. This example shows how it is necessary to do more than open up spaces for new conditions of possibility. The point is to explore these new spaces by doing the detailed empirical research that is necessary to see how alternative social orders and world orders are being visualized in the present, examples being the Islamic State's utopian Caliphate, a revived Chinese world order, Russian Eurasianism, and participatory surveillance on the Web.

Although it is now common to present China's alternative world order as a source of "emancipation" from the problems of "Western modernity," *Sensible Politics* does not figure Chinese and Asian concepts, practices, and experiences as an "alternative" that will solve the problems of contemporary IR. Recent studies have shown how Qing dynasty China (1644–1911), rather than simply being a victim of Western imperialism, was itself a colonial empire that worked in ways similar to other contemporaneous empires.[52] As we will see in Chapter 7, map-making was

[51] Zhang Yimou, dir., *Changcheng* [The Great Wall] (Legendary Pictures, 2016).
[52] Peter C. Perdue, "China and Other Colonial Empires," *Journal of American-East Asian Relations* 16:1–2 (2009):85–103.

an important part of this imperial competition for glory and territory; in the early modern period France, Russia, and China simultaneously employed cartography for state-building and empire-building.[53] In this coeval clash of empires, imperial map-making in Qing China (finished in 1712) actually preceded that in Bourbon France (1744) and tsarist Russia (1745).[54]

While much critical IR deconstructs how European visual images served as tools of imperialism, this book aims to move beyond postcolonial IR's understanding of China (and the non-West) simply as a victim of imperialism and beyond critical IR's fascination with Euro-America, the nation-state, and neoliberal capitalism. Rather, it considers if and how Chinese and Asian visual images and artifacts were imperial performances. The purpose of exploring the Chinese and Asian "alternatives," once again, is not "emancipation" from Eurocentrism, but to show how Chinese, Korean, and Russian maps, for example, creatively engage in world-making by visualizing power and authority in ways that enforce particular world orders.

The East/West dynamic dyad, therefore, does not define a set of problems and solutions, so much as it examines the productive tensions that emerge in the political relations of various performances of social-ordering and world-ordering. Attention to, for example, Chinese concepts, practices, and experiences doesn't just fill in the empirical "gap" noted by Mirzoeff in his *Introduction to Visual Culture*. I hope it also presents an oblique entry into a nuanced appreciation of sensible politics itself. The book thus does discuss 9/11, but in Chapter 10 rather than on page one, and rather than using it to frame issues in Chapter 10's introduction, New York's September 11 Museum and Memorial is discussed in the chapter's conclusion in terms of the civility/martiality dynamic generated by an analysis of Japanese, Chinese, and French imperial gardens.

Once again, the aim is not to provide either a general theory or a comprehensive survey of visual IR. Rather, the goal is to set aside the imperatives of high theory for a more modest set of concepts, conventions, and practices that some media theorists call "medium theory."[55] The analysis thus proceeds through the deployment of odd conceptual frames and strange juxtapositions that hope to provide oblique views of events, practices, and experiences. *Sensible Politics's* more artisanal mode of theorizing thinks of concepts in terms of dynamic dyads—visible/visual, center/

[53] Jordan Branch, *The Cartographic State: Maps, Territory, and the Origins of Sovereignty* (New York: Cambridge University Press, 2014), p. 72; Peter C. Perdue, *China Marches West* (Cambridge, MA: Harvard University Press, 2005), pp. 442–461; Hostetler, *Qing Colonial Enterprise*; Steven Seegel, *Mapping Europe's Borderlands: Russian Cartography in the Age of Empire* (Chicago: University of Chicago Press, 2012); Magnus Fiskesjö, "The Legacy of the Chinese Empires: Beyond 'the West and the Rest,'" *Education About Asia* 22:1 (2017):6–10.

[54] Branch, *Cartographic State*, 157–158; Hostetler, *Qing Colonial Enterprise*; Yee, "Chinese Maps in Political Culture," 92.

[55] W. J. T. Mitchell, "Medium Theory: Preface to the 2003 *Critical Inquiry* Symposium," *Critical Inquiry* 30:2 (2004):324–335; Mirzoeff, *The Right to Look*, xv.

periphery, concealing/revealing, loosening/tightening—that often grow out of the practical conventions that guide picture-taking, film-making, map-making, veil-wearing, wall-building, garden-building, and Web-surfing. The purpose of exploring both dynamic dyads and conventions is to make sense of the social construction of the visual and appreciate the visual performance of the social—and of the international. In other words, it is necessary not to simply deconstruct how visual artifacts reflect social, political, and economic power relations; we also need to consider how they can visually provoke and perform new and different social, political, and economic relations that engage in social-ordering and world-ordering practices.

Conclusion

Rather than see visibility and visuality as opposing strategies, Chapter 3 argues that both are valuable for an analysis of sensible politics. Instead of seeing visibility/visuality as an exclusive binary opposition, it considers them a dynamic dyad that is relational, contextual, contingent, and fluid. The chapter explores the East/West dyad to develop this approach in ways that problematize visual IR's Eurocentrism. It examines concepts, practices, and experiences from China to argue that an inclusion of non-Western sources is not just an empirical issue, but one of theory and method. It uses comparative political theory to decenter (but not necessarily discard) critical IR discourse that characteristically generalizes from Euro-American examples. The chapter introduces a set of dynamic dyads—inside/outside, Civilization/barbarism, civility/martiality—that are developed in later chapters. In this way, our understanding of social theory and visual international politics benefits from exploring both the "social construction of the visual" and the "visual performance of social orders and world orders."

PART II

VISUAL IMAGES

Part I, "Visibility/Visuality: A Framework for Analysis," provided a detailed discussion of how to critically analyze the sensible politics of visual IR. It presented an analytical framework to both understand the meaning of visuals and appreciate their affect. In particular, it explained how the visibility strategy is useful for tracing the "social construction of the visual," while the visuality strategy is useful for appreciating the "visual construction of the social"—and the visual performance of the international. It argued that we need to think of visibility and visuality not as binary opposites, but as a dynamic dyad that is relational, contextual, contingent, and fluid. Part I showed how sensible politics is provoked and performed through the productive tension of dynamic dyads such as visibility/visuality, ideology/affect, and images/artifacts.

While Part I examined theoretical debates, Part II, "Visual Images," more directly addresses trends in visual IR research through chapters that examine the aesthetic turn in IR (Chapter 4), visual securitization (Chapter 5), and ethical witnessing (Chapter 6). Part II uses the framework of visuality/visibility and ideology/affect to analyze how a range of images—photographs, documentary films, feature films, online videos, and visual art—engage in visual IR. In Chapters 5 and 6, it introduces the cultural governance/resistance dynamic dyad to probe questions of how to respond to war and violence.

The goal of Part II is to explore how visual culture studies and visual IR have used the visibility strategy to deconstruct visual images in order to reveal their hidden ideology. It argues that while exploring important issues, this research agenda is also limited by its hermeneutic mode of analysis and by its narrow focus on Euro-American images of security, war, and atrocity. It seeks to push beyond this verbally-inflected mode of analysis to see not just what images mean, but what they can "do" in provoking affective communities of sense. Part II thus employs comparative analysis and critical aesthetics to juxtapose concepts, practices, and experiences from different times and places.

Many of the examples considered in Part II highlight the necessity of expanding from visual IR to appreciate sensible politics. The audio-visuality of films and the tactility of art installations both show how visual international politics is a multisensory experience. Three-dimensional sculptures and art installations also provoke questions about visual IR's focus on images that lead us to the analysis of the sensible politics of visual artifacts, material modalities, and sensory spaces explored in Part III.

4

Methods, Ethics, and Filmmaking

Introduction

This chapter uses the experience of documentary filmmaking to autoethnographically explore research methods and ethics for sensible politics and visual IR. It locates its analysis in the "aesthetic turn" in critical IR, to compare different modes of analysis: empiricism, hermeneutics, and critical aesthetics. But it also suggests that an appreciation of visual IR needs to look beyond the aesthetic turn's focus on language and representation to explore what visual images can "do" that is different from the written word. Hence, the chapter engages in a "visualizing turn" to examine filmmaking as a theory-making activity that joins the metatheoretical with the practical in its consideration of the sensible politics of the everyday. The goal is to see what knowledge production can "mean" and what it can "do," especially when it provokes new sites and senses of international politics, including new and different "affective communities of sense."

While writing the first draft of this chapter on methods and ethics, I started working on a documentary film, *toilet adventures* (2015, 15 min.), which addresses the politics of shit in China.[1] It uses the on-camera testimonials of over a dozen participants recounting their first impressions of China to explore the very mundane personal experience of going to the bathroom in the People's Republic of China (PRC). I thought it would be an entertaining way to chart how people encounter the unknown through a bodily function that is both intimate and universal. In this way, I hoped to creatively address some of the self/Other issues at the cutting edge of critical IR: the role of person-to-person relations, the importance of the everyday, and the value of emotions and embodied knowledge.[2] Indeed, the founder of

---

[1] The film is posted at William A. Callahan, "Toilet Adventures in China: A Film about Transnational Encounters," Australia National University: The China Story (August 25, 2015) https://www.thechinastory.org/2015/08/toilet-adventures-in-china-making-sense-of-transnational-encounters/ (accessed July 23, 2018). In 2015, *toilet adventures* was shortlisted for a major award by the UK's Arts and Humanities Research Council.

[2] Emma Hutchison, *Affective Communities in World Politics: Collective Emotions After Trauma* (Cambridge, UK: Cambridge University Press, 2016); Michael J. Shapiro, *Studies in Trans-Disciplinary*

Sensible Politics. William A. Callahan, Oxford University Press (2020). © Oxford University Press.
DOI: 10.1093/oso/9780190071738.001.0001

feminist IR, Cynthia Enloe, explains that to get a critical bottom-up understanding of international politics, we need to switch from research in the halls of power to take "notes in a brothel, a kitchen, or a latrine."[3]

The goal of the film thus was to provide a nuanced view of encounters with the unknown—in this case, Chinese public toilets—and show how different people addressed this alien situation, often with good humor; there was a lot of laughing as people recounted their uncomfortable experiences. Such laughter highlights what documentary filmmaking offers that is different from text-based studies, audio-recorded interviews, and written analysis of existing films—namely, an appreciation of the power of the nonlinear, nonlinguistic, and nonrepresentational aspects of knowledge, the laughs, sighs, shrugs, cringes, and tears that are provoked in the on-camera interview process, which then can be edited into an engaging set of images that in turn can produce laughs, cringes, and tears in the film's audience. Indeed, audience reactions are unpredictable; while I see *toilet adventures* as a serious film about vulnerability, it was celebrated at a film festival as a comedy.[4]

In this way, filmmaking provides an exemplary method for showing both the visibility strategy of what knowledge production can "mean" as a social construction of the visible and the visuality strategy of what it can "do" as a visual provocation of the social. Because films can viscerally move us in different ways from verbal texts, we need to appreciate them not just in terms of their ideological-value, but also in terms of their affect-work: not just what they mean, but also how they can move us and connect us, both as individuals and as collectives. This chapter thus builds on Part I's exploration of theory and method to probe how filmmaking is not merely a research "tool" but is also an innovative method that raises important ethical issues.[5]

Method: After the Aesthetic Turn (New York: Routledge, 2013); Roland Bleiker, David Campbell, and Emma Hutchison, "Visual Cultures of Inhospitality," *Peace Review* 26:2 (2014):192–200; Cynthia Enloe, "The Mundane Matters," *International Political Sociology* 4:5 (2011):446–462; Roland Bleiker and Emma Hutchison, eds., "Forum: Emotions and World Politics," special issue, *International Theory* 6:3 (2014):490–594.

[3] Enloe, "The Mundane Matters," 446.

[4] Riga Pasaules Film Festival, Riga, Latvia (April 26–28, 2018).

[5] See Andy Lawrence, *Filmmaking for Fieldwork: An Ethnographer's Handbook* (Manchester, UK: University of Manchester Press, forthcoming); Elena Barabantseva and Elizabeth Dauphinee, "*Border People*: Editor's Interview with Elena Barabantseva," *Journal of Narrative Politics* 4:2 (2018):58–64; Elena Barabantseva and Andy Lawrence, "Encountering Vulnerabilities through 'Filmmaking for Fieldwork,'" *Millennium* 43:3 (2015):911–930; Sophie Harman, "Making the Invisible Visible in International Relations: Film, Co-Produced Research and Transnational Feminism," *European Journal of International Relations* (2017):1–23; Sophie Harman, "Film as Research Method in African Politics and International Relations: Reading and Writing HIV/AIDS in Tanzania," *African Affairs* 115:461 (2016):733–750; Gillian Rose, *Visual Methodologies: An Introduction to Researching with Visual Materials*, 4th ed. (London: Sage, 2016); Luc Pauwels, *Reframing Visual Social Science: Towards a More Visual Sociology and Anthropology* (Cambridge, UK: Cambridge University Press, 2015); Roy Germano, "Analytic Filmmaking: A New Approach to Research and Publication in the Social Sciences," *Perspectives*

This innovative method looks to feminist IR theory's focus on "the personal as the international" to stretch IR beyond its preoccupation with geopolitics, security, war, and terrorism.[6] To explore international politics in terms of the sensible politics of self/Other relations in the everyday, it probes the ideology/affect dyad to juxtapose the methods and ethics of empiricism, hermeneutics, and critical aesthetics.

Certainly this topic risks descending into the cliché of middle-class people experiencing structural poverty for the first time in the "Third World," for example, Montezuma's revenge or Delhi belly. Such funny stories are political in the sense that they distinguish insiders from outsiders; there is always "the butt of the joke," in this case China, India, or Mexico. The interviews thus tended to reaffirm dominant ways of formulating problems: the discourses of "Orientalism" and "Science," with their attendant and interrelated hierarchical distinctions of East/West and backward/advanced.[7] Indeed, in one sense the film is merely one more illustration of the culture war of China versus the West that raged during the Cold War and continues in the twenty-first century to turn difference into Otherness for both sides. It also illustrates China's current odd position in both being a potential "threat" as the world's second largest economy and military, and bearing the enduring "backward" image of the world's largest developing nation that still faces many "hygienic modernity" challenges.[8]

Hence it is not strange that some viewers of early versions of *toilet adventures* drew ideological conclusions from it, such as that China is a dirty, backward place that is essentially different from the modern West. While participants and audiences were generally very enthusiastic about China and its recent economic success, at the same time many still felt that the PRC is defined by what one participant called its "lavatorial aspects"—and this was not meant as a compliment.[9] Hence while making the film, I felt a persistent concern with the ethical problem of "fairness" to my analytical subject (i.e., China), as well as to individual interview participants: I

on Politics 12:3 (2014):663–676; Rens van Munster and Casper Sylvest, "Documenting International Relations: Documentary Film and the Creative Arrangement of Perceptibility," *International Studies Perspectives* 16 (2015):229–245; Rens van Munster and Casper Sylvest, eds., *Documenting World Politics: A Critical Companion to IR and Non-Fiction Film* (London: Routledge, 2015); Wesley Shrum, Ricardo Duque, and Timothy Brown, "Digital Video as Research Practice: Methodology for the Millennium," *Journal of Research Practice* 1:1 (2005):1–19.

[6] Cynthia Enloe, *Bananas, Beaches and Bases: Making Feminist Sense of International Politics*, 2nd ed. (Berkeley: University of California Press, 2014).

[7] See Elena Barabantseva, "In Pursuit of an Alternative Model? The Modernisation Trap in China's Official Development Discourse," *East Asia* 29 (2012):63–79.

[8] Gonçalo Santos, "Technological Choices and Modern Material Civilization: Reflections on Everyday Toilet Practices in Rural South China," in *Anthropology and Civilizational Analysis: Eurasian Explorations*, edited by Johann Arnason and Chris Hann (Albany: State University of New York Press, 2018), p. 262.

[9] Interview, August 8, 2014.

had legal permission to use the interviews, but was it fair to present them—and China at large—in a less than favorable light?

In this sense, the making of *toilet adventures* provides a good case study of methods and ethics for research films when the purpose is less to document the truth and more to engage in analysis. It helps show how filmmaking can provide innovative methods for the study of international politics, especially when we think of foreign policy as a matter of self/Other relations.[10] The filmmaking process also can show how methods and ethics are entangled in interesting and unexpected ways— for example, how one's ethical position becomes even more complicated when conducting a "domestic ethnography" that films friends and family.[11]

The first section of this chapter provides a critical analysis of IR methods and of methodologies for visual culture. Following from Part I, it locates the analysis in the positivist/post-positivist debates that animate critical IR and visual cultural studies to do two things: (1) appreciate the methodological shifts from empiricism to hermeneutics to a "critical aesthetic" mode of analysis and (2) argue that analysis of visual international politics also needs to shift from its focus on ideology to appreciate affect.[12]

While in many ways the first section unpacks the impact of the aesthetic turn in IR on studies of visual international politics,[13] the second section explores what could be called IR's visual turn. As we saw in Chapter 1, the aesthetic turn characterizes most critical analysis of visual culture and visual international politics and is guided by a strong "hermeneutics of suspicion" toward the power of images. But rather than follow the aesthetic turn's focus on the power of language and the politics of representation, this chapter also explores what visual images can "do" that is different from the written word.

---

[10] David Campbell, *Writing Security: United States Foreign Policy and the Politics of Identity*, rev. ed. (Minneapolis: University of Minnesota Press, 1998); R. B. J. Walker, *Inside/Outside: International Relations as Political Theory* (Cambridge, UK: Cambridge University Press, 1993); William E. Connolly, *Identity\Difference: Democratic Negotiations of Political Paradox*, expanded ed. (Ithaca, NY: Cornell University Press, 2002), pp. 36–63.

[11] Michael Renov, *The Subject of the Documentary* (Minneapolis: University of Minnesota Press, 2004), pp. 216–229.

[12] Brian Massumi, *Parables for the Virtual: Movement, Affect, Sensation* (Durham, NC: Duke University Press, 2002); Brian Massumi, *Politics of Affect* (Cambridge, UK: Polity, 2015); William F. Schroeder, "On Cowboys and Aliens: Affective History and Queer Becoming in Contemporary China," *GLQ: A Journal of Lesbian and Gay Studies* 18:4 (2012): 425–452; Rune S. Andersen, Juha A. Vuori, and Can E. Mutlu, "Visuality," in *Critical Security Methods: New Frameworks for Analysis*, edited by Claudia Aradau, Jef Huysmans, Andrew Neal, and Nadine Voelkner (New York: Routledge, 2014), pp. 85–117.

[13] Roland Bleiker "The Aesthetic Turn in International Political Theory," *Millennium: Journal of International Studies* 30 (2001):509–533; Roland Bleiker, *Aesthetics and World Politics* (London: Palgrave Macmillan, 2012).

Hence the second section engages in a "visual turn"—which is perhaps better described in the verbal as a "visualizing turn" because it stresses filmmaking as a theory-making activity that joins the metatheoretical with the practical. As Gilles Deleuze declares, "[T]he great directors of cinema . . . must also be compared with thinkers."[14] The chapter thus explores what documentary filmmaking can "do" by critically recounting the methods of research film production. Although such autoethnography can appear self-indulgent to those who desire analysis that is objective and rigorous, this chapter follows Morgan Brigg and Roland Bleiker to suggest that we need to employ a different set of criteria to evaluate autoethnographic discussions of filmmaking.[15] Rather than looking for objectivity and generalizability as the guiding criteria, this method values creativity in the sense of generating new sites and senses of international politics:[16] the role of person-to-person relations, the importance of the everyday, and the value of emotions and embodied knowledge. In this way, the *toilet adventures* film and this chapter each explore how affect theory's shift of attention from "facts" to "feelings" can inform our understanding of international politics. Rather than engage in a comprehensive survey of visual social science methodology,[17] this chapter has the more modest goal of seeing how researchers can use filmmaking as a method. The aim is to see what knowledge production can "mean" and what it can "do," especially when it provokes new sites and senses of international politics as self/Other relations.

Admittedly, writing about filmmaking is an uneasy strategy that raises many contradictions—that is, using a linear and representational mode to discuss non-linear and nonrepresentational methods. It is noteworthy that two leading IR filmmakers—James Der Derian and Cynthia Weber—both generally avoid academic discussions of their methods. Weber's book-length description of how she came to make the " 'I Am an American': Portraits of Post-9/11 US Citizens" suite of films is as much a personal travelogue as it is a critical analysis.[18] As in her films, the book's images provoke analysis as much as the written text. Der Derian's essays and interviews about *Human Terrain* are fascinating for how they deliberately refuse to discuss methods; rather than look to the director to define the film's meaning, the point is to watch it, then discuss it.[19]

[14] Gilles Deleuze, *Cinema I: The Movement-Image*, translated by Hugh Tomlinson and Barbara Habberjam (London: Bloomsbury, 1986), p. xiii.

[15] Morgan Brigg and Roland Bleiker, "Autoethnographic International Relations: Exploring the Self as a Source of Knowledge," *Review of International Studies* 36:3 (2010): 779–798; also see Roland Bleiker, "Visual Autoethnography and International Security: Insights from the Korean DMZ," *European Journal of International Security* (forthcoming 2019).

[16] See van Munster and Sylvest, "Documenting International Relations."

[17] See Pauwels, *Reframing Visual Social Science*.

[18] Cynthia Weber, *"I Am an American": Filming the Fear of Difference* (Chicago: University of Chicago Press, 2011).

[19] James Der Derian, "Now We Are All Avatars," *Millennium* 39:1 (2010):181–186; James Der Derian, "War Becomes Academic: Human Terrain, Virtuous War and Contemporary Militarism," in

Alongside these two worthy approaches, this chapter follows other research filmmakers who more deliberately describe and analyze the filmmaking process as an innovative method for producing knowledge in IR.[20] In my case, film production and chapter-writing definitely informed each other. But in the end, the film and the chapter are actually about two different things: the film explores issues of self and Other on the toilet in China, while the chapter focuses on the theoretical, methodological, and ethical possibilities provided by filmmaking. For many of the reasons discussed in this chapter—including that filmmaking offers a different form of knowledge than that produced by writing texts—this chapter does not seek to reproduce the film's content in written form. Neither is *toilet adventures* a "film adaptation" of the written chapter that is geared to disseminate its research results; rather, the film and the chapter are both designed to stand alone as original research.[21] Hence, it may be helpful to read the chapter alongside watching the film.

The Aesthetic Turn: Visual Culture Methodologies and IR Methods

Since Roland Bleiker declared the aesthetic turn in IR theory in 2001,[22] much has been written about the need to resist the rational methods and the linear teleological narratives that frame our understanding of ourselves and the world. He called for IR to more directly address the interpretive aspects of politics and suggested that we look at poetry, art, and film as alternative sources to understand IR.

Although many scholars now employ visual images in their analysis, few directly discuss research methods for visual international politics.[23] Hence it is helpful to

---

Militarism and International Relations: Political Economy, Security, Theory, edited by Anna Stavrianakis and Jan Selby (London: Routledge, 2013), pp. 59–73.

[20] Lawrence, *Filmmaking for Fieldwork*; Barabantseva and Dauphinee, "*Border People*: Editor's Interview with Elena Barabantseva"; Barabantseva and Lawrence, "Encountering Vulnerabilities"; Harman, "Making the Invisible Visible in International Relations"; Harman, "Film as Research Method"; van Munster and Sylvest, "Documenting International Relations"; Germano, "Analytic Filmmaking"; Shrum, Duque, and Brown, "Digital Video as Research Practice."

[21] Germano, "Analytic Filmmaking," 667. For using filmmaking as a dissemination strategy, see Rose, *Visual Methodologies*, 330–356.

[22] Bleiker, "The Aesthetic Turn."

[23] Andersen, Vuori, and Mutlu, "Visuality"; Harman, "Making the Invisible Visible in International Relations"; Cerwyn Moore and Chris Farrands, "Visual Analysis," in *Critical Approaches to Security: An Introduction to Theories and Methods*, edited by Laura J. Shepherd (London: Routledge, 2013), pp. 221–235; David Shim, *Visual Politics and North Korea: Seeing Is Believing* (London: Routledge, 2013); Lene Hansen, "Theorizing the Image for Security Studies: Visual Securitization and the Muhammad Cartoon Crisis," *European Journal of International Relations* 17:1 (2011):51–74; Roland Bleiker, "Pluralist Methods for Visual Global Politics," *Millennium* 43:3 (2015):872–890.

examine how scholars use visual images in their analysis more generally: for example, David Campbell's analysis of photography, humanitarianism, and genocide; Cynthia Weber's books that use films to discuss IR theory and US foreign policy; James Der Derian's work on the "military-industrial-media-entertainment network"; and geographers' consideration of the visual in "critical geopolitics."[24] Even fewer people actually make films as a method for considering international politics.[25]

To explore research methods for visual international politics, then, it is helpful first to separate analysis into the two cognate fields: visual cultural studies and IR. Certainly there is much discussion of methodology in the social sciences, as well as new attention to methods in IR.[26] However, there is less discussion of methodology in visual cultural studies. Gillian Rose's *Visual Methodologies: An Introduction to Research with Visual Materials* stands out as an example of a theoretically-sophisticated, practical handbook of research methods. In line with postpositivist IR theory, her goal is not to find the singular correct "truth" about visual images, but to "ground . . . interpretations in careful empirical research of the social circumstances in which they are embedded."[27] Rose thus develops a "critical visual methodology" by considering the "cultural significance, social practices, and power relations" that are embedded in each image, with the aim of challenging mainstream ways of seeing, understanding, and acting.[28] This multifaceted research method is helpful because it targets both the factual/explanatory and the embodied/affective

---

[24] David Campbell, "Geopolitics and Visuality: Sighting the Darfur Conflict," *Political Geography* 26:4 (2007):357–382; Cynthia Weber, *International Relations Theory: A Critical Introduction* (New York: Routledge, 2013); Cynthia Weber, *Imagining America at War: Morality, Politics and Film* (London: Routledge, 2006); James Der Derian, *Virtuous War: Mapping the Military-Industrial-Media-Entertainment Network* (New York: Routledge, 2009); Gearóid Ó Tuathail, *Critical Geopolitics* (Minneapolis: University of Minnesota Press, 1996); Fraser MacDonald, Rachel Hughes, and Klaus Dodds, eds., *Observant States: Geopolitics and Visual Culture* (New York: I. B. Taurus, 2010).

[25] See Cynthia Weber, "'I Am an American': Portraits of Post-9/11 US Citizens" (2007), https://www.iamanamericanproject.com (accessed August 23, 2019); Weber, *"I Am an American": Filming the Fear of Difference*; James Der Derian, David Udris, and Michael Udris, *Human Terrain: War Becomes Academic* (Bullfrog Films, 2011); James Der Derian and Phillip Gara, *Project Z: The Final Global Event* (Bullfrog Films, 2015); Elena Barabantseva, "Border People," *Journal of Narrative Politics* 4:2 (2018), https://jnp.journals.yorku.ca/index.php/default/article/view/87/88 (accessed August 22, 2019); Elena Barabantseva, *British Born Chinese* (Manchester, UK: AllRightsReversed, 2015); Sophie Harman and Leanne Welham, *Pili* (Kuonekana Films Ltd., 2017).

[26] Claudia Aradau, Jef Huysmans, Andrew Neal, and Nadine Voelkner, eds., *Critical Security Methods: New Frameworks for Analysis* (New York: Routledge, 2014); Alan Bryman, *Social Research Methods* (Oxford: Oxford University Press, 2012); Shapiro, *Trans-Disciplinary Method*; Laura J. Shepherd, ed., *Critical Approaches to Security: An Introduction to Theories and Methods* (London: Routledge, 2013); Bleiker, "Pluralist Methods."

[27] Rose, *Visual Methodologies*, xxi.

[28] Rose, *Visual Methodologies*, xxii.

role of images, which is discussed more later in the chapter. The question here is not (just) how images look and what ideologies they reveal, but what they can "do" in the sense of an active notion of what visceral affect they can provoke.[29]

In its later editions, *Visual Methodologies* ventures into the social sciences to see how researchers can answer questions not only by examining images, but also by making them, for example, by taking photographs and making films.[30] Rose laments that there is little dialogue between these social scientists and visual culture specialists and commends anthropologists and geographers for experimenting with making images in order to consider the nonrepresentational and nonlinear aspects of social life. She explores this in chapters on "making images as research data" and "using images to disseminate research findings."[31] Interestingly, Rose notes that many of these photographic projects are deliberately involved in "social reform" campaigns that explore the experience of "marginalized or disempowered people and places: children, the homeless."[32]

The goal of such "social reform" films is to make invisible people more visible, according to the "visibility strategy" discussed in Chapter 1. While the aesthetic turn generally concentrates on criticizing empiricism's rationalist methodology to allow space for hermeneutics's interpretive strategy,[33] it is important to note that both positivist and postpositivist filmmakers are concerned with using research films to make the invisible more visible. For example, Roy Germano's documentary film *The Other Side of Immigration* develops a positivist method to reveal the true causes of Mexican migration to the United States.[34] Germano's arguments are interesting because they come from an unexpected quarter. While positivist social science is hegemonic in North America, research filmmaking is dominated by postpostivist anthropologists and sociologists. Germano feels compelled to defend positive social science's assumptions and approaches against what he sees as a lack of scientific rigor in documentary filmmaking. He thus offers a systematic "analytic filmmaking" model that has the capacity to produce knowledge that is more "accurate and complete."[35]

Standard documentary filmmakers, Germano explains, see themselves as storytellers who follow idiosyncratic characters on a journey. Their method is to edit films to highlight the stories of such "engaging characters" by building "narrative tension" in a three-act narrative arc.[36] Analytic filmmaking, on the other hand, is

---

[29] Rose, *Visual Methodologies*, 9–10, 21.

[30] Rose, *Visual Methodologies*, 15–16.

[31] Rose, *Visual Methodologies*, 307–329, 330–356.

[32] Rose, *Visual Methodologies*, 328.

[33] See, for example, Bleiker, *Aesthetics*, 1–47.

[34] Germano, "Analytic Filmmaking"; Roy Germano, dir., *The Other Side of Immigration* (RG Films, 2010).

[35] Germano, "Analytic Filmmaking," 663.

[36] Germano, "Analytic Filmmaking," 664.

not character-driven, but theory-driven; it is "guided by rigorous social scientific standards" to produce "a logical explanatory narrative that sheds light on the causal processes that underlie some social or political outcome."[37]

While anthropologists delight in telling entertaining stories about "eccentrics and outsiders," analytical filmmaking is different:

> (1) it emphasizes the general over the particular; (2) it engages in original theoretical inquiry and nomothetic explanation over descriptive storytelling and character development; (3) it is categorically nonfictional and privileges accuracy above all else; and (4) it advances positive arguments based on theory and evidence rather than normative arguments based on opinion, emotion, and dramatization.[38]

To accomplish this, Germano develops a model that looks to three core concepts: video data, theoretical pillars, and strategic reiteration. His discussion of "video data" sees the camera as a tool that objectively records and stores audio-video information. Research questions guide the gathering of data from interviews and observational footage, which is then edited into an engaging social science film according to the logic of "theoretical pillars" (rather than according to episodes in the journey of a particular person). To build a causal argument, Germano employs "strategic reiteration," in which film clips of different people doing or saying similar things are edited together to present conclusions that are generalizable. Utilizing these three concepts— video data, theoretical pillars, and strategic reiteration—analytic filmmaking is able to "systematically unpack causal processes or present new evidence from an original social scientific study."[39] The resulting documentary films can properly draw universal conclusions that in turn are more impactful with policymakers.[40]

Germano's methodology, and its (mis)characterization of "documentary film," generated much critical discussion at a panel hosted by the journal *Perspectives on Politics*.[41] One of the main critiques was that analytic filmmaking is an exemplary

---

[37] Germano, "Analytic Filmmaking," 666.

[38] Germano, "Analytic Filmmaking," 665.

[39] Germano, "Analytic Filmmaking," 670.

[40] Germano, "Analytic Filmmaking," 663.

[41] Sunita Parikh, "Analytic Filmmaking and the Persistence of Narrative: A Response to Roy Germano," *Perspectives on Politics* 12:3 (2014):677–679; Dvora Yanow, "I Am Not a Camera: On Visual Politics and Method, A Response to Roy Germano," *Perspectives on Politics* 12:3 (2014):680–683; Jeffrey L. Gould, "Analytic Filmmaking as Social Scientific Research: A Response to Roy Germano," *Perspectives on Politics* 12:3 (2014):684–685; Henry Farrell, "The Woodgrain of the Chessboard: A Response to Roy Germano," *Perspectives on Politics* 12:3 (2014):686–687; Davide Panagia, "*Cinéma vérité* and the Ontology of Cinema: A Response to Roy Germano," *Perspectives on Politics* 12:3 (2014):688–690; Roy Germano, "Analytic Filmmaking: A Response to Critics," *Perspectives on Politics* 12:3 (2014):691–694.

case of what Michael J. Shapiro calls empiricism's "pre-Kantian slumber," in which "experience is engendered by what appears."[42] Here, seeing is believing, and as with analytic filmmaking, the researcher's job is to explain the data by "systematically achieving representations of experience by using reliable (that is repeatable) techniques of observation" and representation.[43] The reality-effect of film is strong because images are seen as empirically reflecting objective truth.[44] Thus in analytical filmmaking data are gathered and represented to make visible the invisible "causal processes that underlie some social or political outcome."[45] The purpose is to inform public debate and policymaking; in Germano's case, rather than seeing illegal immigration as a problem at the US-Mexico border, his film reveals the hidden political-economic factors that push migration from Mexican villages that are actually far from the US border.[46] *The Other Side of the Border* thus is an exemplary case of empiricist research film methodology, especially in its focus on ideology (i.e., social science truth) over affect.

Alongside analytic filmmaking, hermeneutic strategies are also used to make research films that can likewise work as social reformist "campaign videos" to make visible the invisible for popular and policymaking audiences.[47] Among critical IR research films, Sophie Harman and Leanne Welham's feature film *Pili* stands out because it employs transnational feminist theory and creative filmmaking methods to make "the invisible visible in international relations," in this case poor Tanzanian women who live with HIV/AIDS.[48] By presenting "a combination of moving images that allows women to be multidimensional and express themselves in their own language and movement," this project builds on the experiences of Tanzanian women to challenge the "skinny white men" aesthetic of HIV/AIDS.[49]

In many ways, *Pili* is an example of what Germano is trying to counter; as a feature film, it not only blurs the fact/fiction distinction, but actually celebrates its dramatic fictional approach to the social journey of an individual as an innovative way of giving voice to an under-represented group. Rather than posit abstract and universal research questions, *Pili*'s filmmaking process is an active construction of knowledge that defers to the concrete, contextualized experiences of particular women. The story and the script were developed by working closely with groups of

---

[42] Shapiro, *Studies in Trans-Disciplinary Method*, 1.

[43] Michael J. Shapiro, *Cinematic Geopolitics* (London: Routledge, 2009), p. 5.

[44] Michael J. Shapiro, *The Politics of Representation: Writing Practices in Biography, Photography and Policy Analysis* (Madison: University of Wisconsin Press, 1988), p. 124.

[45] Germano, "Analytic Filmmaking," 666.

[46] Germano, *The Other Side of Immigration*; Germano, "Analytic Filmmaking."

[47] W. J. T. Mitchell, *What Do Pictures Want? The Lives and Loves of Images* (Chicago: University of Chicago Press, 2005), p. 350.

[48] Harman, "Making the Invisible Visible in International Relations"; Harman and Welham, *Pili*.

[49] Harman, "Film as Research Method," 737; Harman, "Making the Invisible Visible in International Relations," 9, 11; Harman and Welham, *Pili*.

women in rural Tanzania, many of whom then acted in the film.[50] While Germano dismisses such people as "eccentrics and outsiders," *Pili* allows them to bear witness to the complex experience of living with HIV/AIDS. Rather than strive for objectivity or mimesis, *Pili*'s hermeneutic strategy sees research filmmaking as "a dramaturgical affair, with roles and stages, costumes and cueing."[51] Hence as a film and as a research method, *Pili* engages in the social construction of the visual; it makes visible the invisible in a creative way reminiscent of John Grierson's definition of documentary film as the "creative treatment of actuality."[52]

The result of this hermeneutic project is a co-produced feature film that engages popular and policymaker audiences in the South and the North. Screenings were sponsored by the United States Agency for International Development (USAID) in rural Tanzania and by public health providers in rural England; the shared goal was to encourage people to overcome the social stigma of admitting being HIV positive and thus take advantage of available medical treatment.[53] Through the film, and its participatory production process that puts Tanzanian women in the frame, passive victims are turned into active citizens.

Weber's suite of "'I Am an American': Portraits of Post-9/11 US Citizens" films similarly uses a hermeneutic strategy to make visible people who are hidden by America's patriotic diversity citizenship discourse. These short films engage popular and policymaking audiences by playing off a popular Ad Council PSA, "I am an American," which celebrated the diversity of the United States in the wake of the 9/11 attacks. The Ad Council's goal was to promote tolerance of diversity—especially for Muslim-Americans—and to unify the nation; the PSA ended with America's national motto: *E Pluribus Unum* ("Out of Many, One"). Weber's film project uses a similar format but explores a different set of participants to show who is left out of the frame: "the son of an immigrant without papers, a political refugee *from* the US, a person wrongly accused of being a terrorist spy." In the end, she concludes that the United States has always been fragmented, and her films each finish with the reworked motto: *Ex Uno, Plures* ("From One, Many").[54]

In this sense, "'I Am an American': Portraits of Post-9/11 US Citizens" is exemplary of analysis of self/Other relations in international politics. The various stories are each tragic in their own way, which is shown not only through the information conveyed, but also through the participants' silences, tone of voice, and facial expressions. Indeed, a large part of the work of the films is done through visuals and nonverbal sound, such as establishing shots at gravesites, military memorials, the US-Canada border, and the US-Mexico border. The films thus work by showing

[50] Harman, "Film as Research Method," 733.

[51] Shrum, Duque, and Brown, "Digital Video as Research Practice," 8–9.

[52] John Grierson, "The Documentary Producer," *Cinema Quarterly* 2 (1933):8.

[53] Sophie Harman, Q&A after screening of *Pili* (London: LSE, November 29, 2018).

[54] Weber, "'I Am an American': Portraits of Post-9/11 US Citizens."

how participants are concerned, bewildered, disappointed, and disillusioned that the United States is not living up to its ideals.

Like many social science research film projects, "'I Am an American': Portraits of Post-9/11 US Citizens" thus seeks to make disempowered subjects more "visible" so their problems can be addressed through the mobilization of progressive reform movements.[55] This is part of a common polemic in visual international politics that seeks to criticize the "War on Terror" more generally, thus reproducing mainstream IR's focus on sovereign state power in the international system.[56] Although Weber explains that her films aim to "suggest the possibility for new mobilizations of affect, aesthetics, and politics,"[57] when push comes to shove, ideology trumps affect. For example, when Minuteman founder Chris Simcox used Weber's film about him to raise funds for his US Senate campaign, Weber removed the film from the Internet and forbade Simcox from using it "at any time for any reason in any form whatsoever" because this constituted a "flagrant violation" of her politics.[58]

While the ethically-charged research of these films by Germano, Harman, and Weber is admirable for provoking political discussion, such a sharp focus on social and political problems can also limit visual methodology to certain forms of identity politics and partisan politics. As Shapiro argues, cinema is valuable because it allows us "to *think* rather than pursue a particular interest," as do many social reform–themed research films.[59] This challenge to identity politics enables a methodological shift from the social reform films' oppositional stance of "disgust" and "disillusion"—which can actually reaffirm the reigning political system—to think again in ways that "disrupt" dominant discourses, create "dissensus" and "discord," and thus "displace" institutional forms of recognition to open up spaces for new political thinking.[60] While the aesthetic turn generally concentrates on criticizing empiricism to allow space for interpretation,[61] Shapiro questions both empiricism's focus on representation and hermeneutics's focus on disclosure to advocate a post-empiricist, post-hermeneutic mode of inquiry that poses the question of power by emphasizing the forces (languages, genres, apparatuses) that are involved in the production of presence.[62]

[55] Gillian Rose, "On the Relation Between 'Visual Research Methods' and Contemporary Visual Culture," The *Sociological Review* 62:1 (2014):24–46.

[56] Weber, *Imagining America*; Der Derian, "Now We Are All Avatars"; MacDonald, Hughes, and Dodds, *Observant States*.

[57] Cynthia Weber, '"I Am an American': Protesting Advertised 'Americanness,'" *Citizenship Studies* 17:2 (2013):288.

[58] Weber, *"I Am an American": Filming the Fear of Difference*, 187.

[59] Shapiro, *Cinematic Geopolitics*, 4.

[60] Shapiro, *Cinematic Geopolitics*, 4–5.

[61] See, for example, Bleiker, *Aesthetics*, 1–47. Bleiker's mimetic/aesthetic distinction is much like Shapiro's empiricist/hermeneutic distinction.

[62] Shapiro, *Trans-Disciplinary Method*, 4, 3.

This critical attitude is "aesthetic" in two senses. It shifts from the normal objects of scrutiny in IR (official documents, elite interviews, survey data, and so on) to artistic genre (novels, music, films, and so on) in order to challenge the epistemological certainties of the other modes of inquiry. Rather than offering a traditional model of explanation or interpretation, artistic genres provide a "heterogeneous assemblage" that can arrest common sense.[63] Films are valuable not necessarily for their narrative content, but for their visuality; when we think visually in this way, we can appreciate how a "film's landscape and close-up face and body shots carry the burden of its political thinking."[64] Here the film's "cuts and juxtapositions throw the reader back on her-/himself to provoke critical reflection rather than allow for mere recognition or understanding."[65] This post-hermeneutic approach to sensible politics engages in "sense-making" that no longer looks to meaning or reference.[66] Sensible politics emerges not through representation, but through juxtaposition, montage, and mis-en-scène.[67] Shapiro thus encourages us to "avoid argument-marking meta-statements" in order to allow "juxtapositions [to] carry much of the burden of the analyses."[68] Here we move from an empiricist/hermeneutic process of making subjects more "visible" to the critical aesthetic mode of exploring the "visuality" of how images (and sounds) themselves can "do" things beyond narrative, representation, and interpretation.[69] This is what is meant by the shift in evaluative criteria from "generalizability" to "creativity" for research methods.

The critical aesthetic mode of inquiry thus is less interested in representing facts and making interpretations than it is in seeing how artistic genre can provoke new affective communities of sense. Here we encounter the second sense of aesthetics, which stresses "the pre-linguistic, embodied, or feeling-based aspect of perception."[70] "Affect," as we saw in Chapter 2, is a broad and contested concept.[71] It generally seeks to shift critical focus from facts to feelings; from stable individual identity to multiple flows of encounter; from texts to nonlinear, nonlinguistic, and nonrepresentational genres; and from abstract rational knowledge to embodied forms of knowledge. Rather than test the truth-value of data, it seeks to appreciate

---

[63] Bleiker, "Pluralist Methods."

[64] Shapiro, *Trans-Disciplinary Method*, 23.

[65] Shapiro, *Trans-Disciplinary Method*, 29.

[66] Shapiro, *Trans-Disciplinary Method*, 29.

[67] Deleuze, *Cinema I*, 33–34; Jacques Rancière, *The Emancipated Spectator*, translated by Gregory Elliott (London: Verso, 2011), p. 67.

[68] Shapiro, *Trans-Disciplinary Method*, 31.

[69] Rose, "On the Relation," 36–41.

[70] Shapiro, *Trans-Disciplinary Method*, 15.

[71] Massumi, *Parables for the Virtual*; Schroeder, "On Cowboys and Aliens"; Gregory J. Seigworth and Melissa Gregg, "An Inventory of Shimmers," in *The Affect Theory Reader*, edited by Melissa Gregg and Gregory J. Seigworth (Durham, NC: Duke University Press, 2010), pp. 1–25; Sarah Ahmed, *The Cultural Politics of Emotion* (Edinburgh: Edinburgh University Press, 2004).

the "cringe-value" of heterogeneous visceral encounters. The critical aesthetic mode here is not about what symbols mean, but rather embodies what experiences can "do" and thus moves from ideology to affect. Affect theory addresses a tension between emotion and affect, seeing emotion as the internal subjective content of the individual, while affect emerges as a social experience as bodies connect. Affect thus is a complex concept that is useful for appreciating how audio-visual images can move and connect people both individually and collectively.

As we saw in the discussion of visual culture methodology, affect theory looks to image genres, particularly film and television.[72] Indeed, film in particular activates affective communities of sense through "its possibility to connect subjects, filmmaker and audience through a shared understanding of the emotion, frustrations, confusion, and struggles of everyday life."[73] William Schroeder offers an exemplary analysis of affect work when he considers the strange and unexpected feelings produced in China by Ang Lee's *Brokeback Mountain* (2005). Many commentators expected Lee's film to have limited impact in China even among gay and lesbian audiences due to its unfamiliar setting and strange language (i.e., cowboys speaking English). Hence scholars were surprised when broad audiences in China—both gay and straight—embraced the film, in what came to be known as "Brokeback Fever."[74]

Many viewers identified with a character who had to sacrifice love for duty, which is a common experience in China for both gay and straight people, who are torn between the filial duty of heterosexual marriage and reproduction, on the one hand, and the romantic freedom to pursue their own desire, on the other. The film appealed to a wide variety of Chinese viewers, therefore, not because it was familiar in content (white homosexual cowboys), but because of its affective resonance: the shared experience of sacrifice and forbearance. Schroeder argues that this is not simply a "Chinese" appropriation of a "Western" story; *Brokeback Mountain* actually was successful because it resonates through an experience of liminality that connects gay and straight people, Chinese and Americans, and Brokeback Mountain and the world.[75]

For some, the very alien-ness of the story and the setting created space for an affective connection at the visceral level: "that excess, which might be best described as 'giddiness' and which I suggest is at its most striking or potentiating when derived from the disorientation associated with connecting with the strange."[76] Through this contingent affective experience, the film created space for people to be both "queer" and "Chinese" in ways that jammed established discourses of identity, locality, and history.[77]

[72] Massumi, *Parables for the Virtual*, 27.
[73] Barabantseva and Lawrence, "Encountering Vulnerabilities," 929.
[74] Chris Berry, "The Chinese Side of the Mountain," *Film Quarterly* 60:3 (2007):32–37.
[75] Schroeder, "On Cowboys and Aliens," 432.
[76] Schroeder, "On Cowboys and Aliens," 440.
[77] Schroeder, "On Cowboys and Aliens," 447.

Elena Barabantseva's *British Born Chinese* film engages in a similar shift. In early drafts, the film explored the racial bullying that two pre-teen ethnic Chinese boys suffered in Northern England. But as the film project's participatory action research method developed, the two boys resisted the limitations of such racialized identity categories to express more complex social experiences of vulnerability that exceed racial categories.[78] Both *Brokeback* and *British Born Chinese* thus go beyond the guiding binaries of identity politics (e.g., East/West, gay/straight) to create new sites and senses for international encounters. In this way they move from ideology to affect.

This section has juxtaposed empiricist, hermeneutic, and critical aesthetic methodological strategies to argue that more attention to visual images is helpful for realizing some of the goals of the aesthetic turn, in particular, suggesting ways to resist the rational methods and the linear teleological narratives that frame our understanding of ourselves and the world. It also pushes further to argue that employing a critical aesthetic mode helps to shift analytical attention from issues of identity and ideology to an appreciation of affective communities of sense that move and connect people.

The Visualizing Turn: Making Movies, Making Theory

Theorists of the critical aesthetic mode and of critical visual methodology generally focus more on "reading" found images than on "making" new images.[79] This is an outgrowth of the suspicion of state and corporate powers' manipulation of images as a mode of cultural governance. Deconstructing the visuality of war thus is a major concern, especially with the growth of state and corporate surveillance activities since 9/11.[80]

This section, however, argues that the visualizing turn of research filmmaking provides a useful method for IR analysis because (1) filmmaking provides a method for shifting from ideological issues to explore affective experience that is nonlinear, nonlinguistic, and nonrepresentational; and (2) it is particularly helpful for examining the sensible politics of self/Other relations, especially the role of person-to-person relations, the importance of the everyday, and the value of emotions and embodied knowledge. By exploring these themes, this section more deliberately

---

[78] Barabantseva and Lawrence, "Encountering Vulnerabilities," 926–927; Barabantseva, *British Born Chinese.*

[79] Shapiro, *Trans-Disciplinary Method*; Rose, *Visual Methodologies*, 318.

[80] MacDonald, Hughes, and Dodds, *Observant States*; Shapiro, *Cinematic Geopolitics*; Der Derian, *Virtual War*; David Lyon, *The Culture of Surveillance: Watching as a Way of Life* (Cambridge, UK: Polity Press, 2018). Also see Chapter 11 of this book.

moves away from what films can mean to see what filmmaking can "do" in the sense of provoking new sites and senses of international politics.

Since issues of self/Other relations in foreign climes are likewise explored in the cognate field of visual anthropology, it is helpful to consider the three approaches examined in the first section alongside discussions of ethnographic filmmaking methods.[81] But rather than summarize and critique debates in visual anthropology, this section employs them to frame the examination of the methods used in making *toilet adventures*. This section thus engages in autoethnography to critically describe the issues confronted in the production of a research film. By dealing with filmmaking at both the metatheoretical level and the practical level, we can see how film-production can profitably inform theory-production.[82]

As Brigg and Bleiker's discussion of autoethnography shows, such self-referentiality is still controversial in the social sciences.[83] They suggest that while autoethnographers need not be judged according to the standard social science criteria of objectivity and generalizability, to avoid accusations of self-indulgence, they still need to locate their research within a specific knowledge community. If we locate this chapter's research in the cognate communities of visual international politics and visual anthropology, then we can further explore how the visualizing turn in IR allows researchers to value creativity in the sense of generating new sites and senses of international politics. The remainder of this section examines what filmmaking can "do" by discussing (1) how issues of the international politics of the everyday were confronted in pre-production, (2) how issues of the IR of person-to-person relations were addressed in production, and (3) how the sensible politics of emotion and embodied knowledge were negotiated in post-production editing.

[81] Barabantseva and Lawrence, "Encountering Vulnerabilities"; Lawrence, *Filmmaking for Fieldwork*; Sarah Pink, ed., *Advances in Visual Methodology* (London: Sage, 2012); Paul Henley, "Are You Happy? Interviews, 'Conversations', and 'Talking Heads' as Means of Gathering Oral Testimony in Ethnographic Documentary," in *Film und Interview: Volkskundliche und ethnologische Ansatze zu Methodik un Analyse*, edited by Joachim Wossidlo and Ulrich Roters (Berlin: Waxmann Verlag, 2003), pp. 51–67; Paul Henley, "On Narratives in Ethnographic Film," in *Reflecting Visual Ethnography: Using the Camera in Anthropological Research*, edited by Metje Postma and Peter Ian Crawford (Hoejbjerg: Intervention Press 2006), pp. 376–401; Renov, *The Subject of the Documentary*; Malin Wahlberg, *Documentary Time: Film and Phenomenology* (Minneapolis: University of Minnesota Press, 2008); Marcus Banks, *Visual Methods in Social Research* (London: Sage, 2001).

[82] See Wahlberg, *Documentary Time*, x; Deleuze, *Cinema I*, xiii.

[83] Brigg and Bleiker, "Autoethnographic International Relations"; Bleiker, "Visual Autoethnography and International Security."

Pre-Production: Selecting Cinematic Topics and Sources for the International Politics of the Everyday

The *toilet adventures* project actually started at a personal level. My maternal great uncle was a businessman in Shanghai from 1924 to 1949,[84] and my father was in Qingdao and Shanghai as a sailor in the US Navy in 1946–1947. I thought it would be interesting to compare their stories; then like others,[85] I became interested more generally in the experience of non-Chinese who over the past century have chosen to live in China. Until quite recently, the border between China and the rest of the world was very high—legally, politically, culturally, and symbolically. People who crossed—going either direction—entered a strange new world of the unknown.[86] *Toilet adventures* thus is part of a much larger film project, "Digging to China," which examines how people construct their self through very personal everyday encounters when they become the Other while abroad.[87]

By the time *toilet adventures* was made in 2015, this project included nearly one hundred on-camera interviews with participants aged between 2 and 107 years old, from mainland China, Taiwan, Hong Kong, the United States, the United Kingdom, France, Thailand, India, Germany, Switzerland, Spain, Canada, Denmark, Belarus, Australia, and Mexico. The main interview question was "what was your first impression of China" for non-Chinese participants, and "what was your first impression of [country X]" for Chinese participants. The logic of this project is that the personal everyday experiences of non-Chinese in China (and Chinese outside the PRC) embody "foreign policy" in the sense of encounters with the foreign, the strange, and the unknown, where the personal is the international.[88]

The interviews were simple but open-ended and thus provided a mass of material to work with. As discussed previously, one way to negotiate complicated material is to employ the "classical" narrative mode of a three-act drama that follows the protagonist on an experiential journey.[89] Weber's "'I Am an American': Portraits of Post-9/11 US Citizens" films, for example, follow characters through the "typical

---

[84] See Bill Callahan, dir., *An American in Shanghai* (2016, 22 min.), which is posted at William A. Callahan, "An American in Shanghai: Then and Now," Australia National University: The China Story (September 28, 2016) https://www.thechinastory.org/2016/09/an-american-in-shanghai-then-and-now/ (accessed July 23, 2018).

[85] See Kin-ming Liu, ed., *My First Trip to China* (Hong Kong: Muse, 2012).

[86] See Bill Callahan, dir., *You Can See CHINA from Here* (2018, 14:35 min.) https://vimeo.com/169046223 (accessed July 26, 2018).

[87] See a selection of films at Bill Callahan, "Digging to China," https://vimeo.com/album/4040464 (accessed July 26, 2018).

[88] Enloe, *Bananas, Beaches and Bases*; Campbell, *Writing Security*; Jacques Derrida and Anne Dufourmantelle, *Of Hospitality*, translated by Rachel Bowlby (Stanford, CA: Stanford University Press, 2000).

[89] See Toni de Bromhead, *Looking Two Ways: Documentary's Relationship with Cinema and Reality* (Aarhus, Denmark: Intervention Press, 1996), pp. 35–67; Lawrence, *Filmmaking for Fieldwork*.

arc of normal life before 9/11, how 9/11 changed the character's life for better or usually worse, [and] how this change was adjusted to or resolved."[90] Der Derian likewise explains how *Human Terrain* is a character-driven film because "it makes it easier for the audience to identify and understand a complex issue."[91]

But unlike Germano's narrow understanding of anthropological filmmaking in terms of character-led, three-act narrative arcs, there are other ways to organize a documentary. Since no single character stood out in my project, I thought making an "episodic film" that explores a theme from multiple perspectives, but without the backbone of a single character arc,[92] would be a more effective way of using film to explore the sensible politics of the everyday. The *toilet adventures* theme actually jumped out in the first interviews of the "Digging to China" project in 2011; Thai and American women, in particular, went out of their way to recount their "suffering" with toilets in China.[93] Following the episodic mode, the film is emplotted not according to a chronological beginning/middle/end,[94] but through a nonlinear affective movement inspired by the five stages of grief—denial, anger, bargaining, depression, and acceptance—which are reworked in *toilet adventures* as shock, fear, bargaining, struggle, and acceptance.

Toilets provide a good hook because, on the one hand, everyone has to use them, and on the other, it is still generally taboo to discuss toilet activities.[95] Toilet experiences thus provide what Malin Wahlberg describes as a "frame-breaking" experience:[96] discussing it is defamiliarizing, first for the interview participant, and then for the audience. Such frame-breaking experiences are not natural, but are "manufactured" by the filmmaker in order to call social codes into question. For example, when recalling how a group of Chinese women watched her take a pee in a public toilet, an American professor declared, "It was as if I wasn't alone, and usually going to the bathroom should be a solo activity."[97] Well, maybe not—as another participant explained, pissing and shitting can also be a collective social activity that is widely discussed. Hence, rather than simply illustrating quirky eccentricities, frame-breaking shows how odd experiences can reveal norms among film participants, filmmakers, and the audience.

Toilet experiences thus provide a good topic because they break the frame of modern/Western/bourgeois propriety, both in terms of explanatory meaning and

---

[90] Weber, "'I Am an American': Protesting Advertised 'Americanness'," 286.

[91] Der Derian, "War Becomes Academic," 60.

[92] de Bromhead, *Looking Two Ways*, 69–79.

[93] Interview, January 9, 2011.

[94] Henley, "On Narratives in Ethnographic Film."

[95] See Kathinka Frøystad, "Failing the Third Toilet Test: Reflections on Fieldwork, Gender and Indian Loos," *Ethnography* (October 15, 2018):1–19, https://doi.org/10.1177/1466138118804262 (accessed August 23, 2019).

[96] Wahlberg, *Documentary Time*, 44.

[97] Interview, July 5, 2014.

in terms of affective experience.[98] Indeed, the toilet has provided the hook for critical discussions of Japanese aesthetics, American consumerism, and Chinese "hygienic modernity."[99] Toilets also can join elite and popular experiences of foreign relations. On the one hand, the sovereign power of the self/state includes sovereign control over such mundane bodily functions; a former UK ambassador to China was "grateful" to recall that in his more than eight years' service in the PRC, he "never had to encounter a Chinese toilet *in extremis*, so to speak."[100] On the other hand, recall that Enloe challenges researchers to take "notes in a brothel, a kitchen, or a latrine" in order to get a bottom-up understanding of international politics.[101] Toilets thus provide a rich theme for self/Other relations in the sensible politics of everyday life in ways that highlight the ideology/affect dynamic.

Even so, *toilet adventures* differs from many IR documentaries because its topic is not directly "geopolitical." As we have seen, many critical studies of visual international politics focus on the interplay of stagecraft and statecraft and concentrate on issues of war, security, militarization, and terrorism.[102] The focus of *toilet adventures*, however, shifts to the act of shitting as a more intimate experience in which state-to-state relations are reconstituted as person-to-person relations. Campaigning for better sanitation around the globe is a worthy endeavor; the United Nations has designated November 19 as "World Toilet Day" to highlight this important issue. However, the goal of the film is more modest: to see IR in terms of how people negotiate the messy relations of self and Other while they are abroad, and while they are on the toilet. Rather than focus on the geopolitics of security, it examines how social-ordering and world-ordering processes provoke the personal as the international in affective communities of sense.

Since filming in toilets would be an ethically-problematic approach that would raise a host of sticky issues, I decided to make a "memory film"[103] that uses on-camera interviews and archival images as its main sources. The list of participants for the project started with colleagues, friends, and family and quickly expanded to friends of friends and acquaintances of acquaintances (i.e., the snowball sampling method). In this sense, on-camera testimonial interviews appeal to standard methods of qualitative analysis described by Germano: it is a matter of getting a

---

[98] Wahlberg, *Documentary Time*, 51.

[99] Junichiro Tanzaki, *In Praise of Shadows* (London: Vintage Books, 2001), pp. 8–12; Francesca Bray, "American Modern: The Foundation of Western Civilization" (2000) http://www.anth.ucsb.edu/faculty/bray/toilet/index.html (accessed January 3, 2015); Santos, "Technological Choices."

[100] Interview, July 25, 2014.

[101] Enloe, "The Mundane Matters," 447.

[102] Weber, *Imagining America at War*; MacDonald, Hughes, and Dodds, *Observant States*, 10; Barabantseva and Lawrence, "Encountering Vulnerabilities," 914.

[103] See Douglas MacDougall, "Films of Memory," in *Transcultural Cinema* (Princeton, NJ: Princeton University Press, 1998), pp. 231–244.

broad representative sample, then accurately recording and representing their information.[104]

But it was actually dissatisfaction with the reliability of elite interviews that ultimately led me to the method of staging formal on-camera interviews. The Chinese state and its policymaking procedures are highly opaque, and it is difficult to get reliable information from using standard interview techniques. Officials and academics in the PRC generally are suspicious of "foreigners" and wary of providing them with information on "sensitive" topics such as foreign relations. This is a common problem with fieldwork, which is exacerbated in the Chinese context, where people risk being imprisoned for providing information to foreigners.[105] For example, on the PRC's "National Security Day" in 2018, a propaganda cartoon warned patriotic Chinese to be suspicious of foreign professors, who were characterized as spies.[106] Elite interviews, as I argue at length elsewhere, are a problematic method for researching international politics in China.[107]

Visual anthropologists have a different objection to the use of interviews in documentary filmmaking. Ethnographic filmmaking training often downplays instruction in interview techniques because, as in ethnography more generally, such films "should be about showing not telling. That is we should be interested in showing how our subjects actually lived their lives rather than giving them the opportunity to tell us how they did so."[108] Formal on-camera interviews thus are viewed with "suspicion" by many visual anthropologists, largely due to problems of reliability and accuracy.

The *toilet adventures* project, however, returns to the elite interview method, but with a different objective. Rather than using the interview hermeneutically to extract secret information from participants, the purpose is to appreciate the contours of participants' on-camera testimonials as a "performance." As with the visualizing turn more generally, here we switch from evaluating interviews in terms of their "truth-value"—that is, whether or not they provide accurate and complete information—to appreciate their affect-work: Can they provoke new sites and senses of international politics? Hence alongside asking the "what happened" questions

[104] Ruth Blakely, "Elite Interviews," in *Critical Approaches to Security: An Introduction to Theories and Methods*, edited by Laura J. Shepherd (London: Routledge, 2013), pp. 158–168; Germano, "Analytic Filmmaking."

[105] See Maria Heimer and Stig Thogerson, *Doing Fieldwork in China* (Copenhagen: NIAS Press, 2006).

[106] "Anquan zai wo xin: 4–15 Guojia anquan ri zhuanti (2): 'Gongmin fangfan zhengzhi shentou' xuanchuan manhua" [Security in my heart: April 15 National Security Day special (2): "Prevent political penetration of citizens" propaganda comics], Sohu (April 13, 2018) http://www.sohu.com/a/228225702_391364 (accessed July 23, 2018).

[107] William A. Callahan, *China Dreams: 20 Visions of the Future* (New York: Oxford University Press, 2013), pp. 4–5.

[108] Henley, "Are You Happy?," 53.

characteristic of standard rationalist methodology, interviews pay particular attention to the "how did it make you feel" questions to probe the affective dynamics of embodied knowledge. Paul Henley argues that interviews can do much more than reveal facts; as a multisensory practice, they can "reveal cultural conventions of speaking, gesture and storytelling . . . like a theatrical performance."[109]

Thinking of on-camera interviews in terms of performativity also highlights how the categories that we use to understand international politics are not merely socially-constructed, but come into being through the "visual performance of the international." Here we are shifting from requiring objectivity, to value issues of subjectivity, otherness, and ethics.[110] In terms of topics and sources, then, research filmmaking provides an innovative method for research on nonlinear and nonrepresentational topics, and the sensible politics of bodily performativity in everyday life.

Production: Hospitality-as-Method for Exploring Person-to-Person IR

Filmmaking is a relational process, in which you don't just read books, but also interact very directly with various participants in person-to-person relations.[111] It thus provides an interesting method for theoretically-engaged fieldwork that highlights the relationality of knowledge.[112] Filmmaking's reliance on person-to-person relations thus raises a particular set of ethical and methodological issues.

To address issues of Otherness in on-camera interviews, it is helpful to employ an ethic of hospitality-as-method. Although it may seem like a "natural conversation between two people,"[113] an interview is not an encounter between equals. In both the actual interview and post-production editing, the agenda is set by the researcher, and there is "no parity of exposition" in the sense of "self-revealing testimony by the interviewer."[114] One way to critique this unequal situation is to make it more equal in the sense of negotiating the research agenda with the participant.[115] This is what Harman does through co-production and what Barabantseva and Lawrence do through participatory action research methods.

Another strategy is to acknowledge the hierarchy and employ an ethic of hospitality. Hospitality, of course, means different things in different contexts and

[109] Henley, "Are You Happy?," 57.

[110] Wahlberg, *Documentary Time*, xi, xvii.

[111] See Barabantseva and Lawrence, "Encountering Vulnerabilities"; Harman, "Film as Research Method."

[112] See Brigg and Bleiker, "Autoethnographic International Relations."

[113] Germano, "Analytic Filmmaking," 668.

[114] Henley, "Are You Happy?," 51.

[115] Renov, *The Subject of the Documentary*, 122–124; Rose, *Visual Methodologies*, 332–37.

traditions, for example in Greek and Chinese philosophy.[116] Immanuel Kant's essay "Perpetual Peace" continues to make hospitality an issue for cosmopolitan global politics, while Emmanuel Levinas and Jacques Derrida use the concept to address local and global encounters with the Other.[117]

If we can delink hospitality from the Kantian metanarrative of cosmopolitanism that dominates IR, then a more Hellenistic shared meaning emerges: it is the person-to-person relation of welcoming the stranger as a guest. In this situation, the host is in a superior position to provide hospitality to the stranger, either as an unconditional right or as a conditional duty. The stranger's main obligation is to be a proper guest; as Benjamin Franklin quipped, "Guests, like fish, begin to smell after three days." Derrida argues that even in conditional hospitality, the stranger still has some power, in the sense that the host can become hostage to the guest.[118] Hence, "hospitality," "host," and "hostage" are in a dynamic, contingent relationship.

Although the topic of *toilet adventures* is provocatively frame-breaking, the interviews for the broader "Digging to China" project relied on hospitality in its various forms. One of the main tasks was to build rapport with participants. For these interviews, I generally chose participants whom I had known for years—and sometimes decades. They were colleagues, friends, teachers, students, and family. Hence, many of the interviews started from a sense of intimacy and trust, which of course raised a peculiar set of ethical issues. It's one thing to deal with the macro-level postcolonial ethical issues provoked by a "white American man" (like me) filming "China"; it's something else entirely when you are filming a "domestic ethnography" that includes your mother and mother-in-law.[119] While such issues of methods and ethics certainly arise in standard interview-based fieldwork, they take on an added dimension in filmmaking because people tend to be even more protective of their visual image than of their spoken and written words. As one participant put it: "Don't make me look stupid."[120]

The relations of hospitality thus involve what Michael Renov calls "co(i) mplication" because they are complicated in ways that co-implicate the subject/ object identities of the researcher and the participant.[121] On the one hand, the researcher is the host because she or he sets the agenda and makes editing decisions. But on the other, participants act as the host by welcoming the researcher into their

[116] Julian Pitt-Rivers, "The Law of Hospitality," *HAU: Journal of Ethnographic Theory* 2:1 (2012 [1977]):501–517; James Hevia, *Cherishing Men from Afar: Qing Guest Ritual and the Macartney Embassy of 1793* (Durham, NC: Duke University Press, 1994).

[117] Emmanuel Levinas, *Totality and Infinity*, translated by Alphonso Lingis (Pittsburgh: Duquesne University Press, 1969); Derrida and Dufourmantelle, *Of Hospitality*.

[118] Derrida and Dufourmantelle, *Of Hospitality*, 109, 123–124; also see Pitt-Rivers, "The Law of Hospitality."

[119] Renov, *The Subject of the Documentary*, 216–229.

[120] Interview, July 25, 2014.

[121] Renov, *The Subject of the Documentary*, 218.

homes and offering their testimony. Indeed, one of the problems of testimonials is that the participant can "hijack" the interview to lead it in a different direction, which in effect holds the filmmaker hostage.[122] This is particularly problematic in a domestic ethnography, where the filmmaker has to keep "tacking between inside and outside" in order to maintain both familial harmony and scholarly distance.[123]

At the same time, it is easy for the researcher to abuse this hospitality. Certain participants—students and Asian friends in particular—likely feel more obligated to accept the request for the interview. Furthermore, the clips used for *toilet adventures* are actually taken from interviews about something else: people's experiences on their first trips abroad. Participants thus may be surprised to see that out of their hour-long interview, I have chosen the fifteen seconds when they talked about their most intimate and embarrassing episode.

While researchers are required to gain informed consent from participants during the interview, this legal requirement is not necessarily sufficient. It is better to see consent as a "rolling process" rather than a "one-off event."[124] Researchers thus can be good hosts by taking their participant-guests' feelings into account in the finished product—but without becoming hostage to any across-the-board post-production approval. The method of hospitality thus requires an ethic of care and a sense of intersubjective reciprocity.[125]

Although this discussion of hospitality-as-method may appear to be a list of problems, such co(i)mplicated on-camera interviews can provide rich views of a participant's multilayered performance of both rational knowledge and affective experience. It thus explores the dynamic of person-to-person relations in ways that generate new sites and senses of international politics.

Post-production: Editing-as-Critique for Affective IR

In one sense, filmmaking is even more linear than essay-writing. The first step in the online editing process is to copy all of the relevant film clips onto a timeline, which teleologically proceeds from beginning to end. Editing typically, then, is less the practice of creating, than it is of cutting and trimming. In a way, it actualizes Michel Foucault's dictum: "Knowledge is not for knowing: knowledge is for cutting."[126]

---

[122] Henley, "Are You Happy?," 57.

[123] Renov, *The Subject of the Documentary*, 218; Der Derian, "Now We Are All Avatars," 185–186.

[124] Rose, *Visual Methodologies*, 327; Pauwels, *Reframing Visual Social Science*, 265.

[125] Kate Nash, "Documentary-for-the-Other: Relationships, Ethics and (Observational) Documentary," *Journal of Mass Media Ethics* 26:3 (2011):224; Carol Gilligan, *In a Different Voice: Psychological Theory and Women's Development* (Cambridge, MA: Harvard University Press, 1982); Renov, *The Subject of the Documentary*, 219.

[126] Michel Foucault, "Nietzsche, Genealogy and History," in *The Foucault Reader*, edited by Paul Rabinow (New York: Pantheon, 1984), p. 88.

But in another way, film editing is a much more complex way of producing knowledge than writing essays. The timeline itself is just the spine of the story, to which numerous layers of visual image and sound can be attached. Wahlberg employs the analogy of film and music to explain how editors need to skillfully conduct multiple elements,[127] which is much like how a conductor directs the many instruments of the orchestra. The musical analogy is also useful for understanding the temporal dimension of editing, in which the editor plays with the order, duration, and frequency of film clips to produce visual rhythm.[128] Episodic films such as *toilet adventures* need to pay particular attention to rhythm, because their narrative coherence appeals to the repetition of similar experiences rather than to the progressive journey of a character arc. Here the tremors of affect are produced through the montage of images and the juxtaposition of interview film clips.[129]

In *toilet adventures*, clips from over a dozen interviews conducted between 2011 and 2014 in China, Thailand, the United States, and the United Kingdom are edited together to create a rhythmic, crosscut conversation around common themes. At key points in the film, two separate people talking about a similar experience are edited together in a parallel montage, whose fast crosscuts build suspense and produce affect.[130] Examining one of the film's edited-interplays can illustrate this technique. Two women—Wannapa, a PhD with the Ministry of Public Health in Thailand who did her fieldwork in rural China, and Miriam, an American historian who studies the politics of public health in Maoist China—explain their experiences of Chinese public toilets in the 1990s:

WANNAPA: I would like to go to toilet, we have to go to the public toilet. I don't know how to do, and I don't know . . .

MIRIAM: I went into the bathroom. There were cubicle-like stalls, back to back to back down the middle. They were all squat toilets—

W: —with very, very low walls, low walls. But no door—

M: —the barriers between these cubicles came about breast high. So you could stare down the entire row of ladies squatting at the toilets.

W: And then I saw something dirty, smelly—

M: —the stench of the place, as is normal, was outrageous. The cleanliness, we won't even speak of that.

W: —so I have to walk and look, look, look and go into the last one, the last one.

M: I squatted to do my business and I had this very peculiar feeling. It was as if I was not alone.

---

[127] Wahlberg, *Documentary Time*, 64.

[128] Wahlberg, *Documentary Time*, ix, 66.

[129] Deleuze, *Cinema I*, 33–61.

[130] Deleuze, *Cinema I*, 34–36.

w: I tried to do something, but I could not even sit down, because I saw so
many accumulated faeces, faeces. As well as I saw the maggots, a lot of
maggots. . . .

M: I sort of look up, and I am surrounded. There is an entire group of Chinese
ladies who are peering down to see if my butt is as white as my face is.

w: —so I just walk away, and told my professor that I can't do it. (Laughter)
I couldn't do it.

M: —and I eventually get out there as quick as I can, not only because of the
stink but because the observation was intense.

w: (Sigh)

The participants here provide plenty of facts to answer the "where," "when," and
"how" questions to make visible the hidden toilet experience in rural China. But
the main point is affect: the cringe-factor that we see on the participants' faces
when they recall coming face-to-face with a dirty, smelly squat toilet for the first
time; the anxiety about catching infectious disease; the uncomfortable laughs provoked when the private becomes public; and the cathartic relief when the experience is complete. These two different experiences are edited together in a rhythmic
montage in which "juxtapositions carry much of the burden of the analyses"; the
film thus can "avoid meta-statements" that efface affect in favor of explanation and
interpretation.[131] Reading this transcript while watching the film also shows what
documentary filmmaking's entangled, multilayered visualization of nonlinguistic
and nonrepresentable experiences of Otherness and vulnerability can "do" that
is different from textual analyses of international politics. Wannapa and Miriam
are both internationally-respected experts in the field of public health in China.
However, the key moment for me is not the story or the analysis, but the audio-
visual intensity of Wannapa's heart-felt sigh. At screenings of *toilet adventures*,
audiences likewise have affectively responded at key points with uneasy laughs
and sighs.

Like the Chinese reception of *Brokeback Mountain*, the experience—and
the storytelling—is interesting not in spite of being exotic (and here perhaps
Orientalized), but just because it is exotic. Here Der Derian's notion of diplomacy as interpersonal "estrangement"—rather than state-to-state "engagement"—is actualized, again and again, through affect in various participants'
experiences of Chinese toilets.[132] It is a matter in which *l'étranger*—Derrida's
discussion of the "foreign" and/as the "strange"[133]—takes shape when people
choose to be the Other. Affect here is not simply evoking emotion, but

---

[131] Shapiro, *Trans-Disciplinary Method*, 31.

[132] James Der Derian, *On Diplomacy: A Genealogy of Western Estrangement* (Oxford: Blackwell, 1987).

[133] Derrida and Dufourmantelle, *Of Hospitality*, 3ff.

appreciating "the unpredictability of the virtual" in a nonlinear "connection be-tween multiple places and times, [that] challenges ideology's power to arbitrate meaning."[134]

Alongside this affect-work, the fourth chapter of the film, "struggle," shifts back to the explanatory/interpretive mode by putting non-Chinese participants' toilet adventures in the context of the PRC's recent history of public health campaigns, which continue to promote a form of "hygienic modernity" that values both sanitary progress and political disciplining.[135] (Indeed, public toilets are now part of China's surveillance state, using facial recognition technology to fight toilet paper theft.)[136] Here the editing method shifts from fast-cut jux-taposed "conversations" to longer monologue testimonials that provide histor-ical analyses of ideological campaigns, rather than personal memories of private encounters. As in many "memory films," the editing here employs visual archives that run parallel to the auditory testimony:[137] a public health PSA on spitting and public health campaign posters from the 1950s and 1960s.[138] Yet even these "propaganda posters" provide much more than simply the facts; as a montage they evoke feeling through images and slogans that connect individual health to family health, to public health, and finally to the health of socialism and the health of the Chinese nation (see figure 4.1). The images from visual archives thus can be understood as a performance that evokes affect rather than simply as evidence that proves an analytical or an ideological point.

Editing therefore can serve as critique.[139] Its techniques, especially fast-cut juxtapositions and image montages, can be used as part of the visuality strategy to create a multisensory affective register. Through editing, face-to-face conversations can be produced that highlight emotional and sensorial knowledge practices. Editing-as-critique is also helpful for examining the uneasy relation between ide-ology and affect.

Conclusion

As Kimberly Hutchings noted in her critical summation of *Millennium*'s 2014 con-ference on method, methodology, and innovation in IR, producing knowledge is

---

[134] Schroeder, "On Cowboys and Aliens," 427.

[135] Santos, "Technological Choices."

[136] Benjamin Haas, "Wiping Out Crime: Face-scanners Placed in Public Toilet to Tackle Loo Roll Theft," *The Guardian* (March 20, 2017) https://www.theguardian.com/world/2017/mar/20/face-scanners-public-toilet-tackle-loo-roll-theft-china-beijing (accessed, July 26, 2018).

[137] Henley, "On Narratives in Ethnographic Film"; MacDougall, "Films of Memory."

[138] National Institutes of Health, "Chinese Public Health Posters" exhibit (2006) http://www.nlm.nih.gov/hmd/chineseposters/introduction.html (accessed July 28, 2014).

[139] Also see Lawrence, *Filmmaking for Fieldwork*.

Figure 4.1 "To fully carry out a patriotic public health movement" (1963). Source: National Institutes of Health, USA[140]

a messy business. Guided by the conceptual dyads of visibility/visuality and ideology/affect, this chapter argues that documentary filmmaking allows researchers to "do" a range of things that call into question standard modes of representation. In particular, it shows how on-camera testimonials, in which people recount their uncomfortable experiences while in public toilets in China, can provide a different kind of knowledge: a nonlinear, nonlinguistic, and/or nonrepresentational mode of knowledge, which manifests itself in the intensities of laughs, cringes, sighs, and tears rather than in the accuracy of facts or the persuasiveness of interpretations. This method is employed to explore three sets of issues that animate the sensible politics of self/Other notions in IR: the role of person-to-person relations, the importance of the everyday, and the value of emotions and embodied knowledge. These themes are examined through an autoethnographic account of the making of *toilet adventures*, which utilized on-camera interviews not just to gather the ideological "facts" of people's experiences, but also to illustrate the affective politics of

---

[140] "Dali kaizhan aiguo weisheng yundong" [To fully carry out a patriotic public health movement] (1963), Chinese Public Health Posters exhibit, (National Institutes of Health, 2006) https://www.nlm.nih.gov/hmd/chineseposters/images/1200/DSC_4052.jpg (accessed on December 20, 2018). This poster adds another layer of analysis because it has text in both Chinese and Korean languages; it was produced by and for ethnic Korean Chinese people.

the estrangement, the giddiness, and thus the excess evoked by such experiences. Rather than test the truth-value of data, the film seeks to appreciate the "cringe-value" of heterogeneous visceral encounters that move and connect people. Indeed, *toilet adventures* shows how bowel movements can provoke emotional movement and even political mobilization.

Research filmmaking thus provides a good method for exploring the intricacies and intensities of how sensible politics works through self/Other relations, especially as state-to-state relations interact with people-to-people relations through experiences of hospitality, estrangement, intimacy, and vulnerability. In this way, the chapter pushes the empiricist/hermeneutic debate of the aesthetic turn toward a visualizing turn in IR to show how documentary filmmaking provokes new sites and senses of international politics. The goal is to demonstrate how documentary filmmaking provides an exemplary method for showing what knowledge production can "do," rather than what it can mean.

While much critical IR analysis has a hard time gaining traction with mainstream audiences and policymakers, award-winning films by Der Derian, Harman, and Weber show that non-specialists have an easier time engaging with a well-crafted research film. This appeal to creative methods of critique is not limited to documentary filmmaking; similar multisensory methods can be used in research to produce (rather than just analyze) cartoons, collages, photo essays, performance art, and other multisensory media.[141]

One of the main thrusts of the chapter is to shift from framing international politics in terms of ideology to appreciate its affective register. This is not simply a theoretical argument, but a political intervention. At the beginning of this chapter, I suggested that *toilet adventures* is complicit in the reproduction of the dominant discourses of "Orientalism" and "Science," with their attendant hierarchical distinctions of East/West and backward/advanced. In many ways the film plays into stereotypes of China as an exotic place that, although achieving much progress, is still "behind" the "advanced" West. But the chapter also aims to take a critical view of such "ideological" arguments, to suggest that we should examine the affective work that documentary films can do. Shifting from the ideological polemic of East/West to the affective register of self/Other relations here can produce a critical opening.[142] As we saw in Schroeder's discussion of *Brokeback Mountain* and in Barabantseva's *British Born Chinese* film, the heterogeneous encounters seen in *toilet adventures* jam any simple Chinese/non-Chinese binary division to create new sites

[141] See Bleiker, "Visual Autoethnography and International Security"; Saara Särmä, "Collaging Iranian Missiles: Digital Security Spectacles and Visual Online Parodies," in *Visual Security Studies: Sights and Spectacles of Insecurity and War*, edited by Juha A. Vuori and Rune Saugmann Andersen (London: Routledge, 2018), pp. 114–130.

[142] See Allen Chun, *Forget Chineseness: On the Geopolitics of Cultural Identification* (Albany: State University of New York Press, 2017), pp. 16–17.

and senses of international politics. Rather than treating "China/non-China" as a contradiction in need of resolution, audio-visual media provokes a new set of affective communities of sense. The *toilet adventures* documentary film project thus both reinscribes and resists dominant discourses by refiguring them in a strange place: Chinese toilets.

Throughout the chapter I have employed the rhetoric of "shifts": from facts to feelings, from texts to nonrepresentational genres, from ideology to affect, and from the aesthetic turn to the visualizing turn. But the discussion of film production methods underlines claims made in Chapter 3 that, perhaps, it is better to think in terms of a rhetoric of juxtaposition, mixture, and montage, such as that exemplified in the Maoist public health posters that mix facts and feelings, written texts and images, and abstract concepts with embodied forms of knowledge (see figure 4.1). In this way, to employ Levinas's critique of rational knowledge, the visualizing turn of documentary filmmaking can provide "a mode of thought better than knowledge" for understanding international politics.[143]

---

[143] Quoted in Renov, *The Subject of the Documentary*, 148; also see Nash, "Documentary-for-the-Other."

5

Visualizing Security, Order, and War

Because the Islamic State (IS) used media as a key part of its strategy, accounting for its rise (and fall) is not just a matter for traditional IR. Even after defeat on the ground in Iraq and Syria, IS continued to produce visual media products to promote itself as a virtual Caliphate.[1] In 2014–2017 IS invested scarce resources in production houses and communications platforms to wage war through images: online videos, Twitter, Instagram and Facebook posts, and glossy online magazines. It thus used the stagecraft of visuals as statecraft, to literally produce a sovereign state that is also a utopian state:[2] the Caliphate that "is not just a political entity but also a collective religious obligation (*wajib kifa'i*), a means to salvation."[3]

While Chapter 4 examined the critical aesthetic opportunities offered by research filmmaking, this chapter returns to more traditional IR topics to ask: How is the visible essential not only for thinking about war in the twenty-first century, but also for waging it? What can visuals tell us about security, social-ordering, and world-ordering? To consider these issues, Chapter 5 explores the examples of (1) the North Korea-US national security event provoked by the feature film *The Interview* (2014) and (2) the Islamic State's use of images on social media to hail people in Europe, North America, and within IS itself.

---

[1] Mia Bloom and Chelsea Daymon, "Assessing the Future Threat: ISIS's Virtual Caliphate," *Orbis* (Summer 2018):372–388; Charlie Winter and Jade Parker, "Virtual Caliphate Rebooted: The Islamic State's Evolving Online Strategy," Lawfare blog (January 7, 2018) https://www.lawfareblog.com/virtual-caliphate-rebooted-islamic-states-evolving-online-strategy (accessed October 24, 2018); Fawaz A. Gerges, *ISIS: A History* (Princeton, NJ: Princeton University Press, 2016); Abel Bari Atwan, *Islamic State: The Digital Caliphate* (London: Saqi Books, 2015); Aaron Y. Zelin, "Picture Or It Didn't Happen: A Snapshot of the Islamic State's Official Media Output," *Perspectives on Terrorism* 9:4 (2015):89.

[2] Fraser MacDonald, Rachel Hughes, and Klaus Dodds, "Introduction," in *Observant States: Geopolitics and Visual Culture*, edited by Fraser MacDonald, Rachel Hughes, and Klaus Dodds (New York: I. B. Taurus, 2010), p. 9; Roxanne L. Euben, "Spectacles of Sovereignty in Digital Time: ISIS Executions, Visual Rhetoric and Sovereign Power," *Perspectives on Politics* 15:4 (2017):1024.

[3] Gerges, *ISIS*, 28.

Sensible Politics. William A. Callahan, Oxford University Press (2020). © Oxford University Press.
DOI: 10.1093/oso/9780190071738.001.0001

Unlike other areas of IR, which tend to ignore visuals, in critical security studies there has been much discussion of the role of images.[4] Here the international politics of visual images is seen as an example of "securitization," and this chapter compares securitization's hermeneutic strategy with the broader and more nuanced considerations provided by the cultural governance/resistance dynamic. Chapter 5 seeks to go beyond framing visuality and violence in terms of a "war of images" to see how visuals can affectively provoke utopian social order and world order in a battle of visualities. In this way, it considers how visuality has been key to waging war; the ideas, concepts, and technologies of visual images and modern warfare are entangled.[5] Chapter 5 thus argues that it is helpful to complement the visibility strategy's hermeneutic approach of "reading" visual securitization with the visuality strategy's attention to how images can actively provoke affective communities of sense that complicate what can (and cannot) be seen, said, thought, and done.

Visual Securitization

The main mode of understanding the overlap of visual culture and international relations is securitization theory. Securitization theory, also known as the Copenhagen school, argues that security is "not an objective condition, but is the outcome of a specific social process."[6] Security issues thus are a social construction, in which the issue is constituted—"securitized"—as an existential threat that requires emergency measures beyond normal political procedures and public debate.[7] This is an intersubjective process, wherein the issue is successfully securitized "only if and when the audience accepts it as such."[8]

---

[4] The critical security studies research on visual IR is substantial; recent exemplary works include Roland Bleiker, ed., *Visual Global Politics* (New York: Routledge, 2018); Juha A. Vuori and Rune Saugmann Andersen, eds., *Visual Security Studies: Sights and Spectacles of Insecurity and War* (New York: Routledge, 2018).

[5] See Paul Virilio, *War and Cinema: The Logistics of Perception* (New York: Verso, 1989); Nicholas Mirzoeff, *The Right to Look: A Counterhistory of Visuality* (Durham, NC: Duke University Press, 2011); Antoine J. Bousquet, *The Eye of War: Military Perception from the Telescope to the Drone* (Minneapolis: University of Minnesota Press, 2018).

[6] Michael C. Williams, "Words, Images, Enemies: Securitization and International Politics," *International Studies Quarterly* (2003) 47:513. Williams is critically summarizing Barry Buzan, Ole Wæver, and Jaap de Wilde, *Security: A New Framework for Analysis* (Boulder, CO: Lynne Rienner, 1998), pp. 21–35; also see Frank Möller, "Photographic Interventions in Post 9/11 Security Policy," *Security Dialogue* 38:2 (2007):179–196; Stuart Croft, *Securitizing Islam: Identity and the Search for Security* (Cambridge, UK: Cambridge University Press, 2012); Axel Heck and Gabi Schlag, "Securitizing Images: The Female Body and the War in Afghanistan," *European Journal of International Relations* 19:4 (2012):891–913.

[7] Buzan et al., *Security*, 24.

[8] Buzan et al., *Security*, 25.

Securitization theory looks to speech-act theory to argue that language does more than describe events; it can actively constitute a new social reality. In *How to Do Things with Words*, J. L. Austin examines how judges employ language to pass judgment, for example, condemning a person to death or marrying a couple.[9] Judith Butler has extended Austin's analysis to argue that identity is not essential but performative; she looks to drag queens to show how gender is not a scientific category but a social performance.[10]

Securitization theory builds on Austin's and Butler's arguments to show how security is a social performance that works through speech-acts; a president declaring war would be an exemplary case. For a securitization speech-act to be effective, it needs to satisfy two criteria: (1) it must follow conventional procedures (in this case the constitutional rules for declaring war), and (2) the securitizing actor must occupy the proper social or political position of authority (in this case the presidency).[11] Hence, here only a country's political leader can declare war, and only if that person follows the proper procedure. It is common for securitization theorists to stress that "securitizing actors" need not be official political leaders, and the referent object need not be the state, while still acknowledging that "[c]ommon players in this role are political leaders, bureaucracies, governments, lobbyists, and pressure groups" that seek to speak on behalf of the state.[12]

International politics is likewise "desecuritized" through authoritative statements, such as political leaders declaring a truce or signing peace treaties. The goal for critical analysis is to find ways to problematize securitization activities and encourage "desecuritization" in the sense of "the shifting of issues out of emergency mode and into the normal bargaining processes of the political sphere."[13] Desecuritization thus seeks to persuade security actors and audiences by providing alternatives to securitization, such as by promoting more nuanced engagements with the Other through "peace" photographs and films.[14] For example, Bill Anders's iconic *Earthrise* photograph (1968, figure 5.1) was used by many groups to envision a world united

---

[9] J. L. Austin, *How to Do Things with Words* (Oxford: The Clarendon Press, 1962); Buzan et al., *Security*, 26–27.

[10] Judith Butler, *Gender Trouble: Feminism and the Subversion of Identity* (New York: Routledge, 2006); Buzan et al., *Security*, 40; Croft, *Securitizing Islam*, 84.

[11] Buzan et al., *Security*, 32; Williams, "Words, Images, Enemies," 525.

[12] Buzan et al., *Security*, 40, 36. For analysis that takes a broader view of security actors and objects, see Croft, *Securitizing Islam*, 73–109; Heck and Schlag, "Securitizing Images."

[13] Buzan et al., *Security*, 4.

[14] Michael J. Shapiro, *Cinematic Geopolitics* (New York: Routledge, 2009), pp. 1–2; Frank Möller, *Visual Peace: Images, Spectatorship, and the Politics of Violence* (New York: Palgrave Macmillan, 2013); Möller, "Photographic Interventions"; Frank Möller, "From Aftermath to Peace: Reflections on a Photography of Peace," *Global Society* 31: 3 (2017):315–335; Nicholas Mirzoeff, *How to See the World* (New York: Pelican Books, 2015), pp. 3–5.

Figure 5.1 Bill Anders, *Earthrise* (1968). Courtesy NASA

in peace and harmony, rather than one divided by nations or ideologies.[15] This approach accords with the visibility strategy's social constructivism and is hermeneutic in the sense that we need to " 'read' the rhetorics of securitizing acts."[16] An issue thus isn't successfully securitized until it is read, understood, and supported by an audience.

Since it relies on "speech-acts" and rhetoric, securitization theory's focus on written and verbal texts seems like an odd choice for analysis of visual images. In 2003 Michael C. Williams therefore challenged securitization theory to expand beyond its narrow focus on verbal texts and political elites to address "the dynamics of security in a world where political communication is increasingly bound with images and in which televisual communication is an essential element of communicative action."[17]

---

[15] Ian Sample, "Earthrise: How the Iconic Image Changed the World," *The Guardian* (December 24, 2018) https://www.theguardian.com/science/2018/dec/24/earthrise-how-the-iconic-image-changed-the-world (accessed January 2, 2019).

[16] Williams, "Words, Images, Enemies," 527; Buzan et al., *Security*, 26.

[17] Williams, "Words, Images, Enemies," 527.

Lene Hansen's work on "visual securitization" provides a robust response to Williams's challenge.[18] International relations here needs to address the growing presence of visual images due to rapid advances in digital technology that allow a greater range of actors to influence opinion-making and policy-making in international politics, especially through the rapid dissemination of visual images as seen in the global real-time coverage of 9/11.

Exploring how the "Muhammad cartoon crisis" in 2005 provided a securitization challenge to Danish foreign and domestic policy, Hansen argues that visual images securitize in different ways from speech-acts. On the one hand, Hansen follows the verbalist trend in securitization theory to highlight how visual images cannot speak for themselves and in particular cannot speak foreign policy. Images need people to interpret them through spoken and written texts in an intertextual process wherein texts do not stand alone, but are part of a network of inter-reference.[19] She argues this by examining how we need to understand the original twelve "Muhammad cartoons" in various intertextual contexts: first the context of the original Danish-language publication in Copenhagen's *Jyllands-Posten* newspaper in 2005, and then how the securitization crisis escaped this context when (often selected) cartoons were re-published abroad in different intertexts and contexts. Hansen also expands beyond "intertextuality" to argue that we need to understand images in terms of "intervisuality," in which iconic images often point to other iconic images; for example, during the Balkans war "photos of emaciated Bosnian prisoners . . . invoked the icon of the Nazi concentration camp."[20] In this way, images can become securitized through the dynamics of self/Other relations that construct friends and enemies. Hansen thus asks whether the "Muhammad cartoons" demonized, belittled, or ignored Muslims as a whole—which is a securitizing problematic—or whether they just targeted violent jihadists, which could be seen as normal politics.[21]

Hansen's most interesting analysis examines how images' immediacy, circulability, and ambiguity challenge securitization theory's understanding of international politics. Immediacy here refers to time; through twenty-four-hour cable news programs, the Internet, and social media platforms such as Instagram, images can appear very quickly. The temporal immediacy is also an emotional immediacy;

---

[18] Lene Hansen, "Theorizing the Image for Security Studies: Visual Securitization and the Muhammad Cartoon Crisis," *European Journal of International Relations* 17:1 (2011):51–74; Lene Hansen, "How Images Make World Politics: International Icons and the Case of Abu Ghraib," *Review of International Studies* 41:2 (2015):263–288; Lene Hansen, "Reading Comics for the Field of International Relations: Theory, Method and the Bosnian War," *European Journal of International Relations* 23:3 (2016):581–608.

[19] Hansen, "Theorizing the Image for Security Studies," 54. For more analysis of the politics of the "Muhammad cartoon crisis," see Jytte Klausen, *The Cartoons That Shook the World* (New Haven, CT: Yale University Press, 2009).

[20] Hansen, "Theorizing the Image for Security Studies," 55.

[21] Hansen, "Theorizing the Image for Security Studies," 63–64.

iconic images, especially of death and violence, can provoke a more direct and immediate response from the viewer. This immediate response is both rational in the sense that photographs are seen as reflections of the truth, and emotional because images of human faces can provoke identification with greater humanity.[22]

Hansen argues that the decentered and rapid circulation of images through modern media technologies problematizes "securitization theory's rather traditional notion of securitizing actors as political elites," in which "security is constituted through an 'if–then' sequence where the[ir] constitution of threats legitimizes the adoption of emergency measures."[23] As we saw in Chapter 2, the "Europe in 2035" maps made a large security splash, even though they were not produced by an official source as part of official policy. The "Muhammad cartoon crisis" also shows how the continual circulation of images kept reconstituting the security crisis: first in 2005, then in 2008, and again in 2015. Hansen acknowledges that texts circulate and re-circulate like this, but the nonverbal nature of images means that they can more easily "transcend linguistic boundaries" and thus reach a broader and more diverse audience both locally and globally.[24]

This broader distribution of images across linguistic boundaries highlights Hansen's third factor, ambiguity; because "different audiences might 'see' the same image, they are unlikely to 'read' it in the exact same way."[25] She also sees ambiguity in the sense that images are often focused on individuals, whereas securitization engages a collective; this is why it is important for the securitizing actor to have authority as the representative of a collective political or social group. Hansen thus argues that there is an "interpretive gap" between the individuals in the image and the collective. More important, while verbal securitization generally promotes a specific policy response, visual securitization can raise a set of problems but rarely provides a policy-relevant answer.[26]

Although Hansen's analysis might seem to raise a set of problems, she argues that this should not disqualify visual securitization. Rather than be a theoretical problem, these questions can be addressed through analysis of specific empirical case studies. In other words, the question is not whether visual images are securitized or not, but *how* they are securitized.[27] Hansen's analysis thus underlines "the powerful conflict potential of the visual."[28] Rather than a process of securitization/desecuritization, we have seen a continual re-securitization of the cartoons, Danish foreign policy, and Muslims in Europe and elsewhere.

[22] Hansen, "Theorizing the Image for Security Studies," 56.
[23] Hansen, "Theorizing the Image for Security Studies," 57.
[24] Hansen, "Theorizing the Image for Security Studies," 57.
[25] Hansen, "Theorizing the Image for Security Studies," 57.
[26] Hansen, "Theorizing the Image for Security Studies," 58.
[27] Hansen, "Theorizing the Image for Security Studies," 62.
[28] Hansen, "Theorizing the Image for Security Studies," 68.

Securitizing *The Interview*

Hansen's analysis is interesting and important because it moves from the usual examples of visual securitization—journalistic photographs of war, violence, and atrocity—to analyze editorial cartoons, which more than documenting an event that needs to be witnessed, also critically engage with the political issues that visual images can performatively provoke. Cartoons are also helpful because they illustrate the ambiguity of images, often employing strategies of satire, irony, and polysemy that are easily lost in translation.[29] Even so, editorial cartoons are intentionally created to be "serious" political and moral commentary; that's why they are on the op-ed page.[30]

Yet what do we do when the securitizing images are not meant to be serious or even political? *The Interview* (2014), a feature film that was described as a "tepid, uninspired, and often crude comedy,"[31] presents an interesting case of how visual culture can get securitized in unexpected and unintentional ways.[32] In terms of narrative content, *The Interview* is very political; it tells the story of how the CIA recruits an elite American journalist to poison North Korean leader Kim Jong-un during an exclusive interview in Pyongyang. In the end, the assassination attempt fails. Still, after Kim starts to launch a nuclear attack against the United States, he is killed in a strange battle against the new alliance of the American journalists and North Korea's head of propaganda.

The film highlights real-life geopolitical tensions by putting the interview in the context of North Korea's growing nuclear arsenal, which includes ballistic missiles that can reach the United States. Since political assassination is one of North Korea's modi operandi—including the assassination of Kim's half-brother Kim Jong-nam in Malaysia in 2017—it's not surprising that Pyongyang took notice.[33] When the film's trailer came out in June 2014,[34] North Korea's official news agency demanded that President Barack Obama stop the film because North Korea saw it as an act of terrorism and war. Then North Korea's UN ambassador sent a letter to the secretary-general, likewise denouncing the film:

---

[29] Hansen, "Theorizing the Image for Security Studies," 59–60.

[30] See Klaus Dodds, "Steve Bell's Eye: Cartoons, Geopolitics and the Visualization of the 'War on Terror,'" *Security Dialogue* 38:2 (2007):157–177.

[31] Steve Erickson, "Voyeurs in the Hermit Kingdom: The Interview and Other Films on North Korea," *Cineaste* 40:2 (2015):37.

[32] Seth Rogen and Evan Goldberg, dir., *The Interview* (Sony Pictures Entertainment, 2014).

[33] The United States also targets some of its enemies' leaders. See Euben, "Spectacles of Sovereignty in Digital Time," 1020; James P. Farwell, "Jihadi Video in the 'War of Ideas,'" *Survival* 52:6 (2010):140.

[34] *The Interview: Official Trailer no. 2* (2014) https://www.youtube.com/watch?v=frsvWVEHowg.

To allow the production and distribution of such a film on the assassination of an incumbent head of a sovereign state should be regarded as the most undisguised sponsoring of terrorism as well as an act of war.... The United States authorities should take immediate and appropriate actions to ban the production and distribution of the aforementioned film; otherwise, it will be fully responsible for encouraging and sponsoring terrorism.[35]

In response to North Korea's threatening complaints, the head of Sony Pictures Entertainment talked to a North Korea expert at RAND Corporation and to contacts in the US State Department. The RAND researcher felt that the film could have a positive regime-change effect in North Korea if DVDs were smuggled in from South Korea; he thus advised against toning down the film. The State Department assured Sony executives that North Korea's bark was worse than its bite and stressed that "entertainers are free to make movies of their choosing, and we are not involved in that." Still, under pressure from Sony executives, the release date of the film was delayed, and the Kim Jong-un death scene was toned down.[36] The news was not all bad for *The Interview*; it was rescheduled for release on Christmas Day 2014 as a holiday blockbuster.

Fast-forward to November 2014; a group called Guardians of Peace hacked Sony to protest the film's imminent release. At first this was framed as an economic crime and a social problem; the attack wiped Sony's computers, leaked upcoming films, published embarrassing emails, and threatened people who worked at Sony. There were serious economic consequences; the value of Sony shares dropped by more than 10 percent. It then became a violent crime issue when the Guardians of Peace threatened to attack American cinemas if they screened *The Interview*:

We will clearly show it to you at the very time and places "The Interview" be shown, including the premiere, how bitter fate those who seek fun in terror should be doomed to. Soon all the world will see what an awful movie Sony Pictures Entertainment has made. The world will be full of fear. Remember the 11th of September 2001. We recommend you to keep

---

[35] "North Korea Complains to UN about Film Starring Rogen, Franco," Reuters (July 9, 2014) https://UK.Reuters.com/article/UK-NorthKorea-UN-Film/North-Korea-complains-to-UN-about-film-starring-Rogen-Franco-idukkbn0fe21b20140709 (accessed October 20, 2018).

[36] Tatiana Siegel, "Sony Altering Kim Jong Un Assassination Film 'The Interview,'" *The Hollywood Reporter* (August 13, 2014) https://www.hollywoodreporter.com/news/sony-altering-kim-jong-assassination-725092 (accessed August 23, 2018); William Boot, "Sony Emails Say State Department Blessed Kim Jong-un Assassination in 'The Interview,'" *Daily Beast* (December 17, 2014) https://web.archive.org/web20141217180144/http://www.thedailybeast.com/articles/2014/12/17/exclusive-sony-emails-allege-u-s-govt-official-ok-d-controversial-ending-to-the-interview.html   (accessed August 23, 2018).

yourself distant from the places at that time. (If your house is nearby, you'd better leave.)[37]

Sony thus decided to not release the film in December 2014, primarily because cinema chains refused to screen it.

After the film's cancellation, the US government got involved. Up to this point, the North Korean government had securitized the film by criticizing it in official media and through a letter to the United Nations. After the Guardians of Peace—a hacker organization that was traced to North Korea—threatened the American theater-going public, the White House declared it a national security issue. Obama first scolded Sony for being weak in the face of the challenge, then declared, "We cannot have a society in which some dictator someplace can start imposing censorship here in the United States." The secretary of the Department of Homeland Security's statement was even more securitizing: "The cyberattack against Sony Pictures Entertainment was not just an attack against a company and its employees. It was also an attack on our freedom of expression and way of life."[38] Washington's response to this existential crisis was diplomatic through targeted economic sanctions, and military because it reportedly cut off North Korea from the Internet for a day. This is noteworthy, because it was the first time the United States had treated cyberattacks as a security issue rather than as an economic issue of protecting intellectual property rights.[39]

The strange story of *The Interview* is a good example of visual securitization. It exemplifies the two criteria necessary for securitization: properly credentialed security actors (a North Korean ambassador and an American president) working according to established rules and procedures (a letter to the United Nations and official government statements). The film and the responses of various audiences also show the self/Other dynamic involved in constructing friends and enemies. Curiously, this visual securitization was done primarily through verbal and textual interventions; by the end of December 2014 only the trailer was available for general viewing, and none of the security actors had actually seen the film, let alone a broader audience. This process shows how an issue can move from corporate

---

[37] Quoted in Boot, "Sony Emails."

[38] Quoted in David E. Sanger, Michael S. Schmidt, and Nicole Perlroth, "Obama Vows a Response to Cyberattack on Sony," *New York Times* (December 19, 2014) https://www.nytimes.com/2014/12/20/world/fbi-accuses-north-korean-government-in-cyberattack-on-sony-pictures.html (accessed August 22, 2018); also see Josh Eells, "Seth Rogen's 'Interview': Inside the Film North Korea Really Doesn't Want You to See," *Rolling Stone* (December 17, 2014) http://www.rollingstone.com/culture/features/seth-rogen-interview-north-korea-controversy-cover-story-20141217 (accessed October 20, 2018).

[39] Sanger, Schmidt, and Perlroth, "Obama Vows."

security to national security; as we've seen, the film was securitized by both sides as North Korea versus America.

But what happened is more complicated than that, and these complications undermine the logic of securitization theory. First, this event shows how people from outside the political elite can be sucked into national security politics. The film was co-written and co-directed by Seth Rogen and Evan Goldberg, who are not known for serious or artistic filmmaking. Rather, they are famous for making movies that appeal to the male teenage demographic's interest in casual sex and gross bodily functions. Rogen was bewildered at North Korea's threats, posting on Twitter: "People don't usually wanna kill me for one of my movies until after they've paid 12 bucks for it." If we see the film as a political satire, the targets are American journalism and US foreign policy as much as North Korea's dictator.[40] Progressive elites such as George Clooney tried to organize actors and directors to defend *The Interview* as a matter of freedom of expression, but he was unsuccessful, perhaps because many saw it as a bromance movie rather than as a serious political film worthy of political activism.[41] In other words, Rogen and Goldberg are not worthy members of the political and cultural elite, whose work requires defending.

Moreover, neither Rogen nor Goldberg is American; they are both proudly Canadian, and much of the movie was filmed in their hometown of Vancouver. Although based in Los Angeles, Sony Pictures Entertainment is part of the larger Japanese multinational corporation Sony, and the Tokyo headquarters weighed in to tone down the excesses of the film after North Korean complaints in summer 2014. How then can we say that the film is part of securitization if neither the filmmakers nor the company is clearly "American"? Certainly some would point to Sony's discussions with RAND Corporation and the US State Department to argue that *The Interview* was part of US foreign policy and propaganda.[42] But since Sony ultimately didn't follow their advice, to me it suggests that something else was going on.

If we return to Hansen's new modalities of visual securitization, we can see how *The Interview* confirms that the circulation of images through modern media technologies challenges securitization theory's rather traditional notion of securitizing actors as political elites. As the movie shows, now we have non-elite producers of

---

[40] See Brian McNair, "*The Interview*: Schnarking, Nob Jokes and the Right to Cause Gross Offence," *Journalism Practice* 9:3 (2015):452–454.

[41] David Carr, "How the Sony Hacking Became a Horror Movie," *New York Times* (December 22, 2014); an online discussion of *The Interview* situation among East Asian politics specialists came to a similar conclusion.

[42] For similar arguments about Hollywood-Pentagon collusion, see David Campbell, "Cultural Governance and Pictorial Resistance: Reflections on the Imaging of War," *Review of International Studies* 29 (2003):60; James Der Derian, *Virtuous War: Mapping the Military-Industrial-Media-Entertainment Network* (New York: Routledge, 2009).

security images, the intentionality and policy-relevance of which is hard to establish, if it exists at all. Here, comedians become security actors who are on a par with political leaders. Rather than security being the image's objective, the goals are aesthetic (Is it a funny movie?) and financial (ticket sales). Securitization thus is an unintended consequence of the film. Rather than the image representing a securitizing event, the film itself has become the securitizing event—and it is not entirely clear who is securitizing whom.

The immediacy argument is also problematic. Although the trailer was available online, the film itself was not immediately available to watch. The main motivation for securitization actually was the "invisibility" of the film, rather than its immediate visibility. After Sony canceled its theater release, people couldn't see it at all. *The Interview* was eventually released for online streaming, and Rogen joked that North Korea's complaints were a great marketing campaign; in the end the film made a small profit. As we saw with the Muhammad cartoon crisis, the securitization of cultural products can spin out of control and last for a long time. The cartoons were first controversial in 2005, then in 2008, and again in 2015. *The Interview* film was not an intentional securitization issue, and as we saw, it took months to get securitized.

The film, however, is a good example of Hansen's discussion of the political ambiguities provoked by comedy: audiences can read the same image differently. In the United States *The Interview* was a low-brow comedy, while in North Korea it was seen as an outrageous security threat. The film was offensive because it attacked the sacred image of the North Korean leader. Pyongyang's response then attacked America's sacred value of free speech. Hence irony, satire, and humor—modes that are not easily translated—spur the possibility of multiple readings of the film, much as they did for the Muhammad cartoons. While declarations of war are clear examples of using language to securitize international relations, images don't work in the same way; as Hansen argues, we have to interpret images on a case-by-case basis.

But is this a sufficient response to the problems raised in arguments for visual securitization? Or are the problems too serious to salvage securitization theory? Even with recent modifications that look to the impact of non-state actors such as the mainstream media,[43] the theory is very state-centric and elitist, and assumes an if-then relationship between existential threats and securitization. It works fine to make sense of international politics seen in terms of elite political actors representing states. But it doesn't work so well in the messy world of popular culture and cyberspace. Hence, while Hansen argues that visual securitization is an empirical issue rather than a theoretical problem, what if the theory is the problem? While we could keep spinning verbal yarns to make sense of images and foreign policy, it is helpful to look elsewhere to make sense of the visual international politics of violence and war. In other words, it is necessary to switch from the visibility strategy's

---

[43] See Croft, *Securitizing Islam*, 73–109; Heck and Schlag, "Securitizing Images."

hermeneutic approach of reading visual securitization to visuality strategy's attention to the broader issues of how images can actively provoke affective communities of sense that complicate what can (and cannot) be seen, said, thought, and done

Images of War and Peace

While securitization theory sees "security" as an unstable discourse that needs to be socially constructed, it relies on a certain stability of the state, sovereignty, and the image. Actors securitize the image on behalf of the state in a recognized process, or an image is securitized and the state has to respond. But what if we turn the question around to query the stability of the state, sovereignty, and the image? Here we move from analyzing the social construction of the visual as a security problem (as Hansen does for the Muhammad cartoons, and I do for *The Interview*) to see how an unstable visuality constructs the state and sovereignty as contingent events. Theoretically, we are moving from documenting securitization as a foreign policy-making practice to tracing patterns of sensible politics that work in the different registers of social-ordering and world-ordering.

On the first page of her path-breaking book *On Photography*, Susan Sontag similarly declared that photographs do not simply represent the world, but also change the way we see it and act in it: "In teaching us a new visual code, photographs alter and enlarge our notions of what is worth looking at and what we have a right to observe. They are a grammar and, even more importantly, an ethics of seeing."[44] More recently, Sontag argued that the torture activities at Abu Ghraib were "deeply informed by photography" in the sense that they were "created precisely to be photographed."[45] The visual here is not a photographic representation of war, violence, and atrocity that people need to respond to in a humanitarian or ethical mode.[46] As we saw with *The Interview*, representation and interpretation aren't always the best ways to see how images work and what they do.

Rather than help us make visible official state-centric (upper-case) "Foreign Policy," critical attention to images helps us to visualize how the social relations of everyday life—what David Campbell calls the non-official (lower-case) "foreign

[44] Susan Sontag, *On Photography* (New York: Penguin, 1977), p. 3.

[45] Jonathan Finn, "Seeing Surveillantly: Surveillance as Social Practice," in *Eyes Everywhere: The Global Growth of Camera Surveillance*, edited by Aaron Doyle, Randy Lippert, and David Lyon, 67–80 (London: Routledge, 2012), p. 70; Susan Sontag, "Regarding the Torture of Others," *New York Times Magazine* (May 4, 2014) https://www.nytimes.com/2004/05/23/magazine/regarding-the-torture-of-others.html (accessed October 20, 2018).

[46] For example, see Judith Butler, *Frames of War: When Is Life Grievable?* (London: Verso, 2016). Also see discussion in Chapter 6.

policy" of self/Other relations[47] can produce the state, sovereignty, and war. As argued in Chapter 2, the visuality strategy's goal is not necessarily to evaluate official foreign policy or analyze image wars. As Jacques Rancière explains, images "do not simply supply weapons for battles ... [Rather, they] help sketch new configurations of what can be seen, what can be said and what can be thought and, consequently a new landscape of the possible."[48]

Visual international politics is not simply a current events issue that is the outcome of advances in digital technology over the past few decades; visuality, war, and peace have been interwoven for centuries, if not longer. And it's not simply a question of visual technology aiding war. As Nicholas Mirzoeff argues, the history of warfare is also the history of visuality: "Battlefields were visualized first in the mind's eye of the general; then from the air by balloons, aircraft, satellites and now drones."[49]

Before Napoleon, war was a small-scale battle between elites. After Napoleon, modern war became a new kind of political event that required mass armies and thus popular support.[50] In the 1860s, the American Civil War was the first modern war, and one of the first wars to be photographed; its industrial warfare used mechanized weapons, which caused over half a million casualties. It was total war with total destruction—General Sherman's "March to the Sea" scorched-earth campaign (1864) devastated Georgia between Atlanta and Savannah—and this wholesale destruction was duly recorded in photographs that intervisually evoke images of destroyed Syrian cities in the 2010s (see figure 5.2).[51]

As such Civil War photographs show, modern warfare challenged the pre-industrial mode of understanding conflict, which was based on historical paintings. Benjamin West's iconic painting *The Death of General Wolfe* (1770, figure 5.3) was the "summary image" of the French and Indian War (1754–1763).[52] The general is a symbolic hero, who represents the sovereign (but not the nation). An assemblage of soldiers and civilians, both Europeans and Native Americans, collectively witness his death to record the heroic tragedy of the British military victory.

But as the Civil War photographs show, the camera changed what counted as historical record; its images are not as dramatic. This was for technical reasons: in

[47] David Campbell, *Writing Security: United States Foreign Policy and the Politics of Identity*, rev. ed. (Minneapolis: University of Minnesota Press, 1998), p. 68.

[48] Jacques Rancière, *The Emancipated Spectator*, translated by Gregory Elliott (London: Verso, 2011), p. 103.

[49] Mirzoeff, *How to See the World*, 15.

[50] Alan Trachtenberg, *Reading American Photographs: Images as History, Matthew Brady to Walker Evans* (New York: Hill and Wang, 1989), p. 75; Virilio, *War and Cinema*.

[51] George N. Barnard, *Photographic Views of Sherman's Campaign* (1866), p. 101. This book can be viewed at Duke University Library, https://idn.duke.edu/ark:/87924/r39p2wj24 (accessed May 29, 2019).

[52] Trachtenberg, *Reading American Photographs*, 74.

Figure 5.2 George N. Barnard, *City of Atlanta GA No. 2* (1866). Source: George N. Barnard, *Photographic Views of Sherman's Campaign* (1866), p. 101.

the nineteenth century, the camera needed long exposure times, so photographers couldn't capture images of war at the height of conflict. Hence, as key Civil War photographs show, images of war became rotting corpses after battle rather than the general's heroic action during battle. Many iconic Civil War photos were staged: photographers moved corpses around to get the desired effect, in a practice that continues today.[53] The iconic photos of World War II victory—the American flag-raising at Iwo Jima and the Soviet flag-raising in Berlin—were staged after the fact. They thus provoke the iconoclastic critique of photography and film discussed in Chapter 1: Do they represent the objective truth? Or does manipulating dead bodies mean that photographs are dangerous because they provoke emotion in order to manipulate the public?[54]

Beyond issues of authenticity, Paul Virilio argues that war is the logistics of perception in general, in which politics is about (visual) targeting.[55] It's not simply a

[53] Trachtenberg, *Reading American Photographs*, 73.

[54] See Butler, *Frames of War*; MacDonald, Hughes, and Dodds, *Observant States*.

[55] Virilio, *War and Cinema*, 4.

Figure 5.3 Benjamin West, *The Death of General Wolfe* (1770). Courtesy National Gallery of Canada

question of visual technology aiding war. As Mirzoeff argues, "visuality is not war by other means: it is war."[56] James Der Derian explains that at both the micro-level of chemistry and the macro-level of economics, war and cinema are intimately entangled; the same chemical is used in explosives and celluloid filmstrips, the same technology for motion picture cameras and for airplane machine guns, and similar "modes of representation and destruction [are] organized to represent, see, and kill the enemy while securing and seducing the citizen have converged in dual economies of sight and might."[57] To frame is to target, and to target is to attack; for the military, it is an act of war to lock on another country's ship or plane as a target.[58]

To chart out the complex relations between visuality and war, particularly when they assert the stateliness of IS's new Caliphate, the dynamic of cultural governance and resistance is useful.[59] Rather than taking the "nation" for granted as an actor in

[56] Mirzoeff, *The Right to Look*, 6.

[57] James Der Derian, "After-image," in *Documenting World Politics: A Critical Companion to IR and Non-Fiction Film*, edited by Rens van Munster and Casper Sylvest (London: Routledge, 2015), pp. 226–227.

[58] Bousquet, *The Eye of War*; Rey Chow, *Entanglements, or Transmedial Thinking about Capture* (Durham, NC: Duke University Press, 2012), pp. 1–12.

[59] Michael J. Shapiro, *Methods and Nations: Cultural Governance and the Indigenous Subject* (New York: Routledge, 2004).

a rational calculus, Michael J. Shapiro sees the nation as a set of unstable social relations that take on coherence through cultural governance. This cultural governance looks to Michel Foucault's understanding of power as a productive force that is generated by contingent social relationships, rather than as a set of juridical practices of sovereignty that restrict action.[60] Shapiro argues that while for the early-modern state sovereignty relied on "military and fiscal initiatives," by the nineteenth century these "coercive and economic aspects of control have been supplemented by a progressively intense cultural governance . . . aimed at making territorial and national/cultural boundaries coextensive."[61] But Shapiro does not simply chart out the productive power of state-led cultural governance; his critical approach also shows how resistance can emerge through other modalities of expression—films, journals, diaries, novels, and counter-historical narratives—that "challenge the state's coherence-producing writing performances."[62] As we see in the next section, alongside its coercive rituals of sovereignty (military campaigns and public executions), IS uses videos to create a utopian state—the Caliphate—by making people feel moved by it and connected to it in an affective community of sense.

Visualizing the Islamic State

The Islamic State sees media not simply as an outlet for propaganda, but as a "battlefield" that is nearly as important as the military battlefield: as the title of an official IS handbook puts it, *O Media Worker, You Are a Mujahid!*[63] While Salafi-jihadi movements have utilized media technologies to creatively distribute their messages for decades, IS is noteworthy for both the high quality of its visual products and its effective use of social media technology to disseminate them.[64] In addition to its

---

[60] Michel Foucault, "Governmentality," in *The Foucault Effect: Studies in Governmentality*, edited by Graham Burchell, Colin Gordon, and Peter Miller (London: Harvester Wheatsheaf, 1991), pp. 87–104.

[61] Shapiro, *Methods and Nations*, 34.

[62] Shapiro, *Methods and Nations*, 49; Campbell, "Cultural Governance and Pictorial Resistance."

[63] Quoted in Marwan M. Kraidy, "The Projectilic Image: Islamic State's Digital Visual Warfare and Global Networked Affect," *Media, Culture & Society* 39:8 (2017):1197; also see Abu Bakr Naji, *The Management of Savagery: The Most Critical Stage Through Which the Umma Will Pass*, translated by William McCants (Cambridge, MA: John M. Olin Institute for Strategic Studies at Harvard University, May 23, 2006).

[64] Anne Stenersen, "A History of Jihadi Cinematography," in *Jihadi Culture: The Art and Social Practices of Militant Islamists*, edited by Thomas Hegghammer (New York: Cambridge University Press, 2017), pp. 108–127; Attila Kovács, "The 'New Jihadist' and the Visual Turn from al-Qa'ida to ISIL/ISIS/Da'ish," *Bitzpol Affairs* 2:3 (2015):47–69; Simone Molin Friis, "'Behead, Burn, Crucify, Crush': Theorizing Islamic State's Public Displays of Violence," *European Journal of International Relations* 24:2 (2018):243–267; Simone Molin Friis, "'Beyond Anything We Have Ever Seen': Beheading Videos and the Visibility of Violence in the War against ISIS," *International Affairs* 91:4 (2015):725–746; James

main production sites—the al-Hayat Media Center and the al-Furqan Foundation for Media Production—IS spent scarce resources to develop a decentralized network of thirty-three local media bureaus. According to one source, between January 2014 and August 2016 IS produced more than nine thousand video products.[65] Its media strategy, which worked to both recruit fighters and intimidate enemies, was quite successful; by 2017, more than thirty thousand people had traveled to join the Islamic State.[66]

Moreover, IS media has been a key site for analysis of visual international politics and securitization, with particular attention to the visuality of its execution videos. The political violence of beheading was not new, but its global visibility through IS videos certainly was a new development. While some criticize American and British leaders for treating IS as a unique case that demanded new and different policies, US secretary of defense Chuck Hagel's lament that it presented a threat "beyond anything we have ever seen" is correct in the sense that previously such political violence was not *seen* by such a global audience.[67]

To understand this new global media strategy, Roxanne L. Euben, Simone Molin Friis, and Sara Monaci have each analyzed key IS videos in which people are beheaded or burned alive.[68] Rather than look for the political meaning of the videos as "tactics" in order to craft proper policy responses, Euben argues that we need to examine how the videos "work" as visual modes of violence that "constitute visceral power."[69] The task is less hermeneutic (to trace the social construction of the visual) and more critically aesthetic, to appreciate the creative visual construction of the

P. Farwell, "The Media Strategy of ISIS," *Survival* 56:6 (2014):49; Euben, "Spectacles of Sovereignty in Digital Time"; Farwell, "Jihadi Video in the 'War of Ideas'"; Kraidy, "The Projectilic Image"; Sara Monaci, "Explaining the Islamic State's Online Media Strategy: A Transmedia Approach," *International Journal of Communication* 11 (2017):2842–2860; Charlie Winter, *Documenting the Virtual "Caliphate"* (London: Quilliam Foundation, 2015); Brendan I. Koerner, "Why ISIS Is Winning the Social Media War," *Wired* (April 2016), https://www.wired.com/2016/03/isis-winning-social-media-war-heres-beat/ (accessed August 23, 2019); Axel Heck, "Images, Visions and Narrative Identity Formation of ISIS," *Global Discourse* 7:2/3 (2017):244–259 ; Axel Heck, "The Struggle for Legitimacy of the Islamic State—Facts, Myths, and Narratives," in *Political Storytelling: From Fact to Fiction* edited by Frank Gadinger (Duisburg: Käte Hamburger Kolleg/Centre for Global Cooperation Research, 2016), pp. 81–88.

    65 Kraidy, "The Projectilic Image," 1199.
    66 Monaci, "Explaining the Islamic State's Online Media Strategy," 2857; Koerner, "Why ISIS Is Winning."
    67 Friis, "'Beyond Anything We Have Ever Seen,'" 736; Euben, "Spectacles of Sovereignty in Digital Time," 1009; Brian Mello, "The Islamic State: Violence and Ideology in a Post-Colonial Revolutionary Regime," *International Political Sociology* 12 (2018):139–155.
    68 Euben, "Spectacles of Sovereignty in Digital Time"; Friis, "'Beyond Anything We Have Ever Seen'"; Monaci, "Explaining the Islamic State's Online Media Strategy"; Kraidy, "The Projectilic Image."
    69 Euben, "Spectacles of Sovereignty in Digital Time," 1007.

social and of the international. Indeed, Euben argues that the "videos are verbally parsimonious, using images, quick cuts, composition, blocking, pacing, resolution, sound/silence, camera angles, dress, and casting, to 'speak' as much as words."[70] These visual artifacts work less through instrumental rationality and more through affective resonance, in resonance's literal sense of "evoking a response."[71] As Kraidy explains, in execution videos, images "do not represent an object, but rather are part of an operation," that "connect[s] processes, events and bodies."[72] Like *Sensible Politics*'s approach, Euben argues that an appreciation of the nonverbal and nonnarrative audio-visual politics of these execution videos allows us to "document how visual images can reshape interpretive frameworks that, in turn, reconstitute the realm of what is politically thinkable and doable."[73]

What is newly "politically thinkable and doable" in these execution videos? It is the founding of the Islamic State as the Caliphate. In an argument shared with other analysts, Euben sees execution videos as political rituals meant to constitute the sovereign power of the Islamic State as the Caliphate.[74] Here she follows Foucault's analysis of sovereignty as the power over death, in which political legitimacy is produced through the public spectacle of executing the human body.[75] The focus of such executions, either in eighteenth-century France or the twenty-first-century Middle East, is not on the executioner or the executed. Rather, it is on the audience (both local and global) that is hailed by the ritualized spectacle to recognize and swear allegiance to the ruling state power.[76] Kraidy explains that "[t]he video showcases IS as a state," while Mello declares that "violent execution videos produce in this public faith in the status and power of the Islamic State."[77] The execution videos thus are not simply "random brutality," but are a visual practice that produces sovereign power through the production and circulation of the videos.[78] The videos

---

[70] Euben, "Spectacles of Sovereignty in Digital Time," 1018.

[71] Euben, "Spectacles of Sovereignty in Digital Time," 1026; also see Monaci, "Explaining the Islamic State's Online Media Strategy," 2854; Kraidy, "The Projectilic Image," 1198; Farwell, "Jihadi Video in the 'War of Ideas,'" 127; Koerner, "Why ISIS Is Winning."

[72] Kraidy, "The Projectilic Image," 1198.

[73] Euben, "Spectacles of Sovereignty in Digital Time," 1009; Friis, "'Behead, Burn, Crucify, Crush,'" 245.

[74] Euben, "Spectacles of Sovereignty in Digital Time," 1010, 1020; Mello, "The Islamic State," 143–145; Monaci, "Explaining the Islamic State's Online Media Strategy," 2856; Kraidy, "The Projectilic Image," 1202.

[75] Michel Foucault, *Discipline and Punish: The Birth of the Prison*, translated by Alan Sheridan (London: Allen Lane, 1977), p. 24; Euben, "Spectacles of Sovereignty in Digital Time," 1010; Friis, "'Behead, Burn, Crucify, Crush,'" 251; Mello, "The Islamic State," 143–145.

[76] Euben, "Spectacles of Sovereignty in Digital Time," 1021; Mello, "The Islamic State," 144.

[77] Kraidy, "The Projectilic Image," 1202; Mello, "The Islamic State," 145; also see Euben, "Spectacles of Sovereignty in Digital Time"; Friis, "'Behead, Burn, Crucify, Crush,'" 258–260; Monaci, "Explaining the Islamic State's Online Media Strategy," 2856.

[78] Friis, "'Behead, Burn, Crucify, Crush,'" 248.

don't just engage in securitizing enemies—or even in provoking the United States and the United Kingdom to securitize the Islamic State[79]—but through cultural governance, they also actively provoke social orders and world orders as affective communities of sense.

IS Utopian Public Service Announcements

Much of the analysis of the execution videos concerns whether (or not) they present IS as a dystopia of overwhelming savagery, characterized by beheadings, slavery, and other examples of extreme violence. Kraidy, for example, argues that while "Hollywood, for the most part, seeks to impart enjoyment, IS seeks to inflict pain."[80] Euben explains that the beheading videos work to enact "retaliatory humiliation . . . not by way of explicit argument, but through the visual inscription of impotence upon male bodies whose public subjugation and abjection is symbolically converted into that of the American nation."[81] Such conclusions are drawn from close analysis of IS's violent films; Friis, for example, spent two years studying 985 IS videos of public violence, including an "in-depth analysis of 185 of the group's execution videos."[82]

But execution videos are only one genre in IS's video repertoire. Its media centers have also produced a host of what could be characterized as PSAs that present IS as a utopian project, an actually-existing Caliphate. The strategy of previous Islamic terrorist groups, including al-Qaeda, focused on creating chaos, with the Caliphate as a vague goal for the long-term future. According to James Farwell, such groups thus presented a "wholesale failure to define an alternative vision of the society they wish to create."[83] On the other hand, IS's videos work to create the Caliphate in the here-and-now, as a utopian project that hails Muslims throughout the world.

According to Charlie Winter's analysis, most of IS's media products— 52.7 percent—can be characterized as "utopian," focusing on issues of governance, morality, justice, economy, physical infrastructure, and social welfare.[84] In addition to tearing down the ancien regime, videos show how IS also engages in

---

[79] See Friis, "'Beyond Anything We Have Ever Seen,'" 736; Euben, "Spectacles of Sovereignty in Digital Time," 1009; Mello, "The Islamic State."

[80] Kraidy, "The Projectilic Image," 1205.

[81] Euben, "Spectacles of Sovereignty in Digital Time," 1010.

[82] Friis, "'Behead, Burn, Crucify, Crush,'" 246.

[83] Farwell, "Jihadi Video in the 'War of Ideas,'" 148.

[84] Winter, *Documenting the Virtual "Caliphate"*, 30; also see Stenersen, "A History of Jihadi Cinematography," 125; Bloom and Daymon, "Assessing the Future Threat," 378; Jeu Delemarre, "*Dabiq*: Framing the Islamic State" (MA thesis, Radboud University Nijmegen, 2017) https://theses.ubn.ru.nl/bitstream/handle/123456789/4718/Delemarre%2C_J.F.M._1.pdf?sequence=1 (accessed October 13, 2018).

state-building, society-building, and world-building.[85] What is most interesting about the IS media strategy is that it works not just to create a sovereign "state" (as previously argued), but to create a utopian one that is "Islamic"; one of the main tasks of IS media products is to "persuade all Muslims [that] battling to restore a caliphate is a religious duty."[86]

While many scholars focus on the savagery of public violence, here I follow those who look at the sensible politics of everyday life in warzones. In this way, we can see how the Islamic State engages in "rebel governance" to assert itself as a legitimate state not only through military conquest, but also through social welfare provision.[87] Here it is like other rebel states—for example, Sri Lanka, Columbia, and Sudan— that gained civilian support through social welfare projects, thus "performing the state . . . within the routines and patterns of everyday life."[88] In Syria, it has long been the state's job to provide social welfare to the population, including free health care and subsidized oil and food. Indeed, during the Syrian civil war, hospitals and bakeries have been strategic sites both in the sense that rival regimes (the Assad regime, the Kurdish YPG, the Free Syrian Army, and armed Islamist groups including IS) have competed for civilian loyalty by devoting scarce resources to hospitals and bakeries, and in the sense that the Assad regime and IS deliberately destroyed hospitals and bakeries to undermine their rivals.[89] The war thus is not just between armed groups, but also takes place in everyday life struggles.

The rest of this section examines the visuality of war through PSAs that celebrate IS's rebel governance of a utopian society. In particular, it examines IS videos about health and food. For these videos, the search for legitimacy switches from the sovereign's power over death (which characterizes late-medieval/early modern European politics), to what Foucault sees as the modern administrative state's biopolitical project of nurturing populations. He argues that in the modern era "the function of pastoral power has spread far beyond the church to inform the state's

---

[85] Mello, "The Islamic State," 147; Kraidy, "The Projectilic Image," 1195; Bloom and Daymon, "Assessing the Future Threat," 379; Delemarre, "*Dabiq*," 38; Heck, "The Struggle for Legitimacy of the Islamic State," 84.

[86] Farwell, "The Media Strategy of ISIS," 49.

[87] José Ciro Martínez and Brent Eng, "Stifling Stateness: The Assad Regime's Campaigns Against Rebel Governance," *Security Dialogue* 49:4 (2018):235–253; José Ciro Martínez and Brent Eng, "Struggling to Perform the State: The Politics of Bread in the Syrian Civil War," *International Political Sociology* 11 (2017):130–147; Alex Jeffrey, *The Improvised State: Sovereignty, Performance and Agency in Dayton Bosnia* (London: John Wiley & Sons, 2012); David Brenner, *Rebel Politics: A Political Sociology of Armed Struggle in Myanmar's Borderlands* (Ithaca, NY: Cornell University Press, 2019), pp. 13–28.

[88] Martínez and Eng, "Struggling to Perform the State," 131; Martínez and Eng, "Stifling Stateness," 237, 238.

[89] See Martínez and Eng, "Stifling Stateness"; Martínez and Eng, "Struggling to Perform the State."

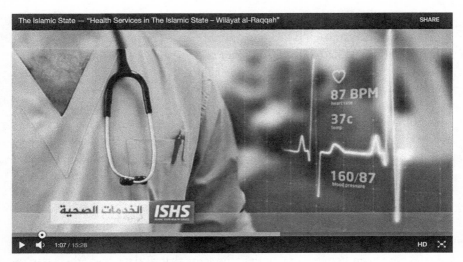

Figure 5.4 Screenshot of *Health Services in The Islamic State* (2015).

modes of managing society."[90] Here the theo-political state administers not just the spiritual needs of its population, but also the population's everyday material and cultural needs. These PSAs show the day-to-day rebel governance of society; but as creative products themselves, they are an important part of cultural governance in ways that are both very pious and very modern (and very modernistic). They hail audiences both within the IS and outside it, in a battle of visualities that looks to the sensible politics of everyday life.

While IS stresses that it is completely different from European secular states, its video *Health Services in the Islamic State* (2015) exhibits interesting parallels with the West.[91] Indeed, the Islamic State Health Service logo (ISHS) will be familiar to people in the United Kingdom; it closely mirrors that of the National Health Service (NHS) (see figure 5.4). The video starts in the hermeneutic style of a pious doctor at Al-Raqqah General Hospital explaining how the IS's Health Service worked to overcome obstacles to benefit the people, and thus produces the legitimacy of the Islamic State. To prove how the ISHS is working at a global level that

[90] Michel Foucault, "Afterword: The Subject and Power," in *Michel Foucault: Beyond Structuralism and Hermeneutics,* edited by Hubert L. Dreyfus and Paul Rabinow (New York: The Harvester Press, 1982), p. 214; also see Foucault, "Governmentality."

[91] *Health Services in the Islamic State—Wilāyat al-Raqqah* (April 24, 2015) https://jihadology.net/ ?s=health+service (accessed September 3, 2018). The script of this video was translated from Arabic by a professional translation company. For discussion of the Islamic State Health Service, see Aymenn Jawad Al-Tamimi, "The Archivist: Critical Analysis of the Islamic State's Health Department" (August 27, 2015) https://jihadology.net/2015/08/27/the-archivist-critical-analysis-of-the-islamic-states-health-department/ (accessed October 19, 2018).

includes specialized care, the video gives the viewer a tour of the hospital, which is also a medical school. Certainly the hospital is caring for war casualties, but the head doctor stresses that the intensive care unit also works to heal people with "injuries from car accidents, poison, burns, trauma, brain damage, nerve damage, and surgical complications."[92] The video thus makes visible the virtuous pastoral work done by the Islamic State.

Here the verbal information is complemented by visual affect-work: we see injured and sick people being cared for, including heart-wrenching clips of little children and old people. Actually, the affect-work precedes the ideological work; the first minute of the fifteen-minute film is an audio-video collage of film clips from around the hospital set to the beat of an EKG beep (the graph of which is animated over the images; see figure 5.4) and the harmony of a pious *anashid* (an a cappella religious song).[93] It is a music video in a fast-cut MTV style that edits together clips of ambulances, doctors in scrubs, and premature infants in incubators in ways that stylistically reference Western medical TV dramas. The video's introduction ends with the music fading out, focusing first on an ambulance racing up to the hospital, and then on paramedics rushing the injured person into the emergency room.

The head doctor's testimony and the tour of the wards are both done with high production values; like with the execution videos, the Health Service video employs multiple cameras, "quick cuts, composition, blocking, pacing, resolution, sound/silence, camera angles, dress, and casting, to 'speak' as much as words."[94] But here, rather than using violence to medievally-mutilate the human body as a means of asserting the sovereign power over death, the video uses high-tech life-saving techniques to heal human bodies in the IS as a biopolitical utopia. While many analyze the ideology of IS videos to probe their effectiveness in recruiting warriors, this video uses affective work to attract life-giving medical professionals to the IS utopia. Numerous doctors invite their medical colleagues in the West to join the multinational ISHS and thus pledge allegiance to the Islamic State. As an Australian doctor pleads:

> [I have] a message that I would want to send out to any brothers or sisters still in living in the West who are considering coming. I swear it was a

---

[92] For a description of how the health service worked in a two-tiered system that favored IS cadres over the general public, see Ghaith Abdul-Ahad, "How the People of Mosul Subverted ISIS 'Apartheid,'" *The Guardian* (January 30, 2018) https://www.theguardian.com/cities/2018/jan/30/mosul-isis-apartheid (accessed October 26, 2018).

[93] For more on the politics of singing *nasheen*, see Nelly Lahoud, "A Capella Songs (Anashid) in Jihadi Culture," in *Jihadi Culture: The Art and Social Practices of Militant Islamists*, edited by Thomas Hegghammer, 42–62 (New York: Cambridge University Press, 2017); Thomas Hegghammer, "Non-military Practices in Jihadi Groups," in *Jihadi Culture: The Art and Social Practices of Militant Islamists*, edited by Thomas Hegghammer (New York: Cambridge University Press, 2017), pp. 188–189.

[94] Euben, "Spectacles of Sovereignty in Digital Time," 1018.

decision I was very very happy I made. . . . Everything lived up to my ex-
pectations completely. And we really need your help, any little thing gives
the local people who are truly suffering a lot of benefit. . . . God willing, see
you soon.

The video ends much as it began, with a collage of images from the Al-Raqqah
General Hospital, except this time the images stress not crisis, but happiness and
contentment: the doctors who were interviewed in the video are shown in slow motion smiling and laughing, crosscut with clips of vulnerable infants who are under
their care, against the catchy soundtrack of an *anashid*. The IS here is a productively
healthy utopia full of people working together for the good life and succeeding in
pious triumph; the IS flag waves in the video's upper left corner.[95] As an artifact
of creative cultural governance, this video works to exhort various audiences—
primarily from outside IS—to support the Islamic State as a legitimate utopian state.

Videos of the IS's administration of food are also good examples of rebel governance, cultural governance, and biopolitical utopia. Actually, it's a bit more complicated because the two films—*Food Security* and *Administration of Bakeries and
Ovens*—show a tension between securitization and cultural governance.[96] *Food
Security*, not surprisingly, starts with military security issues: a black and white clip
of President Obama announcing airstrikes against IS, then black and white images
of war and destruction from the IS point of view.[97] The video is narrated with a declaration of IS's goal "to protect its soldiers, borders, and to protect the Muslims."

However, this protection is not only a military project; it is pastoral in the sense
of protecting food security. The video soon switches (as in *The Wizard of Oz*) from
black and white to color images of a combine harvesting wheat, underlining how
farmers are warriors in the battle to "maintain and expand" IS. The film then engages
in a fascinating PSA tour of the food industry in Ḥalab province. Although not exactly a statement of "Organic IS,"[98] it does present a "farm-to-table" process video
of life in the Islamic State. It visually traces how wheat is grown and harvested, then
ground into flour, which is then made into dough that is, in turn, baked to make pita

---

[95] Also see Gerges, *ISIS*, 228; Bloom and Daymon, "Assessing the Future Threat," 379.

[96] *Food Security: Aspects from the Work of the Agriculture Administration in the Province—Wilāyat
Ḥalab* (November 10, 2015) https://jihadology.net/2015/11/10/new-video-message-from-the-
islamic-state-food-security-aspects-from-the-work-of-the-agriculture-administration-in-the-province-
wilayat-ḥalab/ (accessed October 19, 2018); *Administration of Bakeries and Ovens in Wilāyat al-Raqqah*
(August 15, 2015) https://jihadology.net/2015/08/15/new-video-message-from-the-islamic-state-
administration-of-the-bakery-and-ovens-in-wilayat-al-raqqah/ (accessed October 19, 2018). The
scripts of these videos were translated from Arabic by a professional translation company.

[97] Interestingly, for ideological reasons, the video does not mention how the Assad regime was actually bombing IS bakeries. See Martínez and Eng, "Struggling to Perform the State," 138.

[98] Thanks to Katharine Millar for the phrase "Organic IS."

Figure 5.5 Screenshot of *Administration of Bakeries and Ovens* (2015).

bread. The clips show how this pita bread is stacked, weighed, bagged, and loaded onto a truck for distribution. As the narrator explains, "[T]he Administration of Mills and Bakeries takes responsibility for delivering bread to the homes of Muslims in remote villages and far areas." But actually, the narration is moot, because we see the trucks going down long, dusty roads to deliver bread to happy and grateful families (which has parallels with the production and distribution of the video itself). The video presents life in IS as "paradise" in the sense of an Islamic garden (based on the Garden of Eden) that is well-irrigated and full of flora and fauna, sweet honey, juicy fruits, and crunchy nuts.[99] The off-screen narrator concludes, "The province of Ḥalab had what other provinces had: food security. And this is due to God's grace and his luck, thank you God for what you have graced us with."

The other food PSA, *Administration of Bakeries and Ovens in Wilāyat al-Raqqah*, is even more interesting because the verbal-ideological aspect seems to be an afterthought. The first two minutes of this five-minute video are a series of audio-video clips that show the bakery production of pita bread in even more detail than in *Food Security*, without any narration at all. It is a well-crafted video that uses all the techniques discussed previously to produce a PSA/music video that is not only informative but aesthetically-pleasing (see figure 5.5). This process video style of visualizing how things are made is an effective (and affective) way of addressing audiences both inside and outside the Islamic State. This style is also popular in other countries, where bakery process videos are used to move and connect

[99] See Emma Clark, *Underneath Which Rivers Flow: The Symbolism of the Islamic Garden* (London: Prince of Wale's Institute of Architecture, 1996).

audiences for projects as diverse as welfare for adults with learning disabilities in Edinburgh and Muslim Uyghurs in concentration camps in Northwest China.[100] In these examples, as well as in IS videos, populations perform bread-making as happy and healthy participants in a greater (utopian) project.

In *Administration of Bakeries and Ovens*, the narrator appears on-screen quite late (and soon disappears behind the b-roll of bakery-process clips). Importantly, he explains that IS is concerned with not only the quantity of food, but also its quality: "As for the quality of bread in the bakeries of the Islamic State, praise to God, where we have standards for the quality of the bread, high-quality standards for bread." Like a proper pastoral state, these quality control mechanisms guarantee the safety of bread and other necessary foodstuffs. By producing food through rebel governance, IS produces power through cultural governance. Once again, these videos show that IS is not simply a sovereign state that gains legitimacy through its control over death, but is at the same time a biopolitical state that nurtures the life of its growing and expanding population. As the health and food videos show, this biopower is both pious and modern, and it produces IS as a legitimate utopian state: the twenty-first-century Caliphate. Like the health video, the food videos are examples of creative cultural governance that works to exhort specific audiences to support IS's utopian social-ordering and world-ordering projects.

These films are disseminated through IS's global multimedia network, which includes promotion on top-ten video lists and prominent tie-in articles in its flagship glossy monthly magazine *Dabiq*.[101] This intervisuality among different platforms produces a "global networked affect"[102] of IS as not simply a sovereign state that relies on savage violence, but also a biopolitical utopia where people viscerally feel at home. IS videos thus provide a good example of the audio-visual as an affective mode that "does" things through cultural governance. This utopian social-ordering and world-ordering project moves and connects people first emotionally to support IS, then materially when they, like the Australian doctor, migrate to the Islamic State to live the good life in the Caliphate. These PSAs hailed audiences both inside IS, to cultivate loyalty and legitimacy among the civilian population, and outside IS, to attract pious professionals to join the utopian project. Rather

---

[100] The Edinburgh film is Yasmin Fedda, *Breadmakers* (2007) https://vimeo.com/21718544 (accessed October 22, 2018); the Chinese film is *Zhulao fangtan* [Building the foundation], Focus Interview, Chinese Central Television Channel 13 (October 16, 2018) http://tv.cctv.com/v/v1/VIDEVvr9aq34SsDMrB6IRGnh181016.html (accessed October 22, 2018).

[101] For example, see "Report: Health Care in the Khilafah," *Dabiq* 9 (May 2, 2015):24–26; "10 Videos Selected from the Wilayat of the IS," *Dabiq* 9 (May 2, 2015):33; "10 Videos Selected from the Wilayat of the IS," *Dabiq* 12 (November 18, 2015):63. For IS memes, see https://knowyourmeme.com/search?q=islamic+state.

[102] Kraidy, "The Projectilic Image," 1198.

than being an issue of security or securitization, IS videos show how cultural governance in warzones can provoke new social orders and world orders as affective communities of sense.

Conclusion

This chapter explores the connections among visuality, security, order, and war. It compares securitization and cultural governance as two approaches to appreciating the political workings of images. Securitization theory is useful for unpacking how visual images can shape foreign policy events through their immediacy, circulation, and ambiguity. But the chapter uses the security crisis provoked by the feature film *The Interview* to question securitization's focus on the state, official elites, and the close relationship between existential threats and security problems. It then outlines how cultural governance can better address the political problems provoked in less official spaces, such as popular culture and cyberspace, which has implications for the wider issues of social-ordering and world-ordering. In this way, the chapter shows, on the one hand, the visibility strategy's hermeneutic approach to reading visual securitization, and on the other, the visuality strategy's attention to the broader issues of how images can actively provoke affective communities of sense that complicate what can (and cannot) be seen, said, thought, and done.

To push beyond the visibility strategy's ideological questions, the chapter examines the audio-visual affective politics of Islamic State videos. It argues that IS is a strong example of cultural governance; between 2014 and 2019, the world witnessed the creation (and then destruction) of a sovereign state. This was not simply a military conquest of territory; IS devoted scarce resources to building legitimacy through rebel governance and media products, including professional-quality videos that were disseminated through a global affect network. In critical security studies, analysts have shown how the extreme violence of IS videos works to assert sovereignty through control over death. This chapter argues that we also need to look beyond the shock of savage violence to see how IS videos work through the pastoral politics of cultural governance to create a biopolitical utopia. Certainly we can understand IS PSAs in terms of securitization, such as food security. But I argue that the broader conceptual framework of cultural governance allows us to better appreciate IS as a utopian project of social-ordering and world-ordering that produces new affective communities of sense.

But what about resistance? Cultural governance theory follows Foucault to argue that where there is power, there is resistance. Yet as a theo-political totalitarian state, within IS there was very little space for cultural resistance. Resistance forces certainly didn't have access to the video equipment and expertise necessary to make counter-PSAs (e.g., Cynthia Weber's *I Am an American* videos, discussed in Chapter 4). Although there was state-led and popular resistance to IS from outside the Caliphate,[103] resistance within IS was limited to everyday activities for survival.[104] This shows a conceptual weakness shared by securitization and cultural governance: both assume that there is political space for cultural activity within or alongside the polity.[105] But this space is not evident in many revolutionary, funda-mentalist, authoritarian, or totalitarian states, where critics are either dissidents (who are silenced) or establishment intellectuals (who parrot the party line).

The next chapter develops the resistance factor of the cultural governance/re-sistance dynamic through an analysis of artistic work done by dissidents fighting the state and by international refugees who address transnational flows of people.

---

[103] See Koerner, "Why ISIS Is Winning."

[104] See Abdul-Ahad, "How the People of Mosul Subverted ISIS 'Apartheid.' "

[105] See Saloni Kapur and Simon Mabon, "The Copenhagen School Goes Global: Securitisation in the Non-West," *Global Discourse* 8:1 (2018):1–4.

6

Visual Art, Ethical Witnessing, and Resistance

Introduction

As we saw in the introduction's discussion of Europe's refugee crisis in summer 2015, the photograph of the dead toddler Alan Kurdi didn't just illustrate the dangers facing migrants. It also actively did things, including moving German chancellor Angela Merkel to allow over one million refugees into her country. To many, this was evidence of the CNN-Effect, in which images drive policy; that is, the spectacle of suffering and vulnerable people, displayed originally on twenty-four-hour cable news programs and now on popular YouTube and social media sites, is able to mobilize the viewing public—and ultimately their political leaders—to respond to injustice.[1] This is an example of how photojournalism works as an ethical witness to move and connect people—here Western citizens, Middle Eastern migrants, and European political leaders—to excite political action. Conversely, there are many examples of atrocities that go unanswered on the global stage unless and until they are illustrated by powerful images: the Rwandan genocide (1994), torture at Abu Ghraib prison (2004), and over one million Muslims in concentration camps in Northwest China (2017–present).

How are we to understand the role of images in global politics? What do they mean, and what can they do? Can visual art serve as a site of resistance to cultural governance? And are viewers just passive spectators who reproduce hegemonic power, or can they be emancipated spectators who can ethically witness injustice in creative ways that provoke new affective communities of sense? The previous chapter introduced the concept of "cultural governance" to analyze how state and

---

[1] Warren P. Strobel, "The CNN Effect," *American Journalism Review* (May 1996) http://ajrarchive. org/article.asp?id=3572 (accessed December 20, 2018); Piers Robinson, *The CNN Effect: The Myth of News Foreign Policy Intervention* (London: Routledge, 2002); Piers Robinson, "Media Empowerment vs. Strategies of Control: Theorizing News Media and War in the 21st Century," *Zeitschrift fur Politik* 4 (2014):461–479.

Sensible Politics. William A. Callahan, Oxford University Press (2020). © Oxford University Press.
DOI: 10.1093/oso/9780190071738.001.0001

corporate power productively creates sovereignty, legitimacy, and power by creating and managing supportive forms of culture and identity. But cultural governance does not exhaust political possibility, because there are opportunities for resistance to state and corporate powers' imaginings of legitimacy. Resistance here does not necessarily take place in political institutions (e.g., political parties at home and international organizations abroad), but also can emerge through other modalities of expression—films, journals, diaries, novels, and counter-historical narratives—that "challenge the state's coherence-producing writing performances."[2] This cultural governance/resistance dynamic assumes that there are alternative cultural spaces within or alongside the polity, that is, civil society. But as we saw in Chapter 5, this space for resistance is not obvious in many revolutionary, fundamentalist, authoritarian, or totalitarian states. Hence, to complement Chapter 5's examination of the cultural governance of PSAs from the Islamic State, this chapter considers how images—especially visual art—can engage in resistance to cultural governance through an ethical witnessing that resists authoritarian state oppression and transnational atrocities.

To trace these issues, the chapter analyzes the work of Ai Weiwei, a world-famous artist-activist whose work ideologically resists China's authoritarian party-state in both the traditional sense of liberal resistance to authoritarian state oppression and the hermeneutical sense, in which it is necessary to decode his work for its "meaning" as a social construction of the visual. The chapter then considers how resistance can take shape through the "visual provocation of the social"—and of the global. Ai's documentary film *Human Flow* (2017) is analyzed to see how it expands from a critique of China's domestic oppression to visualize the oppression of refugees on a global scale in a creative way that can mobilize transnational affective communities of sense. The chapter thus considers how visual art can serve as an "ethical witness" to resist reigning political regimes, and how it also can excite affective communities of sense to creatively resist reigning political aesthetics. Ai Weiwei's experience also shows how resistance—even that of a world-famous artist—still relies to a large extent on what the state will allow; in 2015, Ai was forced into exile, where he no longer focuses his critique on China.

While the previous chapter explored how war and violence must be appreciated for their aesthetic nature, this chapter flips the aesthetics/politics dynamic to explore how things that we normally view as aesthetic—here visual art—are also very political. Actually, both the Islamic State PSA videos and Ai's *Human Flow* are dealing with the same issue: the massive movement of people to and from Syria and Iraq. While the Islamic State videos considered in Chapter 5 aimed to attract

---

[2] Michael J. Shapiro, *Methods and Nations: Cultural Governance and the Indigenous Subject* (New York: Routledge, 2004), p. 49; David Campbell, "Cultural Governance and Pictorial Resistance: Reflections on the Imaging of War," *Review of International Studies* 29 (2003):57–73.

Muslim migrants to the utopian Caliphate, Ai's *Human Flow* traces the horrors of people trying to escape from Syria and Iraq. In this way, Ai's visual art can be seen as a mode of resistance not just to European (anti-)migration regimes, but also to the Islamic State's cultural governance project.

Photojournalism, Witnessing, and Ethics

Discussion of the role of images in "witnessing" links the disciplines of international relations and media and communications. Debates center around how audiences react to graphic images of violence, trauma, and pain, either as passive voyeurs or as active witnesses. After World War I, there was much hope that the shocking images of military violence provided by the new mass medium of photography would convince the general public to oppose war. While Virginia Woolf's *Three Guineas* is famous for raising the issue of gender and IR, here it is also important because it discusses the politics of images: the power of photographs to raise awareness and the responsibility of the viewer to respond. As Woolf describes, during the Spanish Civil War the Republican government sent packets of grisly photos—twice a week—to sympathetic viewers in Europe and America. These graphic images aimed to mobilize support for their cause: "photographs of more dead bodies, of more ruined houses, to call forth an answer, and an answer that will give you, Sir, the very help that you require."[3] Woolf thus employs a mimetic understanding of knowledge as the "mirror of nature," in which photographs reflect the unvarnished truth of the horrors of war: "Those photographs are not an argument; they are simply a crude statement of fact addressed to the eye."[4] This is an early version of what we now call the CNN-Effect: as in the 1930s, in the twenty-first century you need a visual image to transform local political violence into a global political event.[5]

However, the Frankfurt school, and later critics such as Susan Sontag, warned that images can be dangerous. Rather than appreciating how images could support progressive causes, as in the Spanish Civil War, they look to the contemporaneous example of how Leni Riefenstahl's documentary films—*Triumph of the Will* (1935) and *Olympia* (1938)—mobilized popular support for the Nazi Party.[6] Here photographs do not reflect the truth; rather, the films' aesthetic spectacle manipulates the masses. Walter Benjamin thus concluded that "[f]ascism is the

---

[3] Virginia Woolf, *Three Guineas* (London: Hogarth Press, 1938), pp. 10, 39. Also see Susan Sontag, *Regarding the Pain of Others* (New York: Penguin, 2003).

[4] Woolf, *Three Guineas*, 10.

[5] Rune Saugmann Andersen, "Videos," in *Making Things International 1: Circuits and Motion*, edited by Mark B. Salter (Minneapolis: University of Minnesota Press, 2015), p. 260.

[6] Susan Sontag, "Fascinating Fascism," *New York Review of Books* (February 6, 1975):1–20; Susan Sontag, *On Photography* (New York: Penguin, 1977).

introduction of aesthetics into political life," and "[a]ll efforts to render politics aesthetic culminate in one thing: war."[7] In the twenty-first century, such photographs and videos are part of state-led campaigns to justify war to Euro-American audiences as a humanitarian duty.[8]

This "hermeneutics of suspicion" recalls arguments about the relationship of word and image discussed in Chapter 1: while photographs shock us, narratives make us understand.[9] Images emotionally manipulate people into reproducing hegemonic power as passive voyeurs; hence, following the visibility strategy's hermeneutics mode, the critic's job is to look behind the image and iconoclastically reveal the institutional power that supports it. The CNN-Effect thus is a ruse; rather than showing the democratizing power of widely distributed topical images, such visual campaigns are evidence of the elite manipulation of our emotions.[10] While for Woolf it is the duty of humanity to witness and react to the horrors presented in photographs, for others photographs and films work as propaganda to manipulate what the masses think, and how they feel.[11]

To critique this iconoclastic approach that sees spectators as passive voyeurs, Robert Hariman and John Louis Lucaites explain how a more active notion of witnessing has emerged.[12] Rather than appeal to the photograph as a technology that reflects the truth, however, this approach appeals to photography (warts and all) as a "vital technology of democratic citizenship" that can serve as "a mode of experience, a medium for social thought, a public art" that is "a boon for human understanding and solidarity."[13] Here spectatorship does not look to reflection or

---

[7] Walter Benjamin, "The Work of Art in the Age of Mechanical Reproduction," in *Illuminations: Essays and Reflections*, edited by Hannah Arendt (New York: Schocken Books, 1968), p. 241.

[8] Lilie Chouliaraki, "The Humanity of War: Iconic Photojournalism of the Battlefield, 1914–2012," in *Visual Security Studies: Sights and Spectacles of Insecurity and War*, edited by Juha A. Vuori and Rune Saugmann Andersen (New York: Routledge, 2018), pp. 71–90; Robinson, "Media Empowerment vs. Strategies of Control"; Piers Robinson, "CNN Effect," in *Visual Global Politics*, edited by Roland Bleiker (London: Routledge, 2018), pp. 62–67.

[9] Sontag, *Regarding the Pain of Others*, 80.

[10] Robinson, "Media Empowerment vs. Strategies of Control"; Robinson, "CNN Effect."

[11] Sontag, *Regarding the Pain of Others*.

[12] Robert Hariman and John Louis Lucaites, *The Public Image: Photography and Civic Spectatorship* (Chicago: University of Chicago Press, 2016), pp. 1–28. Also see Jacques Rancière, *The Emancipated Spectator*, translated by Gregory Elliott (London: Verso, 2009); Jacques Rancière, *The Politics of Aesthetics: The Distribution of the Sensible*, translated by Gabriel Rockhill (London: Continuum International Publishing Group, 2004); Susie Linfield, *Cruel Radiance: Photography and Political Violence* (Chicago: University of Chicago Press, 2010); Ariella Azoulay, *Civil Imagination: A Political Ontology of Photography*, translated by Louise Bethlehem (London: Verso, 2012); Lilie Chouliaraki, *The Ironic Spectator: Solidarity in the Age of Post-humanitarianism* (Cambridge, UK: Polity Press, 2013); Judith Butler, *Frames of War: When Is Life Grievable?* (London: Verso, 2016); Frank Möller, *Visual Peace: Images, Spectatorship, and the Politics of Violence* (London: Palgrave MacMillan, 2013).

[13] Hariman and Lucaites, *The Public Image*, 2, 3.

manipulation, but is a "civic capability" that is learned and critically discussed.[14] As Jacques Rancière argues:

> Being a spectator is not some passive condition that we should transform into activity. It is our normal situation. We also learn and teach, act and know, as spectators who all the time link what we see to what we have seen and said, done and dreamed.[15]

Spectatorship thus is not understood as a reaction to images, as in the CNN-Effect, but is figured as a social relationship that is an "affective alignment."[16]

The "ethical witness" thus shifts from being the victim of elite manipulation to being an "emancipated spectator," an "ironic spectator," and a "participant witness," who can actively resist the cultural governance of state and corporate power.[17] And it's not just the human witness who is active, but also the image itself: as Judith Butler explains: "The photo is not merely a visual image awaiting interpretation: it is itself actively interpreting, sometimes forcibly so."[18] While the iconoclastic approach employs the visibility strategy's hermeneutics of suspicion to deconstruct ideological meaning, active witnessing is better explained in terms of the visuality strategy's appreciation of how affect-work can provoke communities of sense that complicate what can (and cannot) be seen, said, thought, and done.

The dynamic relation of visibility and visuality, ideology and affect, and active and passive witnessing is helpfully shown in Roland Bleiker and Amy Kay's comparison of how two styles of documentary photography—humanitarian and pluralist photography—represent HIV/AIDS in Africa.[19] Humanitarian photography is done by professional photojournalists who fly in to document the violence of wars and humanitarian crises for a Euro-American audience. These aren't realist images that seek to reflect reality, but activist images that aim to make invisible suffering more visible, such as Ed Hooper's iconic photograph of a Ugandan mother and her baby in the last stages of an AIDS-related illness. Humanitarian photographs hope to "serve as a catalyst for positive change" by evoking compassion in the viewer.[20]

Still, such photos are problematic because they tend to universalize and homogenize Africans into nameless, passive victims. The activism also risks reproducing

---

[14] Hariman and Lucaites, *The Public Image*, 14.

[15] Rancière, *The Politics of Aesthetics*, 17.

[16] Hariman and Lucaites, *The Public Image*, 15.

[17] Rancière, *The Emancipated Spectator*; Chouliaraki, *The Ironic Spectator*; Möller, *Visual Peace*.

[18] Butler, *Frames of War*, 71; also see W. J. T. Mitchell, *What Do Pictures Want? The Lives and Loves of Images* (Chicago: University of Chicago Press, 2005).

[19] Roland Bleiker and Amy Kay, "Representing HIV/AIDS in Africa: Pluralist Photography and Local Empowerment," *International Studies Quarterly* 51 (2007):139–163.

[20] Bleiker and Kay, "Representing HIV/AIDS in Africa," 141.

the hierarchy of postcolonial power relations in a politics of pity wherein helpless Africans rely on Euro-American saviors. Although humanitarian photography may successfully raise funds for charity—and even change government policy—such images often reinforce existing self/Other relations that separate the safe Euro-American "here" from the dangerous African "there."

To critique how humanitarian photography generates passive victims and passive spectators, Bleiker and Kay consider how "pluralist photography" encourages dialogue among active subjects and active spectators. Rather than look to iconic photos taken by outsiders that tend to homogenize Africa, they explore the example of a photography project in Ethiopia that involved HIV/AIDS-affected children. Here the children were given cameras and asked to tell their own stories through pictures. The result was an exhibition of the day-to-day experience of "living with HIV-AIDs," rather than dying from it (as seen in humanitarian photographs). Bleiker and Kay argue that such pluralist photography was empowering for the children and even moved policy in Ethiopia. As well as treating the photographic subjects as active agents, the resulting photo exhibit was designed to activate the audience; viewers were encouraged to add their own letters and pictures to the children's photos. Rather than the foreign subject and the local object, the participatory process produced a "creative and safe space for dialogue" among active self-photographers and emancipated spectators.[21] Witnessing here is not simply the reaction of the Euro-American spectator to images of disaster in Africa, but creates an interactive social relation that moves, connects, and changes people in many places.

Bleiker and Kay's analysis of pluralistic photography exhibits is also interesting because it jams the distinction between photojournalism and visual art. Indeed, parallel to the discussion of the resistance potential of photojournalism is a robust debate about the relation of visual art, world politics, and resistance.[22] Rather than dealing with issues of authenticity—such as whether or not the image is manipulated—visual art addresses the entanglement of aesthetics, politics, and

[21] Bleiker and Kay, "Representing HIV/AIDS in Africa," 157; also see Möller, Visual Peace, 19.

[22] Alex Danchev, On Art and War and Terror (Edinburgh: Edinburgh University Press, 2011); Roland Bleiker, Aesthetics and World Politics (London: Palgrave Macmillan, 2012); Meg McLagan and Yates McKee, eds., Sensible Politics: The Visual Culture of Nongovernmental Activism (New York: Zone Books, 2012); Christine Sylvester, Art/Museums: International Relations Where We Least Expect it (London: Routledge, 2008); Alex Danchev, "Witnessing," in Visual Global Politics, edited by Roland Bleiker (London: Routledge, 2018), pp. 332–338; David Campbell and Michael J. Shapiro, "Guest Editor's Introduction: Securitization, Militarization and Visual Culture in the Worlds of Post-9/11," Security Dialogue 38:2 (2007):131–137; Alex Danchev and Debbie Lisle, "Introduction: Art, Politics, Purpose," Review of International Studies 35:4 (2009):775–779; Kia Lindroos and Frank Möller, eds., Art as Political Witness (Leverkusen: Barbara Budrich, 2016); Möller, Visual Peace; Jill Bennett, Empathic Vision: Affect, Trauma, and Contemporary Art (Stanford, CA: Stanford University Press, 2005); Alex Danchev and R. B. J. Walker, eds., "Art and Politics," special issue, Alternatives: Global, Local, Political 31:1 (2006):1–104.

ethics. It considers how works of art that serve as an ethical witness can creatively challenge prevailing conceptions of social order and world order, and even offer "innovative solutions."[23]

Following from analysis in previous chapters, Chapter 6 uses the visibility/ visuality dynamic to explore the international politics of visual art. The visibility strategy examines the meaning of art by considering how, as a "social construction of the visual," art can resist oppression through witnessing, and the visuality strategy explores how art can provoke new affective communities through a "visual provocation of the social"—and of the global.[24] The visibility strategy works to make invisible ideology more visible, while the visuality strategy looks to how affect-work can create new communities of sense and thus new ways of seeing, feeling, and perhaps doing. As Rancière explains, "[I]mages are the object of a twofold question: the question of their origin (and consequently their truth content) and the question of their end or purpose, the uses they are put to and the effects they result in."[25] Visual art as a mode of resistance here works in complementary ways: on the one hand, it acts ideologically as a witness to atrocities in order to speak truth to power, while on the other it works affectively to creatively excite new affective communities of sense.

To trace this ideology/affect dynamic, the chapter examines how tragedy and vulnerability are represented in art that mixes the visual and the visceral. There is a long tradition of this in European art, perhaps starting with medieval Christian art, and seen in modern times in Goya's *Disasters of War* (1810–1820) and Picasso's *Guernica* (1937).[26] Indeed, we should note that visual art can be even more successful than photojournalism; a copy of *Guernica* now hangs in the UN Headquarters in New York, where it is seen as a general anti-war statement.

However, this chapter strays from the Western canon to see the interaction of art, politics, and resistance in the visual art of Ai Weiwei. The point is not to provide a non-Western riposte to art/politics analysis that is dominated by analysis of art from Europe and America. As we will see, in some ways Ai is the embodiment of the comparative political theory dynamic discussed in Chapter 3; his creative combination of modern, traditional, Euro-American, Chinese, and Middle Eastern concepts, practices, and experiences jams any East-West binary opposition. The chapter explores the interplay of ideology and affect to see how visual art can serve as a "witness" to resist reigning political regimes, as well as how it can provoke affective community that creatively resists reigning political aesthetics.

---

[23] Bleiker, *Aesthetics and World Politics*, 1, 10–13.

[24] Mitchell, *What Do Pictures Want?*, 343.

[25] Rancière, *The Politics of Aesthetics*, 20.

[26] See Liu Quan, "Nanmin yu yishu" [Refugees and art], *Meishu guancha* no. 2 (2017):147–150; Möller, *Visual Peace*, 9; Danchev, "Witnessing," 332; Bennett, *Empathic Vision*, 35.

Witnessing as Ideological Resistance

In the past decade, Ai Weiwei has burst out from his limited role of Chinese artist to become a key artist-activist on the global stage. He first gained international fame as the artistic consultant for Beijing's "Bird's Nest" Olympic stadium; just before the 2008 Olympics, however, Ai became infamous for denouncing the stadium as China's "fake smile" to the world. In October 2010 Ai fascinated the art world with his *Sunflower Seeds* exhibit at London's Tate Modern art gallery; before the exhibit closed in May 2011, Ai became a global political figure when he was arrested by the Chinese government on April 3, 2011. Following his release in June 2011 after eighty-one days of illegal detention, Ai continued to intrigue, outrage, and entertain audiences in China and around the world. In response to the controversy around US mass surveillance operations, Ai argued that by invading people's privacy "the US is behaving like China."[27] After years of post-detention harassment by China's party-state, in 2015 Ai moved into self-imposed exile in Berlin, where he continued to produce noteworthy art—and activism.

Ai Weiwei is famous for crossing boundaries, especially the boundary between art and politics. His activities explore the limits of what is acceptable in China in terms of both political action and aesthetic taste: in 2000 he co-organized an exhibit in Shanghai called *Fuck Off*, and more recently his nude photos were denounced as pornography both by the police and in the court of public opinion.[28] He thus is a polarizing figure among both artistic and nonartistic audiences, who delights in making people—both friends and enemies—feel uncomfortable. His main friend, promoter, and defender in the West, Swiss art collector and former ambassador to China Uli Sigg, warned Ai "to be careful. Don't let them mix your position as an artist and a political activist" because " 'political art' is not a good word."[29] After Ai was illegally detained in April 2011, a critic in one of China's official newspapers complained that Ai's art "confounds the boundary between the artistic and the political; in fact, he uses it to engage in political activities."[30]

Ai's work as an activist-artist thus is noteworthy not because it is "new." His critique of China's politics and society is actually part of a broad and ongoing debate about the moral crisis that China faces after four decades of economic reform and opening up. In other words, China's New Left, traditionalists, and liberals are all

[27] Ai Weiwei, "NSA Surveillance: The US Is Behaving Like China," *The Guardian* (June 11, 2013) https://www.theguardian.com/commentisfree/2013/jun/11/nsa-surveillance-us-behaving-like-china (accessed April 11, 2019).

[28] See Hua Tianxue, Ai Weiwei, and Feng Boyi, eds., *Bu hezuo fangshi-Fuck Off* [An uncooperative approach-Fuck Off] (Shanghai: Eastlink Gallery, 2000).

[29] Ai Weiwei, interview with the author in Beijing (May 27, 2013).

[30] Liu Yiheng, "Ai Weiwei zhen mianmu: Wu wan yishujia—wu du ju quan" [The true face of Ai Weiwei: Five play artist—five poisons] *Wenhui Bao* (April 15, 2011).

worried about the "values crisis" presented by what they call China's new "money-worship" society.[31] Intellectuals from across the political spectrum thus are engaged in what Chinese call "patriotic worrying" (*youhuan yishi*); they feel that it is their job to ponder the fate of the nation and to find the correct formula to solve China's problems.[32]

Ai's contribution to this debate is straightforward: he feels that the PRC is a corrupt authoritarian state, and the country can only be saved if the government respects freedom of expression and the rule of law.[33] As he wrote in his blog: "Return basic rights to the people, endow society with basic dignity, and only then can we have confidence and take responsibility, and thus face our collective difficulties. Only rule of law can make the game equal, and only when it is equal can people's participation possibly be extraordinary."[34] Ai thus sees China's dictatorial state as the problem.[35] As he wrote in *The Guardian*, "[E]very day in China, we put the state on trial."[36] In one tweet he declares, "Every delight we have on Twitter is a death of dictatorship and totalitarianism," while in another he states, "Evil exists to test our courage."[37] Ai thus figures politics as a Manichean struggle of good versus evil, in which the heroic dissident fights the cruel state.[38]

Ai thus shares many political values with Nobel laureate Liu Xiaobo, who likewise questioned Beijing's authoritarian rule. In his co-authored "Charter '08" manifesto, Liu argued that the Chinese people need to "embrace universal human values, join the mainstream of civilized nations, and build a democratic system."[39] Yet Ai's style and tactics are quite different. Liu acted like a classic twentieth-century

---

[31] See William A. Callahan, *China Dreams: 20 Visions of the Future* (New York: Oxford University Press, 2013); Liu Mingfu, *Zhongguo meng: Hou Meiguo shidai de daguo siwei zhanlue dingwei* [The China dream: The great power thinking and strategic positioning of China in the post-American era], 2nd ed. (Beijing: Zhongguo youyi chuban gongsi, 2013); Xu Jilin, *Dangdai Zhongguo de qimeng yu fan-qimeng* [Enlightenment and anti-enlightenment in contemporary China] (Beijing: Shehui kexue wenxian chubanshe, 2011).

[32] Gloria Davies, *Worrying about China: The Language of Chinese Critical Inquiry* (Cambridge, MA: Harvard University Press, 2007); Liu, *Zhongguo meng*.

[33] Ai Weiwei, interview with the author.

[34] Ai Weiwei, *Ai Weiwei's Blog: Writings, Interview, and Digital Rants, 2006–2009*, edited and translated by Lee Ambrozy (Cambridge, MA: MIT Press 2011), pp. 181–182.

[35] For a different view of Ai's ideology, see Christian Sorace, "China's Last Communist: Ai Weiwei," *Critical Inquiry* 40:2 (2014):396–419.

[36] Ai Weiwei, "Every Day in China, We Put the State on Trial," *The Guardian* (April 15, 2013) https://www.theguardian.com/commentisfree/2013/apr/15/ai-weiwei-china-state-on-trial (accessed April 11, 2019).

[37] Ai, *Ai Weiwei's Blog*, September 3, 2009, and August 3, 2009.

[38] See Richard Curt Kraus, *The Party and the Arty in China: The New Politics of Culture*. Lanham, MD: Rowman & Littlefield, 2004), p. 1.

[39] Liu Xiaobo, *No Enemies, No Hatred: Selected Essays and Poems*, edited by Perry Link, Tianchi Martin-Liao, and Liu Xia (Cambridge, MA: Harvard University Press, 2012), p. 301.

dissident: he drafted manifestos demanding political change, acted in rationally earnest ways—and, in 2017, he tragically died in prison. "Charter '08," which landed Liu in jail for "state subversion," reads like a five-year plan for rational democratic reform in China.

Ai, however, takes a twenty-first-century approach to resistance that blurs art, life, politics, and activism. Rather than writing earnest essays that demand rational governance, Ai appeals to people's outrage, mocks the government, and works primarily through the Internet to witness the party-state's oppression. This often takes the form of an ideological campaign for government transparency and accountability that is expressed through his visual art.[40] Although he has always been political in the sense of demanding freedom of expression, Ai was moved to intervene more directly in politics by the official corruption exposed by China's Wenchuan earthquake in 2008. Like many public intellectuals in the PRC, Ai was critical of the official response to the earthquake.[41] Noticing that public schools often suffered more damage than surrounding buildings, many people felt that the schools had collapsed due to substandard construction stemming from official corruption. After the government refused to investigate, Ai enlisted hundreds of volunteers in what he called a "Public Citizen Investigation Project" to ethically witness the combination of state and private corruption that had produced this tragedy.[42]

Using techniques similar to those of the Forensic Architecture group,[43] this citizens' investigation eventually compiled and published a list of the names of the 5,212 children who were killed in the earthquake. As a project of building civil society, the process of the investigation itself was important; as Ai explains, "[I]t became a symbol or some kind of testimony to show how an individual can cast against the whole system."[44] Ai and his team eventually shamed the government into releasing its own list of 5,335 names. Again blurring the line between art and politics, Ai turned this tragedy into visual art. The *Wall of Names*, which lists the name, gender, age, and school of each of the 5,212 victims in Chinese and English, was exhibited as artwork.[45] Ai's massive mosaic *Remembering* (2009), exhibited at Munich's Haus der Kunst, lined up nine thousand school bags to spell out one mother's reaction to her daughter's death: "She lived happily on this earth for seven

[40] See Giorgio Strafella and Daria Berg, "'Twitter Bodhisattva': Ai Weiwei's Media Politics," *Asian Studies Review* 39:1 (2015):138–157.

[41] See Christian Sorace, "China's Vision for Developing Sichuan's Post-Earthquake Countryside: Turning Unruly Peasants into Grateful Urban Citizens," *China Quarterly* 218 (2014):404–427.

[42] Ai Weiwei, interview with the author.

[43] See Eyal Weizman, *Forensic Architecture: Violence at the Threshold of Detectability* (Cambridge, MA: Zone Books, 2017).

[44] Ai, quoted in Tim Marlow, "Ai Weiwei in Conversation," in *Ai Weiwei* [Exhibition catalogue], edited by Tim Marlow and John Tancock, 17–29 (London: Royal Academy of Arts, 2015), p. 22.

[45] See Marlow and Tancock, *Ai Weiwei*, 136–143.

years." Ai also straightened out 150 tons of twisted steel rebar that had been salvaged from the Wenchuan ruins, which was exhibited in orderly piles as *Straight* at the 2013 Venice Art Biennale.[46] Ai thus uses visual art to highlight the party-state's lack of accountability, including the literal counting of dead children. To fight the crookedness of official corruption that had led to the collapsed school buildings, Ai straightened out the mangled rebar taken from the ruins of those buildings.

Through his nude photography, Ai also promotes witnessing, visibility, and transparency in a more playful way that blends art, politics, and life. Many Chinese artists and intellectuals visited Ai during his New York sojourn (1981–1993). At that time he always carried a camera, and he often persuaded his friends to pose nude in public with him: Ai and Yan Li are smilingly nude in a now-iconic photo at the World Trade Center Plaza (1985).[47] After his release from detention in 2011, Ai used nudity to poke fun at China's political leadership. *Grass Mud Horse Covering the Middle* is a photograph of a naked Ai covering his genitals with a stuffed animal, which Ai posted on the Internet. Its title invokes the word-play (*e'gao*) used to resist the keyword-based online censorship of China's Great Firewall; "Grass Mud Horse Covering the Middle" is a homophone for "Fuck your mother, Communist party central committee."[48] Ai also returned to his New York habits; in 2011 four activists wanted a photograph with Ai to commemorate their visit to his studio in Beijing. Ai suggested that they take off their clothes, and the result is a nude photograph of him with these four women, *One Tiger, Eight Breasts*, which was posted on the Internet. The Chinese police reacted by accusing Ai and his photographer of spreading pornography online, and then China's netizens responded in support of free artistic expression by posting online naked photos of themselves.[49] As with the citizen's investigation of accountability after the Wenchuan earthquake, here Ai brought together a diverse group of artists and activists to protest the party-state's

---

[46] Marlow and Tancock, *Ai Weiwei*, 128–141.

[47] Bei Ling, "Grin and Bare It," *South China Morning Post Magazine* (August 28, 2011); also see Feng Xiaogang, "Queshao ni, Niuyue biande pingyong" [Without you, New York is mediocre], *Xingfu* no. 8 (2015):3–5. For the nude photograph with Yan Li at the World Trade Center, see Bei Ling, "Der nackte Bürger Ai Weiwei," *Frankfurter Allgemeine* (May 14, 2011) http://www.faz.net/aktuell/feuilleton/bilder-und-zeiten-1/die-new-yorker-jahre-der-nackte-buerger-ai-weiwei-1638007.html (accessed May 19, 2018). Strangely, none of Ai's nude photos are included in Ai Weiwei, *Niuyue 1983–1993/New York 1983–1993* (Berlin: DISTANZ Verlag, 2011).

[48] Leah Goldman, "Check Out Revolutionary Artwork from Ai Weiwei, the Guy Who Has China Under House Arrest," *Business Insider* (June 23, 2011) http://www.businessinsider.com/ai-weiwei-art-2011-6?op=1&IR=T (accessed May 19, 2018).

[49] Jonathan Watts, "Ai Weiwei Investigated over Nude Art," *The Guardian* (November 18, 2011) https://www.theguardian.com/artanddesign/2011/nov/18/ai-weiwei-investigation-nude-art (accessed May 19, 2018); Tania Branigan, "Ai Weiwei Supporters Strip Off as Artist Faces 'Porn' Investigation," *The Guardian* (November 21, 2011) http://www.guardian.co.uk/world/2011/nov/21/ai-weiwei-porn-investigation-naked (accessed May 19, 2018).

lack of transparency. To protest the opaqueness of the state, Ai witnessed its invisibility through the hypervisibility of nude photography.

Ai Weiwei's eighty-one-day illegal detention also provoked audio-visual art that engaged in ethical witnessing. Some of it is playful; Ai's debut music video *Dumbass* is a foul-mouthed mockumentary about his time in detention.[50] But other work is more serious. *S.A.C.R.E.D.* is a six-part installation of half-scale dioramas in iron boxes; it uses the themes of Supper, Accusers, Cleansing, Ritual, Entropy, and Doubt to reproduce the scene of Ai's illegal detention in a cheap hotel room.[51] This artwork exemplifies both the invisibility of being held in secret detention and the hypervisibility of being under constant surveillance by a team of guards. The themes of nudity and surveillance are combined in *Cleansing*, which witnesses how Ai was forced to take a shower under the watchful gaze of two (fully clothed) guards.[52] The exhibit also addresses issues of witnessing and spectatorship at a structural level; in the art gallery, people can only see into *S.A.C.R.E.D.*'s six boxes through small, awkwardly-placed holes. Hence viewers are turned into voyeurs who are complicit with China's surveillance state. *S.A.C.R.E.D.* thus is interesting not simply as a visual image that represents politics; this three-dimensional visual artifact is a multisensory space that active spectators can performatively witness through sight, sound, and touch.

In this way, Ai's visual art exemplifies how ethical witnessing can work through the visibility strategy: he works hard to expose the violence and corruption of the party-state. His goal, like that of Czech dissident and later president Vaclav Havel, is to "Live in Truth."[53] Because spectators are called upon to decode the clever meaning of Ai's artwork, viewers must work as active witnesses to creatively reproduce the visibility strategy's hermeneutic urge to speak truth to power. Moreover, Ai's art doesn't just seek to represent other people's pain and suffering. Since Ai himself is a target of party-state oppression, his approach recalls "pluralistic photography" because it involves active participant witnessing to bridge the gap between inside and outside, subject and object.

Art, Exile, and Global Witnessing

Up until his illegal detention in 2011, Ai's work focused almost entirely on China and the oppression of the party-state. His art exhibits generally showed Chinese

---

[50] Tania Branigan, "Dumbass: Ai Weiwei Releases Heavy Metal Music Video," *The Guardian* (May 22, 2013) https://www.theguardian.com/artanddesign/2013/may/22/dumbass-ai-weiwei-music-video (accessed April 11, 2019).

[51] Marlow and Tancock, *Ai Weiwei*, 210–215.

[52] Marlow and Tancock, *Ai Weiwei*, 215.

[53] Vaclav Havel, *Living in Truth* (New York: Faber & Faber, 1987).

things to the world: a hundred million ceramic sunflower seeds in London or thousands of children's backpacks in Munich. While Ai was celebrated in China for his art and design work in the 2000s,[54] after 2009 he more or less disappeared from the mainland's Chinese-language media, which was restricted by the censorship regime from even criticizing his work.

At the same time, Ai received support and praise from the artistic and activist communities outside of China. After his release from detention, Ai was named one of *Foreign Policy*'s "100 Top Global Thinkers of 2011" and made the short list for *Time* magazine's "Person of the Year 2011." *GQ* profiled him as China's "photographer, architect, gambler, orchestrator of installations, organizer of happenings, troublemaker, mad tweeter."[55] In 2012 Elton John dedicated his concert in Beijing to Ai, while in 2013 Ai's detention ordeal was dramatized on the London stage in "#aiww: The Arrest of Ai Weiwei." The coup de grace was when *ArtReview* chose Ai as the "most powerful artist in the world."[56] Still, after his release in 2011, Ai was worn down by the strain of four years of quasi-house arrest, artistic and political censorship, and threats against his family. His experience also shows how resistance—even that of a world-famous artist—still relies to a large extent on what the state will allow.

This combination of push and pull factors finally motivated Ai to accept Germany's offer to set up a studio in Berlin. Once the Chinese government returned his passport in 2015, Ai moved into self-imposed exile. But this European exile was not a totally new experience. Actually, Ai has spent most of his life in exile.[57] Soon after Ai was born in 1957, his family was sent into internal exile on the harsh borderlands of the PRC because Ai's father, the famous communist poet Ai Qing, had criticized Mao and the Communist Party. The family only returned to Beijing in 1976 as the Maoist period drew to a close.

After living for five years in Beijing, Ai was frustrated by the restrictions on artistic expression in China, and in 1981 he went to study in the United States. After dropping out, Ai bummed around Manhattan as an illegal alien, doing odd jobs and hanging out with visiting Chinese artists, filmmakers, and poets while shooting more than ten thousand photographs.[58] He returned to Beijing in 1993 to see his sick father and was based in China until 2015. Hence Ai has only spent seventeen of his sixty-odd years not in exile. Living in Xinjiang, Beijing, New York, and Berlin

---

[54] See "2006 niandu yishujia" [Artists of the year 2006], *Dangdai yishu yu tuozi* no. 2 (2007):8.

[55] Wyatt Mason, "The Danger Artist," *GQ* (December 2011):218.

[56] "The Power 100," *ArtReview* (October 2011) http://www.artreview100.com/power-100-lists-from-2002-through-2008/2011/ (accesses July 15, 2013).

[57] See Ian Boyden, "Not Yet Not Yet Complete: An Interview with Ai Weiwei, Part 3: Exile and the Consequences of Hope," *China Heritage Quarterly* (October 28, 2018) http://chinaheritage.net/journal/exile-and-the-consequences-of-hope-ai-weiwei-interview-part-3/ (accessed April 11, 2019).

[58] Ai, *Niuyue 1983–1993*; Bei, "Grin and Bare It"; Feng, "Queshao ni."

thus has informed his comparative artistic approach, which appeals to a combination of modern, traditional, European, American, and Chinese concepts, practices, and experiences.

It is not strange, then, that Ai Weiwei made *Human Flow* (2017), a film about the current global refugee crisis. This epic film, which British journalist Jon Snow described as "amazing, agonizing, and very beautiful,"[59] addresses the massive challenge of the world's sixty-five million refugees. Like Ai's art-activism in China, the message of *Human Flow* is very clear: we need to look beyond national borders and national interests to appreciate the refugee problem as a global issue of humanity that demands a global solution.[60] Ai's goal in this film is not simply ideological—to inform people about the inhumane conditions of refugees—but also affective, to provoke a transnational community of sense that would creatively do something to help refugees. As one of Ai's colleagues explains, the film "reminds us that in this crisis, we have to look, we have to feel, we have to not accept the status quo and we have to change it."[61] Ai likewise states that "[t]here is no language to describe this crisis. I am trying to see what is the role of civilization and human nature, how they treat these refugees, how they spread the most basic values and human dignity."[62] In other words, the CNN-Effect of providing information for rational discussion of policy options is not enough; *Human Flow* engages active ethical witnessing beyond language to creatively move people to act in new affective communities of sense.

To understand the global artistry of *Human Flow*, it is helpful to see how it employs the visibility strategy to ideologically speak truth to power and invokes the visuality strategy to affectively excite new communities of sense. In this way, we consider how the film's ethical witnessing blurs distinctions between local/national/global, word/image, individual/collective, rational/aesthetic, ideology/affect, and visibility/visuality. The visual international politics of the refugee crisis, globalization, and national borders has generated rich academic analysis,[63] and this section

---

[59] Jon Snow said this as the host of a panel discussion on Ai's film, which can be seen in the "Extras" section of the *Human Flow* DVD.

[60] See "Nationality and Borders Are Barriers to Our Intelligence and Imagination" (interview with Ai Weiwei), *New Perspectives Quarterly* (Fall 2017):35–39; "7 Questions: Ai Weiwei," *Time* (October 23, 2017):112; *Human Flow* final press notes (2017) https://www.humanflow.com/press-kit/ (accessed May 23, 2018).

[61] Diane Weyerman in *Human Flow* final press notes, 4.

[62] "Gen pai zhengzheng yinian, zhe bu jilupian jijiang jiekai Ai Weiwei wei nanmin zuole shenme" [After filming a full year, this documentary reveals what Ai Weiwei has done for refugees], *ArtsBJ* (June 28, 2017) http://www.artsbj.com/show-19-550253-1.html (accessed May 31, 2018).

[63] See David Campbell, "Geopolitics and Visuality: Sighting the Darfur Conflict," *Political Geography* 26 (2007):357–382; Bleiker and Kay, "Representing HIV/AIDS in Africa"; Roland Bleiker, David Campbell, Emma Hutchison, and Xzarina Nicholson, "The Visual Dehumanisation of Refugees," *Australian Journal of Political Science* 48:4 (2013):398–416; Lilie Chouliaraki and Myria Georgiou, "Hospitability: The Communicative Architecture of Humanitarian Securitization at Europe's Borders," *Journal of Communication* 67:2 (2017):159–180. Also see Chapter 7 in this book.

utilizes these arguments to consider the limitations of *Human Flow*. The goal is to see how effective the film is as a humanitarian consciousness-raising project and as an activity-provoking, pluralistic performance.

Local/National/Global

Human Flow is interesting because it not only criticizes nationalism and territorial borders, but also aims to efface such borders in its presentation. Although people in the film are categorized according to their citizenship for bureaucratic reasons, *Human Flow* forces viewers to actively visualize less national and more global identities, spaces, and experiences. While national police certainly are shown guarding national borders, most of the film presents the plight of migrants, who are often a multinational/transnational group of contingent travelers. Likewise, most of the expert testimony offered in the film is from people who work for the United Nations and transnational aid groups. Ai's stated purpose is to efface national boundaries, and this is done by deliberately problematizing these different geographical scales through the journey to twenty-three countries and over forty refugee camps: "At times during the film, the viewer may be disoriented, [and] not know which country or camp he or she is in. Yet this sensation is integral to the film."[64]

Yet the film risks reproducing the hackneyed logic of a package holiday that overwhelms the audience. One reviewer felt that the film's "patchwork construction can make it hard to determine exactly which particular crisis you're in at any given moment. The colors of land, skin and sky are often all you have to go on."[65] In other words, it is like a Grand Tour of suffering that merges numerous horrible experiences in ways that can make spectators passive rather than active.[66] Like humanistic photojournalism, it risks reaffirming the hierarchical division of a safe "here" in Euro-America from a dangerous "there" in refugee camps. Interestingly, because of its appeal to global humanity, there is not a clear Other or enemy in this film. It is certainly critical of European (and Western) policing, apathy, and complicity. But since this is the target audience, it is not constructed as the Other to the refugee self. Indeed, Ai's country of residence—Germany, which let in over one million refugees in 2015—comes off as a welcoming place.

[64] Andrew Cohen in *Human Flow* final press notes, 11.

[65] Robbie Collin, "Human Flow Review: Ai Weiwei's Refugee Documentary Weighs on Your Heart Like a Cannonball" (December 8, 2017) https://www.telegraph.co.uk/films/0/human-flow-review-ai-weiweis-refugee-documentary-weighs-heart/ (accessed May 17, 2018).

[66] Debbie Lisle, *Holidays in the Danger Zone* (Minneapolis: University of Minnesota Press, 2016); Rodanthi Tzanelli, "Schematising Hospitality: Ai WeiWei's Activist Artwork as a Form of Dark Travel," *Mobilities* 13:4 (2018):520–534.

Word/Image: Words

Although the film does not have a voice-over to guide the story, it works according to a particular combination of word and image. In place of an authoritative narrator, it liberally employs on-screen text to provide statistics, definitions, and explanations. These provide a rational argument for why refugees matter, the scale of the crisis, and background information about particular camps and situations. At times this includes a twenty-four-hour-news-channel-type ticker-tape that scrolls (Western media) headlines across the lower third of the screen. Texts also include a series of interviews with refugees and international experts that once again give factual meat and emotional spice to the film's episodic narrative. Interestingly, the on-screen text is more than empirical facts; to add emotional depth to the rational argument, it also displays poems from local and regional writers.[67]

Word/Image: Images

While words and verbal testimony are plentiful, most of the film's political work is done by images, nonverbal sound, and editing.[68] For example, *Human Flow* starts off with an image of a boat rocking gently in the deep blue sea. Filmed from a drone far above and accompanied by evocative music, the scene is more beautiful than agonizing: the bright orange dots (which we later recognize as people in life jackets) look cute against the aquamarine canvas. It is only when the drone descends that we see the precarious position of the people in this overloaded boat. A police boat comes alongside, and the refugees come ashore on Lesbos island in Greece. At this point Ai Weiwei appears, filming the scene with his smartphone. Next we witness Ai offering hot tea and a reflector blanket to a tired and wet man who has come from Iraq (see figure 6.1).

The cinematography of this opening scene is repeated numerous times in the film to ethically witness a visual mixture of collectives and individuals, who are general and specific, abstract and material (see figure 6.2). It is common in documentary films to choose an individual and follow that person on a journey, either to show the person's individual idiosyncrasies or to represent the general experience of a collective.[69] Ai, however, explains that he didn't want to choose between the faceless mass of the collective and the unique experience of the individual; his purpose

---

[67] For a discussion of the aesthetics and politics of poetry, see Bleiker, *Aesthetics and World Politics*.

[68] Peter Bradshaw, "Human Flow Review—Ai Weiwei Surveys Shocking Plight of Migrants on the Move," *The Guardian* (December 7, 2017) https://www.theguardian.com/film/2017/dec/07/human-flow-review-ai-weiwei-migration-documentary (accessed May 17, 2018); Michael J. Shapiro, *Studies in Trans-Disciplinary Method: After the Aesthetic Turn* (New York: Routledge, 2013), p. 31; Chapter 4 in this book.

[69] See Andy Lawrence, *Filmmaking for Fieldwork: An Ethnographer's Handbook* (Manchester, UK: University of Manchester Press, forthcoming).

Figure 6.1 Selfie of Ai offering tea and a blanket to a refugee, *Human Flow* (2017). Courtesy *Human Flow*

was to "get more knowledge on a global scale. Not making a film about one family or one person, but global scale to see the humanity, the human flow."[70]

This appeal to the collective has echoes in Ai's earlier artistic work: 100 million porcelain *Sunflower Seeds* (London, 2010–2011), 9,000 backpacks in *Remembering* (Munich, 2010); the 5,212 names in the *Wall of Names* of Wenchuan victims (London, 2015); and 150 tons of straightened rebar in *Straight* (Venice, 2013). And now in *Human Flow* there were more than 40 forty camps in 23 countries. Many of the film's sections begin with a drone's-eye-view establishing shot that shows wide landscapes and seascapes. Again, as the drone descends, the view shifts from the abstract to the material, the aesthetic to the social, and the collective to the individual. One scene starts far above an abstract pattern that evokes Islamic geometric design; as it descends, a refugee camp of orderly tents in the desert takes shape. Then we see things moving around like ants, and finally we see them emerge as people, including young children, who cheer the drone as it hovers just above them. The transition from collective to individual, however, is incomplete; since the images are captured from above, we don't clearly see specific people's faces.

---

[70] Ai with Snow, *Human Flow* "Extras" section.

Figure 6.2 Drone's-eye view of a refugee camp, *Human Flow* (2017). Courtesy *Human Flow*

After these establishing shots that highlight the shared experience of global humanity, the film offers a series of images of individuals. As well as witnessing how people encounter challenging situations, the film also shows them doing things in everyday life: cooking food, checking and charging mobile phones, and playing. The film thus employs a "pluralistic" strategy that presents refugees not just in life-or-death crises, but also as ordinary people who do ordinary things in daily life. Everyday life also is where Ai again enters *Human Flow* as a character; we see him grilling meat, getting a haircut, giving a haircut, and taking selfies with refugees. While he is buying vegetables, we see how Ai and the vendor are able to viscerally communicate without verbal language through comical gestures. Here we are shown that refugees are just like "us" in Euro-America—and could be us. In one scene, Ai offers to exchange passports and homes with a Syrian man in a camp: "Next time you are Ai Weiwei. Exchange tent for studio in Berlin. . . . I respect you."

There are also numerous scenes in which people are filmed doing nothing—standing against a white backdrop in a tent, or after their interviews. Here they are filmed in long takes in an artistic video portrait that shows the emotional contours of individual people. This aesthetic sense is highlighted by the evocative music that is added in over muted background noise from the camp. These dignified video still-lifes are complemented by portraits of movement: a small child running frantically in tight circles in a confined room, and later a horse running in a tight circle in a small urban space under the guidance of a groom. Such visual rhymes combine the joy and frustration of going nowhere, fast.[71]

The images in the word/image dynamic affirm how audio-visual art serves as an active ethical witness that both provides ideological information and provokes affective communities of sense.

Rational/Aesthetic and Ideology/Affect

In general, the film appeals to the aesthetic and emotional movement of evocative audio-video images more than to the rational and ideological argument of facts. Although it tells a chronological story of Syrian, Iraqi, and Afghan refugees making their way to Europe before the borders closed in 2015–2016, the film lacks a linear narrative. It is more of an artistic collage and cinematic montage of images of fear, joy, frustration, and boredom.[72] As one critic explains:

[71] See Malin Wahlberg, *Documentary Time: Film and Phenomenology* (Minneapolis: University of Minnesota Press, 2008), pp. ix, 66.

[72] On the political aesthetics of montage and collage, see Gilles Deleuze, *Cinema I: The Movement-Image*, translated by Hugh Tomlinson and Barbara Habberjam (London: Bloomsbury, 1986); Sylvester, *Art/Museums*.

[W]hile most documentaries would opt to zero in on a handful of case studies, Human Flow makes a virtue of its vastness, and roves freely between displaced communities—Syrians, Kenyans, Rohingya—in search of both spiky specificity and common ground. It spends no more than a minute or two with any one group, and after someone disappears, they don't come back.[73]

This collage is not only of different refugee groups, but also of "text, faces, ideas, facts, emotions, landscapes and human bonds,"[74] which work together to show the diverse individual and collective elements of the global refugee crisis. Although some of the scenes seem forced—for example, the odd interchange between the US border patrol police officer and Ai at the US-Mexico border—in general the film works to create a broad and deep feeling about the necessity for action. The film here goes beyond promoting ideology to excite a new global affective community of sense.

Human Flow thus ethically witnesses the migration crisis through an interesting mix of the visibility strategy and the visuality strategy. It makes visible the often invisible challenges faced by refugees, and it also is a film that aims to "do" something by provoking new relations in an audio-visual (re)construction of transnational communities of sense. This activism was seen at both the film's world premiere at the Venice International Film Festival (2017) and its British/Irish premiere at 120 cinemas that was followed by a live simulcast interactive panel discussion with Ai Weiwei. *Human Flow* is a consciousness-raising and activity-provoking performance that is like an extended PSA, complete with injunctions to do something: contact your member of parliament! Donate to charity organizations through this URL link! At the end of the panel discussion Ai Weiwei bowed to the ecstatic cheers of the various audiences, perhaps provoking new social-ordering and world-ordering.

At my university, I have screened *Human Flow* to students in class and to a diverse audience at a public event, and it provoked an ecstatic response from both groups. Indeed, one student told the class that seeing the film in 2017 changed his life; it showed the power of artistic documentary films and thus inspired him to study filmmaking as a mode of political activism. This exemplifies Alex Danchev's emancipatory view of art/politics: "[C]ontrary to popular belief, it is given to artists, not politicians, to create a new world order."[75]

[73] Collin, "Human Flow Review."

[74] *Human Flow* final press notes, 14.

[75] Alex Danchev, *On Good and Evil and the Grey Zone* (Edinburgh: Edinburgh University Press, 2016), p. 91.

Too Far?

For some, however, the film is problematic. Although Ai says that the purpose of the film is not to follow one family or one person, it actually does follow Ai on his own personal journey of discovery. Whereas in his earlier work Ai positioned himself as the rebel of Chinese art,[76] now he presents himself as the Chinese savior of humanity. He gives refugees tea and blankets, he consoles a woman who has had an emotional break-down during an interview, and he even pretends to be a refugee by offering his passport—which he quickly takes back.[77]

Sometimes the film is compelling, but at other times it is like Marie Antoinette's performance as a milkmaid at the Versailles dairy. Ai was criticized for an earlier refugee-themed photograph, in which he appropriated the image of the dead toddler Alan Kurdi by lying down on the beach in a similar way.[78] While it is common to criticize Europeans and Americans for appropriating the experience of people of color, here we have an example of the Chinese savior mentality, also known as the "Yellow Man's Burden."[79] Although the lingering gaze of the camera can "humanize" suffering people,[80] it also risks becoming a "colonial gaze."[81] And as mentioned previously, the colossal scale of the film risks morphing the experience to one of the Grand Tour of dark travel.[82]

[76] See William A. Callahan, "Citizen Ai: Warrior, Jester, and Middleman," *Journal of Asian Studies* 73:04 (2014):899–920.

[77] Peter Bradshaw, "Human Flow Review – Ai Weiwei Surveys Shocking Plight of Migrants on the Move," *The Guardian* (December 7, 2017) https://www.theguardian.com/film/2017/dec/07/human-flow-review-ai-weiwei-migration-documentary (accessed May 17, 2018).

[78] "Artist Ai Weiwei Poses as Aylan Kurdi for India Today Magazine," *India Today* (February 1, 2016) https://www.indiatoday.in/india/story/artist-ai-weiwei-poses-as-aylan-kurdi-for-india-today-magazine-306593-2016-02-01 (accessed April 11, 2019); Ian Boyden, "Not Yet Not Yet Complete: An Interview with Ai Weiwei, Part 4, The Conditions of Empathy," *China Heritage Quarterly* (October 28, 2018) http://chinaheritage.net/journal/the-conditions-of-empathy-ai-weiwei-interview-part-5/ (accessed April 11, 2019); Mette Mortensen, "Constructing, Confirming, and Contesting Icons: The Alan Kurdi Imagery Appropriated by #humanitywashedashore, Ai Weiwei, and *Charlie Hebdo*," *Media, Culture & Society* 39:8 (2017):1142–1161.

[79] See Pal Nyri, "Yellow Man's Burden: Chinese Immigrants on a Civilizing Mission," *The China Journal* no. 56 (2006):83–106; Chenchen Zhang, "Racism and the Belt and Road in CCTV's Spring Festival Gala," *The Diplomat* (February 23, 2018) https://thediplomat.com/2018/02/racism-and-the-belt-and-road-in-cctvs-spring-festival-gala/ (accessed January 19, 2018).

[80] See Zito Madu, "The Unflinching Humanity of Ai Weiwei's *Human Flow*," *GQ* (March 27, 2018) https://www.gq.com/story/ai-weiwei-human-flow-radical-empathy (accessed May 17, 2018).

[81] See Frantz Fanon, *Black Skin, White Masks* (New York: Grove Press, 2008); Malek Alloula, *The Colonial Harem* (Minneapolis: University of Minnesota Press, 1986). The colonial gaze is also explored in Chapter 8.

[82] Collin, "Human Flow Review"; Tzanelli, "Schematising Hospitality."

This beautiful and agonizing film risks aestheticizing the suffering: the camera is fascinated with the bright orange life jackets and the deep blue sea.[83] Individual refugees are largely nameless and voiceless in similar ways to what was critically discussed previously as the "humanitarian" style of photography.[84] Visualizing refugees as masses of faceless people crammed onto a boat—rather than individuals with faces—is problematic politically and ethically. According to an article by Roland Bleiker, David Campbell, Emma Hutchison, and Xzarina Nicholson, this is a common strategy for dehumanizing refugees, treating them more as a security threat than as "a humanitarian crisis that involves grievable lives requiring compassion."[85]

Finally, it seems odd that China is invisible in a film about the global refugee crisis. On the one hand, China is a major source of refugees in the world, and on the other it is one of the most anti-refugee places in the world; according to an online poll, 97 percent of the Chinese public opposes receiving any refugees at all.[86] Beijing is commonly criticized both for sending North Koreans back across the border to face certain punishment and for not allowing dissidents, Uyghurs, and Tibetans to leave the PRC. Ai actually mentions North Korea in one of the interviews promoting the film, but only to criticize a "Western mentality": "I've seen people who escape North Korea and cannot accept the Western lifestyle. Don't take the Western lifestyle as the natural, absolute condition."[87] Interestingly, this criticism of Western hypocrisy, which shifts attention away from the sources of the refugee problem in North Korea and China, chimes with the message promoted by the CCP's Propaganda Department. This is not a one-off; in exile, Ai focuses his activism on global issues, rather than on the Chinese party-state. For example, although he lived in Xinjiang for over twenty years, Ai has been relatively quiet about the PRC's mass "re-education" camps there. Ai's global resistance activities in exile thus are still shaped by the party-state back in China. And as mentioned previously, Germany, Ai's home at the time of the film project, also comes out looking pretty good.

Human Flow thus shows how Ai Weiwei has followed the lead of China's state-owned enterprises to "go global."[88] While many political dissidents become irrelevant in exile because they still focus on the authoritarian state back home, Ai has

---

[83]   Bradshaw, "Human Flow Review."

[84]   Bleiker and Kay, "Representing HIV/AIDS in Africa"; Ryan Woods, "Crisis and Confusion: A Review of Human Flow by Ai Weiwei," *Geopolitics and Security* (February 12, 2018) https://rhulgeopolitics.wordpress.com/2018/02/12/crisis-and-confusion-a-review-of-human-flow-by-ai-weiwei/ (accessed May 30, 2018).

[85]   Bleiker et al., "The Visual Dehumanisation of Refugees," 413.

[86]   See Li Ruohan, "97% of Chinese Would Reject Receiving Refugees: Online Poll," *Global Times* (June 20, 2018) http://www.globaltimes.cn/content/1107731.shtml (accessed August 27, 2018).

[87]   "Nationality and Borders," 39.

[88]   See David Shambaugh, *China Goes Global: The Partial Power* (New York: Oxford University Press, 2013).

successfully recast both his art and his activism to adapt to his latest Euro-American exile experience. Rather than being simply an individual artist creating individual works, Ai has expanded to work as a director who orchestrates artistic and cinematic works on an epic scale, including both a hundred million items in *Sunflower Seeds* and thousands of people in dozens of countries and camps in *Human Flow*. The film is interesting because it works hard to provide objective facts for rational discussion at the same time that it tantalizingly excites affective communities. And as my students' experience shows, for some the film moves beyond passive spectatorship to connect and move people to actually "do" ethical witnessing in new affective communities of sense.

Conclusion

This chapter has three interrelated objectives: first, to explore how visual art can act as a site of resistance to cultural governance; second, to consider how this resistance can take the form of ethical witnessing; and third, to see how this analysis can be enabled by the visibility/visuality and ideology/affect dynamic dyads. It thus joins debates in critical theory, media and communications, and IR about what photographs (and other images) mean and what they can do. This also involves probing what spectatorship means and what it does: Are viewers passive voyeurs who are manipulated by the image into reproducing hegemonic power? Or can they be active, emancipated spectators who can ethically witness injustice in creative ways that provoke new affective communities?

To explore these issues, the chapter considers the work of artist-activist Ai Weiwei. As a Chinese artist struggling against a communist party-state, Ai might seem like an idiosyncratic example who does not explain much else. But Ai is an interesting case for a number of reasons. His living and work experience in China, America, Europe, and refugee camps enables him to creatively combine modern, traditional, Euro-American, Chinese, and Middle Eastern concepts, practices, and experiences. As a long-time exile who has felt the sharp boot of the party-state on his own body, Ai doesn't just represent other people's suffering; his art shows how he can ethically witness his own oppression as a collective experience. Ai's concern with transparency and accountability—as seen in his experiments with nude photography and the half-scale model of his prison—shows how one can resist an authoritarian state as an ethical witness. Indeed, the *S.A.C.R.E.D.* dioramas aren't just something that people look at. In the gallery, viewers have to experience them in three dimensions, as voyeurs looking through small holes that offer only partial views. (Part III will further explore how visual artifacts work as both two-dimensional representations and as performances in material modalities and multisensory spaces.) Moreover, *Human Flow* is not simply a visual image; it is an audio-visual image that uses sight and sound to create affective communities of sense.

Finally, *Human Flow* shows how Ai is not simply a "Chinese artist"; this creative juxtaposition of his personal refugee experience with those of a range of other refugees works hard both ideologically and affectively to give information about the horrible situation migrants face, while at the same time provoking new social-ordering and world-ordering activities. This is a transnational form of audio-visual resistance that problematizes the cultural governance of a world divided into nation-states. Still, Ai's shift from a very visible resistance to the Chinese party-state to a global activism in which China is much less visible shows how his resistance is still shaped by the cultural governance of the PRC. Chapter 6 thus highlights the need to appreciate the dynamic tension that entangles cultural governance and resistance.

PART III

VISUAL ARTIFACTS AND SENSORY SPACES

Part II examined how visual IR and visual culture studies analyze visual international politics in terms of aesthetics, securitization, and witnessing. It argued that this research is limited by its hermeneutic mode of analysis and by its narrow focus on Euro-American images of security, war, and atrocity. To critique this tendency, Part II used the visibility/visuality and ideology/affect dynamics to move beyond assessing what images mean to see what they can "do" in provoking affective communities of sense. Part II ended with an analysis of activist films and art installations, which are more than simply visual images.

Part III builds on this discussion of visual image analysis to make three critical moves: (1) expand from visual images to appreciate visual artifacts as material modalities and sensory spaces; (2) examine the interplay among the verbal, the visual, and the multisensory; and (3) engage in comparative political theory by developing conceptual dyads from different times and places. These three interventions are useful for a more detailed analysis and appreciation of visual IR, and they are also useful interventions into the broader disciplines of social theory and international politics.

By the end of Part II, the analysis of activist films and art installations showed what is different about visual artifacts and multisensory experiences. This analysis overlaps with critical IR's analysis of memorials, monuments, museums, architecture, and landscapes. Yet while much of this analysis turns visuals into texts for discursive analysis, Part III works to appreciate maps, veils, walls, gardens, and cyberspace as visual and multisensory artifacts via the critical aesthetics mode.

On the one hand, the definition of "artifact" is simple; as Caitlin Hamilton explains, etymologically it refers to a thing made (*fatto*) with skill (*arte*).[1] Artifacts thus aren't natural objects, but are human-made and thus embody social relations. On the other hand, artifacts can also range from the small and self-contained to the very large and complex, from things that you can hold in your hand, such as a map or a veil, to things that are difficult for humans to comprehend as a single entity, such as the Great Wall of China or the Internet.

There is also the issue of agency and intent. The craftsperson who draws a map, sews a veil, constructs a wall, builds a garden, or uses social media certainly has intent and thus shapes the meaning of those artifacts. But as we saw with the "Europe in 2035" maps, artifacts can also provoke new social orders and world orders far beyond the imagination or intent of any particular actor. Those maps gained meaning and value not just in their production, but also through their circulation and exchange in various affective communities of sense. As one of my students reminded me, while maps are images that you read, they are also artifacts that you touch—and that can touch you viscerally when they spark the attraction (and revulsion) of patriotic themes. Here maps, veils, walls, and gardens aren't simply two-dimensional representations of things that demand critical interpretation; as three-dimensional spatiotemporal artifacts, they are the things, events, and spaces that people can experience and perform as participants, rather than just as observers. To appreciate a wall or a garden, looking at it is not enough; you have to performatively "walk it" as an active participant.[2] This experience certainly is visual, but it is also multisensory; you touch and smell maps and veils, while walls and gardens are sites of sight, sound, touch, smell—and even taste.

While many people see artifacts as "objects" that take on meaning through human agency and interpretive understanding, Part III follows Jane Bennett to consider how material artifacts can have agency—material vitality—to mean things and do things separate from human understanding. They have "*Thing-Power*: the curious ability of inanimate things to animate, to act, to

---

[1] Caitlin Hamilton, "The Everyday Artefacts of World Politics: Why Graphic Novels, Textiles and Internet Memes Matter in World Politics" (PhD dissertation, University of New South Wales, 2016), p. 37.

[2] See Michel de Certeau, *The Practice of Everyday Life* (Berkeley: University of California Press, 1984), pp. 91–110.

produce effects dramatic and subtle."[3] Artifacts thus can do things "in excess of human meanings, designs, or purposes they express or serve."[4] Much as W. J. T. Mitchell argues that pictures themselves can have the agency to desire,[5] Part III examines how artifacts can mean and do things as part of a human-nonhuman assemblage. Such assemblages have their own energy, as "living, throbbing confederations" of bodies that are moved and connected in affective communities of sense.[6] Walls and gardens therefore aren't just individual objects, but are artifactual assemblages that gather together heterogeneous material modalities in sensory spaces.

As artifacts, walls, gardens, and the Internet are a site, an institution, an enactment, an encounter—and an ideology. While Raymond Williams discusses politics and culture in terms of "structures of feeling," artifacts can be appreciated as "infrastructures of feeling" in which politics is represented, performed, and experienced in affective communities of sense. For example, in the Palestinian feature film *Omar* (2013), the West Bank barrier is not presented as an insurmountable material and ideological barrier; rather, the wall is a site, an institution, an enactment, an encounter that Omar performatively surmounts on his everyday visits to his girlfriend.[7] Omar's experience thus exemplifies the sensible politics of artifacts, which work through both multisensory experiences and the pragmatic everydayness of crossing a border (or wearing a veil, or surfing the Web).

While it might be easy to accept maps and walls as artifacts, what about cyberspace: Isn't it a nondimensional virtual space that we (primarily) see on two-dimensional screens? As Kathleen Brennan explains, the Internet is an assemblage of artifacts that includes "devices, computers, cell phones, and tablets; telephone lines, fiber-optic cables, cellular networks, and satellites"; server farms, power grids, companies, and governments; and the software that runs these devices, as well as the protocols that connect them.[8] In Part III we see how such artifactual assemblages are moving, shifting, connecting,

---

[3] Jane Bennett, *Vibrant Matter: A Political Ecology of Things* (Durham, NC: Duke University Press 2010), p. 6.

[4] Bennett, *Vibrant Matter*, 20. Also see Mark B. Salter, ed., *Making Things International 1: Circuits and Motion* (Minneapolis: University of Minnesota Press, 2015).

[5] W. J. T. Mitchell, *What Do Pictures Want? The Lives and Loves of Images* (Chicago: University of Chicago Press, 2005).

[6] Bennett, *Vibrant Matter*, 23.

[7] Hany Abu-Aasad, dir., *Omar* (ZBROS, 2013).

[8] Kathleen P. J. Brennan, "Memelife," in *Making Things International 1: Circuits and Motion*, edited by Mark B. Salter (Minneapolis: University of Minnesota Press, 2015), p. 244.

attracting, and repelling as part of social-ordering and world-ordering. Artifacts thus are both social constructions and provoke social relations.

To summarize, Part III examines visual artifacts and sensory spaces to trace their ideological meaning and appreciate how they move and connect bodies and things. It is common for visual analysis to criticize discursive analysis, and for multisensory analysis to criticize ocular-centrism, as if there were only one true vector from which to engage in politics. Although Part III primarily focuses on the visual and the multisensory, it aims to consider the interplay among the verbal, the visual, and the multisensory. It starts and ends with artifacts—maps and cyberspace—that complicate the verbal/ visual and image/artifact distinctions, in ways that develop the political analysis of multisensory space. The point is not to get rid of texts (or images), but to decenter discursive analysis to see how it works with and against the visual and other senses. *Sensible Politics* thus works to appreciate politics in terms of a complex multisensory ecology.

Part III's third intervention is to broaden and deepen comparative political theory strategies through an elaboration of the dynamic dyads developed in Part II (visibility/visuality, ideology/affect, and cultural governance/resistance) and to introduce and develop a new set of dyads that emerge from a broad range of visual and multisensory experiences: making maps, wearing a veil, building a wall, enjoying a garden, surfing the Web. The new dyads include center/periphery for maps (Chapter 7), concealing/ revealing for women's fashion (Chapter 8), loosening/tightening for walls (Chapter 9), and civility/martiality for gardens (Chapter 10). Part III's consideration of women's fashion and surveillance turns the question of visual IR around: not just how things look, but how you are seen—and how you perform—especially in relation to the male gaze, white/colonial gaze, and surveillant gaze.

Part III, again, deliberately juxtaposes the familiar and the strange, with chapters switching from hard politics to high aesthetics and back again, as well as back and forth between iconic sites and everyday experience. Once more, the chapters in this section stress how Asian and Middle Eastern visual artifacts provide important concepts, practices, and experiences that aid us in understanding sensible politics both beyond Eurocentrism and within Euro-America.

Part III thus engages with visual IR, new materialism, the practice turn, and other critical movements; but its analysis is not reducible to any one of them. Some of the concepts employed—for example, the visual artifact— are unwieldy and open to contestation, but that can be a strength rather than a weakness. In a way Part III, and *Sensible Politics* as a whole, engages with IR's abstract arguments (e.g., envisioning world order, mapping the discursive field, unveiling the truth, building conceptual bridges, and tearing down ideological walls) by materializing these metaphors through an examination of how such infrastructures of feeling actually work to create (and destroy) affective communities of sense.

7

Maps, Space, and Power

In IR, maps characteristically are used to clearly and accurately represent the territorial borders between nation-states in the Westphalian international system. Although this mimetic understanding of maps has been questioned by cartographers for some time, since the 1980s critical cartography has gone further, arguing that maps are social constructions that reflect broader political and cultural agendas. Rather than simply look to mathematical techniques to understand maps, here maps are seen as texts that need to be deconstructed with the tools of semiotics and/or literary criticism.[1] In other words, critical cartography engages in a robust practice of the "visibility strategy" that treats maps as "social constructions of the visual."

But as *Sensible Politics*'s analysis suggests, cartography is more than a social construction that draws sovereign borders to mark the inside from the outside. Following the visuality strategy, cartography can also creatively visualize social order and world order.[2] The "Europe in 2035" maps considered in Chapter 2 graphically show how maps not only mean things, but can do things; although they were made by a Ukrainian horror novelist, these maps ended up shaping discussions in Russia and Euro-America of the future size and shape of Eurasia.[3] In a similar way, maps have been a crucial part of how the Islamic State (IS) visualizes the Caliphate (see Chapter 5). For a broad spectrum of Islamists, the Sykes-Picot map (1916) is figured as the "problem" because it was drawn by British and French diplomats

[1] See J. B. Harley, "Deconstructing the Map," *Cartographica* 26 (1989):1–20; Gearóid Ó Tuathail, *Critical Geopolitics* (Minneapolis: University of Minnesota Press, 1996), pp. 1–20; Benedict Anderson, *Imagined Communities: Reflections on the Origin and Spread of Nationalism*, rev. ed. (New York: Verso, 2006), pp. 170–178; Walter D. Mignolo, *The Darker Side of the Renaissance: Literacy, Territoriality, and Colonization* (Ann Arbor: University of Michigan Press, 1995); Cordell D. K. Yee, "Chinese Cartography among the Arts: Objectivity, Subjectivity, Representation," in *The History of Cartography*, Vol. II, Book II, *Cartography in the Traditional East and Southeast Asian Societies*, edited by J.B. Harley and David Woodward (Chicago: University of Chicago Press, 1994), pp. 128–169.

[2] See W. J. T. Mitchell, *What Do Pictures Want? The Lives and Loves of Images* (Chicago: University of Chicago Press, 2005), pp. 343ff.

[3] See Chapter 2; Frank Jacobs, "What Russia Could Look Like in 2035 If Putin Gets His Wish," *Foreign Policy* (June 4, 2014) http://foreignpolicy.com/2014/06/04/what-russia-could-look-like-in-2035-if-putin-gets-his-wish/ (accessed June 6, 2017).

Sensible Politics. William A. Callahan, Oxford University Press (2020). © Oxford University Press.
DOI: 10.1093/oso/9780190071738.001.0001

to divide up the Ottoman Caliphate.[4] Indeed, one of the early IS English-language videos, *There Is No Life without Jihad*, shows IS fighters from the United Kingdom and Australia rejecting the border that divides Iraq and Syria, that is, the Sykes-Picot line.[5] In 2014, just as the IS was declaring itself the Caliphate, new maps circulated on the Internet that offered IS's unified transnational Caliphate as the twenty-first-century solution to the problem of Sykes-Picot division. Such maps consolidate the Caliphate into a contiguous territory joining the Iberian peninsula and North Africa in the West with India, Central Asia, and Western China in the East.[6] According to these arguments, the Caliphate is not conquering new territories but is visualizing the "reconquest" of Islamic "lost territories"; Russian irredentist maps likewise reclaim the "lost territories" of the Soviet Union.

As with the "Europe in 2035" maps, the origin and source of the IS world map is unclear. And like with the European maps, this both matters and doesn't matter. The visibility strategy tells us to find the original source; before it was circulated by reputable news organizations, the IS world map came from (now familiar) right-wing conspiracy sites. We thus should be wary of this map and interrogate it as an example of "fake news." But like the "Europe in 2035" maps, the IS world map matters because it took on a life of its own, exciting activity both in support of IS as a righteous Caliphate and against it as an aggressive empire. As Steven Seegel argues for similar mapping struggles in the borderlands of Central Eastern Europe in the nineteenth and twentieth centuries, cartography provides a language of both cultural governance and resistance, which are often entangled.[7]

To explore this dynamic, Chapter 7 considers how maps "do" things as visual artifacts, especially when they are empire-maps and world maps that engage in social-ordering and world-ordering. It proposes the new concept "map-fare" to see not only how maps are a social construction, but also how maps visually construct the social. This active map-fare dynamic allows us to examine how as visual artifacts maps provide an interface between word and image that can creatively perform—and not merely represent—world orders. Map-fare is particularly important during times of global transformation; as Jordan Branch argues, the now-familiar concepts

[4] Malise Ruthven, "The Map ISIS Hates," *New York Review of Books* (June 25, 2014) http://www.nybooks.com/blogs/nyrblog/2014/jun/25/map-isis-hates/ (accessed November 1, 2018).

[5] *There Is No Life without Jihad*, al Hayat Media Center (June 19, 2014) https://jihadology.net/2014/06/19/al-hayat-media-center-presents-a-new-video-message-from-the-islamic-state-of-iraq-and-al-sham-there-is-no-life-without-jihad/ (accessed April 18, 2019).

[6] See Aaron Y. Zelin, "Colonial Caliphate: The Ambitions of the 'Islamic State,'" Jihadology (July 8, 2014) https://jihadology.net/2014/07/08/the-clairvoyant-colonial-caliphate-the-ambitions-of-the-islamic-state/ (accessed August 17, 2018).

[7] Steven Seegel, *Mapping Europe's Borderlands: Russian Cartography in the Age of Empire* (Chicago: University of Chicago Press, 2012), p. 2. Also see Nancy Lee Peluso, "Whose Woods Are These? Counter-Mapping Forest Territories in Kalimantan, Indonesia," *Antipode* 27:4 (1995):383–406.

and practices of the international system of sovereign states were first envisioned through the mathematical maps that emerged in sixteenth-century Europe.[8] And this is not a unique case. Carl Schmitt famously argued, "Every new age and every new epoch in the coexistence of peoples, empires, and countries, of rulers and power formations of every sort, is founded on new spatial divisions, new enclosures, and new spatial orders of the earth."[9]

Chapter 7 thus considers how map-fare works in the twenty-first century's current global transformation, and in particular, how the center/periphery logic of early-modern Chinese empire-maps is visually shaping Beijing's current promotion of a post-Westphalian world order. The chapter argues that center/periphery entails more than nationalizing imperial space by re-drawing single-line, inside-outside boundaries; rather, map-fare shows how empires expand and contract in their visualization of new social orders and world orders. Map-fare thus is about more than ideas and representations; as with the Russian and IS irredentist examples mentioned previously, cartography is pushing Beijing to "rejuvenate China" by recovering "lost territories" like those in the South China Sea. This is one way of achieving Chinese president Xi Jinping's "China Dream" of "the great rejuvenation of the Chinese nation."[10] The chapter thus concludes that we need to understand maps as active interventions that can shape global politics, because such map-fare combines word and image, and images and artifacts, to visualize and promote particular (imperial) world orders.

This chapter makes these broad theoretical arguments through the examination of a specific case: Chinese maps that contain a U-shaped line that digs deep into the South China Sea abutting the littoral states of maritime Southeast Asia (see figure 7.1). The South China Sea is a security flashpoint that brings together a rising China, a retrenching United States, and Southeast Asian countries scrambling to deal with this shifting situation. Maps are a key factor in the South China Sea disputes. They are used in warfare to reclaim maritime space, including China's building of new military bases on lost territory that has been "reclaimed" through the terraforming of land reclamation. Maps are also used in "lawfare"— the use of law as a weapon in strategic competition[11]—to (re)claim sovereignty in international tribunals.[12] Indeed, the deliberations of the United Nations Law

---

[8] Jordan Branch, *The Cartographic State: Maps, Territory, and the Origins of Sovereignty* (Cambridge, UK: Cambridge University Press, 2014).

[9] Carl Schmitt, *The Nomos of the Earth in the International Law of the Jus publicum Europaeum*, translated by G. L. Ulmen (New York: Telos, 2003 [1950]), p. 79.

[10] Xi Jinping, *The Governance of China*, [Vol. 1] (Beijing: Foreign Languages Press, 2014), p. 57.

[11] See Charles J. Dunlap Jr., "Lawfare 101: A Primer," *Military Review* 97 (2017):8–17.

[12] Anne Hsiu-An Hsiao, "China and the South China Sea 'Lawfare,'" *Issues & Studies* 52:2 (2016):3; cf. Gao Zhiguo and Bing Bing Jia, "The Nine-Dash Line in the South China Sea: History, Status, and Implications," *The American Journal of International Law* 107:1 (2013):98–124.

Figure 7.1 Chinese U-shaped line map on PRC passport (2016). Courtesy Anonymous

of the Sea (UNCLOS) Arbitral Tribunal of the Permanent Court of Arbitration (2016) on the South China Sea could be seen as a battle between maps: China's historical U-shaped line map, on the one hand, and the Philippines's geographical map of its exclusive economic zone and its geological map of its continental shelf, on the other. As the tribunal's award in 2016 showed, the geographical and geological maps legally trumped the historical map: China's U-shaped line was declared incompatible with international law under UNCLOS.[13]

While legally moot, the U-shaped line map lives on in Chinese institutions—and in the Chinese imagination. The image of the map of China with the U-shaped line in figure 7.1 is a picture of a visa page in the PRC's high-tech e-passport (first issued in 2012). Strangely, the U-shaped line is very ambiguous, both on the passport map, where it is a light watermark, and in Beijing's official policy statements. The PRC has never clearly defined the exact location coordinates of the line, what it means legally and politically, or even its proper name; it is also known as the nine-dash line, the eleven-dash line, and the ten-dash line. Although it appears to clearly mark an international boundary, Beijing's U-shaped line is fascinating because it calls into question both the empiricist function of maps—to accurately represent the earth's surface—and hermeneutic understanding of the image: Just what does it mean? Neither Beijing's top government officials nor its top international lawyers have clear answers to questions about the location and the meaning of this cartographic marking.[14]

This chapter argues that the U-shaped line is ambiguous because it emerges out of an alternative way of envisioning the world. Rather than being a mathematical map—such as the Philippines's geographical and geological maps—the U-shaped map comes from the more normative and aesthetic map-making practice of early-modern China. To show this, the chapter examines four empire-maps/world maps, each of which exemplifies particular cartographic practices and worldviews: (1) All-under-the-Heavens maps from Qing dynasty China (1644–1911 CE) visualize the center/periphery logic of the Sinocentric tributary system; (2) Ch'oenhado from Choson dynasty Korea (1392–1910 CE) exemplify both this center/periphery dynamic and resistance within it; (3) Civilization/barbarism maps from the Song dynasty (960–1279 CE) use an analogous cultural logic to reclaim "lost territories"; and (4) lost territories maps from twentieth-century China combine the center/periphery and lost territories visualizations to assert the proper size and shape of modern China.

These particular maps were chosen for this discussion for two reasons. First, the Chinese government and prominent state-intellectuals tell us to look to such

[13] Permanent Court of Arbitration (PCA), "Award: PCA Case No 2013-19: In the Matter of the South China Sea Arbitration between the Republic of the Philippines and the People's Republic of China" (The Hague: Permanent Court of Arbitration, July 12, 2016) https://pca-cpa.org/wp-content/uploads/sites/175/2016/07/PH-CN-20160712-Award.pdf (accessed July 6, 2017).

[14] State Council, "China Adheres to the Position of Settling Through Negotiation the Relevant Disputes Between China and the Philippines in the South China Sea" (Beijing: State Council Information Office, July 13, 2016) http://www.fmprc.gov.cn/mfa_eng/zxxx_662805/t1380615.shtml (accessed July 5, 2017); Gao and Jia, "The Nine-Dash Line in the South China Sea"; Jianming Shen, "China's Sovereignty over the South China Sea Islands: A Historical Perspective," *Chinese Journal of International* 94 (2002):94–157.

maps as evidence for Beijing's expansive claims in the South China Sea.[15] While the "Europe in 2035" maps and the IS world maps come from unofficial sources, the four maps analyzed in this chapter are either official maps or popular maps from reputable sources. Second, each of these maps exemplifies a particular historical worldview and envisions a specific world order. The chapter argues that these maps intervisually resonate with each other to provoke "affective communities of sense"[16] that celebrate imperial expansion, lament lost territories, and fight to recover them. These four maps thus excite analogous views of the world, and thus worldviews, that call into question the Westphalian mapping that draws inside/outside boundaries. Although the South China Sea is a key security issue, these maps are about more than sovereignty, security, and where to properly draw boundaries.[17] Rather than see Chinese maps as traditional and European ones as modern,[18] the chapter argues that this set of maps exemplifies and promotes a center/periphery worldview that developed in parallel to the Westphalian inside/outside world order and is (re) gaining popularity and power in the twenty-first century.

Chapter 7 thus is not primarily concerned with proving (or disproving) Beijing's claims to the South China Sea. Rather than seek to present incontrovertible evidence to buttress arguments of rational causality that yield generalizable conclusions, the chapter is interested in looking at correlations among these popular and powerful maps to see how they provoke concepts and feelings of the Chinese imaginary that, in turn, produces such U-shaped line maps. This is not a chronological argument about a developing sensibility; instead, it is more conceptual in the sense of recognizing the shimmers and the resonance, and the intertextuality and the intervisuality, of these important maps. While other chapters focus on the visual over the textual, this chapter takes seriously the important dynamic of word and image. Yet rather than looking to a text to discipline the image, it follows Roland Bleiker's analysis of poetry in world politics to appreciate how texts can also be creative and aesthetic,

---

[15] State Council, "China Adheres to the Position," para 21; Shen, "China's Sovereignty over the South China Sea Islands," 126–127; Gao and Jia, "The Nine-Dash Line in the South China Sea."

[16] Emma Hutchison, *Affective Communities in World Politics: Collective Emotions after Trauma* (Cambridge, UK: Cambridge University Press, 2016); Jacques Rancière, "Contemporary Art and the Politics of Aesthetics," in *Communities of Sense: Rethinking Aesthetics and Politics*, edited by Beth Hinderliter, William Kaizen, Vered Maimon, Jaleh Mansoor, and Seth McCormick, 31–50 (Durham, NC: Duke University Press, 2009), p. 31.

[17] Suisheng Zhao, "China and the South China Sea Arbitration: Geopolitics Versus International Law," *Journal of Contemporary China* 27:109 (2018):1–15; Bill Hayton, "The Modern Origins of China's South China Sea Claims: Maps, Misunderstanding and the Making of China's Maritime Geobody," *Modern China* 45:2 (2019):127–170.

[18] Branch, *The Cartographic State*. Branch here over-interprets the sources that argue that European practices replaced Chinese cartography. Richard J. Smith provides a more nuanced view of the interplay of European and Chinese cartography. See Richard J. Smith, *Mapping China and Managing the World: Culture, Cartography and Cosmology in Late Imperial Times* (New York: Routledge, 2012).

offering meanings and feelings in a different register.[19] This chapter analyzes maps as two-dimensional visual images and also appreciates how they work as three-dimensional visual artifacts, material modalities, and sensory spaces that have what Jane Bennett calls "*Thing-Power*: the curious ability of inanimate things to animate, to act, to produce effects dramatic and subtle."[20]

Although most of these maps are now available online, previously they were experienced as material artifacts and sensory spaces. The Qing dynasty map is huge, taking up eight large scrolls; the Korean wheel map is part of an atlas that people leafed through; the Song dynasty map is carved on a large stone stele; and China's twentieth-century maps were either fold-out maps in books or large maps designed to be hung on classroom walls. These maps thus were things that people touched and smelled, as well as saw; the Song dynasty map is actually a rubbing of the stele. The Qing map was made for decorative display, to viscerally demonstrate the power of the emperor.[21] This overlap of word and image, and of image and artifact, exemplifies how cartography is about much more than drawing sovereign borders to mark the inside from the outside, because it engages in the creative experience of visualizing social order and world order.[22]

The twenty-first century is witnessing many challenges to the liberal international order, and again, as Schmitt writes, each new era requires a new spatial division. It is common in critical IR to celebrate "alternatives" to the hegemonic liberal order as emancipatory transformations that are themselves the focus of little critical engagement. For example, it is now popular to present China's alternative world order as a source of "emancipation" from the problems of "Western modernity." All too often, such critiques figure the problem of "Western imperialism" not in terms of "imperialism" itself, but only its Western form.[23] Rather than simply being a victim of Western imperialism, recent studies have shown how Qing dynasty China was itself a colonial empire that worked in ways similar to other contemporaneous empires.[24] This chapter thus does not figure Chinese cartography as an "alternative" that will

---

[19] Roland Bleiker, *Aesthetics and World Politics* (London: Palgrave Macmillan, 2012).

[20] Jane Bennett, *Vibrant Matter: A Political Ecology of Things* (Durham, NC: Duke University Press 2010), p. 6. Emphasis in original.

[21] Craig Clunas, *Pictures and Visuality in Early Modern China* (London: Reaktion Books, 1997), pp. 78–80.

[22] See Seegel, *Mapping Europe's Borderlands*.

[23] For example, see Martin Jacques, *When China Rules the World: The End of the Western World and the Birth of a New Global Order*, 2nd ed. (London: Penguin, 2012); Zhao Tingyang, *Tianxia de dangdaixing: Shijie zhixu de shijian yu xiangxiang* [Tianxia's contemporary relevance: Practice and imagination for world order] (Beijing: Zhongxin chubanshe, 2016).

[24] See Peter C. Perdue, "China and Other Colonial Empires," *Journal of American-East Asian Relations*, 16:1–2 (2009):85–103; Laura Hostetler, *Qing Colonial Enterprise: Ethnography and Cartography in Early Modern China* (Chicago: University of Chicago Press, 2001); Seegel, *Mapping Europe's Borderlands*.

solve the problems of contemporary IR. Rather, it analyzes how "new and different" alternatives are often based on re-imaginings of hierarchical imperial orders that work according to their own often violent center/periphery dynamics. The analysis presented in this chapter thus is about more than China and the South China Sea. It hopes to encourage a robust critical engagement with alternative cartographies and their alternative world orders—as seen in the Islamic State's invocation of the Caliphate (Chapter 5) and Russian appeals to "Eurasian" space (Chapter 2)— especially when these alternative world orders invoke past imperial cartographies.

Map-fare

Much as "lawfare" provides a new optic on the politics of warfare, this chapter proposes the concept "map-fare" to highlight the visual politics of maps. Here maps do not merely reflect or represent reality, but can actually "do" things to transform the world. While J. L. Austin and the securitization theorists discussed in Chapter 5 examine how people "do things with words,"[25] here I switch that idea around to consider how maps "do" things to political leaders, public intellectuals, and the general public. Like Austin's "performative utterances," maps not only describe things but are themselves performances that "do" legal and material things; the Republic of China's (ROC) first official map in 1912 was "issued for enforcement."[26] Likewise, the Sykes-Picot map (1916) was not description; rather, it enacted a new regional order by dismantling the Ottoman Caliphate in order to expand the French and British empires.

China's infamous U-shaped line map certainly is a mathematical representation of the region that has institutional power; since 1992, all maps of the PRC are legally required to include it.[27] Yet the U-shaped line is also an aesthetic creation of spatial identity that seeks to produce affective communities of sense. The passport map, for example, doesn't just excite Chinese pride; it provoked anger in Southeast Asia, with a Vietnamese official declaring, "I think it's one very poisonous step by Beijing among their thousands of malevolent actions. When Chinese people visit Vietnam we have to accept it and place a stamp on their passports."[28] Many

[25] J. L. Austin, *How to Do Things with Words* (Oxford: The Clarendon Press, 1962); Branch, *The Cartographic State*, 36.

[26] "Zhonghua minguo ditu," in *Zhonghua mingguo yuannian lishu* [Almanac of the first year of the Republic of China] (Hunan yanshuo zongke yin, 1912).

[27] "Law on Territorial Waters, Adjacent Areas," Beijing: Xinhua, FBIS-China (February 28, 1992):2; translated in British Broadcasting Corporation, *Summary of World Broadcasts* (November 28, 1992):C1/1-2.

[28] Jamil Anderlini and Ben Bland, "China Stamps Passports with Sea Claims," *Financial Times* (November 21, 2012) https://www.ft.com/content/7dc376c6-3306-11e2-aabc-00144feabdc0 (accessed June 6, 2017).

postcolonial (including post-Soviet) nation-states have serious "cartographic anxi-eties" that move them to legally and martially promote and enforce national maps.[29] Here a map is "not merely space or territory." As Thongchai Winichakul explains, a map is a living and breathing "geobody" that is "a component of the life of a nation. It is a source of pride, loyalty, love, . . . hatred, reason, unreason."[30] As we see in this chapter regarding China's imperial cartography, maps are living, breathing things that expand and contract. As mass-produced visual artifacts, maps thus are more than mathematical representations of "reality." Here the national/imperial map becomes a logomap—the national map as an icon that is separate from the con-text of neighboring territories—that works as a visual icon to mobilize the masses (and the elite). In this way, maps do not only tell us about the inside-outside geo-politics of international borders; when they inscribe space as a geobody, maps are visualizations of "power, duty, and emotion" that can move and connect people in affective communities of sense.[31]

These examples remind us that maps are not merely mathematical reflections of the earth's surface, but are also ideological and aesthetic. The Chinese character for map, *tu* (图, which is also used in Korean and Japanese) speaks to this double-coded science/art understanding: as a noun, *tu* means a picture, a diagram, a chart, a table, and a map, while as a verb it means to anticipate, to hope, to scheme, to plan, to plot against, and even to covet.[32] Cartography according to the nominal-*tu* engages in the ideological-work of "visibility": which territories, countries, states, and peoples are included on the map, and which are excluded. In the South China Sea disputes, this would inform where to draw the boundary to divide up maritime territories. Cartography according to the verbal-*tu*, however, deals with the affect-work of "visu-ality": how to creatively envision different world orders. For the disputes, this would inform whether people understand the issues in terms of Westphalian-style maps that mathematically plot single-line, inside-outside boundaries between sovereign

[29] See Franck Billé, "On China's Cartographic Embrace: A View from Its Northern Rim," *Cross-Currents* no. 21 (2017):1–21; Seegel, *Mapping Europe's Borderlands*.

[30] Thongchai Winichakul, *Siam Mapped: A History of the Geo-body of a Nation* (Honolulu: University of Hawaii Press, 1994), p. 17; also see Anderson, *Imagined Communities*, 170–178; Hayton, "The Modern Origins of China's South China Sea Claims."

[31] Cordell D. K. Yee, "Reinterpreting Traditional Chinese Geographical Maps," in *The History of Cartography*, Vol. II, Book II, *Cartography in the Traditional East and Southeast Asian Societies*, edited by J. B. Harley and David Woodward (Chicago: University of Chicago Press, 1994), p. 67.

[32] Nathan Sivin and Gari Ledyard, "Introduction to East Asian Cartography," in *The History of Cartography*, Vol. II, Book II, *Cartography in the Traditional East and Southeast Asian Societies*, edited by J.B. Harley and David Woodward (Chicago: University of Chicago Press, 1994), p. 25; Cordell D. K. Yee, "Chinese Maps in Political Culture," in *The History of Cartography*, Vol. II, Book II, *Cartography in the Traditional East and Southeast Asian Societies*, edited by J. B. Harley and David Woodward (Chicago: University of Chicago Press, 1994), p. 79; Hostetler, *Qing Colonial Enterprise*, 3; also see Ó Tuathail, *Critical Geopolitics*, 2.

nation-states, or in terms of the more expansive—and more ambiguous—notions of center/periphery territoriality seen in empire-maps/world maps.

Maps thus are not simply auxiliaries that illustrate history and politics, because they can actively perform world order. As mentioned previously, Branch argues that mapping is

> closely linked to societal norms and ideas: how mapmakers depict the world shapes map users' view of the world. . . . [Maps thus] serve to embody, shape, and reshape map users' ideas about the world in which they live, even to the point of altering goals they are pursuing with the help of these cartographic tools.[33]

Through a careful analysis of the shift in map-making concepts and conventions, Branch shows how the empty homogeneous space depicted on the mathematical maps that emerged in early-modern Europe shaped leaders' "fundamental ideas about political rule."[34] The new maps transformed the concepts and practices of world order, shifting from the overlapping non-cartographic forms of authority characteristic of medieval Europe toward a cartographic understanding of world order as a collection of distinct sovereign states separated by clear line boundaries. This conceptual transformation was not the plan of the map-makers; rather, it was an unintended consequence of new techniques of mapping the world. Such mapping conventions produced what Martin Heidegger critically describes as the "age of the world picture," which "does not mean a picture of the world but the world conceived and grasped as a picture."[35] Hence, rather than a singular "world-mirroring," here even mathematical cartography's world-picturing functions as "world-making."[36]

Starting in the sixteenth century, Europe used more mathematical maps, both to conquer the world and to create the world map to carve up the globe into sovereign territories divided by exclusive line boundaries. Walter D. Mignolo argues that cartography here not only shaped the material politics of claiming imperial space and sovereignty, but also worked to "colonize the imagination" of both the conquered and the conquerors.[37] While much critical cartography deconstructs how European world maps served as tools of Western imperialism, this chapter moves beyond critical IR's understanding of China (and the non-West) simply as a victim of imperialism and its fascination with Euro-America, the nation-state, and neoliberal

---

[33] Branch, *The Cartographic State*, 36.

[34] Branch, *The Cartographic State*, 6.

[35] Martin Heidegger, *The Question Concerning Technology, and Other Essays* (London: Garland Publishing, 1997), p. 130; also see Mitchell, *What Do Pictures Want?*, xiv.

[36] Mitchell, *What Do Pictures Want?*, xv; John Agnew, *Geopolitics: Re-visioning World Politics*, 2nd ed. (New York: Routledge, 2003), pp. 15–16.

[37] Mignolo, *The Darker Side of the Renaissance*, 218.

capitalism. Indeed, in the early-modern period France, Russia, and China simul-taneously employed cartography for state-building and empire-building.[38] In this coeval clash of empires, imperial map-making in Qing China (finished in 1712) ac-tually preceded that in Bourbon France (1744) and tsarist Russia (1745).[39] Hence this chapter considers if and how Chinese cartography was an imperial performance, and if and how Chinese maps were able to "colonize the imagination" of both the periphery and the center in East Asia. The purpose of exploring the Chinese "al-ternative," once again, is not "emancipation" from Eurocentrism, but to show how Chinese maps creatively engage in map-fare by visualizing power and authority in ways that perform and enforce particular world orders—including revived imperial world orders.

The Cartography of China's Alternative World Orders

If maps don't just illustrate geopolitics, but performatively "do" things, what did late imperial/early-modern Chinese maps "do"? Rather than promote exclusive sover-eign statehood, maps in East Asia visualized a different form of world order: the center/periphery logic of Sinocentric tributary system. This is seen in All-under-the-Heavens maps (Tianxia tu, Ch'eonhado, Tianxia quantu, Tianxia zongtu) that were popular in East Asia during China's Qing dynasty (1644–1912 CE).

Although the Jesuits helped the Qing court produce the first mathematical-survey-based, comprehensive map of the empire in the early eighteenth century, this map and its technique did not exclusively shape either general cartographic trends or worldviews in China.[40] In fact, All-under-the-Heavens maps, which were very popular from the seventeenth century up to the beginning of the twentieth century, emerged as an alternative view of the world. Figure 7.2 is a hybrid map that provides accurate readings of China's East and Southeast coast, but fantastic visions of China's periphery.[41] While on Westphalian maps Vietnam is a narrow North-South territory, here it is presented as a narrow East-West strip along China's southern underbelly. The Malay peninsula also takes a different shape as a tiny cape labeled Siam (i.e.,

[38] Branch, *The Cartographic State*, 72; Peter Perdue, *China Marches West* (Cambridge, MA: Harvard University Press, 2005), pp. 442–461; Hostetler, *Qing Colonial Enterprise*; Seegel, *Mapping Europe's Borderlands*; Magnus Fiskesjö, "The Legacy of the Chinese Empires: Beyond 'the West and the Rest,'" *Education About Asia* 22:1 (2017):6–10.

[39] Branch, *The Cartographic State*, 157–158; Hostetler, *Qing Colonial Enterprise*; Yee, "Chinese Maps in Political Culture," 92.

[40] See Hostetler, *Qing Colonial Enterprise*; Smith, *Mapping China*; Clunas, *Pictures and Visuality in Early Modern China*, 80.

[41] "DaQing wannian yitong tianxia quantu" [Perpetual All-under-the-Heavens Map of the Unified Great Qing Empire] (1811) (Washington, DC: Library of Congress) https://lccn.loc.gov/gm71005018 (accessed July 8, 2017).

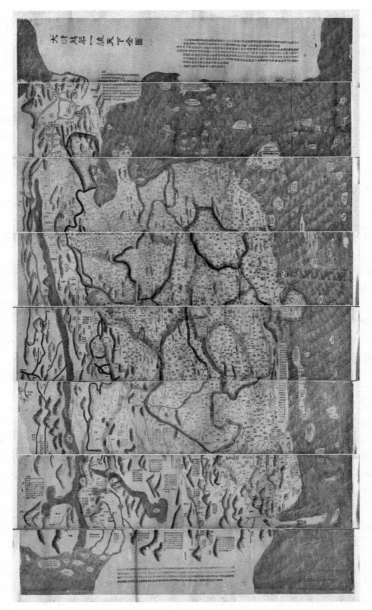

Figure 7.2 Perpetual All-under-the-Heavens Map of the Unified Great Qing Empire (1811). Courtesy Library of Congress

Thailand). Cartographic conventions here are not regulated by the scalar plotting and the clear inside-outside border divisions that are employed to divide empty homogeneous space into separate sovereign territories. Rather, the map visualizes the center/periphery logic characteristic of imperial China. Pre-modern empire-maps actually were world maps, on which it is not clear where China ends and the rest of the world begins.[42] This is because the normative Chinese geography was organized around the Son of Heaven (i.e., the emperor) at the center, with power (and Civilization) radiating out toward the periphery of vassals, tributes, and barbarians.[43]

Perpetual All-under-the-Heavens Map of the Unified Great Qing Empire employs these cartographic conventions to place the Qing dynasty at the center, surrounded by vassal states; such maps thus work to assert and affirm China's tributary system as a hierarchical network that joined the emperor, overlords, and vassals. Here Korea, Vietnam, and Siam are represented not merely for geographical reasons, but for political and historical ones; the textual cartouches describe these countries as vassal states, listing when and how they came to China to offer tribute. Power here works centripetally, with barbarians "turning toward civilization" by coming to China to learn "elegance and etiquette."[44] Such maps promoted an elaborate vocabulary of "imperial condescension,"[45] in which Korea and Vietnam are praised for being loyal vassals, while Japan is chastised for its past as a "country of dwarf pirates." Although mainstream histories of cartography trace the gradual disappearance of text from mathematical maps,[46] Chinese cartography is interesting because it foregrounds the complementary relationship between word and image.[47] As philosopher Wang Bi (226–249 CE) writes, "Image is what brings out meaning; word is what clarifies image."[48] Images and words thus are used to promote the tributary system's hierarchical network of overlords and vassals on All-under-the-Heavens maps, where the "foreign ministry" was the Board of Rites and the Board of Barbarians, and diplomacy took the form of the "guest ritual."[49]

It would be a mistake, however, to suggest that territory didn't matter, or that China was not an expansionist colonial empire. Over the course of the Qing dynasty's first century, China's land territory more than doubled in size. All-under-the-Heavens

---

[42] Smith, *Mapping China*, 48.

[43] See Yee, "Chinese Maps in Political Culture," 76.

[44] Smith, *Mapping China*, 78, 76.

[45] Smith, *Mapping China*, 78.

[46] See Branch, *The Cartographic State*, 55.

[47] Yee, "Chinese Cartography among the Arts," 128.

[48] Quoted in Cordell D. K. Yee, "Space and Place: Ways of World-making," in *Space & Place: Mapmaking East and West, Four Hundred Years of Western and Chinese Cartography*, edited by Cordell D. K. Yee et al. (Exhibition Catalogue for the Library of Congress) (Annapolis, Maryland: St. John's College Press, 1996), p. 11.

[49] See Dittmar Schorkowitz and Chia Ning, eds., *Managing Frontiers in China: The Lifanyuan and the Libu Reconsidered* (Leiden: Brill, 2017).

maps thus visualized the changing size and shape of the Chinese empire. China here is not fixed or eternal, but is a living, breathing geobody, whose new conquests required new maps. A common preface to such maps declared: "The land ruled by the present dynasty is unprecedented in its extent."[50] Indeed, many of the places marked as "lost territories" on twentieth-century Chinese maps are celebrated as "gained territories" on All-under-the-Heavens maps.[51] In general, even as the East Asian world order was challenged by European powers in the nineteenth century, these empire-maps plotted a particular view of the proper Sinocentric world order. The map in figure 7.2 thus is exemplary because it engages in map-fare. It doesn't merely illustrate the ideology of mathematical maps by plotting borders and listing territories. As map-fare, it visualizes the aesthetic conventions of empire: center/periphery in its figuration of the Sinocentric tributary system as an affective community of sense.

This is not simply a historical argument. Over the past two decades, many Chinese officials and scholars have rediscovered the Sinocentric world order, which they present as a model for global governance in the twenty-first century. Indeed, "periphery diplomacy"—which places China at the center—is one of the new trends in Chinese foreign policy.[52] The All-under-the-Heavens system and the tributary system are specifically promoted as peaceful alternatives to the Westphalian world order not just by scholars, but by Chinese leader Xi Jinping himself.[53] For example, Xi recently discussed the valuable lessons of China's idealized imperial history with other national leaders, telling US president Donald Trump that Korea used to be part of China, and Philippines president Rodrigo Duterte that the South China Sea has been Chinese "since the Ming dynasty" (1368–1644 CE).[54] And most importantly, the Chinese state and its top international law judges and scholars all point to All-under-the-Heavens maps examined in this section as evidence for the PRC's claim to expansive maritime sovereignty in the South China Sea.[55]

---

[50] Quoted in Smith, *Mapping China*, 74.

[51] Joanna Waley-Cohen, "Changing Spaces of Empire in Eighteenth-Century Qing China," in *Political Frontiers, Ethnic Boundaries and Human Geographies in Chinese History*, edited by Nicola Di Cosmo and Don J. Wyatt (London: RoutledgeCurzon, 2003), p. 333.

[52] See Xi, *Governance of China*, vol. 1, 315ff.

[53] See "Xi Jinping: Tuidong gongjian 'Yidai yilu' zoushen zoushi zaofu renmin" [Promoting the "One Belt and One Road" to together build a deeper and better benefit for the people], Beijing: Xinhua (August 27, 2018) http://cpc.people.com.cn/n1/2018/0827/c64094-30254137.html (accessed December 5, 2018); Zhao, *Tianxia de dangdaixing*.

[54] "Official Downplays Report of War Threats from China," *Bangkok Post* (May 23, 2017):5.

[55] State Council, "China Adheres to the Position," para 21; Shen, "China's Sovereignty over the South China Sea Islands," 126–127; Gao and Jia, "The Nine-Dash Line in the South China Sea."

Alternative Alternative World Orders in Korean Maps

"Ch'eonhado" is the Korean pronunciation of the Chinese characters for All-under-the-Heavens Map. As figure 7.3 shows, it is colloquially called a "wheel map" because it charts the world according to concentric land and sea rings.[56] It offers an even more graphic visualization of the imperial center/periphery logic of the Sinocentric world order: the central continent of China and Korea is surrounded by peripheral

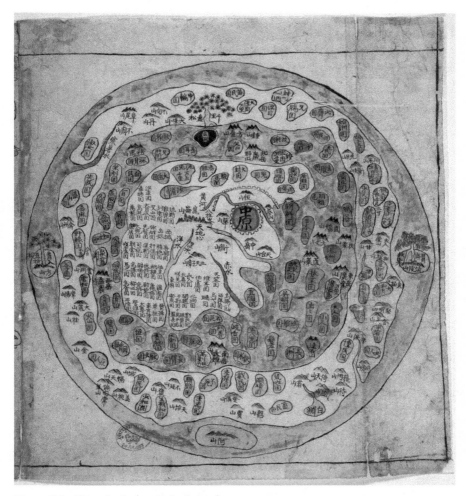

Figure 7.3 Ch'eonhado (ca. 19th century). Courtesy © British Library Board, Maps.33.c.13

[56] "Ch'onhado" (ca. 19th century) [All-under-the-Heavens Map] (London: British Library, Maps.33.c.13).

rings of countries and peoples, both exotic and mythological. As on Chinese All-under-the-Heavens maps, this world map marks neither clear land borders nor accurate island shapes. Places were marked with cartouches, with the territorial size of the country dependent on its importance to the empire. On the outer land ring, all the places are fantastical, based on Chinese literary sources, including the *Classic of Mountains and Seas* (*Shanhai jing*), an ancient Chinese text in which geography, ethnography, and mythology collide.[57] The Ch'eonhado's intertextuality/intervisuality exemplifies how the texts actually come onto the map to explain the mysteries of the Sinocentric periphery in terms of a set of fantastic countries: "the country of the tree people," "the country of the hairy people," and "the country of the righteous and harmonious."[58]

This map is not a one-off; dozens of Ch'eonhado were made between the seventeenth and nineteenth centuries. So what did Ch'eonhado "do" for Koreans? From the fifteenth century, Koreans could produce mathematically accurate maps. In a way, Ch'eonhado are part of a positivist cartography; typically, they were the first maps in an atlas, followed by maps of China, Japan, the Ryukyu islands (i.e., Okinawa), Korea, and finally Korea's provinces and towns. But like the All-under-the-Heavens maps, Ch'eonhado both shape strategic and commercial objectives and serve to satisfy cultural and emotional desires. This popular cartographic genre exemplifies the center/periphery logic of the Sinocentric tributary system: China as the "Central Plain" (Zhongyuan) is the center of both Civilization and territory; Korea is close by as the number one tributary state; and Japan (which was seen as Korea's main military threat) is presented as smaller than Korea, pushed away to China's Southeast.[59]

Ch'eonhado thus provide a strong example of map-fare. This imperial cartography "colonized the imagination" of both the periphery and the center; these Korean maps present an even more Sinocentric view of the world—and worldview—than similar Chinese All-under-the-Heavens maps.

Ch'eonhado are not simply an example of East Asian curiosities. As Seegel argues for similar mapping struggles in the borderlands of Central Eastern Europe, cartography provides a language of both power and protest, which are often intertwined.[60] In other words, Ch'eonhado also were employed by Koreans in map-fare to creatively resist the cultural governance of the Chinese state.

---

[57] See *Shan Hai Ching: Legendary Geography and Wonders of Ancient China* (Taipei: Committee for Compilation and Examination of the Series of Chinese Classics, 1985).

[58] Quoted in Gari Ledyard, "Cartography in Korea," in *The History of Cartography*, Vol. II, Book II, *Cartography in the Traditional East and Southeast Asian Societies*, edited by J. B. Harley and David Woodward (Chicago: University of Chicago Press, 1994), p. 257.

[59] Ledyard, "Cartography in Korea," 258.

[60] Seegel, *Mapping Europe's Borderlands*, 2.

Much of Korean history narrates resistance to Chinese expansionism, which helps explain South Korean anger at Xi Jinping's declaration in 2017 that Korea used to be part of China. Although the atlas's map of China was produced during the Qing era(1644–1911), Chinese space is visualized on these maps according to the previous Ming dynasty's (1368–1644) administrative divisions.[61] Using the logic of Sinocentric Civilization/barbarism relations, Koreans resisted the Qing primarily because they felt that these "barbaric" Manchurians had usurped the throne from the Ming dynasty, which was properly-Confucian and properly Han-Chinese. These maps thus were geographical, but also nostalgic and aspirational; they actively resisted the Qing by plotting the map of China according to the normative order that used to exist, and which the Koreans hoped would soon be restored.[62] While the *Perpetual All-under-the-Heavens Map of the Unified Great Qing Empire* (1811) presented the hegemonic view of China's tributary system, the Ch'eonhado show how alternative visualizations can arise within this world order; by changing the "visibility" of the Chinese map to exclude the Qing and include the Ming, Korean atlases affectively provoked the "visuality" of an alternative affective community of sense. Unlike the Chinese All-under-the-Heavens maps, Korean atlases do not show expanding territoriality but resistance to it. Power is generated here in different, even more visual ways; in this Sinocentric cartography, the periphery has power to choose its preferred center. Ch'eonhado thus flourished during the Qing dynasty as a fantastic view of a properly-ordered, alternative world order.

Lost Territories Maps in Twelfth-Century China

The Ch'eonhado's visualization of the restoration of the proper normative order is not exceptional; it has interesting resonances with Chinese cartography during the Southern Song dynasty (1127–1279 CE). Among the dozens of empire-maps/world maps produced in the Song, the most famous is the *Map of Civilization and Barbarians* (*Huayi tu*, 1136 CE).[63] As figure 7.4 shows, it gives a broad, idealized visualization of the Chinese realm. Much like the All-under-the-Heavens/Ch'eonhado maps that came five centuries later, it employs the cartographic convention of center/periphery, rather than the clear line boundaries of inside-outside. This map

---

[61] See "Ch'eonhado" (ca. 1800) [All-under-the-Heavens Map] (Washington, DC: Library of Congress) https://lccn.loc.gov/93684246 (accessed April 19, 2019).

[62] Ledyard, "Cartography in Korea," 238, 267.

[63] "Huayi tu" (1136 CE) [Map of Civilization and barbarism] (Washington, DC: Library of Congress) https://lccn.loc.gov/2002626771 (accessed July 8, 2017). Although some argue that we should translate ancient terms such as "Yi" as "foreigner" rather than "barbarian," this argument misses the point that in such a hierarchical world order, outsiders are by definition barbarians. See, for example, Lydia H. Liu, *The Clash of Empires: The Invention of China in Modern World Making* (Cambridge, MA: Harvard University Press, 2004).

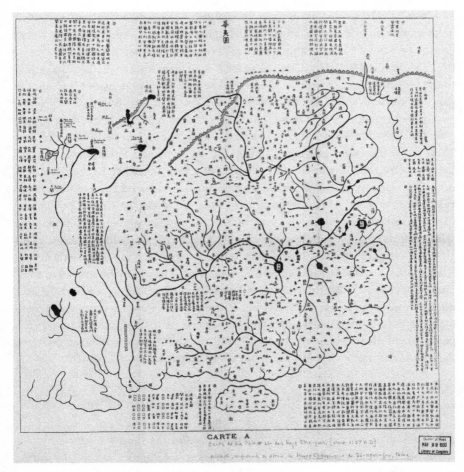

Figure 7.4 Map of Civilization and Barbarians (1136 CE). Courtesy of Library of Congress

provides a total view of the Chinese empire from the Great Wall in the North to Hainan island in the South. The Western frontier is fascinating because here textual and pictorial information slowly peters out as the map traces the origins of the continent's great rivers. There are numerous textual notes on the map to explain the geography of China, as well as the particulars of its neighbors. Like the tributary system's hierarchical order, this map charts global politics not as "international relations," but in terms of cultural and moral judgments: Civilization and barbarism. The center/periphery system in China maps onto the Civilization/barbarism distinction, which is not merely cultural but also spatial. Many empire-maps/world maps were not named according to specific dynasties, but with more general names that highlight China as the center of Civilization; for example, the Central Cultural Florescence (Zhonghua), the Central Kingdom (Zhongguo), and the Central Plain

(Zhongyuan). Barbarism, on the other hand, was visualized in idealized form according to the four cardinal points: Eastern-Yi, Western-Rong, Northern-Di, and Southern-Man.[64]

The *Map of Civilization and Barbarians* is noteworthy because it presents neither the actual territory of the reigning Song dynasty nor that of its powerful neighbors. The map was produced during a violent (global) transformation, in which the Song dynasty lost significant territory. After decades of struggle, in 1141 the Song signed a peace treaty to formally recognize Jin dynasty control over Northern China—that is, territory north of the Yangtze and Huai Rivers. None of the many empire maps of the Southern Song period, however, plotted the territory of both the Song and Jin dynasties.[65] Rather, the *Map of Civilization and Barbarians* shows the Song ruling over all of China, and all of the world. That the map in figure 7.4 is carved on a stone stele underlines its work as a visual artifact, and also its didactic purpose. But rather than instructing people on the actual borders of the Song empire, the purpose is to provoke an affective community of sense. As a commentary on a similar map from the 1190s made clear, such maps "were intended as an illustration for future Song emperor (Ningzong, r. 1194–1224 CE) of how much land had been lost to the northern invaders, and as a reminder of the sovereign's responsibility to reunite the empire."[66] This was not simply a battle between nation-states over where to properly draw national boundaries, but an all-out struggle between Civilization and barbarism: the Jin dynasty was ruled by Jurchens, whom many Han Chinese dismissed as barbaric. The rich vocabulary of imperial condescension that we saw in the Qing dynasty map here is quite crude; those who are not Chinese-Civilized are branded as "barbarian."

Like the image/word dynamic of Ch'eonhado and the *Classic of Mountains and Seas*, Song dynasty cartography was intertextual as well as intervisual. In the *Map of Civilization and Barbarians* the aesthetic of verisimilitude animates both poetry and map-making,[67] as both creative modes long for a truth that is not quite there. Along with instructing emperors, "the sight of the map of the empire" also "struck grief" into many Southern Song intellectuals, who then wrote poems to lament lost territories.[68] One cartographic-literary activist expressed his outrage in a poem called "Reflections on the Past":

> This lowly functionary is overcome by solitary anger
> By the nightly window frame, tears flowing, I look at the map.[69]

---

[64] Smith, *Mapping China*, 48.

[65] Hilde de Weerdt, "Maps and Memory: Readings of Cartography in Twelfth- and Thirteen-Century Song China," *Imago Mundi* 61:2 (2009):164.

[66] Smith, *Mapping China*, 55.

[67] Yee, "Chinese Cartography among the Arts," 133.

[68] de Weerdt, "Maps and Memory," 145.

[69] Quoted in de Weerdt, "Maps and Memory," 159.

Another map-fare poet was more programmatic:

> I carefully examined a map of the empire,
> I'd rather see it once more implemented on the ground.[70]

Empire-maps were evocative because their idealized normative view of the unified empire clashed with people's raw experience of a partitioned kingdom. Map-fare here involves more than providing rational information, or even a persuasive rhetoric. It provokes positive and negative visceral reactions because the map-poetry dynamic provides a "performative structure of geopolitical practices and their affective foundations."[71] Through this vibrant affective community of sense, the lost North was experienced as an open wound on the geobody that generated "territorial phantom pain."[72] This map/poetry (image/word) dynamic was a popular mode of radical political critique that demanded the recovery of lost territories.

Once again, China is a living, breathing geobody that expands and contracts. While the eighteenth-century All-under-the-Heavens maps charted an expanding empire's growing domain of tributary states, here Song dynasty maps of Civilization and barbarism visualized the opposite situation of a contracting territoriality. After being beaten by a "barbaric" foe, cartography worked to visualize lost territories that needed to be restored. Maps here are not meant to reflect reality on the ground, but to "do" something according to the verbal meaning of *tu*-map: they show how emperors and poets "coveted" lost Northern territories and "schemed" to restore lost glory through recovering them. Like the Republic of China's first official map (1912), these twelfth-century empire-maps were "issued for enforcement" to rejuvenate China.

Lost Territories in the Twentieth Century

Chinese maps of lost territories re-emerged at various points in Chinese history, most notably in the first half of the twentieth century. Like the Song dynasty, modern China faced an existential crisis, with fears that imperialist powers from Europe, the United States, and Japan would soon carve up China "like a melon." When the Qing dynasty fell in 1911, it was not at all clear where "China" began or ended and what territories were "Chinese" and what weren't. Chinese atlases from the early twentieth century, for example, characteristically state that the new republic (founded in 1912) needed national maps to know just what it was ruling.

---

[70] Quoted in de Weerdt, "Maps and Memory," 159.

[71] Gearóid Ó Tuathail in Gearóid Ó Tuathail, Monika K. Baar, and Steven Seegel, "Mapping Europe's Borderlands: Russian Cartography in the Age of Empire," *Nationalities Papers* 42:3 (2014):551.

[72] Billé, "On China's Cartographic Embrace," 5.

There was considerable debate about how to even ask this question, because of the tension between the broad Sinocentric notion of territorial domain seen in All-under-the-Heavens maps and the mathematical notion of homogeneous space that asserted exclusive single-line, inside-outside boundaries between nation-states.[73]

The Republic of China's first official map (*Zhonghua minguo ditu*, 1912) exemplifies the tension between the two cartographic visualizations: as the republic's first constitution declared, "the sovereign territory of the Republic of China continues to be the same as the domain of the former Empire."[74] This simply begs the question of defining the domain of the Qing dynasty—which as we have seen relies on a different way of visualizing the world. The ROC map also continues the imperial trend of marking territories according to China's tributary system with historical notes about the evolving relationship. However, rather than celebrating the glories of an expanding empire, it laments the loss of tributary states to other powers, noting how, for example, Korea and Taiwan used to be "on our country's map" and now are Japan's territories.[75] From 1912 to the 1940s, dozens of maps and atlases were published that graphically inscribed China's "lost territories" (*sangshi lingtu, sangdi*).

Map of China's Lost Sovereign Land and Maritime Territories (1927; figure 7.5) is typical of maps published at this time.[76] It is a fold-out map in the appendix of Xie Bin's popular *History of China's Lost Territories*. On the one hand, the map deals with "visibility" issues: it marks China's "lost territories" that were stolen by European and Japanese imperial regimes. This is done through color-coding: "totally" lost territories are colored in green, while territories that are now "shared" with another power are marked in orange, with the year of each territory's loss marked in bright red textual notes. The map includes inset charts that list the name of each lost sovereign land territory and of each lost sovereign maritime territory. The lost sovereign land territory chart lists thirty-four places in terms of three categories: fifteen "homeland territories" (*benguo*), including Sakhalin Island and Taiwan; fifteen tributary states (*fanshu*), including Korea, Vietnam, Afghanistan, and the Sulu Islands (now in the Philippines); and four "territorial concession territories" (*zujiedi*),

[73] See Thongchai, *Siam Mapped*; William A. Callahan, *Contingent States: Greater China and Transnational Relations* (Minneapolis: University of Minnesota Press, 2004), 57ff.; William A. Callahan, *China: The Pessoptimist Nation* (Oxford: Oxford University Press, 2010), pp. 91–125.

[74] *"Constitutional Compact of the Chung Hua Min Kuo,"* *Peking Daily News* (May 1, 1914); also see Chapter 1 and Chapter 3 in this book.

[75] "Zhonghua minguo ditu," no page.

[76] Xie Bin, "Zhongguo sangshi lingtu linghai tu" [Map of China's lost sovereign land and maritime territories], in *Zhongguo sangdishi* [History of China's lost territories] (Shanghai: Zhonghua shuju, 1927). Also see a different style of lost territories map in the 1925 edition of the same book: Xie Bin, "Zhongguo sangshi lingtu linghai tu," in *Zhongguo sangdishi* [History of China's lost territories] (Shanghai: Zhonghua shuju, 1925). This edition was reissued in 2014 with a poor reproduction of the map: Xie Bin, *Zhongguo sangdishi* [History of China's lost territories] (Shanghai: Sanlian shujian, 2014 [1925]).

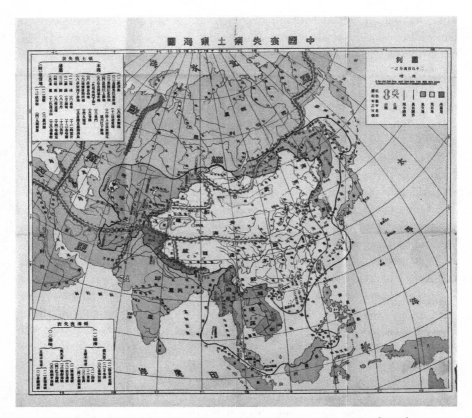

Figure 7.5   Map of China's Lost Sovereign Land and Maritime Territories (1927).
Source: Xie Bin, *Zhongguo sangdishi*

including Hong Kong's New Territories.[77] The lost territories map thus engages in
the issues of "visibility" by marking territories that need to be recovered from imperial powers. As we see later in the chapter, the maps employ the cartography of
Chinese colonial imperialism to accomplish this recovery. Although one might be
sympathetic to China's recovery of lost territories such as Taiwan or Hong Kong,
what about the other places listed on this map, which were decolonized to become
now-familiar independent sovereign nation-states in Central Asia, South Asia,
Southeast Asia, and Northeast Asia? Here the problem of "Western imperialism"
is not "imperialism" itself, but only its Western form; as this map suggests, the preferred solution is a reconstituted Chinese empire.

---

[77] A concession is a territory within a country that is administered by an entity other than the state
that holds sovereignty over it.

Lost territories maps also address "visuality" issues. Although they appear to be modern mathematical maps with scalar plotting and clear inside-outside boundaries, they also promote the Sinocentric center/periphery logic of China's imperial tributary system. Like Ch'eonhado, the lost territories map in figure 7.5 employs two sets of rings to reclaim vast territories. What these places have in common is a history of presenting tribute to the Chinese court. Hence, although it is not explicitly declared, such maps of lost territories are organized according to the center/periphery, Civilization/barbarian cartography of China's expansive imperial domain seen on early-modern and pre-modern maps. Similar claims to lost land and maritime territories are made in maps of China's national humiliation (*Zhongguo guochi tu, Zhonghua guochi tu*), dozens of which were published between the 1910s and 1940s.[78] Indeed, one of the most popular maps, the *Map of China's National Humiliation,* more or less copies the "lost territories" map, which is not surprising as it was published in the same year by the same publisher.[79] Lost territories maps thus were not exceptional, but were part of mainstream debates about the ideal normative size and shape of Republican China. These maps were often produced to hang on classroom walls to instruct students; they were artifacts that you could touch, and that would touch you.

As in the Song dynasty, the purpose of such maps is the "righteous restoration" of lost territories. The textual prefaces attached in the margins of many of these maps, for example, explain that their purpose is to "mark the glorious borders of the reign of the Qianlong emperor [1735–1796], and the timing and extent of territories that were later lost."[80] The didactic message of the cartography of expansive rings of lost territories is clear: since China has "lost more than half its territory," it is necessary to "compile a geographical record of the rise and fall of our country in order to craft a government policy to save it."[81] By the middle of the twentieth century, the image of China at the center of the imperial rings of lost territories had become a logomap—an image separated from its context—that sparked calls for a restoration of lost glory through the recovery of lost territories.[82] The wounded geobody thus moved and connected people in affective communities of sense that demanded action.

[78] See Callahan, *China,* 98–111.

[79] "Zhongguo guochi ditu" [Map of China's national humiliation] (Shanghai: Zhonghua shuju, 1927).

[80] "Zhonghua guochi jianming yutu" [Concise map of Chinese national humiliation] (Nanjing: Jiangsu Military Surveying Department, 1928).

[81] Jia Yijun, *Zhongguo guochi dilixue* [Geography of China's national humiliation] (Beiping: Wenhua xueshe yinxing, 1930), p. 1.

[82] For example, see Yu Guozhen, *Jin bainian waijiao shibai shi* [History of the past century's diplomatic defeats] (Shanghai: Shijie shuju, 1929), cover.

This genre of lost territories maps engages in map-fare in two ways. First, there is a resonance between twentieth-century maps of lost territories and eighteenth-century maps that celebrate imperial China's military conquests and tributary system. While the tributary states and barbarians are marked as "loyal vassals" and "gained territories" on eighteenth-century All-under-the-Heavens maps, in the twentieth century they are marked as "lost territories." These lost territories maps thus graphically transformed the blurred boundaries and overlapping authority of the All-under-the-Heavens system into a campaign to embrace a diverse set of lost territories as the "homeland territories" of the modern Chinese nation-state. Second, as in the Song dynasty, these maps worked in an intertextual/intervisual dynamic wherein cartographically-themed poetry, songs, art, and theater performances affectively provoked Chinese citizens to reclaim lost glory through reclaiming lost territories.[83]

Chinese Cartography and the South China Sea

As China's economic, political, and military power has grown, there have been calls in the PRC for Beijing to use its new influence to recover lost territories. At the turn of the twenty-first century, the return of Hong Kong (1997) and Macau (1999) to Chinese sovereignty was seen in the PRC as the return of lost territories and was celebrated in a special atlas, *Maps of Modern China's Century of National Humiliation*, as well as through hundreds of specially-commissioned cartographic poems.[84] The return of these territories to Chinese sovereignty thus was much more than a diplomatic or ideological victory. It also was affect-work that re-membered the geobody that had been dismembered, moving and connecting people in the PRC to celebrate the territories' "return to the warm embrace of the fatherland."[85] According to an influential Chinese scholar-official, the lesson of this returned territory/restored glory dynamic is irredentist; while "welcoming the return of Hong Kong and Macau to the fatherland, we also look forward to perfect resolution of other historical legacies."[86]

Alongside this celebration, however, another group of less official activists in China lament how territories continue to be lost under the PRC. While some point to

---

[83] See Zhichi, ed., *Guochi* [National humiliation] (Shanghai: Zhichishe, 1915); Wu Gongxiong, ed., *Huitu guochi yanyi* [Drawings of the romance of national humiliation] (Shanghai: Shijie shuju, 1922).

[84] *Jindai Zhongguo bainian guochi ditu* [Maps of the modern China's century of national humiliation] (Beijing: Renmin chubanshe, 1997/2005); Feng Yitong, "Bu qude huhao, chonggao de shixin" [Unyielding call, noble poetic heart], *Nanjing shifan zhuankexiao xuebao* 16:1 (2000):1–4; Callahan, *China*, 91–125.

[85] See Billé, "On China's Cartographic Embrace," 15.

[86] Lu Yiran, "Jindai Zhongguo sangshi lingtu zhihuigu" [A review of modern China's lost territories], *21 shiji*, no. 1 (1997):63.

this peaceful resolution of land border disputes as evidence of China's non-coercive use of diplomacy,[87] others calculate that 4.31 million square kilometers of sovereign national territory has been lost under the CCP's leadership of China.[88] The current map and list of territories lost since the PRC was founded in 1949 includes maritime territories in the South China Sea lost to the Philippines, Vietnam, Malaysia, Indonesia, and Brunei.

Hence, in China the South China Sea disputes are seen by both officials and activists as "lost territories" that need to be recovered, and the U-shaped line is the "scheme" to bring them back onto China's map. But the situation is more complex than that, and Chapter 7's final section explains how the U-shaped line and China's claims in the South China Sea are issues of both visibility (i.e., where to correctly draw the line boundary to reclaim maritime sovereignty) and visuality (i.e., what cartographic conventions to use in creating, promoting, and recovering maritime space). This section thus goes back to the four exemplary empire-maps/world maps previously considered to trace how the Spratly Islands and the U-shaped line came onto China's national map. While it weighs evidence of Beijing's claims, the purpose of the discussion here is more to probe the aesthetic resonances that link these historical maps with the U-shaped line, in ways that have mobilized affective communities of sense to claim the South China Sea as a lost territory.

Visibility

As mentioned previously, the Chinese government instructs viewers to examine All-under-the-Heavens maps for conclusive evidence of Chinese sovereignty over the South China Sea and the Spratly Islands.[89] As the *Map of Civilization and Barbarism* shows, Chinese maps typically see Hainan Island (which is just off the continental coast) as the southern extreme of China. Hence it is noteworthy that maritime features beyond Hainan are marked on the southern margin of the *Perpetual All-under-the-Heavens Map of the Unified Great Qing Empire* (1811): "reefs of 10,000 li" and "embankment for 10,000 li."[90] Yet such maps are unable to serve as reliable evidence to support China's sovereign claim, for two reasons. First, although "reefs of 10,000 li" is supposed to represent the Paracel Islands, and "embankment for 10,000 li" the Spratlys, on other similar maps they are called the opposite, or "reefs of 1000 li" and "embankment for 1000 li." Hence none of these names—reefs for 10,000

---

[87] See M. Taylor Fravel, *Strong Borders, Secure Nation: Cooperation and Conflict in China's Territorial Disputes* (Princeton, NJ: Princeton University Press, 2008).

[88] See, for example, "1949 to Now, China Has Lost over 4 Million Square Kilometers of Sovereign Territory?" (April 12, 2015) http://blog.sciencenet.cn/blog-3017-881866.html (accessed July 5, 2017).

[89] State Council, "China Adheres to the Position."

[90] A *li* is equal to one-third of a mile.

li, reefs for 1000 li, embankment for 10,000 li, embankment for 1000 li—has any stable reference. Second, even if the toponyms were stable, it is difficult to determine where China ends and the rest of the world begins on such maps. To address such interpretive problems, one key commentator explains that "these ancient maps lack precision due to limitations on map drawing techniques."[91]

But when we look at a recently discovered, more "mathematically accurate" maritime map from the Ming dynasty (ca. 1609), a different set of problems arises.[92] While the All-under-the-Heavens maps are designed to perform dynastic magnificence and the Sinocentric world order, this Chinese map—named "Mr. Selden's Map" after the person who donated it to Oxford University—was a route-map designed to facilitate the maritime trade that joined China with East and Southeast Asia. Like many maps of the period, it actually is an assemblage, in the sense that it combines a set of individually drawn maps of China, the South China Sea, Japan, and Taiwan into a more comprehensive map. Unfortunately the relevant placement of the various continental and island features is not quite right. But when aligning the Selden map with GIS coordinates of key features, Timothy Brook and his team were able to reconstruct the map to be remarkably accurate in terms of the scale and position of the features. To get this more accurate rendering, they disassembled and reassembled the map's various component maps, and the result shows that a large part of the South China Sea is missing from the reconstituted map.[93]

Brook suggests that this large swathe of the South China Sea is missing because the shallow waters of the reef-dotted sea were seen by mariners as a "navigational hazard" and thus a risk for shipwreck and piracy, to be avoided. As one historical source warns, the South China Sea reefs are as "tortuous as a long snake lying in the sea. . . . One would be safe to avoid it, and dangerous to come across it."[94] It is likely that if the area was occupied at all, residents were sea nomads and fisher folk from local Malay seafaring groups.[95] Brook thus concludes that although some might think that Selden's map provides evidence for China's "claim to sovereignty over any rock in this sea, [d]eclaring sovereignty wasn't what sailors or mapmakers were doing in this part of Asia in the seventeenth century. These were islands that nobody wanted."[96]

In a way, this Ming dynasty map plots the opposite of the U-shaped line: rather than include the South China Sea on the map to mark maritime sovereign claims,

---

[91] Shen, "China's Sovereignty over the South China Sea Islands," 128.

[92] Timothy Brook, *Mr. Selden's Map of China: The Spice Trade, a Lost Chart, and the South China Sea* (London: Profile Books, 2015).

[93] Brook, *Mr. Selden's Map of China*, 166–167, plate 26.

[94] Quoted in Shen, "China's Sovereignty over the South China Sea Islands," 116–117.

[95] Bill Hayton, *The South China Sea: The Struggle for Power in Asia* (New Haven, CT: Yale University Press, 2014), pp. 1–28.

[96] Brook, *Mr. Selden's Map of China*, 167.

large parts of the sea are deliberately excluded from Selden's map because the sea's reefs presented a set of problems for maritime commerce. While Xi explained to Duterte that the South China Sea has been Chinese since the Ming dynasty,[97] this Ming dynasty map actually does not include much of the South China Sea itself.

Neither the U-shaped line nor the Spratly Islands are marked on the Korean Ch'eonhado or the Song dynasty *Map of Civilization and Barbarism*. As we have seen, the peripheries of such maps characteristically envisioned fantastic places and exotic humanoid creatures. However, the South China Sea and something similar to the U-shaped line do appear on lost territories maps from the early twentieth century. The *Map of China's Lost Sovereign Land and Maritime Territories* (1927) is interesting for two reasons: (1) for the first time, its title stresses maritime territories alongside land territories, and (2) it includes an inset chart that lists lost sovereign maritime territories. Notably, the chart laments the total loss of the Sea of Okhotsk, the Sea of Japan, and the Bay of Bengal and worries about China's partial sovereignty over the Bohai Gulf, the Yellow Sea, the East [China] Sea, and "China's South Sea"—that is, the South China Sea. On such maps, China's southern extreme is extended from Hainan Island to the Paracel Islands, which are marked on lost territories maps as the "Xisha" islands. The Spratly Islands are not marked at all on lost territories maps. Indeed, the outer ring on lost territories maps does not mirror the U-shaped line; it does not include all of the South China Sea, and actually veers West to exclude the Spratlys area (discussed further later in the chapter).

Hence, the exemplary maps examined in this chapter show that the U-shaped line and the Spratly Islands were not issues for China until the twentieth century. While the Chinese government asserts that the disputed territories have been China's "since ancient times," the sudden appearance of the South China Sea as a territorial issue is confirmed by a close analysis of the historical and diplomatic texts of the twentieth century.[98]

Visuality

While twentieth-century controversies over the South China Sea do not present clear evidence of Chinese sovereignty, they do show how PRC elites were developing a "maritime consciousness," as opposed to China's traditional continental consciousness. It is common to understand China's new interest in the seas as a modern phenomenon, tied to its emergence as a nation-state in the early twentieth century

---

[97] "Official Downplays Report of War Threats from China," 5.

[98] Hayton, "The Modern Origins of China's South China Sea Claims"; Chris P. C. Chung, "Drawing the U-Shaped Line: China's Claim in the South China Sea, 1946–1974," *Modern China* 42:1 (2016):38–72.

and as a rejuvenated great power in the twenty-first century.[99] But as the four exemplary empire/world maps show, that interest also grew out of early-modern and pre-modern practices of cartography in China. The U-shaped line resonates with the Sinocentric rings of the lost territories maps. Indeed, in the 1930s and 1940s some of the same people were involved in charting lost territories and the creating the U-shaped line.[100] Moreover, the expansive rings of the lost territories maps visually resonate with the center/periphery cartography that characterizes All-under-the-Heavens maps and Ch'eonhado.

To understand the cartography of lost territories, then, one needs to appreciate how Ch'eonhado provoke power, duty, and emotion through the cartography of concentric rings. On the exemplary lost territories map (1927; figure 7.5), the outer ring is marked as the "boundary of maritime territory during the Qianlong era." This outer line is interesting for what it includes and what it excludes. It includes the Ryukyu Islands and Taiwan, but it excludes Japan and, as noted previously, it does not trace the area in the South China Sea now defined by the U-shaped line. Rather, south of Taiwan the ring veers west before hooking around to include the Sulu Islands, northern Borneo, Singapore, the Malay Peninsula, and the Andaman Islands before going back onshore to claim Burma. This is certainly an odd collection of maritime territories. To understand how this outer ring functions more according to a center/periphery dynamic than an inside-outside distinction, the All-under-the-Heavens maps are helpful. What these places have in common is a history of presenting tribute to the Chinese court. Recall that China's All-under-the-Heavens maps visualized the tributary system, in which authority and power grew out of people-to-people relations as much as through territorial claims. Indeed, recent arguments for Chinese sovereignty look to historical texts to chart how people from the South China Sea presented tribute to China; however, it is hard to map such scattered textual references to any particular place.[101] Features in the South China Sea thus are not marked on Chinese maps, because no loyal vassals from there came to Beijing to present tribute to the emperor. As with the geobody, the focus was on moving people rather than stable territory. Either no one lived on these reefs, or they were home to people who actively resisted centralized imperial authority. Much like James C. Scott's argument for mountains in *The Art of Not Being Governed*, such maritime navigational hazards attracted outlaws—pirates,

---

[99] See Hayton, "The Modern Origins of China's South China Sea Claims"; Chung, "Drawing the U-Shaped Line."

[100] Bai Meichu, *Zuixin Zhonghua minguo gaizao quantu* [The atlas of the Republic of China, with the latest corrections] (Beiping: Jianshe tushuguan, 1930); Zheng Ziyue, *Nanhai zhudao dili zhilu* [Geography of the South Sea Islands] (Shanghai: Shangwu yinshuguan, 1947); Hayton, "The Modern Origins of China's South China Sea Claims, 158–163; Chung, "Drawing the U-Shaped Line," 50.

[101] See Shen, "China's Sovereignty over the South China Sea Islands"; Gao and Jia, "The Nine-Dash Line in the South China Sea."

sea nomads, transient fisher folk—who thrived outside the tributary system.[102] Yet since they were not tributes, they were not on the map. If they are not included on the map as loyal vassals, then even according to Beijing's own imperial visualization, it is difficult for China to make a sovereign claim.

Finally, it is important to note how current explanations of Chinese sovereignty employ a harsh vocabulary of "imperial condescension," like that seen in the Song dynasty. Although Southeast Asian seafarers have plied the South China Sea for millennia, their experience is largely excluded from Chinese explanations. When their experience is included, it is according to the hierarchical logic of the tributary system and Civilization/barbarian relations. Vietnamese claims to the South China Sea are dismissed as illegitimate because "Vietnam remained a tributary to China until 1884" and thus according to Beijing could not make its own sovereign territorial claims.[103] According to this logic, which comes from All-under-the-Heavens maps, none of China's neighbors would be able to make any sovereign territorial claims to their own homeland territory, let alone to maritime space.

The explanations also employ the logic of the *Map of Civilization and Barbarism*; strangely for a twenty-first-century legal text, Chinese arguments actually describe the ancestors of rival claimants as "barbarians."[104] In this way, the current legal arguments visualize the South China Sea disputes in terms of the cartographic conventions of All-under-the-Heavens Maps and Maps of Civilization and Barbarism. This visualization clearly includes China as the sovereign center of Civilization, while erasing the activities of people on China's periphery. The periphery here is like that on Ch'eonhado, a fantastic place of odd humanoid creatures who although entertaining, lack political agency.

What started out as a vision of a fantastic space on the outer margins of the Chinese imagination is now seen as sovereign territory that demands to be recovered and defended; a recent billboard in Beijing pictures an uninhabitable reef in the South China Sea with the caption "Chinese sovereign territory, even an inch will not be ceded!!!"[105] In other words, map-fare traces how countries (e.g., China, Russia, and IS) can recover lost glory through recovering lost territories.

---

[102] James C. Scott, *The Art of Not Being Governed: An Anarchist History of Upland Southeast Asia* (New Haven, CT: Yale University Press, 2009); Hayton, *The South China Sea*.

[103] Gao and Jia, "The Nine-Dash Line in the South China Sea," 113.

[104] Shen, "China's Sovereignty over the South China Sea Islands," 103, 104, 118; Gao and Jia, "The Nine-Dash Line in the South China Sea," 100.

[105] See the image in Andrew Chubb, "Did China Just Clarify the Nine-Dash Line?" *East Asia Forum* (July 14, 2016), http://www.eastasiaforum.org (accessed June 6, 2017).

Conclusion

In a broad sense, the U-shaped line exemplifies the warfare and lawfare issues of one of history's greatest "sea grabs."[106] Beijing's approach to the South China Sea is worrying the PRC's neighbors to the north: in Mongolia and the Russian Far East, there are concerns that China will use the logic of lost territories to demand a revision of previously-settled borders. While the "rigidity" of nation-state maps is generally challenged in critical cartography, here the ambiguity of imperial cartography provokes the concern in Asia that a "spatially liquid" China will "seep into its neighbors."[107] The "living, throbbing" geobody thus can be threatening.[108]

But as the chapter's critical examination of Chinese cartography shows, the U-shaped line is better appreciated as "map-fare": it visually performs a creative world-ordering transformation that provokes particular affective communities of sense. Beijing's reaction to the UNCLOS award in 2016 demonstrates how it feels that multilateral international law is not the appropriate means for addressing questions of the PRC's territoriality. Although the South China Sea is a key security flashpoint, the issue is about more than where to properly draw boundaries. As the maps considered in this chapter show, the region is envisioned according to the social-ordering and world-ordering of the Chinese geobody.

This is part of a broader trend in which the All-under-the-Heavens system is promoted as an alternative to what is seen as the "failed system" of American hegemony. Through a set of creative practices—ranging from making maps, to writing poetry, to terraforming brand new islands—this map-fare covets, plans, and schemes to put the South China Sea and the Spratly Islands onto China's map, and thus into China's geobody.

Maps thus are more than texts that represent the natural and the social worlds. In addition to deconstructing how maps are a social construction of the visual, it is necessary to appreciate how maps are a visual construction of the social—and of the imperial. As this chapter shows, we need to appreciate maps as active interventions that can shape global politics, because such "map-fare" combines word and image, and image and artifact, to visualize particular (imperial) world orders that provoke particular affective communities of sense. In this case, the center/periphery and geobody logic of empire-maps set the conventions both for understanding the modern territoriality of the PRC and for restoring China's proper normative size and shape. Hence cartography is about much more than drawing sovereign borders

---

[106] Howard W. French, *Everything Under the Heavens: How the Past Helps Shape China's Push for Global Power* (New York: Alfred A. Knopf, 2017), pp. 54–55.

[107] Billé, "On China's Cartographic Embrace," 4.

[108] Bennett, *Vibrant Matter*, 23.

to mark the inside from the outside, because it creatively engages in visualizing social order and world order.

While critical IR scholars might welcome this challenge to the Westphalian international system, we should recognize how Beijing looks to an idealized notion of its own (often violent) imperial center/periphery system to make these claims. Once again, the problem of "Western imperialism" is not "imperialism" itself, but only its Western form. Since Eurocentrism here is replaced by Sinocentrism, Chinese cartography does not present an "emancipation" from unequal and unjust power relations. Rather, its alternative world order presents a rival hierarchical system that has its own set of codes and conventions, inclusions and exclusions, and problems and solutions.

China is not alone in challenging the inside-outside cartography of the Westphalian international system with an expansive map-fare of center/periphery that generates world orders. While neoliberal capitalism sought to deterritorialize space away from sovereign states, the twenty-first century is witnessing a resurgence of transnational imperial cartographies that work to visualize and recover lost territories, for example, the IS Caliphate and Russia's "Eurasianism." This chapter looks beyond critical IR's fascination with Euro-America, the nation-state, and neoliberal capitalism to provide a model for analyzing how revived cartographic conventions are visually transforming the normative model of world order, often toward coercively hierarchal models.

8

The Sartorial Engineering of Race, Gender, and Faith

Introduction

NiqaBitch Shakes Paris is a short video that follows two young women walking around Paris dressed in niqab, which conceals their faces and upper bodies, along with hot pants and high heels that reveal their bare legs (see figure 8.1).[1] The video shows how this perambulatory performance shook Paris; it literally stopped traffic, turning people's gazes. NiqaBitch—which combines *niqab*, the French term for a full-face veil, with the American slang "bitch"—excited confusion, as well as appreciation; the video shows how the women get "thumbs up" support from many on the street and even a request for a fun photo from the policewoman at France's Ministry of Immigration and National Identity. In addition to providing information about the French veil ban that came into force six months later in 2011, *NiqaBitch Shakes Paris* provokes a visceral reaction from people on the street, as well as from the police who guard France's national identity.

This outrageous video shows how the visual can performatively provoke the entangled issues of gender, race, and faith. Clothes here are more than functional garments; they are multisensory artifacts that have cultural, religious, and political significance. As Frantz Fanon writes in "Algeria Unveiled":

> The way people clothe themselves, together with the traditions of dress and finery that custom implies, constitutes the most distinctive form of a society's uniqueness, that is to say the one that is the most immediately perceptible . . . through written accounts and photographic records or

[1] *NiqaBitch Shakes Paris* (2010) http://vimeo.com/15747849 (accessed February 23, 2018).

Sensible Politics. William A. Callahan, Oxford University Press (2020). © Oxford University Press. DOI: 10.1093/oso/9780190071738.001.0001

Figure 8.1 NiqaBitch Shakes Paris (2010). Courtesy NiqaBitch

motion pictures. In the Arab world, for example, the veil worn by women is at once noticed.[2]

In *NiqaBitch Shakes Paris*, the contradiction between veiling the face and upper body, on the one hand, and wearing hot pants and high heels, on the other, graphically displays female bodies as an exemplary site of the negotiation of visibility/invisibility. It also suggests the open-ended nature of this concealing/revealing dynamic. Although it is common to either "whole-heartedly support" or "resolutely denounce" the practice of veiling, the video does not provide a clear political statement. It seems to criticize the French state's criminalization of the veil, but it also suggests that taking the veil is not the answer, either.[3] This strategy of moral ambiguity is also manifest in a film by my students, *Awrah: Uncovering the Covered* (2017), in which a young woman in London concludes from her own experience: "I'd say that my relationship with my hijab has been quite turbulent."[4]

As Fanon and NiqaBitch both attest, sartorial practices are political performances, and this chapter explores their visual politics by juxtaposing two modes of visibility/invisibility: taking the veil and participating in beauty pageants. The international

[2] Frantz Fanon, "Algeria Unveiled," in *A Dying Colonialism* (New York: Grove Press, 1965), p. 35. Also see Banu Gökarıksel and Anna Secor, "The Veil, Desire, and the Gaze: Turning the Inside Out," *Signs* 40:1 (2014):177–180.

[3] NiqaBitch, "Hot Pants and Niqabs: NiqaBitch Stroll through Paris," *Monthly Review* (October 13, 2010) http://mrzine.monthlyreview.org/2010/niqabitch131010.html (accessed February 23, 2018).

[4] Su'ad in Abi Steadman, Hayley Rabet, and Lamisa Khan, dir., *Awrah: Uncovering the Covered* (2017) https://vimeo.com/channels/ir318/208667693 (accessed February 23, 2018).

politics of veiling is manifest; it is not much of an exaggeration to state that the veil is "the most politicized piece of fabric in the world."[5] Beauty pageants are also sites of international politics, in the sense that sending a national beauty queen to the Miss Universe pageant confirms a state's sovereignty in international society in ways that are analogous to sending an ambassador to the United Nations. Indeed, in 2003 the People's Republic of China's (PRC) first national beauty queen was recognized by the US government as "Miss China, going to Miss Universe Contest" on her visa to attend the pageant in Puerto Rico.[6]

As previous chapters have shown, *Sensible Politics* is interested in the interplay of politics and aesthetics. Since it is not controversial to see veils and beauty pageants as aesthetic practices of women's fashion, the goal in this chapter is to consider how veiling and beauty pageantry are important as experiences of the political and social negotiation of concealing and revealing. In this way, veiling and beauty pageantry are also key sites of visibility and visuality—that is, as social constructions of the visible and visual constructions of the social. Although common sense might tell us that veiling is about concealing and beauty pageantry is about revealing, both strategies make women hypervisible: paradoxically, up-veiling's invisibility tactic often also makes the female body hypervisible in public.

The chapter thus uses the conceptual dynamic of concealing/revealing to analyze how various groups—women and men, Muslims and non-Muslims, states and corporations—expend considerable resources negotiating, performing, legislating, policing, and resisting such sartorial engineering practices.[7] It first decodes how these sartorial practices take on meaning in a set of social and political contexts: namely, as the choice of many women as individuals and through the discursive structures of the male gaze and the colonial gaze that can govern these choices. Along with beauty pageantry, taking the veil exemplifies Judith Butler's argument that "woman" is not a natural category, but rather a social experience that emerges from the performance of dressing up and acting like a woman.[8] While much of the debate is located in Europe and the Middle East and is framed by the East/West distinction, the chapter juxtaposes these sites with China, a non-Western country that uses the sartorial engineering projects of both de-veiling and beauty pageantry to creatively police its own Muslim minority groups. The discussion thus shows how structures and agents are mutually constituted through cultural governance and resistance.

[5] James Leibold and Timothy Grose, "Islamic Veiling in Xinjiang: The Political and Societal Struggle to Define Uyghur Female Adornment," *China Journal* no. 76 (2016):78.

[6] Elisabeth Rosenthal, "Here She Comes! (Will China Ever Be the Same?)," *New York Times* (July 16, 2002); also see William A. Callahan, *Cultural Governance in Pacific Asia* (New York: Routledge, 2006), pp. 1–4.

[7] Timothy Grose coined the phrase "sartorial engineering."

[8] Judith Butler, *Gender Trouble: Feminism and the Subversion of Identity* (New York: Routledge, 2006).

Finally, the chapter considers how up-veiling and beauty pageantry not only create ideological meaning, but also can excite affective communities of sense. Analyses of the veil characteristically turn this material object into a symbolic discourse and then use hermeneutic methods—for example, interpreting the Qur'an and/or French law[9]—to uncover its hidden ideology and thus reveal its true meaning. Alongside this hermeneutic analysis that seeks to define and deconstruct the veil, Chapter 8 explores what happens when we take seriously the materiality of veils as multisensory artifacts that are seen and touched. The goal is to appreciate veils and beauty pageants as visual artifacts and sensory spaces in which sensible politics is represented, performed, and experienced through more embodied, affective, and everyday encounters on the local, national, and world stages. "Sensible" here not only means "what can be sensed," but also "what makes sense" in the pragmatic politics of everyday life.[10] As we will see, women learn how to move and feel differently when they up-veil, de-veil, re-veil, and participate in beauty pageants. The chapter thus employs the visuality strategy to examine how these sartorial performances visually construct the social and the international: you don't just take the veil, the veil also takes you, in a politics that is creative as well as disciplinary. To put it another way, if "hijab" means partition and up-veiling is a performance at the intersection of invisibility and hypervisibility, then such sartorial practices exemplify Jacques Rancière's "(re)partition of the sensible."[11]

While it is common to draw conclusions that either support or denounce veiling and beauty pageantry, this chapter is more interested in appreciating how such material sartorial performances push us to think visually and feel visually in unexpected ways. Chapter 8 thus analyzes veiling and beauty pageantry to explore two areas: (1) the visual international politics of race, gender, and faith; and (2) visual artifacts and bodily experiences as sites of ideology and affect. Certainly we should be careful in our analysis.[12] In addition to provoking controversy, veils and beauty pageants themselves present an uneasy juxtaposition; they are not opposites, and

[9] See Mona Eltahawy, *Headscarves and Hymens: Why the Middle East Needs a Sexual Revolution* (London: Weidenfeld & Nicolson, 2015), pp. 36–38; Christian Joppke, *Veil: Mirror of Identity* (Cambridge, UK: Polity, 2009); Nick Hopkins and Ronni Michelle Greenwood, "Hijab, Visibility and the Performance of Identity," *European Journal of Social Psychology* 43 (2013):438; Leibold and Grose, "Islamic Veiling in Xinjiang," 78; Louise Bourgeois in Steadman et al., *Awrah*.

[10] Davide Panagia, *The Political Life of Sensation* (Durham, NC: Duke University Press, 2009), p. 3. Also see Meg McLagan and Yates McKee, eds., *Sensible Politics: The Visual Culture of Nongovernmental Activism* (New York: Zone Books, 2012).

[11] Eltahawy, *Headscarves and Hymens*, 36; Jacques Rancière, *The Politics of Aesthetics: The Distribution of the Sensible*, translated by Gabriel Rockhill (London: Continuum International Publishing Group, 2004).

[12] For a discussion of how my positionality as a "white male American" might impact the analysis, see the preface. In this chapter I aim to problematize the male gaze and the white/colonial gaze by taking seriously the concepts, practices, and experiences offered by feminist theory and Middle Eastern and Asian studies.

there is considerable diversity and slippage within both practices.[13] But this jux-taposition provides an interesting entry into broader debates within global visual politics. The chapter's conclusion considers the wider theoretical and international politics of sartorial engineering to ask whether veiling, as a performance of both invisibility and hypervisuality, marks the limits of visual international politics. In other words, this chapter hopes to shake up visual international politics, much as NiqaBitch shakes up Paris.

Up-veiling and Beauty Pageantry as Individual Choices

As noted, it is not an exaggeration to say that taking the veil constitutes one of the most provocative political and cultural statements in the world today. Reactions are strong, both in defense of veiling and attacking it, and these reactions are expressed in personal space, community space, national space, and global space. Taking the veil is not only a religious practice; it is also a social practice of spe-cific women at specific times and places. Veiling is also a concept in the sense that post-Enlightenment political thought focuses on issues of invisibility and visibility, concealing and revealing, dark iron curtains and bright transparency, and veiling and unveiling. As we saw in Chapter 6, artist-activist Ai Weiwei protests the lack of official transparency in China through the body politics of getting naked by himself and with friends. Veiling offers a different strategy. As the French guerrilla artist Princess Hijab explains:

> What's interesting about the niqab is that it isolates the person wearing it, while at the same time here in the Western world—especially in France— it puts you in the spotlight. That's the contradiction, by wishing to disap-pear from the public sphere, you're far more visible. You take possession of the public space. It's an empowering piece of clothing, but it can also be frightening.[14]

In the post-ideological era, such empowering/frightening visual performances can produce essentialized self/Other relations, which in turn can excite the dy-namics of identity/difference: gender, race, and religion. A woman recently described how when she wears hijab on the streets of London, people assume that

---

[13] This chapter employs a broad sense of "veil" and "veiling" to "indicate an Islamic system of mod-esty in dress" (Gökariksel and Secor, "The Veil, Desire, and the Gaze," 178).

[14] Princess Hijab in *Princess Hijab's "Veiling Art"*, Al Jazeera English (July 6, 2010) http://www.youtube.com/watch?v=h0GLv-HzJFc (accessed February 23, 2018).

Figure 8.2 A "white British Muslim convert". Courtesy Amena Amer

she is "Arab," while she describes herself as a "white British Muslim convert."[15] As she explains, "People outside the Muslim community have a hard time believing I'm white. It's like I can't be white and Muslim. If I didn't wear the hijab they wouldn't have a problem accepting I'm white" (see figure 8.2). Veiling here is a visual performance that marks communities of race and religion in the sensible politics of everyday sartorial practice; it is a choice, an assertion of a woman's "cultural sovereignty" at the personal level.

In the short video *Awrah: Uncovering the Covered*, young Muslim women in London also describe up-veiling in terms of personal choice: "I started wearing hijab in secondary school. It was completely my choice. Most people think girls get forced into it, but for me my family were quite open. I decided to wear it. For me it's a quite personal decision."[16] Likewise, another woman uses "choice" to explain why she no longer takes the veil: "So I started wearing it from age 5. When you're that young you sort of do as your parents say. So I never had a choice, I never wanted to wear it. In the same way, I didn't want 'not' to wear it. I stopped wearing it when I was 19. I think the reason is I sort of fell out of love with the idea that a woman needed to wear a hijab to be modest."[17]

---

[15] Amena Amer, "A White British Muslim" (London: LSE Research Festival Exhibition, 2015) http://eprints.lse.ac.uk/63004/ (accessed February 23, 2018).

[16] Nadine Othman in Steadman et al., *Awrah*.

[17] Su'ad Abdi in Steadman et al., *Awrah*; also see Mina Hoti in Steadman et al., *Awrah*.

The choice to take the veil in the twenty-first century does not necessarily mean an assertion of tradition over modernity. Rather, it is often an expression of "global Islamic *haute couture*," which is part of a larger global "movement to construct alternative, sometimes specifically Islamic and transnational, versions of modernity."[18] The rise of "modest fashion," in which beautiful clothes do not reveal much skin, is an important part of this trend because it both questions the hegemonic European view of beauty and provides an alternative; London Fashion Week is now complemented by London Modest Fashion Week. The choice to take the veil and to conceal the body thus can be an aesthetic expression of individuality that is celebrated (and commodified) by the global modest fashion industry.[19]

With modest fashion, the aesthetics of concealing/revealing seen in up-veiling overlaps with that of beauty pageants. While the popularity of beauty pageants is waning in Euro-America, they are still quite popular in Asia.[20] Certainly socialist countries such as Vietnam and China generally shared the Euro-American feminist view of beauty pageants as spectacles of bourgeois decadence and Western corruption. But by 2003 both Vietnam and China had held their first national beauty contests.[21] Initially, Chinese officials were suspicious even of this inaugural pageant. But after the first Miss China's success in the Miss Universe 2002 pageant—she came in third—many Chinese people caught the beauty pageant bug, and contests started to proliferate throughout the country.[22] After the Miss China pageant received the official blessing in 2003, the new enthusiasm did not stop with national pageantry; the Chinese state aggressively (and successfully) lobbied to host the Miss World pageant in December 2003. For the first time an international beauty pageant was broadcast nationwide on China's state-controlled television. The contest was so successful (Miss China again came in third) that the Miss World pageant has returned to China on a regular basis.

[18] Leibold and Grose, "Islamic Veiling in Xinjiang," 101; also see Banu Gökariksel and Anna Secor, "Between Fashion and Testtür: Marketing and Consuming Women's Islamic Dress," *Journal of Middle East Women's Studies* 6:3 (2010):119.

[19] See Reina Lewis, *Muslim Fashion: Contemporary Style Cultures* (Durham, NC: Duke University Press, 2015); Reina Lewis, ed., *Modest Fashion: Styling Bodies, Mediating Faith* (London: I. B. Taurus, 2013); Jennifer Heath, "Introduction," in *The Veil: Women Writers on Its History, Lore, and Politics*, edited by Jennifer Heath (Berkeley: University of California Press, 2008), p. 11; Nafisa Bakkar in Steadman et al., *Awrah*.

[20] Laura Mulvey, "The Spectacle of the Vulnerable: Miss World, 1970," in *Visual and Other Pleasures*, 2nd ed. (New York: Palgrave Macmillan, 2008), pp. 3–5; Deborah L. Madsen, "Performing Community through the Feminine Body: The Beauty Pageant in Transnational Contexts" (presented at University of Zurich, October 2005) http://sigmao2.blogspot.co.uk/2009/01/lecture-presented-at-university-of_08.html (accessed February 3, 2018).

[21] "Beauty Pageants Gaining Popularity in China," *China Daily* (August 16, 2003); Rosenthal, "Here She Comes!"; Seth Myans, "Vietnam: Beauty in the Eye of the Government," *New York Times* (March 28, 2002); Callahan, *Cultural Governance in Pacific Asia*, 1–4.

[22] "Miss China Beauty Pageant Opens," *China Daily* (January 21, 2005).

As with up-veiling, participating in a beauty contest is seen as a matter of personal choice. Some Chinese women see the pageants as a new measure of their skills: "I believe that while I win in university entrance examinations, I can also win in beauty contests," reasoned an elite student at Beijing University.[23] Similarly, in Thailand, Lily Chaweewan Chongsakjarenkul explains, "I believe I was crowned Miss Thailand China Cosmos [2013] because of my wisdom."[24] Taking the veil and participating in beauty pageants thus are not seen by participants as traditional or backward activities; rather, highly educated young women choose such activities as part of being modern.[25]

In the 1990s beauty queens even became part of the "women's rights" movement in Thailand; public discussion of equal rights was provoked by a high-profile divorce case involving a former Miss Thailand/Miss Universe.[26] The general uproar at the unfair treatment of a woman who had represented Thailand generated a political debate that eventually led to an amendment in Thailand's 1997 Constitution that guaranteed equal rights for women and men. Thus, it is not surprising that in 2016 Lily declared: "I am a beauty queen, and I'm a feminist. I'm for human rights, and women's rights. . . . I support children's and women's rights, to help them to be independent, and not dependent on men, like it was a hundred years ago."

Likewise, when scholars and public intellectuals analyze why women take the veil (or not), the consensus is that it is a matter of individual choice, a matter of personal sovereignty that is inviolable.[27] Lila Abu-Lughod thus argues that Euro-Americans should stop "obsessing" about the veil, because Muslim women do not need saving. Moreover, she argues that Western analysts should stop using general categories such as "Muslim women" altogether, because they characteristically are

---

[23] "Beauty Pageants Gaining Popularity in China."

[24] Author's interview with Lily Chaweewan Chongsakjarenkul in Bangkok, Thailand (December 2016); also see NJ Survey, "Do You Agree with Beauty Pageants?," *The Nation Junior* (Bangkok) 2:42 (May 1–15, 1994):22; Kawalpreet Kaur, "It Takes Brains to Be Beautiful," *The Nation Junior* (Bangkok) 2:26 (September 1–15, 1993):26.

[25] Lewis, *Muslim Fashion*, 12ff.; Lila Abu-Lughod, *Do Muslim Women Need Saving?* (Cambridge, MA: Harvard University Press, 2013), pp. 17–18, 39–40; Wolfgang Wagner, Ragini Sen, Risa Permandadeli, and Caroline S. Howarth, "The Veil and Muslim Women's Identity: Cultural Pressures and Resistance to Stereotyping," *Culture & Psychology* 18:4 (2012):536.

[26] Opas Boonlom, "High-stakes Divorce Case Sparks Women's Rights Debate," *The Nation* (Bangkok) (February 15, 1995):A8.

[27] Abu-Lughod, *Do Muslim Women Need Saving?*; Martha C. Nussbaum, *The New Religious Intolerance: Overcoming the Politics of Fear in an Anxious Age* (Cambridge, MA: Harvard University Press, 2012); Ayaan Hirsi Ali, *The Caged Virgin: An Emancipation Proclamation for Women and Islam* (New York: Free Press, 2006); Yasmin Alibhai-Brown, *Refusing the Veil* (London: Biteback Publishing, 2014). Eltahawy, *Headscarves and Hymens*; Heath, *The Veil*; Joan Wallach Scott, *The Politics of the Veil* (Princeton, NJ: Princeton University Press, 2007); Wagner et al., "The Veil and Muslim Women's Identity"; Hopkins and Greenwood, "Hijab, Visibility and the Performance of Identity," 438.

recruited to justify the West's imperialist actions.[28] A contemporary example of this is Laura Bush's speech in November 2001 that invoked saving women as justification for the US invasion of Afghanistan: "The fight against terrorism is also a fight for the rights and dignity of women."[29] Postcolonial feminists, however, turn the question around to ask why white men (and women) continually feel the need to save brown women from brown men.[30]

Governance by the Male Gaze and the Colonial Gaze

Against the robust defense of personal agency just discussed, post-Marxist critical analysis looks to how these individual choices are shaped by the social and political structures of patriarchy. In a general sense this is part of structural governance of both the state and transnational capital. In a more specific sense it looks to how women's visibility is determined by the "male gaze," whereby "men act and women appear."[31] The woman is the "bearer, not maker, of meaning"; hence we do not have "images of women, but images as women," with women concealing and revealing their bodies for the pleasure of men.[32] In 1970 the London Women's Liberation Workshop's intervention in the Miss World contest was a graphic illustration of both the workings of the male gaze and resistance to it.[33] Outside the Royal Albert Hall, the venue of the Miss World contest, hundreds of activists demonstrated against beauty pageants, which were criticized as "cattle markets." Protestors countered the male gaze's objectification of women by chanting "We're not beautiful, we're not ugly, we're angry!" Inside the hall, they disrupted the televised proceedings with a cascade of leaflets, smoke bombs, stink bombs, and flour bombs. The

[28] Abu-Lughod, *Do Muslim Women Need Saving?*; see also Heath, *The Veil*; Wagner et al., "The Veil and Muslim Women's Identity," 523.

[29] Laura Bush, "The Weekly Address Delivered by the First Lady" (November 17, 2011) http://www.presidency.ucsb.edu/ws/?pid=24992 (accessed February 23, 2018).

[30] Abu-Lughod, *Do Muslim Women Need Saving?*, 33. This idea originally comes from Gayatri Chakravorty Spivak, "Can the Subaltern Speak?," in *Colonial Discourse and Postcolonial Theory: A Reader*, edited by Patrick Williams and Laura Chrisman (London: Harvester Wheatsheaf, 1994), p. 53.

[31] Laura Mulvey, "Visual Pleasure and Narrative Cinema," in *Visual and Other Pleasures*, 2nd ed. (New York: Palgrave Macmillan, 2009), pp. 14–27; John Berger, *Ways of Seeing* (London: Penguin Books, 1972), p. 47.

[32] Mulvey, "Visual Pleasure and Narrative Cinema," 15; Mitchell, *What Do Pictures Want?*, 35; Teresa de Lauretis, *Alice Doesn't: Feminism, Semiotics and Cinema* (Bloomington: Indiana University Press, 1984), p. 149.

[33] Mulvey, "The Spectacle of the Vulnerable." In 1968 Women's Liberation protested against the Miss America Pageant using similar methods and language; see Maxine Leeds Craig, *Ain't I a Beauty Queen? Black Women, Beauty and the Politics of Race* (Oxford: Oxford University Press, 2002), pp. 3–5.

pageant's male judges and journalists were pelted with tomatoes, lettuce, and other rotten vegetables.[34] Activists thus engaged in a war of images on international television, fighting one spectacle—women parading in swimsuits—with another: "This was our moment to tell the whole world about feminism."[35] The protest's spectacle was designed to literally reclaim the gaze for women by disrupting the television broadcast.

In a similar way, the "white gaze," works to make non-Europeans visible in specific hierarchal ways: "For not only must the black man be black; he must be black in relation to the white man." Fanon tells the story of how when he was on a train in France, a white child cried out: "Look, a Negro! . . . Mama, see the Negro! I'm frightened!"[36] Fanon's reaction to "being dissected under white eyes" was to be "*fixed*" in "shame and self-contempt," as if photographed by the white gaze.[37] National beauty pageants can similarly provoke controversy when an "visible minority" is chosen to represent the nation; racist reactions were provoked in 2017 when an ethnically Filipino woman was crowned Miss Belgium, in 2005 when the first Muslim woman was crowned Miss England, in 1996 when a black woman was selected to be Miss Italy, and so on.[38] These are not just individual cases, but show the workings of what W. E. B. Du Bois called "The Color Line" in (inter)national identity construction projects.[39] The white gaze thus is related to the "colonial gaze," in which the Occident figures the Orient as part of imperial self/Other relations: the West is strong, masculine, rational, and scientific only when contrasted against the East as weak, feminine, mysterious, and exotic.[40]

The entangled tension of gender and race in beauty pageants becomes clearer when we see how they have been instrumental in nation-building and state-

---

[34] Sally Alexander, "Miss World: My Protest at 1970 Beauty Pageant," BBC World Service: Witness (March 5, 2014) http://www.bbc.co.uk/news/av/magazine-26437815/miss-world-my-protest-at-1970-beauty-pageant (accessed February 23, 2018); Jo Robinson, "Miss World Protest," British Library (no date) http://www.bl.uk/learning/histcitizen/sisterhood/clips/bodies-minds-and-spirits/body-experience/143246.html (accessed February 23, 2018); also see Beatrix Campbell, "Another World," *The Guardian* (November 19, 2010) https://www.theguardian.com/lifeandstyle/2010/nov/19/feminists-disrupted-miss-world-tv (accessed February 23, 2018).

[35] Robinson, "Miss World Protest."

[36] Frantz Fanon, *Black Skin, White Masks* (New York: Grove Press, 2008), pp. 82–83, 84; also see Malek Alloula, *The Colonial Harem* (Minneapolis: University of Minnesota Press, 1986).

[37] Fanon, *Black Skin, White Masks*, 87; emphasis in original.

[38] "Newly-crowned Miss Belgium Faces Racist Abuse Online," *The Straits Times* (January 20, 2018) http://www.straitstimes.com/world/europe/newly-crowned-miss-belgium-faces-racist-abuse-online (accessed February 23, 2018); "First Muslim Miss England Crowned," BBC News (September 4, 2005) http://news.bbc.co.uk/1/hi/england/4212412.stm (accessed February 23, 2018); Celestine Bohlen, "Que Pasa, Miss Italy?," *New York Times* (September 15, 1996).

[39] W. E. B. Du Bois, *The Souls of Black Folk* (New York: New American Library, 1903), p. 19.

[40] See Edward Said, *Orientalism* (New York: Vintage, 2004).

building.[41] As I explain in detail elsewhere,[42] in the 1930s the Miss Siam contest—Thailand was called Siam until 1939—was an important part of nation-building and state-building. After the overthrow of the absolute monarchy in 1932, the new civilian and military elite cultivated political legitimacy for the new constitutional monarchy through a constitution festival, which included the first Miss Siam pageant on Constitution Day in 1934. As Supatra Kopkijsuksakul explains, Miss Siam served as a "media of entertainment to attract the attention of people to come to the Constitutional Festival" because the contest itself "promoted democracy by selecting a beauty to grace the constitution."[43] The pageant was organized by a newly created section of the Interior Ministry called the "Office of the Miss Siam Pageant," which made searching for beautiful women an official duty of (male) government officials. The responsibilities of Miss Siam included not only the expected charity work and entertainment activities, but also attending parliamentary functions and promoting state policy.[44] Hence the pageant was a site of nation-building and state-building in which the hereditary king was replaced by a beauty queen who was chosen by the people and worked for the nation.

The Interior Ministry's Office of the Miss Siam Pageant also highlighted the international importance of the beauty queen: "Miss Siam is the representative of Thai women to show the world that Siam has Miss Siam who is as beautiful as the beauty queens of other countries."[45] In 1965 Miss Thailand won the Miss Universe pageant, and the director of the Tourist Authority of Thailand directly linked beauty pageant success with Bangkok's foreign policy goal of securing further security guarantees from the United States in the context of the Vietnam War.[46] The Miss Siam pageant thus used the visual spectacle of beautiful women to craft the new Thai nation and the modern Thai state for both domestic and foreign policy. It also shows how the male gaze of the Thai administrative state was able to mobilize women and men as active national citizens (as opposed to loyal royal subjects).

Beauty pageants in Jamaica show an even more complex entanglement of the male gaze and the colonial gaze. As Rochelle Rowe explains, Jamaican elites in government and the media very deliberately employed beauty pageants to build a proper postcolonial identity.[47] The Miss Jamaica contest was first held in 1929. But

[41] See Craig, *Ain't I a Beauty Queen?*, 5; Lewis, *Muslim Fashion*, 5.

[42] See William A. Callahan, "Beauty Queens, National Identity and Transnational Politics," in *Cultural Governance and Resistance in Pacific Asia*, 43–70.

[43] Supatra Kopkijsuksakul, "Kan Prakuat Nangsao Thai (B.E. 2477–2530)" [Miss Thailand contest: 1934–1987] (master's thesis, Thammasat University, Bangkok, 1988), p. 49. Many thanks to Sumalee Bumroongsook for alerting me to Supatra's thesis and translating key passages.

[44] Supatra, "Kan Prakuat Nangsao Thai," 118.

[45] Quoted in Supatra, "Kan Prakuat Nangsao Thai," 59.

[46] Supatra, "Kan Prakuat Nangsao Thai," 158.

[47] Rochelle Rowe, "'Glorifying the Jamaican Girl': The 'Ten Types—One People' Beauty Contest, Racialized Femininities, and Jamaican Nationalism," *Radical History Review* 103 (2009):36–58.

Miss Ebony   Miss Mahogany   Miss Satinwood   Miss Allspice   Miss Sandalwood   Miss Golden Apple   Miss Jasmine   Miss Pomegranate   Miss Lotus   Miss Appleblossom

A spectrum of Jamaican beauty displayed before a cannon of Fort Charles, Port Royal. 'Ten types one people' was the heading of this contest, run in 1955 as part of the 'Jamaica 300' celebrations

Figure 8.3 "Ten Types—One People" pageant winners (1955). Source: Peter Abrahams, *Jamaica: An Island Mosaic* (London: The Stationery Office, 1957). Courtesy The Stationery Office

this beauty queen did not represent Jamaica very well; the pageant was a private affair run by the island's upper-class, white, British planters and merchants, who typically chose their daughters to be the beauty queen.[48] In 1955 a rival beauty pageant emerged as part of the "Jamaica 300" festival that commemorated the island's three centuries as a British colony. Rather than directly compete with Miss Jamaica by crowning a rival beauty queen, the contest offered a new postcolonial way to visualize Jamaica. The "Ten Types—One People" pageant was designed to find and display beauties according to ten racial and ethnic categories, such as "Miss Apple Blossom" for women of European parentage, "Miss Allspice" for women of part Indian parentage, and "Miss Ebony" for women of black complexion (see figure 8.3).[49] Interestingly, while most beauty pageants choose a single person to represent the nation—such as Miss Jamaica—this contest simultaneously crowned ten beauty queens, and Miss Ebony was equal to Miss Apple Blossom. The pageant was seen as progressive because it not only encouraged black and colored women to participate,

[48] Rowe, " 'Glorifying the Jamaican Girl,' " 40.
[49] Rowe, " 'Glorifying the Jamaican Girl,' " 44.

it also created space for them to win. Young women in Jamaica thus "embraced the beauty contest format as a new means of challenging racial discrimination."[50]

This model of mixed-race national identity was not just for beauty pageants; the "Ten Types" pageant directly influenced the idea of a "racially harmonious" Jamaica, as seen in the slogan for the country's independence in 1962: "Out of Many, One People."[51] The duties of Jamaica's beauty queens were not confined to domestic nation-building. Soon after independence in 1962, the Miss Jamaica Nation pageant was created to celebrate black beauty queens. Its winner went to Africa as an "unofficial cultural ambassador" to share experiences with other new countries that were emerging from the British empire.[52]

As in Thailand, Jamaican pageants were organized by men; the new middle-class colored and black elite likewise "scour[ed] the countryside for Jamaica's hidden beauties."[53] The male gaze also reproduced the white/colonial gaze, as the Ten Types winners all "conform to a recognizable Western ideal. The selected beauty queens were all, unsurprisingly, slim and petite in frame"[54] (see figure 8.3). The criticism that the global beauty pageant industry reproduces European ideals of beauty rings true in Thailand as well. In 1984 the organizer of the Miss Thailand pageant noted that "[w]e must admit that the world is shrinking, and these changes affect Miss Thailand too. She cannot be sweetly beautiful as she used to be. She must be good in her figure, her personality and her language."[55] In the 1990s Euro-American beauty standards were promoted by the pageant's corporate sponsors: Colgate Palmolive, Catalina swimsuits, and Revlon makeup.[56] One reaction to such a foreign imposition is resistance to the West and its colonial gaze, as we saw with the global movement for modest fashion.[57] But in Thailand pageant organizers decided to adapt to the new international standard in order to better compete on the world stage. For example, while Miss Thailand 1994 looked great in the context of her Thai

---

[50] Rowe, " 'Glorifying the Jamaican Girl,' " 48. This is also the logic behind the Miss Black America Beauty pageant, which was launched in the United States in 1968 by the NAACP (Craig, *Ain't I a Beauty Queen?*, 3–6).

[51] Rowe, " 'Glorifying the Jamaican Girl,' " 53, 44, 36–37; also see M. Cynthia Oliver, *Queen of the Virgins: Pageantry and Black Womanhood in the Caribbean* (Jackson: University Press of Mississippi, 2009).

[52] Rowe, " 'Glorifying the Jamaican Girl,' " 49; also see Craig, *Ain't I a Beauty Queen?*, 45–64.

[53] Rowe, " 'Glorifying the Jamaican Girl,' " 43.

[54] Rowe, " 'Glorifying the Jamaican Girl,' " 44; also see Craig, *Ain't I a Beauty Queen?*, 5, 16.

[55] See Supatra, "Kan Prakuat Nangsao Thai," 246.

[56] Chin Ampornratana, Secretary to the Managing Director of BBTv Color Channel 7, interview with the author in Bangkok (October 27, 1994).

[57] For example, see Craig, *Ain't I a Beauty Queen?*, 5–6, 24–26; Madsen, "Performing Community through the Feminine Body"; M. G. G. Pillai, "West's Idea of Beauty Ignores Rest of the World," *Bangkok Post* (February 22, 1995):5.

rivals, Thai commentators concluded that she did poorly on the global stage at the Miss Universe pageant because she was too short.

Patterns of the male gaze and the colonial gaze emerge in different ways with the veil in revolutionary Algeria. Fanon's arguments in "Algeria Unveiled" show how the veil was seen as a strategic weapon in the resistance against the French colonial state. The veil here is not a constant of either tradition or modernity, because the "attitude toward the veil underwent modifications during the revolution."[58] Fanon first narrates the "traditional" role of the veil in traditional Algeria, as a sartorial practice that protected women in their preferred home life. The French colonial state, he explains, pictured Algerian women as "humiliated, sequestered, [and] cloistered" and worked to de-veil them in the name of emancipation. France's real objective, according to Fanon, was to "convert the woman, [by] winning her over to foreign values," which would "destroy [the] structure of Algerian society [and its] capacity for resistance."[59]

Initially, France's de-veiling strategy produced resistance because it "strengthened traditional patterns of behavior" among Algerian women.[60] But as the revolution progressed, the issues shifted from the grand ideologies of identity politics to the sensible politics and pragmatic tactics of revolutionary action. Indeed, the veil evolved from being the sign of traditional modesty to be deployed as revolutionary armament. According to Fanon, originally women were excluded from the liberation struggle.[61] Hence he praises them for sacrificing their modesty for the revolution by going outside the home and outside the Casbah to carry messages and guns under the cover of their veils. Fanon then praises women for sacrificing their modesty even more when they are required to change into "Western" clothes—short skirts, sleeveless dresses—so as to move more freely in the European part of Algiers. Interestingly, Gillo Pontecorvo's *The Battle of Algiers* (1966) visualizes Fanon's arguments by showing how veiled women could pass through checkpoints more easily; after that strategy was discovered, Algerian women de-veiled to deliver bombs to the European city.[62]

The film visualizes this transformation from modest to "European" by showing three women de-veiling, cutting their hair, applying make-up, dressing in short skirts, and as Pontecorvo explains, "generally assuming the look of the French women."[63]

---

[58] Fanon, "Algeria Unveiled," 47.

[59] Fanon, "Algeria Unveiled," 39, 37.

[60] Fanon, "Algeria Unveiled," 49.

[61] This point is contested; Minne argues that women were involved in resistance from the very beginning. See Daniele Djamila Amarane Minne, "Women at War," *Interventions* 9:3 (2007):340–349.

[62] Gillo Pontecorvo, dir., *The Battle of Algiers* (Casbah Film, 1966). For a discussion of the relation between Fanon's "Algeria Unveiled" and Pontecorvo's film, see Lindsey Moore, "The Veil of Nationalism: Frantz Fanon's 'Algeria Unveiled' and Gillo Pontecorvo's *The Battle of Algiers*," *Kunapipi* 25:2 (2003):56–73.

[63] Gillo Pontecorvos, dir., *Return to Algiers* (1992) https://youtu.be/tQvOeJ11iRA (accessed February 23, 2018); also see Minne, "Women at War."

Figure 8.4 De-veiled woman in *The Battle of Algiers* (1966).

The scene's strong audio drumbeat highlights that these women aren't dolling up for a date, but are arming to do battle. Figure 8.4 shows how this new sartorial performance enables a new body politics: the young woman in a sleeveless dress distracts French soldiers by flirting with them. As Fanon explains, "Carrying revolvers, grenades, hundreds of false identity cards or bombs, the unveiled Algerian woman moves like a fish in Western waters. The soldiers, the French patrols, smile at her as she passes, complements on her looks are heard here and there, but no one suspects that her suitcases contain the automatic pistol which will presently mow down four or five members of one of the patrols."[64] Then once this de-veiling strategy had run its course—that is, when French troops started to target immodest "Westernized" Algerian women—partisans re-veiled to conceal messages and arms under the folds of their revolutionary garments. As Fanon concludes, "[T]he veil was resumed, but stripped once and for all of its exclusively traditional dimension."[65]

Both Fanon and the film employ the visibility strategy, wherein the veil is a tactical tool that is deployed and withdrawn. As Fanon explains, "Removed and reassumed again and again, the veil has been manipulated, transformed into a technique of camouflage, into a means of struggle."[66] This is an exemplary case of the female body as the site of the dynamic politics of revealing and concealing. Yet although the anti-colonial arguments are strong, Fanon and the film both employ a paternalistic view of women. By manipulating both the male gaze and the colonial gaze for what is

[64] Fanon, "Algeria Unveiled," 58.
[65] Fanon, "Algeria Unveiled," 63.
[66] Fanon, "Algeria Unveiled," 61.

seen as the greater good of national liberation, un/veiling in revolutionary Algeria certainly was deployed for political resistance. But it also was a mode of what could be called a postcolonial male gaze. Hence veiling and beauty pageantry are used in similar ways by the new middle-class elite in Thailand, Jamaica, and Algeria to mobilize women in nation-building projects run by men, primarily for men. In other words, women's liberation was secondary to national liberation.[67] Malek Alloula's *The Colonial Harem* raises similar issues; the postcolonial critique of the postcards' combination of the colonial gaze and the male gaze is sharp. But reproducing images of naked Algerian women also provoked feminist criticism because it uncritically recycled the male gaze: men are still using images of women for their projects.[68]

State-led Cultural Governance and Resistance

As the previous section showed, sartorial politics is not merely a personal choice, but can be conditioned by the patriarchal politics of the male gaze and the imperial politics of the colonial gaze. The sartorial performances of veiling and beauty pageantry mobilize women to participate in nation-building, state-building, and even corporate brand-building. The locus of these activities has been moving from state policy to transnational corporate marketing strategies as part of a neoliberal trend since the 1970s.[69] Yet we also need to appreciate how state-led cultural governance has been reasserting itself—often simultaneously with corporate-led cultural governance—both in prescribing dress codes in some Middle Eastern countries and in proscribing them in some European countries. This section fleshes out how the choices women make in concealing and revealing their bodies are shaped by the state's radical intervention in the sensible politics of the everyday, which in turn excites collective and individual performances of resistance to state and corporate power. Here we turn from analysis informed by choice and structured by gazes to examine how structures and agents are mutually constituted through cultural governance and resistance.[70]

Saudi Arabia and Iran do not agree about much, but both have official dress codes for women and morality police to enforce them. According to Iran's Islamic establishment, the "hijab is protection from sin" for both women and men, and

---

[67] Moore, "The Veil of Nationalism"; Minne, "Women at War"; also see Craig, *Ain't I a Beauty Queen?*, 14.

[68] For example, see Mieke Bal, "The Politics of Citation," *Diacritics* 21:1 (1991):25–45.

[69] See Callahan, "Beauty Queens, National Identity and Transnational Politics."

[70] For a discussion of cultural governance, see Michael J. Shapiro, *Methods and Nations: Cultural Governance and the Indigenous Subject* (New York: Routledge, 2004); David Campbell, "Cultural Governance and Pictorial Resistance: Reflections on the Imaging of War," *Review of International Studies* 29 (2003):57–73; Callahan, *Cultural Governance and Resistance in Pacific Asia.*

the morality police see themselves as a "kind of hijab for the society of the Islamic Republic."[71] Rather than being an obstacle to public life, here the veil provides women with "security" to enable them to enter the public sphere, especially when society is seen as a space haunted by dangerous moral temptations.[72] Indeed, for many veils provide the security of a "mobile home," and to de-veil is to publicly reveal oneself as "naked."[73] The cultural logic also appeals to global self/Other relations: "pious Iran" versus "the Great Satan" of America. Sometimes it is directly invoked in international politics; in 2015 Iran's reformist president Hassan Rouhani was criticized for the loosening of morality rules as a way to attack his government's nuclear agreement with the Group of Six world powers.[74] Yet even within Iran, such fundamentalism lends itself to ridicule; as one young woman criticized the morality police: "[W]hat right do you have to say whether my hijab is proper or improper? Can you show me the hijab-o-meter they issued you when you took this job?"[75]

In *Headscarves and Hymens*, Mona Eltahawy recounts her personal experience of up-veiling and de-veiling in the wider context of everyday life in Egypt, London, and Saudi Arabia.[76] Many women celebrate the veil in terms of emancipation and security and criticize white Western feminists for exacerbating Islamophobia through their misunderstanding of the practice.[77] Thus when Eltahawy asks, "Why do you hate us?," one expects a similar East versus West argument. Eltahawy, however, reframes the issue to Arab men hating Arab women. For her, the veil is a concrete expression of patriarchal power relations, in which women are seen as the "walking embodiment of sin," and "clerics [are] obsessed with female orifices."[78] In this legalistic practice of the male gaze, morality police are not promoting piety, but rather cynically using their power to commit sexual harassment. At Islam's holiest site in Saudi Arabia, the veil didn't protect Eltahawy; rather, it actually enabled the police

---

[71] Marketa Hulpachova, "Hijab: A Woman's Rite of Passage in Iran," *The Guardian* (December 19, 2013) https://www.theguardian.com/world/iran-blog/2013/dec/19/iran-hijab-islamic-veil (accessed February 23, 2018); "Rouhani Clashes with Iranian Clergy over Women Arrested for 'Bad Hijab,'" *The Guardian* (May 27, 2015) https://www.theguardian.com/world/iran-blog/2015/may/27/iran-hijab-rouhani-versus-senior-clergy-enforcement (accessed February 23, 2018); also see Eltahawy, *Headscarves and Hymens*, 49.

[72] See Heath, *The Veil*; Eltahawy, *Headscarves and Hymens*, 34–35; Wagner et al., "The Veil and Muslim Women's Identity," 531; Hopkins and Greenwood, "Hijab, Visibility and the Performance of Identity," 444.

[73] Abu-Lughod, *Do Muslim Women Need Saving?*, 36; Eltahawy, *Headscarves and Hymens*, 46; Heath, "Introduction," 2, 14; Fanon, "Algeria Unveiled," 42, 43, 45.

[74] "Rouhani Clashes with Iranian Clergy."

[75] Cited in "Rouhani Clashes with Iranian Clergy."

[76] Eltahawy, *Headscarves and Hymens*.

[77] Abu-Lughod, *Do Muslim Women Need Saving?*; Scott, *The Politics of the Veil*; Heath, "Introduction," 1–2; Wagner et al., "The Veil and Muslim Women's Identity"; Hopkins and Greenwood, "Hijab, Visibility and the Performance of Identity."

[78] Eltahawy, *Headscarves and Hymens*, 10.

officer to grope her anonymously.[79] Likewise, the Islamic Republic's "cultural revolution," described in Marjane Satrapi's graphic novel *Persopolis*, shows how sartorial politics can be very personal and very threatening; debate among Iranian women was not between East and West, but between "the veil" and "freedom."[80]

Veiling is also politically charged in France. Curiously, much as in Iran and Saudi Arabia, the French state appeals to legally-defined dress codes to control veiling. In 2004 it banned girls from wearing headscarves in public schools, then in 2011 banned public burqa-wearing. Veil politics invaded the beaches in summer 2016 with the ban on burkinis—a modest-style swimsuit—in many French coastal resort towns.[81] Supporters of the veil bans argued that the veil is problematic not just as a practice, but conceptually as well; it poses a challenge both to the liberal ideological order of French secularism (*laïcité*, laicity) and to the liberal world order in the global war on terror. As in the feminist protest against Miss World in 1970, this concern was expressed in terms of "women's rights" and figured veils as a sign of female submission to the patriarchal culture of Islam. While many girls and women in France argued that they had freely chosen veiling, the counter-argument was that one cannot have free choice in such a male-dominated culture and society. Muslim girls, according to this logic, needed to be saved from their families and their community.

Here French feminists' resistance to what they see as the "male gaze" of Islamic patriarchy meets the resistance of some Muslim women to what they see as the "colonial gaze" of white French women.[82] This is not the first time that there has been a tension between anti-sexism and anti-racism movements. Intersectional politics also erupted at the Miss World pageant in 1970. The London Women's Liberation Workshop mocked the winner, Jennifer Hosten, for her "conventionality," yet Hosten explained that the contest gave her "opportunities to travel, study and work that, as a black woman from Grenada, she might otherwise not have had."[83] The tension had been even more manifest in 1968, when (predominantly white) feminists protested in Atlantic City against the Miss America pageant to fight sexism, while just down the boardwalk the NAACP launched the first Miss Black America pageant to fight racism.[84]

---

[79] Eltahawy, *Headscarves and Hymens*, 50–51.

[80] Marjane Satrapi, "The Veil," in *Persopolis* (London: Vintage, 2008).

[81] See Angelique Chrisafis, "French Mayors Refuse to Lift Burkini Ban Despite Court Ruling," *The Guardian* (August 28, 2016) https://www.theguardian.com/world/2016/aug/28/french-mayors-burkini-ban-court-ruling (accessed February 23, 2018).

[82] See Johanna Gullberg, "The Republic of Difference: Feminism and Anti-racism in the Parisian *Banlieues*" (PhD dissertation, Stockholm University, 2016).

[83] Mulvey, "The Spectacle of the Vulnerable," 3; Robinson, "Miss World Protest."

[84] Craig, *Ain't I a Beauty Queen?*, 3–22.

Back in France, debates about the veil ban often invoke a "clash of civilizations" logic that sees Islamic values and Western values as incompatible.[85] While it is popular to criticize Samuel P. Huntington's monolithic view of culture, a leading Muslim cleric actually agrees that Islam and laicity are incommensurable.[86] French president Jacques Chirac thus saw the headscarf as a "kind of aggression," and a state commission concluded that veils were part of Islam's "permanent guerrilla war against laicity."[87] This concern was not just domestic, but is part of a global visual economy of veiling: some feared that "the experience of Iran was about to be imported into France."[88] Indeed, this French concern over a cultural and political invasion of Islamism was the topic of Michel Houellebecq's novel *Submission* (2015).[89] Veil bans thus were criticized by many for exemplifying a deeper Islamophobic racism.[90]

Globally, many Muslims saw France's veil bans as an attack on Islam as a whole. Indeed, the crusade against the veil has Orientalist overtones. As we have seen, conquering the East by de-veiling Muslim women is a recurring Western male fantasy from the colonial period, which continues in the present. While the Muslim clerics may see unveiled women as "naked," this unveiling/naked dynamic is also found in paintings by Manet, Renoir, Matisse, and Picasso.[91] In the realm of popular culture, colonial Algeria produced a whole genre of postcards for French soldiers that showed unveiled women as naked.[92] More recently, the veil—and unveiling—has been a popular topic for cartoons in *Playboy* magazine.[93]

As in Iran and Saudi Arabia, where morality police see the absence of veils as a threat to moral order and social order, in France veiling has become a matter of cultural sovereignty, cultural governance, and resistance to it. Iranians resist by challenging the veil, and in France women resist by veiling. But the veil has also become a site of art, fashion, and satirical intervention in France. Princess Hijab uses graffiti art "to spark debates about fundamentalism and feminism" by drawing veils with a black marker pen on fashion posters in the Paris Metro (see figure 8.5).[94] As she

---

[85] Samuel P. Huntington, *The Clash of Civilizations and the Remaking of World Order* (New York: Simon & Schuster, 1996).

[86] Joppke, *Veil*, 31, 112–123.

[87] Cited in Joppke, *Veil*, 4, 47.

[88] Scott, *The Politics of the Veil*, 176.

[89] Michel Houellebecq, *Submission* (London: William Heinemann, 2015).

[90] Scott, *The Politics of the Veil*; Heath, *The Veil*.

[91] Heath, "Introduction," 14.

[92] Alloula, *The Colonial Harem*; also see Fanon, "Algeria Unveiled," 45.

[93] Faegheh Shirazi, *The Veil Unveiled: The Hijab in Modern Culture* (Miami: University Press of Florida, 2001), pp. 39–61; also see Heath, "Introduction," 11.

[94] Angelique Chrisafis, "Princess Hijab: Underground Resistance," *The Guardian* (November 11, 2010)   http://www.theguardian.com/artanddesign/gallery/2010/nov/10/princess-hijab-graffiti-france-metro (accessed February 23, 2018); Annelies Moors, "NiqaBitch and Princess Hijab: Niqab Activism, Satire and Street Art," *Feminist Review* 98 (2011):128–135; *Princess Hijab's "Veiling Art"*.

Figure 8.5 Visual cultural resistance by Princess Hijab. Source: Anonymous artist, *The Guardian*

explains, "When I see an interesting billboard or model that I find unusually arresting, I feel the impulse to hijabize, . . . to draw a black veil on the model."[95] This "hijabization" of public images not only questions the role of the state in everyday sartorial practices, but also targets the "visual terrorism" of the advertising industry for promoting a consumerist view of life and politics.[96]

As we saw at the beginning of this chapter, two young women who call themselves NiqaBitch protested against France's veil bans through a video of themselves walking around Paris dressed in niqab that concealed their faces and upper bodies, along with hot pants and high heels that revealed their bare legs. The video shows how they get "thumbs up" support from many on the street as they walk around central Paris, pausing at many government buildings. The audio-visual experience

---

[95] Princess Hijab in *Princess Hijab's "Veiling Art"*.
[96] Cited in Moors, "NiqaBitch and Princess Hijab," 134.

underlines both the fun and the protest: the video is edited to the rhythm of the Beastie Boys anthem that declares, "If you don't like it, then hey fuck you!"[97]

Interestingly, their reception at France's Ministry of Immigration and National Identity is mixed: the policeman guarding this site tells them to move along, while the policewoman engages them in a conversation that highlights the sensible politics of the everyday:

> POLICEWOMAN: I love your outfit, is it to do with the new law?
> NIQABITCH: Yes, we want to de-dramatize the situation.
> POLICEWOMAN: It's brilliant. Can I take a photo?

Here timing was crucial; when the law went into effect six months later, the same policewoman would be obliged to fine them for the same veiling activity.

Princess Hijab's guerrilla art and NiqaBitch's performance art are both fascinating sites of resistance that mix the sacred and the secular to question how sensible politics works in France. Power here is expressed by state control over visual practice, specifically legally prescribing a sartorial performance. Likewise, we have two examples of young women visually expressing their protest against state control over their everyday lives. They show how veils work as material artifacts to performatively provoke affective communities of sense: "Operating within a visual field that requires little linguistic competence and using Internet infrastructures to circulate their work, they are able to reach a global public."[98] Both cultural governance and resistance thus are more than local, as they are part of a global political-economy of visual images and multisensory artifacts.

The debate over veiling/unveiling in Europe and the Middle East can be summarized as debates between women and men and between East and West. Many supporters of veiling see it as a practice that positively distinguishes Eastern/Islamic/Arabic communities from Western ones. Many critics of veiling call for the liberation of all women from patriarchy. This figuration makes a certain amount of sense when the debate is located in Europe and the Middle East. But what happens when we relocate it to China, a non-Western country whose Northwest frontier is home to the Muslim Uyghur ethnic group? How does it complicate the notions of Islamic modernity as an alternative to the West, as well as struggles within liberalism?

In many ways the situation in Northwest China offers the familiar cultural governance/cultural resistance dynamic that we saw in France. Veils were not a major issue until the 2000s, when Uyghur women started re-veiling as part of the global

---

[97] NiqaBitch, *NiqaBitch Shakes Paris*; Nesrine Malik, "NiqaBitch Unveil Themselves in Paris," *The Guardian* (October 7, 2010); NiqaBitch, "Hot Pants and Niqabs."

[98] Moors, "NiqaBitch and Princess Hijab," 128–129.

Islamic revival that includes the global Islamic modest fashion trend.[99] Beijing became particularly concerned about this visual artifact after 2009, as riots erupted in Xinjiang between Uyghurs and Han Chinese. "Islam" in Xinjiang thus was increasingly understood as a foreign threat to China's national security and cultural sovereignty, while the veil was seen as a visual provocation of what Beijing calls the "Three Evil Forces" of separatism, extremism, and terrorism.[100]

As in Iran and France, visual performances and sensible politics are seen as a legitimate site for state intervention. Sartorial engineering as a mode of cultural governance is not new in China. During the Cultural Revolution (1966–1976), people were obliged to wear the military-inspired Mao suit. In 2001 the "Han clothing movement" emerged as a grassroots nativist movement to resist what is seen as the Manchu "bastardization" of Chinese civilization.[101] While sartorial engineering in Xinjiang is a local issue, it is also located in the global visual politics of national security. The concern is foreign terrorism, and the goal is social stability along China's long Central Asian frontier. Since 2011 the veiling practices of Uyghur women have been a topic of intense study by Han men and women in the party-state.[102] The concern is that vulnerable women are being "brainwashed" into wearing the veil by foreign fundamentalists and their local supporters. De-veiling thus is presented as an issue of women's liberation, which has the added benefit of fighting the "Three Evil Forces."[103]

In addition to proscribing veils, in 2011 the Xinjiang government launched a five-year, $8 million Beauty Engineering Project to prescribe the proper attire for the veil-free "new style woman": a multicolored *ätläs-fabric* dress, a doppa hat, and braided hair (see figure 8.6).[104] As an official newspaper explains:

---

[99] Lewis, *Muslim Fashion.*

[100] See Zunyou Zhou, "Chinese Strategy for De-Radicalization," *Terrorism and Political Violence* (June 9, 2017):1–23, https://doi.org/10.1080/09546553.2017.1330199; Leibold and Grose, "Islamic Veiling in Xinjiang," 80; Maya Wang, *"Eradicating Ideological Viruses": China's Campaign of Repression Against Xinjiang's Muslims* (New York: Human Rights Watch, 2018).

[101] See Kevin Carrico, *The Great Han: Race, Nationalism and Tradition in China Today* (Stanford, CA: Stanford University Press, 2017).

[102] See Jin Wei, "Burqas, Hijabs and Beards in the Governance of Xinjiang," University of Nottingham, China Policy Institute Blog (April 29, 2015) http://blogs.nottingham.ac.uk/chinapolicyinstitute/2015/04/29/regulating-burqas-hijabs-and-beards-to-push-or-pull/ (accessed December 11, 2017); James Leibold, "Surveillance in Xinjiang: Ethnic Sorting, Coercion, and Inducement," *Journal of Contemporary China* (May 31, 2019):1–15, https://doi.org/10.1080/10670564.2019.1621529.

[103] Leibold and Grose, "Islamic Veiling in Xinjiang," 89.

[104] See Xinjiang Uyghur Autonomous Regional Government, "Liangli gongcheng: Zuo liangli nuxing, zhanda mei Xinjiang" [Beauty Engineering Project: Make beautiful women, display a beautiful Xinjiang], http://www.ts.cn/special/2011_Beautiful/node_93130.htm (accessed December 11, 2017); Leibold and Grose, "Islamic Veiling in Xinjiang," 89ff.

Figure 8.6 Official mural for the Beauty Engineering Project, Kashgar. Source: BBC, "The Colourful Propaganda of Xinjiang" (January 12, 2015) http://www.bbc.co.uk/news/world-asia-china-30722268 (accessed December 11, 2017).

> Veils and long robes block a women's splendor and beauty.... Women represent the love and beauty of the world and they should personify beauty and serve as emissaries of love. Wrapping oneself up is not only not beautifying, it can also destroy one's body and mind. One's heart and soul can wither due to long periods in the dark.[105]

While fashion is a site of cultural resistance in France, it is a site of cultural governance in Xinjiang, where the official Xinjiang Women's Federation organizes fashion shows that encourage women to "expose their pretty face and allow their beautiful hair to flow free."[106] The *People's Daily* also celebrates such sartorial engineering: "The audience enjoyed a visual feast with charming models wearing dresses that are both ethnic and fashionable."[107] The goal is to "make beautiful women, to

---

[105] Quoted in Leibold and Grose, "Islamic Veiling in Xinjiang," 89–90.

[106] "Xinjiang Promotes Beauty Project in Communities," http://womenofchina/html1/projects/project/15/2485-1.htm; "'Beauty Project' Garment Design Competition Held in Xinjiang," *People's Daily* (November 5, 2015) http://en.people.cn/n/2015/1105/c98649-8971893.html (accessed December 11, 2017); United Front Work Department of the Chinese Communist Party Central Committee, "Xinjiang nuxing 'liangli gongcheng' wu zhounian chengguo zhan zai Kashen juban" [An exhibition for the five-year anniversary of the Xinjiang Women's "Beauty Engineering Project" held in Kashgar], Tianshan wang (June 27, 2016) http://www.zytzb.gov.cn/tzb2010/S1824/201606/016b28c620d94cd8bb3a9bca81bca197.shtml (accessed December 11, 2017); Jin, "Burqas, Hijabs and Beards"; Leibold and Grose "Islamic Veiling in Xinjiang," 89–90.

[107] "'Beauty Project' Garment Design Competition."

display a beautiful Xinjiang."[108] The Beauty Engineering Project reaped benefits at the national level in 2013, when Mikray, a non-veiled Uyghur woman, won the Miss China beauty pageant and went on to be a top model for Beauty Engineering Project–style attire.[109] This sartorial engineering also gained international exposure in 2012 in the China-Eurasia Expo's fashion show, which is now held every other year in Xinjiang's capital city, Urumqi.

Certainly in China there is a wide range of resistance to both up-veiling and de-veiling. As James Leibold and Timothy Grose show, some Uyghur agree that veils are an improper import from the Arab world, and some women complain that they have been pressured by their husbands to veil. However, rather than see it as foreign and backward, many Uyghur women celebrate veiling as an important activity in global Islam's modern cosmopolitan modest fashion.[110] The Chinese case also shows the problems of cultural sovereignty in both domestic and international politics. Beijing responds to threats to cultural sovereignty not just by controlling national identity by prescribing what (not) to wear to be "Chinese," but by controlling ethnic/religious identity by positively defining the proper ethnic dress for Uyghur women. Here material visual culture (i.e., the veil) is not simply a problem; as the Beauty Engineering Project shows, an alternative material visual culture is the solution. In a fascinating twist, the Beauty Engineering Project brings together the two modes of concealing and revealing juxtaposed in this chapter—veils and beauty pageants—in ways that resonate with NiqaBitch, Princess Hijab, and modest fashion.

Beijing's strategy thus is interesting because it combines the Iranian proscription of female fashion with the French prescription of female fashion: the visual culture of the veil is presented as the problem, and the visual culture of an alternative "authentic" sartorial form is presented as the solution. Rather than relying on just legal measures to ban veils, as in France, Beijing looks to its own kind of morality police. In the early 2010s tens of thousands of party cadres were sent around Xinjiang to urge women to discard the "regressive fad" of veiling. This campaign was positive in the sense that women who de-veiled were rewarded with cash prizes. It was negative in the sense that the party cadres created intelligence files to monitor uncooperative

---

[108] Xinjiang Uyghur Autonomous Regional Government, "Beauty Engineering Project."

[109] Huang Lina, "Nu daxuesheng mire ayi: He shijian saipao de jianzhi mote" [Female college student Mikray: Part-time model who races against time], Tianshan wang (March 7, 2015) http://news.hexun.com/2015-03-07/173835037.html (accessed December 11, 2017); Kubanjan Samat, dir., *Bainian qian Zhongguo Xinjiang 13 ge diqu fushi* [Clothing in 13 regions of Xinjiang, China from one hundred years ago] (September 3, 2017) https://www.youtube.com/watch?v=SVJCKrg6JG8&featu re=youtu.be (accessed December 11, 2017); "Gaoqing: Motezhe Xinjiang nuxing 'liangli gongcheng' fuzhuang douyan" [HD: Models of Xinjiang women's Beauty Engineering Project], Zhongguo xinwen wang (November 6, 2015) http://leaders.people.com.cn/n/2015/1106/c58278-27785534.html (accessed December 11, 2017).

[110] Leibold and Grose, "Islamic Veiling in Xinjiang," 98–100.

women. Likewise, citizens who reported veiled women to the authorities were rewarded, and stores that sold cloth suitable for making veils were penalized.[111]

While the Beauty Engineering Project generally focused on persuasion, in 2015 the banning of public veil-wearing in Urumqi signified the shift to a much more coercive strategy.[112] The party-state's tactics also include the "Marrying-up and Becoming Kin" campaign, which mobilizes Han Chinese cadres to go and live with Uyghur families in order to promote "inter-ethnic mingling" and "ethnic harmony."[113] Through such intense everyday surveillance, Uyghur women are disciplined to de-veil and wear approved clothing. After Xi Jinping intensified the crackdown in 2017—declaring that China needs to build a "Great Wall of Iron" in Xinjiang[114]—the situation became a humanitarian disaster. More than one million people, or over 11 percent of Xinjiang's adult Muslim population, have been incarcerated in "re-education camps" for things such as having a long beard or wearing a veil.[115] Although these anti-veiling/pro-new-ethnic-clothing campaigns aim to win the hearts and minds of Muslim women, one consequence is the fraying of Xinjiang's social fabric. As James Leibold explains, such surveillance and control creates mistrust beyond target groups, causing "husbands to mistrust their wives; sisters their brothers; Uyghurs other Uyghurs; and Party officials one another."[116] This assault on Muslims in China continues, and Chapter 11 examines its surveillance politics.

Like other countries, the Chinese party-state seeks to nail down the meaning of the veil through official definition and moral policing, and as in other countries, the more it seeks to enforce a stable meaning, the more up-veiling/de-veiling resistance it creates. Once again, culture, visuality, and global politics bleed into each other. But the Chinese experience complicates the East/West framing of the debate in unexpected ways, making us think again about the proper role of visual images and multisensory artifacts in state/society relations. Finally, this experience shows how China is not able to escape the political problems that we usually trace to "the West."

---

[111] Jin, "Burqas, Hijabs and Beards"; Leibold and Grose, "Islamic Veiling in Xinjiang," 95.

[112] "The City of Urumqi Prohibition on Wearing Items That Mask the Face or Robe the Body," translated by Timothy Grose and James Leibold (February 4, 2015) http://www.chinafile.com/reporting-opinion/features/city-urumqi-prohibition-wearing-items-mask-face-or-robe-body (accessed April 19, 2019).

[113] Leibold, "Surveillance in Xinjiang," 11; Darren Byler and Timothy Grose, "China's Surveillance Laboratory," Dissent (October 31, 2018) https://www.dissentmagazine.org/online_articles/chinas-surveillance-laboratory (accessed March 87, 2019).

[114] "China's Xi Calls for 'Great Wall of Iron' to Safeguard Restive Xinjiang," Reuters (March 10, 2017) https://www.reuters.com/article/us-china-security-xinjiang-idUSKBN16H04J (accessed April 19, 2–19).

[115] Adrian Zenz, "'Thoroughly Reforming Them Towards a Healthy Heart Attitude': China's Political Re-education Campaign in Xinjiang," Central Asian Survey 38:1 (2019):122.

[116] Leibold, "Surveillance in Xinjiang," 14.

Beijing's focus on "beauty" as the measure of female value underlines how this national security project is ordered by the "male gaze." It is also culturally governed by China's own "colonial gaze," which promotes Han Chinese beauty standards in Xinjiang. Indeed, there is a long history of Chinese men fantasizing about "conquering" Uyghur women as part of imperial governance, and Uyghur women are now being encouraged to build inter-ethnic harmony by marrying Han men.[117]

Conclusion: Visibility and Visuality in Veiling and Beauty Pageantry

This chapter explores the complex body politics of race, gender, and faith through the unlikely juxtaposition of veiling and beauty pageantry. It employs the conceptual dynamic of concealing/revealing to analyze how various groups—women and men, states and corporations—expend considerable resources negotiating, performing, legislating, policing, and resisting such sartorial practices. Using examples from Europe, the Middle East, and Asia, Chapter 8 first decodes how they take on meaning as an individual choice, then how the discursive structures of the male gaze and the colonial gaze can structure these choices. It then examines state projects of sartorial engineering to consider how structures and agents are mutually constituted through cultural governance and resistance.

As we have seen, it is hard to nail down the meaning of the veil; it means different things to different people, in different times and places. Many analysts thus conclude that we should not be "obsessed" with veiling because it distracts us from the real issues of the day: the physical violence and poverty suffered by women,[118] racism in the West,[119] and the political contradictions that define the liberal polity.[120] Such analysis replays many of the ideological arguments of the twentieth century, in which visual images were seen by many critical scholars as a distraction from the true nature of class, race, and humanity in the ideologies of communism, fascism, and liberal democracy. Rather than seek to clarify the essence of these grand ideological narratives, we need to appreciate that the provocation of veiling and beauty pageants shows how politics can move us in visceral ways in affective communities of sense.

[117] See James A. Millward, "A Uyghur Muslim in Qianlong's Court: The Meaning of the Fragrant Concubine," *Journal of Asian Studies* 53:2 (1994):427–458; Darren Byler, "Uyghur Love in a Time of Interethnic Marriage," SupChina (August 7, 2019) https://supchina.com/2019/08/07/uyghur-love-in-a-time-of-interethnic-marriage/ (accessed August 23, 2019).

[118] Heath, "Introduction," 14.

[119] Abu-Lughod, *Do Muslim Women Need Saving?*; Scott, *The Politics of the Veil*; Heath, *The Veil*; Lewis, *Muslim Fashion*.

[120] Joppke, *Veil*.

Awrah, the video about young London women's experience of up-veiling and de-veiling, is interesting because it is more than the text. While these women discuss the very serious topics of faith, belonging, and politics, the video shows them not as ideologues, but as people who have fun in the sensible politics of everyday life. The protest at the 1970 Miss World pageant shows activists' visceral revulsion to this sexist spectacle in ways that complement the meaning of their powerful slogan: "We're not beautiful, we're not ugly, we're angry!" NiqaBitch's mixed experience at France's Ministry of Immigration and National Identity seems to exemplify Rancière's political aesthetics. The policeman literally "polices" the hegemonic partition of the sensible by telling the women to move along, nothing to see here. The policewoman, on the other hand, repartitions the sensible to highlight the levity and the gravity of their visual performance: "I love your outfit, is it to do with the new law? . . . Can I take a photo?"

The analysis of taking the veil and competing in beauty pageants suggests that these activities make participants move and feel differently. On the one hand, veiling and beauty pageantry provoke nonverbal reactions that make people see women differently. As a young woman in London recounts: "The first thing that you see when you look at me is my headscarf. So automatically you know that I'm Muslim. Even before I even say anything to you."[121] In a similar way, Lily declares, "I'm not a typical beauty queen-type. I believe I was crowned Miss Thailand China Cosmos [2013] because of my wisdom."[122]

But rather than focus on the viewer's experience and thus limit our analysis to visibility/invisibility as a problem to be overcome, it is also important to highlight women's multisensory bodily experiences, especially when veiling and beauty pageantry make them move and feel differently. As Fanon and *The Battle of Algiers* show, up-veiling, de-veiling, and re-veiling make women move and feel in new ways, for a new body politics. In "Algeria Unveiled," Fanon discusses women and the veil not just in terms of tactics (as considered earlier in the chapter), but in terms of bodily transformation. Behind the veil, he notes, women are at home physically, socially, and bodily: "The veil covers the body and disciplines it, tempers it. . . . The veil protects, reassures, isolates."[123] To leave the home unveiled, young women needed to "overcome inner resistances" because of the hostile reaction from men who saw unveiled women as "naked."[124] *The Battle of Algiers* visualizes this uneasy conversion from modest to activist by showing how thoughtful women are when they de-veil, cut their hair, apply make-up, and change into short skirts. Importantly, there is no dialogue in this scene; the characters thus do not tell us how they feel, instead showing us what they can do.[125]

---

[121] Nafisa Bakkar in Steadman et al., *Awrah*; also see Eltahawy, *Headscarves and Hymens*, 35.
[122] Interview with Lily Chaweewan Chongsakjarenkul.
[123] Fanon, "Algeria Unveiled," 59.
[124] Fanon, "Algeria Unveiled," 52–53.
[125] Minne, "Women at War," 347.

This transformation is not just of the body, but of bodily movements, such as learning a new way to walk: "Having been accustomed to confinement, her body did not have the normal mobility before a limitless horizon of avenues, of unfolded sidewalks, of houses, of people dodged or bumped into."[126] To overcome this, the new revolutionary woman "quickly has to invent new dimensions for her body, new means of muscular control. She has to create for herself an attitude of unveiled-woman-outside."[127] The successful transformation is astounding for Fanon: "The shoulders of the unveiled woman are thrust back with easy freedom. She walks with a graceful, measured stride, neither too fast nor too slow. Her legs are bare, not confined by the veil, given back to themselves, and her hips are free."[128] As we saw with the woman flirting at the checkpoint, the confident body politics of the newly de-veiled women is clear in *The Battle of Algiers* (see figure 8.4). Fanon concludes that through this experience, the Algerian woman "relearns her body, re-establishes it in a totally revolutionary fashion. This new dialectic of the body and of the world is primary in the case of one revolutionary woman."[129] The point here is not that women are "emancipated" when they de-veil. Rather, these experiences show how women can be empowered through both up-veiling and de-veiling performances, because "the necessities of combat give rise in Algerian society to new attitudes, to new modes of action, to new ways."[130]

Certainly we should be careful about drawing strong conclusions from Fanon's "Algeria Unveiled"; it is a polemical work about women written by a man for a liberation struggle that was dominated by men.[131] A recent survey of young women's experiences of taking the veil in Britain thus is helpful for exploring how you don't just take the veil; the veil takes you, too, in a social performance of sensible politics.[132] On the one hand, the survey confirms the experience of the "white British Muslim convert" seen at the beginning of the chapter: women up-veil to have their faith recognized on the street by other Muslims in a shared affective community of sense.[133] And as in revolutionary Algeria, the veil is used by women "to manage the degree to which men (Muslim and non-Muslim) oriented to them in terms of their physical attractiveness."[134] More important, many young Muslim women reported how taking the veil changed their behavior; because you are seen as an "ambassador of Islam, . . . you have to watch your own etiquette."[135] Numerous people reported

---

[126] Fanon, "Algeria Unveiled," 49.
[127] Fanon, "Algeria Unveiled," 59.
[128] Fanon, "Algeria Unveiled," 58.
[129] Fanon, "Algeria Unveiled," 59.
[130] Fanon, "Algeria Unveiled," 64; also see Moore, "The Veil of Nationalism," 60.
[131] For a critical view see Minne, "Women at War"; Moore, "The Veil of Nationalism."
[132] Hopkins and Greenwood, "Hijab, Visibility and the Performance of Identity."
[133] Hopkins and Greenwood, "Hijab, Visibility and the Performance of Identity," 441.
[134] Hopkins and Greenwood, "Hijab, Visibility and the Performance of Identity," 443.
[135] Hopkins and Greenwood, "Hijab, Visibility and the Performance of Identity," 443.

that visibility as a Muslim woman helped them to avoid the temptations of boys and liquor at university:

> It's weird how [up-veiling] changes your whole you know thinking and stuff. It's quite good. And it's good in the way that you, before doing something, when you've got a hijab on you actually think twice you know whereas if I didn't wear hijab I would just do whatever.[136]

The veil thus works to encourage self-monitoring and self-discipline.[137] While this survey concludes that veils are an identity performance for British Muslims, we can also highlight the productive body politics provoked by veils. More than changing thinking, veils are also shaping and changing bodily performances in ways similar to those described by Fanon and seen in *The Battle of Algiers*.

This productive sensible politics of body performance likewise emerges in beauty pageantry. On the one hand, when conducting interviews I found that beauty queens do not like to be filmed without the armor of their gown, sash, and crown. On the other hand, as part of the pageantry process contestants learn how to move and act differently. Lily described her four weeks' training for the Miss Thailand Chinese Cosmos pageant as "boot camp," which was highlighted as a segment of the contest's television broadcast.[138] In my own filmed interview with Lily, she shares this bodily knowledge by teaching her friends how to properly smile, walk, and pose.

The feature film *Miss Congeniality* (2000) and the experience of Areeya Chumsai (Miss Thailand 1994) both confirm the parallel body politics of beauty pageants and military training. In *Miss Congeniality* the main character, Gracie, is forced to transform herself from a highly-trained FBI agent into a highly-trained beauty queen. The film shows how she painfully (and comically) learns how to wear a tight dress, walk in high heels, and lose weight for the pageant. In the end, Gracie successfully learns how to walk and act like a "lady," who admires the "discipline" of her fellow contestants.[139] Areeya pursued the opposite trajectory: after training to transform herself from a journalist into a beauty queen in 1994, in 1998 she took a job teaching at Thailand's military academy that required her to go to an actual boot camp. Like Gracie learning to wear a tight dress, Areeya explains how she "felt powerful and

---

[136] Hopkins and Greenwood, "Hijab, Visibility and the Performance of Identity," 444–445.

[137] Also see Gökarıksel and Secor, "The Veil, Desire, and the Gaze," 188–190.

[138] See *Miss Thailand Chinese Cosmos 2013, Part 2/7*, Bangkok: Channel 7 TV (July 18, 2013) https://www.youtube.com/watch?v=XotXQt1ALcY (accessed February 23, 2018).

[139] Donald Petrie, dir., *Miss Congeniality* (Castle Rock, 2000); Madsen, "Performing Community through the Feminine Body," 3–5.

proud" learning how to properly wear the army uniform. Likewise, she describes the muscle-memory that recruits have to develop to be able to properly salute superior officers.[140] In conversation with her boot camp comrades, Areeya also describes the bodily training in terms of wearing shoes:

> "What's the difference between the Army and the pageant, [Areeya]?"
> "The difference between high heels and combat boots," I said.
> "What's the similarity then?"
> "Both give you sore feet."[141]

As these embodied performances show, it is difficult to reduce analysis of veiling and beauty pageantry to an accurate representation of visibility/invisibility. The negotiations of concealing and revealing seen in such visual artifacts and bodily experiences—in public pageantry and public veiling, as in public diplomacy—produce an excess of meaning beyond what can be expressed in words and encapsulated in ideology. Here we go beyond hermeneutics to appreciate veils as material artifacts and pageants as affective experiences, both of which "do" politics through more embodied, affective, and everyday encounters on the local, national, and world stages. Hence, rather than reveal the truth-value of de/veiling and beauty pageantry, we can appreciate the affect-work, the uneasy excitement, and the heterogeneous encounters provoked in such affective communities of sense.

Even so, veils are a challenge not only to the liberal polity, but also to larger ethical debates. Consider how, on the one hand, Jacques Derrida encourages us to provide unconditional hospitality that welcomes the "Other" into our homes, without either judging them or seeking to convert them to the self.[142] On the other hand, Emmanuel Levinas stresses how we must not simply tolerate difference but actively engage it through person-to-person, face-to-face, eye-to-eye encounters.[143] Roland Bleiker, David Campbell, and Emma Hutchison likewise conclude that to have an ethical relation with refugees as people, we need to see their faces, up close and in person.[144]

---

[140] Areeya Chumsai, *Muat Pop* [Lt. Pop] (English title: *Boot Camp*) (Bangkok: Future Publishing, 1998), pp. 25–26.

[141] Areeya, *Muat Pop*, 113.

[142] Jacques Derrida and Anne Dufourmantelle, *Of Hospitality*, translated by Rachel Bowlby (Stanford, CA: Stanford University Press, 2000).

[143] Emmanuel Levinas, *Totality and Infinity* (Pittsburgh, PA: Duquesne University Press, 1969).

[144] Roland Bleiker, David Campbell, and Emma Hutchison, "Visual Cultures of Inhospitality," *Peace Review* 26:2 (2014):192–200.

But what of the veil: Does it deny this ethical encounter in the public square? Are veiled women actually judging non-veiled women as impious?[145] Or does it mean that we need to think about the limits that the visual poses on global politics? This tension between moral certainty (i.e., the piety of the religious, secular, Left, or Right) and moral ambiguity is examined in more detail in Chapter 9's discussion of the sensible politics of walls.

[145] Eltahawy, *Headscarves and Hymens*; Gökarıksel and Secor, "The Veil, Desire, and the Gaze"; Heath, *The Veil*; Lewis, *Modest Fashion*.

9

Walls as Barriers, Gateways, and the Sublime

It's going to be a big, fat, beautiful wall!

—Donald J. Trump[1]

A person who thinks only about building walls, wherever they may be, and not building bridges, is not Christian.

—Pope Francis[2]

As Donald J. Trump's presidential campaign graphically showed, walls are a hot topic; he promised to build a serious wall along the US-Mexico border—and to get Mexico to pay for it. On his visit to Mexico in 2016, Pope Francis responded to Trump's wall call by declaring that building walls is morally repugnant, while building bridges is the "Christian" way.

Like the pope, many critical intellectuals argue that such walls are not just a political problem, but a moral problem. Wendy Brown's *Walled States, Waning Sovereignty*, for example, examines the theoretical politics of wall-building in the United States and Israel and concludes that these walls are both ineffective and immoral; they don't really keep foreigners out, and they actually produce a xenophobic identity within America and Israel.[3] With few exceptions,[4] such criticism reflects the

[1] Michael Finnegan, "It's Going To Be a Big, Fat, Beautiful Wall!," *Los Angeles Times* (June 3, 2016) http://www.latimes.com/politics/la-na-pol-trump-california-campaign-20160602-snap-story.html (accessed December 22, 2017).

[2] Jim Yardley, "Pope Francis Suggests Donald Trump Is 'Not Christian,' " *New York Times* (February 18, 2016) http://www.nytimes.com/2016/02/19/world/americas/pope-francis-donald-trump-christian.html (accessed December 22, 2017).

[3] Wendy Brown, *Walled States, Waning Sovereignty* (New York: Zone Books, 2014).

[4] See, for example, Timothy W. Luke, "Design as Defense: Broken Barriers and the Security Spectacle at the US-Mexico Border," in *Building Walls and Dissolving Borders: The Challenges of Alterity, Community and Securitizing Space*, edited by Max O. Stephenson and Laura Zanotti (Burlington, VT: Ashgate, 2014), pp. 115–131; John Williams, "Territorial Borders, International Ethics and Geography: Do Good Fences Still Make Good Neighbours?," *Geopolitics* 8:2 (2003):25–46.

Sensible Politics. William A. Callahan, Oxford University Press (2020). © Oxford University Press.
DOI: 10.1093/oso/9780190071738.001.0001

tone of discussions of border walls not just in the academy,[5] but also among public intellectuals in newspapers, magazines, radio/TV, and popular nonfiction.[6]

Indeed, the radical critique of walls as ineffective barriers that exclude vulnerable people on morally repugnant grounds is compelling. But rather than be satisfied with this moral critique, Chapter 9 seeks not only to problematize the "political piety" of moral judgments of walls as "good," but also to interrogate the political piety of denouncing them as "evil."[7] As George W. Bush's post–September 11, 2001 "axis of evil" foreign policy narrative showed, such moralizing "rhetoric is an 'analytical cul-de-sac' that prevents rather than encourages understanding."[8] It tends to close down discussion and thus reproduce the politics of domination.

This chapter, however, seeks to understand walls in a different register as visual artifacts and sensory spaces that embody political negotiations and experiences. While morality is singular and cannot be negotiated—walls are either "good" or "evil"—once we recognize walls as sites of negotiation, then we likewise recognize that they can be renegotiated, which is a productive understanding of politics itself. Indeed, here we switch from partisan campaigning to figure politics in terms of cultivating a "critical attitude" of self-reflection that goes beyond "merely serving particular social segments or disempowered groups." Rather than stake out political positions, the goal here is to "displace institutionalized forms of recognition with *thinking*. To think (rather than to seek to explain) in this sense is to invent and apply conceptual frames and create juxtapositions that disrupt and/or render historically contingent accepted knowledge practices." Discussion thus can explore "a challenge to identity politics in general, . . . even those on which some social movements are

---

[5] See, for example, Eyal Weizman, *Hollow Land: Israel's Architecture of Occupation* (London: Verso, 2007); Thomas Nail, *Theory of the Border* (New York: Oxford University Press, 2016); Yara Sharif, *Architecture of Resistance: Cultivating Moments of Possibility within the Palestinian/Israeli Conflict* (London: Routledge, 2017); Max O. Stephenson and Laura Zanotti, eds., *Building Walls and Dissolving Borders: The Challenges of Alterity, Community and Securitizing Space* (Burlington, VT: Ashgate, 2014); Elisabeth Vallet, ed., *Borders, Fences and Walls: State of Insecurity?* (Burlington, VT: Ashgate, 2014); Mohammad A. Chaichian, *Empires and Walls: Globalization, Migration, and Colonial Domination* (Leiden: Brill, 2014); Reece Jones, *Border Walls: Security and the War on Terror in the United States, India and Israel* (London: Zed Books, 2012).

[6] See, for example, Tom Vanderbilt, "The Walls in Our Heads," *New York Times* (November 4, 2016) http://www.nytimes.com/2016/11/06/opinion/sunday/the-walls-in-our-heads.html (accessed April 27, 2019); James West, "Donald Trump Loves the Great Wall of China: Too Bad It Was a Complete Disaster," *Mother Jones* (March 3, 2016) http://www.motherjones.com/politics/2016/03/great-wall-china-donald-trump (accessed April 27, 2019); Marcello Di Cintio, *Walls: Travels along the Barricades* (London: Union Books, 2013).

[7] For a discussion of political piety, see Michael J. Shapiro, *The Politics of Representation: Writing Practices in Biography, Photography, and Policy Analysis* (Madison: University of Wisconsin Press, 1988), p. 130.

[8] Roland Bleiker, *Aesthetics and World Politics* (London: Palgrave Macmillan, 2012), p. 72.

predicated."[9] The aim is to see how the walls are not simply physical barriers that exclude disadvantaged groups, but also "work" to produce political meaning and political affect—and not necessarily the meanings and feelings that we've come to expect.

Walls are key sites of visibility and visuality, where the visibility/visuality dynamic builds on W. J. T. Mitchell's argument that we need to do more than trace the "social construction of the visual," because we also need to pay attention to the "visual construction of the social"—and of the international.[10] In other words, it is necessary to not simply deconstruct how walls reflect social, political, and economic power relations; we also need to consider how they can visually produce new and different social orders and world orders. This chapter thus develops *Sensible Politics*'s argument that visuals need to be appreciated not just in terms of their ideological-value, but also in terms of their affect-work: not just what they mean, but also how they can move us and connect us, as individuals and collectives in "affective communities of sense."[11]

To do this, Chapter 9 juxtaposes the American and Israeli walls with the Great Wall of China, the massive physical infrastructure that is celebrated in the PRC as the positive symbol of the Chinese nation.[12] Mao Zedong told his compatriots: "You aren't really a hero [*haoHan*] until you've climbed the Great Wall." China's national anthem sings: "Arise, ye who refuse to be slaves!/With our flesh and blood, let us build our new Great Wall!" In 1984 Deng Xiaoping declared "Love our China, restore our Great Wall."[13] As we will see, the Great Wall is promoted as a symbol of the PRC's morally superior "defensive" foreign policy and as evidence that China has never invaded any other country.[14] The Great Wall thus is more than China's

---

[9] Michael J. Shapiro, *Studies in Trans-Disciplinary Method: After the Aesthetic Turn* (New York: Routledge, 2013), pp. 8, xv, 8.

[10] W. J. T. Mitchell, *What Do Pictures Want? The Lives and Loves of Images* (Chicago: University of Chicago Press, 2005), p. 343ff.

[11] See Emma Hutchison, *Affective Communities in World Politics: Collective Emotions after Trauma* (Cambridge, UK: Cambridge University Press, 2016); Brian Massumi, *Parables for the Virtual: Movement, Affect, Sensation* (Durham, NC: Duke University Press, 2002); Jacques Rancière, "Contemporary Art and the Politics of Aesthetics," in *Communities of Sense: Rethinking Aesthetics and Politics*, edited by Beth Hinderliter, William Kaizen, Vered Maimon, Jaleh Mansoor, and Seth McCormick (Durham, NC: Duke University Press, 2009), p. 31.

[12] See, for example, Huang Hua, "Renovating the Great Wall," *China Today* 43:8 (August 1994):12–13.

[13] Quoted in Carlos Rojas, *The Great Wall: A Cultural History* (Cambridge, MA: Harvard University Press, 2010), pp. 135, 131, 143.

[14] Liu Dexi, "Zhongguo de fazhan yu waijiao zhengce de zouxiang" [Trends in China's development and foreign policy], *Guoji zhengzhi yanjiu* (2015) http://study.ccln.gov.cn/fenke/zhengzhixue/zzzgwj/163609.shtml (accessed April 27, 2019); Arthur Waldron, "Scholarship and Patriotic Education: The Great Wall Conference, 1994," *China Quarterly* no. 143 (1995):843–850.

national heritage; it is "global cultural heritage" that exemplifies a morally good for-eign policy of peace.[15]

The Great Wall juxtaposition thus can help us to challenge received wisdom—both conservative and critical—about border walls. Rather than reflections of clear territorial or social boundaries, the walls here are multiple and contingent artifacts that function more as complex sites of flow than as absolute barriers. Franz Kafka's short story "The Great Wall of China" discusses the Wall's piecemeal, jigsaw-like construction process as a critique of singular coherent narratives; wall-building here creates more gaps than barriers.[16] "The Great Wall of China" story thus shows how walls can take on meaning through creative destruction—discontinuous construc-tion, destruction, and reconstruction—that animates more fluid inside/outside dynamics.[17]

The Great Wall presents an interesting spatial (i.e. non-Western) juxtaposi-tion; it also shows how walls vary in meaning temporally. A century ago the Great Wall was understood in China as a monument to the wastefulness of tyrannical emperors and/or as a useless ruin that didn't border anything.[18] In the twenty-first century it is taken for granted that the Great Wall is morally good as a symbol of peace that benefits humanity.[19] This wall's unstable historical meaning can provoke odd questions: In a hundred years, will Trump's Great Wall likewise be celebrated around the world as the symbol of a defensive foreign policy that is morally exem-plary? This outrageous idea recalls the shock Michel Foucault experienced when he encountered the strange categories of a Chinese encyclopedia (as imagined by Borges): "the stark impossibility of thinking *that*."[20]

Certainly these walls are different: the US-Mexico barrier marks an actual inter-state border, while the Great Wall of China is an archeological ruin and historical curiosity that doesn't mark sovereign space. Yet when figured as an infrastructure of feeling, the Great Wall can tell us much about human relations. It also can tell us

---

[15]   Cheng Dalin, "The Great Tourist Icon," in *The Great Wall of China*, edited by Claire Roberts and Geremie R. Barmé (Sydney: Powerhouse Publishing, 2006), p. 26.

[16]   Franz Kafka, *The Complete Short Stories* (London: Vintage, 2005), pp. 235–249.

[17]   Also see Sharif, *Architecture of Resistance*, xv, 8.

[18]   See Arthur Waldron, *The Great Wall of China: From History to Myth* (Cambridge, MA: Cambridge University Press, 1990), p. 155; Rojas, *The Great Wall*, 5; Claire Roberts, "China's Most Famous Ruin," in *The Great Wall of China*, edited by Claire Roberts and Geremie R. Barmé (Sydney: Powerhouse Publishing, 2006), p. 16; Julia Lovell, *The Great Wall: China Against the World, 1000 BC–AD 2000* (New York: Grove Press, 2006).

[19]   At this point, analyses of the Great Wall often note the West's influence in the rebirth of the Great Wall as a positive symbol in the twentieth century (see Waldron, *The Great Wall of China*, 203ff.; Rojas, *The Great Wall*; Roberts and Barmé, *The Great Wall of China*; Lovell, *The Great Wall*). I do not recount this argument for two reasons: (1) I am interested in Chinese understandings of the Great Wall, and (2) this Western-centric approach tends to devalue Chinese agency in understanding the Great Wall.

[20]   Michel Foucault, *The Order of Things* (New York: Pantheon, 1970), p. xv (emphasis in original).

about how people relate to the material culture of massive projects as visual artifacts and sensory spaces that provoke affective responses—even exciting the sublime. Indeed, the Great Wall keeps appearing at China's borders as a sign of sovereign power. The sign shown in figure 9.1 is noteworthy because its stylized Great Wall

Figure 9.1 Immigration counter at Haikou International Airport, China (2016). Courtesy William A. Callahan

marks the border in Hainan Island, historically China's Southern extreme, which is thousands of miles away from the Great Wall itself.

The first part of the chapter thus uses the counter-example of the Great Wall of China to deconstruct the ideology of post–Cold War walls like the US-Mexico barrier. It probes this juxtaposition to show how (1) walls actually can be instruments of security policy that is rationally sound, and (2) wall-building in both China and the United States emerges from prior moral judgments that continue to produce the moral problems of exclusion. While critical IR generally understands walls in terms of the tension between absolute barriers at sovereign borders and neoliberalism's unrestrained flows of goods and capital, Chapter 9 employs the new conceptual framework of "gaps" to explore how walls work as gateways that are neither completely closed nor completely open.

Critical borders studies scholars have profitably explored how borders are not static and can take on meaning through movement and flows: borders here are no longer just at the edge of the nation-state, but are complex sites of flows, often throughout society.[21] Interestingly, however, this research agenda has not been applied to analyze border walls, which characteristically are figured as static barriers that ineffectively impede flows from without, while creating xenophobic homelands within.[22] In other words, in critical border studies walls generally are presented as a "problem" that needs to be "solved." This chapter, however, employs the "gaps" concept to explore how walls themselves can be productive sites of movement, flows, and exchange that complicate problem/solution figurations.

While the first section employs the "critical juxtaposition" of the Great Wall of China and the "conceptual frame" of gaps to rethink border politics, the next section explores another conceptual frame to understand walls in a different register; specifically, it switches from a hermeneutic approach to a critical aesthetic mode that values detailed empirical study and creative visual analysis of sensible politics. The goal is to appreciate the visuality and materiality of walls as nonnarrative sites of visceral provocation, moving from ideology to affect.[23] Explorations of visuality thus often shift attention away from the state and official foreign policy-making to see how foreign affairs emerge through local, transnational, and unofficial self/

[21] The literature on critical borders studies is substantial. For exemplary texts see David Newman, "On Borders and Power: A Theoretical Framework," *Journal of Borderlands Studies* 18:1 (2003):13–25; Reece Jones, Corey Johnson, Wendy Brown, Gabriel Popescu, Polly Pallister-Wilkins, Alison Mountz, and Emily Gilbert, "Interventions on the State of Sovereignty at the Border," *Political Geography* 59 (2017):1–10; Corey Johnson, Reece Jones, Anssi Paasi, Louise Amoore, Alison Mountz, Mark Salter, and Chris Rumford, "Interventions on Rethinking 'the Border' in Border Studies," *Political Geography* 30 (2011):61–69; Louise Amoore and Alexandra Hall, "Border Theatre: On the Arts of Security and Resistance," *Cultural Geographies* 17:3 (2010):299–319.
[22] See, for example, Jones, *Border Walls*.
[23] For a detailed discussion of ideology and affect, see Chapters 1, 2, and 4.

Other relations: the sensible politics of everyday encounters with walls as barriers and gateways.

To explore this critical aesthetic strategy, the chapter discusses short films about border walls and gateways, specifically Cynthia Weber's pair of *We Are Not Immigrants* films from the US-Mexico border and a Tecate beer advertisement that aired in September 2016 during the US presidential campaign.[24] Here walls aren't necessarily either the problem or the solution; rather, the goal is to encourage a greater appreciation of their political complexity and moral ambiguity as gateways that govern flows of goods, capital, ideas, and people.[25] By problematizing political piety (both conservative and critical), the chapter hopes to understand walls as visual and multisensory experiences that work in a different register as active embodiments of political debate—and of political resistance. The chapter thus further develops the idea of visual artifacts as multisensory spaces and infrastructures of feeling that move and connect people in affective communities of sense.

The Great Wall, of course, is not the only example that one could use to interrogate current criticism of post–Cold War walls.[26] This chapter examines Chinese examples because that is my particular area of expertise. But as the comparative analysis of walls will show, this research deploys unexpected juxtapositions and new conceptual frames to call into question any Orientalist regionalization of international studies. Indeed, the hope is that this chapter will generate further studies of the sensible politics of walls that will explore examples from other times and places.

Deconstructing the Wall

Walls are interesting because they are physical and symbolic sites of inclusion and exclusion that mark the inside from the outside. As discussed in earlier chapters, inside/outside is the guiding distinction for IR: it marks the division between domestic politics and international politics that is not only territorial but also social. "Inside" denotes safety, law, and sovereignty, while "outside" marks danger, violence, and anarchy.[27] This order-inside/wilderness-outside view of social life can be seen in an eighteenth-century silk painting of the Great Wall (see figure 9.2).[28]

---

[24] Cynthia Weber, dir., *We Are Not Immigrants* (18 minutes), screened at the Visual International Politics workshop at LSE (June 13, 2016); *Tecate Beer Wall Advertisement*, YouTube (September 2016) https://www.youtube.com/watch?v=nXYM_zBVF7Q (accessed August 23, 2019).

[25] See Michael J. Shapiro, *For Moral Ambiguity: National Culture and the Politics of the Family* (Minneapolis: University of Minnesota Press, 2001); Bleiker, *Aesthetics and World Politics*, 68.

[26] See, for example, Chaichian, *Empires and Walls*.

[27] R. B. J. Walker, *Inside/Outside: International Relations as Political Theory* (Cambridge, UK: Cambridge University Press, 1993). Also see Gaston Bachelard, *The Poetics of Space* (Boston: Beacon Press, 1964), pp. 211–231.

[28] Also see Roberts and Barmé, *The Great Wall of China*, 184.

Figure 9.2 Inside and outside the Gate of Mountains and Seas (1760). Courtesy Collection of National Palace Museum

The inside/outside distinction also emerged in 1961 when East Germany constructed the Berlin Wall, which it saw as an "anti-fascist wall," to distinguish what it saw as its morally superior socialist "experiment" from West Berlin's morally corrupt capitalist "tumor."[29] This territorial division soon came to symbolize for both sides the global Cold War ideological division between the East and the West. Likewise, when the Berlin Wall came down in 1989, it was seen as a sign that the Cold War was over. This led to declarations of the end of history, the end of ideology, and a brave new borderless world. In the neoliberal era of globalization, nations are not divided by walls, but joined by unrestrained transnational flows of goods and capital.

Why, then, do countries keep building walls? Since the fall of the Berlin Wall in 1989, dozens of new walls have been built, not just in the United States and Israel, but also both inside the European Union and at its edges, as well as in the Middle East, Africa, South Asia, and East Asia. The end of the Cold War thus did not result in the final victory of neoliberalism and the "End of History"; rather, exclusive nationalism erupted first in many post-communist states, and now in the Brexit-Trump era in liberal democratic states as well. Walls thus work as barriers to separate people, in what some see as a "disease" and others as "apartheid."[30]

As Brown and others argue, these new walls speak to a number of contradictions. First, walls don't work very well as a security strategy; the technologies of artillery and airpower have made walls obsolete as a military strategy. In World War II, the Germans just went around the Maginot Line to invade France, and then the Allies

---

[29] Greg Eghigian, "Homo Munitus: The East Germans Observed," in *Socialist Modern: East German Everyday Culture and Politics*, edited by Katherine Pence and Paul Betts (Ann Arbor: University of Michigan Press, 2007), p. 49.

[30] Di Cintio, *Walls*, 11; Sharif, *Architecture of Resistance*, 15, 26, 63, 130; Weizman, *Hollow Land*, 10.

breached the Nazi's Atlantik Wall, designed to seal off the continent. The US and Israeli walls do not really "work" either; they are functionally ineffective as barriers and are very expensive.[31]

Rather than seeing walls as something that states have built since ancient times, Brown argues that new walls in the twenty-first century are a new general phenomenon that lays bare the unique contradictions of our era.[32] While rationally we should see walls as a waste of time and money, Trump's populist election campaign showed that they are very popular with the general public. For Brown, walls thus exemplify a crisis of sovereignty peculiar to the neoliberal era, in which sovereignty has become unhinged from the state and has been relocated to transnational capital and transnational religious activity.[33]

Many would counter that the new walls exemplify the global politics of the post-9/11 era: a re-securitization of the state and a rapid expansion of sovereign state power, not just in the United States, but globally.[34] While Euro-America is addressing the problems of neoliberalism, China, for example, is pursuing a combination of two illiberal ideologies—socialism and Confucianism—in what some call the neo-socialist ideology, which cultivates expanded state power both at home and abroad.[35] This post–Cold War expansion of sovereign state power includes building the "Great Firewall of China" to control cyberspace, as well as a new wall along the PRC's external border with North Korea designed to keep out refugees.[36]

But Brown is not persuaded by this argument: we are in what she calls the "post-Westphalian" era, in which transnational capitalism uses the state to generate profits, while transnational religious groups are the main threat to state security. New walls thus exemplify the post-Westphalian shift in IR from state-to-state conflict to transnational flows of goods, capital, ideas, and people. People here are not acting as agents of the nation-state, but as individuals and groups who cross borders as migrants, refugees, and terrorists: Mexican border-crossers are not pursuing Mexican state policy, and BP (formerly British Petroleum) doesn't act in the interests of Great Britain when it spills/drills for oil in the Gulf of Mexico.

Brown argues that the new walls are not really meant to be material barriers, but are symbolic and ideological performances designed to deal with popular anxieties about the loss of sovereign power. It's a complicated argument, but in general, Brown sees walls as sites of "pure interdiction" that contradict liberalism's commitment to openness.[37] They are a site of "hypocrisy" where liberal states break the law

---

[31] See Brown, *Walled States*, 32; Weizman, *Hollow Land*, 161; Jones, *Border Walls*; Nail, *Theory of the Border*.

[32] Brown, *Walled States*, 7–8.

[33] Brown, *Walled States*, 21ff.

[34] See, for example, Jones, *Border Walls*.

[35] See Frank Pieke, *Knowing China* (Cambridge, UK: Cambridge University Press, 2016).

[36] See Chapter 11.

[37] Brown, *Walled States*, 25; also see Jones, *Border Walls*, 181.

to enforce the law; to stop illegal immigrants, states build walls that actually require them to break other laws.[38] Hence walls exemplify the crisis of the liberal values of "universal inclusion, equality, liberty, and the rule of law."[39]

This is a technical, economic, and political issue, but for Brown and many others wall-building ultimately is a moral issue: the wall is a blank screen upon which people project their anxieties over the erosion of state sovereignty.[40] Walls thus aren't a material expression of sovereign power, but rather an ideological sign of the loss of power and a loss of sovereignty. Instead of asserting strength, walls are a symptom of vulnerability and anxiety. They don't really keep foreigners out and actually produce a racist and xenophobic homeland within. Recall how Trump declared the necessity of walls when he announced his presidential candidacy: "When Mexico sends its people, they're not sending their best. They're sending people that have lots of problems, and they're bringing those problems with them. They're bringing drugs. They're bringing crime. They're rapists."[41]

Walls thus are less physical constructions than they are symbolic social borders that need to be deconstructed according to the visibility strategy for the proper understanding of their hidden ideology. Brown here employs a robust example of hermeneutic analysis to reframe walls from concrete material infrastructure to be symbolic sites of the "bordering process." The goal for hermeneutics is to trace patterns of signification and thus show "how the text can be understood in terms of the hidden content it discloses."[42] For visual international politics, the visibility strategy's hermeneutic mode is useful for revealing who is left out of political debates: who is visible inside the frame, and who is invisible outside; who is included inside the wall, and who is excluded outside the wall. Walls here are like visual images and artifacts more generally, which take on meaning through "social construction." Indeed, one of the hermeneutic mode's key contributions is highlighting—often visually—the plight of vulnerable people on the Other side of the wall. As in much of critical IR, the target of criticism is the sovereign state, and walls are prime examples of its exclusionary security practices. The political subject is not the citizen but the migrant, and walls are illusions that hide dominant ideology.[43]

---

[38] Brown, *Walled States*, 39–40, 101.

[39] Brown, *Walled States*, 72.

[40] Brown, *Walled States*, 73; Weizman, *Hollow Land*; Vallet, *Borders, Fences and Walls*; Stephenson and Zanotti, *Building Walls and Dissolving Borders*.

[41]   Fred Imbert, "Donald Trump: Mexico Going to Pay for Wall," CNBC (October 28, 2015) http://www.cnbc.com/2015/10/28/donald-trump-mexico-going-to-pay-for-wall.html (accessed December 22, 2017).

[42] Shapiro, *Studies in Trans-Disciplinary Method*, 29–30.

[43] See Nail, *Theory of the Border*, 13ff.

Figure 9.3 Ana Teresa Fernández, *Borrada* (2010). Courtesy Gallery Wendi Norris

The goal here is emancipation: to demolish the ideological, social, and physical walls that separate humans from each other. Indeed, one of the strategies for resisting the US-Mexico barrier is to artistically tear down the wall; for example, Mexican-American artist Ana Teresa Fernández "erases the border" by painting the wall with the landscape that it blocks (see figure 9.3).[44] Walls, as an overwhelmingly visual policing of social distinctions, both exemplify social exclusion and distract us from the truth of power as domination.

To draw such conclusions, Brown looks to a few Western examples to make a general argument about sovereignty and its demise.[45] She is clear about not being concerned with the specifics of particular walls—indeed, her passing reference to the Great Wall of China locates it in the wrong region: South Asia rather than East Asia.[46] While Brown doesn't see the need to look beyond her Western liberal democratic examples, she suggests that "someone should."[47]

[44] Ana Teresa Fernández, "Borrando La Frontera—Erasing the Border" (2010) http://anateresafernandez.com/borrando-la-barda-tijuana-mexico/ (accessed April 27, 2019). Sharif also artistically resists the West Bank barrier by using collages to "break all boundaries" (Sharif, *Architecture of Resistance*, 8).

[45] Brown, *Walled States*, 78.

[46] Brown, *Walled States*, 74.

[47] Brown, *Walled States*, 78.

Accepting Brown's invitation, this chapter looks to Chinese experiences as examples of a different relation to walls as markers of community and security. While walls are an insult to liberal society, they are very popular in China:

> "Wall" is what makes China, wall makes the city of Beijing, the Imperial City, the Forbidden City, and all subsidiary units down to country town, village, and private home. Give any Chinese some loose bricks and he will build a wall, a gate, and hire a gatekeeper to prevent an outsider from entering. . . . The Great Wall is the symbol of China par excellence.[48]

Indeed, as the classical Chinese philosopher Xunzi explains: "Wherein lies that which makes humanity human? I say it lies in humanity's possession of boundaries."[49]

The Great Wall thus is not simply a site of military architecture; it is a site of identity politics that informs the definition of Chinese foreign policy as "defensive."[50] The main security problem for pre-modern China was from the Central Eurasian steppe, and guarding the border along the Great Wall was a common solution. China's military intellectuals still argue that "without the Great Wall, China could never have survived as a unified state (Rome, it was pointed out, perished at the hands of barbarians)."[51] The Great Wall, in this popular narrative, is exemplary because it shows how China did not expand, but merely sought to defend itself from foreign armies that attacked from the North. Responding in 2016 to the US Defense Secretary's description of Beijing's actions in the South China Sea as "building a Great Wall of self-isolation," the spokesman for China's Ministry of National Defense explained, "[A]s those who study Chinese history know, the Great Wall itself is a defensive strategy. It was built to keep out the cruel oppression of invaders, not friendly envoys or free trade."[52] The Great Wall thus is taken as concrete evidence that China has never invaded any other country—and never will.[53] It also exemplifies the PRC's long-standing ideological position of non-interference in the domestic politics of other countries.

As well as a sign of defense, the Great Wall is also a symbol of diplomacy. In 1974 the PRC gave the United Nations a massive thirty-six-by-sixteen-foot silk tapestry of the Great Wall, which now hangs in the UN headquarters in New York.

---

[48] Jeffrey F. Meyer, *The Dragons of Tiananmen: Beijing as a Sacred City* (Columbia: University of South Carolina Press, 1991), p. 4.

[49] Quoted in Rojas, *The Great Wall*, xvii.

[50] See Liu, "Zhongguo de fazhan."

[51] Waldron, *The Great Wall of China*, 847.

[52] "Mei wumie wojian[:] 'ziwo guali de changcheng'[;] Guofangbu: Zhongguo pengyou bian tianxia" [US slander: We have built "a Great Wall of self-isolation"; Ministry of National Defence: We have friends all over the world], *Cankao xiaoxi wang* (July 1, 2016) http://www.cankaoxiaoxi.com/china/20160701/1214020.shtml (accessed December 22, 2017).

[53] See Liu, "Zhongguo de fazhan"; Huang, "Renovating the Great Wall."

Figure 9.4 Chinese ambassador presents Great Wall tapestry to Foreign Ministry of
Pakistan (2014). Source: Embassy of the People's Republic of China in the Islamic Republic of
Pakistan

Great Wall tapestries also hang in the reception rooms of China's embassies abroad,
as well as in the entrance hall of the foreign ministry of one of Beijing's key allies,
Pakistan (see figure 9.4).[54] Visiting world leaders regularly make a pilgrimage to the
wall; in 1972 Richard Nixon declared, "This is a great wall and it had to be built by
a great people," while in 2009 Barak Obama mused that it is "magical."[55] The Great
Wall thus is "not just China's national treasure, but shared or global cultural heritage."[56] Rather than being a moral problem, the Great Wall is offered as a moral
solution, again and again, not just for China, but for the world.

China here is neither exotic nor unique. The Great Wall actualizes the standard
textbook concept of sovereignty, in which one of the sovereign state's necessary

---

[54] "Sun Weidong dashi xiang Bajisitan waijiaobu zengsong 'Wanli Changcheng' guatan"
[Ambassador Sun Weidong presents "Great Wall" tapestry to the Foreign Ministry of Pakistan],
Embassy of the People's Republic of China in the Islamic Republic of Pakistan (February 7,
2014) http://pk.chineseembassy.org/chn/zbgx/t1126157.htm (accessed April 27, 2019). Also see
Zhou Rong, "Ba-Zhong youyi rutong wanli changcheng" [The friendship between Pakistan and China
is like the Great Wall], *Guangming ribao* (February 8, 2014) http://epaper.gmw.cn/gmrb/html/2014-
02/08/nw.D110000gmrb_20140208_3-08.htm (accessed April 27, 2019).

[55] See Rojas, *The Great Wall*, 1.

[56] Cheng, "The Great Tourist Icon," 26.

tasks is to guard its territorial borders—otherwise it is not sovereign.[57] When asked about Trump's wall plans in 2017, Mexico's economy minister stated that "[t]he US is a sovereign nation and if the US decides to build a wall on the southern border, it's their sovereign decision. We may like it or not . . . [but] we have to respect the sovereign act of a nation."[58]

The judgment of inefficiency—for example, that people can always climb over or tunnel under walls—also misunderstands the logic of walls as a security strategy: they are not meant to provide a hermetic seal, but to be part of a multidimensional strategy that includes patrols, drones, remote sensors, and other forms of surveillance.[59] The goal is not complete security, but "good enough" security.[60] As the architect of the US wall built after 2006, Homeland Security Secretary Michael Chertoff, explains, "a *fence is part of a whole strategy*. A fence by itself is not going to work, but in conjunction with other tools, it can help."[61] While it is common to deconstruct the "rationality" of realist foreign policy claims, this suggests that it is also necessary to deconstruct critics' claims of the wall's "irrationality." In other words, if it is broadly rational to safeguard one's national borders, why is the US-Mexico barrier so controversial?

Brown cannot appreciate the rationality of walls because she is employing a singular, absolute, and complete version of sovereignty that is taken from a survey of classical and contemporary political theory.[62] In IR theory, however, there are more nuanced notions of borders and sovereignty. While the argument about the post-Westphalian erosion of sovereignty assumes that sovereignty was ever solid, R. B. J. Walker argues that sovereignty has never been stable and has always been problematic.[63] The problems of sovereignty thus are not simply post-Westphalian, but pre-Westphalian, and Westphalian too. Westaphalian sovereignty thus is an ideal that is never realized—but this is not necessarily seen as a failure of the system as a whole. Rather than speak of containment and impermeable barriers, it is common

---

[57] See, for example, Robert Jackson and Georg Sorenson, *Introduction to International Relations*, 6th ed. (Oxford: Oxford University Press, 2016), p. 4; John Baylis, Steve Smith, and Patricia Owens, eds., *The Globalization of World Politics: An Introduction to International Relations*, 5th ed. (Oxford: Oxford University Press, 2011), pp. 23–24.

[58] Dana Afina, "Mexico Economy Minister Talks NAFTA, Border Wall in Detroit Visit," Mlive News (March 4, 2017) http://www.mlive.com/news/detroit/index.ssf/2017/03/mexico_economic_official_detro.html (accessed April 27, 2019); also see Irasema Coronado, "Towards the Wall between Nogales, Arizona and Nogales, Sonora," in *Borders, Fences and Walls: State of Insecurity?*, edited by Elisabeth Vallet (Burlington, VT: Ashgate, 2014), pp. 261–262.

[59] See Weizman, *Hollow Land*; Sharif, *Architecture of Resistance*.

[60] Luke, "Design as Defense," 120.

[61] Quoted in Ronald Rael, "Border Wall as Architecture," in *Borders, Fences and Walls: State of Insecurity?*, edited by Elisabeth Vallet (Burlington, VT: Ashgate, 2014), p. 278.

[62] Brown, *Walled States*, 22ff.

[63] Walker, *Inside/Outside*, 179.

for critical IR theorists to recognize sovereignty as partial, overlapping, graduated, and even an experience of "organized hypocrisy."[64] Even so, it still is the job of the state to defend its borders—otherwise it is not sovereign. Thus the Great Wall of China can help us to rethink the politics and the morality of the US wall to reframe it as a defensive act.[65]

If we step away from a condemnation of walls as immoral sites of separation, then we can examine not just what they mean, but what they can "do." Rather than simply condemning exclusion, the Chinese practice of walling encourages us to look more closely at how the inside/outside distinction works as a "bordering process":[66]

> Traditionally [the Great Wall] marks off the "sacred land" (*shenzhou*) from the rest of the world. Walls are important to the Chinese because, over and above practical considerations (preventing thievery, resisting attack, and the like), the wall is the line clearly drawn between what is significant and what is insignificant, what is powerful and what is not powerful, who is kin and who is stranger, what is sacred and not sacred.[67]

Understanding inside/outside as a complex and contingent relation is popular in critical IR literature,[68] and it is even more central to Chinese political discourse as *nei/wai*.[69] As discussed in previous chapters, conceptual dyads such as *nei/wai*-inside/outside are key to social life in China, organizing relations among individuals, families, and clans, and all the way up to relations between different peoples and different states. Rather than function according to the fixed binary distinctions characteristic of Enlightenment modernity, such dyads are relational, contextual, contingent, and fluid, with a productive tension between the ideal and lived

[64] See, for example, Siba N'Zatioula Grovogui, *Sovereigns, Quasi Sovereigns, and Africans* (Minneapolis: University of Minnesota Press, 1996); William A. Callahan, *Contingent States: Greater China and Transnational Relations* (Minneapolis: University of Minnesota Press, 2004); Aihwa Ong, "Graduated Sovereignty in Southeast Asia," *Theory, Culture, and Society* (2000) 17(4):55–75; Stephen D. Krasner, *Sovereignty: Organized Hypocrisy* (Princeton, NJ: Princeton University Press, 1999).

[65] See Williams, "Territorial Borders."

[66] See Newman, "On Borders and Power"; Nail, *Theory of the Border.*

[67] Meyer, *The Dragons of Tiananmen*, 4.

[68] See Walker, *Inside/Outside*; R. B. J. Walker, *Out of Line: Essays on the Politics of Boundaries and the Limits of Modern Politics* (New York: Routledge, 2016).

[69] See Lien-sheng Yang, "Historical Notes on the Chinese World Order," in *The Chinese World Order: Traditional China's Foreign Relations* edited by John King Fairbank, 20–33 (Cambridge, MA: Harvard University Press, 1968); Ge Zhaoguang, *Lishi Zhongguo de nei yu wai: Youguan "Zhongguo" yu "zhoubian" gainian de zai chengqing* [Inside and outside in historical China: Re-clarifying the concepts of "Middle Kingdom" and "periphery"] (Hong Kong: Chinese University Press, 2017).

experience.[70] Indeed, while much critical analysis of walls focuses on etymological definitions and canonic texts,[71] what is most interesting about these Chinese dyads is the general *lack* of stable canonic definition; there is no orthodoxy, and the dyads' contingent flexibility demands that we make sense of each dynamic through continual interpretive practice.[72]

Civilization/barbarism (*Hua/yi*) and loosening/tightening (*fang/shou*) are two other conceptual dyads that are key to understanding how walls work. Loosening/tightening is a contemporary Chinese concept used to describe the nonlinear and non-progressive exercise of power seen in the PRC.[73] Although *fang/shou* generally describes a cycle of loosening and tightening of state control over society, often it was not so much a chronological shift from loose to tight, and then back to loose again, as doing both simultaneously. As Deng Xiaoping declared, successful governance requires "grasping with both hands" (*liangshou zhua*), with one hand grasping Beijing's economic policy of "reform and opening," and the other grasping political stability.[74]

Such dynamic dyads resonate with Foucault's concept of "governmentality" because they shift us away from a blunt understanding of politics as the juridical power to say "no," toward a more nuanced sense of power as productively generated by social relationships.[75] The issue thus is "no longer that of fixing and demarcating the territory, but of allowing circulations to take place, of controlling them, sifting the good and the bad, ensuring that things are always in movement."[76] Governmentality and loosening/tightening thus help us to shift from seeing walls as sovereign barriers that separate and exclude the outside from the inside to appreciating how walls also can function as productive sites that regulate flows according to degrees of loosening/tightening. The governmentality of flows, which functions according

[70] Thomas A. Metzger, *Escape from Predicament: Neo-Confucianism and China's Evolving Political Culture* (New York: Columbia University Press, 1977), p. 84; also see David L. Hall and Roger T. Ames, *Thinking Through Confucius* (Albany: State University of New York Press, 1987).

[71] Brown, *Walled States*; Nail, *Theory of the Border*.

[72] See Oleg Benesch, "National Consciousness and the Evolution of the Civil/Military Binary in East Asia," *Taiwan Journal of East Asian Studies* 8:1 (2011):165.

[73] See Richard Baum, *Burying Mao: Chinese Politics in the Age of Deng Xiaoping* (Princeton, NJ: Princeton University Press, 1994), p. 5ff.

[74] See Yang Fengcheng, ""Liangshou zhua" de yuanqi, neihan yu yanbian" [The origin, meaning and evolution of "grasp with both hands"] *Guangming ribao* (February 23, 2011) http://news.ifeng.com/history/shixueyuan/detail_2011_05/23/6567879_0.shtml (accessed December 22, 2017).

[75] See Michel Foucault, "Governmentality," in *The Foucault Effect: Studies in Governmentality*, edited by Graham Burchell, Colin Gordon, and Peter Miller (London: Harvester Wheatsheaf, 1991), pp. 87–104.

[76] Michel Foucault, *Security, Territory, Population: Lectures at the College de France, 1977–1978* (London: Palgrave Macmillan, 2007), p. 65.

to a loosening/tightening dynamic, thus is quite different from neoliberalism's unrestrained flows of capital and goods.

As in earlier chapters, here we resist the geopolitical container-style organization of knowledge-production, in which the choice is between the "modern West" and "traditional China."[77] Rather than replacing "Eurocentric" concepts with "Sinocentric" ones, the chapter explores the political dynamics of walls through an assemblage of concepts that are Chinese, Euro-American, traditional, and contemporary. The goal here is to use Chinese concepts, examples, and experiences as a critical juxtaposition that problematizes the moralized discourse of walls as good or evil and opens up space for a more nuanced appreciation of what walls can "do" as visual images and artifacts.

The Great Wall of China, therefore, is not simply a defensive act. Like many walls, it was built to mark a moral distinction. It wasn't built to defend an interstate border; rather, it was employed to operationalize another dynamic dyad, the Civilization/barbarism distinction (*Hua/yi*), that governed pre-modern China's political, moral, and literary discourse.[78] Rather than just being exemplary post-Westphalian phenomena, walls here are also pre-Westphalian events. To put it another way, we need to recognize how post–Cold War IR theory was not simply dominated by globalists. It also witnessed the backlash of essentialized identity politics, exemplified by Samuel P. Huntington's "clash of civilizations" thesis. Clash of civilizations is not simply a post–Cold War phenomenon; in many ways, it reproduces a pre-modern notion of international politics that continues to be very popular in China and other non-Western countries.[79] However, rather than following Huntington to distinguish between different civilizations, Chinese texts characteristically distinguish between Civilization and barbarism. Indeed, the word for Civilization (*Hua*) is the same as the word for "Chinese." Civilized China only takes shape when it is distinguished from barbarism, with "China being internal, large, and high and barbarians being external, small and low."[80] This is not simply an ancient understanding; prominent Chinese scholars still argue that border walls, including the Great Wall, are "an indicator of settled social development, generally termed 'civilization.'"[81]

---

[77] See Leigh Jenco, *Changing Referents: Learning Across Space and Time in China and the West* (New York: Oxford University Press, 2015).

[78] See Yang, "Historical Notes"; Joseph MacKay, "The Nomadic Other: Ontological Security and the Inner Asian Steppe in Historical East Asian International Politics," *Review of International Studies* 42 (2016):471–491.

[79] See, for example, Wang Jisi, "Huntingdun tiaoqi de lunzhan jiang chaoyue shikong" [The debate provoked by Huntington transcends time and space], *Shijie zhishi* no. 3 (2009) https://user.guancha.cn/main/content?id=66738 (accessed August 23, 2019).

[80] Yang, "Historical Notes," 20.

[81] See Bruce Gordon Doar, "Delimited Boundaries and Great Wall Studies," in *The Great Wall of China*, edited by Claire Roberts and Geremie R. Barmé (Sydney: Powerhouse Publishing, 2006), pp. 122, 123ff.

The Great Wall was an important part of policing this hierarchical and moralized social distinction. It was built to guard China from nomadic pastoralists of the Central Eurasian steppe. Although nomads regularly banded together into large armies, they generally did not present a state-to-state challenge to China, so much as the ecological conflict between settled farmers who formed states and mobile pastoralists who occasionally banded into confederations.[82] Wall-building then emerged from a Civilization/barbarism distinction that violently creates, targets, and attacks the nomadic pastoralists as an invading barbaric horde. These political and moral distinctions could be harsh; the orthography of classical Chinese categorizes many nomads as "animals" rather than as fellow humans. Although the Chinese language changed to include them as humans in the mid-twentieth century, the sub-human barbarian image remains prominent: Zhang Yimou's feature film *The Great Wall* (2016) sees the threat on the other side of the wall as green-blooded, man-eating monsters.[83]

Thus China's hierarchical, exclusive, and morally superior understanding of walls is familiar. The Great Wall of China is a pre-Westphalian example of a strategy designed to address the security challenge of mobile non-state peoples, rather than interstate territorial conflict. As Ai Weiwei's film *Human Flow* (2017) shows, twenty-first-century walls likewise are designed to manage the post-Westphalian transnational challenge of flowing people rather than to mark fixed territory. Like Central Eurasian nomadic pastoralists, people at the US border—migrants, refugees, smugglers, and terrorists—are largely unorganized, and do not act on behalf of a state. Hence the Great Wall's Civilization/barbarism distinction resonates with Trump's racialist description of Mexicans as barbaric criminals rather than as vulnerable migrants: "They're bringing drugs. They're bringing crime. They're rapists."

While the Great Wall of China's defensive foreign policy goal can be rationally exemplary, when probed more deeply its moral problems emerge. The division between Civilized people and barbarians often became a racially-exclusive policing of the distinction between Han and non-Han social groups. Indeed, even Mao's famous quotation about Chinese going to the Great Wall reflects this: *haoHan* means "hero" and "good fellow," but it also means "good Chinese"—and "good Han." Strangely, the wall that provokes moral outrage in the United States and Israel becomes the key to China's exceptionalist moral superiority.

Hence this juxtaposition of walls can help us to understand US and Chinese foreign policy in new ways. On the one hand, the Chinese experience allows us to see walls as instruments of a security policy that is rationally sound: it is the sovereign

---

[82]   See Owen Lattimore, *Inner Asian Frontiers of China* (New York: American Geographical Society, 1940). For a more complex view see MacKay, "The Nomadic Other."

[83]   Zhang Yimou, dir., *Changcheng* [The Great Wall] (Legendary Pictures, 2016).

state's job to guard its borders, otherwise it is not sovereign. But because the Chinese discourse of Civilization/barbarism is broadly analogous to the racialist distinctions that support the US wall, the Great Wall of China has moral problems as well. It is common to figure non-Western experience as either completely the same or completely different—that is, as derivative sites of "modernization" or as exotic alternatives. But this comparative political theory-style of analysis shows how the juxtaposition of walls from different times and places can yield fruitful—and unexpected—insights.

From Singular Barrier to Contingent Gateway

Critiques of the US-Mexico barrier and Israel's West Bank barrier often rely on a singular notion of walls, in both time and space. Walls have been here since the beginning of time as expressions of Western civilization and/or Judeo-Christian theology that mark out sacred from secular space.[84] Here sovereignty is absolute, and borders are unproblematic, single-line boundaries. The US-Mexico barrier is figured as a singular, coherent, linear, and unitary wall that sits exactly on the border, ranging from the Pacific Ocean in San Diego to the Gulf of Mexico in Texas.

Curiously, this unitary wall-scape is shared by supporters and critics alike. Supporters seek to build such an international hermetic seal, yet because the wall does not measure up to this unitary absolute singularity, critics declare it technically, economically, politically, and morally "ineffective." Thus gaps are a problem for both groups. They need to be sealed for supporters, while for critics they are evidence of the deadly consequences of the wall's failure: gaps in the wall redirect people from urban crossings toward the high desert plateau, which generates greater costs in terms of higher fees paid to human traffickers, as well as a higher death rate among migrants.[85] According to this argument, it's all or nothing: walls are located along 100 percent of the border and work 100 percent of the time—or they are useless.[86]

The Great Wall of China generates similar discussions of unity and multiplicity, continuity and gaps. The textbook description of the Great Wall portrays it as a sign of the nation's power, unity, and longevity.[87] The Great Wall was built by China's first unified dynasty, and the Wall as a whole is presented as unified and continuous in space and time: it is thousands of miles long and thousands of years old, the largest and longest structure built by human beings, and the only man-made structure visible from outerspace. As mentioned previously, the Great Wall exemplifies the

---

[84] See Brown, *Walled States*; Nail, *Theory of the Border*.
[85] Brown, *Walled States*, 38; Nail, *Theory of the Border*, 21, 172–176, 189.
[86] Brown, *Walled States*, 24; Vallet, *Borders, Fences and Walls*.
[87] See Rojas, *The Great Wall*, 2–3.

timeless history of a defensive foreign policy: despite substantial historical experience to the contrary, we are constantly told that China has never invaded any other country—and never will.

Upon closer examination, it turns out that none of these statements is true. The current wall was built by the Ming dynasty five centuries ago and was rebuilt by the PRC starting in 1952.[88] It is neither continuous nor visible from outerspace. There are dozens of sections of the wall that do not line up into a single-line barrier (like with from San Diego to Brownsville, Texas). Until recently, we didn't even know the wall's basic statistics; China's State Bureau of Surveying and Mapping completed the first archeological survey of the Great Wall in 2012, concluding that it is a massive 21,196.18 kilometers in length.[89] But this survey raises more questions than answers because measuring the Great Wall is more than an empirical question; it is an epistemological problem in the sense that any definition of the Great Wall is unstable.[90] There is no single continuous Great Wall; rather, there are dozens of discontinuous and overlapping walls, built at different times, by different peoples, for different purposes. Scholars deal with this epistemological instability in various ways: some use different terms to refer to the wall in different eras, while others simply pluralize the term: the Great Walls of China.[91]

Likewise, the Great Wall's morality is neither singular nor unitary. Until the twentieth century, it was seen in folk culture as an immoral artifact of the brutal tyranny of the first emperor of the Qin dynasty (221–206 BCE). One of China's most popular folk tales, the story of Lady Meng Jiang, describes the wall as a site of cruelty and suffering because it is built on the bones of conscripted laborers.[92] The Great Wall here is immoral not because it excluded vulnerable Others, but because it brutalized Chinese subjects.

Instead of seeking a more precise measurement of the Great Wall and thus asserting its unity and coherence in time and space, Carlos Rojas argues that we should celebrate its gaps, and use them to engage in a critical view of identity, territoriality and politics.[93] Historically speaking, walls were not clear markers of Civilization/barbarism. Han Chinese built walls against each other in the Warring States period (475–221 BCE), and non-Han built their own walls to guard against Han in various periods.[94] Rather than reflections of clear territorial or social

---

[88] Waldron, *The Great Wall of China*, 217.

[89] Xinhua, "China's Great Wall Is 21,196 km Long: Survey" (June 5, 2012) http://news.xinhuanet.com/english/china/2012-06/05/c_131632790.htm (accessed April 27, 2019).

[90] Rojas, *The Great Wall*, 17.

[91] See Rojas, *The Great Wall*, xiv; Claire Roberts and Geremie R. Barmé, "Introduction," in *The Great Wall of China*, edited by Claire Roberts and Geremie R. Barmé (Sydney: Powerhouse Publishing, 2006), p. 11; Waldron, *The Great Wall of China*.

[92] Waldron, *The Great Wall of China*, 201–203.

[93] Rojas, *The Great Wall*, 13ff.

[94] Rojas, *The Great Wall*, 68–69.

boundaries, the walls here are multiple and contingent artifacts. As previously suggested, Kafka's short story "The Great Wall of China" appreciates the creative power of disjuncture by showing how wall-building creates more gaps than barriers. Walls thus take on meaning through creative destruction: discontinuous construction, destruction, and reconstruction that animates more fluid loosening/tightening, inside/outside, and Civilization/barbarism dynamics. The Great Wall of China thus can be experienced as an indeterminate challenge to the unitary and essentialized master narratives of identity, culture, and territory—and hence a challenge to abstract binary notions of sovereignty, borders, and walls.

Therefore, rather than understand walls as barriers that separate countries, territories, and populations, it is helpful to understand them as gateways that can join them.[95] Indeed, a popular Chinese idiom for inside or outside the Wall is actually inside or outside the gate or pass: *guannei, guanwai*. Alongside its work as military architecture, the Great Wall was a site of meeting and exchange. At the wall, China and its Northern neighbors fostered peaceful relations through trade, in which nomadic pastoralists exchanged horses for Chinese grain, metalwork, and handicrafts.[96] As a former Chinese foreign minister explains:

> the Great Wall of China, while safeguarding the Chinese people, also served as a meeting point for economic and cultural exchange between China and the countries on the other side [that] . . . increased its friendly relations with other nations.[97]

The silk painting of the Great Wall in figure 9.2 thus helps us to question assumptions we have about walls as immoral barriers. It was made by a Korean artist and presented by the Korean ambassador to the Qing emperor as a tributary gift. This image is painted from two perspectives: inside and outside the gate. But rather than painting the "outside" of wall in protest—as often happens at the US-Mexico barrier and Israel's West Bank barrier—this pair of paintings is a vassal state's celebration of the sovereign power and cultural magnificence of the Chinese emperor as the Son of Heaven. In 2014 Beijing reasserted such wall-themed friendship diplomacy by giving its key ally, Pakistan, a silk painting of the Great Wall that hangs in the foyer of Pakistan's foreign ministry (see figure 9.4).

Certainly gateways can include harsh checkpoints that actualize (im)moral judgments of self and Other: Checkpoint Charlie, the Palestinian checkpoints, and the US-Mexico border. However, instead of understanding walls simply as blunt instruments of sovereign juridical power, it is helpful to think of power as

---

[95] See Newman, "On Borders and Power"; Williams, "Territorial Borders"; Nail, *Theory of the Border*.

[96] See MacKay, "The Nomadic Other."

[97] Huang, "Renovating the Great Wall," 12–13.

productively generated by social relationships. In this way, "Israeli checkpoints, or the 'Separation Wall' [i.e. the West Bank Barrier], are no longer perceived as spaces of division and fragmentation, but can also be recaptured as 'bridges' that connect invisible networks, space of livelihood, or collective spaces to dream."[98] Hence, rather than be examples of barriers to neoliberalism's unrestrained flows of goods and capital, here walls can also provoke the new political dynamic of governmentality, where power is produced through the loosening/tightening of flows of goods, capital, ideas, and people.

Indeed, the first major wall-building project on the US-Mexico border was not called "Operation Barrier" but "Operation Gatekeeper" (1994). Although it is common to declare that the US wall is evidence of a progressive militarization of the border, Luke argues that when compared with other countries, the United States is actually an "underwalled state."[99] Actually, the wall itself tightens and loosens according to political season. The wall mandated by the Secure Fence Act (2006) was never completed; the Obama administration suspended construction in 2010 when the project ran out of funds.[100]

Of course the border is tightening now with Trump's call to build a big, beautiful wall. But even here the moral arguments falter: when the Trump administration put out a call for bids to "design and build several prototype wall structures," 10 percent of the responding contractors were Hispanic. According to *The Guardian*, after some soul-searching many Mexican-American contractors put moral issues aside and treated the wall as a business opportunity: "My goal is to build a wall so I can make enough money so we can turn this thing around and tear down the wall again."[101]

Instead of being the site of "pure interdiction," here walls as gateways are contact zones, sites of markets and exchange where entry and exit are managed through the loosening/tightening dynamic. In the Palestinian feature film *Omar* (2013), for example, Omar's love-life is regulated according to the loosening/tightening dynamic of the West Bank barrier that he has to climb over to visit his girlfriend.[102] While Omar certainly engages in armed resistance to Israeli occupation, the wall here is treated not as an absolute barrier but as one of the many features that he has to creatively negotiate to get from here to there in the sensible politics of everyday life. While contemporary critics see walls as a moral problem of clear divisions, where all selves are xenophobic in their division from the Other, attention to this

[98] Sharif, *Architecture of Resistance*, 8.
[99] Luke, "Design as Defense," 116.
[100] Luke, "Design as Defense," 121.
[101] Julia Carrie Wong, "One in 10 Firms Bidding for Trump's Mexico Wall Project Are Hispanic-Owned," *The Guardian* (March 11, 2017) https://www.theguardian.com/us-news/2017/mar/11/mexico-border-wall-hispanic-owned-construction-companies?CMP=Share_iOSApp_Other (accessed December 22, 2017).
[102] Hany Abu-Aasad, dir., *Omar* (ZBROS, 2013).

loosening/tightening dynamic shows how the power, unity, and even morality of the wall is produced at its gaps. Rather than being evidence of "hypocrisy,"[103] the wall's contradictions are fruitful as ambiguous and multiple experiences of governmentality. The wall is not a simple moral outrage; rather, it is a new economic and political opportunity that has been provoked by a recalibrated governmentality of flows.

From Textualizing the Wall to Visualizing the Wall

In China, wall-building characteristically arose from a hermeneutic approach to international politics. Pre-modern China is famous for its meritocratic civil service, which valued ethical and literary knowledge over hereditary lineage. But this otherwise admirable policy employed textual modes of knowledge production over other ways of experiencing the world, which in turn produced particular political problems. Scholar-officials often discussed the Great Wall through texts and images that invoked the moralized Civilization/barbarism distinction described above. As we saw in Chapter 7, the oldest extant map of China, the *Map of Civilization and Barbarians* (*Huayi tu*; 1136 CE), famously includes the Great Wall as the proper unitary boundary between Civilized China and the barbaric North (see figure 7.4). The problem with this very detailed map—and with much pre-modern Great Wall discourse—is that it is based on textual references, rather than on fieldwork-based ethnographic or geographic surveys.[104] Indeed, empirical research at the Great Wall was impossible at that time because Northern China was governed by the semi-nomadic Jurchen Jin dynasty (1115–1234 CE). The hermeneutic mode, which relied on moralized distinctions between Civilization and barbarism, thus tragically narrowed the options for Chinese foreign policy to the containment or the extermination of nomads as "barbarians."[105]

The Chinese problem of textualizing the wall can help us to understand the weaknesses of current critiques of twenty-first-century walls. Brown's main argument is not based on experience, interviews, or fieldwork; rather, as a political theorist she examines classical and contemporary texts for a conceptual discussion of walls and sovereignty. Yet this detailed theoretical analysis also shows the weakness of abstract discussion: while thick descriptions of specific events show the messiness of walls, hermeneutics reproduces the problems of binary oppositions that add up to singular unity: self/Other, inside/outside, and so on. As previously mentioned, Brown posits the US wall as a single continuous structure that goes from beginning to end, and then criticizes it for not living up to this ideological standard.[106]

---

[103] Brown, *Walled States*, 101.
[104] Waldron, *The Great Wall of China*, 24, 32.
[105] Waldron, *The Great Wall of China*, 37; also see Rojas, *The Great Wall*, 73.
[106] Brown, *Walled States*, 30.

To explain the illusory power of walls, Brown recalls the story of the Wizard of Oz,[107] who appeared to be an awesome sovereign until Toto tore away the curtain to reveal an anxious and vulnerable man. This illustrates the workings of hermeneutic interpretation, which aims to trace patterns of signification and thus reveal hidden ideology. The lesson here is that walls themselves are secondary, "a derivative phenomenon" that is the product of deeply embedded social contradictions.[108] The focus on reading walls as "texts" reflects critical theory's suspicion of images and other visual artifacts.[109] It is the job of critical scholars, according to the hermeneutic mode of analysis, to deconstruct how state and corporate power use images to manipulate the general public.[110] Brown's text is exemplary in its negative view of visuality; walls are criticized as "stages," "spectacles," and "screens" that powerful people use to "theatricalize and spectacularize" sovereignty in a "ritualistic performance" that disguises hegemonic power and hides true ideological intentions.[111] Walls thus are less physical constructions than symbolic borders that are socially constructed and thus need to be deconstructed for proper understanding.

Certainly we can gain much by treating walls as "texts" to see how they function as narratives of national identity and resistance to it. But rather than just understand them as representations of narratives of sovereignty, identity, and security, a "critical aesthetic" mode of analysis helps us to see walls as a collection of nonnarrative and nondiscursive sites constructed to provoke emotions—pride, awe, disgust, outrage, and sadness—that are themselves political performances. Thus, if the chapter's first shift of conceptual frame is from figuring walls as absolute barriers to see them as gateways of governmentality, then the second shift is from hermeneutic textual analysis to a critical aesthetic mode that values detailed empirical study and creative analysis of walls as visual artifacts and sensory spaces.

When we speak of "aesthetics" in global politics, we are not discussing a theory of beauty but are more concerned with styles of ordering that raise ethical questions.[112] The shift from exclusive binary oppositions to relational dyads seen in this book is one example of a critical aesthetic approach to probing the global politics of walls. While critics commonly figure walls as screens that hide true meaning and hegemonic ideology, this critical aesthetic strategy treats visuality as an opportunity, in which screens and other visual sites are valued for their potential to excite affective

---

[107] Brown, *Walled States*, 25.

[108] Nail, *Theory of the Border*, 21; also see Sharif, *Architecture of Resistance*, 192.

[109] See Mitchell, *What Do Pictures Want?*, 342.

[110] Mitchell, *What Do Pictures Want?*, 32–33; Brown, *Walled States*, 74–75; Stephenson and Zanotti, *Building Walls and Dissolving Borders*.

[111] See, for example, Brown, *Walled States*, 26, 39, 70, 73, 90, 91, 92, 93, 104, 130.

[112] Jacques Rancière, *The Politics of Aesthetics: The Distribution of the Sensible*, translated by Gabriel Rockhill (London: Continuum International Publishing Group, 2004); Bleiker, *Aesthetics and World Politics*; Shapiro, *Studies in Trans-Disciplinary Method*.

communities of sense. In such a critical aesthetic mode, we move from seeing walls as material and/or symbolic barriers between pre-existing spaces to figure them as not simply partitions of space (e.g., territorial borders), but multisensory experiences of sight, sound, touch, and smell that (re)partition the see-able, the say-able and the think-able.[113] Resistance is not necessarily found in the emancipation of a wall-free, borderless world—for example, the liberal victory of demolishing the Berlin Wall. Rather, resistance works in a different register that emerges through more nuanced repartitions the sensible that create new political dynamics, as well as new political problems. Politics here emerges less in the formal arenas of the struggle for state power than in the broader sense of provoking affective communities of sense that complicate what can (and cannot) be seen, said, thought, and done.

While Raymond Williams discusses politics in terms of "structures of feeling," here we can appreciate walls as "infrastructures of feeling." The critical aesthetic strategy thus is helpful for understanding the Great Wall as a nonnarrative and non-discursive artifact and experience. For many it is an "[a]we-inspiring fragment of something much larger, more complex and contradictory"; the Great Wall is often described as a magnificent dragon gracefully flowing through the steep hills and deep valleys of Northern China.[114] According to Brown's understanding, however, twenty-first-century walls are awesome only in a negative way: the US wall is a "behemoth," while the Israeli wall "snakes" rather than dances through the hills.[115] These contemporary walls thus are examples of the hegemonic militarized power of "shock and awe."[116]

The Great Wall, on the other hand, can excite the sublime. Immanuel Kant uses a beautiful/sublime distinction to explore judgment, where the beautiful refers to "the form of an object, which consists in having boundaries." The object is beautiful here because it is harmonious and thus is pleasurable within accepted measures of judgment. The sublime, however, appeals to the "momentary arrest of our inter-pretive faculties" that excites a shock that can be both horrible and pleasurable.[117] While the beautiful inspires "restful contemplation," the sublime excites movement, a vibration "quickly alternating attraction towards, and repulsion from, the same Object."[118] The sublime thus can emerge through a relational mode of creative/

[113] Rancière, *The Politics of Aesthetics*, 63.

[114] Roberts, "China's Most Famous Ruin," 25; see interviews in Bill Callahan, dir., *Great Walls: Journeys from Ideology to Experience* (Wildwood Films, 2019), screened at LSE Festival, London (March 2, 2019) https://vimeo.com/billcallahan/great-walls (accessed August 23, 2019).

[115] Brown, *Walled States*, 8.

[116] Brown, *Walled States*, 104.

[117] Immanuel Kant, *The Critique of Judgment*, translated by J. H. Bernard (Amherst, NY: Prometheus Books, 2000), p. 102. Also see Michael J. Shapiro, *The Political Sublime* (Durham, NC: Duke University Press, 2018); Michael J. Shapiro, "The Sublime Today: Re-partitioning the Global Sensible," *Millennium* 34:3 (2006):657–681; Bleiker, *Aesthetics and World Politics*, 67–83.

[118] Kant, *The Critique of Judgment*, 120.

destruction. A violent thunderstorm is an experience of the mathematical sublime; it is so "absolutely large" that it causes us to turn inward, encouraging critical reflection.[119] In the dynamic sublime, we "recognize the fearfulness of nature without fearing it" and so elevate our imagination beyond the boundaries of common sense.[120] The Great Wall does not have the destructive power of a violent storm, but it does work on a massive scale. Even in its fragmented state, the wall's spatial and temporal expanse cannot be comprehended as an individual experience. As Rojas explains, the "great" in the Great Wall is the sublime: first as the symbol of territorial, ethnic, and historical boundaries, and then as the experience of boundlessness; it is thousands of miles long and thousands of years old.[121]

To understand how walls can be sublime, it is helpful to change our perspective from analyzing the wall in terms of its verticality—that is, the hermeneutic project of giving voice to vulnerable others on the Other side of the wall—to horizontally look along the wall itself.[122] Here we not only can see the clear inside-outside boundary between Civilization and barbarism, but also can experience the sublime boundlessness of the wall dancing its way through the hills like a mystical dragon. Chinese artist Cai Guo-Qiang's Project to Extend the Great Wall (1993; see figure 9.5) was an explosive public art event that celebrates the mystical nature of the wall.[123] While Fernández paints a peaceful landscape on the US-Mexico barrier to "erase the border" (see figure 9.3), Cai's pyrotechnic art lights up the night sky to violently extend the western terminus of the Great Wall by ten kilometers. Cai's art thus speaks to the violent creative/destruction and the awe-inspiring boundary/boundlessness of the sublime wall.

The sublime thus does not provide emancipation from the "moral problem" of walls; rather, it allows us to appreciate their affect-work as material performances and multisensory spaces that can excite politics in a different register. Much like Kant's understanding of the sublime as "ever being alternatively attracting and repelling,"[124] China's most famous modern writer, Lu Xun, concludes: "The Great Wall of China: a wonder and a curse."[125]

[119] Kant, The Critique of Judgment, 46.
[120] Kant, The Critique of Judgment, 118; Shapiro, "The Sublime Today," 664.
[121] Rojas, The Great Wall, 14.
[122] For a similar approach to borders, see Rumford, Cosmopolitan Borders, 39–54.
[123] See Takehisa Araki, dir., Cai Guo-Qiang: Project to Add 10,000m to the Great Wall of China—Project for Extraterrestrials No. 10 (Cai Studio, 1993); Rojas, The Great Wall, 20–22. A clip of this film can be seen at the end of Callahan, Great Walls.
[124] Kant, The Critique of Judgment, 57.
[125] Quoted in Geremie R. Barmé, "Prince Gong's Folly," in The Great Wall of China, edited by Claire Roberts and Geremie R. Barmé (Sydney: Powerhouse Publishing, 2006), p. 248.

Figure 9.5 Cai Guo-Qiang, *Project to Extend the Great Wall of China by 10,000 Meters: Project for Extraterrestrials No. 10* (1993). Courtesy Cai Studio

Visibility and Visuality at the US-Mexico Barrier

This section re-visions walls in ways that appreciate the productive tension between hermeneutics and critical aesthetics, narrative and nonnarrative, ideology and affect, and the quotidian everyday and the boundless sublime, ultimately understanding sensible politics in terms of visibility and visuality.

Weber's pair of *We Are Not Immigrants* (2016) films about the US-Mexico border exemplify such productive tensions. One film is narrative and the other is nonnarrative. Both address questions of visibility and visuality: the visibility of who is (not) allowed to cross the border, and the visuality of the anger, frustration, fear, (and occasional joy) of the sensible politics of everyday border-crossing experiences.[126] In many ways, Weber's films illustrate critical theorists' hermeneutic analysis: they show the progressive militarization of the US-Mexico border and the moral problems this barrier creates for disempowered people who need to cross the wall. It is an ethnographic approach in the traditional sense; the first film explores the experience of people from the Pascua Yaqui Nation, a Native American tribe whose community has been divided by the border's arbitrary barrier. One of the indigenous community's leaders, José Matus, makes a verbal critique—"We are not

---

[126] Also see Sharif, *Architecture of Resistance*; Abu-Aasad, *Omar*.

Figure 9.6 Negotiating a border wall. Courtesy Cynthia Weber

immigrants!"—and narrates the injustice produced by the wall that separates him from his cousins on the Other side of the border.[127]

But the film also offers a visual critique, showing Matus not just at the boundary of the United States and Mexico, but at the wall between his sovereign indigenous nation and the sovereign nation-state of the United States. Rather than being an imposing wall that is an outrage to liberalism, this wall is 2.5 meters high and has an open and unguarded gate. Matus shows its fluidity by stepping inside and outside the border of his indigenous community, in an expression of his own sovereignty (see figure 9.6). As with the Great Wall of China, it is the gaps that produce meaning—and a meaning that is not singular but ambiguous. As for many indigenous groups, here claiming and performing sovereignty is the goal rather than the problem.

The second film in the *We Are Not Immigrants* pair is nonnarrative and nonlinear. It is designed for display in an art gallery and employs three side-by-side screens that flash in and out; sometimes three images are screened in parallel, but at other times only one or two are shown. It works according to an aesthetic of loosening/tightening: the three 4:3 aspect ratio spaces enact the openness of a broad landscape that typifies the high desert, but the flashing black spaces also point to tightening. The film has an affective rhythm, but no linear narrative; it is designed to be screened in a loop, so there is no beginning or end. Scenes from the first film of the frightening experience of crossing the border are reproduced here: we see big,

---

[127] Also see Cynthia Weber, *"I Am an American": Filming the Fear of Difference* (Chicago: University of Chicago Press, 2011), pp. 78–84.

armed, border patrol officers "policing" the border by demanding documents, again and again, with a coercively official politeness.

But there are new clips as well, which provoke affect in different ways. Indeed, both films highlight how the wall is not the site of "pure interdiction," but a gateway of governed flows that is a site of exchange, play, and enjoyment. One sequence shows a party at the border, complete with a Tecate beer tent and children playing volley-ball over the wall, while a border patrol SUV drives by on the American side. The experience thus can be sublime: the horrible police state alongside a pleasurable fiesta where the wall is as much a gateway as a barrier. While Brown is very serious about the ideology of the wall, here *We Are Not Immigrants* allows a more ambiguous and creatively sublime appreciation of what the wall can do. Indeed, it shows how walls not only separate people but can bring them together as "a catalyst to promote cross-border cooperation."[128]

With the nastiness of Trump's wall-policy in mind, this argument is difficult to sustain. Walls are still an expression of post-sovereign and post-Westphalian power that is a moral outrage. Still, Trump's wall-building campaign has provoked interesting reactions. Alongside Pope Francis's serious moral chastising of Trump, a Mexican beer commercial offers a creative critique that is both sharp and playful. It starts with the familiar bird's-eye view of the US-Mexico barrier as an ominous monument to racist separation; snaking through the extreme frontier of the Tecate desert, it is sublimely terrible.[129] The narrator declares in a menacing tone, "It's time for a wall, a tremendous wall, the best wall!," with the film showing four Mexicans and four Californians confronting each other at the wall. The ad then dramatically shifts perspective in terms of both tone and scale. The wall, it turns out, is only two feet high. The narrator declares with glee: "The Tecate Beer Wall. A wall that brings us together. This wall might be small, but it's going to be YUGE!" The Mexican and Californian men go from mutual enmity to mutual amity, with hugs, handshakes, and fist-bumps. The awesome wall is brought down to earth and re-visioned on a more human scale, as a long thin table that facilitates beer drinking. More important, the Mexicans share their Tecate beer, and the Californians jump over the wall in celebration to join the party on the Other side. As in Weber's second *We Are Not Immigrants* film, the party at the border involves drinking Tecate beer in a playful, affective community of sense.

Certainly we can see this as another example of the post-Westphalian/post-sovereign era: the transnational corporation Heineken, which owns Tecate beer, employed the global PR firm Saatchi and Saatchi to set the political agenda in terms of buying more beer.[130] In a confirmation of the commercial nature of the video,

[128]   Coronado, "Towards the Wall," 265.

[129]   See *Tecate Beer Wall Advertisement*. Also see "Mexican Beer Brand Mocks Trump's Wall in Brilliant Ad," *The Huffington Post* (September 28, 2016) http://www.huffingtonpost.com/entry/tecate-ad-beer-wall-trump_us_57ec5fb3e4b024a52d2cd2b3 (accessed December 22, 2017).

[130]   See "Mexican Beer Brand."

Heineken USA refused to give me permission to use the Tecate ad in my *Great Walls* film because, they explained, they need to maintain absolute control over their brand.

But I think that this playful, thirty-second ad is fruitfully pregnant with reversals and contradictions. And it is even political in the sense of partisan campaigning; it premiered in September 2016 during the first presidential debate on Fox News, Univision, and Telemundo. More important, it shows "play" in the sense of both ludic action and flexible plasticity; the wall brings together as well as separates.[131] It creatively combines visibility and visuality in a multidimensional sensory experience that needs to be not only unpacked for political meaning, but also appreciated for political affect. Rather than political piety, here we have moral ambiguity at the wall.

Conclusion

It is common to criticize post–Cold War walls, especially the US-Mexico barrier and Israel's West Bank barrier, as ineffective and immoral. Chapter 9, however, problematizes such arguments by using the unlikely juxtaposition of the Great Wall of China and the conceptual dynamics of gaps and loosening/tightening to explore (1) how walls can be a rational security policy, (2) how they are not simply barriers but can be complex gateways for flows, and (3) how walls are not simply texts waiting to be decoded: they are also sites of nonnarrative and nonlinear affective experience that can even excite the sublime.

While many critical theorists understand twenty-first-century walls in terms of the tension between "pure interdiction" at sovereign borders and neoliberalism's unrestrained flows of goods and capital, this chapter refigures walls as gateways that are neither completely closed nor completely open and thus function through a loosening/tightening governmentality of flows. Rather than merely being an issue of security and foreign policy, walls thus can provoke new dynamics of social-ordering and world-ordering. By putting moral questions to the side for a moment, the chapter aims to understand walls in a different register as sublime experiences of horror and wonder. Walls here are more than visual images whose ideology demands deconstruction; they are also visual artifacts, multisensory spaces, and infrastructures of feeling that move and connect people in unexpected affective communities of sense.

---

[131] See Sharif, *Architecture of Resistance*, xv, 13.

Gardens in Diplomacy, War, and Peace

Introduction

Chapter 10 continues the exploration of how visual artifacts can be sensory spaces and infrastructures of feeling that provoke unexpected affective communities of sense. It examines gardens as social constructions of social-ordering and world-ordering that both shape and participate in international politics. As multisensory artifacts, gardens are a site where both political elites and ordinary people perform the sensible politics of everyday life. In particular, Chapter 10 questions understandings of international politics that employ the peace-war binary, to argue that the "civility/martiality" dynamic dyad is more helpful for understanding such social-ordering and world-ordering performances. It juxtaposes historical gardens from Japan, China, and France to flesh out the dynamics of "civility/martiality." The chapter looks to my experience in garden-building to examine how aesthetic conventions and practical techniques excite ideology and affect in two national war memorial sites: the Nanjing Massacre Memorial in China and the Yasukuni Shrine in Japan. The chapter's conclusion shows how we can use this analytical framework to better understand (and feel) the sensible politics of other key national memorial spaces, such as the National September 11 Museum and Memorial in New York. As with picture-taking, film-making, map-making, veil-wearing, and wall-building, here garden-building is theory-building: by producing new sites and sensibilities, it creatively shapes our understanding of international politics.

To explore these arguments, it is helpful to examine a twenty-first-century diplomatic controversy. On December 26, 2013, Japanese prime minister Shinzo Abe visited the Yasukuni Shrine in Tokyo to commemorate his country's war dead. A few days later Liu Xiaoming, China's ambassador to the United Kingdom denounced Abe's visit in London's *Daily Telegraph*:

> In the Harry Potter story, the dark wizard Voldemort dies hard because the seven horcruxes, which contain parts of his soul, have been destroyed. If militarism is like the haunting Voldemort of Japan, the Yasukuni Shrine in

Sensible Politics. William A. Callahan, Oxford University Press (2020). © Oxford University Press.
DOI: 10.1093/oso/9780190071738.001.0001

Tokyo is a kind of horcrux, representing the darkest parts of that nation's soul. Last week, in flagrant disregard of the feelings of his Asian neighbors, Shinzo Abe, the Japanese prime minister, paid homage at the Yasukuni Shrine.[1]

Liu here is voicing a reasonable concern that Abe is remilitarizing Japan; indeed, the Yasukuni Shrine is a controversial site because it enshrines the souls of thousands of war criminals. China and South Korea are particularly critical when Japan's leaders visit the shrine because they are still mourning the atrocities committed by imperial Japan.

Discussions of the Yasukuni Shrine thus characteristically frame it as an issue of "Japanese nationalism," "East Asian international relations (IR)," and/or the problems of "history and memory."[2] Ambassador Liu's intervention is interesting because it points in new directions. Certainly his invocation of Harry Potter follows the trend in IR that values popular culture as an innovative approach to international politics.[3] Importantly for this chapter, Liu's criticism of Abe's visit to the Yasukuni Shine also highlights gardens as sites of international politics; the Shrine is not simply a memorial, it is also a garden park.[4] While "peace gardens" as a site for relaxation are now common in everyday urban life,[5] how can we understand the international politics of gardens that actively celebrate war? This chapter thus follows the Chinese ambassador's lead to explore how gardens can be "unexpected places" for the sensible politics of diplomacy, peace, and war in a general sense,[6] and how the Yasukuni Shrine in particular demands to be interpreted as a peace/war garden.

Although gardens are a popular location for diplomatic performances—such as the Treaty of Versailles—analysis of the international politics of gardens itself

---

[1] Liu Xiaoming, "China and Britain Won the War Together," *Daily Telegraph* (January 1, 2014) http://www.telegraph.co.uk/comment/10546442/Liu-Xiaoming-China-and-Britain-won-the-war-together.html (accessed June 3, 2017).

[2] See Jeff Kingston, "Awkward Talisman: War Memory, Reconciliation and Yasukuni," *East Asia* 24 (2007):295–318; Akiko Takenaka, *Yasukuni Shrine: History, Memory, and Japan's Unending Postwar* (New York: Columbia University Press, 2015).

[3] See Iver Neumann and Daniel H. Nexon, eds., *Harry Potter and International Relations* (London: Rowman & Littlefield, 2006).

[4] See Mashima Mitsuhide, *Yasukuni no Shiki* [Four seasons at the Yasukuni Shrine] (Tokyo: Kindai Publishing Company Mashima, 2008).

[5] See Alex McClimens, Stuart Doel, Rachel Ibbotson, Nick Partridge, Elaine Muscroft, and Lesley Lockwood, "How Do the 'Peace Gardens' Make You Feel? Public Space and Personal Wellbeing in City Centre Sheffield," *Journal of Urban Design* 17:1 (2012):117–133.

[6] See Christine Sylvester, *Art/Museums: International Relations Where We Least Expect It* (London: Routledge, 2008); Debbie Lisle, *Holidays in the Danger Zone: Entanglements of War and Tourism* (Minneapolis: University of Minnesota Press, 2016); Xavier Guillaume, Rune S. Andersen, and Juha A. Vuori, "Paint It Black: Colours and the Social Meaning of the Battlefield," *European Journal of International Relations* 22:1 (2015):49–71.

is under-researched in IR. Serious research is generally located in the humanities and professional schools of art history, social history, and landscape architecture.[7] Among social scientists, geographers and sociologists have devoted the most attention to the topic, using gardens to interrogate relations of space, nature, culture, and power.[8] This chapter builds on these interdisciplinary trends to examine how gardens—like battlefields[9]—are contingent social constructions that shape and participate in international politics. Gardens here are a site, an institution, an enactment, an encounter—and an ideology. In addition to analyzing gardens as ideological sites of symbolic power, the chapter also appreciates them as concrete visual artifacts, sensory spaces, and infrastructures of feeling in which diplomacy, war, and peace are represented, performed, and experienced through more embodied, affective, and everyday encounters.[10] The aim of the chapter, then, is to highlight how peace-war becomes intelligible and thus is enacted or appropriated, in part through garden performances that employ the visibility strategy (the social construction of the visual) and/or the visuality strategy (the visual construction of the social).

To develop a framework for exploring the sensible politics of gardens, the chapter first locates its analysis in the following interrelated theoretical contexts— Jacques Rancière's "distribution of the sensible," Michel Foucault's "heterotopia,"

---

[7] See Wang Yi, *Zhongguo yuanlin wenhua shi* [The cultural history of Chinese gardens] (Shanghai: Renmin chubanshe, 2014); Geremie R. Barmé, "The Garden of Perfect Brightness: A Life in Ruins," *East Asian History* 11 (1996):111–158; Geremie R. Barmé, "Beijing, a Garden of Violence," *Inter-Asia Cultural Studies* 9:4 (2008):612–639; Craig Clunas, *Fruitful Sites: Garden Culture in Ming Dynasty China* (Durham, NC: Duke University Press, 1996); Martin Jay, "No State of Grace: Violence in the Garden," in *Sites Unseen: Landscape and Vision,* edited by Harris Dianne Suzette and D. Fairchild Ruggles (Pittsburgh, PA: University of Pittsburgh, 2011), pp. 45–60; Wybe Kuitert, *Themes in the History of Japanese Garden Art* (Honolulu: University of Hawai'i Press, 2002); Wybe Kuitert, *Japanese Gardens and Landscapes, 1650–1950* (Philadelphia: University of Pennsylvania Press, 2017); Wybe Kuitert, "Borrowing Scenery and the Landscape That Lends—The Final Chapter of Yuanye," *Journal of Landscape Architecture* 10:2 (2015):32–43; Ron Henderson, *The Gardens of Suzhou* (Philadelphia: University of Pennsylvania Press, 2013).

[8] See Zygmunt Bauman, *Legislators and Interpreters: On Modernity, Post-modernity and Intellectuals* (Oxford: Oxford University Press, 1987); Zygmunt Bauman, *Modernity and the Holocaust* (Ithaca, NY: Cornell University Press, 1989); Hong-key Yoon, "Two Different Geomentalities, Two Different Gardens: The French and the Japanese Cases," *GeoJournal* 33:4 (1994):471–477; Chandra Mukerji, *Territorial Ambitions and the Gardens of Versailles* (Cambridge, UK: Cambridge University Press, 1997); Chandra Mukerji, "Space and Political Pedagogy at the Gardens of Versailles," *Public Culture* 24:3 (2012):509–534; Timothy W. Luke, "The Missouri Botanical Garden: Reworking Biopower as Florapower," *Organization and Environment* 13:3 (2000):305–321; Gibson Burrell and Karen Dale, "Utopiary: Utopias, Gardens and Organizations," *The Sociological Review* 50:1 (2002):106–127; McClimens et al., "How Do the 'Peace Gardens' Make You Feel?"

[9] See Guillaume, Andersen, and Vuori, "Paint It Black," 2.

[10] Judith Butler, *Gender Trouble: Feminism and the Subversion of Identity* (New York: Routledge, 2006); Cynthia Enloe, "The Mundane Matters," *International Political Sociology* 5:4 (2011):447–450; Lisle, *Holidays in the Danger Zone,* 22.

and the hybrid concept "civility/martiality"—to understand gardens as a dynamic performance of "cultural governance/resistance." It then examines the (in)visibility of gardens as sites of international politics, using examples from China and Japan to show that gardens already are diplomatic spaces. Next, the chapter looks to Versailles and China's Garden of Perfect Brilliance to consider the political visuality of gardens. It examines how gardens, rather than being simply another place for standard state-centric diplomacy, can serve as spaces for the creative, sensible politics of social-ordering and world-ordering, as well as sites of resistance. In this sense, gardens are not simply visible as political sites; they enact an international politics of visuality because the gardens themselves "do" things through cultural governance performances that are often nonnarrative and nondiscursive.[11] The next section employs my garden-building experience to examine how aesthetic conventions and practical techniques actively create affective communities of sense in the Yasukuni Shrine in Tokyo and the Nanjing Massacre Memorial in China. The conclusion argues that we can use this analytical framework to better understand (and feel) the multisensory politics of other key national memorial spaces, such as the National September 11 Museum and Memorial in New York.

Certainly it is common to think of gardens as sites of unchanging, essential national identity: "The" Chinese Garden or "The" Japanese Garden. Critical analysis then would treat gardens as "texts" to see how they function as narratives of national identity and resistance to it. But this can be problematic because gardens themselves are alive, always growing and changing. These visual artifacts are also sensory spaces and infrastructures of feeling that are built, destroyed, and rebuilt, as well as real property that is bought, sold, occupied, and confiscated.[12] Furthermore, as sensory spaces, gardens allow us not only to observe IR, but also to participate in sensible politics.

Hence, rather than just understand gardens in terms of a unified narrative of culture, nature, and order, a critical aesthetic approach to international politics helps us to see these gardens as an assemblage of nonnarrative and nondiscursive scenes constructed to provoke emotions—pride, awe, disgust, outrage, loss, and sadness— that are themselves political performances. Here garden-building can be theory-building; by producing new affective communities of sense, it creatively shapes our understanding of international politics.

---

[11] See Michael J. Shapiro, *Studies in Trans-Disciplinary Method: After the Aesthetic Turn* (New York: Routledge, 2013); Kuitert, *Japanese Gardens and Landscapes*; Li Xiaodong and Felicia Lim, "Poetics of Gardening: A Holistic Approach Towards Chinese Landscape Cultivation Based on the Case Study of Yuan Ye," *Studies in the History of Gardens and Designed Landscapes* 24:3 (2004):229–249.

[12] Clunas, *Fruitful Sites*; Tobie Meyer-Fong, "Civil War, Revolutionary Heritage, and the Chinese Garden," *Cross-Currents: East Asia History and Culture Review* 13 (2014):75–98.

Aesthetics, Politics, and Gardening

This discussion of the sensible politics of gardens is again located in the "aesthetic turn" of international studies.[13] It argues that the issues of diplomacy, war, and peace can be profitably explored through an assemblage of conceptual dynamics: utopia/dystopia/heterotopia, (re)distribution of the sensible, cultural governance/resistance, and civil/military.

It is common to see gardens as a utopian space: a peaceful place, a blissful island of apolitical serenity, in which people engage in contemplation, play, and sensuous enjoyment. In both Persian and Greek, "paradise" comes from the word for a walled garden.[14] As we saw in Chapter 5, the Islamic State's *Food Security* video used garden images to evoke the new Caliphate as a utopian paradise.[15] Interestingly, in his discussion of utopia and heterotopia, Michel Foucault points directly to gardens. Utopian spaces, according to Foucault, are "fundamentally unreal spaces . . . sites with no real place."[16] Heterotopia, however, can be radical because it is "capable of juxtaposing in a single real place several spaces, several sites that are in themselves incompatible."[17] Heterotopia is a hybrid place where multiple spaces are simultaneously represented, contested, and inverted. Foucault's examples of heterotopia are colonies, brothels, prisons, cemeteries, ships—and gardens. Here, heterotopia is involved in projects of social-ordering and world-ordering; Foucault is particularly fascinated by the garden as heterotopia because it "is the smallest parcel of the world and then it is the totality of the world. . . . [It is] a sort of happy, universalizing heterotopia."[18]

Botanical gardens, for example, are a heterotopic mix of incompatible plants that juxtapose incommensurable ecosystems: alpine plants in lowland London and desert plants in rain-forest Singapore.[19] Heterotopia, then, is an interesting concept because it disrupts any search for singular meaning. Rather than engage in critique that appeals to simple reversals, such as utopia and dystopia, examining gardens as heterotopic experiences can jam such binary oppositions. This approach is useful because it encourages us to understand space aesthetically in terms of multiple, overlapping, and contingent dynamics, such as utopia/dystopia/heterotopia.

[13]   See Roland Bleiker, *Aesthetics and World Politics* (New York: Palgrave Macmillan, 2012); Roland Bleiker, "Pluralist Methods for Visual Global Politics," *Millennium* 43:3 (2015):872–890; Shapiro, *Studies in Trans-Disciplinary Method*.

[14]   Burrell and Dale, "Utopiary"; McClimens et al., "How Do the 'Peace Gardens' Make You Feel?," 124–125; Henderson, *The Gardens of Suzhou*, xi, 6.

[15]   *Food Security: Aspects from the Work of the Agriculture Administration in the Province—Wilāyat Ḥalab* (November 10, 2015) https://jihadology.net/2015/11/10/new-video-message-from-the-islamic-state-food-security-aspects-from-the-work-of-the-agriculture-administration-in-the-province-wilayat-ḥalab/ (accessed October 19, 2018).

[16]   Michel Foucault, "Of Other Spaces," *Diacritics* 16:1 (1986):24.

[17]   Foucault, "Of Other Spaces," 25.

[18]   Foucault, "Of Other Spaces," 26.

[19]   See Luke, "The Missouri Botanical Garden."

When we speak of "aesthetics" in international politics, we are not discussing a theory of beauty but are more concerned with styles of ordering that raise ethical questions.[20] Rancière argues that we need to understand aesthetics as a specific "distribution of the sensible": "the delimitation of spaces and times, of the visible and the invisible, of speech and noise, that simultaneously determines the place and the stakes of politics as a form of experience."[21] Politics, then, is found not just in the struggle for institutional power, but also in the configuration of space and sensibility that provokes social-ordering and world-ordering, especially in affective communities of sense. Politics thus takes shape either in "policing" the hegemonic distribution of the sensible or in challenging it through dissensus, a redistribution of the sensible that "disrupt[s] the relationship between the visible, the sayable, and the thinkable."[22] Politico-aesthetics here is very active, a heterotopic performance that takes in all senses of material experience.[23]

As heavily-designed spaces that forge particular relations between the see-able, hear-able, smell-able, taste-able, and touch-able,[24] gardens are exemplary distributions of the sensible. Still, the politics of material modalities and visual artifacts is often overlooked, even in critical IR, because of their indirect impact on international politics; this chapter, however, argues that gardens can shape international politics in a broader way by provoking affective communities of sense that complicate what can (and cannot) be seen, said, thought, and done.[25]

To chart out the ethical workings of such sensible politics, the dynamic of cultural governance and resistance is useful.[26] Cultural governance looks to Foucault's

---

[20] David L. Hall and Roger T. Ames, *Thinking Through Confucius* (Albany: State University of New York Press, 1987); Jacques Rancière, *The Politics of Aesthetics: The Distribution of the Sensible*, translated by Gabriel Rockhill (London: Continuum International Publishing Group, 2004); Jacques Rancière, *The Emancipated Spectator*, translated by Gregory Elliott (London: Verso, 2009); Bleiker, *Aesthetics and World Politics*; Shapiro, *Studies in Trans-Disciplinary Method*.

[21] Rancière, *The Politics of Aesthetics*, 13. There are two equally valid ways to translate Rancière's phrase: "partition of the sensible" and "distribution of the sensible." In previous chapters on veils and walls, "partition of the sensible" was useful because it highlights the work of barriers. Here, "distribution of the sensible" is a better translation because it addresses the politics of multidimensional sensory spaces.

[22] Rancière, *The Politics of Aesthetics*, 63.

[23] Butler, *Gender Trouble*; Rancière, *The Politics of Aesthetics*, 40–41; Lisle, *Holidays in the Danger Zone*, 21.

[24] Kuitert, *Themes in the History of Japanese Garden Art*; Kuitert, *Japanese Gardens and Landscapes*, 314.

[25] Jacques Rancière, "Contemporary Art and the Politics of Aesthetics," in *Communities of Sense: Rethinking Aesthetics and Politics*, edited by Beth Hinderliter, William Kaizen, Vered Maimon, Jaleh Mansoor, and Seth McCormick, 31–50 (Durham, NC: Duke University Press, 2009), p. 31; Rancière, *The Politics of Aesthetics*.

[26] Michael J. Shapiro, *Methods and Nations: Cultural Governance and the Indigenous Subject* (New York: Routledge, 2004).

understanding of power as a productive force that is generated by contingent social relationships, rather than as a set of juridical practices of sovereignty that restrict action.[27] Hence, instead of taking the "nation" for granted as an actor in a rational calculus, Michael J. Shapiro sees the nation as a set of unstable social relations that take on coherence through cultural governance rather than just through "military and fiscal initiatives."[28] Shapiro explains that alongside hegemonic cultural governance, resistance can emerge through other modalities of expression: films, journals, diaries, novels, counter-historical narratives—and gardens.[29] Cultural governance here is analogous to Rancière's policing of the distribution of the sensible, and resistance emerges through dissensus, a redistribution of the sensible.[30]

Finally, this section considers how the peace-war distinction is informed by the civil-military distinction. As Ambassador Liu's newspaper article shows, the PRC regularly presents itself as a "peaceful civilization"—especially in relation to what it sees as the "remilitarization" of Japan. Tokyo likewise proudly points to postwar Japan's "Peace Constitution" and worries about China's growing military capability. But "militarism" refers to more than the accumulation of military hardware; as Martin Shaw explains, it is better understood as "the penetration of social relations in general by military relations."[31] Indeed, while the common liberal narrative of social progress sees society civilizing the military, often the interaction results in the militarization of society.[32]

I would like to expand this consideration of civil-military relations to see how civil and military can work together aesthetically in the distribution of the sensible in war/peace gardens. IR theory's standard view of "civil" and "military" sees them as separate and distinct camps "pitched in opposition to each other" in a struggle for power.[33] To see how civil and military work aesthetically in war/peace gardens, it is helpful to examine how the civil-military distinction takes shape in another political

---

[27] Michel Foucault, "Governmentality," in *The Foucault Effect: Studies in Governmentality*, edited by Graham Burchell, Colin Gordon, and Peter Miller, 87–104 (London: Harvester Wheatsheaf, 1991).

[28] Shapiro, *Methods and Nations*, 34.

[29] Shapiro, *Methods and Nations*, 49.

[30] See Shapiro, *Studies in Trans-Disciplinary Method*, xv, 30–31.

[31] Martin Shaw, "Twenty-First Century Militarism: A Historical-Sociological Framework," in *Militarism and International Relations: Political Economy, Security, Theory*, edited by Anna Stavrianakis and Jan Selby (New York: Routledge, 2013), p. 20; also see Christopher R. Hughes, "Militarism and the China Model: The Case of National Defense Education," *Journal of Contemporary China* 26:103 (2017):54–67.

[32] Samuel P. Huntington, *The Soldier and the State: The Theory and Politics of Civil-Military Relations* (Cambridge, MA: Harvard University Press, 1957), p. 466; Paul Virilio, *Speed and Politics: An Essay on Dromology* (New York: Semiotext(e) Foreign Agents Series, 1986), p. 62.

[33] Huntington, *The Soldier and the State*, 80–86; Peter D. Feaver, "The Right to Be Right: Civil-Military Relations and the Iraq Surge Decision," *International Security* 35:4 (2011):90.

space: imperial China's *wen/wu* dynamic. *Wen* generally means "literary," "civilian," and "civilization," while *wu* generally means "physical," "military," and "martial."[34] The two concepts certainly can be understood as opposites, but not necessarily in the sense of the mutually exclusive binary opposition of "either civil or military." *Wen/wu* does not necessarily contrast the roles of different autonomous actors, such as the soldier and the civilian.[35] Likewise, *wen/wu* does not map easily onto gendered distinctions: feminine-civil and masculine-martial.[36] Rather, the ideal person in pre-modern China, Japan, and Korea harmonized a dynamic balance of civility and martiality, as both a poet and a warrior. World-ordering, national governance, family relations, and personal self-cultivation were all guided by this quest to harmonize the complementary opposites of literary and martial performances.[37] As Kam Louie explains, this civil/military dynamic is going global through East Asian popular culture.[38]

The main point here is not the (neo)Orientalist one that East Asia provides an "exotic" alternative, fundamentally different from "Western civilization." Following from earlier chapters, here we resist any geopolitical container-style organization of knowledge-production in which the choice is between the "modern West" and "traditional China."[39] Rather than replacing "Eurocentric" concepts and experiences with "Sinocentric" ones, this chapter explores how discussions of civil/military relations in different social and historical spaces can generate theoretical consensus and dissensus.

Here the argument is that civil/military is much more than a categorical distinction or a struggle between the autonomous camps of civilians and soldiers. It builds on critical IR's critique of the binary oppositions that characterize Enlightenment thought and disciplinary IR[40] to see civility/martiality as a contingent conceptual dynamic. This dynamic governs the performances of social-ordering and world-ordering in ways that can provide a more nuanced understanding of questions of diplomacy, war, and peace. The point is not simply to sort national identities as "peaceful" or "militarist," but to see how each new event (national day parade, treaty

---

[34] Kam Louie, *Theorising Chinese Masculinity: Society and Gender in China* (Cambridge, UK: Cambridge University Press, 2002), p. 10.

[35] Huntington, *The Soldier and the State*; Feaver, "The Right to Be Right."

[36] Louie, *Theorising Chinese Masculinity*, 9–11.

[37] Louie, *Theorising Chinese Masculinity*, 11, 15–17; Oleg Benesch, "National Consciousness and the Evolution of the Civil/Military Binary in East Asia," *Taiwan Journal of East Asian Studies* 8:1 (2011):133–137.

[38] Kam Louie, *Chinese Masculinities in a Globalizing World* (London: Routledge, 2015), p. 121.

[39] See Leigh Jenco, *Changing Referents: Learning Across Space and Time in China and the West* (New York: Oxford University Press, 2015); Diego von Vacano, "The Scope of Comparative Political Theory," *Annual Review of Political Science* 18 (2015):465–80.

[40] See R. B. J. Walker, *Inside/Outside: International Relations as Political Theory* (Cambridge, UK: Cambridge University Press, 1993); Shapiro, *Studies in Trans-Disciplinary Method*.

signing, military battle—and garden experience) needs to be evaluated in terms of how it performs the civility/martiality dynamic. Indeed, what is most interesting about this dynamic is its *lack* of a stable canonic definition; there is no orthodoxy, and its contingent flexibility demands that we make sense of civil/military relations through continual interpretive practice.[41]

As this section has argued, these conceptual dynamics share a common aesthetic approach that helps us to highlight how international politics takes shape through social relations, sensibility, experience, and performativity. These contingent dynamics resonate with each other in complex ways as an assemblage that offers no stable account of causality. For the sake of this chapter's analysis of the international politics of gardens, they constitute a framework for examining how gardens can act as exemplary sites where the civility/martiality dynamic takes shape as a heterotopic experience of particular (re)distributions of the sensible. Such (re)distributions of the sensible, in turn, generate cultural governance and resistance that are not simply visual experiences, but are visual/multisensory performances.

Before employing these complementary theoretical dynamics to examine how gardens create affective communities of sense, it is necessary to explore the ideological politics of the visibility/invisibility of gardens in IR.

Gardens as Political and Diplomatic Spaces

The Yasukuni Shrine and the Nanjing Massacre Memorial are not isolated examples of gardens as sites of international politics. Since the turn of the twentieth century, gardens have been an important part of public diplomacy for both China and Japan. Their goal was ideological: to use gardens as a mode of cultural governance to present their countries to the West as "civilized" and "peaceful" nations worthy of international respect— and thus not as targets of military intervention.[42] One of the first Japanese gardens built abroad was commissioned by Tokyo as Japan's official national pavilion at the Chicago World's Fair in 1893. This Japanese stroll garden was a state-directed social construction of the visual, and it was very popular, successfully presenting Japan as an exotic, civilized country that was not a threat. In 1910 the British and Japanese governments organized the Japan-British Exhibition in London to celebrate the two countries' new military alliance; it also was designed to convince the British public that Japan was not a backward country. In addition to showing Japan's modern manufactures, the exhibit displayed a traditional Japanese garden, The Garden of Peace.[43]

---

[41] See Benesch, "National Consciousness and the Evolution of the Civil/Military Binary in East Asia," 165; Louie, *Chinese Masculinities in a Globalizing World*.

[42] See Kuitert, *Japanese Gardens and Landscapes*, 144–148.

[43] Kotaro Mochizuki, *Japan To-day: A Souvenir of the Anglo-Japanese Exhibition Held in London, 1910* (Tokyo: Liberal News Agency, 1910).

After World War II, one of the ways that the United States and Japan pursued reconciliation was through gardens. The Japanese embassy in Washington, D.C., includes the Ippakutei tea house garden, which is open to the public each spring. Ippakutei, which means "Century Tea House," was built in 1960 to commemorate a century of US-Japan relations. Many cities in the United States have a Japanese garden park, often cooperatively built though sister-city diplomacy.[44] Indeed, the Japanese pavilion in Chicago was rebuilt in the 1960s with donations from the Japanese city of Osaka and is now called the Osaka Garden. Likewise, the Portland Japanese Garden in Oregon (dedicated in 1963, opened in 1967) was part of a prominent move toward reconciliation through cultural exchange at the local level.[45] As Portland's mayor explained in 1962: "This Garden will provide the citizens of Portland with an area of great beauty and serenity and at the same time represent a warm, understandable link to Japan."[46]

Chinese gardens are also popular around the world and are likewise part of diplomatic reconciliation.[47] After the United States and China normalized diplomatic relations in 1979, the first cultural exchange project was to build a Chinese garden for the Metropolitan Museum of Art in New York.[48] This garden-building was part of Beijing's general re-engagement with the world that had started in 1978 with Deng Xiaoping's reform and opening policy. By 1998 more than thirty-five Chinese gardens had been built in fourteen countries.[49] As its plan to build a $100 million Chinese garden in Washington's US National Arboretum shows, Beijing continues to see gardens as a suitable investment for influence abroad.[50] Japan and China have thus recruited gardens into their public diplomacy strategies as examples of state-led cultural governance. As in many hegemonic distributions of the sensible, gardens employ seemingly apolitical activities for very ideological aims. The success of

[44] Bruce Taylor Hamilton, *Human Nature: The Japanese Garden of Portland, Oregon* (Portland: Japanese Garden Society of Oregon, 1996), pp. 89–90.

[45] Hamilton, *Human Nature*, 1, 89–93.

[46] Quoted in Hamilton, *Human Nature*, 91.

[47] See Stephen McDowall, "Cultivating Orientalism," *International Institute for Asian Studies Newsletter* 73 (2016):12 http://iias.asia/the-newsletter/article/cultivating-orientalism (accessed June 3, 2017).

[48] Alfreda Murck and Wen Fong, "A Chinese Garden Court: The Astor Court at the Metropolitan Museum of Art," *The Metropolitan Museum of Art Bulletin* 38:3 (1980–1981):61.

[49] Joseph Cho Wang, *The Chinese Garden* (New York: Oxford University Press, 1998), p. 61; McDowall, "Cultivating Orientalism."

[50] Adrian Higgins, "China Wants a Bold Presence in Washington—So It's Building a $100 million Garden," *Washington Post* (April 27, 2017) https://www.washingtonpost.com/lifestyle/style/china-wants-a-bold-presence-in-washington--so-its-building-a-100-million-garden/2017/04/27/a334ef18-2b61-11e7-be51-b3fc6ff7faee_story.html?hpid=hp_hp-cards_hp-card-lifestyle%3Ahomepage%2Fcard&utm_term=.0026e5aa6e80 (accessed June 3, 2017).

this strategy can be seen at the UNESCO world headquarters in Paris, where global humanity's Garden of Peace is a Japanese garden.[51]

Strangely, both China's and Japan's public diplomacy strategies involve an odd recycling of Orientalist discourse that is now deployed by Asian states rather than by the Euro-American metropole.[52] But such diplomatic gardens are not merely directed at foreign audiences; as we see in the next section, as state-sponsored social constructions of the visible, gardens are a site of cultural governance (and resistance) for both domestic and foreign policy performances.

Gardens as Sites of Social-Ordering and World-Ordering

Louis XIV (r. 1643–1715) was known to have an overwhelming passion for two things: building and war. The result of both passions is the world's most famous imperial garden at the Palace of Versailles. With its geometrical design, Versailles is the best example of French formal gardens embodying the Enlightenment ideology of order, rationality, and logic. As Chandra Mukerji explains, Versailles was not simply a pleasure garden, but rather a site of cultural governance.[53] French formal gardens functioned as "social laboratories," where economic power was translated into political power.[54] The garden at Versailles was thus France-writ-small, a virtual world in which the French monarch's control over the garden embodied the French state's control over nature—and its control over society.[55] The geometric patterns at Versailles were not simply aesthetically pleasing but served to integrate diverse elements—in the garden and in French society—to reflect the hierarchies of the new centralized state.[56] As such, it is an example of Rancière's politico-aesthetics: Versailles's new relation of the visible, the say-able, and the think-able asserted a redistribution of the sensible in an affective community of sense suitable for imperial France.

[51] UNESCO, "Garden of Peace" (n.d.) http://webarchive.unesco.org/20151215223006// (accessed June 3, 2017).

[52] See Kuitert, *Japanese Gardens and Landscapes*; Clunas, *Fruitful Sites*; McDowall, "Cultivating Orientalism."

[53] Mukerji, *Territorial Ambitions*; Mukerji, "Space and Political Pedagogy."

[54] Mukerji, *Territorial Ambitions*, 32.

[55] Mukerji, *Territorial Ambitions*; Mukerji, "Space and Political Pedagogy"; David L. Hall and Roger T. Ames, "The Cosmological Setting of Chinese Gardens," *Studies in the History of Gardens and Designed Landscapes* 18:3 (1998):81; Greg M. Thomas, "Yuanming Yuan/Versailles: Intercultural Interactions between Chinese and European Palace Cultures," *Art History* 32:1 (2009):119.

[56] Mukerji, *Territorial Ambitions*, 9; Thomas, "Yuanming Yuan/Versailles"; Yoon, "Two Different Geomentalities, Two Different Gardens."

Here, Louis XIV was engaging in what Zygmunt Bauman calls the "gardening impulse," which is not just about gardens, but entails broader notions of governance. While in pre-modern Europe the ruling class functioned as "game-keepers" to keep peasants off their estates, by the early modern period the ruling class worked as "gardeners" to regulate the environment and society.[57] Bauman thus argues that the gardening impulse works to violently set *"apart useful elements destined to live and thrive, from harmful and morbid ones, which ought to be exterminated."*[58] This scientific view of social ordering informs the modern administrative state, which Bauman calls the "gardening state," in applying the violent logic of the gardening impulse to sort humanity into useful elements to be nurtured and harmful ones to be exterminated.[59]

The violence of the gardening state was not merely metaphorical. The baroque landscape of Versailles was constructed by military engineers to reflect the Sun King's martial values; the garden's battlement-style walls supported the king's hierarchal view of society.[60] Louis XIV thus integrated civility and martiality in a redistribution of the sensible that built France as a modern administrative "gardening state."

The cultural governance of Versailles also worked through garden itineraries written by Louis XIV himself; nobles, the bourgeoisie, and even peasants were invited to perform the garden by walking it in particular ways. Importantly, these tours instructed people to look at a series of views "developed as systems for showing the park, not explaining it."[61] The promenades thus were a nonnarrative and nondiscursive performance designed to surprise and delight—that is, a visuality of the sensible politics affect rather than the visibility of the discursive politics of ideology.[62] These garden visits were also a diplomatic activity: the state organized tours to impress distinguished foreigners. The goal was to display the French state's cultural and technical power, as well as its geographical and civilizational reach. Indeed, many modernizing monarchs around the world emulated Louis XIV's model of cultural governance by building their own Versailles-like gardens, such as Peter the Great's Peterhof Palace in St. Petersburg and the Bang Pa-In Palace in Thailand.[63] As a project of the gardening state's social-ordering and world-ordering,

---

[57] Bauman, *Legislators and Interpreters*, 52.

[58] Bauman, *Modernity and the Holocaust*, 70 (emphasis in original).

[59] Bauman, *Modernity and the Holocaust*, 13. Also see Luke, "The Missouri Botanical Garden"; Barmé, "Beijing, a Garden of Violence"; Jay, "No State of Grace."

[60] Mukerji, *Territorial Ambitions*, 15, 39ff.; Jay, "No State of Grace," 50.

[61] Mukerji, *Territorial Ambitions*, 13.

[62] Mukerji, "Space and Political Pedagogy"; Michel de Certeau, *The Practice of Everyday Life* (Berkeley: University of California Press, 1984), pp. 91–110.

[63] Paul Keenan, "The Summer Gardens in the Social Life of St Petersburg, 1725–1761," *Slavonic and East European Review* 88:1/2 (2010):153; *Bang Pa-In Palace* (Bangkok: Royal Household Bureau, 2003).

Versailles actively integrated civility and martiality to produce "France" for natives and foreigners alike.[64]

Like Louis XIV, China's Qianlong emperor (r. 1735–1796) had a passion for battles and gardens.[65] He is well known for doubling the territorial expanse of the empire and for expanding the size of the Beijing's Summer Palace—the Garden of Perfect Brilliance (Yuanming yuan)—and these two activities are related.[66] The Qianlong emperor certainly enjoyed the Garden of Perfect Brilliance as a pleasure garden, a place to rest and recuperate after his long military campaigns and elaborate imperial tours.[67] While it is common to see gardens as a refuge from the demands of political life,[68] the Garden of Perfect Brilliance was a site of imperial administration and governance, that, like Versailles, was a diplomatic space. While Louis XIV engaged in Westphalian interstate diplomacy at Versailles, the Garden of Perfect Brilliance embodied the hierarchical diplomacy of tributary relations in the Chinese world order: vassal states came to the garden to present tribute to the Son of Heaven (i.e., the emperor).[69] Indeed, this tribute from China's Asian neighbors often included garden-building materials such as exotic plants, ornamental stones, and strange beasts.[70] European diplomats also met the emperor in the garden; when British envoy Lord Macartney went to China in 1793, he first visited the Throne Room of the Garden of Perfect Brilliance to offer gifts to the court.[71]

The Garden of Perfect Brilliance was not simply one coherent utopian garden; it is better understood as a heterotopic redistribution of the sensible that integrated a "massive complex of gardens, villas, government buildings, landscapes and vistas, [that] drew on many elements of fantasy, of garden and scenic design, of cultural myth and imaginative practice."[72] This heterotopic assemblage combined civility

---

[64] Mukerji, *Territorial Ambitions*, 37.

[65] Maggie Keswick, *The Chinese Garden: History, Art, and Architecture*, 2nd rev. ed. (London: Frances Lincoln, 2003), p. 92; Thomas, "Yuanming Yuan/Versailles," 118.

[66] Barmé, "The Garden of Perfect Brightness"; Anne-Marie Broudehoux, *The Making and Selling of Post-Mao Beijing* (New York: Routledge, 2004), pp. 46–47.

[67] Thomas, "Yuanming Yuan/Versailles."

[68] See McClimens et al., "How Do the 'Peace Gardens' Make You Feel?"

[69] The tributary system was a hierarchical network of overlords and vassals centered on the Chinese emperor in Beijing. It was a strong example of political aesthetics in the sense that the "foreign ministry" was the Board of Rites and the Board of Barbarians, and diplomacy took the form of the "guest ritual." See Dittmar Schorkowitz and Chia Ning, eds., *Managing Frontiers in China: The Lifanyuan and the Libu Reconsidered* (Leiden: Brill, 2017). Also see Chapter 7 of this book.

[70] Keswick, *The Chinese Garden*, 45, 169; Thomas, "Yuanming Yuan/Versailles," 116.

[71] See Thomas, "Yuanming Yuan/Versailles."

[72] Barmé, "The Garden of Perfect Brightness," 113.

and martiality in interesting ways: the Qianlong emperor brought back gardening ideas from both his military campaigns and his imperial tours.[73]

The Garden of Perfect Brilliance thus functions both as a condensed version of the best gardens of the empire and as the Sinocentric world order's particular distribution of the sensible. The Qianlong emperor's main imperial residence in the Garden of Perfect Brilliance was the Garden of the Nine Realms, Clear and Calm,[74] which according to garden historian Wang Yi was the exemplary imperial garden.[75] In this "peace garden" (i.e., "Clear and Calm"), the emperor could survey the world in microcosm, with the mythological integration of the "nine realms" alluding to the legendary unification of China—and the unification of the world.[76] As with Foucault's garden heterotopia, the Garden of the Nine Realms "is the smallest parcel of the world and then it is the totality of the world. . . . [It is] a sort of happy, universalizing heterotopia."[77] And as at Versailles, military engineers constructed the imperial garden as a redistribution of the sensible that reproduced the expanding territoriality of the Qing dynasty, as well as the enduring hierarchy of the Sinocentric world order.[78]

The Qianlong emperor's gardening practice was much like that in Bauman's gardening state, which views "the society it rules as an object of designing, cultivating and weed-poisoning."[79] As the Qianlong emperor put it: "When I find pleasure in orchids, I love righteousness; when I see pines and bamboo, I think of virtue; when I stand beside limpid brooks, I value honesty; when I see weeds, I despise dishonesty."[80] The Qianlong emperor thus showed his control over nature and society through garden-building, much as Louis XIV did at Versailles.[81]

Interestingly, Mao Zedong used a similar "gardening state" logic in the mid-twentieth century. In 1956 Mao encouraged intellectuals to criticize the new socialist government when he called on them to "[l]et one hundred schools of thought contend, and one hundred flowers bloom." Ai Qing, the famous communist poet and father of Ai Weiwei, responded with a prose poem, "The Gardener's Dream." In this dream, hundreds of different kinds of flowers criticize the gardener for only cultivating roses. Upon awakening, the gardener realizes that "his world is too narrow. With no point of comparison, many ideas will become confused."

---

[73] Broudehoux, *The Making and Selling of Post-Mao Beijing*, 49–50; Meyer-Fong, "Civil War, Revolutionary Heritage, and the Chinese Garden," 89.

[74] Thomas, "Yuanming Yuan/Versailles," 126.

[75] Wang, *Zhongguo yuanlin wenhua shi*, 158.

[76] Barmé, "The Garden of Perfect Brightness," 117; Broudehoux, *The Making and Selling of Post-Mao Beijing*, 53; Wang, *Zhongguo yuanlin wenhua shi*, 158–162.

[77] Foucault, "Of Other Spaces," 26.

[78] Wang, *Zhongguo yuanlin wenhua shi*, 269–308. Also see Chapter 7.

[79] Bauman, *Modernity and the Holocaust*, 13.

[80] Quoted in Keswick, *The Chinese Garden*, 191.

[81] Thomas, "Yuanming Yuan/Versailles."

He thus concludes that to have a "kingdom of many fragrances" he needs to "let all flowers bloom in their own time."[82]

Although "The Gardener's Dream" is a characteristic act of resistance to state-led cultural governance, China's head gardener Mao was not amused. In 1957 Ai and his family (including newborn Ai Weiwei) were sent into internal exile as part of the Anti-Rightist Campaign, and they would only be allowed to return to Beijing in 1976. This crack-down also used gardening metaphors in ways that reproduced Bauman's gardening impulse: Mao told Communist cadres to distinguish between "fragrant flowers" and "poisonous weeds" in order to "weed out the old so that the new may flourish."[83] Again, this was not just a metaphor; as Ai Qing's experience shows, there were serious consequences that continue to shape the work of artist-activist Ai Weiwei.[84]

The gardening state is at work again in China with the current crackdown in Xinjiang on Uyghurs and other Muslim groups, which has interned over one million people in "re-education camps." This mass campaign treats Islam as a "disease,"[85] and the extrajudicial incarceration of over 11 percent of Xinjiang's adult population was justified by a Chinese official in terms of the gardening impulse: "You can't uproot all the weeds hidden among the crops in the field one by one—you need to spray chemicals to kill them all. Reeducating these people is like spraying chemicals on the crops. That is why it is a general reeducation, not limited to a few people."[86]

Back in the early modern period, at about the same time that grand imperial gardens were being built in China and France, expansive stroll gardens emerged in Japan. After unifying war-torn Japan at the beginning of the Edo period (1603–1868), one of the ways that the Shogun military leader safeguarded the new order was to require nobles to maintain two residences, one in their home province and another in the imperial capital (where their families were being held "hostage"). Yet the shogunate did more than use centralized military control to create social order. It employed cultural governance as the "sponsor of the imperial imagination"; elite competition for status and privilege worked largely through nonviolent means, including the construction by nobles of elaborate gardens in both the provinces and

---

[82] Ai Qing, "The Gardener's Dream," in *Ai Qing: Shi Xuan/Selected Poems*, edited by Eugene Chen Eoyang, 208–210 (Beijing: Foreign Languages Press, 1982), pp. 209, 210.

[83] Quoted in Barmé, "Beijing, a Garden of Violence," 621.

[84] See Chapter 6.

[85] Maya Wang, *"Eradicating Ideological Viruses": China's Campaign of Repression Against Xinjiang's Muslims* (New York: Human Rights Watch, 2018).

[86] "Chinese Authorities Jail Four Wealthiest Uyghurs in Xinjiang's Kashgar in New Purge," Radio Free Asia (January 5, 2018) https://www.rfa.org/english/news/uyghur/wealthiest-01052018144327.html (accessed April 20, 2019). Also see Edward Schwarck, "The Failure of China's Security Policy in Xinjiang," Royal United Services Institute, *Newsbrief* (January 11, 2019) https://rusi.org/sites/default/files/20190111_newsbrief_vol39_no1_schwarck_web.pdf (accessed April 20, 2019).

the capital.[87] By the early nineteenth century, there were more than one thousand stroll gardens in the capital alone.[88]

Edo stroll gardens worked much like the Garden of Perfect Brilliance: they were built to embody ideal social worlds, but in a heterotopic way that typically mixed references to Chinese and Japanese classical texts and popular vistas. Like the Qianlong emperor's heterotopic garden, they functioned as "theme parks" that offered a sequence of fantastic scenes rather than a singular master narrative.[89] Edo stroll gardens thus combined previous Japanese garden styles on their expansive landscaped grounds, including tea house gardens and temple gardens. The development of Japanese garden styles over the past fifteen hundred years was quite complex;[90] at the risk of over-generalization, one can say that temple and tea house gardens were developed during periods of military rule for leaders who sought to cultivate a civility/martiality dynamic as a means of cultural governance.[91]

Because Japan had little international contact in the Edo period, the focus of cultural governance in the garden was less on diplomacy and more on constructing and maintaining social order, on the one hand, and fantastic world orders, on the other. The large gardens were vibrant social sites for entertaining the shogun, the emperor, and other elites in affective communities of sense;[92] much like in France and China, people performed the gardens by walking around a central pond on a path that revealed (and concealed) a series of carefully cultivated views. Many of these Edo stroll gardens did not survive into Japan's modern period (1868–present). Those that did survive were often transformed into public parks; Korakuen in Okayama prefecture is an interesting example because it balances the civility of a stroll garden with the martiality of a castle, which rises above the garden as a "borrowed view."[93] As a gardening convention, the borrowed view plays with the inside/outside distinction to include the outside landscape (e.g., a view of Mt. Fuji) in the viewer's vista in ways that transgress the boundaries of the walled garden.

Back in China, in addition to working as sites of entertainment and diplomacy, gardens were also the site of war. Indeed, the Garden of Perfect Brilliance was itself a battlefield during the Second Opium War (1856–1860): British and French troops looted the palace of its treasures, and then burnt it down. The Second Opium War is important because it still plays a central role in China's national identity

---

[87] Kuitert, *Themes in the History of Japanese Garden Art*, 165.

[88] Kuitert, *Japanese Gardens and Landscapes*, 7.

[89] Kuitert, *Japanese Gardens and Landscapes*, 16; Marc P. Keane, *Japanese Garden Design* (Tokyo: Tuttle, 1996), pp. xi, 39.

[90] See Kuitert, *Themes in the History of Japanese Garden Art*; Kuitert, *Japanese Gardens and Landscapes*; Keane, *Japanese Garden Design*.

[91] See Kuitert, *Themes in the History of Japanese Garden Art*, 151–157.

[92] Kuitert, *Japanese Gardens and Landscapes*, 7.

[93] Kuitert, *Japanese Gardens and Landscapes*, 6–7.

narrative as a brutal clash of civilizations or, more to the point, as a prime example of how Chinese civilization—the imperial garden—was destroyed by European "barbarians."[94]

But as Geremie R. Barmé explains, the situation was more complicated than that. The war had been raging on and off since 1856.[95] In 1860 the British and French sent an official delegation to Beijing hoping to negotiate permanent diplomatic recognition from China. "After numerous prevarications, bluffs and acts of deception" by the Qing court, the latter imprisoned the thirty-nine members of the delegation in the Garden of Perfect Brilliance. They were held hostage and "subsequently tortured. Of their number eighteen died and, when their bodies were eventually returned to the Allied forces in October 1860, even the liberal use of lime in their coffins could not conceal the fact that they had suffered horribly before expiring."[96]

British and French forces discussed various ways to respond to this outrage. One option was to burn down the capital city, as new dynasties typically did in China.[97] Another strategy for the British and French was to attack the imperial garden rather than the city; the looting and torching of the Garden of Perfect Brilliance was designed to inflict pain on the Manchu imperial court rather than on the general Chinese public. In a way this can be seen as a properly Chinese reaction; Chinese armies often destroyed Chinese gardens as part of war campaigns. During the contemporaneous Taiping Rebellion (1850–1864), gardens were targeted for looting and burning by both sides in this civil war, and less than 10 percent of the fabulous gardens of central China survived this conflict.[98]

Rather than simply framing the destruction of the Garden of Perfect Brilliance as a military action, we thus can see the attack on the garden as a redistribution of the sensible that resisted China's cultural governance. It was seen not as an act of vengeance, but as an act of "justice" that would punish what the Europeans saw as China's corrupt and barbaric regime.[99] Instead of pure martial barbarism, the Franco-British strategy is a curious combination of civility and martiality. On the one hand, the garden was built to embody the Sinocentric hierarchy's particular distribution of the sensible. If we take seriously political aesthetics in France, then we should in China, too: much like the cultural governance of promenades at Versailles, diplomats in Beijing were obliged to recognize China's hierarchical worldview as they performed

[94] Haiyan Lee, "The Ruins of Yuanmingyuan: Or, How to Enjoy a National Wound," *Modern China* 35:2 (2009):155–190.

[95] Barmé, "The Garden of Perfect Brightness."

[96] Barmé, "The Garden of Perfect Brightness," 131.

[97] See Pierre Ryckmans, "The Chinese Attitude towards the Past," *China Heritage Quarterly* 14 (2008)   http://www.chinaheritagequarterly.org/articles.php?searchterm=014_chineseattitude.inc&issue=014 (accessed June 3, 2017).

[98] Meyer-Fong, "Civil War, Revolutionary Heritage, and the Chinese Garden," 79.

[99] Barmé, "The Garden of Perfect Brightness," 132–133; Keswick, *The Chinese Garden*, 57; Thomas, "Yuanming Yuan/Versailles," 27.

the imperial garden on official visits. On the other hand, the looting and burning of the garden was a political performance, a violent redistribution of the sensible that was figured as an act of resistance to the Sinocentric world order's affective community of sense. It was a key event in the redistribution of the sensible that asserted an alternative "standard of civilization": the Westphalian system of the liberal world order.[100]

Indeed, the Garden of Perfect Brilliance continues to function as a powerful site of cultural governance; this major educational tourist destination works to exemplify both China's sophisticated civilization and the barbarism of Western imperialism.[101] But that does not exhaust its impact in terms of either ideology or affect: in the twenty-first century, Beijing's Old Summer Palace has been rebuilt as a historical theme park at which people create their own meanings through the active interpretive practice of walking the grounds in unpredictable ways.[102] The Garden of Perfect Brilliance is thus a heterotopic distribution of the sensible and a visual/multisensory construction of the international that continues to combine civility and martiality in entangled ways; it is both a palace and prison, a site of diplomacy and torture, peace and war, civilization and barbarism, cultural governance—and resistance.

France and China have recruited gardens into public diplomacy as an expression of cultural governance for the performance of both domestic and foreign policy. Likewise, dissensus in gardens is neither new nor rare. During China's Yuan and Ming dynasties (1271–1644 CE), for example, gardens actually flourished as a mode of resistance. Scholar-officials turned to garden-building after they resigned in protest at what they saw as "immoral government," or after they were fired. While imperial gardens such as the Garden of Perfect Brilliance engaged in cultural governance, private literati gardens offered a redistribution of the sensible as alternative affective communities of sense, in which marginalized scholar-officials could control things in their own utopia.[103] This was not simply a private protest against official oppression; China's literati gardens characteristically were open to visits from elites on tour and to peasants during festivals. The best example is the aptly-named

---

[100] See Gerritt Gong, *The Standard of "Civilization" in International Society* (Oxford: Oxford University Press, 1984); Erik Ringmar, *Liberal Barbarism: The European Destruction of the Palace of the Emperor of China* (New York: Palgrave MacMillan, 2013).

[101] See Lee, "The Ruins of Yuanmingyuan."

[102] Barmé, "The Garden of Perfect Brightness"; Lee, "The Ruins of Yuanmingyuan"; Rancière, *The Emancipated Spectator*; William A. Callahan, *China: The Pessoptimist Nation* (Oxford: Oxford University Press, 2010).

[103] Murck and Fong, "A Chinese Garden Court," 1–9; Clunas, *Fruitful Sites*, 51–52; Keswick, *The Chinese Garden*, 121, 117, 123; Henderson, *The Gardens of Suzhou*, 12–13; Wang, *Zhongguo yuanlin wenhua shi.*

Artless Administrator's Garden, which is the largest and one of the most popular in Suzhou, a key site of traditional gardens in China.[104]

Gardens of Peace, War, and Civility/Martiality

The previous section's discussion of examples from France, China, and Japan demonstrates how gardens are part of a long and complex international historical sociology of social-ordering and world-ordering. Its focus on the historicity and sociality of gardens as spatiotemporal sites of diplomacy, war, and peace can help us to analyze the sensible politics of our two controversial examples: the Yasukuni Shrine and the Nanjing Massacre Memorial. While they are typically understood as modern war memorial sites, this section shows how both the Nanjing Massacre Memorial and the Yasukuni Shrine were actually designed as gardens and are often experienced as gardens.[105] While earlier sections have used international historical sociology to show how gardens, as social constructions of the visual, are sites of ideology, this section follows my own Japanese garden design experience[106] to explore how the aesthetic conventions and practical techniques of garden-building can excite affect. The argument is that this set of practices engages in a visual/multisensory construction of the social that can provoke cultural governance and resistance. The aim is not only to see how the memorials convey facts and figures, but also to show how they use garden-building conventions to produce political meaning and political affect—and not necessarily the ideologies and feelings that we've come to expect. While the hermeneutic search for meaning highlights the visibility of gardens, an appreciation of gardens as performances evokes their visuality as affective communities of sense.

Therefore, to understand these memorials as distributions of the sensible that creatively combine civility and martiality, it is helpful to survey the aesthetic regime, that is, the aesthetic conventions and practical techniques, of Chinese and Japanese garden-building.[107] As the Chinese gardening manual *Yuan Ye* (1631 CE) tells us, "There are no

[104] Clunas, *Fruitful Sites,*, 22–59; Keswick, *The Chinese Garden*; Henderson, *The Gardens of Suzhou*, 33–42; Meyer-Fong, "Civil War, Revolutionary Heritage, and the Chinese Garden," 80–81, 84.

[105] See Qi Kang, *QinHua Rijun Nanjing datusha yunan tongbao jinianguan* [The Monument Hall to compatriots murdered in the Japanese military invasion of China] (Shenyang: Liaoning daxue kexue jishu chubanshe, 1999); Mitsuhide, *Yasukuni no Shiki*; *Precinct Map* (Tokyo: Yasukuni Shrine, no date) http://www.yasukuni.or.jp/english/precinct/index.html (accessed June 3, 2017); Meyer-Fong, "Civil War, Revolutionary Heritage, and the Chinese Garden," 86–87.

[106] In autumn 2010, I attended the two-week intensive seminar "The Japanese Garden" at the Research Center for Japanese Garden Art and Historical Heritage, Kyoto University of Art & Design, https://www.kyoto-art.ac.jp/en/academics/research/japanese-garden-art/ (accessed April 20, 2019).

[107] See Yoon, "Two Different Geomentalities, Two Different Gardens"; *Sakuteiki: Visions of the Japanese Garden; A Modern Translation of Japan's Gardening Classic*, translated by Jiro Takei and Marc

fixed rules in garden creation; it all depends on what the landscape lends."[108] As with "civility/martiality," there is no orthodoxy in garden-building; one of the first things that garden designers learn is that there is no recipe or checklist for building the correct "Chinese garden."[109] Rather, a garden is judged by how it combines five elements— rocks, water, architecture, plants, and poetry—according to the aesthetic conventions of irregularity, asymmetry, variety, and rusticity.[110] Unlike French formal gardeners who remake the environment, Chinese garden designers often defer to the site to take advantage of the environment's natural contours and borrowed views. Certainly they still shape the site; according to *Yuan Ye*, gardening is the process of "digging ponds and piling rocks for mountains."[111] This underlines the need to construct an aesthetic balance between rocks and water, which is seen as a symbolic balance between magical mountains and sacred lakes. This aesthetic balance is not simply of natural elements, because gardens also often integrate aspects of high culture. Chinese gardens character- istically contain poetic inscriptions and architectural follies.[112]

Rather than having the precise geometry of French formal gardens, Chinese and Japanese gardens thrive on the aesthetic experience of irregularity. A common fea- ture is the zig-zag bridge, which questions the rational desire to go from here to there. Often bridges join not just different material places, but different ideological and affective spaces, leading us from one world to another.[113] Walls are another im- portant feature, but rather than perform as absolute barriers, they work like veils to both conceal and reveal.[114] As master gardener Shen Fu (1763–1808 CE) explains, Chinese garden-building employs the heterotopic art of deception: "showing the large in the small and the small in the large, providing for the real in the unreal world and for the unreal in the real."[115] Unlike with visual images, in which authenticity is a major issue, when we treat gardens as visual artifacts and multisensory spaces, then manipulation is actually valued as a way of making the strange familiar and the familiar strange. Like the civility/martiality dynamic, garden-building is a con- tingent social/visual construction, a heavily-designed distribution of the see-able,

P. Keane (Tokyo: Tuttle Publishing, 2001); Ji Cheng, *Yuan Ye Tushuo* (Jinan: Shandong huabao chubanshe, 2004); Kuitert, *Themes in the History of Japanese Garden Art*; Kuitert, *Japanese Gardens and Landscapes*; Henderson, *The Gardens of Suzhou*; Li and Lim, "Poetics of Gardening."

[108] Kuitert, "Borrowing Scenery and the Landscape That Lends," 35; Ji, *Yuan Ye*, 257.

[109] See Kuitert, *Themes in the History of Japanese Garden Art*; Kuitert, *Japanese Gardens and Landscapes*.

[110] Yoon, "Two Different Geomentalities, Two Different Gardens"; Hall and Ames, "The Cosmological Setting of Chinese Gardens"; Keswick, *The Chinese Garden*; Ji, *Yuan Ye*.

[111] Ji, *Yuan Ye*, 56.

[112] Ji, *Yuan Ye*, 76–103; Henderson, *The Gardens of Suzhou*, 21–29.

[113] See Yoon, "Two Different Geomentalities, Two Different Gardens."

[114] Hall and Ames, "The Cosmological Setting of Chinese Gardens," 175–178; Keswick, *The Chinese Garden*, 138, 146–148; Ji, *Yuan Ye*, 179–193. Also see Chapters 8 and 9.

[115] Quoted in Wang, *The Chinese Garden*, 34.

hear-able, smell-able, and touch-able, and thus of the say-able, the think-able, and the do-able.

Japanese gardens grew out of Chinese gardens, which were introduced from Korea in the sixth century CE.[116] While Chinese gardens employ five elements, Japanese gardens generally look to three elements: water, stones, and plants.[117] But once again, the dynamic of the garden lies in the way it is designed, rather than in its design elements. Japan's medieval gardening classic text, the *Sakuteiki*, opens with the declaration that gardening is "the art of setting stones."[118] It values the harmonic interplay between two-dimensional planes (ponds, raked sand, walls, and fences) and three-dimensional volumes (especially rocks and clipped plants).[119] There is always a tension between awe at nature's wildness and the need for human control,[120] which is very similar to the civility-martiality dynamic. Gardens in both China and Japan thus don't focus on flowers and plants; they are more conceptual, as an interplay of style and content that excites affective experiences in a (re)distribution of the sensible. As visual constructions of the social (and of the international), Chinese and Japanese gardens are a site of the visuality strategy: in this case, the multisensory construction of social order and world order as affective communities of sense.

Nanjing Massacre Memorial Hall

The Nanjing Massacre Memorial is the most popular museum in China. It commemorates the victims of atrocities committed by the imperial Japanese army when it invaded the Chinese capital in 1937.[121] The Massacre Memorial is thus the closest thing China has to an official war memorial; indeed, in 2014 Chinese president Xi Jinping went there to declare China's first "National Memorial Day."[122] It receives over five million visitors per year, primarily students on school trips but also an increasing number of domestic tourists. Over the May Day holiday in 2011, for example, it was packed with families, as well as a few young dating couples.

[116] Yoon, "Two Different Geomentalities, Two Different Gardens," 447; Keane, *Japanese Garden Design*, 10.

[117] Yoon, "Two Different Geomentalities, Two Different Gardens"; Keane, *Japanese Garden Design*, 38.

[118] *Sakuteiki*, 151.

[119] Keane, *Japanese Garden Design*, 16–18, 137; Hall and Ames, "The Cosmological Setting of Chinese Gardens," 180–181.

[120] See Luke, "The Missouri Botanical Garden"; *Sakuteiki*, 151, 191–192; Burrell and Dale, "Utopiary."

[121] The Memorial Hall of the Victims in Nanjing Massacre by Japanese Invaders (no date) http://www.nj1937.org/en/index.htm (accessed January 8, 2017); Kirk Denton, *Exhibiting the Past: Historical Memory and the Politics of Museums in Postsocialist China* (Honolulu: University of Hawaii Press, 2014), pp. 133–152.

[122] Xinhua New Agency, "President Xi Attends China's First State Memorial Ceremony for Nanjing Massacre Victims" (December 13, 2014) http://news.xinhuanet.com/english/china/2014-12/13/c_133851995.htm (accessed June 3, 2017).

The Nanjing Massacre Memorial Hall is an award-winning series of structures. The Memorial Hall's main exhibit is in a "tomb-like" underground history museum that commemorates the victims of wartime atrocities by graphically telling the horrific story of rape, murder, looting, and destruction. While the museum works to nail down the meaning of the memorial as singular and dystopic—militarist Japan attacking civilized China—the overall style of the memorial space is more of a heterotopic distribution of the sensible. It was designed by top architect Qi Kang, who felt his mission was to express the "social and national feelings" of the Nanjing Massacre by "embodying the historical disaster in the entire design of the environment."[123] To do this, Qi mixed the design styles of socialist realism, classical Chinese gardens, and Japanese public architecture.[124] His task was to generate an affective atmosphere using landscape gardening techniques "to give visitors a true representation of what happened in history. In a word, buildings, grounds, walls, trees, slopes and sculptures were essential elements not to be neglected."[125] The memorial has been built in four phases to commemorate the fortieth and seventieth anniversaries of the end of World War II and the sixtieth and seventieth anniversaries of the Nanjing Massacre. It thus is a heterotopic assemblage that contains many different gardens, and this chapter focuses on two of them.

The *Disaster in Jinling [Nanjing]* public sculpture opened in 1997 as part of phase two (see figure 10.1); since its organizing themes are "pain" and "hatred," it focuses sharply on what is seen as China's unfinished historical business with Japan.[126] This monumental sculpture shows a scene of violence and tragedy, in which Chinese people suffered during Japan's invasion of Nanjing, which resulted in a huge death toll and the destruction of one-third of the city's buildings. The site includes a massive decapitated man's screaming head, the frantically outstretched arm of a buried-alive victim, and a city wall that has been mutilated by artillery fire. Qi's aim here is for the memorial sculpture to be "resonant with the wails and shrieks of the dead."[127]

But on second glance, the *Disaster in Jinling* also employs many classical Chinese garden-building conventions (see figure 10.2). As Qi explains, "In design, Chinese gardens came to mind, which is a sort of concentration of nature, with mountains and pavilions put in a limited ensemble."[128] When the memorial is viewed from this oblique angle, different meanings emerge.[129] It has the familiar mix of water, rocks,

[123] Qi, *QinHua Rijun*, 12.
[124] Qi, *QinHua Rijun*, 16, 124–125.
[125] Qi, *QinHua Rijun*, 13.
[126] Qi, *QinHua Rijun*, 16.
[127] Qi, *QinHua Rijun*, 17.
[128] Qi, *QinHua Rijun*, 16.
[129] Rancière, *The Emancipated Spectator*, 111ff; Geoffrey Whitehall and Eric Ishiwata, "The International Aesthetic of the Yasukuni Jinja and the Yushukan Museum," in *The New Violent Cartography: Geo-Analysis after the Aesthetic Turn*, edited by Sam Okoth Opondo and Michael J. Shapiro (New York: Routledge, 2012), pp. 234–247.

Figure 10.1 Disaster in Jinling, Nanjing Massacre Memorial (2017). Courtesy Wikimedia

Figure 10.2 Disaster in Jinling, close up (1999). Source: Qi, *QinHua Rijun Nanjing datusha yunan tongbao jinianguan*

Figure 10.3 Peace Tower (2009). Courtesy Wikimedia

and architecture, and there is a harmonic dynamic between the water-like gravel in the front and the mountain-like wall in the rear. The sculptures of a dismembered head and a clawing arm resemble a Chinese garden's ornamental stones. The bullet-ridden city wall, inscribed with the official number of victims—300,000 dead—is much like a garden's symbolic mountain range inscribed with classical poetry. Finally, the curved bridge takes visitors over a river of gravel to a different affective space that has vibrant pine trees that evoke virtue and eternal life.[130] Hence, *Disaster in Jinling* is not simply a memorial; it is a Chinese garden that visually excites feelings of anger, loss, and remembrance in a particular affective community of sense.[131]

The second example is Peace Square, which opened in 2007 to mark the seventieth anniversary of the Nanjing Massacre. It has a long reflecting pool at the center on an East-West axis, a landscaped garden to the south, and a bas-relief wall to the north. The focus of Peace Square is on Peace Tower at the West end of the reflecting pool; the tower integrates three "peace symbols" into one sculpture: a woman who both carries a child and releases a dove (see figure 10.3). Rather than a Chinese garden, Peace Square is a more generic, modern garden-park. Still, it uses some Chinese aesthetic conventions to conceal and reveal the view;[132] to enter the garden,

---

[130] See Keswick, *The Chinese Garden*, 191; Henderson, *The Gardens of Suzhou*.

[131] See Meyer-Fong, "Civil War, Revolutionary Heritage, and the Chinese Garden," 86–87; Emma Hutchison, *Affective Communities in World Politics: Collective Emotions After Trauma* (Cambridge, UK: Cambridge University Press, 2016), p. 128.

[132] Keswick, *The Chinese Garden*, 28, 37.

Figure 10.4 Peace through strength (2013). Courtesy Wikimedia

you have to first pass through a very dark commemoration hall before coming out into the bright light that reveals the beautiful scene of the reflecting pool with the Peace Tower at the end. Once again, the garden bridge leads you from the dark horrors of war to the bright sunshine of peace.

But what kind of "peace" is presented in this garden?[133] China's military victory over Japan is displayed by the bugling soldier, whose boot stands on a Japanese helmet and sword (see figure 10.4). As the sculpture shows, this garden embodies a particular civility/martiality dynamic: peace through strength. Behind the bugler is a large bas-relief *Wall of Victory* that records how the Communist Party heroically led the Chinese people to employ military force to triumph over Japan. Peace here is seen as the result not of mutual understanding, but of military strength.

---

[133] For a discussion of what counts as a "peace image," see Frank Möller, *Visual Peace: Images, Spectatorship, and the Politics of Violence* (London: Palgrave Macmillan, 2013).

While Qi Kang's goal is to foster peace and promote reconciliation through garden-style landscape architecture, the memorial's particular distribution of the sensible works to produce feelings of fear, outrage, and hate. Peace here is experienced not in terms of nonviolence or reconciliation, but in terms of a celebration of overwhelming military force and invocations of raw emotion. This peace-war dynamic was underlined in 2002 when a plan to rename the massacre memorial the "Nanjing International Peace Center" generated outrage among the Chinese public. After it was found that 80 percent of Nanjing residents opposed the plan, it was dropped.[134] In 2015 the memorial opened an annex dedicated to a new exhibit, *Three Victories: The Victory of the Anti-Fascist War in the China Theater and Judging the Historical Truth of Japan's War Crimes*.[135] Hence, in China the cultural governance of anti-Japanese historiography and militarized peace is hegemonic, allowing only limited space for resistance.[136]

Even so, there are opportunities for people to performatively experience the garden in ways that resist state-led cultural governance. For example, teenagers on a date are likely to be engaging in their own redistribution of the sensible. Back at Peace Square, during my visit in 2011 resistance emerged through an unintentional use of a Chinese garden-building convention. Behind the Peace Tower is an impious "borrowed view": the sacred (socialist) patriotism of the site is violated by the (capitalist) profanity of the billboard for Jinsheng International Property (see figure 10.3).

Yasukuni Shrine

Like most national war memorials, the Yasukuni Shrine in central Tokyo commemorates the sacrifice of people who died for their country.[137] The souls of fallen soldiers are enshrined at this Shinto temple, which is sponsored by the Japanese emperor (see figure 10.5). It is also a controversial place, because in 1978 the souls of fourteen "Class A" war criminals and 5,700 "Class B and C" war criminals were secretly enshrined there.[138] Hence, as the Chinese ambassador's intervention described previously shows, there was outrage when Prime Minister Shinzo Abe visited the Yasukuni Shrine in 2013.

---

[134] Huang Ying, "80% Nanjing Citizens Strongly Opposed to Rename 'Nanjing Massacre Memorial Hall,'" *People's Daily* (March 26, 2002) http://en.people.cn/200203/25/eng20020325_92780.shtml (accessed January 21, 2019).

[135] The Memorial Hall of the Victims in Nanjing Massacre.

[136] See William A. Callahan, "Identity and Security in China: The Negative Soft Power of the China Dream," *Politics* 35:3–4 (2015):216–229.

[137] See Jenny Edkins, *Trauma and the Memory of Politics* (Cambridge, UK: Cambridge University Press, 2003), pp. 57–110.

[138] Kingston, "Awkward Talisman"; Takenaka, *Yasukuni Shrine*.

Figure 10.5 Yasukuni Shrine, Tokyo (2004). Courtesy Wikimedia

To many in East Asia, the Yasukuni Shrine is not a utopian site for national heroes but a dystopian site that celebrates wartime atrocities. Abe's visit thus provoked a general concern about the return of Japanese militarism and was seen as part of his reinterpretation of Japan's Peace Constitution to expand the role of the military.[139] The Yusukan Museum, which is on the grounds of the shrine and guides mainstream understandings of this memorial, shows that there is cause for concern. The museum's tour of Japanese history, with its scenes of war, death, and martial commemoration, glorifies Japan as both a heroic warrior nation and an unrepentant victim.[140] The Yusukan Museum thus embodies a distribution of the sensible that serves to police the meaning of the Yasukuni Shrine and of the Japanese nation according to a stable linear narrative of patriotic coherence and unity.[141]

But there is more to the Yasukuni Shrine than the Yusukan Museum; in many ways, the shrine is an Edo stroll garden that juxtaposes different elements and

---

[139] Marie Thorsten, "Soft-Hard Power Convergence and Democracy in Abe's Japan," in *Power in Contemporary Japan*, edited by Gill Steel (London: Palgrave, 2016), pp. 239–262.

[140] See *Record in Pictures of Yushukan* (Tokyo: Kindai Publishing Co., 2009).

[141] See Edkins, *Trauma and the Memory of Politics*; Whitehall and Ishiwata, "The International Aesthetic of the Yasukuni Jinja."

styles.[142] To enter, you can pass through Japan's largest shrine gate and promenade up the central path through landscaped gardens complete with statuary, stone lanterns, religious out-buildings, and market stalls. After passing through another gate, you enter the "Inner Garden," a temple garden that is dominated by Yasukuni's Main Shrine and also contains other temple and tea house gardens: behind the shrine is the Sacred Pond Garden, which includes three tea house gardens.[143]

When recognized as a heterotopic garden park that combines civility and martiality, the Yasukuni Shrine complex can accommodate meanings and feelings that resist the militarism of the Yushukan Museum. To put it another way, there is more than one way to experience the shrine. Most people outside Tokyo only see the shrine when it is a site of key national events, especially the militarist and pacifist demonstrations sparked by the visits of leading politicians on important event days. But for people who live and work in the neighborhood, the shrine has different meanings that are not exhausted by the war-peace binary opposition. While it is a sacred imperial shrine, it is also a space of rambling everydayness. People crisscross it as part of their everyday activities, creating different meanings as they walk.[144] Much like Louis XIV's Versailles, the shrine is a space of visual/multisensory performances of cultural governance that excite particular affective communities of sense. But unlike Versailles, it is also a site of resistance to both militarism and its opposite, pacifism. It is a sacred space and a hypernationalist site, but it is also a short cut, a place for a smoke or to eat lunch on a sunny day (see figure 10.6).[145] Unlike the Nanjing Massacre Memorial, which is mostly contained behind high walls, the Yasukuni Shrine, like many urban peace gardens, is a crossroads for pedestrian traffic at the heart of the city.[146]

Walking in Tokyo, Yasukuni Shrine is a fascinating YouTube video that records the experience of simply walking through the shrine and thus performing this Japanese stroll garden via an impious itinerary.[147] The video was a response to a film made of the hypernationalist crowds that gathered in 2006 to cheer on Prime Minister Junichiro Koizumi's controversial visit to the Yasukuni Shrine on August 15, the day that Japan marks the end of World War II. The YouTube video aims to show how the Yasukuni Shrine has meanings beyond hypernationalism and militarism. Importantly, it does this without any narration, letting the images and sounds of partisan contestation and everyday life do the political work.

---

[142] See Mitsuhide, *Yasukuni no Shiki*; Kuitert, *Japanese Gardens and Landscapes*, 1–44, 247–307.

[143] See *Precinct Map*.

[144] See de Certeau, *The Practice of Everyday Life*, 91–110; Enloe, "The Mundane Matters."

[145] Whitehall and Ishiwata, "The International Aesthetic of the Yasukuni Jinja."

[146] See McClimens et al., "How Do the 'Peace Gardens' Make You Feel?," 122; Keenan, "The Summer Gardens in the Social Life of St Petersburg," 154.

[147] Egawauemon, *Walking in Tokyo, Yasukuni Shrine*, YouTube (August 18, 2008) http://www.youtube.com/watch?v=Ew9AllEWehM (accessed June 3, 2017).

Figure 10.6 Yasukuni Shrine, Sacred Pond Garden (2016). Source: Koinsky, Flickr

The video starts off outside the shrine grounds in the midst of a political demonstration complete with banners, activists with loudspeakers, and helicopters circulating overhead. It offers the perspective of an ordinary visitor, walking in the front gate and up the main pedestrianized avenue of the Yasukuni Shrine, performing it as an Edo stroll garden. It is fascinating to see—and hear—the multisensory experience evolve from partisan politics to the politics of everyday life. The people walking the site shift from activists outside the gate to a human assemblage on the shrine grounds: salarymen (white-collar workers), students, families, tourists, and shoppers all out for a stroll. The sound of the loudspeakers and helicopters is gradually overwhelmed by the screech of crickets, the murmur of private conversation, and music from the temple. Surely some people are going to the Yusukan Museum, but that is not the focus of this film. Others pause to experience the sacred space, while yet another set of people traverse the site as a crossroads between here and there. In this way, meaning is actively constructed in perambulative performances worthy of de Certeau's practice of everyday life and Rancière's emancipated spectator.[148]

This nonnarrative film thus encourages us to change the question from "what" is the meaning of the Yasukuni Shrine to "when" and "where" are the meaning of the shrine? If we find the film's perambulative performance meaningful, then we can appreciate the Yasukuni Shrine as an Edo stroll garden that creatively resists the state-led cultural governance that frames politics in terms of war versus peace. Rather than allow the Yusukan Museum to determine the ideology of the experience, we can look to the Sacred Pond Garden at the back of the shrine to reframe our understanding of it as a site of life, reflection, and other possibilities (see figure 10.6). Still, one of my visual IR students was outraged at this analysis, which he criticized as normalizing Japanese militarism. He stated that instead of walking the shrine in impious ways, "as a Korean, it's my duty to burn down the Yasukuni Shrine."

Yet to redistribute the sensible and thereby resist cultural governance, I argue that it is not necessary to burn down China's imperial garden, as the Anglo-French forces did in 1860, or to torch the Yasukuni Shrine now. People can resist state-led cultural governance simply by experiencing the garden as a heterotopia that redistributes the sensible dynamic of civility and martiality in performances that not only counter militarism, but also resist the war-peace framing of international politics. In this way, the garden experience moves from ideology to affect, and from questions of visibility to performative experiences of visuality that excite affective communities of sense.

---

[148] de Certeau, *The Practice of Everyday Life*, 91–114; Rancière, *The Emancipated Spectator*; Enloe, "The Mundane Matters."

Conclusion

This chapter explores the contingent social and visual workings of key gardens to make two main arguments. First is the visibility/invisibility argument: gardens are "unexpected spaces" for the international politics of social-ordering and world-ordering, which in turn impact issues of diplomacy, war, and peace. Second is the visuality argument: to understand the sensible politics of gardens, it is necessary to take an aesthetic approach to IR that appreciates visual artifacts as heterotopic (re) distributions of the sensible that can embody new visual/multisensory performances of cultural governance and resistance. Specifically, the chapter questions how we categorize the Nanjing Massacre Memorial and the Yasukuni Shrine as "peace gardens" or "war gardens" to explore how they function as distributions of the sensible that embody particular civility/martiality dynamics. As we have seen, such (re) distributions of the sensible, in turn, can generate cultural governance and resistance. Gardens here are infrastructures of feeling that provoke unexpected affective communities of sense.

Rather than performing a simple reversal to see the Nanjing Massacre Memorial as a war garden and the Yasukuni Shrine as a peace garden, this analysis aims to shake loose such binary distinctions and iconic images to better appreciate the creative play in the civility/martiality dynamic.[149] Such oblique interventions underline how war memorials, gardens, and other unexpected spaces of IR are not stable containers of ideology, but instead need to be actively (re)interpreted as multisensory performances of cultural governance and resistance. As noted, what is most interesting about the civility/martiality dynamic is its *lack* of a stable canonic definition; there is no orthodoxy. Likewise, for garden-building in China and Japan, there is no canonic recipe for building the correct garden; rather, garden design generally defers to the site and to other specific factors. The contingent flexibility of the civility/martiality dynamic and garden-building strategies thus demands that we make sense of the sensible politics of gardens through continual interpretive practice and performative experience.

This chapter addresses East Asian international politics because that is my particular area of interest and expertise. But as the example of Versailles shows, this research deploys unexpected juxtapositions and new concepts to call into question any (neo)Orientalist regionalization of international studies. Indeed, the hope is that this research will generate further studies of the international politics of gardens that will explore examples from other times and places. For example, what sense can we make of the National September 11 Museum and Memorial in New York, which embodies a particular civility/martiality dynamic in its heterotopic distribution of the sensible? On the one hand, the official museum seems to follow the distribution

---

[149] See Rancière, *The Emancipated Spectator*, 48–49.

of the sensible seen at the Nanjing Massacre Memorial. Both provoke raw emotions through their intimate connection to death: the Massacre Memorial is built on the site of a mass grave, and thousands of people died a violent death at Ground Zero. Both underground museums seek to stabilize the meaning of the tragedy (and the identity of the nation) by assigning the roles of villains and victims in a tragically heroic narrative.[150]

On the other hand, rather than being walled-off like the Nanjing Massacre Memorial, the above-ground 9/11 memorial is open, like the Yasukuni Shrine. As a key hub in New York's mass transportation system, it is even more of a crossroads that people traverse going from here to there in everyday life, as well as on particular pilgrimages. Michael Arad's *Reflecting Absence* memorial is radically open: twin voids that controversially reproduce the gaping wound in the cityscape as a pair of black holes. Like the Japanese stroll garden, this water garden is open to multiple interpretations as a site of life, death, and rebirth.[151]

As this exploratory discussion suggests, the 9/11 memorial is ripe for further analysis; it can be profitably analyzed as a garden heterotopia that redistributes the sensible dynamic of civility and martiality in performances of cultural governance and resistance. It highlights how, as infrastructures of feeling, memorials and gardens are not just visual experiences but are entangled performances that provoke affective communities of sense. As visual artifacts, material modalities, and sensory spaces, gardens allow us to not only observe IR, but also participate in international politics. Like picture-taking, film-making, map-making, veil-wearing, and wall-building, here garden-building is theory-building: by producing new sites and sensibilities, it creatively shapes our understanding of IR.

[150] See Allison Blais and Lynn Rasic, *A Place of Remembrance, Updated Edition: Official Book of the National September 11 Memorial* (New York: National Geographic, 2015).

[151] See G. Roger Denson, "Michael Arad's 9/11 Memorial 'Reflecting Absence': More Than a Metaphor or a Monument," *Huffington Post* (September 9, 2011) http://www.huffingtonpost.com/g-roger-denson/michael-arads-911-memoria_b_955454.html (accessed June 3, 2107); Blais and Rasic, *A Place of Remembrance*; Marita Sturken, "The Objects That Lived: The 9/11 Museum and Material Transformation," *Memory Studies* 9:1 (2016):13–26; Michael J. Shapiro, *The Political Sublime* (Durham, NC: Duke University Press, 2018), pp. 166–167.

11

Visibility, Visuality, and Mass (Self)Surveillance

Governments of the Industrial World, you weary giants of flesh and steel, I come from Cyberspace, the new home of Mind. On behalf of the future, I ask you of the past to leave us alone. You are not welcome among us. You have no sovereignty where we gather. . . . We are creating a world where anyone, anywhere may express his or her beliefs, no matter how singular, without fear of being coerced into silence or conformity.

—John Perry Barlow
"A Declaration of the Independence of Cyberspace" (1996)[1]

Devotedly keeping watch over heaven and earth every day,
Taking up our mission as the sun rises in the East,
Innovating every day, embracing the clear and bright,
Like warm sunshine moving in our hearts,
Unified with the strength of all living things,
Devoted to turning the global village into the most beautiful scenery.
Internet superpower! The Internet is where glorious dreams are.
Internet superpower! From the distant cosmos to our longed-for home.
Internet superpower! Tell the world that the China Dream is lifting up the great China.

Internet superpower! Each of us represents our country to the world.

—"Cyberspace Spirit"
Anthem of the Cyberspace Administration of China (2015)[2]

As the first quotation declares, the Internet, as a free-wheeling, transnational civil society, promised to emancipate us from authoritarian states and conservative

---

[1] John Perry Barlow, "A Declaration of the Independence of Cyberspace" (February 8, 1996) https://www.eff.org/cyberspace-independence (accessed June 2, 2018), quoted in Alexander Klimburg, *The Darkening Web: The War for Cyberspace* (New York: Penguin Press, 2017), p. 14.

[2] *"Cyberspace Spirit,"* Cyberspace Administration of China, YouTube (February 2015) https://www.youtube.com/watch?v=-QlNjvWlWZk (accessed June 3, 2018).

Sensible Politics. William A. Callahan, Oxford University Press (2020). © Oxford University Press.
DOI: 10.1093/oso/9780190071738.001.0001

societies. In 2000 US president Bill Clinton echoed this view when he mocked China's effort to control the Internet: "Good luck! That's sort of like trying to nail Jell-O to the wall." As debates over the Arab Spring of 2011 show, Internet platforms such as Facebook and Twitter can play an important part in mobilization and social change in authoritarian states. This certainly has been seen in Beijing as a pertinent example of the Internet's potential threat to regime stability in the PRC.[3]

More recently, however, surveillance scandals about the Internet have burst into the news on a regular basis. In 2013 there was global outrage after Edward Snowden revealed the massive size and scope of PRISM (Personal Record Information System Methodology), the global data mining project run by the US National Security Agency (NSA) and the Five Eyes intelligence alliance (US, UK, Canada, Australia, New Zealand).[4] In 2017–2018, again, there was concern about how Cambridge Analytica had worked with social media platforms to influence the 2015 Brexit referendum in the United Kingdom and the 2016 Trump election in the United States.

As these examples show, surveillance is not just an issue for authoritarian states. It is also a problem in liberal democracies and emerges in the overlapping private/public sphere of local, national, and transnational spaces, with battles over transparency, regulation, and sovereignty on the global stage. Surveillance thus is an issue of visibility: it characteristically becomes visible when it generates moral panic. Otherwise, to be effective surveillance itself is largely invisible, whether it is parents monitoring their children's social media activity, Facebook tracking your "likes," or a state spying on foreign rivals—and its own citizens.

Cybersecurity for individuals, companies, and nation-states is certainly a serious issue. But rather than just raising questions of security, surveillance also provokes questions of order. Chapter 11 thus turns the question of visibility around—not just what we see, but how we are seen in various gazes and how we perform in various spaces—to explore how surveillance engages in social-ordering and world-ordering in the twenty-first century. Following previous chapters, the chapter examines surveillance in terms of the ideological-work of what it means and the affect-work of what it does—and even what it desires.[5]

Surveillance thus is another profitable site for analysis using the visibility/visuality dynamic, in which the visibility strategy works to make more visible the

[3] Shaun Breslin, "China and the Arab Awakening," *ISPI Analysis* 140 (2012):1–8.

[4] See Zygmunt Bauman, Didier Bigo, Paulo Esteves, Elspeth Guild, Vivienne Jabri, David Lyon, and R. B. J. Walker, "After Snowden: Rethinking the Impact of Surveillance," *International Political Sociology* 8 (2014):121–144.

[5] Didier Bigo, "Security, Surveillance, and Democracy," in *Routledge Handbook of Surveillance Studies*, edited by Kirstie Ball, Kevin D. Haggerty, and David Lyon (New York: Routledge, 2014), p. 282; Jonathan Finn, "Seeing Surveillantly: Surveillance as Social Practice," in *Eyes Everywhere: The Global Growth of Camera Surveillance*, edited by Aaron Doyle, Randy Lippert, and David Lyon (London: Routledge, 2012), pp. 67–80; W. J. T. Mitchell, *What Do Pictures Want? The Lives and Loves of Images* (Chicago: University of Chicago Press, 2005).

invisible ideological distinctions of security/freedom, public/private, and democratic/authoritarian, while the visuality strategy looks at how affect-work can create a new way of seeing, feeling, and perhaps doing in communities of sense. It is important to make visible the largely invisible artifacts of surveillance—Internet infrastructure, hidden cameras, and algorithms—and it is also important to appreciate the visuality of how people now "see surveillantly" in sensory spaces as a "social practice [that] requires a self-reflexive look at our own willingness and desire to watch, record and display our lives and the lives of others."[6] As Kathleen P. J. Brennan explains, the Internet is a "visual realm" wherein images emotionally connect people first, who then search for information.[7]

Admittedly, analysis of the visual international politics of surveillance is an odd way to conclude Part III, "Visual Artifacts." Cyberspace doesn't really fit into the distinction between two-dimensional visual images and three-dimensional visual artifacts. But this chapter looks at surveillance in terms of the interplay of three-dimensional surveillance infrastructure and online images and experiences. Together they produce a multisensory social space for ideological work and affective performances. As with walls and gardens, here a visual artifact is more than a "thing": it is a social space that is human-designed and performative. The Internet thus is an infrastructure of feeling that provokes a range of affective communities of sense.

This chapter develops the visibility/visuality and ideology/affect conceptual dynamics through the juxtaposition of surveillance concepts, practices, and experiences in Europe, the United States, and China. These examples are at times unwieldy, showing how surveillance doesn't readily fit into established categories; because of the dearth of analysis on surveillance in China, there is more discussion of that country.[8] The chapter argues that while it's common to look at airports to see the future of security and surveillance practices,[9] we actually need to look to China—and specifically at the Social Credit System and the cyber-police state in Xinjiang—to appreciate how surveillance practice works through an entangled ecology of surveillance, sousveillance, and co-veillance, which I call "inter-veillance."

---

[6] Finn, "Seeing Surveillantly," 79; David Lyon, *The Culture of Surveillance: Watching as a Way of Life* (Cambridge, UK: Polity Press, 2018), pp. 113ff.

[7] Kathleen P. J. Brennan, "Memelife," in *Making Things International 1: Circuits and Motion*, edited by Mark B. Salter (Minneapolis: University of Minnesota Press, 2015), pp. 244, 252.

[8] For a discussion of the problem of the lack of surveillance studies beyond Euro-America, see James Leibold, "Surveillance in Xinjiang: Ethnic Sorting, Coercion, and Inducement," *Journal of Contemporary China* (May 31, 2019):2, https://doi.org/10.1080/10670564.2019.1621529 (accessed August 23, 2019).

[9] See Mark B. Salter, *Politics at the Airport* (Minneapolis: University of Minnesota Press, 2008); Lyon, *The Culture of Surveillance*, 61–71; Debbie Lisle, *Holidays in the Danger Zone* (Minneapolis: University of Minnesota Press, 2016).

This is not just a matter of domestic politics in China, because the PRC is exporting its hardware and software of surveillance and control through its massive infrastructure development projects, which in turn increasingly impact governance norms on the Internet.[10] But the sensible politics of surveillance is not simply an ideological battle between (Western) freedom and (Chinese) order; similar technologies are exciting similar performances in affective communities of sense around the world, especially on social media. The chapter thus compares how surveillance provokes censorship, self-discipline, and creative social-ordering in China, the United States, and Europe. While the epigraphs at the beginning of the chapter suggest that critical politics requires either resisting state control or asserting state control, Chapter 11 considers how both democratic and authoritarian countries see surveillance in terms of social and moral order. The conclusion is that surveillance provokes political and moral questions rather than technical or cultural issues, and that it is important to move beyond questions of cybersecurity to appreciate surveillance as a social-ordering and world-ordering process that excites affective communities of sense.

Surveillance Studies and Visual International Politics

Surveillance studies emerged in the 1960s as the sociological study of domestic policing issues. Scholarly interest in international surveillance was later provoked by the US government's high-tech response to terrorism after 9/11, and especially after the global scale of data mining by the NSA and Five Eyes was revealed in 2013. While it is common to focus on the United States—many publications frame their analysis in terms of post-9/11 and post-Snowden[11]—we should remember that the United Kingdom and China compete for recognition as the world's most surveilled societies. Britain's CCTV monitoring system, which was pioneered in the City of London's "Ring of Steel" project, was developed after the Irish Republican Army started targeting England in the 1980s; the Great Firewall of China was set up to block democracy soon after China hooked up to the Internet in 1994.[12] Since

---

[10] See Office of the Leading Group for the Belt and Road Initiative, *Building the Belt and Road: Concept, Practice and China's Contribution* (Beijing: Foreign Languages Press, May 2017), pp. 27–28; James Griffiths, *The Great Firewall of China: How to Build and Control an Alternative Version of the Internet* (London: Zed, 2019).

[11] See Lyon, *The Culture of Surveillance*; Bauman et al., "After Snowden"; Louise Amoore, "Vigilant Visualities: The Watchful Politics of the War on Terror," *Security Dialogue* 38:2 (2007):215–232; Rex Troumbley, "Colonization.com: Empire Building for a New Digital Age," *East-West Affairs* 1:4 (2013):93–107.

[12] Eric Lipton, "To Fight Terror, New York Tries London's 'Ring of Steel,'" *New York Times* (July 24, 2005), p. C3; Geremie R. Barmé and Sang Ye, "The Great Firewall of China," *Wired* (June 1, 1997) https://www.wired.com/1997/06/china-3/ (accessed June 23, 2018); State Council Information

these projects preceded 2001, they are best not understood as a "reaction" to US threats; indeed, after 9/11 the United States actively tried to learn from London's surveillance experience.[13] While surveillance studies characteristically focus on Europe and North America, we also need to appreciate China as an influential source of concepts, policies, and experiences for the visual international politics of surveillance.

Pundits often assume that all surveillance is bad, yet the discipline of surveillance studies actually highlights its Janus-faced character, analyzing the "negative" state/corporate invasions of privacy as well as the potentially positive activity of "good gazing" for the care of the other.[14] The two epigraphs sketch not only the parameters of debates about cyberspace, but also their normative moral arguments. On the one hand, we have the cyber-utopian demand for a free and democratic space beyond nations on the global Internet superhighway, and on the other, we have the cyber-dystopia of authoritarian state power that demands cyber-sovereignty and cyber-surveillance on distinct national intranets. Of course these views can be seen from an alternative perspective: the Chinese party-state sees democracy and civil society as existential threats, and a "clean and righteous" national Internet is not only an instrumental political tactic for regime security but also a normative moral goal.[15]

Although China's surveillance project seems to be an issue of human rights in Chinese society, like the rest of the Chinese political-economy, it is actually "going global."[16] This was made clear to me in 2012 when I was living in Singapore: upon returning from a visit to the PRC, my mobile phone's Chinese SIM card automatically sent me a text message from the Chinese foreign ministry instructing me to obey the local laws and act in a "civilized" manner. People who use Chinese apps abroad now take the PRC's surveillance, filtering, and censorship regime with them to other countries.[17] China's surveillance dynamic thus spreads around the world

Office, "The Internet in China" (June 8, 2010) http://www.gov.cn/english/2010-06/08/content_1622956.htm (accessed May 30, 2018).

[13] Lipton, "To Fight Terror," C3.

[14] Lyon, *The Culture of Surveillance*, 17, 194–196; Gary T. Marx, *Windows on the Soul: Surveillance and Society in an Age of High Technology* (Chicago: University of Chicago Press, 2016), p. xv; David Lyon, Kevin D. Haggerty, and Kirstie Ball, "Introducing Surveillance Studies," in *Routledge Handbook of Surveillance Studies*, edited by Kirstie Ball, Kevin D. Haggerty, and David Lyon (New York: Routledge, 2014), p. 3.

[15] "China's Xi Says Ideology Work 'Absolutely Correct' Amid Trade Row Criticism," Reuters (August 22, 2018) https://www.reuters.com/article/us-china-politics-idUSKCN1L71CG (accessed March 7, 2019).

[16] See David Shambaugh, *China Goes Global: The Partial Power* (New York: Oxford University Press, 2013).

[17] See Lotus Ruan, Jeffrey Knockel, Jason Q. Ng, and Masashi Crete-Nishihata, "One App, Two Systems: How WeChat Uses One Censorship Policy in China, and Another Internationally," The Citizen Lab (November 30, 2016) https://citizenlab.ca/2016/11/wechat-china-censorship-one-app-two-systems/ (accessed May 10, 2018).

through both individual smartphones and state-led Internet infrastructure invest-ment projects such as Beijing's Cyber Silk Road initiative (discussed more later in the chapter).[18] Indeed, its aggressive research and development strategy, cou-pled with its weak commitment to privacy and the rule of law, has made China the "global leader in surveillance technologies and practices."[19] This is not just an issue of hardware and software; alongside Russia, China is presenting itself to the world as the future of the Internet's global norms and governance.[20]

Most analyses look to technology and security to consider how surveillance practices generate meaning and sort people. This chapter also appreciates surveillance as an affective social performance of social-ordering and world-ordering, in what David Lyon calls the interactive "culture of surveillance."[21] While framing the issues in terms of culture rather than technology allows for a more aesthetic appreciation of the politics of surveillance, "culture" itself raises a different set of issues. It is popular to understand Chinese actions in terms of an East/West conceptual scheme, wherein negotiable po-litical issues are quickly converted into fixed identity positions. Indeed, it is common to argue that Chinese civilization frames the issues in terms of order/chaos rather than in terms of public/private and security/freedom; as the former head of the PRC's Cyberspace Administration of China explained, "[T]he more we pursue freedom, the more we require order."[22]

To avoid (self)Orientalism's problems of essentialized identity, this chapter develops Michel Foucault's and Gilles Deleuze's models of social-ordering: so-ciety of sovereignty, society of discipline, and the networked society of control.[23] It juxtaposes these three social models to examine how each enacts what Jacques

---

[18] See Office of the Leading Group, *Building the Belt and Road*, 27–28; Griffiths, *The Great Firewall of China*.

[19] Leibold, "Surveillance in Xinjiang," 2.

[20] Office of the Leading Group, *Building the Belt and Road*, 27–28; Adam Segal, "When China Rules the Web: Technology in Service of the State," *Foreign Affairs* (August 13, 2018) https://www.foreignaffairs.com/articles/china/2018-08-13/when-china-rules-web (accessed March 15, 2019).

[21] Lyon, *The Culture of Surveillance*.

[22] Lu Wei, "Speech at the 13th China Online Media Forum" (October 30, 2013), translation avail-able at http://chinacopyrightandmedia.wordpress.com/2013/10/30/siio-director-outlines-eight-objectives-for-online-media/ (accessed June 3, 2018).

[23] Galloway explains that Deleuze's control society is analogous to Manuel Castell's network so-ciety; thus I combine the concepts as "networked society of control." Gilles Deleuze, "Postscript on the Societies of Control," *October* 59 (1992):3–7; for application of this idea to the Internet, see Alexander Galloway, *Protocol: How Control Exists after Decentralization* (Cambridge, MA: MIT Press, 2006), p. 24; Wendy Hui Kyong Chun, *Control and Freedom: Power and Paranoia in the Age of Fiber Optics* (Cambridge, MA: MIT Press, 2006), pp. 7–9. For an application of this to surveillance studies, see Greg Elmer, "Panopticon—Discipline—Control," in *Routledge Handbook of Surveillance Studies*, edited by Kirstie Ball, Kevin D. Haggerty, and David Lyon (New York: Routledge, 2014), pp. 21–29.

Rancière calls a distinct "repartition of the sensible":[24] wall-building in sovereignty society, the Panopticon in disciplinary society, and interactive performances of multidirectional "inter-veillance" in networked control society. While it is common to see these as distinct historical epochs—with the state-led surveillance of the Panopticon and Big Brother being replaced by a neoliberal performance of "surveillance capitalism"[25]—this chapter follows Foucault in appreciating how "new techniques do not replace, erase, or exclude those that currently exist, but rather penetrate, permeate, infiltrate, and dovetail into them."[26] As we will see, China's Social Credit System is working to integrate the societies of sovereignty, discipline, and networked control by interactively scoring individuals through a big data sharing system that takes advantage of government tracking, e-commerce activity, and social media performances to watch, filter, censor, reward, punish—and amuse—everyone all the time.

Binary Surveillance in the Society of Sovereignty

In *Discipline and Punish*, Foucault discusses the disciplinary society by contrasting it with the society of sovereignty. France's seventeenth-century reaction to leprosy exemplifies the surveillance strategy of the sovereignty society, because it asserted a strict binary division. Once the very visible signs of leprosy—the corrosion of the body—were seen, lepers were made invisible by quarantining them outside the body politic. These "rituals of exclusion" produced a pure society by isolating impurities in separate institutions. At this time, those with other visible signs of difference such as insanity were likewise exiled to institutions that were outside the purview of the pure society.[27]

In the nineteenth and twentieth centuries, surveillance similarly targeted outsiders who were seen as a threat to the health of society—criminals, political activists, and spies—and was regulated through the legal framework of target first, track later. The opening credits of season one of *The Wire* illustrate the limited,

---

[24] Jacques Rancière, *The Politics of Aesthetics: The Distribution of the Sensible*, translated by Gabriel Rockhill (London: Continuum International Publishing Group, 2004), p. 63. For more discussion of "(re)partition of the sensible," see Chapters 2, 9, and 10.

[25] Lyon, *Culture of Surveillance*, 145; Marx, *Windows on the Soul*.

[26] Michel Foucault, *"Society Must Be Defended": Lectures at the Collège De France, 1975–6*, translated by David Macey, edited by Mauro Bertani and Alssandro Fontana (New York: Picador, 2003), pp. 241–242.

[27] Michel Foucault, *Discipline and Punish: Birth of the Prison*, translated by Alan Sheridan (New York: Pantheon, 1977), pp. 198, 195–200; Michel Foucault, *History of Sexuality*, Vol. 1, *An Introduction*, translated by R. Hurley (New York: Pantheon, 1978), pp.135–136; also see Gilles Deleuze, *Foucault*, translated by Sean Hand (Minneapolis: University of Minnesota Press, 1988), pp. 25–44.

juridical, and deliberate nature of surveillance, showing images of the warrant necessary for wiretapping the phones of specific criminal suspects, individual police
eavesdropping on phone conversations, individual police photographers, a helicopter overseeing the neighborhood, and the grainy images of an early generation
of CCTV cameras. The program also shows resistance to such targeted surveillance;
as in the Intifada's low-tech response to Israel's high-tech occupation, in *The Wire* a
young man throws a stone to crack the lens of a CCTV camera.[28] The sovereignty
society maintained social order through a binary division that protected the inside
of a healthy polity through the surveillance and control of a select group of people
who were quarantined as a threat to social purity.

China also has a history of maintaining the sovereignty society through a binary
form of targeted surveillance, although in the PRC it was not so legalistic. Criminals
and dissidents were individually surveilled through filtering their mail and tapping
their telephones, as well as through visual surveillance; their information was compiled in personal files (*dang'an*) that recorded their political activities and infractions.
The Great Firewall of China employs information and communications technology
(ICT) in a more modern example of the surveillance prerogatives of the society of sovereignty.[29] Indeed, since 2010 the party-state has justified its cybersecurity actions in
terms of defending China's "Internet sovereignty" in order to "create a healthy and harmonious Internet environment."[30]

The Great Firewall is a complex set of procedures and technologies that accomplish a broad range of tasks; this section discusses its quarantining functions. The
first email sent from China, on September 14, 1987, proudly proclaimed: "Across

[28] *The Wire* (2002) https://www.youtube.com/watch?v=E1ABR4UpDSU (accessed June
10, 2018).

[29] For discussion of China's censorship and Internet policies, see Margaret E. Roberts,
Censored: Distraction and Diversion Inside China's Great Firewall (Princeton, NJ: Princeton
University Press, 2018); Griffiths, *The Great Firewall of China*; Xiao Qiang, "The Road to Digital
Unfreedom: President Xi's Surveillance State," *Journal of Democracy* 30:1 (2019):53–67; Lotus Ruan,
When Winner Takes It All: Big Data in China and the Battle for Privacy, Australian Strategic Policy
Institute, Report No. 5/2018 (May 2018); Samantha Hoffman, *Social Credit: Technology-enhanced
Authoritarian Control with Global Consequences*, Australian Strategic Policy Institute, Report No. 6/
2018 (June 2018); Florian Schneider, *China's Digital Nationalism* (New York: Oxford University
Press, 2018); Jacques deLisle, Avery Goldstein, and Guobin Yang, eds., *The Internet, Social Media,
and a Changing China* (Philadelphia: University of Pennsylvania Press, 2016); Amy Chang, *Warring
State: China's Cybersecurity Strategy* (Washington, DC: Center for a New American Security, December
14, 2014); "The Great Firewall: The Art of Concealment," *The Economist* (April 6, 2013) https://
www.economist.com/special-report/2013/04/06/the-art-of-concealment (accessed June 26, 2018);
Guobin Yang, ed., *China's Contested Internet* (Copenhagen: NIAS Press, 2015); Rebecca MacKinnon,
Consent of the Networked: The Worldwide Struggle for Internet Freedom (New York: Basic Books, 2012).

[30] State Council, "The Internet in China"; Min Jiang, "Authoritarian Informationalism: China's
Approach to Internet Sovereignty," *SAIS Review* 30:2 (2010):71–89.

the Great Wall we can reach every corner in the world."[31] But after China joined the Internet in 1994, the party-state began building what became known as the Great Firewall of China to restrict users' access to ideas and information from outside the PRC. It employs software first developed by Western companies such as Sun Microsystems and Cisco Systems to filter the Internet in a similar way to how parents can regulate their children's Web-surfing and corporations manage the online activity of their staff.[32] It uses the logic of defending the youth and fighting pornography to likewise restrict access to "politically exciting ideas."[33]

In 2010 the PRC's "Internet in China" white paper took a broad view of forbidden topics of discussion:

> No organization or individual may produce, duplicate, announce or disseminate information having the following contents: being against the cardinal principles set forth in the Constitution; endangering state security, divulging state secrets, subverting state power and jeopardizing national unification; damaging state honor and interests; instigating ethnic hatred or discrimination and jeopardizing ethnic unity; jeopardizing state religious policy, propagating heretical or superstitious ideas; spreading rumors, disrupting social order and stability; disseminating obscenity, pornography, gambling, violence, brutality and terror or abetting crime; humiliating or slandering others, trespassing on the lawful rights and interests of others; and other contents forbidden by laws and administrative regulations.[34]

The list's first restricted topic shows that these problems are political rather than legal or social: the Chinese constitution's "cardinal principles" require that the PRC be a socialist country led by the Chinese Communist Party (CCP). It thus is a matter of regime security to guard the CCP's legitimacy by blocking access to "foreign" content that the party-state deems "harmful."[35] The Great Firewall is the world's most advanced national firewall, policing the Internet's sensible gateways into China since 1996. Much like France's late-medieval leprosy strategy, it is the party-state's job to regulate cyberspace in order to protect Chinese citizens from impure and harmful thoughts, including "heresy, pornography, violence, and terror."[36]

---

[31] "How Does China Censor the Internet?," *The Economist* (April 22, 2013) https://www.economist.com/the-economist-explains/2013/04/21/how-does-china-censor-the-internet (accessed June 4, 2018).

[32] Barmé and Sang, "The Great Firewall of China"; Troumbley, "Colonization.com."

[33] See Richard Curt Kraus, *The Party and the Arty in China: The New Politics of Culture* (Lanham, MD: Rowman & Littlefield, 2004), p. 93; State Council, "The Internet in China."

[34] State Council, "The Internet in China."

[35] Barmé and Sang, "The Great Firewall of China"; Roberts, *Censored*.

[36] State Council, "The Internet in China."

The Great Firewall of China thus blacklists unacceptable sites associated with the Dalai Lama, the Tiananmen massacre, Taiwanese independence, Falun Gong, and other hot button issues. It likewise blocks many foreign media outlets such as the *New York Times*. There also is a sophisticated filtering mechanism that bans keywords in browser searches and increasingly in email and social media messages.[37] This is done by hand and by automation; the Chinese government distributes a list of forbidden "sensitive words" (*minggan ci*) to Chinese Internet firms, and the Cyberspace Administration of China employs more than sixty thousand personnel to directly police the Web.[38] (The number of official censors is an estimate; it keeps growing.) Often the result of a "sensitive word" search is invisible, producing an error message stating that the desired web page is not available. Likewise, the sender is not alerted when an out-going message is deleted. As virtual China has become more visual through online photos and videos, the Great Firewall has adapted to filter and censor visual images as well as text.[39] The scale is staggering: between 1 and 10 percent of all social media posts are removed by censors.[40]

Yet where there is power there is resistance. Like the Great Wall of China, the Great Firewall of China is a blunt instrument for producing sovereignty by excluding foreign influence. Internet-savvy people in China use VPNs to "jump the Great Firewall" and get access to the global Internet. Activists can resist the censorship system that targets "sensitive words" by engaging in *e-gao* wordplay. Artist-activist Ai Weiwei and his friends jam the filters by using homophones for Chinese words, as well as words in English. When the #MeToo (#我也是/#WoYeShi) social media movement was blocked in China, it then proliferated as "Rice Bunny-*Mi tu*" because those characters sound like "Me Too" in English. But in this cat-and-mouse game, the censors always seem to win; "Rice Bunny" was quickly banned.[41] Since

---

[37] See Qiang, "The Road to Digital Unfreedom"; Juha Antero Vuori and Lauri Paltemaa, "The Lexicon of Fear: Chinese Internet Control Practice in Sina Weibo Microblog Censorship," *Surveillance and Society* 13:3/4 (2015):400–421; Schneider, *China's Digital Nationalism*.

[38] See "Collecting Sensitive Words: The Grass-Mud Horse List," *China Digital Times*, https:// chinadigitaltimes.net/2013/06/grass-mud-horse-list/ (accessed June 26, 2018); Roberts, *Censored*, 104, 150–189; Nathan Vanderklippe, "Unpublished Chinese Censorship Document Reveals Sweeping Effort to Eradicate Online Political Content," *Globe and Mail* (June 3, 2018) https://www. theglobeandmail.com/world/article-unpublished-chinese-censorship-document-reveals-sweeping-effort-to/ (accessed June 4, 2018); Klimburg, *The Darkening Web*, 271.

[39] See Jeffrey Knockel, Lotus Ruan, Masashi Crete-Nishihata, and Ron Deibert, "(Can't) Picture This: An Analysis of Image Filtering on WeChat Moments," The Citizen Lab (August 14, 2018) https:// citizenlab.ca/2018/08/cant-picture-this-an-analysis-of-image-filtering-on-wechat-moments/ (accessed September 15, 2018); Vanderklippe, "Unpublished Chinese Censorship Document."

[40] Roberts, *Censored*, 151.

[41] Yang, *China's Contested Internet*; Roberts, *Censored*, 162–163; Rogier Creemers, "Cyber China: Upgrading Propaganda, Public Opinion Work and Social Management for the Twenty-First Century," *Journal of Contemporary China* 26:103 (2017):86; Lily Kuo, "From 'Rice Bunny' to 'Back Up the Car': China's Year of Censorship," *The Guardian* (December 31, 2018) https://www.theguardian.

2017 Beijing has been cracking down on VPNs as well, throttling their connections to make them so slow as to be unworkable.[42] One netizen wrote a science-fiction story to parody how banning "sensitive words" is shrinking the Chinese language in Orwellian ways. In the story, the new technology of "GFW Turbo" (i.e., Great Firewall Turbo) becomes self-aware and runs out of control, banning almost the entire Chinese language. By 2025 only one phrase is left: "sensitive word."[43]

By employing a "friction" strategy that imposes costs, in terms of money and/or time, on people who want to jump the wall, the Great Firewall has been quite effective at nudging Chinese users to Internet sites more amenable to the regime.[44] As Margaret E. Roberts concludes, "Small costs of access, not draconian punishments or sophisticated manipulation, can have huge effects on the behaviour of a majority." This strategy also drives a wedge between ordinary people who stay within the Great Firewall and elite dissidents who jump it.[45] While the Great Wall of China acted as a barrier between Civilization and barbarism, the Great Firewall likewise acts as a barrier, quarantining the harmful outside from the purely harmonious inside. Indeed, in reaction to political violence in 2009 between Uyghurs and Han in the Northwest region of Xinjiang, Beijing cut off the region from the Internet and international phone calls for over a year. Starting in 2014, Beijing again restricted much of Xinjiang from international communication that uses the Internet and telephones. While David Lyon and Gary T. Marx tell us that it is unhelpful to think of surveillance in terms of *1984*,[46] Beijing's assertion of Internet sovereignty and the sci-fi story both suggest that the Great Firewall really does work like Orwell's Big Brother.

The Great Firewall of China is the largest and most sophisticated digital boundary in the world.[47] As the head of the Cyberspace Administration of China explained in 2015, it functions according to the sovereign logic of border walls:

> We live in a common online space. This online space is made up of the internets of various countries, and each country has its own independent and autonomous interest in internet sovereignty, internet security and

---

com/world/2018/dec/31/from-rice-bunny-to-back-up-the-car-chinas-year-of-censorship (accessed March 7, 2019).

[42] Qiang, "The Road to Digital Unfreedom," 56.

[43] "GFW de lishi he weilai" [The history and future of the GFW], Zhongguo jiwenwang (May 15, 2013) https://www.bannedbook.org/bnews/fanqiang/20130515/129086.html (accessed June 26, 2018); also see "The Great Firewall," *Economist*.

[44] Roberts, *Censored*, 150–189.

[45] Roberts, *Censored*, 13, 8.

[46] Lyon, *Culture of Surveillance*, 1; Marx, *Windows on the Soul*, xv.

[47] Michael Anti, *Behind the Great Firewall of China*, Ted Talk (July 2012) https://www.ted.com/speakers/michael_anti (accessed June 4, 2018).

internet development. Only through my own proper management of my own internet, [and] your proper management of your own internet … can the online space be truly safe, more orderly and more beautiful.[48]

China's Internet sovereignty argument thus is not just for domestic consumption; it is seen as Beijing's contribution to the global governance of the Internet. At China's World Internet Conference 2015, Xi Jinping told the global audience:

> The principle of sovereign equality enshrined in the Charter of the United Nations is one of the basic norms in contemporary international relations. It covers all aspects of state-to-state relations, and therefore should also apply to cyberspace. We should respect the right of individual countries to independently choose their own path of cyber development and model of cyber regulation, and internet public policies and participate in international cyberspace governance on an equal footing.[49]

Thus, according to Alexander Klimburg, there are "two large internets in the world: the US-oriented global patchwork of around forty-two-thousand-odd interconnecting internets with the largely free flow of information over their networks and services, and the Chinese internet."[50]

Actually, after Snowden's revelations about global data harvesting by the NSA/ Five Eyes, China's idea of Internet sovereignty has become more popular. Brazilian president Dilma Rousseff, for example, used her annual speech at the UN General Assembly in 2013 to criticize the US spying as a "breach of international law" that violated not just the human rights of Brazilian people, but also the national sovereignty of the Brazilian state.[51] In response, Brazil started to build its own national Internet capability, separate from the US networks in terms of both hardware and software.[52] The PRC is a big part of the nationalization of the Internet around the world through Xi's signature project, the Belt and Road Initiative:[53]

[48] Quoted in David Bandurski, "Lu Wei on the 'Dream of the Web,'" China Media Project (February 17, 2015) http://chinamediaproject.org/2015/02/17/lu-wei-on-the-dream-of-the-web/ (accessed June 10, 2018).

[49] Xi Jinping, *The Governance of China*, Vol. II (Beijing: Foreign Languages Press, 2017), pp. 582–583.

[50] Klimburg, *The Darkening Web*, 256.

[51] Julian Borger, "Brazilian President: US Surveillance a 'Breach of International Law,'" *The Guardian* (September 24, 2013) https://www.theguardian.com/world/2013/sep/24/brazil-president-un-speech-nsa-surveillance (accessed June 4, 2018).

[52] Bauman et al., "After Snowden," 129–130; Rachel Brown, "Beijing's Silk Road Goes Digital," Council for Foreign Relations (June 6, 2017) https://www.cfr.org/blog/beijings-silk-road-goes-digital (accessed March 15, 2019).

[53] For the Belt and Road Initiative, see William A. Callahan, "China's 'Asia Dream': BRI and the New Regional Order," *Asian Journal of Comparative Politics* 1:3 (2016):226–243.

We must, with the construction of "One Belt One Road" as juncture, strengthen cooperation with countries along the line and especially developing countries, in areas such as basic network infrastructure construction, the digital economy, cybersecurity, etc., and build a Digital Silk Road for the 21st Century.[54]

Zambia is one of the countries where the PRC is constructing this Digital Silk Road by funding, building, and sometimes managing fiber-optic cables, surveillance systems, and telecommunications networks. Beijing thus isn't exporting just hardware and software, but also the surveillance norms and practices of the sovereignty society; civil society groups in Zambia have complained about increased surveillance and censorship.[55] In this way, the Internet is shifting from being a transnational information superhighway to becoming a collection of national intranets that need to be guarded by the assertion of national Internet sovereignty.

These examples show how the society of sovereignty works according to the state's power to define and exclude the inside from outside and to make the visible invisible. This is an ideological practice that surveils threats deemed to be "foreign" and acts by restricting the flow of "harmful" information, often through censorship and filtering. The video of China's "Cyberspace Spirit" anthem shows how the song is scored to the rhythm of a military march, which is performed by a well-disciplined chorus. This and other evidence shows that Beijing envisions surveillance as a mode of "inspection and control" that works according to a Cold War understanding of local, national, and global politics.[56] The Great Firewall, like the Great Wall of China and France's anti-leprosy strategy, serves as both a barrier against the impure and a gateway to regulate the flow of the healthy; Lu Wei, the first head of the Cyber Administration of China, was known as the "gatekeeper of the Chinese Internet."[57] As the examples from Brazil and Zambia show, this is not just an issue of censorship in China; Beijing is globalizing the Great Firewall through its Cyber Silk Road infrastructure project, which promotes the global governance norm of Internet sovereignty.

---

[54] "Xi Jinping's Speech at the National Cybersecurity and Informatization Work Conference"; also see Office of the Leading Group, *Building the Belt and Road*, 27–28.

[55] Sheridan Prasso, "China's Digital Silk Road Is Looking More Like an Iron Curtain," *Bloomberg* (January 10, 2019) https://www.bloomberg.com/news/features/2019-01-10/china-s-digital-silk-road-is-looking-more-like-an-iron-curtain (accessed January 20, 2019); Joe Parkinson, Nicholas Bariyo and Josh Chin, "Huawei Technicians Helped African Governments Spy on Political Opponents," (August 14, 2019) https://www.wsj.com/articles/huawei-technicians-helped-african-governments-spy-on-political-opponents-11565793017 (accessed August 23, 2019).

[56] Leibold, "Surveillance in Xinjiang," 3–4.

[57] Roberts, *Censored*, 1.

Panoptic Surveillance in the Society of Discipline

While the French state dealt with leprosy through the ritual of excluding visible difference, Paris's response to the plague involved an alternative strategy that worked to make difference more visible in a particular repartition of the sensible. Rather than exiling the afflicted, the state fixed everyone in place through a strict partitioning of space that can still be seen in Paris's arrondissement districts. The purpose was not to enforce a strict inside/outside distinction, as with leprosy, but to regulate the whole society though mass surveillance. This social ordering strategy employs a system of permanent registration and reporting, in which the omniscient and omnipresent power effects a "penetration of regulation into even the smallest details of everyday life."[58] Rather than a massive binary division of people, it called for "multiple separations" to individualize and discipline the population. The disorder of the plague thus was met by a new state-led surveillance society in which power laid "down for each individual his place, his body, his disease and his death."[59] While the anti-leprosy strategy led to the pure sovereign community, the anti-plague strategy produced the disciplinary society.

The Panopticon is the exemplary case of the society of discipline. Jeremy Bentham's model prison, in which the central tower is surrounded by individual cells, produces and enforces power relations according to who is watching whom. The overseer in the central tower can see the inmates in their peripheral cells but cannot be seen by them. According to Foucault, the Panopticon does not have to use coercive power to regulate the inmates; rather, this invisible surveillance produces docile bodies that self-regulate and self-discipline. Disciplinary society is the model for most modern institutions—factories, schools, barracks, and hospitals—which are highly regulated through a non-coercive habitus.

Power here penetrates into each individual's everyday life in a productive way that goes beyond the society of sovereignty's ability to say "no" (i.e., don't look there, don't do that) to create a productive power that tells people where to look and how to act: "Panopticism is the discipline mechanism: a functional mechanism that must improve the exercise of power by making it lighter, more rapid, more effective, a design of subtle coercion for a society to come."[60] It is not simply a power relation of watcher over watched in a unidirectional surveillant gaze; the overseer in the Panopticon is also the object of surveillance in a "landscape that could at any time impart in an individual a likelihood of surveillance."[61] The logic goes beyond Bentham's project "to see without being seen . . . *to impose a particular conduct on a*

---

[58] Foucault, *Discipline and Punish*, 198.
[59] Foucault, *Discipline and Punish*, 197.
[60] Foucault, *Discipline and Punish*, 209.
[61] Elmer, "Panopticon—Discipline—Control," 24.

particular human multiplicity."[62] Visibility does not set people free, but rather "is a trap."[63] It is not a politics of watching (as in sovereignty society), so much as one of being watched, that productively generates identities, institutions, and behaviors.[64] The Panopticon thus offers "not the relations of sovereignty but the relations of discipline"[65] in a society of surveillance.

The society of discipline helps make sense of how ICTs can surveil everyone all the time in twenty-first-century democratic societies. In the sovereignty society, security and police apparatuses worked through "index cards and filing cabinets" to monitor a select, targeted number of criminals, dissidents, and spies who moved in "close-knit and geographically localized communities." Now with computerized record-keeping, individual data are digitized and accumulated in databases that are "mobile, searchable and sharable."[66] In this way, the state can surveil the daily activities of a large number of people; whereas the sovereignty society targets first, and then tracks, the disciplinary society tracks everyone first, and only later targets individuals.[67] Like Foucault's Panopticon of multiple separations, these data-driven surveillance activities engage in "social sorting" to categorize "people into groups, so that the persons themselves can be treated differently, depending on the group."[68] This is the Orwellian/*1984*/Big Brother version of the surveillance society.

The Panopticon also helps explain the NSA's mass surveillance projects. The state mines data from telephone companies, Internet service providers, browsers, search engines, and social media platforms in order to sort out who might be a terrorist threat. It also harvests data by intercepting telephone and online traffic by tapping the Internet's physical infrastructure of cables and switches that serve as gateways to vast regions; cables to Latin America pass through the United States, and Western Europe's cables go through the United Kingdom.[69] More than spying on content, the goal is to visualize large populations in a disciplinary society by mapping social relations. Through cooperation with the expanded Five Eyes network, the NSA was able to achieve a global program of data mining. Although it is illegal for Five Eyes Plus states to spy on their own citizens, the project's data sharing logic was able to circumvent such restrictions: state 1 would spy on state 2's citizens, and vice versa, and then they would share data. But this was not an equal relationship; the NSA's capacity is probably ten times that of any of its partners.[70] The NSA's goal, again, is not

---

[62] Deleuze, *Foucault*, 34 (emphasis in original).

[63] Foucault, *Discipline and Punish*, 200.

[64] Elmer, "Panopticon—Discipline—Control," 27.

[65] Foucault, *Discipline and Punish*, 208.

[66] Lyon, Haggerty, and Ball, "Introducing Surveillance Studies," 4; Lyon, *The Culture of Surveillance*, 5.

[67] Lyon, *The Culture of Surveillance*, 165.

[68] Lyon, *The Culture of Surveillance*, 13.

[69] Bauman et al., "After Snowden," 122.

[70] Bauman et al., "After Snowden," 124–126.

to censor—as in the sovereignty society's regime of inspection and control—but to data mine and data profile in the society of discipline. Still, this activity has led to a significant "chilling" of civil society activity on telephones and on the Web, resulting in self-discipline through self-censorship.[71]

China has cultivated a disciplinary society of surveillance since late imperial times, and in the first four decades of the PRC, surveillance worked through the "work unit" (*danwei*) system.[72] Work units employed military-style organization to unify the Panopticon institutions of factory, school, hospital, and residence with a top-down control of the biopolitics of labor, marriage, and reproduction. Up through the 1980s these institutions produced docile bodies that were self-disciplined by continual surveillance that guided not only your profession, but where you work, where you live, whom you can marry, and if and when you can have a child (and until 2015, what punishment you'd suffer for having more than one child).

The Chinese intranet works in similar ways to produce what Foucault called docile bodies through a lighter and less coercive touch, with the goal of "creat[ing] a predictable political environment."[73] It is "domesticated" in the sense of being both localized and tamed. The Chinese government has worked with private Chinese companies not only to block harmful content through the sovereignty society's Great Firewall, but also to clone popular Internet platforms to create Chinese equivalents. As Chinese activist Michael Anti explains,

> You have Google, we have Baidu. You have Twitter, we have Weibo. You have Facebook, we have Renren. You have YouTube, we have Youku and Tudou. The Chinese government blocked every single international Web 2.0 service, and we Chinese copycat every one.[74]

As figure 11.1 shows, the invisible workings of the Chinese intranet become visible at transnational nodes such as hotel rooms in Beijing, where staff have to explain to non-Chinese visitors how the Great Firewall works—that is, what is allowed and what is not. As Roberts explains, these clone sites can easily nudge Chinese users away from foreign platforms that Beijing finds problematic: "If the functionality of a foreign website can be easily substituted by an unblocked Chinese site, users may be unlikely to spend the time and resources to [jump the Great Firewall to] evade censorship."[75]

---

[71] Lyon, *The Culture of Surveillance*, 59, 65–68; Bauman et al., "After Snowden," 142.

[72] See Michael R. Dutton, *Policing and Punishment in China: From Patriarchy to "the People"* (New York: Cambridge University Press, 1992).

[73] Creemers, "Cyber China," 97.

[74] Anti, "Behind the Great Firewall of China."

[75] Roberts, *Censored*, 183.

Figure 11.1 "Some tips for internet" at a Chinese hotel (2018). Courtesy Mark C. Elliott

Within China, the Great Firewall employs domestic filtering and surveillance to move from the society of sovereignty to the society of discipline. The police use a system of grid-based urban management that includes surveillance through networks of CCTV cameras, mobile devices, number plate recognition, and facial recognition.[76] As Rogier Creemers explains, "[S]urveillance and monitoring moved from *dang'an* [files] and neighborhood informers to cameras, big data algorithms and cloud storage."[77] This combination of police state and surveillance state is at its most extreme in Xinjiang, where through both human-driven and machine-driven systems, surveillance is becoming individualized as with the Panopticon: Uyghurs and other Muslim groups are required to load their smartphones with surveillance apps and tag their vehicles with GPS and RFID devices, as well as to submit to scans for facial recognition, voice recognition, walking gait recognition, and other forms of biometric data (fingerprints, iris scans, DNA gathering, etc.).[78] One of the Xinjiang surveillance state's innovations is to use the big data provided by the mass facial recognition scans to hone the software to better differentiate between ethnic Han Chinese and "ethnic minority" groups such as Uyghurs, Kazahks, and so on.[79] At the same time, the human-driven systems are becoming more intrusive; since 2016 a government program called "Marrying-up and Becoming Kin" has mobilized Han Chinese cadres to go and live with Uyghur families to promote "inter-ethnic mingling" and "ethnic harmony"—through intense day-to-day surveillance that both disciplines everyday life and produces electronic records for data sharing and analysis.[80]

This vast experiment, which is starting to expand to the rest of the PRC, aims not merely to record data for past offenses, but to predict future offenses by sorting people into three categories: "trustworthy," "average," and "untrustworthy."[81] Based on some of these surveillance data, over 11 percent of the adult Muslim population of Xinjiang has been incarcerated in "transformation-through-education" camps since 2017, and the number keeps growing.[82] Needless to say, the surveillance society is producing altered behavior among targeted populations both in China and abroad. Since one of the "risk factors" is making overseas calls, Uyghurs who live abroad report that their relatives in Xinjiang have told them to stop calling and

[76] Leibold, "Surveillance in Xinjiang," 5; Rogier Creemers, "China's Social Credit System: An Evolving Practice of Control," SSRN (May 9, 2018) https://papers.ssrn.com/sol3/papers.cfm?abstract_id=3175792 (accessed June 11, 2018).

[77] Creemers, "Cyber China," 90.

[78] See Leibold, "Surveillance in Xinjiang," 5–8; Darren Byler, "Ghost World," *Logic* no. 7 (2019) https://logicmag.io/07-ghost-world/ (accessed April 20, 2019); Maya Wang, *"Eradicating Ideological Viruses": China's Campaign of Repression Against Xinjiang's Muslims* (New York: Human Rights Watch, 2018).

[79] John Honovich, "Hikvision's Minority Analytics," IPVM (May 8, 2018) https://ipvm.com/reports/hikvision-minority (accessed September 15, 2018).

[80] Leibold, "Surveillance in Xinjiang," 11; Byler, "Ghost World."

[81] Wang, *"Eradicating Ideological Viruses"*, 12; Leibold, "Surveillance in Xinjiang," 2, 11; Byler, "Ghost World."

[82] Adrian Zenz, "'Thoroughly Reforming Them Towards a Healthy Heart Attitude': China's Political Re-education Campaign in Xinjiang," *Central Asian Survey* 38:1 (2019):122.

messaging.[83] This "penetration of regulation into even the smallest details of everyday life" is an example of the "multiple separations" described by Foucault that fix in place each individual in a surveillance society.[84]

Back in the rest of China, Internet platforms actively filter and censor because they are legally required to by the party-state; indeed, the dominance of the main players—Baidu, Alibaba, Tencent—is incumbent on "cooperation with the Chinese government's information management goals." In 2009, for example, Baidu received a "Chinese Internet Self-Discipline Award" for fostering "healthy, harmonious Internet development."[85] Because they can be heavily fined or shut down for non-cooperation, China's private tech companies are uncritical handmaidens of the party-state's information surveillance and social control policy. More to the point, private companies participate because they can gain "influence and profits" in China's growing "security-surveillance complex."[86]

In addition to censoring searches and posts, the state and private Internet service providers employ a total of around two million people to troll critical netizens.[87] This "Fifty-Cent Party"—named after the fee that participants receive for each post—is the largest security organization in the world. Fifty-Centers don't just attack critics of the government; they also spread "positive news" about the CCP's achievements and negative views of foreigners' failures.[88] In an interview with a member of the Fifty-Cent Party, artist-activist Ai Weiwei probed the mechanics of "guiding public opinion." The technique is more than regulating ideological views; it also engages in affect-work by employing the positive governance of "tone of speech, identity and stance of speech" in order to "guide netizens obliquely and let them change their focus without realising it."[89] The scale of public opinion guidance is massive; "about 10 to 20% out of the tens of thousands of comments posted on a forum" are posted by Fifty-Centers.[90] Rather than just being a freelance activity, one of China's new and growing industries involves "censorship factories," in which people go to the

---

[83] Wang, *"Eradicating Ideological Viruses"*. China's high-tech crackdown in Xinjiang is a fast-developing situation; to keep track of this humanitarian crisis, see Uyghur Human Rights Project, "China's 'Re-education'/Concentration camps in Xinjiang," https://uhrp.org/featured-articles/chinas-re-education-concentration-camps-xinjiang (accessed September 15, 2018).

[84] Foucault, *Discipline and Punish*, 198, 197.

[85] Sarah Logan, "The Geopolitics of Tech: Baidu's Vietnam," Internet Policy Observatory (June 15, 2015) http://globalnetpolicy.org/wp-content/uploads/2015/06/Logan-geopolitics-of-tech-Final-6.8.pdf (accessed June 30, 2018):6; MacKinnon, *Consent of the Networked*, 105.

[86] Leibold, "Surveillance in Xinjiang," 3.

[87] This was the estimate in 2013. See Elizabeth C. Economy, *The Third Revolution: Xi Jinping and the New Chinese State* (New York: Oxford University Press, 2018), p. 82.

[88] Ai Weiwei, "Meet the 50-Cent Party," *New Statesman* (October 19–25, 2012):42–45; Roberts, *Censored*, 4–10, 209–210; Creemers, "Cyber China," 98.

[89] Ai, "Meet the 50-Cent Party," 43.

[90] Ai, "Meet the 50-Cent Party," 45.

office to review and censor Web-posts (both texts and images) on behalf of China's ICT companies.[91]

In recent years Xi Jinping has been promoting the "China model for a better social governance system,"[92] which goes beyond the binary censorship of the society of sovereignty. China was helping Brazil, for example, not only to assert Internet sovereignty by building a new South-South infrastructure network to bypass the hardware of US-based cables, but also to clone popular social media platforms to bypass US-based software.[93] Through its Digital Silk Road project, the PRC is exporting its disciplinary society to other countries—for example, Educador, Iraq, Kenya, Mauritius, Morocco, Uganda, Zambia, Zimbabwe—through "safe city"/ "smart city" infrastructure projects that use the PRC's sophisticated surveillance systems to socially order the populations.[94] Chinese companies are using data gathered from countries such as Zimbabwe to further develop facial recognition software beyond the "racial mix" found in China.[95]

These activities all show how the surveillance society in China works to watch, filter, censor, sort, and guide Internet users. As with Foucault's Panopticon, the key is to use a porous style of censorship that is a low-cost, non-coercive, and largely invisible way of "manipulating citizen's incentives so that they choose, rather than are forced, to engage in the desired behaviour."[96] It works in ways that are now familiar

[91]   Li Yuan, "Learning China's Forbidden History, So They Can Censor It," *New York Times* (January 2, 2019) https://www.nytimes.com/2019/01/02/business/china-internet-censor.html (accessed January 20, 2019).

[92]   Qiang, "The Road to Digital Unfreedom," 62; Martin Hala and Jichang Lulu, "The CCP's Model of Social Control Goes Global," The Asia Dialogue (December 20, 2018) http://theasiadialogue.com/2018/12/20/the-ccps-model-of-social-control-goes-global/ (accessed March 7, 2019).

[93]   Bauman et al., "After Snowden," 129–130; see also "Huawei Marine Targets New Submarine Cable for South Africa," *Business Tech* (January 2, 2018) https://businesstech.co.za/news/telecommunications/217541/huawei-marine-targets-new-submarine-cable-for-south-africa/ (accessed June 30, 2018).

[94]   See Paul Mozur, Jonah M. Kessel, and Melissa Chan, "Made in China, Exported to the World: The Surveillance State," *New York Times* (April 24, 2019) https://www.nytimes.com/2019/04/24/technology/ecuador-surveillance-cameras-police-government.html (accessed April 27, 2019); Brown, *"Beijing's Silk Road Goes Digital"*; Byler, *"Ghost World"*; "Video Surveillance as the Foundation of 'Safe City' in Kenya," Huawei (n.d.) https://www.huawei.com/en/industry-insights/technology/digital-transformation/video/video-surveillance-as-the-foundation-of-Safe-City-in-Kenya; (accessed March 15, 2019); Parkinson et al., "Huawei Technicians Helped African Governments Spy on Political Opponents"; Prasso, "China's Digital Silk Road Is Looking More Like an Iron Curtain"; Adrian Shahbaz, *Freedom on the Net 2018: The Rise of Digital Authoritarianism*, Freedom House (October 2018) https://freedomhouse.org/sites/default/files/FOTN_2018_Final%20Booklet_11_1_2018.pdf (accessed March 15, 2019).

[95]   Amy Hawkins, "Beijing's Big Brother Tech Needs African Faces," *Foreign Policy* (July 24, 2018) https://foreignpolicy.com/2018/07/24/beijings-big-brother-tech-needs-african-faces/ (accessed September 15, 2018).

[96]   Roberts, *Censored*, 228.

after the revelations about how Cambridge Analytica was able to guide the votes of people in the United States and the United Kingdom, except that it operates on a much grander scale with a clearer message that comes from the party-state. Recent UK and EU legislation shows how stricter regulatory regimes for "freedom of information," "data protection," and privacy can be key modes of resistance to the state-led surveillance activities of the society of sovereignty.[97] China, on the other hand, uses law and regulation to enforce its disciplinary society. Yet it is more than that, because the party-state sees socially managing the Internet as its moral duty. The PRC's disciplinary surveillance society thus combines attack and misdirection, and censorship and propaganda, to produce a docile, self-regulating body politic.

Performative Inter-veillance in the Networked Society of Control

Surveillance in both the sovereignty society and the disciplinary society is primarily a state-led, top-down activity that either restricts visibility through censorship or guides it through discipline, including self-discipline and self-censorship. The issues are government transparency and individual privacy, and they are sites of the production and reproduction of ideology. Interestingly, neither mode of understanding mass surveillance was able to make sense of the general lack of outrage at Snowden's revelations about democratic governments' massive data mining of their own citizens.[98]

Perhaps this is because the surveyor-surveilled relationship has changed. The main data gatherer is no longer the state, but various private companies: telephone companies, ISPs, Facebook, Google, and so on. Here, the geometric dynamics of surveillance have changed from top-down state surveillance to corporate-led multidimensional and multidirectional surveillance, sousveillance, and co-veillance, which can be summarized as "inter-veillance." Like intertextuality and intervisuality, inter-veillance understands the production of meaning and value as an entangled experience of circulation. This approach also shifts from understanding the Internet as a set of visual artifacts that are controlled by state and corporate power to seeing it as a sensory space that people performatively experience in affective communities of sense. Especially on social media, people are watching each other and performing

---

[97] See Robert Hazell, Ben Worthy, and Mark Glover, *The Impact of the Freedom of Information Act on Central Government in the UK: Does FOI Work?* (New York: Palgrave Macmillan, 2010); Rocco Bellanova, "Digital, Politics, and Algorithms: Governing Digital Data through the Lens of Data Protection," *European Journal of Social Theory* 20:3 (2017):329–347; Russell Brandom, "Everything You Need to Know about GDPR," *The Verge* (May 25, 2018) https://www.theverge.com/2018/3/28/17172548/gdpr-compliance-requirements-privacy-notice (accessed January 3, 2019).

[98] Bauman et al., "After Snowden"; Lyon, *The Culture of Surveillance*, 59.

for each other; as the protagonist in the dystopian novel *The Circle* exclaims, "I want to be seen. I want proof that I existed."[99] Such individual social media performances are for security, but also are for convenience, profit, and amusement. Rather than the surveillance society, here we have "social surveillance."[100] Instead of being sorted by the state according to their ideological principles, people are viscerally moved and connected in their interaction with a range of affective communities of sense.

To make sense of social media's visibility/visuality dynamic, it is helpful to look beyond the disciplinary surveillance society to explore how the networked control society works through individual and collective performances that not only promote ideology but also excite affect. Here, "[t]he story of surveillance . . . [is] less one of technology, government, law or rights, than one of cultural practice."[101] The cultural performative mode of surveillance is not just what social media means or even "does." Indeed, as we saw in Chapter 7, where Chinese maps excited irredentist territorial desires, the questions change to what social media wants and what it desires. Facebook desires more "likes" and "shares" in order to move and connect more virtual bodies in an ever-expanding network. As Nicholas Mirzoeff argues, "[I]f what a picture wants above all is to be seen, what the digitized image wants is to be circulated."[102] Rather than the centrally-organized Panoption, one of Mark Zuckerberg's Facebook cover photos speaks to the multicentered logic of the networked society of control; it is a map of the world in which individual people are linked together in a rhizomatic network.[103] In this "surveillant assemblage,"[104] visual social media such as Instagram work much like Brian Massumi's description of affect as an "intensive force" that emerges through the resonance of connecting virtual bodies at "the intersection of matter, movement, aesthetics, and sensation."[105]

Rather than hiding from surveillance by finding an unobserved corner or asserting the legalistic right of data protection, many people now perform "onlife"

---

[99] Dave Eggers, *The Circle* (New York: Penguin, 2014), p. 485; for a discussion of this novel in terms of surveillance, see Lyon, *The Culture of Surveillance*, 149–172.

[100] Alice Marwick, *Status Update: Celebrity, Publicity and Branding in the Social Media Age* (New Haven, CT: Yale University Press, 2013).

[101] John McGrath, "Performing Surveillance," in *Routledge Handbook of Surveillance Studies*, edited by Kirstie Ball, Kevin D. Haggerty, and David Lyon (New York: Routledge, 2014), pp. 83; Lyon, *The Culture of Surveillance*.

[102] Nicholas Mirzoeff, *The Right to Look: A Counterhistory of Visuality* (Durham, NC: Duke University Press, 2011), p. 290.

[103] Mark Zuckerberg, Facebook cover photo (September 24, 2013) https://www.facebook.com/photo.php?fbid=10101026493146301&set=a.941146602501&type=1&theater (accessed March 15, 2019); Lyon, *The Culture of Surveillance*, 125.

[104] Kevin D. Haggerty and Richard V. Ericson, "The Surveillant Assemblage," *British Journal of Sociology* 51:4 (2000):605–622.

[105] Brian Massumi, *Parables for the Virtual: Movement, Affect, Sensation* (Durham, NC: Duke University Press, 2002), p. 28.

(i.e., with the entanglement of online and offline activities) for security, convenience, profit, and amusement.[106] Performative surveillance thus is user-generated surveillance that is "not just a subject for commentary, but a practice through which subjects reimagine themselves."[107] This is what Jonathan Finn means by "seeing surveillantly" when surveillance is more than a state-driven or corporate-driven Panopticon; it entails "a way of seeing, understanding and engaging with the world around us" that is an interactive, lateral inter-veillance not of passive voyeurs, but of active agents performing in affective communities of sense.[108]

In practical terms, we have shifted from the disciplinary society's "Big Brother" to the networked society of control's "big data," wherein information is monetized and weaponized:

> [T]he kinds of data now circulating in greater volume, velocity, and variety—to use the words often applied to Big Data—than ever are of tremendous interest to a growing range of actors; not just government departments, security agencies and police, but also internet companies, healthcare providers, traffic engineers, city planners, and many more.[109]

The issues shift from the wall-themed discussions of censorship, freedom of information, and data protection (either bring down the wall for transparency or erect a wall for privacy, including the right to be forgotten) to questions of trust and morality.

Although many European scholars compare the strong data protection regime in the EU with the NSA's invasion of the privacy of global citizens, it is better to compare the EU with the PRC. Both systems are technologically advanced and address the more cultural issues of trust and morality. In Europe, trust in government—and trust in the United States—was shaken by the NSA's data mining from private companies (telephone companies, ISPs, browsers, search engines, and Web 2.0 platforms such as Facebook). The response was to build trust by legislating a series of government regulations to limit what governments and companies can do with an individual person's data. The moral arguments considered the issues of transparency, accountability, and freedom in a democratic society.[110] The result is the EU's General Data Protection Regulation, which restricts what governments and

---

[106] Luciano Floridi, ed., *The Onlife Manifesto: Being Human in a Hyperconnected Era* (New York: Springer, 2015).

[107] Lyon, *The Culture of Surveillance*, 5; John McGrath, "Performing Surveillance," 84.

[108] Finn, "Seeing Surveillantly," 67, 76.

[109] Lyon, *The Culture of Surveillance*, 3, 4.

[110] Bauman et al., "After Snowden," 129–130; Klimburg, *Darkening Web*, 80; Floridi, *The Onlife Manifesto*.

Internet companies can surveil, what data they can collect, how long they can hold the data, and how they can share the data.[111]

In China, the issues of trust and morality produced a different response from the government. As in many rapidly developing societies, economic change has produced social dislocation in China. Until recently the PRC had a cash economy in which people and companies were largely invisible to the financial system. One of the results of this is a poorly regulated society in which governmental and commercial scandals are common: poisoned medicines, food, and water; dangerous merchandise; identity theft; official corruption; and so on.[112] These scandals became public through the Internet, especially through the social media of Web 2.0. Chinese netizens also suffered from fraud and blackmail online, making data security a major issue. Indeed, the party-state justified its "real-name registration" policy for mobile phones and Internet identity not through an appeal to national security or ideology, but in order to fight the online fraud that was plaguing ordinary Chinese netizens.[113]

While Europe and the United States address such issues through democratic methods of the free press, representative government, and the regulation of the state and industry, the PRC takes the authoritarian option of using technology to solve political problems. As one commentator asked, "[W]ho needs democracy when you have data?"[114] The Chinese government thus decided to build trust through generating greater transparency and accountability in local government, commerce (especially e-commerce), and society—but not through greater transparency and accountability of the central government and the CCP, and certainly not through independent watchdogs in civil society. Beijing decided to "solve" this problem in a way that promoted its more general social governance goals of building innovative ICT capacity through the Internet Plus project, which, as Chinese premier Li Keqiang explains, aims to "integrate mobile Internet, big data, cloud computing and the Internet of things."[115] Rather than regulating state and corporate power through data protection, Beijing's solution is to have an even more intense program

---

[111] Bellanova, "Digital, Politics, and Algorithms"; Brandom, "Everything You Need to Know about GDPR."

[112] Creemers, "China's Social Credit System," 11–12.

[113] See David Bandurski, "Cashing in on Dystopia: Through a Simple Mobile Transaction, You, Too, Can Be Big Brother," SupChina (January 3, 2017) http://supchina.com/2017/01/03/cashing-in-on-dystopia/; Creemers, "Cyber China," 98.

[114] Christina Larson, "Who Needs Democracy When You Have Data?," MIT Technology Review (August 20, 2018). https://www.technologyreview.com/s/611815/who-needs-democracy-when-you-have-data/ (accessed August 28, 2018).

[115] Li Keqiang, "Report on the Work of the Government (2015)," State Council Information Office (March 5, 2015) "http://english.gov.cn/archive/publications/2015/03/05/content_281475066179954.htm (accessed March 15, 2019).

of surveillance of everyone's everyday life, all the time. The goal is to make the population legible and visible in the logic of governmentality.[116]

There has been some discussion of China's Social Credit System and whether or not it constitutes an Orwellian/Panopticon invasion of privacy.[117] It builds on earlier innovations in Chinese Internet governance, for example, the enforcement of "real-name registration" of all users of mobile telephones, email, and social media. In this way, the activities of individuals and companies are knowable and trackable because they are associated with specific individuals who are the responsible parties; this approach thus "sits at the heart of the effort to connect the vast amount of potentially useful information gathered through individuals' interactions with technology."[118]

The PRC is now building a national program to track, reward, and punish people for their activities, starting with digitizing and sharing information on financial creditworthiness and juridical decisions and expanding to a broader notion of credit that includes economic, social, political—and moral—sincerity and trustworthiness.[119] A detailed "Planning Outline" was published in 2014, with the goal of having a nationwide system in place by the end of 2020.[120] As Creemers describes, the Social Credit System is part of China's "informatization of governance" and involves a three-step process: (1) ensure that individuals are identifiable through ID cards and biometric data so "information about them can be collected, stored, processed, shared, and used"; (2) create databases and platforms to share information; and (3) establish procedures for processing, analyzing, and using the stored information "to generate actionable insights."[121] The Social Credit System thus is an infrastructural and normative project to identify and sort the Chinese population in terms of the political categories of credit and trust. But it is more than a top-down government program; "the 'social' dimension of SCS [Social Credit System] also entails that members of society create the incentives for each other

---

[116] Creemers, "Cyber China"; Creemers, "China's Social Credit System."

[117] See "Big Data, Meet Big Brother: China Invents the Digital Totalitarian State," *Economist* (December 17, 2016) http://www.economist.com/news/briefing/21711902-worrying-implications-its-social-credit-project-china-invents-digital-totalitarian?fsrc=scn/tw_ec/china_invents_the_digital_totalitarian_state (accessed June 28, 2018); Creemers, "China's Social Credit System; Hoffman, *Social Credit*; Sarah Cook, " 'Social Credit' Scoring: How China's Communist Party Is Incentivising Repression," *Hong Kong Free Press* (February 27, 2019) https://www.hongkongfp.com/2019/02/27/social-credit-scoring-chinas-communist-party-incentivising-repression/ (accessed March 7, 2019).

[118] Creemers, "Cyber China," 96.

[119] Creemers, "China's Social Credit System," 1.

[120] State Council, "Guowuyuan: Guanyu yifa shehui xinyong tixi jianshe kuanhua gangyao (2014–2020)" [State Council: Planning outline for the construction of a Social Credit System (2014–2020)], translated on China Copyright and Media (June 14, 2014) https://chinacopyrightandmedia.wordpress.com/2014/06/14/planning-outline-for-the-construction-of-a-social-credit-system-2014-2020/ (accessed June 11, 2018).

[121] Creemers, "China's Social Credit System," 19–22.

to act in the desired manner, without direct intervention of State actors."[122] It is an affective inter-veillance performance on social media, much like that seen in Euro-America—although it goes beyond the symbolic identity experiences to include very material rewards and punishments.[123]

People already face harsh penalties for "spreading rumors, disrupting social order and stability" online; since 2013, if unacceptable speech is retweeted five hundred times or viewed five thousand times, the user can face up to three years in jail. Now the new Social Credit System uses digitized information on financial creditworthiness and juridical decisions to blacklist certain people from certain activities: purchasing air and high-speed train tickets, enrolling their children in private schools, staying in some hotels, and purchasing tickets for entertainment events. The reasoning is instrumental, but also moral—people who owe money for legal judgments should not be allowed to consume luxury items—and by the end of 2018 over twenty-three million air and train ticket purchases had been blocked.[124] It is also political: according to the "Planning Outline," the goal is to "strengthen sincerity in government affairs, commercial sincerity, social sincerity, and judicial credibility construction," while at the same time to "punish insincerity."[125] This is part of the party-state's more general goal of raising the "quality" (*suzhi*) of the population by constructing a "sincerity culture." This massive social engineering project combines China's Confucian-Leninist paternalism with the CCP's "deeply positivist and mechanical view of the world."[126]

At the time of writing (August 2019), there is not yet a national system that combines the data from financial, legal, commercial, social, and political activities; although it may be delayed, the goal is to have the system in place by the end of 2020. There have been protests in China against various pilot schemes that measured and scored individual conduct because they were seen as too invasive.[127] But there are also pilot schemes that have been successful in the eyes of both the central government and local citizens. Simina Mistreanu's in-depth report on a popular

[122] Creemers, "China's Social Credit System," 8.

[123] Cook, "'Social Credit' Scoring"; Gladys Pak Lei Chong, "Cashless China: Securitization of Everyday Life through Alipay's Social Credit System—Sesame Credit," *Chinese Journal of Communication* (March 12, 2019):1–18, https://doi.org/10.1080/17544750.2019.1583261 (accessed August 23, 2019).

[124] Creemers, "China's Social Credit System," 15; Lily Kuo, "China Bans 23m from Buying Travel Tickets as Part of 'Social Credit' System," *The Guardian* (March 1, 2019) https://www.theguardian.com/world/2019/mar/01/china-bans-23m-discredited-citizens-from-buying-travel-tickets-social-credit-system (accessed March 7, 2019).

[125] State Council, "Planning Outline."

[126] Leibold, "Surveillance in Xinjiang," 3.

[127] Creemers, "China's Social Credit System," 10; also see Liu Zhun, "China's Social Credit System Won't Be Orwellian," *Global Times* (November 1, 2016) http://www.globaltimes.cn/content/1015248.shtml (accessed June 28, 2018).

social credit system run in the town of Rongcheng shows how a national system could work. Each resident gets a one-thousand-point score, which is adjusted according to that person's sincerity conduct:

> Get a traffic ticket; you lose five points. Earn a city-level award, such as for committing a heroic act, doing exemplary business, or helping your family in unusual tough circumstances, and your score gets boosted by 30 points. For a department-level award, you earn five points. You can also earn credit by donating to charity or volunteering in the city's program.[128]

The goal, as in the national scheme, is to "allow the trustworthy to roam everywhere under heaven, while making it hard for the discredited to take a single step."[129] Again, this is not simply top-down, state-led surveillance; it works because local people buy into the inter-veillance practice of watching and being watched.[130] It is a gamification of social-ordering, in which people get prizes for participating, including prizes for informing on others.[131]

In the private sector there are parallel developments that are even more participatory and better exploit big data dynamics. For example, Chinese tech-giant Alibaba's "Sesame Credit" tracks people's conduct in terms of credit history, behavior trends, ability to honor agreements, verifiable personal information, and social relationships.[132] It is an opt-in loyalty scheme that calculates a score of between 350 and 950 points to determine a range of rewards and punishments, including a reduction or waiver of fees for products and services such as mobile phones, hotels, and bicycle rentals. In this way it is like a credit card loyalty scheme in the United States. But it is also expanding to facilitate other services, including visa applications and even dating sites; some people list their Sesame Credit score online to attract interest from prospective mates. In a press conference, Sesame Credit's technology director said that people buying diapers would be "seen as more trustworthy than someone playing video games for ten hours per day."[133] Hence, Sesame Credit penalizes users for what it sees as bad social conduct, including a frequent change of address. Like Rongcheng's official pilot scheme, it monetizes trustworthiness, because charitable donations raise your score.[134] It is more than a loyalty scheme

---

[128] Simina Mistreanu, "Life Inside China's Social Credit Laboratory," *Foreign Policy* (April 3, 2018) http://foreignpolicy.com/2018/04/03/life-inside-chinas-social-credit-laboratory/ (accessed June 11, 2018).

[129] State Council, "Planning Outline."

[130] See Genia Kostka, "China's Social Credit Systems and Public Opinion: Explaining High Levels of Approval," *New Media and Society* 21:7 (2019):1565–1593; Chong "Cashless China."

[131] Cook, " 'Social Credit' Scoring."

[132] See Chong "Cashless China."

[133] Creemers, "China's Social Credit System," 22–24.

[134] Creemers, "China's Social Credit System," 23.

because it uses an algorithm to predict each individual's future trustworthy conduct. And it is more than the private sector because China's big tech companies work closely with the party-state.[135] It is likely that Sesame Credit will be a model for China's nationwide social credit system, because only an organization as large and sophisticated as Alibaba would be able to create and run such a system.

At present, the party-state's project is primarily a binary system of blacklisting, rather than a fully integrated system that would use algorithms to sort people, assign numerical scores, and predict future behavior.[136] But as the State Council's "Planning Outline" declares, Beijing's goal is to share data among government bureaucracies, ISPs, browsers, and e-commerce sites to give a full-spectrum view of the sincerity of China's citizenry. As we have seen, a parallel program in Xinjiang shows the party-state's goal for the total surveillance/inter-veillance of online and offline activity that sorts and predicts economic, social, cultural, and political activity.

Creemers has doubts about whether Beijing has the capacity to overcome the various technical and social obstacles facing a fully-integrated Social Credit System.[137] On the other hand, Richard P. Suttmeier argues that Chinese labs, including those involved in developing the PRC's "surveillance state," are successfully "inventing the future."[138] As the Great Firewall shows, with enough investment and effort, you can even nail Jell-O to the wall.

China's Social Credit Scheme is also being applied to non-Chinese companies, and in very political ways. In 2018 China accused United Airlines, Qantas, and other international airlines of "serious dishonesty" for listing Taiwan, Hong Kong, and Macau on their websites as destinations distinct from China. It demanded that all airlines state that these were Chinese territories or risk the penalties associated with blacklisting under the Social Credit System.[139] Although the White House described this situation as "Orwellian," the airlines ultimately complied. Beijing is also exporting its Social Credit System to other countries such as Venezuela, where a single smart card—the "fatherland card"—collects and shares data on medical history, social media activity, political party membership, and whether the person has voted.[140]

[135] See Manya Koetse, "Baihang and the Eight Personal Credit Programmes: A Credit Leap Forward," What's On Weibo (June 10, 2018) https://www.whatsonweibo.com/baihang-and-the-eight-personal-credit-programmes-a-credit-leap-forward/ (accessed September 15, 2018).

[136] Creemers, "China's Social Credit System," 10.

[137] Creemers, "China's Social Credit System," 27–28.

[138] Richard P. Suttmeier, "Inventing the Future in Chinese Labs: How Does China Do Science Today," Asia Dialogue (September 24, 2018) http://theasiadialogue.com/2018/09/24/inventing-the-future-in-chinese-labs-how-does-china-do-science-today/ (accessed November 8, 2018).

[139] Hoffman, *Social Credit*, 5.

[140] ABC News (Australia), "Chinese Telecom Giant ZTE 'Helped Venezuela Develop Social Credit System'" (November 16, 2018) https://www.abc.net.au/news/2018-11-16/

These examples from inside and outside the PRC show how China is engaging in a complex ecology of inter-veillance, including top-down state surveillance, bottom-up sousveillance, and co-veillance of people watching each other. China thus shows how the three models of surveillance in society—sovereignty, discipline, and networked performance—can coexist in a surveillance assemblage under the watch of the party-state. While it is common to declare that the Panopticon era of surveillance is over, the Chinese experience shows how Big Brother can still exist in tension with the Great Firewall and performative inter-veillance in a complex surveillance ecology. Social media and social credit schemes are not successful just because they are imposed in a top-down way by states and/or corporations; people actively buy into such platforms because these affective communities of sense provide security, convenience, profit, and amusement. This infrastructure of feeling thus works in the macro-register of geopolitics and social control, as well as in the micro-register of the onlife sensible politics of the everyday.

Conclusion

It would be easy to draw the ideological conclusion that China's surveillance state threatens the freedom not just of Chinese citizens, but also of people in liberal democratic societies. There is plenty of evidence that the party-state is building a surveillance state in the PRC, as well as a growing corpus of evidence that Beijing is exporting its surveillance infrastructure, concepts, and norms to both authoritarian and democratic countries.

But the chapter also shows that we need to think beyond the framing of issues in terms of the ideological battles of freedom and order, West and East. To do this, the analysis looks to the conceptual dynamics of visibility/visuality and ideology/affect to reconsider the sensible politics of surveillance in terms of Foucault's and Deleuze's models of social ordering: wall-building in sovereignty society, the Panopticon in disciplinary society, and interactive performances of multidirectional "inter-veillance" in networked control society. Rather than simply being a description of historical evolution, Chapter 11's examples from China, the United States, and Europe show how all three social models can overlap and co-exist in the present. The Great Firewall of China exemplifies how the PRC continues to successfully enforce sovereignty society's borders by employing the visibility/invisibility strategy of policing what can and cannot be seen. Disciplinary society and the networked society of control both appeal more to the affect-work of visuality. Rather than simply being top-down, state-centric expressions of restrictive power, surveillance society's logic of self-discipline and networked society's practice of self-realization

chinese-tech-giant-zte-helps-venezuela-develop-fatherland-card/10503736 (accessed March 7, 2019); Mozur et al., "Made in China, Exported to the World"; Griffiths, *The Great Firewall of China.*

both demand active participation in everyone's everyday onlife performances. Here the Internet is an infrastructure of feeling that provokes a range of affective communities of sense.

Importantly, the chapter shows how activities in (authoritarian) China and the (democratic) West differ more in degree than in kind. Similar technologies and concepts are provoking similar performances around the world. Indeed, there is evidence of a growing demand for individual privacy in China, as well as a growing call for regulation in Euro-America. Certainly the epigraphs in this chapter look to the state as the main factor: either the Silicon Valley libertarian model of resisting state control or the China Model of asserting state control. This chapter, however, looks at different models of Internet governance to highlight how the EU's data protection regime stresses the value of individual and social privacy as a moral good, while the PRC's cybersecurity laws and Social Credit System project see social legibility and stability as the moral goal. Again, Beijing's logic is "Who needs democracy when you can have big data?"

The threat to democracy from surveillance is very real, but it cannot be reduced to geopolitics and security: that either the United States or China is the main threat to freedom. The conclusion is that surveillance is a political rather than technical or cultural issue, and that it is important to move beyond questions of cybersecurity to appreciate it as a social-ordering and world-ordering process. The visual politics of surveillance thus is not just about how you are captured by the surveillant gaze. It is also about visualizing what kind of world you want to live in, as well as what kind of world you don't want to see and feel.

PART IV

CONCLUSION

Conclusion

Sensible Politics

Beginnings

Sensible Politics is the product of a number of distinct beginnings: a Filmmaking for Fieldwork class in Manchester in 2011; a Japanese Garden Design class in Kyoto in 2010; and even my PhD dissertation in Hawaii, which looked at the body politics of laughter (as opposed to the psychological/ideational politics of humor) in 1992. The shared motivation for these various activities was to think about politics in terms of ideas and experiences, and meaning and doing. This book's version of the project considers how visual international politics takes shape according to the dynamic dyad of visibility (which looks to ideas, images, representations, and ideology) and visuality (which appreciates experiences, artifacts, performances, and affect).

My interest in sensible politics and visual IR was provoked by numerous experiences of exhilaration and frustration. What is it about Japanese gardens that makes them excite indescribable feelings? What is missing from visual IR research that concentrates on deconstructing Western images of the Other? At first, I addressed this exhilaration/frustration experience as an issue of content and thus embarked on a study of gardens and toilets, for example, as sites of international politics that were not necessarily involved in some East-West or Left-Right conflict. But soon I realized that the issue was more than one of content, because it provokes questions of theory, method, and ethics. At the risk of exhibiting the irrational exuberance of the newly-converted, taking the Filmmaking for Fieldwork course changed my life—or at least it jammed the way I think about meaning, value, and politics.

Like many who study visual IR, I am well-trained in hermeneutics, deconstruction, and the politics of representation. For many years I followed what I call the "visibility strategy," using semiotics and narrative theory to turn political events, artifacts, and processes into texts, which I then analyzed to reveal their hidden

Sensible Politics. William A. Callahan, Oxford University Press (2020). © Oxford University Press.
DOI: 10.1093/oso/9780190071738.001.0001

ideology. This approach is employed in *Sensible Politics* to make visible new sites of IR that add a critical sense to international studies: for example, Chinese toilets; utopian PSAs from the Islamic State (IS); the counter-PSAs of Cynthia Weber's *I Am an American* videos; historical and futuristic empire-maps from Russia, IS, and China; veils and beauty pageants in Europe, the Middle East, and Asia; and gardens in France, China, and Japan.

Many of the chapters speak to each other, and often in unexpected ways. The visuality of borders and the logic of inside/outside distinctions is explored not only through an analysis of the geopolitics of border walls (Chapter 9), but also through an examination of how walling-strategies erupt in less obvious places, for example, how the Great Firewall of China polices cyberspace (Chapter 11), how veil-wearing is seen as a protective/restrictive social barrier (Chapter 8), and even how garden-building generally starts with the construction of a border wall, which is then transgressed through "borrowed views" that look over that barrier (Chapter 10). Once again, the task of the critic is to examine the social construction of the image and employ the hermeneutic mode of analysis to disclose its hidden ideological meaning. The visibility strategy thus follows the "aesthetic turn" in IR to argue that the practice of representation is the site of politics.[1]

Here the researcher must cultivate a critical attitude, and more important, a self-critical attitude. Questions of identity are paramount: gender, race, ethnicity, ability, class, age, sexuality, and so on. Since I am an American white male who studies Asian theory and politics, self-critique meant targeting "The West" for criticism and either promoting the "non-West" as an ethically-superior "alternative" or leaving open the "conditions of possibility" to create space for non-hegemonic voices to develop their own critique.[2] This informed the book's attention to how scopic regimes—the male gaze, the colonial/white gaze, the surveillant gaze—can guide visual IR in elite politics and popular culture. *Sensible Politics* thus uses historically- and socially-informed analysis of non-Western experiences to problematize Eurocentrism in IR in both spatial and temporal terms. As Alex Danchev put it, the

---

[1] See Roland Bleiker, "The Aesthetic Turn in International Political Theory," *Millennium: Journal of International Studies* 30: (2001):510; Michael J. Shapiro, *The Politics of Representation: Writing Practices in Biography, Photography and Policy Analysis* (Madison: University of Wisconsin Press, 1988).

[2] A good example of this strategy is the World Orders Models Project, which supported both the academic journal *Alternatives: Global, Local, Political* and Walker's *Inside/Outside* book project. See R. B. J. Walker, *Inside/Outside: International Relations as Political Theory* (Cambridge, UK: Cambridge University Press, 1993), p. xi; Ranji Kothari, "Editorial Statement," *Alternatives* 1:1 (1975):1–5; Ranji Kothari, "Towards a Just World," *Alternatives* 5 (1979–1980):1–42; "Alternatives: A Journal for World Policy Published," World Policy (no date) https://worldpolicy.org/timeline/1975-alternatives-a-journal-for-world-policy-published/ (accessed January 4, 2019). Also see William E. Connolly, *Identity\Difference: Democratic Negotiations of Political Paradox*, expanded ed. (Ithaca, NY: Cornell University Press, 2002 [1991]); William A. Callahan, *Contingent States: Great China and Transnational Relations* (Minneapolis: University of Minnesota Press, 2004).

point is not just to "think otherwise," but to cultivate a critical aesthetic attitude that is "other-wise."[3]

After engaging for many years in such a hermeneutic analysis of the politics of film, popular culture, and gardens, I thought that learning how films are made and how gardens are built would enhance my research into their hidden ideologies and alternative possibilities. What I found in the Filmmaking for Fieldwork and the Japanese Garden Design courses was actually quite different from what I expected. Filmmaking and garden-building push you to think, feel, and act in a different register and in a more creative than deconstructive mode. As Roland Barthes quipped, such a critique "paints more than it digs."[4] Hence, while film criticism employs the visibility strategy to reveal the "social construction of the visual," filmmaking employs the visuality strategy to creatively engage in the "visual construction of the social"—and the international. In other words, I learned that it is not only necessary to deconstruct how films and gardens reflect social, political, and economic power relations; we also need to consider how making films and building gardens visually constructs new and different social, political, and economic orders.

Because visuals can viscerally move us in different ways than written texts, these practical courses pushed me to appreciate visuals not just in terms of their ideological-value, but also their affect-work: not just what they mean, but also how they make us feel, especially when they move us and connect us in nonverbal, nonlinear, and nonnarrative ways. As we've seen, the visuality strategy works to highlight the broader issues of how visual images and artifacts can actively excite affective communities of sense that complicate what can (and cannot) be seen, said, thought, and done.[5] Here *Sensible Politics* presses beyond the visibility strategy's goal of making visible the invisible ideologies, in order to explore new sensibilities through what Emmanuel Levinas saw as "a mode of thought better than [rational] knowledge."[6]

In learning the aesthetic conventions and practical techniques of film-making and garden-building, I thus learned a different approach to theory and method. To appreciate how the visual/multisensory can provoke new social orders and world orders, this book argues that it is necessary to complement hermeneutics with a critical aesthetic mode of inquiry that (1) involves a switch from the search for meaning

[3] Alex Danchev, *On Art and War and Terror* (Edinburgh: University of Edinburgh Press, 2011), p. 4.

[4] Roland Barthes, "Inaugural Lecture: College de France," in *A Barthes Reader*, edited by Susan Sontag (London: Vintage, 2000), p. 475.

[5] Emma Hutchison, *Affective Communities in World Politics: Collective Emotions after Trauma* (Cambridge, UK: Cambridge University Press, 2016); Jacques Rancière, "Contemporary Art and the Politics of Aesthetics," in *Communities of Sense: Rethinking Aesthetics and Politics*, edited by Beth Hinderliter, William Kaizen, Vered Maimon, Jaleh Mansoor, and Seth McCormick (Durham, NC: Duke University Press, 2009), p. 31.

[6] Emmanuel Levinas, quoted in Michael Renov, *The Subject of the Documentary* (Minneapolis: University of Minnesota Press, 2004), p. 148.

to an appreciation of what visuals can "do" and (2) a switch from privileging the word over the image to appreciate the more uncertain relation of word and image, (3) which enables a shift from the search for ideology to an appreciation of how the visual/multisensory works to move and connect people in affective communities of sense; (4) it thus refocuses the critical gaze from the reformist politics of empowerment to see critique in terms of the social-ordering and world-ordering work involved in actively creating "redistributions of the sensible."[7]

The Filmmaking for Fieldwork course's intensive training in camera-work, light and sound design, and film editing was pivotal because it forced me to think visually rather than in terms of written texts. I'm still learning how to use a montage of evocative images and sounds—rather than a logical chain of statements—to create a critical understanding of international politics. Each year I reproduce this learning experience when we teach students how to make films in a final year undergraduate course, Visual International Politics.[8] This course is practical, and students learn by doing; they get the camera kit on day-one, and ten weeks later they deliver a ten-minute video documentary. To cultivate "active looking" skills—and thus wean students from using words to make meaning—the first assignment is to make a two-minute "silent movie" in which meaning and value emerge from a series of images, rather than from a verbal argument. Interviewing is part of the training, but it comes much later, because in visual ethnography the goal is to see how people live, rather than ask them to explain it. Even so, video interviews are fascinating because they require active listening; people tell you things that they would never say in a normal conversation. As my students' *Awrah: Uncovering the Covered* film and my *toilet adventures* film both show, people share their intimate experiences on-camera, usually without provocation (Chapters 4 and 8).[9]

At the end of the Visual International Politics class, we throw a party and have a mini-film festival to watch each other's films. This experience is also different from seminars in which students present their topics and defend their analyses. Rather than have the students introduce their films, the class watches them, and only then discusses them. The point is not necessarily to make arguments that rationally prove or rhetorically persuade, but to see how viewers respond to the film experience. As my filmmaking teacher, Andy Lawrence, instructs, rather than react to critique (to show that you're right, and they're wrong), it's best to actively watch and listen to audience feedback to see what is working in the film and what isn't. Filmmaking

[7] See Jacques Rancière, *The Politics of Aesthetics: The Distribution of the Sensible*, translated by Gabriel Rockhill (London: Continuum International Publishing Group, 2004).

[8] This course is co-taught will Darren Moon.

[9] Abi Steadman, Hayley Rabet, and Lamisa Khan, dir., *Awrah: Uncovering the Covered* (2017) https://vimeo.com/channels/ir318/208667693 (accessed February 23, 2018); Bill Callahan, dir., *toilet adventures* (August 25, 2015) https://www.thechinastory.org/2015/08/toilet-adventures-in-china-making-sense-of-transnational-encounters/ (accessed July 23, 2018).

thus can foster intimate moving and connecting to promote an ethical community of sense among the subjects, filmmakers, and the audience.[10]

Learning and re-learning how to make films thus has changed the way I think about visuals and politics. Rather than simply treating images as illustrations of a logical argument, thinking visually and feeling visually helped me to appreciate new sensibilities of IR. It also opens up the range of visuals to include three-dimensional visual artifacts—maps, veils, walls, gardens, and cyberspace—that can act as material modalities, sensory spaces, and infrastructures of feeling. Here material objects have "thing-power";[11] they can do things, and make things, as well as mean things. As heavily-designed spaces that forge particular relations between the see-able, hear-able, smell-able, taste-able, and touch-able, walls and gardens are exemplary distributions of the sensible (Chapters 10 and 11). Of course, most people still experience visual artifacts in terms of the visual images of photographs and film. But it works the other way around, too. Visual images can take on material form as artifacts and practical experiences; an important part of "going to the movies" is the collective social experience, and photographic prints are material objects that people produce, exchange, and accumulate in everyday experience. Visual images and artifacts are sites of both ideology and sensibilities of affect.

While finishing this book, the strange tension between ideology and affect erupted once more while I was making *Great Walls: Journeys from Ideology to Experience* (2019), a short film that runs parallel to Chapter 9's consideration of the US-Mexico barrier, the Berlin Wall, and the Great Wall of China.[12] Although the film's narrative was initially organized according to Chapter 9's analytical out-line, the available film clips—both my own ethnographic clips of experiences at the three sites and archive clips of political leaders at these walls—led the project in different directions. First there was the issue of whom to include and whom to exclude. The PRC started rebuilding the Great Wall in 1952 as a tourist site that was designed not just for patriotic Chinese, but also for visiting foreign leaders. Indian prime minister Jawaharlal Nehru was the first foreign leader to visit the Great Wall, during his official trip to China in 1954. But after much archive work with Chinese and Indian sources, I have yet to find any picture of Nehru's visit to the wall. Images of British politicians and royals at the various walls are also hard to locate, as well as being very expensive to use. On the other hand, the US presi-dential library system makes it easy—and cheap—to get high quality photographs

---

[10] Elena Barabantseva and Andy Lawrence, "Encountering Vulnerabilities through 'Filmmaking for Fieldwork,'" *Millennium* 43:3 (2015):929.

[11] Jane Bennett, *Vibrant Matter: A Political Ecology of Things* (Durham, NC: Duke University Press, 2010).

[12] See Bill Callahan, dir., *Great Walls: Journeys from Ideology to Experience* (Wildwood Films, 2019), screened at LSE Festival, London (March 2, 2019) https://vimeo.com/billcallahan/great-walls (accessed August 23, 2019).

and film clips of official visits to walls in Berlin and China, as well as to the US-Mexico border. The wall-themed presidential films are certainly very ideological. John F. Kennedy surveys the Berlin Wall and declares US support for Berliners on both sides (1963). Richard Nixon declares that the Great Wall of China "is a great wall and it had to be built by a great people" (1972). Ronald Reagan condemns the Berlin Wall as the physical manifestation of the Iron Curtain that ideologically divides Europe, famously demanding, "Mr. Gorbachev, tear down this wall!" (1987). Donald J. Trump looks to the Great Wall of China as a model for what he calls the Great Wall of Trump: "2000 years ago, China built the Great Wall of China. And this is a serious wall. . . . They built a wall, think of this: 13,000 miles long, and this is a serious wall" (2016).

Recalling the words of such important wall-themed events clearly highlights ideology. But to appreciate them as affective performances, it's necessary to juxtapose the films to see (and hear) the experiences. It's common to mock Nixon for the silliness of saying that it's really a "great wall." But the film shows the excitement of both Americans and Chinese at this momentous event, when an anti-communist president goes to "Red China" to offer friendship and support. While Nixon is known in the United States as a failed politician who was driven from office, in China he is admired and respected for reaching out across the ideological divide to engage with the PRC. The film clips show Nixon's Chinese hosts smiling and enjoying themselves. Nixon actually concludes that he hopes that neither physical walls nor walls of ideology will divide the peoples of the world. This pivotal event now inspires both high civilization and popular culture; John Adams wrote the *Nixon in China* opera (1987), and Spock says "only Nixon could go to China" as "an old Vulcan proverb" in *Star Trek VI* (1991).

One of the strangest things about making the *Great Walls* film was stumbling upon a pair of long-forgotten official films that record First Lady Pat Nixon dedicating International Friendship Park at the San Diego/Tijuana border—which now is where the thirty-foot-high US-Mexico barrier spills into the Pacific Ocean. In 1972 President Nixon went to China to admire the Great Wall (with Mrs. Nixon by his side), while in 1971 she was at the US-Mexico border speaking fondly of her Mexican neighbors and hoping that the five-foot-tall border fence wouldn't be there much longer (see figure C.1). Again, the words alone don't allow us to appreciate the affective experience. At the ceremony, an army general, who is relinquishing possession of his ocean-side military test range so it can become a state park, is very stiff and formal. Mrs. Nixon, on the other hand, comes across as fun and sincere, playfully joking with friends on both sides of the border. The strangeness of right-wing politicians criticizing walls in China and at the US-Mexico border is compelling. But the main point, once again, is that visual artifacts are sites of multisensory, performative experience in which the personal, the political, and the international collide. The filmmaking experience also shows the "visual/multisensory construction of the international" because I had to edit together clips from two separate

Figure C.1 Patricia Nixon at the US-Mexico border (1971). Courtesy Richard M. Nixon
Presidential Library and Museum

films: one of Pat Nixon giving the speech, and the other of her meeting people and
working the crowds.

The strange collision of Richard Nixon's and Pat Nixon's wall adventures becomes
even stranger when juxtaposed with the film of Chinese artist Cai Guo-Qiang's art
project to *Extend the Great Wall by 10 Kilometers* (1993). This pyrotechnic spectacle
plays with the dynamic dyad of creative/destruction by building a wall through
explosives (see Chapter 9). At first the film seems to display a typical New Year's
Eve fireworks show. But as the monochromatic pyrotechnic display dances over
hills and echoes through valleys, it turns into a bombing campaign—complete with
mushroom clouds—which is greeted by the excited, confused, and haunting cheers
of the local Chinese who have gathered to watch the spectacle.[13] Once again, the visuality strategy encourages us to see walls not simply as sites of ideology that divide
people, but also as spaces where affective experience can move and connect people
in strange ways—even exciting the sublime. Here wall-building and filmmaking
visually construct new and different social orders and world orders as affective

[13] Takehisa Araki, dir., *Cai Guo-Qiang: Project to Add 10,000 m to the Great Wall of China—Project
for Extraterrestrials No. 10* (Cai Studio, 1993). A clip of this film can be seen at the end of Callahan,
Great Walls.

communities of sense. Jacques Rancière thus concludes that politics emerges not through representation, but through mis-en-scène.[14]

This demonstrates the contribution of *Sensible Politics*: its visibility/visuality analytic framework enables visual IR research that is attentive to both ideological meaning and affective experience. It pushes us to think of politics in a different register that is more attentive to the visceral politics of everyday bodily practices, wherein both elites and non-elites creatively participate in affective communities of sense. *Sensible Politics* is about multisensory politics; but it also looks beyond icons and ideology to "what makes sense" in the pragmatic politics of everyday life.

From Self/Other and Inside/Outside to Social-Ordering and World-Ordering

If pressed to make a general conclusion, I think that the book's analysis of visual images and multisensory artifacts shows that it is helpful to figure international politics in terms of social-ordering and world-ordering performances, rather than in terms of self/Other and inside/outside relations. In 1991 William E. Connolly insightfully argued that we need to appreciate global politics in terms of identity\ difference, and in 1993 R. B. J. Walker famously wrote that we need to understand IR in terms of inside/outside.[15] Rather than be limited by a Cold War–style set of East-West and Left-Right options, Connolly figured politics and critique in terms of fostering new "conditions of possibility." While Connolly's and Walker's shared goal was to problematize how we socially draw and enforce such self-Other and inside-outside binary distinctions, much critical IR research focuses on the distinctions themselves, often in ways that have the unintended consequence of essentializing identities rather than loosening the binaries.[16] If constructivism's logic is that national identity determines national interest, which in turn produces foreign policy, then its goal is to explain how Americans are like "this," while Chinese are like "that."[17] Visual securitization and ontological security likewise are concerned with

---

[14] Jacques Rancière, *The Emancipated Spectator*, translated by Gregory Elliott (London: Verso, 2009), p. 67.

[15] Connolly, *Identity\Difference*, 36–63; Walker, *Inside/Outside*.

[16] In later editions and books, Connolly and Walker both recognize this problem. See Connolly, *Identity\Difference*, xiii–xxxi; R. B. J. Walker, *Out of Line: Essays on the Politics of Boundaries and the Limits of Modern Politics* (New York: Routledge, 2016), pp. 1–30.

[17] See, for example, Peter Katzenstein, ed., *Civilizations in World Politics: Plural and Pluralist Perspectives* (New York: Routledge, 2010); David C. Kang, *East Asia Before the West: Five Centuries of Trade and Tribute* (New York: Columbia University Press, 2010); Wang Ban, ed., *Chinese Visions of World Order: Tianxia, Culture, and World Politics* (Durham, NC: Duke University Press, 2017); Martin Jacques, *When China Rules the World: The End of the Western World and the Birth of a New Global Order*, 2nd ed. (London: Penguin, 2012).

critically identifying discursive boundaries to reveal the mainstream identities that they assert. While this search for hegemons and alternatives can be interesting and important, it risks ossifying identity categories—with critique often invoking a simple reversal to show the civilized West as barbaric, for example.[18] Critical IR's "border walls are evil" discourse, as discussed in Chapter 9, is a case in point.

The sense in much of critical IR is that drawing boundaries is an ethical and political problem, and it is the job of analysts to deconstruct inside/outside and self/Other distinctions as representational problems.[19] For example, the solution to the social construction of security—that is, securitization—is desecuritization. My sense of politics, on the other hand, follows that of the classical Chinese philosopher Xunzi: "Wherein lies that which makes humanity human? I say it lies in humanity's possession of boundaries."[20] Rather than pursuing an emancipatory project to erase all boundaries—Reagan telling Gorbachev to tear down the Berlin Wall or the pope telling Trump to build bridges rather than walls—*Sensible Politics* examines how visuals can actively create social order and world order in ways that creatively play with inside/outside and self/Other distinctions. In other words, we move seeing IR in terms of security (and desecuritization) to ordering (and re-ordering), as seen in Rancière's (re)distribution of the sensible.

Rather than focusing critique on the existing liberal world order, and leaving "alternatives" open for others to create, *Sensible Politics* has examined an actual set of post-Western alternatives that are creatively and actively promoted by scholars and policymakers. A detailed study of "non-Western" examples is important because it enriches our understanding of visual international politics. But there is more; visual images and multisensory artifacts from the Middle East, Asia, and China are not simply important, but are different in the sense of pushing critique into a new register. Using the Great Wall of China to critically engage with Trump's wall can help us to shift from a Berlin Wall–inspired understanding of barriers as ideologically evil, to appreciate walls as sites of performative experience that is morally ambiguous—or even morally good (as in China). We often hear about the increasing militarization of civilian society; but *Sensible Politics* looks to East Asian gardens to show how civil/military relations are better appreciated through the shifting civility/martiality dynamic. Because Islamic veils problematize liberal and post-Marxist visions of society as open and transparent, they raise a different set of conceptual issues, suggesting the limits not just of visibility, but also of an ethics that demands

---

[18] Tzvetan Todorov, *The Fear of Barbarians: Beyond the Clash of Civilizations* (Chicago: University of Chicago Press, 2010); Erik Ringmar, *Liberal Barbarism: The European Destruction of the Palace of the Emperor of China* (New York: Palgrave Macmillan, 2013).

[19] Walker, *Out of Line*, 2; Wendy Brown, *Walled States, Waning Sovereignty* (New York: Zone Books, 2014).

[20] Quoted in Carlos Rojas, *The Great Wall: A Cultural History* (Cambridge, MA: Harvard University Press, 2010), p. xvii.

face-to-face relations. While we could see these visual experiences as yet another drawing of inside/outside boundaries of identity/difference, I hope the book has shown the value of treating them as affective assemblages that performatively produce social orders and world orders as affective communities of sense.

The point is not to switch from West to East or to replace Eurocentrism with Sinocentrism, but to loosen up such distinctions to explore sensible politics through an assemblage of concepts that are Chinese, Asian, Islamic, Western, traditional, and contemporary. The book thus uses non-Western concepts, practices, and experiences as a critical juxtaposition to problematize critical IR discourse that characteristically generalizes from Euro-American examples. Once the West is decentered from its hegemonic position in critique, then Euro-American examples can be (re)considered. The purpose of theory thus is not to locate the East/West or friend/enemy boundary, but to loosen up the categories that we use to understand politics and IR.[21] In this way, we can shake loose the hold of iconic images and engage in comparative political theory that problematizes simple reversals and moral equivalences.

Here *Sensible Politics* follows Michel Foucault's consideration of heterotopia, which shies away from a search for singular utopian alternatives, to appreciate the messiness of already-existing alternative social formations: colonies, brothels, prisons, cemeteries, ships, and gardens.[22] Foucault is not promoting such places as normatively good alternatives—not even gardens. Rather, heterotopia is interesting because it allows us to appreciate how each alternative social order has its own set of distinctions, hierarchies, violences, and dreams. Once again, rather than hoping that the non-West will provide answers to the problems of Western modernity, *Sensible Politics* has examined in detail the distinctions, hierarchies, violences, and dreams of how such alternatives are visualized in terms of photos, films, maps, veils, walls, gardens, and cyberspace. It's one thing to open the critical door to new conditions of possibility; it's another to walk through the door to do the detailed empirical research that is necessary to see how alternative social orders and world orders are being visualized in the present: the IS's utopian Caliphate, a revived Chinese world order, Russian Eurasianism, inter-veillance on the Web, and so on.

While there was much hope that the non-West could better address modernity's concern with equality and inclusion, I have instead found different dynamics of hierarchy and exclusion. It's important to criticize Euro-American societies for being hypocritical in their pursuit of equality. But the book has shown that it's also necessary to appreciate how powerful voices in China (and elsewhere) now present "hierarchy" as the answer, the preferred regulatory ideal, that will solve the "problem"

---

[21] For example, see Allen Chun, *Forget Chineseness: On the Geopolitics of Cultural Identification* (Albany: State University of New York Press, 2017); Kevin Carrico, *The Great Han: Race, Nationalism and Tradition in China Today* (Berkeley: University of California Press, 2017).

[22] Michel Foucault, "Of Other Spaces," *Diacritics* 16:1 (1986):22–27.

of equality.[23] In addition to being "Other-wise," it is important to continue critique, and in an ethical manner that avoids simple reversals and moral equivalences.

Theory and Dynamic Dyads

The experience of film school and garden design class also shaped *Sensible Politics*'s conceptual arguments to highlight how theory can be found in odd places and practices, including picture-taking, film-making, map-making, veil-wearing, wall-building, garden-building, and Web-surfing. Rather than engage in high theory to make causal explanations or deconstruct truth-claims, each of the chapters of *Sensible Politics* works to analyze, explain, and experience visual/multisensory IR by inventing and applying new concepts and creating unexpected juxtapositions.[24] Some of the book's odd juxtapositions have already been mentioned in this conclusion: the sartorial engineering of veils and beauty pageants; French, Chinese, and Japanese gardens; and Syrian migrants both in the IS utopian PSAs and in Ai Weiwei's tragic *Human Flows* film. Conceptually, the book looks to the "medium theory" of dynamic dyads—visibility/visuality, ideology/affect, center/periphery, concealing/revealing, loosening/tightening, civility/martiality. This more artisanal mode of theorizing emerges from the practical conventions that guide, for example, the inside/outside framing of picture-taking and film-making (Chapter 4) and the center/periphery relation seen on the All-under-Heavens maps of the Chinese world order (Chapter 7). Rather than function according to the fixed binary distinctions characteristic of Enlightenment modernity, *Sensible Politics* has shown how such dynamic dyads are relational, contextual, contingent, and fluid; their productive tension generates important social-ordering and world-ordering performances. What is most interesting about these dyads is their general *lack* of stable canonical definition; there is no orthodoxy, and the dynamic dyads' contingent flexibility demands that we appreciate each event through continual interpretive practice and affective experience. Likewise, there is no recipe for building a Japanese or Chinese garden.

Hence, as I was learning new filmmaking techniques, I also had to unlearn some familiar analytic modes. While hermeneutics works to problematize conventions and criticize habitus in order to speak truth to power, filmmaking and garden-building actually work by recognizing and respecting aesthetic conventions and practical techniques, while playing with them to make something new and interesting. According to Paul Henley, there are "10 Commandments" for observational

---

[23] See, for example, Yan Xuetong, *Ancient Chinese Thought, Modern Chinese Power* (Princeton, NJ: Princeton University Press, 2011); Qin Yaqing, *A Relational Theory of World Politics* (Cambridge, UK: Cambridge University Press, 2018).

[24] Michael J. Shapiro, *Studies in Trans-Disciplinary Method: After the Aesthetic Turn* (New York: Routledge, 2013), p. 8, xv.

CONCLUSION

filmmaking, including "don't use a tripod" and "don't do formal interviews." The tenth commandment, however, is to ignore the first nine commandments when that's helpful, so long as you ignore them knowingly and in pursuit of making a better film.[25] Rather than emancipation from ideologies and resistance to conventions, here we play with conventions to create new infrastructures of feeling and affective communities of sense. Creative play here thus entails both ludic action and flexible plasticity.

But attention to the visuality strategy and affective-work is not sufficient, either. As each chapter shows, the book's purpose is not to switch from one approach to another—from visibility to visuality, from ideology to affect, from images to artifacts—but to appreciate how sensible politics can come alive in different ways through the productive tension of visibility/visuality, ideology/affect, and images/artifacts. The Visual International Politics class likewise works to combine the visibility strategy and the visuality strategy. Students learn "visual literacy" by cultivating a hermeneutics of suspicion toward images that are produced by state and corporate power. While filmmaking involves the visual construction of the social, in class students use texts to "read" images in order to reveal the social construction of the visual. And this informs students' filmmaking practice; many student films address ideological issues of identity: what it means to be British Asian, how a woman can get elected to Parliament, what it's like to take the veil in London, whom Chinese new year represents, the purpose of International Women's Day, what a beard means for Muslims and non-Muslims, and so on.[26] These films are insightfully ideological in their search for meaning and are also affective in their attention to the visceral sensible politics of everyday experience.

While it is common to respond to the challenges of the "post-truth" era by deconstructing "fake news," the Visual International Politics class shows the value of political critique that creatively produces multisensory artifacts that can move and connect people to form new affective communities of sense, and perhaps different social and world orders. It's not enough to engage in resistance that speaks truth to power by fact-checking the lies (of Brexit, Trump, the Islamic State, and the Chinese Communist Party). Because such resistance is parasitic on the order that it critiques, it thus risks reproducing dominance. The point is not to simply resist domination, but to create a new way of living: "As the saying goes, 'What you resist persists.' Another world is possible, but we can't achieve it through resistance alone."[27] Critique in these student films playfully and creatively engages with finding

[25] See Andy Lawrence, *Filmmaking for Fieldwork: An Ethnographer's Handbook* (Manchester, UK: Manchester University Press, forthcoming).

[26] See "IR318: Visual International Politics," https://vimeo.com/channels/ir318 (accessed January 20, 2019).

[27] Michelle Alexander, "We Are Not the Resistance," *New York Times* (September 21, 2018) https://www.nytimes.com/2018/09/21/opinion/sunday/resistance-kavanaugh-trump-protest.html (accessed January 8, 2019).

a way to wear a veil, run an election campaign, and wear a beard, but in a way that is different from (but not the opposite of) what is expected by those who police the hegemonic distribution of the sensible.

Such student films also show how we need to expand from the focus on the visual to appreciate multisensory IR and verbal/sensory international politics. In the past few years, numerous critical studies have problematized the visual turn in IR in order to highlight the work of other senses. Franck Billé, for example, looks to the haptic politics of the skin to draw attention to the multilayered complexity of both territorial borders and conceptual distinctions.[28] Walker listens to musical harmony to appreciate IR in terms of the scalar politics of verticality.[29] Michelle Weitzel explores the politics of how non-musical sound is used as a weapon by the state, and also as a means of challenging such domination.[30]

The lesson I learn from these interventions is not that we need to fight the new hegemony of visual IR (which many argue), but that it's necessary to appreciate theory and politics as multisensory experiences. To put this another way, the focus on the visual is only a problem (i.e., ocular-centrism) if it marginalizes other ways of feeling; for example, if it silences other voices. The analytical framework developed in *Sensible Politics*—the visibility strategy's analysis of the social construction of the visible and the visuality strategy's appreciation of the visual performance of the international—can also be employed to understand and appreciate the international politics of other senses, for example, the social construction of the audible and the sonic construction of the international. The purpose of visual IR, therefore, is not to create a new hegemonic approach, but as we saw in the book's consideration of walls and gardens (Chapters 9 and 10), to appreciate politics in terms of a complex multisensory ecology.

The focus on visual politics is also heuristic. As we have seen, making "silent films" allows students to escape from the prison-house of language to see other ways of making meaning and value. This attention to how images can create affective atmospheres in a different register, however, does not entail discarding words altogether; films, remember, usually include verbal sounds. Rather, the point is to dethrone language from its hegemonic position in critique and thus enable filmmakers to use words as one of many instruments in the orchestra of multisensory political critique and social-ordering. In this way, the verbal is critically decentered and revalued in order to, once again, probe "the relationship between the visible, the sayable, and the thinkable."[31] Even so, you can still turn anything into a text, a narrative,

---

[28] Franck Billé, "Skinworlds: Borders, Haptics, Topologies," *Environment and Planning D: Society and Space* 36:1 (2018):60–77

[29] Walker, *Out of Line*, 27–30.

[30] Michelle Weitzel, "Audializing Migrant Bodies: Sound and Security at the Border," *Security Dialogue* 49:6 (2018):421–437.

[31] Rancière, *The Politics of Aesthetics*, 63.

and understand most IR issues in terms of securitization. But *Sensible Politics* shows how resisting this urge, to focus on critique as the creative multisensory process of making social orders and world orders as affective communities of sense, can be both interesting and productive.

The institutional challenge for sensory politics is like that for critical IR in general: to gain legitimacy in the academy and in policymaking debates. As disciplines, political science and IR increasingly welcome analysis of visual images and artifacts. The real challenge is to make the multisensory media of films, photo-essays, sound-scapes, and other nonverbal materials count as legitimate academic activities for recruitment, tenure, and promotion. While critical IR has a hard time gaining traction with mainstream audiences and policymakers, award-winning films by IR scholars show that the general public has an easier time engaging with complex issues through a well-crafted research film.[32]

Sensible Politics thus makes important contributions to the new sub-field of visual IR. Many visual IR articles and books conclude by noting what the visual can add to our understanding of international politics, giving us, for example, a better way of understanding security, violence, and peace. *Sensible Politics* does this by highlighting how visual images and multisensory artifacts open up new sites for our appreciation of IR, for example, gardens as sites of diplomacy, war, and peace. Ultimately, however, it is a mistake to see visual IR as a subdiscipline that adds something to already-existing IR debates on war, terrorism, and diplomacy. Rather than "add visuals and stir," the point of *Sensible Politics* is to provide an oblique entry into social theory and international studies that takes advantage of the fascinating work being done in the broader human sciences, as well as in the professional practices of filmmaking and landscape architecture. In addition to offering new sites of IR, the book has explored a range of visceral sensibilities for a nuanced appreciation of multisensory politics that works to understand and feel theory and politics in different registers. As noted in the introduction, the objective of *Sensible Politics* isn't just to convince people cognitively, but also to move and connect us affectively. In other words, its goal is to make us not only think visually, but also feel visually—and creatively act visually for a multisensory appreciation of politics.

---

[32] See, for example, Roy Germano, dir., *The Other Side of Immigration* (RG Films, 2010); Sophie Harman and Leanne Welham, *Pili* (Kuonekana Films Ltd., 2017).

SELECTED BIBLIOGRAPHY

Abu-Aasad, Hany, dir. *Omar* (ZBROS, 2013).

Abu-Lughod, Lila. *Do Muslim Women Need Saving?* (Cambridge, MA: Harvard University Press, 2013).

Agnew, John. *Geopolitics: Re-visioning World Politics*, 2nd ed. (New York: Routledge, 2003).

Ahmed, Sarah. *The Cultural Politics of Emotion* (Edinburgh: Edinburgh University Press, 2004).

Ai Qing. "The Gardener's Dream." In *Ai Qing: Shi Xuan/Selected Poems*, edited by Eugene Chen Eoyang, 208–210 (Beijing: Foreign Languages Press, 1982).

Ai Weiwei. *Ai Weiwei's Blog: Writings, Interview, and Digital Rants, 2006–2009*, edited and translated by Lee Ambrozy (Cambridge, MA: MIT Press, 2011).

Ai Weiwei. *Niuyue 1983–1993/New York 1983–1993* (Berlin: DISTANZ Verlag, 2011).

Ali, Ayaan Hirsi. *The Caged Virgin: An Emancipation Proclamation for Women and Islam* (New York: Free Press, 2006).

Alibhai-Brown, Yasmin. *Refusing the Veil* (London: Biteback Publishing, 2014).

Alloula, Malek. *The Colonial Harem* (Minneapolis: University of Minnesota Press, 1986).

Al-Tamimi, Aymenn Jawad. "The Archivist: Critical Analysis of the Islamic State's Health Department" (August 27, 2015) https://jihadology.net/2015/08/27/the-archivist-critical-analysis-of-the-islamic-states-health-department/.

Amer, Amena. "A White British Muslim" (London: LSE Research Festival Exhibition, 2015) http://eprints.lse.ac.uk/63004/.

Amoore, Louise. "Vigilant Visualities: The Watchful Politics of the War on Terror." *Security Dialogue* 38:2 (2007):215–232.

Amoore, Louise, and Alexandra Hall. "Border Theatre: On the Arts of Security and Resistance." *Cultural Geographies* 17:3 (2010):299–319.

Andersen, Rune S., Juha A. Vuori, and Can E. Mutlu. "Visuality." In *Critical Security Methods: New Frameworks for Analysis*, edited by Claudia Aradau, Jef Huysmans, Andrew Neal, and Nadine Voelkner, 85–117 (New York: Routledge, 2014).

Andersen, Rune Saugmann. "Videos." In *Making Things International 1: Circuits and Motion*, edited by Mark B. Salter, 255–264 (Minneapolis: University of Minnesota Press, 2015).

Anderson, Benedict. *Imagined Communities: Reflections on the Origin and Spread of Nationalism*, rev. ed. (New York: Verso, 2006).

Araki, Takehisa, dir., *Cai Guo-Qiang: Project to Add 10,000m to the Great Wall of China—Project for Extraterrestrials No. 10* (Cai Studio, 1993).

Areeya Chumsai. *Muat Pop* [Lt. Pop] (English title: *Boot Camp*) (Bangkok: Future Publishing, 1998).

Atwan, Abel Bari. *Islamic State: The Digital Caliphate* (London: Saqi Books, 2015).

Austin, J. L. *How to Do Things with Words* (Oxford: The Clarendon Press, 1962).

Azoulay, Ariella. *Civil Imagination: A Political Ontology of Photography*, translated by Louise Bethlehem (London: Verso, 2012).

Bachelard, Gaston. *The Poetics of Space* (Boston: Beacon Press, 1964).

Bai Meichu. *Zuixin Zhonghua minguo gaizao quantu* [The atlas of the Republic of China, with the latest corrections] (Beiping: Jianshe tushuguan, 1930).

Bal, Mieke. "The Politics of Citation." *Diacritics* 21:1 (1991):25–45.

Bandurski, David. "Lu Wei on the 'Dream of the Web.'" China Media Project (February 17, 2015) http://chinamediaproject.org/2015/02/17/lu-wei-on-the-dream-of-the-web/.

Bang Pa-In Palace (Bangkok: Royal Household Bureau, 2003).

Banks, Marcus. *Visual Methods in Social Research* (London: Sage, 2001).

Barabantseva, Elena. "Border People." *Journal of Narrative Politics* 4:2 (2018), https://jnp.journals.yorku.ca/index.php/default/article/view/87/88.

Barabantseva, Elena. *British Born Chinese* (Manchester, UK: AllRightsReversed, 2015).

Barabantseva, Elena. "In Pursuit of an Alternative Model? The Modernisation Trap in China's Official Development Discourse." *East Asia* 29 (2012):63–79.

Barabantseva, Elena, and Elizabeth Dauphinee. *"Border People*: Editor's Interview with Elena Barabantseva." *Journal of Narrative Politics* 4:2 (2018):58–64.

Barabantseva, Elena, and Andy Lawrence. "Encountering Vulnerabilities through 'Filmmaking for Fieldwork.'" *Millennium* 43:3 (2015):911–930.

Barlow, John Perry. "A Declaration of the Independence of Cyberspace" (February 8, 1996) https://www.eff.org/cyberspace-independence.

Barmé, Geremie R. "Beijing, a Garden of Violence." *Inter-Asia Cultural Studies* 9:4 (2008):612–639.

Barmé, Geremie R. "The Garden of Perfect Brightness: A Life in Ruins." *East Asian History* 11 (1996):111–158.

Barmé, Geremie R. "Prince Gong's Folly." In *The Great Wall of China*, edited by Claire Roberts and Geremie R. Barmé, 240–248 (Sydney: Powerhouse Publishing, 2006).

Barmé, Geremie R., and Sang Ye. "The Great Firewall of China." *Wired* (June 1, 1997). https://www.wired.com/1997/06/china-3/.

Barnard, George N. *Photographic Views of Sherman's Campaign* (1866).

Barthes, Roland. *Camera Lucida* (New York: Hill and Wang, 1981).

Barthes, Roland. *Empire of Signs* (New York: Hill and Wang, 1982).

Barthes, Roland. *Image/Music/Text* (New York: Hill and Wang, 1977).

Barthes, Roland. "Inaugural Lecture: College de France." In *A Barthes Reader*, edited by Susan Sontag, 457–478 (London: Vintage, 2000).

Barthes, Roland. *Mythologies* (New York: The Noonday Press, 1972).

Baudrillard, Jean. *Selected Writings*, edited by Mark Poster (Cambridge, UK: Polity, 1988).

Baum, Richard. *Burying Mao: Chinese Politics in the Age of Deng Xiaoping* (Princeton, NJ: Princeton University Press, 1994).

Bauman, Zygmunt. *Legislators and Interpreters: On Modernity, Post-modernity and Intellectuals* (Oxford: Oxford University Press, 1987).

Bauman, Zygmunt. *Modernity and the Holocaust* (Ithaca, NY: Cornell University Press, 1989).

Bauman, Zygmunt, Didier Bigo, Paulo Esteves, Elspeth Guild, Vivienne Jabri, David Lyon, and R. B. J. Walker. "After Snowden: Rethinking the Impact of Surveillance." *International Political Sociology* 8 (2014):121–144.

Baylis, John, Steve Smith, and Patricia Owens, eds. *The Globalization of World Politics: An Introduction to International Relations*, 5th ed. (Oxford: Oxford University Press, 2011).

Bellanova, Rocco. "Digital, Politics, and Algorithms: Governing Digital Data through the Lens of Data Protection." *European Journal of Social Theory* 20:3 (2017):329–347.

Benesch, Oleg. "National Consciousness and the Evolution of the Civil/Military Binary in East Asia." *Taiwan Journal of East Asian Studies* 8:1 (2011):133–137.

Benjamin, Walter. "The Work of Art in the Age of Mechanical Reproduction." In *Illuminations: Essays and Reflections*, edited by Hannah Arendt, 217–251 (New York: Schocken Books, 1968).

Bennett, Jane. *Vibrant Matter: A Political Ecology of Things* (Durham, NC: Duke University Press, 2010).

Bennett, Jill. *Empathic Vision: Affect, Trauma, and Contemporary Art* (Stanford, CA: Stanford University Press, 2005).

Berger, John. *Ways of Seeing* (London: Penguin Books, 1972).

Berry, Chris. "The Chinese Side of the Mountain." *Film Quarterly* 60:3 (2007):32–37.

Bigo, Didier. "Security, Surveillance, and Democracy." In *Routledge Handbook of Surveillance Studies*, edited by Kirstie Ball, Kevin D. Haggerty, and David Lyon, 277–284 (New York: Routledge, 2014).

Bilgin, Pinar, and L. H. M. Ling, eds. *Asia in International Relations: Unlearning Imperial Power Relations* (London: Routledge, 2017).

Billé, Franck. "On China's Cartographic Embrace: A View from Its Northern Rim." *Cross-Currents* no. 21 (2017):1–21.

Billé, Franck. "Skinworlds: Borders, Haptics, Topologies." *Environment and Planning D: Society and Space* 36:1 (2018):60–77.

Blais, Allison, and Lynn Rasic. *A Place of Remembrance, Updated Edition: Official Book of the National September 11 Memorial* (New York: National Geographic, 2015).

Blakely, Ruth. "Elite Interviews." In *Critical Approaches to Security: An Introduction to Theories and Methods*, edited by Laura J. Shepherd, 158–168 (London: Routledge, 2013).

Bleiker, Roland. "The Aesthetic Turn in International Political Theory." *Millennium: Journal of International Studies* 30 (2001):509–533.

Bleiker, Roland. *Aesthetics and World Politics* (London: Palgrave Macmillan, 2012).

Bleiker, Roland. "Visual Autoethnography and International Security: Insights from the Korean DMZ." *European Journal of International Security* (forthcoming 2019).

Bleiker, Roland. "Mapping Visual Global Politics." In *Visual Global Politics*, edited by Roland Bleiker, 1–29 (London: Routledge, 2018).

Bleiker, Roland. "Pluralist Methods for Visual Global Politics." *Millennium* 43:3 (2015):872–890.

Bleiker, Roland, ed. *Visual Global Politics* (New York: Routledge, 2018).

Bleiker, Roland, David Campbell, and Emma Hutchison. "Visual Cultures of Inhospitality." *Peace Review* 26:2 (2014):192–200.

Bleiker, Roland, David Campbell, Emma Hutchison, and Xzarina Nicholson. "The Visual Dehumanisation of Refugees." *Australian Journal of Political Science* 48:4 (2013):398–416.

Bleiker, Roland, and Emma Hutchison, eds. "Forum: Emotions and World Politics," special issue, *International Theory* 6:3 (2014):490–594.

Bleiker, Roland, and Amy Kay. "Representing HIV/AIDS in Africa: Pluralist Photography and Local Empowerment." *International Studies Quarterly* 51 (2007):139–163.

Bloom, Mia, and Chelsea Daymon. "Assessing the Future Threat: ISIS's Virtual Caliphate." *Orbis* (Summer 2018):372–388.

Bousquet, Antoine J. *The Eye of War: Military Perception from the Telescope to the Drone* (Minneapolis: University of Minnesota Press, 2018).

Branch, Jordan. *The Cartographic State: Maps, Territory, and the Origins of Sovereignty* (New York: Cambridge University Press, 2014).

Bray, Francesca. "American Modern: The Foundation of Western Civilization" (2000) http://www.anth.ucsb.edu/faculty/bray/toilet/index.html.

Brennan, Kathleen P. J. "Memelife." In *Making Things International 1: Circuits and Motion*, edited by Mark B. Salter, 243–254 (Minneapolis: University of Minnesota Press, 2015).

Brenner, David. *Rebel Politics: A Political Sociology of Armed Struggle in Myanmar's Borderlands* (Ithaca, NY: Cornell University Press, 2019).

Breslin, Shaun. "China and the Arab Awakening." *ISPI Analysis* 140 (2012):1–8.

Brigg, Morgan, and Roland Bleiker. "Autoethnographic International Relations: Exploring the Self as a Source of Knowledge." *Review of International Studies* 36:3 (2010): 779–798.

Brook, Timothy. *Mr. Selden's Map of China: The Spice Trade, a Lost Chart, and the South China Sea* (London: Profile Books, 2015).

Broudehoux, Anne-Marie. *The Making and Selling of Post-Mao Beijing* (New York: Routledge, 2004).

Brown, Wendy. *Walled States, Waning Sovereignty* (New York: Zone Books, 2014).

Bryman, Alan. *Social Research Methods* (Oxford: Oxford University Press, 2012).

Burrell, Gibson, and Karen Dale. "Utopiary: Utopias, Gardens and Organizations." *The Sociological Review* 50:1 (2002):106–127.

Bush, Laura. "The Weekly Address Delivered by the First Lady" (November 17, 2011) http://www.presidency.ucsb.edu/ws/?pid=24992.

Butler, Judith. *Frames of War: When Is Life Grievable?* (London: Verso, 2016).

Butler, Judith. *Gender Trouble: Feminism and the Subversion of Identity* (New York: Routledge, 2006).

Buzan, Barry, Ole Wæver, and Jaap de Wilde. *Security: A New Framework for Analysis* (Boulder, CO: Lynne Rienner, 1998).

Byler, Darren. "Ghost World." *Logic* no. 7 (2019) https://logicmag.io/07-ghost-world/.

Byler, Darren, and Timothy Grose. "China's Surveillance Laboratory." *Dissent* (October 31, 2018) https://www.dissentmagazine.org/online_articles/chinas-surveillance-laboratory.

Callahan, Bill, dir. *An American in Shanghai* (2016, 22 min.) https://www.thechinastory.org/2016/09/an-american-in-shanghai-then-and-now/.

Callahan, Bill. "Digging to China." https://vimeo.com/album/4040464.Callahan, Bill, dir. *Great Walls: Journeys from Ideology to Experience* (28 minutes). Screened at LSE Festival, London (March 2, 2019).

Callahan, Bill, dir. *toilet adventures* (August 25, 2015) https://www.thechinastory.org/2015/08/toilet-adventures-in-china-making-sense-of-transnational-encounters/.

Callahan, Bill, dir. *You Can See CHINA from Here.* (2018, 14:35 min.) https://vimeo.com/169046223.

Callahan, Bill, dir. *Great Walls: Journeys from Ideology to Experience.* (Wildwood Films, 2019) https://vimeo.com/billcallahan/great-walls.

Callahan, William A. *China: The Pessoptimist Nation* (Oxford: Oxford University Press, 2010).

Callahan, William A. *China Dreams: 20 Visions of the Future* (New York: Oxford University Press, 2013).

Callahan, William A. "China's 'Asia Dream': BRI and the New Regional Order." *Asian Journal of Comparative Politics* 1:3 (2016):226–243.

Callahan, William A. "Citizen Ai: Warrior, Jester, and Middleman." *Journal of Asian Studies* 73:04 (2014):899–920.

Callahan, William A. *Contingent States: Greater China and Transnational Relations* (Minneapolis: University of Minnesota Press, 2004).

Callahan, William A. *Cultural Governance in Pacific Asia* (New York: Routledge, 2006).

Callahan, William A. "Identity and Security in China: The Negative Soft Power of the China Dream." *Politics* 35:3–4 (2015):216–229.

Campbell, David. "Cultural Governance and Pictorial Resistance: Reflections on the Imaging of War." *Review of International Studies* 29 (2003):57–73.

Campbell, David. "Geopolitics and Visuality: Sighting the Darfur Conflict." *Political Geography* 26 (2007):357–382.

Campbell, David. *Writing Security: United States Foreign Policy and the Politics of Identity*, rev. ed. (Minneapolis: University of Minnesota Press, 1998).

Campbell, David, and Michael J. Shapiro. "Guest Editor's Introduction: Securitization, Militarization and Visual Culture in the Worlds of Post-9/11." *Security Dialogue* 38:2 (2007):131–137.

Carrico, Kevin. *The Great Han: Race, Nationalism and Tradition in China Today* (Berkeley: University of California Press, 2017).

Chaichian, Mohammad A. *Empires and Walls: Globalization, Migration, and Colonial Domination* (Leiden: Brill, 2014).

Chang, Amy. *Warring State: China's Cybersecurity Strategy* (Washington, DC: Center for a New American Security, December 14, 2014).

Chen, Kuan-Hsing. *Asia as Method: Toward Deimperialization* (Durham, NC: Duke University Press, 2010).

Cheng Dalin. "The Great Tourist Icon." In *The Great Wall of China*, edited by Claire Roberts and Geremie R. Barmé, 26–32 (Sydney: Powerhouse Publishing, 2006).

Ch'eonhado [All-under-the-Heavens Map] (ca. 1800). (Washington, DC: Library of Congress) https://lccn.loc.gov/93684246.

Choi, Jung-Bong. "Mapping Japanese Imperialism onto Postcolonial Criticism." *Social Identities* 9:3 (2003):325–339.

Chong, Gladys Pak Lei. "Cashless China: Securitization of Everyday Life through Alipay's Social Credit System—Sesame Credit." *Chinese Journal of Communication* (March 12, 2019):1–18, https://doi.org/10.1080/17544750.2019.1583261.

Ch'onhado [All-under-the-Heavens Map] (ca. 19th century). (London: British Library, Maps.33.c.13).

Chouliaraki, Lilie. "The Humanity of War: Iconic Photojournalism of the Battlefield, 1914–2012." In *Visual Security Studies: Sights and Spectacles of Insecurity and War*, edited by Juha A. Vuori and Rune Saugmann Andersen, 71–90 (New York: Routledge, 2018).

Chouliaraki, Lilie. *The Ironic Spectator: Solidarity in the Age of Post-humanitarianism* (Oxford: Polity Press, 2013).

Chouliaraki, Lilie, and Myria Georgiou. "Hospitability: The Communicative Architecture of Humanitarian Securitization at Europe's Borders." *Journal of Communication* 67:2 (2017):159–180.

Chow, Rey. *Entanglements, or Transmedial Thinking about Capture* (Durham, NC: Duke University Press, 2012).

Chun, Allen. *Forget Chineseness: On the Geopolitics of Cultural Identification* (Albany: State University of New York Press, 2017).

Chun, Wendy Hui Kyong. *Control and Freedom: Power and Paranoia in the Age of Fiber Optics* (Cambridge, MA: MIT Press, 2006).

Chung, Chris P. C. "Drawing the U-Shaped Line: China's Claim in the South China Sea, 1946–1974." *Modern China* 42:1 (2016):38–72.

"City of Urumqi Prohibition on Wearing Items That Mask the Face or Robe the Body." Translated by Timothy Grose and James Leibold (February 4, 2015) http://www.chinafile.com/reporting-opinion/features/city-urumqi-prohibition-wearing-items-mask-face-or-robe-body.

Clark, Emma. *Underneath Which Rivers Flow: The Symbolism of the Islamic Garden* (London: Prince of Wale's Institute of Architecture, 1996).

Clunas, Craig. *Fruitful Sites: Garden Culture in Ming Dynasty China* (Durham, NC: Duke University Press, 1996).

Clunas, Craig. *Pictures and Visuality in Early Modern China* (London: Reaktion Books, 1997).

Clunas, Craig. "Reading Wen Zhengming: Metaphor and Chinese Painting." *Word & Image* 25:1 (2009):96–102.

Connolly, William E. *Identity\Difference: Democratic Negotiations of Political Paradox*, expanded ed. (Ithaca, NY: Cornell University Press, 2002).

Coronado, Irasema. "Towards the Wall between Nogales, Arizona and Nogales, Sonora." In *Borders, Fences and Walls: State of Insecurity?*, edited by Elisabeth Vallet, 247–266 (Burlington, VT: Ashgate, 2014).

Craig, Maxine Leeds. *Ain't I a Beauty Queen? Black Women, Beauty and the Politics of Race* (Oxford: Oxford University Press, 2002).

Creemers, Rogier. "China's Social Credit System: An Evolving Practice of Control." SSRN (May 9, 2018) https://papers.ssrn.com/sol3/papers.cfm?abstract_id=3175792.

Creemers, Rogier. "Cyber China: Upgrading Propaganda, Public Opinion Work and Social Management for the Twenty-First Century." *Journal of Contemporary China* 26:103 (2017):85–100.

Croft, Stuart. *Securitizing Islam: Identity and the Search for Security* (Cambridge, UK: Cambridge University Press, 2012).

Curtis, Adam, dir. *Bitter Lake* (London: BBC, 2015).

Curtis, Adam, dir. *The Power of Nightmares* (London: BBC, 2004).

Dali kaizhan aiguo weisheng yundong [To fully carry out a patriotic public health movement] (1963). Chinese Public Health Posters exhibit (National Institutes of Health, 2006) https://www. nlm.nih.gov/hmd/chineseposters/images/1200/DSC_4052.jpg.

Dallmyr, Fred, and Zhao Tingyang, eds. *Contemporary Chinese Political Thought: Debates and Perspectives* (Lexington: University Press of Kentucky, 2012).

Danchev, Alex. *On Art and War and Terror* (Edinburgh: University of Edinburgh Press, 2011).

Danchev, Alex. *On Good and Evil and the Grey Zone* (Edinburgh: Edinburgh University Press, 2016).

Danchev, Alex. "Witnessing." In *Visual Global Politics*, edited by Roland Bleiker, 332–338 (London: Routledge, 2018).

Danchev, Alex, and Debbie Lisle. "Introduction: Art, Politics, Purpose." *Review of International Studies* 35:4 (2009):775–779.

Danchev, Alex, and R. B. J. Walker, eds. "Art and Politics," special issue, *Alternatives: Global, Local, Political* 31:1 (2006):1–104.

DaQing wannian yitong tianxia quantu [Perpetual All-under-the-Heavens map of the Unified Great Qing Empire] (1811). (Washington, DC: Library of Congress) https://lccn.loc.gov/ gm71005018.

Davies, Gloria. *Worrying about China: The Language of Chinese Critical Inquiry* (Cambridge, MA: Harvard University Press, 2007).

de Bromhead, Toni. *Looking Two Ways: Documentary's Relationship with Cinema and Reality* (Aarhus, Denmark: Intervention Press, 1996).

de Certeau, Michel. *The Practice of Everyday Life* (Berkeley: University of California Press, 1984).

de Lauretis, Teresa. *Alice Doesn't: Feminism, Semiotics and Cinema* (Bloomington: Indiana University Press, 1984).

de Weerdt, Hilde. "Maps and Memory: Readings of Cartography in Twelfth- and Thirteen-Century Song China." *Imago Mundi* 61:2 (2009):145–167.

Debord, Guy. *The Society of the Spectacle* (Cambridge, MA: MIT Press, 1995).

Delemarre, Jeu. "*Dabiq*: Framing the Islamic State." MA thesis, Radboud University Nijmegen, 2017.

Deleuze, Gilles. *Cinema I: The Movement-Image*, translated by Hugh Tomlinson and Barbara Habberjam (London: Bloomsbury, 1986).

Deleuze, Gilles. *Foucault*, translated by Sean Hand (Minneapolis: University of Minnesota Press, 1988).

Deleuze, Gilles. "Postscript on the Societies of Control." *October* 59 (1992):3–7.

Deleuze, Gilles, and Felix Guattari. *A Thousand Plateaus: Capitalism and Schizophrenia* (London: Athlone Press, 1996).

Delisle, Guy. *Pyongyang: A Journey in North Korea* (New York: Jonathan Cape, 2006).

deLisle, Jacques, Avery Goldstein, and Guobin Yang, eds. *The Internet, Social Media, and a Changing China* (Philadelphia: University of Pennsylvania Press, 2016).

Denton, Kirk. *Exhibiting the Past: Historical Memory and the Politics of Museums in Postsocialist China* (Honolulu: University of Hawaii Press, 2014).

Der Derian, James. "After-image." In *Documenting World Politics: A Critical Companion to IR and Non-Fiction Film*, edited by Rens van Munster and Casper Sylvest, 223–231 (London: Routledge, 2015).

Der Derian, James. "Now We Are All Avatars." *Millennium* 39:1 (2010):181–186.

Der Derian, James. *On Diplomacy: A Genealogy of Western Estrangement* (Oxford: Blackwell, 1987).

Der Derian, James. *Virtuous War: Mapping the Military-Industrial-Media-Entertainment Network* (New York: Routledge, 2009).

Der Derian, James. "War Becomes Academic: Human Terrain, Virtuous War and Contemporary Militarism." In *Militarism and International Relations: Political Economy, Security, Theory*, edited by Anna Stavrianakis and Jan Selby, 59–73 (London: Routledge, 2013).

Der Derian, James, and Phillip Gara. *Project Z: The Final Global Event* (Bullfrog Films, 2015).

Der Derian, James, David Udris, and Michael Udris. *Human Terrain: War Becomes Academic* (Bullfrog Films, 2011).

Derrida, Jacques, and Anne Dufourmantelle. *Of Hospitality*, translated by Rachel Bowlby (Stanford, CA: Stanford University Press, 2000).

Di Cintio, Marcello. *Walls: Travels along the Barricades* (London: Union Books, 2013).

Dirlik, Arif. *The Postcolonial Aura: Third World Criticism in the Age of Global Capitalism* (Boulder, CO: Westview Press, 1998).

Doar, Bruce Gordon. "Delimited Boundaries and Great Wall Studies." In *The Great Wall of China*, edited by Claire Roberts and Geremie R. Barmé, 119–127 (Sydney: Powerhouse Publishing, 2006).

Dodds, Klaus. "Steve Bell's Eye: Cartoons, Geopolitics and the Visualization of the 'War on Terror.'" *Security Dialogue* 38:2 (2007):157–177.

Du Bois, W. E. B. *The Souls of Black Folk* (New York: New American Library, 1903).

Duara, Prasenjit. *The Crisis of Global Modernity: Asian Traditions and a Sustainable Future* (Cambridge, UK: Cambridge University Press, 2015).

Dugin, Alexander. *Eurasian Mission: An Introduction to Neo-Eurasianism* (London: Arktos Media, 2014).

Dunlap, Charles J., Jr. "Lawfare 101: A Primer." *Military Review* 97 (2017):8–17.

Dutton, Michael R. *Policing and Punishment in China: From Patriarchy to "the People"* (New York: Cambridge University Press, 1992).

Eco, Umberto. *A Theory of Semiotics* (Bloomington: Indiana University Press, 1976).

Economy, Elizabeth C. *The Third Revolution: Xi Jinping and the New Chinese State* (New York: Oxford University Press, 2018).

Edkins, Jenny. *Trauma and the Memory of Politics* (Cambridge, UK: Cambridge University Press, 2003).

Egawauemon. *Walking in Tokyo, Yasukuni Shrine*. YouTube (August 18, 2008) http://www.youtube.com/watch?v=Ew9AllEWehM.

Eggers, Dave. *The Circle* (New York: Penguin, 2014).

Eghigian, Greg. "Homo Munitus: The East Germans Observed." In *Socialist Modern: East German Everyday Culture and Politics*, edited by Katherine Pence and Paul Betts, 37–70 (Ann Arbor: University of Michigan Press, 2007).

Elmer, Greg. "Panopticon—Discipline—Control." In *Routledge Handbook of Surveillance Studies*, edited by Kirstie Ball, Kevin D. Haggerty, and David Lyon, 21–29 (New York: Routledge, 2014).

Eltahawy, Mona. *Headscarves and Hymens: Why the Middle East Needs a Sexual Revolution* (London: Weidenfeld & Nicolson, 2015).

Enloe, Cynthia. *Bananas, Beaches and Bases: Making Feminist Sense of International Politics*, 2nd ed. (Berkeley: University of California Press, 2014).

Enloe, Cynthia. "The Mundane Matters." *International Political Sociology* 4:5 (2011):446–462.

Erickson, Steve. "Voyeurs in the Hermit Kingdom: The Interview and Other Films on North Korea." *Cineaste* 40:2 (2015):37–41.

Euben, Roxanne L. *Enemy in the Mirror: Islamic Fundamentalism and the Limits of Modern Rationalism; A Work of Comparative Political Theory* (Princeton, NJ: Princeton University Press, 1999).

Euben, Roxanne L. "Spectacles of Sovereignty in Digital Time: ISIS Executions, Visual Rhetoric and Sovereign Power." *Perspectives on Politics* 15:4 (2017):1007–1033.

Evans, Jessica, and Stuart Hall, eds. *Visual Culture: The Reader* (London: Sage, 1999).

Fanon, Frantz. *Black Skin, White Masks* (New York: Grove Press, 2008).

Fanon, Frantz. *A Dying Colonialism* (New York: Grove Press, 1965).

Farrell, Henry. "The Woodgrain of the Chessboard: A Response to Roy Germano." *Perspectives on Politics* 12:3 (2014):686–687.

Farwell, James P. "Jihadi Video in the 'War of Ideas.'" *Survival* 52:6 (2010):127–150.

Farwell, James P. "The Media Strategy of ISIS." *Survival* 56:6 (2014):49–55.

Feaver, Peter D. "The Right to Be Right: Civil-Military Relations and the Iraq Surge Decision." *International Security* 35:4 (2011):87–125.

Feng Xiaogang. "Queshao ni, Niuyue biande pingyong" [Without you, New York is mediocre], *Xingfu* no. 8 (2015):3–5.

Feng Yitong. "Bu qude huhao, chonggao de shixin" [Unyielding call, noble poetic heart], *Nanjing shifan zhuankexiao xuebao* 16:1 (2000):1–4.

Fernández, Ana Teresa. "Borrando La Frontera–Erasing the Border" (2010) http://anateresafernandez.com/borrando-la-barda-tijuana-mexico/.

Finn, Jonathan. "Seeing Surveillantly: Surveillance as Social Practice." In *Eyes Everywhere: The Global Growth of Camera Surveillance*, edited by Aaron Doyle, Randy Lippert, and David Lyon, 67–80 (London: Routledge, 2012).

Fiskesjö, Magnus. "The Legacy of the Chinese Empires: Beyond 'the West and the Rest.'" *Education About Asia* 22:1 (2017):6–10.

Fiskesjö, Magnus. "On the 'Raw' and the 'Cooked' Barbarians of Imperial China." *Inner Asia* 1:2 (1999):139–168.

Floridi, Luciano, ed. *The Onlife Manifesto: Being Human in a Hyperconnected Era* (New York: Springer, 2015).

Food Security: Aspects from the Work of the Agriculture Administration in the Province—Wilāyat Ḥalab (November 10, 2015) https://jihadology.net/2015/11/10/new-video-message-from-the-islamic-state-food-security-aspects-from-the-work-of-the-agriculture-administration-in-the-province-wilayat-ḥalab/.

Foster, Hal, ed. *Vision and Visuality* (Seattle: Bay Press, 1988).

Foucault, Michel. "Afterword: The Subject and Power." In *Michel Foucault: Beyond Structuralism and Hermeneutics,* edited by Hubert L. Dreyfus and Paul Rabinow (New York: The Harvester Press, 1982).

Foucault, Michel. *Discipline and Punish: Birth of the Prison*, translated by Alan Sheridan (New York: Pantheon, 1977).

Foucault, Michel. "Governmentality." In *The Foucault Effect: Studies in Governmentality*, edited by Graham Burchell, Colin Gordon, and Peter Miller, 87–104 (London: Harvester Wheatsheaf, 1991).

Foucault, Michel. *History of Sexuality*. Vol. 1, *An Introduction*, translated by R. Hurley (New York: Pantheon, 1978).

Foucault, Michel. "Nietzsche, Genealogy and History." In *The Foucault Reader*, edited by Paul Rabinow, 76–100 (New York: Pantheon, 1984).

Foucault, Michel. "Of Other Spaces." *Diacritics* 16:1 (1986):22–27.

Foucault, Michel. *The Order of Things* (New York: Pantheon, 1970).

Foucault, Michel. *Security, Territory, Population: Lectures at the College de France, 1977–1978* (London: Palgrave Macmillan, 2007).

Foucault, Michel. *"Society Must Be Defended": Lectures at the Collège De France, 1975–6*, translated by David Macey, edited by Mauro Bertani and Alssandro Fontana (New York: Picador, 2003).

Foucault, Michel. *This Is Not a Pipe* (Berkeley: University of California Press, 1982).

Fravel, M. Taylor. *Strong Borders, Secure Nation: Cooperation and Conflict in China's Territorial Disputes* (Princeton, NJ: Princeton University Press, 2008).

French, Howard W. *Everything Under the Heavens: How the Past Helps Shape China's Push for Global Power* (New York: Alfred A. Knopf, 2017).

Friis, Simone Molin. "'Behead, Burn, Crucify, Crush': Theorizing Islamic State's Public Displays of Violence." *European Journal of International Relations* 24:2 (2018):243–267.

Friis, Simone Molin. "'Beyond Anything We Have Ever Seen': Beheading Videos and the Visibility of Violence in the War against ISIS." *International Affairs* 91:4 (2015):725–746.

Frøystad, Kathinka. "Failing the Third Toilet Test: Reflections on fieldwork, Gender and Indian Loos." *Ethnography* (October 15, 2018):1–19, https://doi.org/10.1177/1466138118804262.

Galloway, Alexander. *Protocol: How Control Exists after Decentralization* (Cambridge, MA: MIT Press, 2006).

Gao Zhiguo, and Bing Bing Jia. "The Nine-Dash Line in the South China Sea: History, Status, and Implications." *The American Journal of International Law* 107:1 (2013):98–124.

Ge Zhaoguang. *Lishi Zhongguo de nei yu wai: Youguan "Zhongguo" yu "zhoubian" gainian de zai chengqing* [Inside and outside in historical China: Re-clarifying the concepts of "Middle Kingdom" and "periphery"] (Hong Kong: Chinese University Press, 2017).

Gerges, Fawaz A. *ISIS: A History* (Princeton, NJ: Princeton University Press, 2016).

Germano, Roy. "Analytic Filmmaking: A New Approach to Research and Publication in the Social Sciences." *Perspectives on Politics* 12:3 (2014):663–676.

Germano, Roy. "Analytic Filmmaking: A Response to Critics." *Perspectives on Politics* 12:3 (2014):691–694.

Germano, Roy, dir. *The Other Side of Immigration* (RG Films, 2010).

"GFW de lishi he weilai" [The history and future of the GFW]. Zhongguo jiwenwang (May 15, 2013) https://www.bannedbook.org/bnews/fanqiang/20130515/129086.html.

Gilley, Bruce. "The Case for Colonialism." *Third World Quarterly* (September 8, 2017):1–17.

Gilligan, Carol. *In a Different Voice: Psychological Theory and Women's Development* (Cambridge, MA: Harvard University Press, 1982).

Gliddens, Sarah. *Rolling Blackouts: Dispatches from Turkey, Syria, and Iraq* (New York: Drawn & Quarterly, 2016).

Gökariksel, Banu, and Anna Secor. "Between Fashion and Testtür: Marketing and Consuming Women's Islamic Dress." *Journal of Middle East Women's Studies* 6:3 (2010):118–148.

Gökariksel, Banu, and Anna Secor. "The Veil, Desire, and the Gaze: Turning the Inside Out." *Signs* 40:1 (2014):178–200.

Gong, Gerritt. *The Standard of "Civilization" in International Society* (Oxford: Oxford University Press, 1984).

Gould, Jeffrey L. "Analytic Filmmaking as Social Scientific Research: A Response to Roy Germano." *Perspectives on Politics* 12:3 (2014):684–685.

Grierson, John. "The Documentary Producer." *Cinema Quarterly* 2 (1933):7–9.

Griffiths, James. *The Great Firewall of China: How to Build and Control an Alternative Version of the Internet* (London: Zed, 2019).

Grovogui, Siba N'Zatioula. *Sovereigns, Quasi Sovereigns, and Africans* (Minneapolis: University of Minnesota Press, 1996).

Guillaume, Xavier, Rune S. Andersen, and Juha A. Vuori. "Paint It Black: Colours and the Social Meaning of the Battlefield." *European Journal of International Relations* 22:1 (2015):49–71.

Gullberg, Johanna. "The Republic of Difference: Feminism and Anti-racism in the Parisian Banlieues." PhD dissertation, Stockholm University, 2016.

Habermas, Jürgen. *Time of Transitions,* translated and edited by Max Pensky (Cambridge, UK: Polity Press, 2006).

Haggerty Kevin D., and Richard V. Ericson. "The Surveillant Assemblage." *British Journal of Sociology* 51:4 (2000):605–622.

Hall, David L., and Roger T. Ames. *Anticipating the Han: Thinking Through the Narratives of Chinese and Western Culture* (Albany: State University of New York Press, 1995).

Hall, David L., and Roger T. Ames. "The Cosmological Setting of Chinese Gardens." *Studies in the History of Gardens and Designed Landscapes* 18:3 (1998):175–186.

Hall, David L., and Roger T. Ames. *Thinking Through Confucius* (Albany: State University of New York Press, 1987).

Hall, Stuart, ed. *Representations: Cultural Representations and Signifying Practices* (London: Sage, 1997).

Hamilton, Bruce Taylor. *Human Nature: The Japanese Garden of Portland, Oregon* (Portland: Japanese Garden Society of Oregon, 1996).

Hamilton, Caitlin. "The Everyday Artefacts of World Politics: Why Graphic Novels, Textiles and Internet Memes Matter in World Politics." PhD dissertation, University of New South Wales, 2016.

Hansen, Lene. "How Images Make World Politics: International Icons and the Case of Abu Ghraib." *Review of International Studies* 41:2 (2015):263–288.

Hansen, Lene. "Reading Comics for the Field of International Relations: Theory, Method and the Bosnian War." *European Journal of International Relations* 23:3 (2016):581–608.

Hansen, Lene. "Theorizing the Image for Security Studies: Visual Securitization and the Muhammad Cartoon Crisis." *European Journal of International Relations* 17:1 (2011):51–74.

Hariman, Robert, and John Louis Lucaites. *No Caption Needed: Iconic Photographs, Public Culture, and Liberal Democracy* (Chicago: University of Chicago Press, 2011).

Hariman, Robert, and John Louis Lucaites. *The Public Image: Photography and Civic Spectatorship* (Chicago: University of Chicago Press, 2016).

Harley, J. B. "Deconstructing the Map." *Cartographica* 26 (1989):1–20.

Harman, Sophie. "Film as Research Method in African Politics and International Relations: Reading and Writing HIV/AIDS in Tanzania." *African Affairs* 115:461 (2016):733–750.

Harman, Sophie. "Making the Invisible Visible in International Relations: Film, Co-Produced Research and Transnational Feminism." *European Journal of International Relations* (2017):1–23.

Harman, Sophie, and Leanne Welham. *Pili* (Kuonekana Films Ltd., 2017).

Havel, Vaclav. *Living in Truth* (New York: Faber & Faber, 1987).

Hayton, Bill. "The Modern Origins of China's South China Sea Claims: Maps, Misunderstanding and the Making of China's Maritime Geobody." *Modern China* 45:2 (2019):127–170.

Hayton, Bill. *The South China Sea: The Struggle for Power in Asia* (New Haven, CT: Yale University Press, 2014).

Hazell, Robert, Ben Worthy, and Mark Glover. *The Impact of the Freedom of Information Act on Central Government in the UK: Does FOI Work?* (New York: Palgrave Macmillan, 2010).

Health Services in the Islamic State—Wilāyat al-Raqqah (April 24, 2015) https://jihadology.net/?s=health+service.

Heath, Jennifer, ed. *The Veil: Women Writers on Its History, Lore, and Politics* (Berkeley: University of California Press, 2008).

Heck, Axel. "Images, Visions and Narrative Identity Formation of ISIS." *Global Discourse* 7:2/3 (2017):244–259.

Heck, Axel. "The Struggle for Legitimacy of the Islamic State—Facts, Myths, and Narratives." In *Political Storytelling: From Fact to Fiction*, edited by Frank Gadinger, 81–88 (Duisburg: Käte Hamburger Kolleg/Centre for Global Cooperation Research, 2016).

Heck, Axel, and Gabi Schlag. "Securitizing Images: The Female Body and the War in Afghanistan." *European Journal of International Relations* 19:4 (2012):891–913.

Hegghammer, Thomas, ed. *Jihadi Culture: The Art and Social Practices of Militant Islamists* (New York: Cambridge University Press, 2017).

Hegghammer, Thomas. "Non-military Practices in Jihadi Groups." In *Jihadi Culture: The Art and Social Practices of Militant Islamists*, edited by Thomas Hegghammer, 171–201 (New York: Cambridge University Press, 2017).

Heidegger, Martin. *The Question Concerning Technology, and Other Essays* (London: Garland Publishing, 1997).

Heimer, Maria, and Stig Thogerson. *Doing Fieldwork in China* (Copenhagen: NIAS Press, 2006).

Henderson, Ron. *The Gardens of Suzhou* (Philadelphia: University of Pennsylvania Press, 2013).

Henley, Paul. "Are You Happy? Interviews, 'Conversations', and 'Talking Heads' as Means of Gathering Oral Testimony in Ethnographic Documentary." In *Film und Interview. Volkskundliche und ethnologische Ansatze zu Methodik un Analyse*, edited by Joachim Wossidlo and Ulrich Roters, 51–67 (Berlin: Waxmann Verlag, 2003).

Henley, Paul. "On Narratives in Ethnographic Film." In *Reflecting Visual Ethnography: Using the Camera in Anthropological Research*, edited by Metje Postma and Peter Ian Crawford, 376–401 (Hoejbjerg: Intervention Press 2006).

Herman, Edward S., and Noam Chomsky. *Manufacturing Consent: The Political Economy of the Mass Media* (New York: Pantheon Books, 1988).

Hevia, James. *Cherishing Men from Afar: Qing Guest Ritual and the Macartney Embassy of 1793* (Durham, NC: Duke University Press, 1994).

Hoffman, Samantha. *Social Credit: Technology-enhanced Authoritarian Control with Global Consequences*, Australian Strategic Policy Institute, Report No. 6/2018 (June 2018).

Hopkins, Nick, and Ronni Michelle Greenwood. "Hijab, Visibility and the Performance of Identity." *European Journal of Social Psychology* 43 (2013):438–447.

Hostetler, Laura. *Qing Colonial Enterprise: Ethnography and Cartography in Early Modern China* (Chicago: University of Chicago Press, 2001).

Houellebecq, Michel. *Submission* (London: William Heinemann, 2015).

Hsiao, Anne Hsiu-An. "China and the South China Sea 'Lawfare.'" *Issues & Studies* 52:2 (2016):1–42.

Hua Tianxue, Ai Weiwei, and Feng Boyi, eds. *Bu hezuo fangshi-Fuck Off* [An uncooperative approach-Fuck Off] (Shanghai: Eastlink Gallery, 2000).

Huang Hua. "Renovating the Great Wall." *China Today* 43:8 (August 1994):12–13.

Huayi tu (1136) [Map of Civilization and barbarism (1136)] (Washington DC: Library of Congress) https://lccn.loc.gov/2002626771.

Hughes, Christopher R. "Militarism and the China Model: The Case of National Defense Education." *Journal of Contemporary China* 26:103 (2017):54–67.

Huntington, Samuel P. *The Clash of Civilizations and the Remaking of World Order* (New York: Simon & Schuster, 1996).

Huntington, Samuel P. *The Soldier and the State: The Theory and Politics of Civil-Military Relations* (Cambridge, MA: Harvard University Press, 1957).

Hutchison, Emma. *Affective Communities in World Politics: Collective Emotions After Trauma* (Cambridge, UK: Cambridge University Press, 2016).

Jackson, Robert, and Georg Sorenson. *Introduction to International Relations*, 6th ed. (Oxford: Oxford University Press, 2016).

Jacobs, Frank. "What Russia Could Look Like in 2035 If Putin Gets His Wish." *Foreign Policy* (June 4, 2014) http://foreignpolicy.com/2014/06/04/what-russia-could-look-like-in-2035-if-putin-gets-his-wish/.

Jacques, Martin. *When China Rules the World: The End of the Western World and the Birth of a New Global Order*, 2nd ed. (London: Penguin, 2012).

Jay, Martin. *Downcast Eyes: The Denigration of Vision in Twentieth-Century French Thought* (Berkeley: University of California Press, 1994).

Jay, Martin. "No State of Grace: Violence in the Garden." In *Sites Unseen: Landscape and Vision*, edited by Harris Dianne Suzette and D. Fairchild Ruggles, 45–60 (Pittsburgh, PA: University of Pittsburgh, 2011).

Jeffrey, Alex. *The Improvised State: Sovereignty, Performance and Agency in Dayton Bosnia* (London: John Wiley & Sons, 2012).

Jenco, Leigh. *Changing Referents: Learning Across Space and Time in China and the West* (New York: Oxford University Press, 2015).

Ji Cheng. *Yuan Ye tushuo* (Jinan: Shandong huabao chubanshe, 2004).

Jia Yijun. *Zhongguo guochi dilixue* [Geography of China's national humiliation] (Beiping: Wenhua xueshe yinxing, 1930).

Jia Zhangke. *Smog Journeys*. Beijing: Greenpeace (January 21, 2015) https://www.youtube.com/watch?v=zfF7ZmKMUX0.

Jiang, Min. "Authoritarian Informationalism: China's Approach to Internet Sovereignty." *SAIS Review* 30:2 (2010):71–89.

Jin Wei. "Burqas, Hijabs and Beards in the Governance of Xinjiang." University of Nottingham: China Policy Institute Blog (April 29, 2015) http://blogs.nottingham.ac.uk/chinapolicyinstitute/2015/04/29/regulating-burqas-hijabs-and-beards-to-push-or-pull/.

Jindai Zhongguo bainian guochi ditu [Maps of the modern China's century of national humiliation] (Beijing: Renmin chubanshe, 1997/2005).

Johnson, Corey, Reece Jones, Anssi Paasi, Louise Amoore, Alison Mountz, Mark Salter, and Chris Rumford. "Interventions on Rethinking 'the Border' in Border Studies." *Political Geography* 30 (2011):61–69.

Jones, Reece. *Border Walls: Security and the War on Terror in the United States, India and Israel* (London: Zed Books, 2012).

Jones, Reece, Corey Johnson, Wendy Brown, Gabriel Popescu, Polly Pallister-Wilkins, Alison Mountz, and Emily Gilbert. "Interventions on the State of Sovereignty at the Border." *Political Geography* 59 (2017):1–10.

Joppke, Christian. *Veil: Mirror of Identity* (Cambridge, UK: Polity, 2009).

Kafka, Franz. *The Complete Short Stories* (London: Vintage, 2005).

Kang, David C. *East Asia Before the West: Five Centuries of Trade and Tribute* (New York: Columbia University Press, 2010).

Kant, Immanuel. *The Critique of Judgment*, translated by J. H. Bernard (Amherst, NY: Prometheus Books, 2000).

Kapur, Saloni, and Simon Mabon. "The Copenhagen School Goes Global: Securitisation in the Non-West." *Global Discourse* 8:1 (2018):1–4.

Katzenstein, Peter, ed. *Civilizations in World Politics: Plural and Pluralist Perspectives* (New York: Routledge, 2010).

Keane, Marc P. *Japanese Garden Design* (Tokyo: Tuttle, 1996).

Keenan, Paul. "The Summer Gardens in the Social Life of St Petersburg, 1725–1761." *Slavonic and East European Review* 88:1/2 (2010):134–155.

Keswick, Maggie. *The Chinese Garden: History, Art, and Architecture*, 2nd rev. ed. (London: Frances Lincoln, 2003).

Kingston, Jeff. "Awkward Talisman: War Memory, Reconciliation and Yasukuni." *East Asia* 24 (2007):295–318.

Klausen, Jytte. *The Cartoons That Shook the World* (New Haven, CT: Yale University Press, 2009).

Klimburg, Alexander. *The Darkening Web: The War for Cyberspace* (New York: Penguin Press, 2017).

Knockel, Jeffrey, Lotus Ruan, Masashi Crete-Nishihata, and Ron Deibert. *(Can't) Picture This: An Analysis of Image Filtering on WeChat Moments*. The Citizen Lab (August 14, 2018) https://citizenlab.ca/2018/08/cant-picture-this-an-analysis-of-image-filtering-on-wechat-moments/.

Kostka, Genia. "China's Social Credit Systems and Public Opinion: Explaining High Levels of Approval." *New Media and Society* 21:7 (2019):1565–1593.

Kothari, Ranji. "Editorial Statement." *Alternatives* 1:1 (1975):1–5.

Kothari, Ranji. "Towards a Just World." *Alternatives* 5 (1979–1980):1–42.

Kovács, Attila. "The 'New Jihadist' and the Visual Turn from al-Qa'ida to ISIL/ISIS/Da'ish." *Bitzpol Affairs* 2:3 (2015):47–69.

Kraidy, Marwan M. "The Projectilic Image: Islamic State's Digital Visual Warfare and Global Networked Affect." *Media, Culture & Society* 39:8 (2017): 1194–1209.

Krasner, Stephen D. *Sovereignty: Organized Hypocrisy* (Princeton, NJ: Princeton University Press, 1999).

Kraus, Richard Curt. *The Party and the Arty in China: The New Politics of Culture* (Lanham, MD: Rowman & Littlefield, 2004).

Kuitert, Wybe. "Borrowing Scenery and the Landscape That Lends—The Final Chapter of Yuanye." *Journal of Landscape Architecture* 10:2 (2015):32–43.

Kuitert, Wybe. *Japanese Gardens and Landscapes, 1650–1950* (Philadelphia: University of Pennsylvania Press, 2017).

Kuitert, Wybe. *Themes in the History of Japanese Garden Art* (Honolulu: University of Hawai'i Press, 2002).

Lahoud, Nelly. "A Capella Songs (Anashid) in Jihadi Culture." In *Jihadi Culture: The Art and Social Practices of Militant Islamists*, edited by Thomas Hegghammer, 42–62 (New York: Cambridge University Press, 2017).

Lattimore, Owen. *Inner Asian Frontiers of China* (New York: American Geographical Society, 1940).

"Law on Territorial Waters, Adjacent Areas." Beijing: Xinhua, FBIS-China (February 28, 1992):2; translated in British Broadcasting Corporation, Summary of World Broadcasts (November 28, 1992):C1/1-2.

Lawrence, Andy. *Filmmaking for Fieldwork: An Ethnographer's Handbook* (Manchester, UK: Manchester University Press, forthcoming).

Ledyard, Gari. "Cartography in Korea." In *The History of Cartography*, Vol. II, Book II, *Cartography in the Traditional East and Southeast Asian Societies*, edited by J. B. Harley and David Woodward, 235–344 (Chicago: University of Chicago Press, 1994).

Lee, Haiyan. "The Ruins of Yuanmingyuan: Or, How to Enjoy a National Wound." *Modern China* 35:2 (2009):155–190.

Leibold, James. "Surveillance in Xinjiang: Ethnic Sorting, Coercion, and Inducement." *Journal of Contemporary China* (May 31, 2019):1–15, https://doi.org/10.1080/10670564.2019.1621529.

Leibold, James, and Timothy Grose, "Islamic Veiling in Xinjiang: The Political and Societal Struggle to Define Uyghur Female Adornment." *China Journal* no. 76 (2016):78–102.

Levinas, Emmanuel. *Totality and Infinity*, translated by Alphonso Lingis (Pittsburgh: Duquesne University Press, 1969).

Levinson, Barry, dir. *Wag the Dog* (New Line Cinema, 1997).

Lewis, Reina, ed. *Modest Fashion: Styling Bodies, Mediating Faith* (London: I. B. Taurus, 2013).

Lewis, Reina. *Muslim Fashion: Contemporary Style Cultures* (Durham, NC: Duke University Press, 2015).

Li Keqiang. "Report on the Work of the Government (2015)." State Council Information Office (March 5, 2015) http://english.gov.cn/archive/publications/2015/03/05/content_281475066179954.htm.

Li Xiaodong and Felicia Lim. "Poetics of Gardening: A Holistic Approach Towards Chinese Landscape Cultivation Based on the Case Study of Yuan Ye." *Studies in the History of Gardens and Designed Landscapes* 24:3 (2004):229–249.

Lindroos, Kia, and Frank Möller, eds. *Art as Political Witness* (Leverkusen: Barbara Budrich, 2016).

Linfield, Susie. *Cruel Radiance: Photography and Political Violence* (Chicago: University of Chicago Press, 2010).

Ling, L. H. M. *The Dao of World Politics: Towards a Post-Westphalian, Worldist International Relations* (London: Routledge, 2014).

Lisle, Debbie. *Holidays in the Danger Zone: Entanglements of War and Tourism* (Minneapolis: University of Minnesota Press, 2016).

Lisle, Debbie. "Learning How to See." In *Routledge Handbook of International Political Sociology*, edited by Xavier Guillaume and Pinar Bilgin, 299–308 (London: Routledge, 2016).

Liu Dexi. "Zhongguo de fazhan yu waijiao zhengce de zouxiang" [Trends in China's development and foreign policy], *Guoji zhengzhi yanjiu* (2015), http://study.ccln.gov.cn/fenke/zhengzhixue/zzzgwj/163609.shtml.

Liu, Kin-ming, ed. *My First Trip to China* (Hong Kong: Muse, 2012).

Liu, Lydia H. *The Clash of Empires: The Invention of China in Modern World Making* (Cambridge, MA: Harvard University Press, 2004).

Liu Mingfu. *Zhongguo meng: Hou Meiguo shidai de daguo siwei zhanlue dingwei* [The China dream: The great power thinking and strategic positioning of China in the post-American era], 2nd ed. (Beijing: Zhongguo youyi chuban gongsi, 2013).

Liu Quan. "Nanmin yu yishu" [Refugees and art]. *Meishu guancha* no. 2 (2017):147–150.

Liu Xiaobo. *No Enemies, No Hatred: Selected Essays and Poems*, edited by Perry Link, Tianchi Martin-Liao, and Liu Xia (Cambridge, MA: Harvard University Press, 2012).

Liu Xiaoming. "China and Britain Won the War Together." *Daily Telegraph* (January 1, 2014) http://www.telegraph.co.uk/comment/10546442/Liu-Xiaoming-China-and-Britain-won-the-war-together.html.

Louie, Kam. *Chinese Masculinities in a Globalizing World* (London: Routledge, 2015).

Louie, Kam. *Theorising Chinese Masculinity: Society and Gender in China* (Cambridge, UK: Cambridge University Press, 2002).

Lovell, Julia. *The Great Wall: China Against the World, 1000 BC—AD 2000* (New York: Grove Press, 2006).

Lu Yiran. "Jindai Zhongguo sangshi lingtu zhihuigu" [A review of modern China's lost territories], *21 shiji* no. 1 (1997):60–63.

Luke, Timothy W. "Design as Defense: Broken Barriers and the Security Spectacle at the US-Mexico Border." In *Building Walls and Dissolving Borders: The Challenges of Alterity, Community and Securitizing Space*, edited by Max O. Stephenson and Laura Zanotti, 115–131 (Burlington, VT: Ashgate, 2014).

Luke, Timothy W. "The Missouri Botanical Garden: Reworking Biopower as Florapower." *Organization and Environment* 13:3 (2000):305–321.

Lyon, David. *The Culture of Surveillance: Watching as a Way of Life* (Cambridge, UK: Polity Press, 2018).

Lyon, David, Kevin D. Haggerty, and Kirstie Ball. "Introducing Surveillance Studies." In *Routledge Handbook of Surveillance Studies*, edited by Kirstie Ball, Kevin D. Haggerty, and David Lyon, 1–11 (New York: Routledge, 2014).

Lyotard, Jean-François. *Discourse, Figure*, translated by Antony Hudek and Mary Lyndon (Minneapolis: University of Minnesota Press, 2011).

MacDonald, Fraser, Rachel Hughes, and Klaus Dodds. "Introduction." In *Observant States: Geopolitics and Visual Culture*, edited by Fraser MacDonald, Rachel Hughes, and Klaus Dodds (New York: I. B. Taurus, 2010).

MacDonald, Fraser, Rachel Hughes, and Klaus Dodds, eds. *Observant States: Geopolitics and Visual Culture* (New York: I. B. Taurus, 2010).

MacDougall, Douglas. *Transcultural Cinema* (Princeton, NJ: Princeton University Press, 1998).

MacKay, Joseph. "The Nomadic Other: Ontological Security and the Inner Asian Steppe in Historical East Asian International Politics." *Review of International Studies* 42 (2016):471–491.

MacKinnon, Rebecca. *Consent of the Networked: The Worldwide Struggle for Internet Freedom* (New York: Basic Books, 2012).

Madsen, Deborah L. "Performing Community through the Feminine Body: The Beauty Pageant in Transnational Contexts." Presented at University of Zurich, October 2005.

Marlow, Tim, and John Tancock, eds. *Ai Weiwei* (London: Royal Academy of Arts, 2015).

Martínez, José Ciro, and Brent Eng. "Stifling Stateness: The Assad Regime's Campaigns Against Rebel Governance." *Security Dialogue* 49:4 (2018):235–253.

Martínez, José Ciro, and Brent Eng. "Struggling to Perform the State: The Politics of Bread in the Syrian Civil War." *International Political Sociology* 11 (2017):130–147.

Marwick, Alice. *Status Update: Celebrity, Publicity and Branding in the Social Media Age* (New Haven, CT: Yale University Press, 2013).

Marx, Gary T. *Windows on the Soul: Surveillance and Society in an Age of High Technology* (Chicago: University of Chicago Press, 2016).

Massumi, Brian. *Parables for the Virtual: Movement, Affect, Sensation* (Durham, NC: Duke University Press, 2002).

Massumi, Brian. *Politics of Affect* (Cambridge, UK: Polity, 2015).

McClimens, Alex, Stuart Doel, Rachel Ibbotson, Nick Partridge, Elaine Muscroft, and Lesley Lockwood. "How Do the 'Peace Gardens' Make You Feel? Public Space and Personal Wellbeing in City Centre Sheffield." *Journal of Urban Design* 17:1 (2012):117–133.

McDowall, Stephen. "Cultivating Orientalism." *International Institute for Asian Studies Newsletter* 73 (2016):12.

McGrath, John. "Performing Surveillance." In *Routledge Handbook of Surveillance Studies*, edited by Kirstie Ball, Kevin D. Haggerty, and David Lyon, 83–90 (New York: Routledge, 2014).

McLagan, Meg, and Yates McKee, eds. *Sensible Politics: The Visual Culture of Nongovernmental Activism* (New York: Zone Books, 2012).

McNair, Brian. "*The Interview*: Schnarking, Nob Jokes and the Right to Cause Gross Offence." *Journalism Practice* 9:3 (2015):452–454.

Mello, Brian. "The Islamic State: Violence and Ideology in a Post-Colonial Revolutionary Regime." *International Political Sociology* 12 (2018):139–155.

Memorial Hall of the Victims in Nanjing Massacre by Japanese Invaders. (no date) http://www.nj1937.org/en/index.htm.

Metzger, Thomas A. *Escape from Predicament: Neo-Confucianism and China's Evolving Political Culture* (New York: Columbia University Press, 1977).

Meyer, Jeffrey F. *The Dragons of Tiananmen: Beijing as a Sacred City* (Columbia: University of South Carolina Press, 1991).

Meyer-Fong, Tobie. "Civil War, Revolutionary Heritage, and the Chinese Garden." *Cross-Currents: East Asia History and Culture Review* 13 (2014):75–98.

Mignolo, Walter D. *The Darker Side of the Renaissance: Literacy, Territoriality, and Colonization* (Ann Arbor: University of Michigan Press, 1995).

Millward, James A. "A Uyghur Muslim in Qianlong's Court: The Meaning of the Fragrant Concubine." *Journal of Asian Studies* 53:2 (1994):427–458.

Minne, Daniele Djamila Amarane. "Women at War." *Interventions* 9:3 (2007):340–349.

Mirzoeff, Nicholas. *How to See the World* (New York: Pelican Books, 2015).

Mirzoeff, Nicholas. *An Introduction to Visual Culture*, 2nd ed. (New York: Routledge, 2009).

Mirzoeff, Nicholas. *The Right to Look: A Counterhistory of Visuality* (Durham, NC: Duke University Press, 2011).

Mistreanu, Simina. "Life Inside China's Social Credit Laboratory." *Foreign Policy* (April 3, 2018), https://foreignpolicy.com/2018/04/03/life-inside-chinas-social-credit-laboratory/.

Mitchell, W. J. T. *Iconology: Image, Text, Ideology* (Chicago: University of Chicago Press, 1988).

Mitchell, W. J. T. "Medium Theory: Preface to the 2003 *Critical Inquiry* Symposium." *Critical Inquiry* 30:2 (2004):324–335.

Mitchell, W. J. T. *Picture Theory: Essays on Verbal and Visual Representation* (Chicago: University of Chicago Press, 1995).

Mitchell, W. J. T. *What Do Pictures Want? The Lives and Loves of Images* (Chicago: University of Chicago Press, 2005).

Mitsuhide, Mashima. *Yasukuni no Shiki* [Four seasons at the Yasukuni shrine] (Tokyo: Kindai Publishing Company Mashima, 2008).

Mochizuki, Kotaro. *Japan To-day: A Souvenir of the Anglo-Japanese Exhibition Held in London, 1910* (Tokyo: Liberal News Agency, 1910).

Möller, Frank. "From Aftermath to Peace: Reflections on a Photography of Peace." *Global Society* 31: 3 (2017):315–335.

Möller, Frank. "Photographic Interventions in Post 9/11 Security Policy." *Security Dialogue* 38:2 (2007):179–196.

Möller, Frank. *Visual Peace: Images, Spectatorship, and the Politics of Violence* (London: Palgrave Macmillan, 2013).

Monaci, Sara. "Explaining the Islamic State's Online Media Strategy: A Transmedia Approach." *International Journal of Communication* 11 (2017):2842–2860.

Moore, Cerwyn, and Chris Farrands. "Visual Analysis." In *Critical Approaches to Security: An Introduction to Theories and Methods*, edited by Laura J. Shepherd, 221–235 (London: Routledge, 2013).

Moore, Lindsey. "The Veil of Nationalism: Frantz Fanon's 'Algeria Unveiled' and Gillo Pontecorvo's *The Battle of Algiers*." *Kunapipi* 25:2 (2003):56–73.

Moors, Annelies. "NiqaBitch and Princess Hijab: Niqab Activism, Satire and Street Art." *Feminist Review* 98 (2011):128–135.

Mortensen, Mette. "Constructing, Confirming, and Contesting Icons: The Alan Kurdi Imagery Appropriated by #humanitywashedashore, Ai Weiwei, and *Charlie Hebdo*." *Media, Culture & Society* 39:8 (2017):1142–1161.

Mukerji, Chandra. "Space and Political Pedagogy at the Gardens of Versailles." *Public Culture* 24:3 (2012):509–534.

Mukerji, Chandra. *Territorial Ambitions and the Gardens of Versailles* (Cambridge, UK: Cambridge University Press, 1997).

Mulvey, Laura. *Visual and Other Pleasures*, 2nd ed. (New York: Palgrave Macmillan, 2008).

Murck, Alfreda, and Wen Fong. "A Chinese Garden Court: The Astor Court at the Metropolitan Museum of Art." *The Metropolitan Museum of Art Bulletin* 38:3 (1980–1981):2–64.

Nail, Thomas. *Theory of the Border* (New York: Oxford University Press, 2016).

Naji, Abu Bakr. *The Management of Savagery: The Most Critical Stage Through Which the Umma Will Pass*, translated by William McCants (Cambridge, MA: John M. Olin Institute for Strategic Studies at Harvard University, May 23, 2006).

Nash, Kate. "Documentary-for-the-Other: Relationships, Ethics and (Observational) Documentary." *Journal of Mass Media Ethics* 26:3 (2011): 224–39.

National Institutes of Health. *Chinese Public Health Posters* exhibit (2006) http://www.nlm.nih.gov/hmd/chineseposters/introduction.html.

Neumann, Iver, and Daniel H. Nexon, eds. *Harry Potter and International Relations* (London: Rowman & Littlefield, 2006).

Newman, David. "On Borders and Power: A Theoretical Framework." *Journal of Borderlands Studies* 18:1 (2003):13–25.

Nietzsche, Friedrich. *The Gay Science*, edited by Bernard Williams (Cambridge, UK: Cambridge University Press, [1887] 2001).

NiqaBitch. "Hot Pants and Niqabs: NiqaBitch Stroll through Paris." *Monthly Review* (October 13, 2010) http://mrzine.monthlyreview.org/2010/niqabitch131010.html.

Nussbaum, Martha C. *The New Religious Intolerance: Overcoming the Politics of Fear in an Anxious Age* (Cambridge, MA: Harvard University Press, 2012).

Nyri, Pal. "Yellow Man's Burden: Chinese Immigrants on a Civilizing Mission." *The China Journal* no. 56 (2006):83–106.

Ó Tuathail, Gearóid. *Critical Geopolitics* (Minneapolis: University of Minnesota Press, 1996).

Ó Tuathail, Gearóid, Monika K. Baar, and Steven Seegel. "Mapping Europe's Borderlands: Russian Cartography in the Age of Empire." *Nationalities Papers* 42:3 (2014): 548–557.

O'Grady, Lorraine. "Art Is . . ." (1983/2009) http://lorraineogrady.com/art/art-is/.

Office of the Leading Group for the Belt and Road Initiative. *Building the Belt and Road: Concept, Practice and China's Contribution* (Beijing: Foreign Languages Press, May 2017).

Oliver, M. Cynthia. *Queen of the Virgins: Pageantry and Black Womanhood in the Caribbean* (Jackson: University Press of Mississippi, 2009).

Ong, Aihwa. "Graduated Sovereignty in Southeast Asia." *Theory, Culture, and Society* 17:4 (2000):55–75.

Onuf, Nicholas. *World of Our Making* (Columbia: University of South Carolina Press, 1989).

Ott, Brian L. "Affect." In *Oxford Research Encyclopedia of Communication*, 1–26 (Oxford: Oxford University Press, 2017).

Panagia, Davide. "*Cinéma vérité* and the Ontology of Cinema: A Response to Roy Germano." *Perspectives on Politics* 12:3 (2014):688–690.

Panagia, Davide. *The Political Life of Sensation* (Durham, NC: Duke University Press, 2009).

Parikh, Sunita. "Analytic Filmmaking and the Persistence of Narrative: A Response to Roy Germano." *Perspectives on Politics* 12:3 (2014):677–679.

Pauwels, Luc. *Reframing Visual Social Science: Towards a More Visual Sociology and Anthropology* (Cambridge, UK: Cambridge University Press, 2015).

Peluso, Nancy Lee. "Whose Woods Are These? Counter-Mapping Forest Territories in Kalimantan, Indonesia." *Antipode* 27:4 (1995):383–406.

Perdue, Peter C. "China and Other Colonial Empires." *Journal of American-East Asian Relations* 16:1–2 (2009):85–103.

Perdue, Peter. *China Marches West* (Cambridge, MA: Harvard University Press, 2005).

Permanent Court of Arbitration (PCA). "Award: PCA Case No 2013–19: In the Matter of the South China Sea Arbitration between the Republic of the Philippines and the People's Republic of China" (The Hague: Permanent Court of Arbitration, July 12, 2016) https://pca-cpa.org/wp-content/uploads/sites/175/2016/07/PH-CN-20160712-Award.pdf.

Petrie, Donald, dir. *Miss Congeniality* (Castle Rock, 2000).

Pieke, Frank. *Knowing China* (Cambridge, UK: Cambridge University Press, 2016).

Pink, Sarah, ed. *Advances in Visual Methodology* (London: Sage, 2012).

Pitt-Rivers, Julian. "The Law of Hospitality." *HAU: Journal of Ethnographic Theory* 2:1 (2012 [1977]):501–517.

Pontecorvo, Gillo, dir. *The Battle of Algiers* (Casbah Film, 1966).

Qi Kang. *QinHua Rijun Nanjing datusha yunan tongbao jinianguan* [The Monument Hall to compatriots murdered in the Japanese military invasion of China] (Shenyang: Liaoning daxue kexue jishu chubanshe, 1999).

Qin Yaqing. *A Relational Theory of World Politics* (Cambridge, UK: Cambridge University Press, 2018).

Rael, Ronald. "Border Wall as Architecture." In *Borders, Fences and Walls: State of Insecurity?*, edited by Elisabeth Vallet, 267–278 (Burlington, VT: Ashgate, 2014).

Rancière, Jacques. "Contemporary Art and the Politics of Aesthetics." In *Communities of Sense: Rethinking Aesthetics and Politics*, edited by Beth Hinderliter, William Kaizen, Vered Maimon, Jaleh Mansoor, and Seth McCormick, 31–50 (Durham, NC: Duke University Press, 2009).

Rancière, Jacques. *The Emancipated Spectator*, translated by Gregory Elliott (London: Verso, 2009).

Rancière, Jacques. *The Politics of Aesthetics: The Distribution of the Sensible*, translated by Gabriel Rockhill (London: Continuum International Publishing Group, 2004).

Record in Pictures of Yushukan (Tokyo: Kindai Publishing Co., 2009).

Renov, Michael. *The Subject of the Documentary* (Minneapolis: University of Minnesota Press, 2004).

Ringmar, Erik. *Liberal Barbarism: The European Destruction of the Palace of the Emperor of China* (New York: Palgrave Macmillan, 2013).

Roberts, Claire. "China's Most Famous Ruin." In *The Great Wall of China*, edited by Claire Roberts and Geremie R. Barmé, 16–25 (Sydney: Powerhouse Publishing, 2006).

Roberts, Claire, and Geremie R. Barmé, eds. *The Great Wall of China* (Sydney: Powerhouse Publishing, 2006).

Roberts, Claire, and Geremie R. Barmé. "Introduction." In *The Great Wall of China*, edited by Claire Roberts and Geremie R. Barmé, 10–13 (Sydney: Powerhouse Publishing, 2006).

Roberts, Margaret E. *Censored: Distraction and Diversion Inside China's Great Firewall* (Princeton, NJ: Princeton University Press, 2018).

Robinson, Piers. "CNN Effect." In *Visual Global Politics*, edited by Roland Bleiker, 62–67 (London: Routledge, 2018).

Robinson, Piers. *The CNN Effect: The Myth of News Foreign Policy Intervention* (London: Routledge, 2002).

Robinson, Piers. "Media Empowerment vs. Strategies of Control: Theorizing News Media and War in the 21st Century." *Zeitschrift fur Politik* 4 (2014):461–479.

Rogen, Seth, and Evan Goldberg, dir. *The Interview* (Sony Pictures Entertainment, 2014).

Rojas, Carlos. *The Great Wall: A Cultural History* (Cambridge, MA: Harvard University Press, 2010).

Rorty, Richard. *Philosophy and the Mirror of Nature* (Princeton, NJ: Princeton University Press, 1981).

Rose, Gillian. "On the Relation between 'Visual Research Methods' and Contemporary Visual Culture." *The Sociological Review* 62:1 (2014):24–46.

Rose, Gillian. *Visual Methodologies: An Introduction to Researching with Visual Materials*, 4th ed. (London: Sage, 2016).

Rowe, Rochelle. "'Glorifying the Jamaican Girl': The 'Ten Types—One People' Beauty Contest, Racialized Femininities, and Jamaican Nationalism." *Radical History Review* 103 (2009):36–58.

Ruan, Lotus. *When Winner Takes It All: Big Data in China and the Battle for Privacy*. Australian Strategic Policy Institute, Report No. 5/2018 (May 2018).

Ruan, Lotus, Jeffrey Knockel, Jason Q. Ng, and Masashi Crete-Nishihata, "One App, Two Systems: How WeChat Uses One Censorship Policy in China, and Another Internationally." The Citizen Lab (November 30, 2016) https://citizenlab.ca/2016/11/wechat-china-censorship-one-app-two-systems/.

Ryckmans, Pierre. "The Chinese Attitude towards the Past." *China Heritage Quarterly* 14 (2008) http://www.chinaheritagequarterly.org/articles.php?searchterm=014_chineseattitude.inc&issue=014.

Sacco, Joe. *Palestine* (New York: Jonathan Cape, 2003).

Said, Edward. *Culture and Imperialism* (New York: Vintage Books, 1994).

Said, Edward. *Orientalism* (New York: Vintage, 2004).

Sakuteiki: Visions of the Japanese Garden: A Modern Translation of Japan's Gardening Classic. Translated by Jiro Takei and Marc P. Keane (Tokyo: Tuttle Publishing, 2001).

Salter, Mark B. "Introduction: Circuits and Motion." In *Making Things International 1: Circuits and Motion*, edited by Mark B. Salter, vii–xxii (Minneapolis: University of Minnesota Press, 2015).

Salter, Mark B., ed. *Making Things International 1: Circuits and Motion* (Minneapolis: University of Minnesota Press, 2015).

Salter, Mark B. *Politics at the Airport* (Minneapolis: University of Minnesota Press, 2008).

Santos, Gonçalo. "Technological Choices and Modern Material Civilization: Reflections on Everyday Toilet Practices in Rural South China." In *Anthropology and Civilizational Analysis: Eurasian Explorations*, edited by Johann Arnason and Chris Hann, 259–280 (Albany: State University of New York Press, 2018).

Särmä, Saara. "Collaging Iranian Missiles: Digital Security Spectacles and Visual Online Parodies." In *Visual Security Studies: Sights and Spectacles of Insecurity and War*, edited by Juha A. Vuori and Rune Saugmann Andersen, 114–130 (London: Routledge, 2018).

Satrapi, Marjane. *Persopolis* (London: Vintage, 2008).

Schlag, Gabi, and Anna Greis. "Visualizing Violence: Aesthetics and Ethics in International Politics." *Global Discourse* 7:2-3 (2017):193–200.

Schmitt, Carl. *The Nomos of the Earth in the International Law of the Jus publicum Europaeum*, translated by G. L. Ulmen, (New York: Telos, 2003 [1950]).

Schneider, Florian. *China's Digital Nationalism* (New York: Oxford University Press, 2018).

Schorkowitz, Dittmar, and Chia Ning, eds. *Managing Frontiers in China: The Lifanyuan and the Libu Reconsidered* (Leiden: Brill, 2017).

Schroeder, William F. "On Cowboys and Aliens: Affective History and Queer Becoming in Contemporary China." *GLQ: A Journal of Lesbian and Gay Studies* 18:4 (2012): 425–452.

Scott, James C. *The Art of Not Being Governed: An Anarchist History of Upland Southeast Asia* (New Haven, CT: Yale University Press, 2009).

Scott, James C. *Seeing Like a State: How Certain Schemes to Improve the Human Condition Have Failed* (New Haven, CT: Yale University Press, 1998).

Scott, Joan Wallach. *The Politics of the Veil* (Princeton, NJ: Princeton University Press, 2007).

Seegel, Steven. *Mapping Europe's Borderlands: Russian Cartography in the Age of Empire* (Chicago: University of Chicago Press, 2012).

Segal, Adam. "When China Rules the Web: Technology in Service of the State." *Foreign Affairs* (August 13, 2018) https://www.foreignaffairs.com/articles/china/2018-08-13/when-china-rules-web.

Seigworth, Gregory J., and Melissa Gregg. "An Inventory of Shimmers." In *The Affect Theory Reader*, edited by Melissa Gregg and Gregory J. Seigworth, 1–25 (Durham, NC: Duke University Press, 2010).

Shahbaz, Adrian. *Freedom on the Net 2018: The Rise of Digital Authoritarianism* Freedom House (October 2018) https://freedomhouse.org/sites/default/files/FOTN_2018_Final%20Booklet_11_1_2018.pdf.

Shambaugh, David. *China Goes Global: The Partial Power* (New York: Oxford University Press, 2013).

Shan Hai Ching: Legendary Geography and Wonders of Ancient China (Taipei: Committee for Compilation and Examination of the Series of Chinese Classics, 1985).

Shapiro, Michael J. *Cinematic Geopolitics* (London: Routledge, 2009).

Shapiro, Michael J. *For Moral Ambiguity: National Culture and the Politics of the Family* (Minneapolis: University of Minnesota Press, 2001).

Shapiro, Michael J. *Methods and Nations: Cultural Governance and the Indigenous Subject* (New York: Routledge, 2004).

Shapiro, Michael J. *The Political Sublime* (Durham, NC: Duke University Press, 2018).

Shapiro, Michael J. *The Politics of Representation: Writing Practices in Biography, Photography and Policy Analysis* (Madison: University of Wisconsin Press, 1988).

Shapiro, Michael J. *Studies in Trans-Disciplinary Method: After the Aesthetic Turn* (New York: Routledge, 2013).

Shapiro, Michael J. "The Sublime Today: Re-partitioning the Global Sensible." *Millennium* 34:3 (2006):657–681.

Sharif, Yara. *Architecture of Resistance: Cultivating Moments of Possibility within the Palestinian/Israeli Conflict* (London: Routledge, 2017).

Shaw, Martin. "Twenty-First Century Militarism: A Historical-Sociological Framework." In *Militarism and International Relations: Political Economy, Security, Theory*, edited by Anna Stavrianakis and Jan Selby, 19–32 (New York: Routledge, 2013).

Shen, Jianming. "China's Sovereignty over the South China Sea Islands: A Historical Perspective." *Chinese Journal of International* 94 (2002): 94–157.

Shepherd, Laura J., ed. *Critical Approaches to Security: An Introduction to Theories and Methods* (London: Routledge, 2013).

Shim, David. *Visual Politics and North Korea: Seeing Is Believing* (London: Routledge, 2013).

Shirazi, Faegheh. *The Veil Unveiled: The Hijab in Modern Culture* (Miami: University Press of Florida, 2001).

Shrum, Wesley, Ricardo Duque, and Timothy Brown. "Digital Video as Research Practice: Methodology for the Millennium." *Journal of Research Practice* 1:1 (2005):1–19.

Sivin, Nathan, and Gari Ledyard. "Introduction to East Asian Cartography." In *The History of Cartography*, Vol. II, Book II, *Cartography in the Traditional East and Southeast Asian Societies*, edited by J. B. Harley and David Woodward, 23–31 (Chicago: University of Chicago Press, 1994).

Smith, Richard J. *Mapping China and Managing the World: Culture, Cartography and Cosmology in Late Imperial Times* (New York: Routledge, 2012).

Sontag, Susan. "Fascinating Fascism." *New York Review of Books* (February 6, 1975):1–20.

Sontag, Susan. *On Photography* (New York: Penguin, 1977).

Sontag, Susan. *Regarding the Pain of Others* (New York: Penguin, 2003).

Sontag, Susan. "Regarding the Torture of Others." *New York Times Magazine* (May 4, 2014).

Sorace, Christian. "China's Last Communist: Ai Weiwei." *Critical Inquiry* 40:2 (2014):396–419.

Sorace, Christian. "China's Vision for Developing Sichuan's Post-Earthquake Countryside: Turning Unruly Peasants into Grateful Urban Citizens." *China Quarterly* 218 (2014):404–427.

Spivak, Gayatri Chakravorty. "Can the Subaltern Speak?" In *Colonial Discourse and Postcolonial Theory: A Reader*, edited by Patrick Williams and Laura Chrisman, 53–63 (London: Harvester Wheatsheaf, 1994).

State Council. "China Adheres to the Position of Settling Through Negotiation the Relevant Disputes Between China and the Philippines in the South China Sea" (Beijing: State Council Information Office, July 13, 2016).

State Council. "Guowuyuan: Guanyu yifa shehui xinyong tixi jianshe kuanhua gangyao (2014–2020)" [State Council: Planning outline for the construction of a social credit system (2014-2020)]. Translated on China Copyright and Media (June 14, 2014) https://chinacopyrightandmedia.wordpress.com/2014/06/14/planning-outline-for-the-construction-of-a-social-credit-system-2014-2020/.

State Council Information Office. "The Internet in China" (June 8, 2010) http://www.gov.cn/english/2010-06/08/content_1622956.htm.

Steadman, Abi, Hayley Rabet, and Lamisa Khan, dir. *Awrah: Uncovering the Covered* (2017) https://vimeo.com/channels/ir318/208667693.

Stenersen, Anne. "A History of Jihadi Cinematography." In *Jihadi Culture: The Art and Social Practices of Militant Islamists*, edited by Thomas Hegghammer, 108–127 (New York: Cambridge University Press, 2017).

Stephenson, Max O., and Laura Zanotti, eds. *Building Walls and Dissolving Borders: The Challenges of Alterity, Community and Securitizing Space* (Burlington, VT: Ashgate, 2014).

Strafella, Giorgio, and Daria Berg. "'Twitter Bodhisattva': Ai Weiwei's Media Politics." *Asian Studies Review* 39:1 (2015):138–57.

Strobel, Warren P. "The CNN Effect." *American Journalism Review* (May 1996) http://ajrarchive.org/article.asp?id=3572.

Sturken, Marita. "The Objects That Lived: The 9/11 Museum and Material Transformation." *Memory Studies* 9:1 (2016):13–26.

Supatra Kopkijsuksakul. "Kan Prakuat Nangsao Thai (B.E. 2477–2530)" [Miss Thailand Contest: 1934–1987], Master's thesis, Bangkok: Thammasat University, 1988.

Suttmeier, Richard P. "Inventing the Future in Chinese Labs: How Does China Do Science Today." *Asia Dialogue* (September 24, 2018) http://theasiadialogue.com/2018/09/24/inventing-the-future-in-chinese-labs-how-does-china-do-science-today/.

Sylvester, Christine. *Art/Museums: International Relations Where We Least Expect It* (London: Routledge, 2008).

Tanzaki, Junichiro. *In Praise of Shadows* (London: Vintage Books, 2001).

Takenaka, Akiko. *Yasukuni Shrine: History, Memory, and Japan's Unending Postwar* (New York: Columbia University Press, 2015).

Tazzioli, Martina, and William Waters. "The Sight of Migration: Governmentality, Visibility, and Europe's Contested Borders." *Global Society* 30:3 (2016):445–464.

Tecate Beer Wall Advertisement. YouTube (September 2016) https://www.youtube.com/watch?v=nXYM_zBVF7Q.

There Is No Life without Jihad. al Hayat Media Center (June 19, 2014) https://jihadology.net/2014/06/19/al-ḥayat-media-center-presents-a-new-video-message-from-the-islamic-state-of-iraq-and-al-sham-there-is-no-life-without-jihad/.

Thomas, Greg M. "Yuanming Yuan/Versailles: Intercultural Interactions between Chinese and European Palace Cultures." *Art History* 32:1 (2009):115–143.

Thongchai Winichakul. *Siam Mapped: A History of the Geo-body of a Nation* (Honolulu: University of Hawaii Press, 1994).

Thorsten, Marie. "Soft-Hard Power Convergence and Democracy in Abe's Japan." In *Power in Contemporary Japan*, edited by Gill Steel, 239–262 (London: Palgrave, 2016).

Todorov, Tzvetan. *The Fear of Barbarians: Beyond the Clash of Civilizations* (Chicago: University of Chicago Press, 2010).

Trachtenberg, Alan. *Reading American Photographs: Images as History, Matthew Brady to Walker Evans* (New York: Hill and Wang, 1989).

Troumbley, Rex. "Colonization.com: Empire Building for a New Digital Age." *East-West Affairs* 1:4 (2013):93–107.

Tsygankov, Andrei P., and Pavel A. Tsygankov. "National Ideology and IR Theory: Three Incarnations of the 'Russian Idea.'" *European Journal of International Relations* 16:4 (2010):663–686.

Tzanelli, Rodanthi. "Schematising Hospitality: Ai WeiWei's Activist Artwork as a Form of Dark Travel." *Mobilities* 13:4 (2018):520–534.

UNESCO. "Garden of Peace" (n.d.) http://webarchive.unesco.org/20151215223006//.

Vallet, Elisabeth, ed. *Borders, Fences and Walls: State of Insecurity?* (Burlington, VT: Ashgate, 2014).

van Munster, Rens, and Casper Sylvest. "Documenting International Relations: Documentary Film and the Creative Arrangement of Perceptibility." *International Studies Perspectives* 16 (2015):229–245.

van Munster, Rens, and Casper Sylvest, eds. *Documenting World Politics: A Critical Companion to IR and Non-Fiction Film* (London: Routledge, 2015).

Virilio, Paul. *Speed and Politics: An Essay on Dromology* (New York: Semiotext(e) Foreign Agents Series, 1986).

Virilio, Paul. *The Vision Machine* (Bloomington: Indiana University Press, 1994).

Virilio, Paul. *War and Cinema: The Logistics of Perception* (New York: Verso, 1989).

von Vacano, Diego. "The Scope of Comparative Political Theory." *Annual Review of Political Science* 18 (2015):465–80.

Vuori, Juha A., and Rune Saugmann Andersen, eds. *Visual Security Studies: Sights and Spectacles of Insecurity and War* (New York: Routledge, 2018).

Vuori, Juha Antero, and Lauri Paltemaa. "The Lexicon of Fear: Chinese Internet Control Practice in Sina Weibo Microblog Censorship." *Surveillance and Society* 13:3/4 (2015):400–421.

Wagner, Wolfgang, Ragini Sen, Risa Permandadeli, and Caroline S. Howarth. "The Veil and Muslim Women's Identity: Cultural Pressures and Resistance to Stereotyping." *Culture & Psychology* 18:4 (2012):521–541.

Wahlberg, Malin. *Documentary Time: Film and Phenomenology* (Minneapolis: University of Minnesota Press, 2008).

Waldron, Arthur. *The Great Wall of China: From History to Myth* (Cambridge, UK: Cambridge University Press, 1990).

Waldron, Arthur. "Scholarship and Patriotic Education: The Great Wall Conference, 1994." *China Quarterly* no. 143 (1995):843–850.

Waley-Cohen, Joanna. "Changing Spaces of Empire in Eighteenth-Century Qing China." In *Political Frontiers, Ethnic Boundaries and Human Geographies in Chinese History*, edited by Nicola Di Cosmo and Don J. Wyatt, 324–349 (London: RoutledgeCurzon, 2003).

Walker, R. B. J. *Inside/Outside: International Relations as Political Theory* (Cambridge, UK: Cambridge University Press, 1993).

Walker, R. B. J. *Out of Line: Essays on the Politics of Boundaries and the Limits of Modern Politics* (New York: Routledge, 2016).

Wang Ban, ed. *Chinese Visions of World Order: Tianxia, Culture, and World Politics* (Durham, NC: Duke University Press, 2017).

Wang Jisi. "Huntingdun tiaoqi de lunzhan jiang chaoyue shikong" [The debate provoked by Huntington transcends time and space]. *Shijie zhishi* no. 3 (2009). https://user.guancha.cn/main/content?id=66738.

Wang, Joseph Cho. *The Chinese Garden* (New York: Oxford University Press, 1998).

Wang, Maya. *"Eradicating Ideological Viruses": China's Campaign of Repression Against Xinjiang's Muslims* (New York: Human Rights Watch, 2018).

Wang Yi. *Zhongguo yuanlin wenhua shi* [The cultural history of Chinese gardens] (Shanghai: Renmin chubanshe, 2014).

Weber, Cynthia. *"I Am an American": Filming the Fear of Difference* (Chicago: University of Chicago Press, 2011).

Weber, Cynthia, dir. "'I Am an American': Portraits of Post-9/11 US Citizens" (2007) https://www.iamanamericanproject.com.

Weber, Cynthia. '"I Am an American': Protesting Advertised 'Americanness.'" *Citizenship Studies* 17:2 (2013):278–292.

Weber, Cynthia. *Imagining America at War: Morality, Politics and Film* (London: Routledge, 2006).

Weber, Cynthia. *International Relations Theory: A Critical Introduction* (New York: Routledge, 2013).

Weber, Cynthia. *We Are Not Immigrants* (18 minutes). Screened at the Visual International Politics workshop at LSE (June 13, 2016).

Weitzel, Michelle. "Audializing Migrant Bodies: Sound and Security at the Border." *Security Dialogue* 49:6 (2018):421–437.

Weizman, Eyal. *Forensic Architecture: Violence at the Threshold of Detectability* (Cambridge, MA: Zone Books, 2017).

Weizman, Eyal. *Hollow Land: Israel's Architecture of Occupation* (London: Verso, 2007).

Whitehall, Geoffrey, and Eric Ishiwata. "The International Aesthetic of the Yasukuni Jinja and the Yushukan Museum." In *The New Violent Cartography: Geo-Analysis after the Aesthetic Turn*, edited by Sam Okoth Opondo and Michael J. Shapiro, 234–247 (New York: Routledge, 2012).

Williams, John. "Territorial Borders, International Ethics and Geography: Do Good Fences Still Make Good Neighbours?." *Geopolitics* 8:2 (2003):25–46.

Williams, Michael C. "Words, Images, Enemies: Securitization and International Politics." *International Studies Quarterly* 47 (2003):511–531.

Winter, Charlie. *Documenting the Virtual "Caliphate"* (London: Quilliam Foundation, 2015).

Woolf, Virginia. *Three Guineas* (London: Hogarth Press, 1938).

Wu Gongxiong, ed. *Huitu guochi yanyi* [Drawings of the romance of national humiliation] (Shanghai: Shijie shuju, 1922).

Xi Jinping. *The Governance of China*. Vol. 1 (Beijing: Foreign Languages Press, 2014).

Xi Jinping. *The Governance of China*. Vol. II (Beijing: Foreign Languages Press, 2017).

Xiao Qiang. "The Road to Digital Unfreedom: President XI's Surveillance State." *Journal of Democracy* 30:1 (2019):53–67.

Xie Bin. *"Zhongguo sangshi lingtu linghai tu"* [Map of China's lost sovereign land and maritime territories]. In *Zhongguo sangdishi* [History of China's lost territories] (Shanghai: Zhonghua shuju, 1927).

Xie Bin. *Zhongguo sangdishi* [History of China's lost territories] (Shanghai: Sanlian shujian, 2014 [1925]).

Xu Jilin. *Dangdai Zhongguo de qimeng yu fan-qimeng* [Enlightenment and anti-enlightenment in contemporary China] (Beijing: Shehui kexue wenxian chubanshe, 2011).

Yan Xuetong. *Ancient Chinese Thought, Modern Chinese Power* (Princeton, NJ: Princeton University Press, 2011).

Yang, Guobin, ed. *China's Contested Internet* (Copenhagen: NIAS Press, 2015).

Yang, Lien-sheng. "Historical Notes on the Chinese World Order." In *The Chinese World Order: Traditional China's Foreign Relations*, edited by John King Fairbank, 20–33 (Cambridge, MA: Harvard University Press, 1968).

Yanow, Dvora. "I Am Not a Camera: On Visual Politics and Method: A Response to Roy Germano." *Perspectives on Politics* 12:3 (2014):680–683.

Yee, Cordell D. K. "Chinese Cartography among the Arts: Objectivity, Subjectivity, Representation." In *The History of Cartography*, Vol. II, Book II, *Cartography in the Traditional East and Southeast Asian Societies*, edited by J. B. Harley and David Woodward, 128–169 (Chicago: University of Chicago Press, 1994).

Yee, Cordell D. K. "Chinese Maps in Political Culture." In *The History of Cartography*, Vol. II, Book II, *Cartography in the Traditional East and Southeast Asian Societies*, edited by J. B. Harley and David Woodward, 71–95 (Chicago: University of Chicago Press, 1994).

Yee, Cordell D. K. "Concluding Remarks: Foundations for a Future History of Chinese Mapping." In *The History of Cartography*, Vol. II, Book II, *Cartography in the Traditional East and Southeast Asian Societies*, edited by J. B. Harley and David Woodward, 228–230 (Chicago: University of Chicago Press, 1994).

Yee, Cordell D. K. "Reinterpreting Traditional Chinese Geographical Maps." In *The History of Cartography*, Vol. II, Book II, *Cartography in the Traditional East and Southeast Asian Societies*, edited by J. B. Harley and David Woodward, 35–70 (Chicago: University of Chicago Press, 1994).

Yee, Cordell D. K. "Space and Place: Ways of World-Making." In *Space & Place: Mapmaking East and West, Four Hundred Years of Western and Chinese Cartography* (Exhibition Catalogue for the Library of Congress), edited by Cordell D. K. Yee et al., 7–65 (Annapolis, MD: St. John's College Press, 1996).

Yoon, Hong-key. "Two Different Geomentalities, Two Different Gardens: The French and the Japanese Cases." *GeoJournal* 33:4 (1994):471–477.

Yu Guozhen. *Jin bainian waijiao shibai shi* [History of the past century's diplomatic defeats] (Shanghai: Shijie shuju, 1929).

Zelin, Aaron Y. "Colonial Caliphate: The Ambitions of the 'Islamic State.'" Jihadology (July 8, 2014) https://jihadology.net/2014/07/08/the-clairvoyant-colonial-caliphate-the-ambitions-of-the-islamic-state/.

Zelin, Aaron Y. "Picture Or It Didn't Happen: A Snapshot of the Islamic State's Official Media Output." *Perspectives on Terrorism* 9:4 (2015):85–97.

Zenz, Adrian. "'Thoroughly Reforming Them Towards a Healthy Heart Attitude': China's Political Re-education Campaign in Xinjiang." *Central Asian Survey* 38:1 (2019):102–128.

Zhang Yimou, dir. *Changcheng* [The Great Wall] (Legendary Pictures, 2016).

Zhao, Suisheng. "China and the South China Sea Arbitration: Geopolitics Versus International Law." *Journal of Contemporary China* 27:109 (2018):1–15.

Zhao, Tingyang. "Rethinking Empire from a Chinese Concept 'All-under-Heaven' (Tian-xia)." *Social Identities* 12:1 (2006):29–41.

Zhao Tingyang. *Tianxia de dangdaixing: Shijie zhixu de shijian yu xiangxiang* [Tianxia's contemporary relevance: Practice and imagination for world order] (Beijing: Zhongxin chubanshe, 2016).

Zheng Ziyue. *Nanhai zhudao dili zhilu* [Geography of the South Sea Islands] (Shanghai: Shangwu yinshuguan, 1947).

Zhichi, ed. *Guochi* [National humiliation] (Shanghai: Zhichishe, 1915).

Zhongguo guochi ditu [Map of China's national humiliation]. (Shanghai: Zhonghua shuju, 1927).

Zhonghua guochi jianming yutu [Concise map of Chinese national humiliation]. (Nanjing: Jiangsu Military Surveying Department, 1928).

"Zhonghua minguo ditu." In *Zhonghua mingguo yuannian lishu* [Almanac of the first year of the Republic of China] (Hunan yanshuo zongke yin, 1912).

Zhou, Zunyou. "Chinese Strategy for De-Radicalization." *Terrorism and Political Violence* (June 9, 2017):1–23, https://doi.org/10.1080/09546553.2017.1330199.

INDEX

Figures are indicated by *f* following the page number

For the benefit of digital users, indexed terms that span two pages (e.g., 52–53) may, on occasion, appear on only one of those pages.

aesthetics
  aesthetic turn in IR, 1, 8–9, 37, 61, 64, 66, 68, 72, 88, 243, 304
  Chinese aesthetics, 48–49
  conventions, 160, 239, 241–42, 257–59, 262–63, 305–6, 313–14
  critical aesthetics, 20, 36–44, 45, 46, 47–48, 51, 64, 73–75, 90, 106–7, 214–15, 232–33, 235, 242, 304–6
  political aesthetics, 7, 29, 37, 72, 118–20, 122–23, 138, 144, 160, 180, 204, 244, 249, 255–56, 304–5
  theory, 37, 135, 154–56, 165, 184, 232–33, 243–44, 269, 276, 292
affect
  affective communities of sense, 2, 6–7, 16–17, 35, 36, 40–41, 44, 45, 47, 49–50, 61, 73–74, 75, 79, 88–89, 91, 114–15, 117–18, 121, 123, 130–31, 136, 138–39, 141, 144–45, 152–53, 154–56, 176–77, 198, 203, 207, 232–33, 238, 239, 244, 254, 259, 268, 270, 272–73, 291–92, 299–300, 305–6, 309–10, 313–15, 316
  affect-work, 1–2, 3, 41–43, 50–51, 62–63, 78–79, 80–81, 83–86, 88–89, 91, 107–8, 111–15, 121, 130, 140, 155–56, 163, 170, 207, 210–11, 212–14, 234, 236–38, 250–51, 256, 257, 259, 260, 268, 272–73, 276, 289–90, 292, 295–96, 299–300, 305, 307–10, 311–12, 315–16
  affect theory, 2, 3, 5, 36, 38, 39–42, 44, 45, 47, 65, 66–67, 72, 73–75, 78, 123, 181–82, 303, 305–6, 307, 313–14, 316

Ai Weiwei
  activism, 118–19, 123, 124–30, 133*f*, 137–40, 182, 226, 252–53, 280–81, 289–90
  art, 123, 128–29, 138–39, 140
  Human Flow, 118–19, 130–36, 133*f*, 134*f*, 138–39, 140, 226, 313
autoethnography, 61, 65, 76, 77–88

Barabantseva, Elena, 75, 81, 88–89
Barthes, Roland, 28–29, 38, 44, 47, 305
Bauman, Zygmunt, 250, 252, 253
beauty pageantry, 179–82, 203–4, 206–7, 303–4, 313
  China, 184–85, 199–201, 200*f*, 202–3
  Jamaica, 188–91, 189*f*
  nation-building, 187–88, 192–93, 200*f*
  Thailand, 185, 187–88, 190–91, 204, 206–7
  United Kingdom, 184, 186–87
  United States, 186n33, 190n50, 206–7
  Vietnam, 184
Bennett, Jane, 41–42, 142–43, 152–53
Bleiker, Roland, 65, 66, 76, 121, 122–23, 138, 152–53
Brown, Wendy, 52, 54, 209–10, 216–20, 222–23, 231–32, 233, 237
Butler, Judith, 41–42, 92, 121, 180

Cai Guo-Qiang, 234, 235*f*, 309–10
China
  aesthetics, 48–49
  beauty pageants, 184–85, 199–201, 200*f*, 202–3
  gardens, 247, 248–49, 251–53, 254–57
  Great Firewall, 127–28, 217, 274–75, 278–82, 283, 286–88, 287*f*, 299–300, 304

China (*cont.*)
   Great Wall, 23–24, 55, 142, 163–65, 164*f*,
      211–15, 213*f*, 216*f*, 219, 220–23, 221*f*,
      225–29, 231, 233–34, 235*f*, 236, 238,
      280–81, 283, 307–10, 311–12
   maps, 150*f*, 157, 158*f*, 163, 164*f*, 166, 168*f*
   Nanjing Massacre Memorial, 259–64, 261*f*, 262*f*,
      263*f*, 269–70
   South China Sea, 44, 149–56, 150*f*, 160, 170–76
   surveillance, 273–74, 278–83, 286–91,
      287*f*, 294–99
   veils, 198–203, 200*f*
Civilization/barbarism. *See* dynamic dyads
CNN-Effect, 30–31, 117, 119, 120, 121, 130
comparative political theory, 4, 54–57, 106–15,
   123, 129–30, 215, 223–34, 312
Connolly, William, 310–11
creative politics, 2, 6, 19–20, 24, 25, 32–34, 40,
   56, 61–62, 65, 70–71, 73, 75, 76, 86, 88,
   104–5, 106–7, 108–10, 117–18, 122–23,
   130, 139, 147–48, 153, 154–57, 176–77,
   181, 212, 214–15, 228–29, 237, 241–42,
   257–58, 268, 270, 272–73, 305–6, 311–12,
   313–15, 316
critical aesthetics. *See* aesthetics
cultural governance, 75, 110–11, 112, 114–16, 140,
   186–87, 193–203, 247–56

Danchev, Alex, 136, 304–5
Deleuze, Gilles, 65, 276–77, 299–300
Derrida, Jacques, 81–82, 85–86, 207
distribution of the sensible, 6, 36, 37, 42–43,
   244–46, 244n21, 247, 249, 257, 259, 264,
   269–70, 305–6, 307, 311
dynamic dyads
   center/periphery, 5, 56–57, 149, 151–52,
      153–54, 156–60, 158*f*, 161–65, 161*f*,
      168*f*, 169, 173–75, 176–77, 313
   civility/martiality, 8, 10, 50, 239, 245–47,
      250–52, 254, 255–56, 257–59, 263,
      266, 268, 269–70, 311–12, 313
   Civilization/barbarism, 49–50, 55, 151, 157–59,
      163–66, 164*f*, 169, 171–72, 173, 175, 199,
      224, 225–27, 228–29, 231, 234, 256, 260,
      281, 310–11
   concealing/revealing, 5, 22, 30, 51–52, 56–57,
      178, 179, 180, 182, 184, 186–87, 192–93,
      196–98, 201, 203, 207, 254, 262–63, 313
   creative/destruction, 115, 144–45, 212, 228–29,
      233–34, 235*f*, 309–10
   cultural governance/resistance, 75, 91, 104–5,
      115–16, 117–18, 148, 180, 241–42, 243,
      244–45, 247, 257, 264, 269, 270
   East/West, 3–5, 26–27, 44, 48, 49–50, 51, 57,
      63–64, 74, 75, 88–89, 123, 153–54, 156–57,
      177, 180, 187, 194–95, 198, 202–3, 212,
      216, 219, 225, 226–27, 246, 274, 276, 299–
      300, 303, 304–5, 310–13

ideology/affect, 2, 17, 20, 36, 45, 51, 63, 79, 121,
   123, 135–36, 181–82, 235–38, 273, 292,
   305–6, 307, 308–10, 313, 314
inside/outside, 1, 2, 10, 12–13, 17, 22, 25, 45,
   48–49, 57, 82–83, 114, 128, 147–48, 149,
   151–52, 153, 154–56, 159, 163–65, 167,
   169, 174–75, 177, 212, 215–16, 216*f*, 218,
   223–24, 228–29, 231, 234, 254, 277–78,
   283, 284, 304, 310–13
loosening/tightening, 5, 56–57, 224–25,
   228–31, 236–37, 238, 313
meaning/doing, 7, 16–17, 19–20, 36, 41–42,
   43, 45, 46–48, 61, 62–63, 65, 73–74, 76,
   88, 106–8, 117–18, 123, 139, 147–48, 166,
   223, 272, 303, 305–6, 307
meaning/feeling, 2, 40, 45, 47, 121, 152–53,
   155–56, 181, 204, 207, 210–11, 238, 257,
   266–68, 272, 291–92, 310, 314
self/Other, 1, 2, 12–13, 22, 26–27, 48–50, 54,
   55, 61–63, 64, 65, 66, 71–72, 75–76, 78–79,
   86–89, 94, 98–99, 101–2, 121–22, 131,
   182–83, 187, 193–94, 214–15, 229–31,
   310–13
theory, 5, 17, 50–51, 56–57, 144, 223–25,
   232–33, 303, 309–10, 313
verbal/visual, 6, 20–21, 27–29, 36, 37–38, 44,
   46–48, 93, 98–99, 106–7, 111, 120, 132,
   144, 148–49, 152–53, 159, 161–62, 165–66,
   176–77, 207, 305–6, 308–9, 315–16
visibility/invisibility, 22, 23–24, 100, 128, 179–80,
   181–82, 204, 247, 269, 299–300
visibility/visuality, 2, 7, 19–20, 46–47, 57,
   86–88, 121, 123, 130–31, 139, 203–7, 211,
   235–38, 240–41, 272–73, 292, 299–300,
   303, 310, 314

Enloe, Cynthia, 3, 61–62, 78–79
Euben, Roxanne L., 106–8
everyday life, politics of, 1, 3, 4–5, 6–7, 17, 37, 38,
   40–41, 42–43, 45, 62–63, 65, 75–76, 77–81,
   86–88, 101–2, 109–10, 135, 143, 181,
   182–83, 194–95, 196–98, 202, 207, 230–31,
   235–37, 240–41, 266–68, 270, 284–85,
   287–89, 294–95, 299–300, 307, 310, 314

feeling visually, 2, 11, 32, 45, 181–82, 260–62,
   307, 316
feminist theory, 4–5, 26–27, 61–63, 70–71, 185–87,
   193, 194–95, 196–97
Fernández, Ana Teresa, 219*f*, 219, 234
filmmaking, 6, 39, 56–57, 61, 68–72, 75, 77, 81, 83,
   88, 179, 303, 305–10, 313–14
Foucault, Michel, 44, 47, 83, 104–5, 107–8, 109–10,
   115–16, 212, 224–25, 241–42, 243, 244–45,
   252, 276–77, 284, 285, 288–89, 290–91,
   299–300, 312
framing, 1, 21–25, 23*f*, 26–27, 31, 32, 43, 45, 71,
   78–79, 82, 103–4, 218, 313

France
  cartography, 55–56, 156–57
  gardens, 249–51, 303–4
  veils, 178–80, 195–98

gardens
  China, 247, 248–49, 251–53, 254–57
  civility/martiality (*see* dynamic dyads)
  conventions, 247–56, 257–59
  France, 249–51
  Garden of Perfect Brilliance, 251–52, 254–57, 268
  gardening state, 250–51, 252–53
  heterotopia, 243, 252, 268, 270, 312
  Japan, 247–48, 249, 253–54
  Nanjing Massacre Memorial (*see* China)
  resistance, 256–57, 264, 268
  September 11 memorial, 269–70
  Yasukuni Shrine, 239–40, 264–68, 265*f*,
    267*f*, 269–70
gaze
  colonial, 4–5, 26–27, 137, 144, 180, 186–93,
    195, 202–3, 304–5
  male, 4–5, 26–27, 144, 180, 186–93, 194–95,
    202–3, 304–5
  postcolonial male, 192–93
  surveillant, 128, 144, 272, 284–85, 300, 304–5
  white, 4–5, 26–27, 144, 186–93, 304–5
governmentality, 224–25, 229–31, 232, 238, 294–95
Great Firewall of China. *See* China
Great Wall of China. *See* China
Great Walls. See walls

Hansen, Lene, 29–30, 37–38, 94–95, 96, 99–101
hermeneutics, 20, 27, 32, 34–35, 37, 38–39, 40–41,
    45, 46, 47–48, 51, 62–63, 64, 68, 70–72, 75,
    80–81, 88, 91–101, 110–11, 115, 118, 120,
    121, 128, 151, 181, 207, 218, 231, 232, 234,
    235–36, 257, 303–4, 305–6, 313–14
heterotopia, 243, 252, 268, 270, 312
hospitality, 81, 88, 207
Human Flow. See Ai Weiwei
Hutchison, Emma, 40–41, 138, 207
hypervisuality, 11, 127–28, 180–82, 186, 192*f*,
    193, 204

iconoclasm, 30–31, 35–36, 102–3, 120–21
ideology, 2, 5, 17, 19–20, 22, 29–31, 32–34, 36,
    39–40, 51, 59–60, 64, 69–70, 72, 75, 111,
    123, 143, 181–82, 214, 218, 232, 235, 239,
    240–41, 249, 256, 268, 269, 291, 303–4,
    305–6, 307–8
imperialism
  Chinese, 44, 54, 55–56, 149, 152–54, 155–57,
    161, 165–66, 167–70, 176, 202–3, 245–46,
    249, 286, 303–4
  Western, 21–22, 26–27, 52, 54, 55–56, 153–
    54, 156–57, 166–68, 185–86, 187, 190,
    249, 303–4

infrastructures of feeling, 11, 41–42, 42n48, 45,
    143, 215, 233, 238, 239, 240–41, 242, 269,
    270, 307, 314
inside/outside. *See* dynamic dyads
intertextuality, 37–38, 94, 152–53, 161–62,
    165, 170
intervisuality, 37–38, 44, 94, 102, 114–15, 151–53,
    161–62, 165, 170
inter-veillance, 273, 276–77, 291–300, 312
intimate geopolitics, 1, 4–5, 79
Islamic State
  execution videos, 16, 90, 105–8
  maps, 147–48, 153–54, 177
  rebel governance, 109–15
  utopian PSAs, 108–15, 110*f*, 113*f*, 118–19, 243,
    303–4, 314–15

Jenco, Leigh, 54

Lawrence, Andy, 75, 81, 306–7
Lyon, David, 276, 281

maps
  Chinese, 150*f*, 157, 158*f*, 163, 164*f*, 166, 168*f*
  critical cartography, 21–22, 41–42, 44, 47, 56,
    147–54, 157–59, 313
  empire-maps, 55–56, 148–49, 156–57, 163
  "Europe in 2035," 32–35, 33*f*, 36, 95,
    142, 147–48
  Korean, 160, 161, 161*f*
  Islamic State, 147–48
  lost territories, 147–48, 163, 164*f*, 166, 168*f*
  South China Sea, 44, 150*f*, 170, 171, 173
map-fare, 148–49, 154, 159–60, 162, 166, 170,
    175, 176–77
Massumi, Brian, 39–40, 292
medium theory, 5, 7, 50–51, 54–57, 313
methods
  critical aesthetics, 36, 73–75, 232–33, 304–6
  empiricist, 28–29, 30–31, 37, 43, 66, 68, 70, 72,
    75, 88, 151
  hermeneutics, 27–31, 34–35, 38–39, 70–72,
    91–101, 231, 235–36, 303–4, 305–6,
    313–14
  visual, 66–68, 91, 94–96, 99–102
Mirzoeff, Nicholas, 28, 52, 54, 56, 102, 103–4, 292
Mitchell, W. J. T., 6, 19–20, 30–31, 36, 40–41, 44,
    46–47, 142–43, 211
moral ambiguity, 38, 96, 179, 208, 215, 236, 237,
    238, 311–12
multisensory politics, 2, 6–7, 41–42, 45, 86, 144,
    215, 234, 242, 268, 273, 305–6, 310,
    314–15, 316

Nanjing Massacre Memorial. *See* China
NiqaBitch Shakes Paris. See veils
nonlinear, 2, 5, 11, 35, 39–40, 62, 68, 73–74, 75–76,
    78, 81, 85–88, 224, 236–37, 238, 305

nonnarrative, 2–3, 5, 35, 106–7, 214–15, 232, 233, 236–37, 238, 241–42, 250–51, 268, 305

nonverbal, 2, 5, 6, 40, 71–72, 95, 106–7, 132, 305, 316

North Korea, 90, 138, 217
  The Interview, 96–100
  visual securitization, 98–101

ocular-centrism, 6–7, 27, 31, 45, 144, 315

partition of the sensible, 181, 204, 232–33, 244n21, 276–77, 284

performative politics, 1–3, 5, 6–7, 26–27, 32, 35–37, 42–43, 44, 45, 51, 56–57, 80–81, 86, 92, 96, 109, 128, 136, 142–43, 148–49, 154, 156, 157, 172, 176, 178, 181–83, 193, 198, 205–7, 217–18, 232, 234, 236, 241–42, 246–47, 250–51, 254, 255–57, 264, 266–68, 269–70, 273, 276–77, 291–300, 303, 308–9, 310–12, 315

poetry, 27–28, 48, 50, 66, 132, 152–53, 165–66, 170, 176, 245–46, 252–53, 257–58

populism, 2, 15–16, 34–35, 148, 217, 314–15

positionality, 4–5, 82, 181n, 304–5

postcolonial, 56, 82, 121–22, 154–55, 185–86, 188–90, 192–93

Princess Hijab. *See* veils

PSAs (Public Service Announcements)
  China, 86
  Human Flow (*see* Ai Weiwei)
  I Am an American (*see* Weber)
  Islamic State, 108–15, 110*f*, 113*f*, 117–19, 243, 303–4, 313, 314–15
  Smog Journeys, 40, 41*f*

Qianlong emperor, 169, 174–75, 251–52, 254

Rancière, Jacques
  communities of sense, 40–41
  distribution of the sensible, 6, 37, 47, 102, 123, 241–42, 244, 244n, 245, 249, 309–10, 311
  emancipated spectator, 39, 40–41, 121, 268
  partition of the sensible, 181, 204, 244n, 276–77
  representation, 1, 3, 20–22, 24, 25, 28–30, 42–43, 44, 48, 64, 69–70, 72, 73–74, 80, 86–88, 101, 103–4, 107–8, 121, 128, 139, 143, 303–4, 309–10, 311
  gardens, 241–42, 243
  maps, 147, 148–49, 154–55
  veils, 181, 207
  walls, 232

resistance, 115–16, 118–19, 121, 139, 140, 162, 256–57, 264, 268

securitization, 91–93, 93*f*, 101, 115–16, 154, 217
  visual securitization, 91, 96, 101, 106, 112, 114–16, 310–11, 315–16

self/Other relations. *See* dynamic dyads

sensory spaces, 3, 6–7, 39–40, 42–43, 45, 51, 139, 142–44, 153, 181, 210–11, 212–14, 215, 232, 234, 238, 240–41, 242, 258–59, 272–73, 291–92, 307, 315

September 11
  attacks, 51–52, 56, 71, 77–78, 97–98, 210–11
  memorial, 56, 241–42, 269–70

Shapiro, Michael J., 5, 20, 37, 39, 47, 69–70, 72, 73, 104–5, 245

Social Credit System. *See* surveillance

social-ordering, 2, 4–5, 32, 35–36, 37, 39–40, 44, 45, 49, 50, 56–57, 79, 90, 101, 108, 115, 136, 148–49, 176, 238, 241–42, 243–44, 246–47, 249, 259, 264, 272, 274, 276–77, 284, 297, 299–300, 305–6, 310, 313

Sontag, Susan, 25–26, 101, 119–20

South China Sea, 44, 149–56, 150*f*, 160, 170–76

surveillance
  China, 273–74, 278–83, 286–91, 287*f*, 294–99
  disciplinary society, 284, 287*f*, 299–300
  Europe, 290–91, 293–95
  inter-veillance, 291, 299–300
  networked society of control, 291, 299–300
  Social Credit System, 273, 295–98
  sovereignty society, 277, 299–300
  theory, 274
  United States, 272, 285–86, 293–95, 299–300
  Xinjiang, 287–89

thinking visually, 2, 11, 31, 32, 45, 73–74, 181–82, 307, 316

toilet adventures, 61–62, 63–64, 66, 77, 82–83, 84–89, 306

tu, 47, 155–56

veils, 22, 26–27, 30, 180, 185–86, 207, 258–59, 303–4, 311–12, 313, 314
  affective, 203
  Algeria, 178–80, 191–93, 192*f*, 204–6
  Awrah: Uncovering the Covered, 179, 183, 204, 306
  China, 198–203, 200*f*
  France, 178–80, 195–98
  Iran, 193–94
  NiqaBitch Shakes Paris, 178–80, 179*f*, 196–98
  Princess Hijab, 182, 196–97, 197*f*, 198
  Saudi Arabia, 194–95
  United Kingdom, 179, 182–84, 183*f*, 204, 205–6, 306

verbal/visual. *See* dynamic dyads

visceral politics, 1–2, 5, 7–8, 16, 35, 38, 39–40, 44, 45, 62–63, 67–68, 73–74, 86–88, 106–7, 114–15, 123, 135, 142, 153, 166, 178, 203, 204, 214–15, 291–92, 305, 310, 314, 316

visibility/invisibility. *See* dynamic dyads

visibility/visuality. *See* dynamic dyads

visibility strategy
   art, 120, 121, 123, 128, 130–31, 136
   filmmaking, 62–63
   gardens, 241–42, 247
   maps, 147, 148
   security, 91, 93, 100–1, 115
   surveillance, 272–73
   theory, 1, 2, 6–7, 21, 31, 32, 45, 61, 68, 303–4,
      305, 314, 315
   walls, 218, 235–36
visuality strategy
   art, 123, 130–31, 136
   filmmaking, 62–63, 86, 309–10
   gardens, 241–42, 247, 259
   maps, 147–48, 181
   security, 91, 102, 106–8, 109
   surveillance, 272–73
   veils, 192–93
   theory, 1–3, 6–8, 9–10, 32–34, 35–36, 37–38,
      43, 45, 59, 305, 314, 315
   walls, 236–37
visual
   artifacts, 1–2, 3, 5, 17–18, 19–20, 32–34, 40,
      41–43, 45, 141–45, 303, 305, 307, 308–9,
      310–11, 314–15, 316
      art, 128, 139
      gardens, 239, 241–42, 258–59, 270
      maps, 148–49, 152–53, 154–55, 165,
         169, 176–77
      surveillance, 272–73, 291–92
      veils, 178, 181–82, 198, 207
      walls, 210–11, 212–14, 218, 228–29, 238
   images, 1–2, 3, 5, 15, 16–17, 19–24, 25, 26–31,
      32, 35–36, 37–39, 40, 42–43, 45, 46, 47, 48,
      59–60, 64, 91, 93, 115, 117–18, 139, 152–
      53, 303, 304, 305–6, 307, 314, 315–16
      art, 22–23, 23f, 102–3, 104f, 122–23, 126–27,
         128, 139, 229
      cartoons, 15, 16, 29–30, 80, 88, 94–95, 96,
         100, 196
      affective, 128–39
      film and video, 61, 62, 70, 74, 75, 84, 90, 96,
         106–7, 111, 112, 130–39, 266–68
      iconic, 1–2, 3, 28, 38, 42–43, 92–93, 94–95,
         102–3, 121, 127–28, 155–56, 269, 310, 312
      Internet, 272–73, 280, 292
      maps, 149, 151, 153, 159, 169
      methods, 66–68, 91, 94–96, 99–102
      photographs, 1, 102–3, 103f, 117, 119–23,
         127–28, 133f, 134f

posters, 86, 87f, 89
   walls, 218, 225, 229, 232
   of women, 22–23, 23f, 26–27, 180, 186–87,
      188–91, 189f, 192f, 192–93, 197f, 197–98,
      200f, 203
ethnography, 65, 76, 80, 83, 306
   methods, 66–68, 91, 94–96, 99–102
   securitization, 91, 96, 101, 106, 112, 114–16,
      310–11, 315–16
   visual turn, 61, 64–65, 75–86, 88, 315

Walker, R. B. J., 48–49, 222–23, 310–11, 315
walls
   barriers, 30, 210, 214–15, 216–18, 222–23, 227,
      228–29, 230–31, 238, 258–59, 281, 283,
      304, 311–12
   Berlin Wall, 3, 42–43, 216, 232–33,
      307–8, 311–12
   gateways, 214, 215, 227–31, 237, 238, 279,
      283, 285–86
   Great Wall of China (*see* China)
   Great Walls, 237–38, 307–10
   loosening/tightening (*see* dynamic dyads)
   Project to Extend the Great Wall of China, 234,
      235f, 309–10
   sublime, 212–14, 233–34, 235f, 235, 237,
      238, 309–10
   Tecate Beer Wall Advertisement, 237–38
   US-Mexico barrier, 30, 212–14, 219, 219f, 227,
      229–30, 234, 235–38, 307–9, 309f
   We Are Not Immigrants (*see* Weber)
   West Bank barrier, 30, 143, 227, 229–31, 238
Weber, Cynthia
   I Am an American, 71–72, 77–78, 303–4
   visual methods, 65, 66–67, 71–72,
      77–78, 235–37
   We Are Not Immigrants, 215, 235–37
witnessing, 28–29, 41–42, 70–71, 102, 117–18,
   139, 268
   affective, 128–39
   ideological, 124
   theory, 119
world-ordering, 2, 4–5, 32, 35–36, 37, 39–40, 44,
   45, 49, 50, 56–57, 79, 90, 101, 108, 115,
   136, 148–49, 176, 238, 241–42, 243–44,
   246–47, 249, 259, 264, 272, 274, 276, 300,
   305–6, 310, 313

Yasukuni Shrine. *See* gardens